D1498161

AFRICA'S 'AGITATORS'

JONATHAN DERRICK

Africa's 'Agitators'

*Militant Anti-Colonialism in Africa
and the West, 1918-1939*

Columbia University Press
New York

Columbia University Press
Publishers Since 1893
New York

Copyright © 2008 Jonathan Derrick
All rights reserved

Library of Congress Cataloging-in-Publication Data

Derrick, Jonathan.
  Africa's "agitators": militant anti-colonialism in africa
and the west 1918-1939 / Jonathan Derrick.
    p. cm.
  Includes bibliographical references and index.
  ISBN 978-0-231-70056-6 (cloth : alk. paper)
  1. Africa—Politics and government—20th century. 2. Protest movements—Africa—
History—20th century. 3. Government, Resistance to—Africa—History—20th century.
4. Anti-imperialist movements—Africa—History—20th century. 5. National liberation
movements—Africa—History—20th century. 6. Political activists—Africa—History—20th
century. 7. Political activists—Africa—Biography. 8. Africa—History—1884-1960. I. Title.
  DT29.D47 2008
  322.4096—dc22
                              2008028877

Columbia University Press books are printed on permanent and durable acid-free paper.

c 10 9 8 7 6 5 4 3 2

References to Internet Web sites (URLs) were accurate at the time of writing. Neither the author
nor Columbia University Press is responsible for URLs that may have expired or changed since
the manuscript was prepared.

CONTENTS

ABBREVIATIONS

AEF	Afrique Equatoriale Française
AEMNA	Association des Etudiants Musulmans Nord-Africains
ANC	African National Congress
AOF	Afrique Occidentale Française
APO	African People's Organisation
APS	Aborigines' Protection Society
ARAC	Association Républicaine des Anciens Combattants
ARPS	Aborigines' Rights Protection Society
ASAPS	Anti-Slavery and Aborigines' Protection Society
AWU	African Workers' Union
BSAC	British South Africa Company
BTU	Bathurst Trade Union
CAM	Comité d'Action Marocaine
CDRN	Comité de Défense de la Race Nègre
CGT	Confédération Générale du Travail
CGTT	Confédération Générale du Travail Tunisien
CGTU	Confédération Générale du Travail-Unitaire
CMA	Congrès Musulman Algérien
CPGB	Communist Party of Great Britain
CPSA	Communist Party of South Africa
CPUSA	Communist Party of the United States of America
CRA	Congo Reform Association
ECCI	Executive Committee of the Communist International
ENA	Etoile Nord-Africaine
GENA	Glorieuse Etoile Nord-Africaine
IAH	Internationale Arbeitshilfe (International Workers' Relief)
IAFA	International African Friends of Abyssinia

IASB	International African Service Bureau
ICU	Industrial and Commercial Union (of Africa)
ILD	International Labour Defence
ILO	International Labour Office
ILP	Independent Labour Party
INC	Indian National Congress
ITUC-NW	International Trade Union Committee of Negro Workers
KA	Kikuyu Association
KCA	Kikuyu Central Association
KMT	Kuomintang
KPD	Kommunistische Partei Deutschlands
Kutvu	Kommunisticheskii Universitet Trudiashchikhsia Vostoka (Communist University of the Toilers of the East)
LAI	League Against Imperialism/Ligue Anti-Impérialiste
LAR	League of African Rights
LCP	League of Coloured Peoples
LDH	Ligue des Droits de l'Homme
LDRN	Ligue de Défense de la Race Nègre
LFADCIM	Ligue Française pour l'Accession aux Droits de Citoyen des Indigènes de Madagascar
LNU	League of Nations Union
LPACIIQ	Labour Party Advisory Committees on Imperial and on International Questions
LSI	Labour and Socialist International
LUDRN	Ligue Universelle de Défense de la Race Noire
MOPR	Mezhdunarodnaia Organizatsia Pomoshchi Revolutsioneram (=International Red Aid, International Labour Defense)
NAACP	National Association for the Advancement of Coloured People
NCBWA	National Congress of British West Africa
NCCL	National Council for Civil Liberties
NNDP	Nigerian National Democratic Party
NWA	Negro Welfare Association
NYM	Nigerian Youth Movement
PCA	Parti Communiste Algérien

ABBREVIATIONS

PCF	Parti Communiste Français
PCRM	Parti Communiste de la Région de Madagascar
PPA	Parti du Peuple Algérien
PSOP	Parti Socialiste Ouvrier et Paysan
RILU	Red International of Labour Unions
SANNC	South African Native National Congress
SFIO	Section Française de l'Internationale Ouvrière
SPD	Sozialdemokratische Partei Deutschlands
SRI	Secours Rouge International
UAC	United Africa Company
UDC	Union of Democratic Control
UNIA	Universal Negro Improvement Association
UTN	Union des Travailleurs Nègres
VVS	Vy Vato Sakelika
WASU	West African Students' Union

INTRODUCTION

The history of Africa and Africans under colonial rule was my chosen area of special interest when I researched for a PhD thesis for the University of London in the early 1970s, at the School of Oriental and African Studies. Eventually I defended my thesis "Douala under the French Mandate, 1916 to 1936" in 1979, after research including many interviews with people in Douala who remembered that period, then still quite recent. During my research I found something of which I had had no idea before: that among the Duala people there had been political activists who back in the 1920s, in the French Mandate period, were already calling for self-government. I also found how the French colonial rulers had been concerned about other activists living in Europe at the time. Earlier, as my interest in Africa had developed during my first job, with the *West Africa* weekly, I had learned something about such early anti-colonial protest campaigners as the National Congress of British West Africa and such militants as Marcus Garvey and George Padmore. But I now developed the idea that more could and should be published about those Africans who were opposing colonial rule at its peak, in the 1920s and 30s, and the Westerners who supported them.

Initially I planned a biography of I.T.A. Wallace Johnson, the Sierra Leonean pioneer campaigner against British rule in the inter-war era. But I broadened my scope over the many years in which the project took shape, partly because Wallace Johnson had been thoroughly studied in LaRay Denzer's thesis (Birmingham, 1973), partly because there seemed to be a need for a comprehensive study of early anti-colonialism relating to Africa generally. African nationalism as it developed from the 1940s onwards, leading to independence and beyond, was the subject of plentiful research in many countries; so was the Africans' campaign in South Africa over the same period. But what of the pre-

1

decessors of people like Kwame Nkrumah and Nelson Mandela? They were around—fairly small groups of professional people in Africa and students and campaigners in the West rather than well organised parties, but they were there, criticising or totally rejecting colonialism in Africa or South African white supremacy at a time when those things seemed eternal. But I considered that they were not well enough remembered. There was abundant material in archives, and some scattered around scores of published works and theses, but the story needed to be properly put together. Experts in contemporary African history consistently confirmed this and urged me (I am grateful) to pursue a project which dragged on for years because of the demands of work as a journalist and editor.

The people and events described in the now completed work in these pages had not been neglected by scholars—I am not suggesting that. When I developed my project in the 1970s some theses and books had been completed on the subject. At an early stage there were two valuable theses which (like my own thesis) were never published—Denzer's, and James Spiegler's "Aspects of Nationalist Thought among French-Speaking West Africans 1921-1939" (Oxford, 1968)—and published biographies of Padmore (by James Hooker, 1967) and Kenyatta (by Jeremy Murray Brown, 1972). In the USA Marcus Garvey had never been forgotten and Cronon's biography had appeared in 1955. Those three militants, and many others, were covered in studies of Pan-Africanism, which aroused particularly close scholarly attention leading to the books by Geiss (1968, in English 1974), Langley (1973) and Asante (1977); Esedebe's study of the same subject was to be published later (1994). In 1973 Ras Makonnen's own reminiscences were published. This was one of only a very few personal accounts by one of the activists; Padmore's numerous books said little about himself. However, Nnamdi Azikiwe published his autobiography in 1970.

The early researchers into the anticolonialism of the inter-war years were fortunate to be able to interview some activists of those years, as I was to interview Léopold Moumé Etia, who had been a student activist in Paris in the late 1930s, and others in Douala; there can be few if any still living now, but I interviewed C.L.R. James and the grand old man of British anti-colonialism, Fenner Brockway, in 1984. Later scholars such as myself have been able to study more archival material. Many of the archives relating to the period in Britain and France have been open for decades now, but for the study of the Communist involvement in anti-colonialism in particular, the more recent release of MI5 documents in Britain and, still more, the opening of Comintern archives in Moscow since the collapse of the Soviet Union in 1991 have made valuable new material available. There had however been important studies of the Communist involvement before, notably Wilson's study published in 1974.

In France major studies in the field of the present work appeared in the 1980s. On Algeria, Messali Hadj's own reminiscences were published posthumously in 1982 and Benjamin Stora's biography in 1986. They and the considerably later work by Simon (2003) add up to comprehensive coverage of the Etoile Nord Africaine (ENA), adding to the literature on both the Communist involvement in anticolonialism and the Islamic element (which is also studied in Cleveland's 1985 biography of Shakib Arslan). Oved (1984) has studied the links between Moroccan nationalism and French left-wing parties and has been a most valuable source for this book, which has looked more widely at the relations between European anti-imperialists and African protestors. Most valuable sources, too, have been three French works whose scope resembles that of the present work, by Liauzu (1982), Dewitte (1984), and Biondi (1992).

These are only the most important titles in an abundant literature. And I have to tell the reader straight away that much of what follows is derived from these and scores of other secondary sources. This has mainly been because I have for years been unable to do archival research outside Britain, least of all in Moscow; in addition, there has been very thorough published research in France on the ENA and (by Dewitte) on the black militant movements. But I have considered even so that a *tour d'horizon* like what follows would be useful.

The existing works tell only part of the story. This is of course reasonable as each part can easily fill a book or more than one, but a comparative look at the anticolonial movements of the 1920s and 30s can be a useful addition. Of the existing works, the most comprehensive ones have been those published in France, and deal with the French side only. There is no comprehensive study covering both activists in and from the colonies and European anticolonialists in Britain at that period, though Howe (1993) has studied the European ones; more needs to be studied about the latter in Britain and, even after the work of Oved and Biondi, in France. The studies of political Pan-Africanism deal only with one aspect of anti-colonial activity, and only one of them (by Langley) does justice to the French side—though Edwards' literature-oriented study (2003) devoted mainly to prominent Black people in inter-war France has some valuable information on political activists. Those Pan-Africanism studies mostly concentrate on activity in Europe and the USA—which was very important, and takes up much of the present work, but needs to be related to developments within Africa. That was indeed done by Asante in his unrivalled study of the protests against the Italian invasion of Ethiopia; but more generally, I have sought to show how activities within and outside Africa were related.

Many books on the histories of particular countries have dealt well with the inter-war period—Kimble (1963) on Ghana, Cole (1975) on Lagos, Walshe on South Africa (1970), Lejri on Tunisia (1974), Halstead (1967) and Oved on Morocco, Kamoche (1981) on Kenya, and others. Each covers only one country, which is a handful enough. Biographies, such as those already cited and Bunting (1975) on Kotane and Buhle (1988) on James, have of course looked at the context of the subjects' lives, but this book, which has found the biographies obviously useful sources, adds more on that context.

Some of the published works also need revision at certain points. For example, several were affected by an uncritical acceptance of George Padmore's accounts of his separation from the Communists in the 1930s; I went along with this myself in a paper published earlier (in Chafer and Sackur, 2001), but after a closer look I now suggest in my analysis of this important event (in Chapter Four) that Padmore's recollection was faulty.

A comprehensive work on anticolonial activity by Africans and on behalf of Africa, even if confined to the inter-war period, faces the obvious problem of the sheer size of the subject. However, I have from the start reduced the scope somewhat by concentrating on the more radical, militant people and groups. The more cautious ones calling for reforms are of course mentioned also—the distinction was not clear-cut anyway—but the emphasis is on those whose strong opposition to the colonial system made them "agitators" in the eyes of the authorities. Those authorities had power to restrict the activities of such militants in Africa, but not in Europe or the USA. Much of this book therefore deals with activities in the West, but always emphasising the links with Africa which were close and important. In many parts of Africa some anti-government organisation and activity were possible, including links with activists overseas. For reasons of space alone, developments within any part of Africa have to receive rather summary attention, but they are to be borne in mind throughout the study of the militants in exile.

Even if it is somewhat narrowed down in the way indicated, a comprehensive study covers so much ground that there is no space to do justice to any episode, individual or country. Those studying particular countries or themes will find not enough about them, and have my sympathy. However, they will see their objects of interest in context, inviting comparisons, and see directions in which to pursue further research. Indeed one benefit of a comprehensive study, I hope, will be to encourage closer study of episodes, themes or individuals. I can think quickly of two or three dozen subjects for books contained within this book, and most of those books have not been written. Some could dig further into the Comintern archives in Moscow, already being mined by Professor Risto Marjomaa of the University of Helsinki, Holger Weiss and Fredrik Petersson for their research project on "The Comintern and African Nationalism, 1921-1935". There are many other possible research topics besides.

I owe a great debt to many people who have helped me plan and persevere with this project, and provided useful information, directions and contacts for it, over the years. I mention especially Richard Rathbone, Ralph Austen, Michael Twaddle, Claude Liauzu, Marika Sherwood, Philippe Dewitte, John Lonsdale, Holger Weiss, and my publishers: the late Christopher Hurst, who sadly did not live to see completion of a book he had encouraged, and Michael Dwyer. I have heard with regret that MM. Liauzu and Dewitte, authors of two seminal sources, who looked forward to seeing the completion of my research when I consulted them in Paris, have also died.

I must thank the helpful staff of The National Archives in London and Rhodes House at Oxford. Most of all, I must express my profound appreciation and thanks to my wife Xavérie and my son Bernard, who helped me persevere but must have wondered whether this book would ever be finished. Well, here it is.

1

EMPIRE AND ANTI-EMPIRE

European countries conquered and colonised other continents for five centuries, but there was constant resistance. Africans, Asians, and peoples of the New World, Australasia and the Pacific commonly resisted the initial occupation and often rose in revolt later. From the 19th century some of them used the education brought by Western missionaries and colonisers to voice opposition to imperial rule. And there were commonly some Europeans who opposed their countries' imperialism. They did so for various reasons, quite often based on European self-interest, but not always: there was opposition to imperialism on moral grounds, condemning the seizure and plunder of other parts of the world and the enslavement and oppression of the people there.

Early African resistance and protest

Armed resistance, armed risings after occupation, peaceful protests by local people, protests in Europe and America—there was all this when Britain, France and other European countries partitioned and occupied Africa. The occupation of Africa occurred almost entirely between the late 1870s and the first decade of the 20th century.[1] Only one coun-

---

1   Among the vast literature on the colonial occupation of Africa a few major titles can be mentioned here: J. Hargreaves, *Prelude to the Partition of West Africa*, London: Macmillan, 1963; J. Hargeaves, *West Africa Partitioned*, London/Basingstoke: Macmillan, Vol. I, 1974, vol. 2, 1985; G.N. Sanderson, *England, Europe and the Upper Nile, 1882-1899: A Study in the Partition of Africa*, Edinburgh University Press, 1965; T. Pakenham, *The Scramble for Africa, 1876-1912*, London: Abacus, 1992; L.H. Gann and P. Duignan, *Colonialism in Africa, 1870-1960*, 5 vols., Cambridge University Press, 1975; J. Suret-Canale, *French Colonialism in Tropical Africa 1900-1945*, London: C. Hurst and New

try decisively defeated the European occupation forces—Ethiopia, at the battle of Adowa in 1896, a crushing defeat for Italy. But elsewhere the "unfriendly natives" or "hostile tribesmen" that late-Victorians read about at home often fought back hard, despite the Europeans' superiority in arms with their Maxim and Gatling rapid-fire guns. There was a famous African victory, won by the Zulus, at Isandhlwana in January 1879, followed however by defeat at Ulundi later that year. At the Battle of Omdurman in 1898, 9,000 soldiers of the Mahdist state in the Sudan died, cut down by the modern artillery of the Anglo-Egyptian forces whose own losses were very few. Some kingdoms submitted after a decisive battle, but among some peoples of Africa with no centralised states, such as the Igbos of south-eastern Nigeria, uncoordinated resistance went on for years.

Certainly other Africans were ready to side with the Europeans against local enemies and many fought in the conquering imperial armies or helped enforce colonial rule afterwards. There is nothing unusual in this mixed reaction to occupation—the history of Ireland offers many examples—and resistance was considerable, including many uprisings following the first occupation. Famous uprisings included the "Hut Tax War" in 1898 in the Sierra Leone Protectorate (the area inland from Freetown annexed by Britain two years earlier); the Asante (Ashanti) rising of 1900, for which the fighting queen Yaa Asantewa is remembered; the Bailundo rising of the Ovimbundu people of southern Angola, against the Portuguese, in 1902; the great Maji Maji rising against the Germans in Tanganyika in 1905; the resistance of Abdille Hassan of Somalia, who was called "the Mad Mullah" by the British but was sane enough to go on resisting them and the Italians, who occupied most the country, until 1920; the Herero and Nama risings in South-West Africa, against the Germans, from 1904 to 1907; the Bambatha rising in Zululand in 1906; and the rising of the Shona and Ndebele peoples against the rule of Rhodes' British South Africa Company (BSAC) in Southern Rhodesia in 1896-97.[2] Today African states remember the

---

York: Pica Press, 1971 (translation by T. Gottheiner of *L'Afrique noire*, vol. II: *L'Ere coloniale 1900-1945*, Paris: Editions Sociales, 1964).

2   The plentiful literature on African resistance includes M. Crowder (ed.), *West African Resistance: The Military Response to Colonial Occupation*, London: Hutchinson, 1978; S. Marks, *Reluctant Rebellion: the 1906-8 Disturbances in Natal*, Oxford: Clarendon Press, 1970; H. Drechsler, *"Let Us Die Fighting"*:

early resistance and insurgent leaders as national heroes; former French Guinea recalls in this way Samory, who created his own empire and resisted French occupation for seven years (1891-98), and the Fulani chief Alfa Yaya, who at first collaborated with the occupiers but was later deported, brought back and deported again, and accused (possibly quite falsely) of plotting in 1911.[3]

The risings failed and Britain, France, Germany and King Leopold II of the Belgians, who ruled over the Congo Free State as his own private colony, set about imposing their rule and organising economic exploitation. Extracting profit for the West from the colonies was an overriding aim, as was obvious at the time, not only to Africans—European imperialist politicians like Joseph Chamberlain in Britain and Jules Ferry in France, and other defenders of empire, admitted it proudly. While the imagined prospects for industrial exports to Africa were highlighted during the Scramble, once occupation was completed extraction of raw materials, agricultural and mineral, had priority. Africans had to work to produce these raw materials for export in many ways. Some, especially in West Africa, continued to grow export crops (especially cocoa and groundnuts) on their own smallholdings as before the occupation, and some still did so freely, but often the normal colonial flat-rate taxation was designed not only to raise revenue but to force the "lazy native" to grow crops needed by the Europeans, and there was some direct compulsion to grow certain crops also, especially cotton. Africans could be forced in many ways to work for white settlers who occupied the best African land for themselves, especially in French Algeria from the early 19th century, in Morocco and Tunisia after the French occupation later, and in South Africa, Southern Rhodesia and Kenya.

Nobody can doubt the importance of economic exploitation as a motive for imperialism. There has been debate only about theories of *causation*, i.e. what forces impelled the capitalist, industrialising West to occupy a whole continent in such a short time. On that subject the

---

The Struggle of the Herero and Nama against German Imperialism (1884-1915), London: Zed Press, 1980; T.O. Ranger, chapter 6 ("The Nineteenth Century in Southern Rhodesia"), pp. 142-52, in T.O. Ranger (ed.), *Aspects of Central African History*, London: Heinemann, 1968.

3   Suret-Canale (note 1), pp. 75-6, 78-9; C. Harrison, *France and Islam in West Africa, 1860-1960*, Cambridge University Press, 1988, pp. 74-89.

theory published by J.A. Hobson in 1902 and V.I. Lenin in 1916[4]—that capitalism was obliged to push European states into colonial annexations because it could not find outlets for investment otherwise—has been thoroughly examined and generally found inadequate. But that is irrelevant to the subject of this study. The *fact* of economic exploitation as a primary motive for and consequence of colonial occupation and rule was always obvious to all, and was the main reason for anti-colonialism.

From an early date some of the methods of economic exploitation caused enormous harm and led to protests, such as the massive organised migration of grossly exploited workers for gold mines in South Africa and other mines in Southern Rhodesia and the Congo,[5] and, worst of all, the forced collection of wild rubber in the Congo Free State, a murderous operation lasting for years, and repeated in French Congo (renamed in 1910 French Equatorial Africa, AEF) when Leopold's system was reproduced there from 1899. Even in countries spared this extreme suffering there were often severe impositions—forced labour for building of railways (such as the railway to Kano in Nigeria and the Matadi-Leopoldville railway in the Congo), other forced labour for many purposes, conscription of porters (the hapless "native bearer" of colonial literature), and more—and massive disruption of life.

There is abundant literature on these and other aspects of colonial rule, and this book can only glance at them briefly to recall what the opponents of colonialism were fighting against. Besides the various impositions and cruelties, there was the basic fact of military aggression. One of the Western-educated African elite of the Gold Coast Colony, the pioneer nationalist Joseph Ephraim Casely Hayford (1865-1930), wrote:

---

4   J.A. Hobson, *Imperialism: A Study*, London: George Allen & Unwin (1902, revised ed. 1938); V.I. Lenin, *Imperialism: The Highest Stage of Capitalism*, 1916, republished with Introduction by N. Lewis and J. Malone, London: Pluto Press, 1996.

5   A.H. Jeeves, *Migrant Labour in the South African Mining Economy: The Struggle for the Gold Mines' Labour Supply 1890-1920*, Kingston and Montreal: McGill-Queen's University Press, 1985, e.g. pp. 21-6, 222-35; C. Van Onselen, *Chibaro: African Mine Labour in Southern Rhodesia 1900-1933*, London: Pluto Press, 1976, e.g. pp. 62, 66-7, 74-114.

Talking of markets and rich natural products, there is hardly a European Power which will not fight its way to the possession of spheres of influence which are reputed rich in gold and diamonds, particularly if the country belongs to an aboriginal race that cannot work the Maxim or the Long Tom. The cry of gold calls up the spirit of strife. The love of gold dissipates the love of man; for is not the love of gold the root of all evil? Ah! If it were not for the something which the Aborigines have which the white man wants, but cannot get otherwise than, if need be, by breaking the sixth and eighth Commandments at one spell, how dearly would the white man love his brethren the Aborigines of the waste places of the earth?[6]

Here Casely Hayford was alluding to the Europeans' belief that they were occupying Africa out of humane consideration for its people. This was a widespread belief; Europeans often held that economic exploitation was good for both colonisers and colonised. The anti-imperialists, who were always a minority swimming against a strong tide, had to contend with this conviction and with a confident belief in a superior European civilisation, reinforced by abundant writing about evils in Africa—the slave trade, especially in East Africa; "tribal wars", which were depicted as a common or indeed permanent state ended by the peace of colonialism; the real or alleged crimes of various African rulers, such as the Kings of Asante, Dahomey and Benin, who did preside over ceremonial human sacrifices, and the Khalifa (successor of the Mahdi) of the Sudan; and so on. To the constant evocation of such things Casely Hayford replied:

I do not personally approve of executions and slave-raiding, or of slavery in any shape or form. But what calls for loud protest is, that these should be made a cloak for cant—an apology for the use of the Maxim gun—when all the time the world knows that you are simply taking part in the scramble for the black man's country.[7]

There was a widespread idea that because certain evil things happened in Africa it was the duty of Europeans to march in and stop them, because power meant self-imposed duties towards weaker nations, whatever those nations thought themselves—the "white man's

---

6   J.E. Casely Hayford, *Gold Coast Native Institutions*, 1903, quoted in H.S. Wilson (ed.), *Origins of West African Nationalism*, London: Macmillan, 1969, p. 319.

7   Ibid., p. 333.

burden" (Rudyard Kipling), "*le devoir des races supérieures vis-à-vis des races inférieures*" (Jules Ferry). This merged into widespread murky ideas of the right of the stronger to dominate the weaker, often called "Social Darwinism" and expressed by such writers as Benjamin Kidd (*Social Evolution*, 1894). The belief in a scale of evolution towards "civilisation", a scale on which Africans were seen as very far down, was very general. Even critics of empire were very much influenced by such notions, which, however, were challenged by educated Africans.

While the Scramble for Africa was going on educated Africans were observing and commenting on it. There had been educated people, and highly educated ones, for centuries in Muslim Africa, which had the ancient universities of Qarawiyin in Morocco and al-Azhar in Egypt; the use of the term "educated" to mean "Western-educated" is wrong. But in the modern world order what counted was Western education, such as some Africans received from the 18th century but especially from the 19th, in the four British territories in West Africa occupied then and ruled as Crown Colonies—Sierra Leone, Gold Coast, Lagos and Gambia. Many of the Africans there were mission-educated and had considerable freedoms and opportunities under light-handed colonial rule, which the Sierra Leone Creoles—largely "Recaptives", people freed from slave ships by the Royal Navy after Britain abolished the slave trade in 1807—then regarded as fairly beneficial. The Creole community was a remarkable one that included teachers, clerks, lawyers, doctors, clergymen, editors and writers.[8] Creole traders operated along the West African coast and between there and Britain. Most Creoles were of Yoruba birth, and many settled in Lagos, annexed by Britain in 1861, which was close to their home areas. Some others settled in Gambia. In Gold Coast Colony, annexed in 1874, the Western-educated community had been developing since the 18th century and consisted mainly of indigenous Fante and Ga people, though some Sierra Leone Creoles settled there also; there and in Sierra Leone there were some elite families of part-European descent, but relatively few.

West Africans of this early elite moved, traded and intermarried among the four British coastal colonies and Liberia, where African American

8   C. Fyfe, *A History of Sierra Leone,* Oxford University Press, 1962; L. Spitzer, *The Creoles of Sierra Leone,* Madison and London: University of Wisconsin Press, 1974.

settlers had established their independent Republic in 1847. Along the coast they established their British-cultured and largely Christian communities (though there were always Muslims among them in Lagos), educated themselves and their children—often at Fourah Bay College in Freetown (opened in 1827) or in Britain—and founded newspapers of which the *Sierra Leone Weekly News*, published from 1884 to 1951, was just the most famous of many. Similarly, by the end of the 19th century there were African-owned newspapers in the Gold Coast, such as the *Gold Coast Methodist Times* and the *Gold Coast Independent*, while in Nigeria fifty-one newspapers were launched between 1880 and 1937.[9] Editors and owners of newspapers were among the most prominent elite figures, such as James Bright Davies (1848-1920), born in Freetown, who founded the *Gold Coast Independent* in 1895 and the *Nigerian Times* in Lagos in 1910; and the famous Ghanaian lawyer, journalist, editor, newspaper proprietor, writer and pioneer nationalist J.E. Casely Hayford.

Those elite Africans commonly believed as much as their European mentors in Western civilisation, and commonly thought that disseminating it was what Africa urgently needed. A historian of the early Nigerian press notes,

Themselves products of the missionary movement upon whose arguments of the correlations between Western civilisation and Christianity rested the foundations of their outlook and aspirations, the educated elite saw Christianity as the essential preliminary to the building in West Africa of a nation whose society would be modelled on that of the Western world.[10]

In the Gold Coast Colony Fantes of the elite urged the British to hurry up and occupy the Asante kingdom, the Fantes' traditional enemy and a pagan monarchy shocking to African Christians. However, some Asante princes received Western education with the help of the British; two of them, the brothers John and Albert Owusu Ansah, led the Asantehene's embassy to Britain in 1895, which was helped by, among others, a Gold Coast lawyer living in London, James Hutton

9   F.I. Omu, *Press and Politics in Nigeria 1880-1937*, Longman, 1978, p. 26.
10   Ibid., p. 117.

Brew,[11] but failed to stop the occupation of the Asante kingdom at the end of that year.

Another small community of Western-trained Africans grew up under the impact of Victorian humanitarianism in Cape Colony in South Africa. They had special reasons for accepting British rule, even if it meant self-government run by the local white settlers, since Africans—including also the King of Lesotho (Basutoland) who sought British protection and obtained it in 1868—saw this as at least preferable to the Afrikaners (Boers) who ran the independent inland states of Transvaal and Orange Free State.

France's major early possession in black Africa was in Senegal, where the people of a small coastal area—the "Four Communes" of St Louis, Dakar, Gorée and Rufisque—had fairly free lives like the Creoles in Freetown, though they did not initially have full French citizenship. They were as pro-French as Sierra Leoneans were pro-British. Many West Africans of the coastal communities followed the colonial occupation and worked well for the colonial administrations and firms as junior office workers, as people from Nyasaland, where missionaries had begun working in the 1870s, did over a wide area of Southern Africa, and many of the Duala people of German Kamerun (Cameroon), who had begun accepting Christianity and Western education before their chiefs signed the treaty establishing German rule in 1884, did after that date.

The most respected West African intellectual of his time, Edward Wilmot Blyden (1832-1912), was among the elite figures who approved Western colonialism. Such a combination of strong pride in African ancestry with acceptance of colonialism was quite common, another famous example being the much admired Ghanaian educationist James E.K. Aggrey (1875-1927), who spent much of his career in the USA.[12] Blyden, born in the Virgin Islands, moved in adult life between Sierra Leone and Liberia, belonging to both, during a career as a newspaper editor, Presbyterian clergyman, school principal, diplomat (twice Liberian Minister to the UK), scholar, politician (Liberia's Secretary of State

11   I. Wilks, *Asante in the Nineteenth Century: The Structure and Evolution of a Political Order*, CUP 1975, pp. 203-4, 554, 596-605, 612-13, 625-59.

12   K. King, "James E.K. Aggrey: Collaborator, Nationalist, Pan-African", *Canadian Journal of African Studies* vol. 3 no. 3, 1969, pp. 511-30.

for a time), traveller and writer.[13] His writings showed no opposition to colonisation, and the Americo-Liberian elite to which he belonged was one of the occupying powers in the Scramble for Africa; its state gradually subjugated the indigenous Africans of the hinterland and imposed colonial rule similar to neighbouring British and French rule.[14]

Loyalty to the colonial masters was typical of the elite, yet a common European response to it, and to the indispensable service given by African clerks, was mistrust and contempt for the "educated native". This was a striking feature of the colonial period in Africa; it became pathological at times, as colonial writings reveal. While it had been present earlier, it became more marked at the time of the occupation of the interior regions of Africa. In fact that occupation coincided with new discriminatory measures against Western-educated Africans. While some of these were appointed to Legislative Councils, such as the lawyer and writer John Mensah Sarbah (1864-1910) in 1901 and J.E. Casely Hayford in 1916 in Gold Coast Colony, such appointments provided only a forum for expression of elite views, with no power. In government service the upper administrative ranks were reserved to white people and African professionals were systematically excluded from positions they had been able to hold before. For example, after an inquiry into British West African medical services in 1901, African doctors were placed in a subordinate service with lower rank.[15] In British colonies the employment of educated Africans was under attack in Cape Colony, as well as West Africa, by the 1890s.[16] In Portuguese colonies, too, Africans were confined to the lower levels of government service and their status declined after a time of privilege in the coastal areas long occupied by Portugal.

African elite people resented such measures intensely. They were linked with a major change in the whole colonial system imposed by the

13   H. Lynch, *Edward Wilmot Blyden, Pan-Negro Patriot, 1832-1912*, London: Oxford University Press, 1967, especially chapters 4 and 9.

14   M.B. Akpan, *African Resistance in Liberia: the Vai and the Gola-Bandi*, Bremen: Liberia Working Group, 1988.

15   Spitzer (note 8), pp. 65-8; E.A. Ayandele, *Holy Johnson, Pioneer of African Nationalism, 1836-1917*, New York: Humanities Press, 1970, pp. 175-7; D. Kimble, *Politics in Ghana 1850-1928*, Oxford: Clarendon Press, pp. 97-101.

16   B. Willan, *Sol Plaatje: South African Nationalist 1876-1932*, London: Heinemann, 1984, pp. 30-31.

rapid occupation of most of the continent; the new system, with military conquest and then either direct domination or Britain's "Indirect Rule" through indigenous chiefs, was different in kind from the regime in Freetown or the Four Communes of Senegal. The response of elite Africans to this was not to stop working for the colonial masters, nor to encourage resistance to them. But there was a real sense of grievance and hurt. Some in British West Africa responded by calling for a revival of African culture among their own communities, which had adopted a good deal of British culture.[17] In the late 19th and early 20th centuries a sort of "cultural nationalism" was spread by such people as Blyden and another clergyman, a Nigerian of Recaptive Sierra Leonean parentage, David Brown Vincent, who renounced that name for a Yoruba one, Mojola Agbebi (1860-1917), and gave up European dress.[18]

Such a stance was not necessarily combined with any strong criticisms of colonialism, and West Africans who rejected this cultural nationalism still gave priority to responding to racism and asserting Africans' capacity. This was the elites' major preoccupation; it was a natural and reasonable one, but it led to assertion that Africans were as good as Europeans at everything—including running the white man's empire. To condemn white racism but approve of colonialism may seem contradictory from today's standpoint. But at the time racism seemed the number one concern to people who had adopted Western culture but felt spurned by their Western mentors—even in the institutions that had formed them, for there was the assertion of white supremacy in the Anglican and Methodist missionary churches.[19]

In the changed situation in the Anglican church in West Africa a Sierra Leone Recaptive, James Johnson (c.1838-1917), was still able to become Assistant Bishop of the Niger Delta in 1900. Besides defending Africans' role in church affairs, he was one West African elite figure who spoke out strongly against colonialism. He criticised oppression in the Congo Free State and South Africa, and nearer home protested at the British expedition against Ijebu (his Yoruba family's home kingdom)

---

17   Spitzer (note 8), pp. 16-34.

18   J. Ayo Langley, *Ideologies of Liberation in Black Africa 1856-1970*, London: Rex Collings, 1979, p. 77.

19   See for example Ayandele (note 15), *passim*.

in 1892 and defended resistance by the Ashantis.[20] In London in 1900 he said, "The European Governments have parted [sic] the Continent among themselves—by what law, by what right, I know not. Yes, but they have done it. It is undoubtedly the right of might over right, for they have a stronger power."[21] Other elite criticisms of the partition of Africa regularly appeared in the press. Nigerian newspapers criticised the Berlin Conference of 1884-85 (which set ground rules for the Scramble for African territory), the British expedition against Benin in 1897, and the French invasion of Dahomey in 1892.[22]

Like Bishop James Johnson, many African Christians might resent assertion of white supremacy in church affairs but still remained loyal to the mission-founded churches. But from the late 19th century independent African Christian churches and movements emerged. In South Africa such churches grew up through secession from mission Protestant churches from the 1880s. One founded in Pretoria in 1892 was called the Ethiopian Church, and within a few years the whole independent church movement in South Africa came to be called "Ethiopianism". The name "Ethiopia" was commonly used by African and Diaspora Christians to denote the whole continent, partly in reference to Psalm 67, verse 32: "Ambassadors shall come out of Egypt; Ethiopia shall soon stretch out her hands to God."[23] Other independent churches, not usually called Ethiopian (a term used mainly in southern Africa), spread to many countries, including the Congo and West Africa. In Nigeria the Baptist minister Mojola Agbebi founded a Native Baptist Church, declaring that Christianity in Africa must no longer be attached to European culture; its orientation must be not "London-ward and New York-ward but heaven-ward".[24]

Such movements commonly expressed resentment against missionary rather than colonial government rule, and preached obedience to,

20   Ibid., pp. 89-91, 192-217.

21   Ibid., p. 192.

22   Omu (note 9), pp. 124-7.

23   H. Pretorius and F. Jafta, "'A Branch Springs Out': African Initiated Churches", Ch. 12, pp. 211-26 in R. Elphick and R. Davenport (eds and compilers), *Christianity in South Africa: A Political, Social and Cultural History*, Oxford: James Currey and Cape Town: D. Philip, 1997.

24   S.K.B. Asante, *Pan-African Protest: West Africa and the Italo-Ethiopian Crisis 1934-1941*, London: Longman, 1977, pp. 12-13.

or at least passivity towards authority. But colonial and settler governments saw them as preachers of sedition and revolt. In fact suspicion of Ethiopianism, blamed in particular for the 1906 Natal Zulu rising, became a tangible phobia in South Africa at the beginning of the 20th century,[25] rather like the later phobia about Communism.

Mission-educated Africans were predominant in the early protests against colonial rule, which were quite separate from independent church movements. They constantly invoked Christian principles, especially against racism which was a major spur to protest. Besides protesting at exclusion from the higher ranks of government service, West Coast elite people condemned segregation measures introduced on the pretext of protecting white people against malaria, following the discovery of the link between mosquitoes and malaria by Ronald Ross. In Freetown segregation, initially suggested by Ross himself, led to creation of the whites-only Hill Station residential area early in the 20th century.[26] In Cameroon the Germans developed from 1911 a plan for segregation of the city of Douala, with almost all the Africans—at the time still mainly the indigenous Dualas—moved inland to make way for a modern European zone by the river front. Against strong opposition, the first eviction of a Duala district (Bonanjo, the district of the Bonadoo or Bell section of the Dualas) was carried out in March 1914.[27]

Africans' concern for their rights to their land, which lay behind the Duala protests, was strongly expressed everywhere. In Gold Coast local elite leaders, headed by Mensah Sarbah and the Rev. Samuel Attoh Ahuma (1863-1921), a leading clergyman and editor, formed the Aborigines' Rights Protection Society (ARPS) in 1897 to protest against a Lands Bill suspected of being a means for massive expropriation of African land (though that was probably not planned); it started its own newspaper, the *Gold Coast Aborigines,* edited by Attoh

---

25   Reflected in fiction in *Prester John* (1910) by John Buchan, who had been one of High Commissioner Alfred Milner's select team for the administration of the occupied Transvaal ("Milner's Kindergarten").

26   Spitzer (note 8), pp. 51-63.

27   R. Austen and J. Derrick, *Middlemen of the Cameroons Rivers,* Cambridge University Press, 1999, pp. 128-37. The name of the city is now normally spelt "Douala" and that of the people "Duala".

Ahuma, and organised a delegation to London. The Lands Bill was later withdrawn by Chamberlain.[28]

The Western-educated elite in South Africa was quite numerous by the turn of the century, and not confined to Cape Colony. It was subjected more than its counterparts in other parts of Africa, with the obvious exception of Liberia, to American influence. A number of black South Africans studied in the USA and were in direct contact with the Black American community whose affairs, in any case, were generally followed with interest by Africans then as later. The Scramble for Africa coincided with a deadly offensive against the Black people recently freed from slavery in the Southern USA: steady moves to deprive them of the vote, increasingly rigid "Jim Crow" segregation and discrimination, and constant horrific lynching, continued with impunity and terrorising African Americans into submission—3,224 were lynched between 1899 and 1918. The man who rose to be the most eminent Black American of the time, Booker T. Washington (1856-1915), urged his people to respond to all this by patient collaboration. In his famous speech at Atlanta in September 1895 he said they must avoid politics, accept the facts of white supremacy and segregation, and concentrate on practical education and hard work in order to improve their situation gradually. This was the ethos of the Tuskegee Institute which Washington headed in Alabama. His ideas were strongly contested by other Black American leaders, especially by the historian William Edward Burghardt Du Bois (1868-1963), who joined fellow activists to start the Niagara Movement in 1905 and then the National Association for the Advancement of Coloured People (NAACP) in 1909. Their approach was different: stressing the importance of black citizens having the vote, and aiming through publicity, petitions and organised political efforts to end the disabilities of Black Americans.[29]

The Rev. John L. Dube (1871-1946), from Natal, after study and ordination in the USA helped to launch in 1903 and then edit the first Zulu language newspaper, *Ilanga lase Natal* (The Natal Sun). In 1903,

---

28   Kimble (note 15), chapter IX.

29   John White, *Black Leadership in America: from Booker T. Washington to Jesse Jackson*, London: Longman, 1985, pp. 17-73; R. Wolters, *Du Bois and his Rivals*, Columbia, MO and London: Missouri University Press, 2002, especially pp. 40-76.

also, he founded the Zulu Christian Industrial School, renamed the Ohlange Institute, in conscious emulation of Tuskegee.[30] This was not the only example of Washington's influence in Africa; Tuskegee cooperated in educational schemes in Africa with the approval of the colonial rulers. But it is somewhat surprising that Africans should have been so influenced by the ideas of one who was criticised within his own community for preaching acceptance of a subordinate position; African elite protests against discrimination in government service were closer to the ideas of Du Bois, who said an intellectual "Talented Tenth" should lead the African Americans, and the NAACP.

Africans of the elite spoke up for their people when the reconciliation between British and Boers after the war of 1899-1902 led to the creation of the Union of South Africa as a white-supremacy state in 1910. During the negotiations leading to this union of Cape Colony, Natal, Transvaal and Orange Free State a South African Native Convention met to oppose parts of the draft constitution, and several delegates went to Britain including the prominent journalist and activist John Tengo Jabavu, Alfred Mangena (the first Black South African to qualify as an attorney in his country), the white politician W.P. Schreiner (former Prime Minister of Cape Colony, of the "Cape Liberal" tradition) and Mohandas K. Gandhi, the Indian lawyer who had won fame by leading Indians' protests against discrimination in Transvaal in 1907. The delegates secured no concessions for the non-whites in South Africa, though they added to pressure over the status of Bechuanaland, Basutoland and Swaziland, which were eventually excluded from the new Union.[31] The "colour-blind" franchise in Cape Colony (later Cape Province) was entrenched in the Constitution, but not extended to the other three territories. A few years later M.S. Molema (1892-1965), a Sotho South African doctor who had just graduated at Glasgow University and was to be a prominent activist, wrote:

Unreservedly, the Imperial Government has handed over all South African affairs, including absolute power over natives, to the now entirely self-governing

---

30   E. Hunt Davis Jr, "John L. Dube: A South African Exponent of Booker T. Washington", *Journal of African Studies* (University of California, Los Angeles), vol. 2 no. 4, 1975-76, pp. 497-528.

31   P. Walshe, *The Rise of African Nationalism in South Africa: The African National Congress 1912-1952*, London: C. Hurst & Co., 1970, pp. 22-4.

South Africa. That has removed from the native one sole just court of appeal, the fair and disinterested arbiter.[32]

The government of the Union, under the Boer general Louis Botha, soon introduced a Native Land Bill giving white people the sole right of land ownership over most of the country. To protest against this the South African Native National Congress (SANNC) was founded on 8 January 1912 at a conference at Bloemfontein. Dube became the first President of this party which was to become famous as the African National Congress, and Sol Plaatje (1876-1932), a pioneering African journalist who had owned and edited the newspaper *Koranta ea Becoana* and edited it in 1902-5, became the first Secretary General.[33] They and their colleagues were campaigners of a restrained, respectable and respectful sort, who had no impact on a determined racist regime. The Native Land Act was passed on 20 June 1913, outlawing land ownership for Africans except in "reserves" covering 7.3 per cent of the country's area (with a few small exceptions, and the possibility of some increase later); in the rest of the country sharecropping was outlawed and Africans staying on white agricultural land had to work for its owners for 90 days a year. Hundreds of thousands of people were evicted from their land immediately, with many more to follow; and a regime of repression and segregation was steadily imposed, including, for example, the increasing obligation for Africans to carry passes, to control all their movements.

The SANNC tried to secure some changes by sending a delegation to London in 1914, including Dube and Plaatje.[34] It met the Colonial Secretary, Sir Lewis Harcourt, but its protests achieved nothing, and then war intervened. The statement drafted by Plaatje aroused favourable comment in the British press, and Plaatje, who after war broke out stayed in England until 1917 and addressed many meetings, won widespread sympathy for his people's case;[35] but that was all. Generally,

---

32   M.S. Molema, *The Bantu Past and Present*, Edinburgh: W. Green & Son, 1920, p. 247.

33   Walshe (note 31), pp. 30-40; Willan (note 16), pp. 150-55.

34   Willan (note 16), pp. 168-80; Walshe (note 31), pp. 50-52; R. Whitehead, "The Aborigines' Protection Society and the Safeguarding of African Interests in Rhodesia, 1889-1930", DPhil, Oxford, 1975, pp. 118-69.

35   Willan (note 16), pp. 179-202.

when Africans sent delegations to the colonial capitals, they achieved little beyond sympathy expressed at meetings and in the press. However, such delegations were regularly seen in Europe at that time; the idea that an individual governor was to blame rather than the whole colonial system, and that one could go over his head to the centre of the empire, hoping to find a "fair and disinterested arbiter" there, persisted.

Duala paramount chiefs travelled to Germany in 1902, protesting about the restrictions on their people's produce trading, and one section of the Dualas, Akwa, sent a petition to the Chancellor and the Reichstag in 1905. Mpondo (or Mpundu) Dika, son of the Akwa paramount chief, sent two petitions in 1906 to the Chancellor and later spent some years in Germany, for a time editing a monthly magazine, *Elolombe ya Kamerun* ("the Cameroon Sun"); this was not a militant newspaper, but he did make contacts in Germany on his people's behalf.[36] Later, as the protest against land expropriation mounted, the Duala leaders sent Ngoso Din to Germany as their representative and engaged a German lawyer. Their efforts failed, and while earlier Duala protests may have contributed to the sacking of Governor Puttkamer of Kamerun in 1907,[37] this was a rare success if so. Trusting and backing the "man on the spot" was the rule.

Yet Africans knew that there were sympathisers in Europe, and continued regular efforts to appeal to them. By the early 20th century there were a number of African residents in Western countries, including students but also longer-term residents.[38] Some acted as representatives or spokesmen for their countries—such as Alfred Mangena (1879-1924), when a law student in London, on behalf of the Zulu ruler Dinuzulu—or campaigned about African issues generally.

A Pan-African Conference was organised in London in July 1900 on the initiative of Henry Sylvester Williams, a Trinidadian lawyer, and his African Association founded three years before. This was the first of

---

36   Austen and Derrick (note 27), pp. 107-8, 127-8; A. Rüger, "Die Duala und Der Kolonialmacht 1884-1914", Vol. 2, pp. 184-257 in H. Stöcker (ed.), *Kamerun unter Deutsche Kolonialherrschaft*, Berlin: Rütten und Loening, Vol. 1 1960, Vol. 2 1968.

37   Austen and Derrick (note 27), pp. 106-8; Rüger (note 36), p. 214.

38   See Ray Jenkins, "Gold Coasters Overseas, 1880-1919: With Specific Reference to Their Activities in Britain", *Immigrants and Minorities* Vol. 4 no. 3, November 1985, pp. 5-42.

several Pan-African Conferences, but Pan-Africanism started some time before, not as an organised movement but as a widespread sentiment of solidarity among Africans, West Indians and African Americans. The many studies of Pan-Africanism[39] show that it was propagated especially by people of the Diaspora such as Williams and W.E.B. Du Bois, who attended the 1900 Conference, but a few Africans were there, notably Bishop James Johnson. A number of Caribbean people attended including George Christian and John Alcindor, and some people resident in Britain, notably Samuel Coleridge-Taylor, the British composer (son of a Sierra Leonean doctor, Dr Daniel Taylor, and a white British mother). The gathering examined many aspects of the continent where the partition and occupation were drawing to a close. Colonialist policies in South Africa and the Rhodesias were criticised, and a resolution called on Britain to crown the work of Wilberforce, David Livingstone, and Bishop Colenso (who had stood up for Zulus), by giving as soon as practicable "The rights of responsible government to the Black Colonies of Africa and the West Indies."[40] A Haitian, Benito Sylvain, attended the Conference as a representative of Ethiopia; later, in Rome in 1905, he founded a—quickly forgotten—Catholic organisation aimed at "fighting unjust and unreasonable colour prejudice, safeguarding African natives' legitimate rights against settlers, allowing the Blacks themselves the opportunity to rise by their own strength."[41]

Africans in Europe had particularly good contact with events in the rest of the world, such as India, whose nationalist movement always interested them greatly; the Indian National Congress (INC) was founded in 1885. But literate people back in Africa were in touch with world events also. Africans read with interest of the victory of Japan, a non-

---

39   J.A. Langley, *Pan-Africanism and Nationalism in West Africa 1900-1945*, OUP, 1973; Immanuel Geiss, *The Pan-African Movement*, tr. Ann Keep, London: Methuen, 1974; S.K.B. Asante (note 24); Peter O. Esedebe, *Pan-Africanism: The Idea and the Movement, 1776-1991*, 2nd ed. Washington: Howard University Press, 1994; O.C. Mathurin, *Henry Sylvester Williams and the Origins of the pan-African Movement, 1869-1911*, Westport, CT and London: Greenwood Press, 1976; Paul Gilroy, *The Black Atlantic: Modernity and Double Consciousness*, Cambridge, MA: Harvard UP, 1993, Ch. 3, "'Cheer the Weary Traveller': W.E.B. Du Bois, Germany and the Politics of (Dis)placement", pp. 111-45.

40   Esedebe (note 39), pp. 41-8; Geiss (note 39), pp. 182-92

41   C. Ageron, *L'Anticolonialisme en France de 1871 à 1914*, Paris: Presses Universitaires de France, 1973, p. 37.

European power, over one of the European colonising countries, Russia, in 1905, and in the Gold Coast, Nigeria, Algeria and Madagascar wrote admiringly of Japan's progress. Even more impressive for Africans was the victory of fellow Africans in Ethiopia in 1896.

In 1912 a number of Africans in London joined to start a monthly magazine, the *African Times and Orient Review*. The main sponsor was a Sierra Leonean businessman, J. Eldred Taylor, while other West Africans including Casely Hayford provided financial support, which did not prevent it collapsing in August 1914 soon after going weekly. The editor was a remarkable Egyptian of Sudanese origin, Duse Mohammed Ali (1866-1945).[42] Living mostly in Britain from the age of nine, and working as a playwright, actor and journalist there, he followed the events of his country under British rule, and in 1911 published a strong denunciation of that rule and defence of the Egyptian nationalist cause, *In the Land of the Pharaohs*.[43] Duse wrote of British imperialism generally:

Thus England, in the multiplicity of her conquests, whereby trade is advanced, plutocrats wax rich and opulent, and in the interests of "civilisation" and "Christianisation" of primitive races, and races that are not primitive, who are held in tutelage and subjection "for their moral welfare", so that there may be diamond princes, and cotton kings, and other grades of a most ignoble band of financial aristocrats, is only paving the path of materialism with the agonised groans of human subjugation, at the end of which lies her utter dissolution.[44]

But the *African Times and Orient Review*, though critical of British rule in West Africa, did not adopt the same nationalist tone as Duse used in dealing with his home country.

Before 1914 no sub-Saharan African country had anything like a nationalist party until the SANNC was founded in 1912; but Egypt had the Egyptian National Party founded in 1892 and headed for several years by Mustafa Kamil (1874-1908). A popular party for several years, it called plainly for the British to leave, backed by Kamil's news-

---

42   Geiss (note 39), pp. 221-30; I. Duffield, "The Business Activities of Duse Mohammed Ali", *Journal of the Historical Society of Nigeria* vol. IV no. 4, June 1969, pp. 571-600.

43   Published by Stanley Paul & Co., London, 1911; reprinted 1968 London: Frank Cass, with new introduction by Khalil Mahmud.

44   Ibid., pp. 215-16.

paper *al Liwa'*. After Kamil's early death the National Party—deprived
of French support after the Entente Cordiale of 1904—declined, with
many Egyptians following the rival Constitutional Reform Party while
the Khedive, Abbas Hilmi, distanced himself from the National Party
that he had at first supported. The party and *al Liwa'* continued, but by
1914 the party was no longer so powerful, and its leader, Muhammad
Farid, was in exile.[45]

The Egyptian nationalists proclaimed loyalty to the Ottoman Sultan,
still the nominal overlord of Egypt even though Britain in fact ruled
the country from 1882. Elsewhere in North Africa there was support
for Sultan Abdul Hamid II, encouraged by him, especially in his regular clashes with Western countries. This sentiment, commonly called
"Pan-Islamism", was expressed by Muslim activists such as the Persian Jamal al-Din Afghani and the Egyptian Muhammad Abduh, who
briefly edited a militant newspaper, *Al 'Urwa al Wuqthah*, from Paris
in 1884. Pan-Islamism was particularly aroused in support of the Ottoman Sultan-Caliph, but it could simply be the traditional sentiment of
international Muslim solidarity;[46] it was aroused to an unusual pitch by
the Italian invasion of Ottoman Libya in 1911.

Political pan-Islamism overlapped with the Islamic reform and revival movement that spread over many countries from the late 19th century, a movement for a return to the true principles of Islam which, its
advocates said, should encourage Muslims to adopt all the West's scientific and technological knowledge. That movement's outstanding leader
for some years was Abduh (1849-1905), a scholar, judge and writer
who, after abandoning his earlier militancy, became Mufti of Egypt in
1899; he wrote, "...the unbelievers must be fought with the same means

45   A. Goldschmidt, Jr, "The Egyptian Nationalist Party: 1892-1919", pp. 308-33
      in P.M. Holt (ed.), *Political and Social Change in Modern Egypt: Historical Stud-
      ies from the Ottoman Conquest to the United Arab Republic*, London: Oxford
      University Press, 1968; J. Berque, *Egypt: Imperialism and Revolution*, London:
      Faber & Faber, 1972, pp. 235-8, 248-63.

46   C.C. Adams, *Islam and Modernism in Egypt*, Oxford University Press, 1933,
      pp. 1-13, 58-62, 135-6; Berque (note 45), pp. 214-20; M-S. Lejri, *Evolution
      du mouvement national tunisien*, Vol. 1, Tunis: Maison Tunisienne de l'Edition,
      1974, pp. 23-4, 115-20; N.R. Keddie, "The Pan-Islamic Appeal: Afghani and
      Abdülhamid II", *Middle Eastern Studies* vol. 3 no. 1, October 1966, pp. 46-67;
      Jamal M. Ahmed, *The Intellectual Origins of Egyptian Nationalism*, OUP for
      RIIA 1960, especially Ch. III.

which they employ for fighting against Islam. It is included in this, that one must rival them in our time in the manufacture of cannon and rifles, of warships and airships, and other kinds of implements of war."[47] His influence was profound, and his followers led by the Syrian Rashid Rida, who lived in Egypt and edited the influential journal *Al-Manar* there, developed the Salafiyya movement in several Muslim countries: a movement which aimed at returning to true Islamic teaching, but inevitably encouraged Muslim dissatisfaction with rule by unbelievers in several Islamic countries.

More directly, Abduh's ideas influenced Kamil, who wrote in 1898: "If we examine seriously and attentively the causes of the decadence of the Muslims in all the countries of the world, and of the loss of their independence and greatness, we find that they are no other than our departure far from the sound principles of Islam";[48] and Zaghlul Pasha, who was to lead Egypt to (qualified) independence in 1922. Similar ideas spread in Tunisia before the French occupation in 1881. An elite of leading Muslims favouring reform and modernisation initially accepted French rule. A Parti pour l'Evolution de la Tunisie, commonly called the Jeunes Tunisiens, was founded in 1907 by those elite figures favouring Islamic reform and acceptance of Western learning and science, and started a newspaper, *Le Tunisien*. In 1912 the party's leaders backed a strike by Tunis tram workers, and their leaders Ali Bach-Hamba, editor of *Le Tunisien,* and Abdelaziz al Tha'alibi, editor of the newspaper's Arabic edition, were deported with two others, and martial law was declared, to last for ten years.[49]

Although Algeria was different in legal status, in French eyes, from Tunisia—being considered as three departments of France, Algiers, Oran and Constantine—the situation of the indigenous Muslim people was similar in both countries. In both it was virtually impossible for a practising Muslim to become a French citizen, because the rules required renouncing of Islamic "personal status" so that marriage, inheri-

---

47   Adams (note 46), p. 136; Berque (note 46), pp. 214-20.

48   Moustafa Kamel Pacha, *Egyptiens et Anglais*, Paris: Perrin et Cie, 1906, p. 205.

49   Lejri (note 46), pp. 125-52; S. Zmerli, *Les Successeurs*, Tunis: Maison Tunisienne de l'Edition, 1967 (biographies of leading nationalists); D. Goldstein, *Libération ou annexion: aux chemins croisés de l'histoire tunisienne 1914-1922*, Tunis: Maison Tunisienne de l'Edition, 1978, pp. 17-48.

tance, and other matters of personal life should be governed by French civil law alone; the Tunisian nationalists thought it was apostasy for a Muslim to accept naturalisation on the French terms. The Jeunes Algériens, a group of elite protesters expressing their views from 1909 in the newspaper *L'Islam* and in other newspapers, called for easier French naturalisation (though they were not specific about the Islamic "personal status" question), and for extension of the vote to more Muslims, greater local government representation for Muslims, and reforms in the discriminatory taxation system and in the Indigénat, the special summary penal code applied to Muslim Algerians. These and other demands were expressed by a delegation of Algerians, mostly municipal councillors, to Paris, which was received by Prime Minister Poincaré on 18 June 1912. They were all in the direction of greater integration within France.[50] The French-cultured Jeunes Algériens were suspect to some other Muslims, but from that time on they became more Islamic in outlook under the influence of Emir Khaled (1875-1936), a grandson of the Emir Abdelkader who had fought against the original French occupation. Khaled (of whom more later) had served for years in the French army, and was a most loyal protest leader. But he was denounced by the French-Algerian settlers, and often protests by Muslims—for example, the protests of many Algerians against military conscription—aroused the constant French phobia about Islam.

Other colonial rulers shared that phobia. However loyal Muslim traditional rulers might be, in Northern Nigeria for example, there were always fears of Mahdism—both in the Sudan, where the British had defeated the Mahdist state in 1896-98, and elsewhere—and Pan-Islamism. Both of these were seen as subversive ideologies that might lead "loyal natives" astray, just as Communism was to be seen a few years later. The French were afraid of "Pan-Islamist" agitation from an early stage, for example suspecting a wide Islamic conspiracy linked to Alfa Yaya in Guinea, and their apprehensions mounted during the Turco-Italian war of 1911-12.[51] Some Muslims from other countries did help the Turkish and Libyan resistance where possible.

50   A. Koulakssis and G. Meynier, *L'Emir Khaled premier Za'im? Identité algérienne et colonialisme français*, Paris: Harmattan, 1987, pp. 71-3.
51   Harrison (note 3), pp. 29-117.

The obsessive French idea that Islam was incompatible with French citizenship had effects in Senegal. Among the unique community of a few thousands in the Four Communes which had the vote—electing local councils, a General Council, and a deputy in the French National Assembly—and enjoyed considerable liberty expressed in a free press (especially *La Démocratie du Sénégal*, founded in 1913), an elite of part-African, part-European descent and Catholic faith, the Creoles or *assimilés*, was for long dominant. But the majority in that community were those called the Originaires (or often called *évolués* by the French), Muslims who had the vote and many French citizens' privileges, but not actual citizenship. A decree on naturalisation in French West Africa (Afrique Occidentale Française, AOF) in 1912, as applied by the authorities, made it very difficult for African *sujets* of any religion to become citizens. And the government also took measures to reduce the Senegal *évolués*' privileges.

In response Originaires voters helped secure the victory of Blaise Diagne in elections for a new deputy for Senegal in the French National Assembly, in April-May 1914. After a career in the French colonial Customs service Diagne (1872-1934) stood as the candidate of a political club of teachers, clerks and other Western-educated people, the Jeunes Sénégalais, formed two years earlier.[52] Diagne was the first black African to represent Senegal, the previous deputies having been white or (in the Senegalese sense of that word) Creole.[53] He had been noted as a defender of Africans and troublemaker for his superiors while working for various colonial governments, and as a deputy was to take up Africans' grievances and problems, while many Africans under French rule felt inspired and encouraged by his success. But Diagne saw himself as, and proved to be, a true Frenchman.

---

52 G. Wesley Johnson, *The Emergence of Black Politics in Senegal: The Struggle for Power in the Four Communes, 1900-1920*, Stanford, CA: Stanford University Press, 1971, pp. 119-72; Alice L. Conklin, *A Mission to Civilize: the Republican Idea of Empire in France and West Africa, 1895-1930*, Stanford, CA: Stanford University Press, 1997, pp. 151-5.

53 That is, of mixed European and African parentage. There is no acceptable term in English usage for people of such parentage, as there is in French and Portuguese (*métis, mestiço*). Various terms used at the time described in this book are avoided in these pages. The word "Creole" has various meanings, not the same one in Senegal as in Sierra Leone.

Diagne's loyalty was typical of the elite all over the continent. But choosing to submit to colonial rule and make the best of it did not mean having any illusions about it, or despising African traditions and customs. On the contrary, African writers often sought to defend those, such as Blyden (mentioned earlier), Mensah Sarbah in his books *Fanti Customary Laws* (1897) and *Fanti National Constitutions* (1906), and Attoh Ahuma in *The Gold Coast Nation and National Consciousness* (1911). The early elite communities can be seen as preparing the way for later nationalists, including the radical campaigners of the inter-war years. Even though their members were loud in proclaiming loyalty, and many of them devoted little time to politics anyway, among them a spirit of criticism and dissent always remained. This was clear particularly in their newspapers, which were a thorn in the side of the colonial rulers, in Nigeria and Egypt especially.

But the protest activity, all told, was not very radical. Making demands that would ultimately weaken colonial rule was one thing, radical condemnation to encourage efforts to end colonial rule soon was another. That was to come later.

Europeans against empire

Throughout the centuries of European imperialism there were some Europeans who criticised it. But it needs to be recalled again that many of them opposed colonisation from the viewpoint of the colonising country's self-interest, commonly condemning it as a waste of money and European lives.[54] The present work is interested not in them but in others who condemned enslavement, oppression and robbery of the indigenous peoples. Their commonly recognised and honoured pioneer was Bartolomé de Las Casas, who condemned and tried to stop the genocidal treatment of the Indians in the early years of Spanish rule in the Caribbean, where he spent many years as priest and bishop. The Spanish Dominican theologian Francisco de Vitoria examined the justification for Spanish subjugation of the Indians in terms of Catholic theology, in a series of lectures in 1539, and although his conclusions were

---

54   This is made clear in Marcel Merle's collection of excerpts from anti-colonial writings, *L'anticolonialisme européen de Las Casas à Marx*, Paris: Armand Colin, 1969; but he shows that many writers' arguments and ideas were complex. His selection only goes up to the mid-19th century.

very cautious and academic they effectively condemned colonisation as it had been carried out in Spanish America, declaring that the Indians' paganism was not a justification for aggressive war against them.

The African slave trade can be considered an early and prolonged imperialist operation, and those who condemned the monstrous evils of the slave trade on moral grounds shared the basic idea—of equal rights for all men—of the later anti-imperialists. At first they were isolated individuals, including Quakers in England and North America; one Quaker—Thomas Challeley of Virginia—declared in 1738, referring to the American Indians, "...no people, according to our own principle, which is according to the glorious Gospel of our dear and holy Lord Jesus Christ, ought to take away or settle on other men's land."[55] Campaigning against the slave trade grew rapidly in England in the late 18th century and led to the abolition of the trade by Britain, the greatest slave-trading nation in the previous century, in 1807. Then campaigns were directed against the continued trade in slaves by other European countries, and against the institution of slavery itself, which was abolished in British territories in 1834.

Protests against slavery naturally merged with protests against other ill-treatment, short of actual enslavement, of Africans, Asians and people of the Pacific islands. The Aborigines' Protection Society (APS) was founded in England in 1837. Like the British and Foreign Anti-Slavery Society, founded in 1824, it was a product of Evangelical Christian concern, and the societies' campaigning was allied with the efforts of many Protestant missionary bodies in the 19th century. As missionary and humanitarian societies often held annual May meetings at Exeter Hall in the Strand in London, "Exeter Hall" became a general term for pressure on behalf of African victims of imperialism.

Such pressure was part of the imperialist scene in Queen Victoria's time. When the aggressive phase of imperialism began in the 1870s, there were strong protests by humanitarian and missionary lobbies against, for example, Henry Stanley's expeditions—like marauding military campaigns—which paved the way for Leopold II's rule in the Congo. Under its well known Secretary from 1889 to his death in 1909, Henry Fox-Bourne, the APS made protests, for example, over the

---

55   E.W. Kelsey, *Friends of the Indians 1655-1917*, Philadelphia, 1917, p. 51.

Ijebu expedition of 1892, and publicised many abuses in its journal *The Aborigines' Friend*. These campaigns were continued after the APS was merged with the Anti-Slavery Society in 1909, by the combined Anti-Slavery and Aborigines Protection Society (ASAPS) and its journal, the *Anti-Slavery Reporter and Aborigines' Friend*.[56]

Missionaries were noted critics of ill-treatment of Africans—individually, through their mission societies, and through the humanitarian groups—criticising settlers, notably the Afrikaners, and businesses as well as colonial officialdom and such aggressive empire-builders as Cecil Rhodes. Missions quarrelled with colonial governments on many other issues also, and relations were often poor.[57] Colonial officials and propagandists knew that mission education was teaching Africans to be less docile, and often wanted it restricted or banned; Frederick Lugard's attitude as High Commissioner for Northern Nigeria (1900-7) and Governor-General of unified Nigeria (1912-18) was a noted example. Lugard, Rhodes and Sir Harry Johnston (a leading empire-builder in Nyasaland in particular) were agnostics, and imperialism was not so closely linked with spreading of the Gospel as Africans sometimes thought, such as Mojola Agbebi, a clergyman himself, who in 1902 referred to Christianity as "a religion which points with one hand to skies, bidding you 'lay up for yourselves treasures in heaven', and while you are looking up grabs all your worldly goods with the other hand, seizes your ancestral lands, labels your forests, and places your patrimony under inexplicable legislation."[58] In 1895-96 the Freethinkers of the Third French Republic attacked and defeated the Christian Queen of Madagascar; both French and British colonial rulers defended a *secular* idea of "civilisation".

However, missionaries and other churchmen generally accepted or favoured colonialism. They shared many colonialist attitudes, even towards African Christians. Many European churchmen had the trusting

56   K.D. Nworah, "The Aborigines' Protection Society, 1889-1909: A Pressure Group in Colonial Policy", *Canadian Journal of African Studies* Vol. V no. 1, 1971, pp. 74-91.

57   See e.g. H. Rudin, *Germans in the Cameroons*, Yale University Press, 1938, reprint 1968, pp. 221, 318-19, 376-80, 399-401; John McCracken, *Politics and Christianity in Malawi 1875-1940*, new edition Blantyre: Christian Literature Association in Malawi, 2000, especially pp. 197-225.

58   Quoted in Langley, *Ideologies* (note 18), p. 77.

attitude of Bishop Ingham of Freetown to colonialism: "Money, it is to be feared, is the prime consideration, but a sense of responsibility exists towards the native tribes in and around the colonies and protectorates now in process of formation."[59] Besides telling people always to obey "Caesar" (as churchmen have usually done everywhere), missionaries often told Africans to see colonial rule in particular as a blessing.

But if the missionaries who exposed and condemned and lobbied against forced labour, land expropriation and other ill-treatment commonly favoured a better sort of colonialism, this did not make that work any less valuable at a time when nobody else was defending the African victims. In the Congo Free State missionaries were, for the first few years, mainly responsible for publicising the atrocities that followed the forcible wild rubber collection over huge areas covered by the Domaine de la Couronne, directly owned and controlled by King Leopold, or in the hands of concessionary companies in which the King had shares. Agents of the companies or the state were given unlimited powers and used troops to force people to get every last ounce of rubber from every corner of the forest in huge areas, often by seizing women and children as hostages; troops commonly cut off the hands of people who tried to fight back; millions are estimated to have died.[60] Protestant missionaries took the lead in exposing these crimes in the Congo and the attitude of many Catholic ones was deplorable, though some of them did speak out there and in Cameroon.[61]

An Anglican bishop of Natal, John William Colenso (1814-83), consistently defended the Zulus and condemned British actions, as in a famous sermon after Isandhlwana in January 1879.[62] His advocacy was continued by his children, especially his daughter Harriette (1847-1932), a missionary, who declared in 1897:

59   E.G. Ingham, *Sierra Leone After a Hundred Years*, London: Seeley & Co., 1894, p. 356.

60   E.D. Morel, *Red Rubber*, London, 1906, 3rd Edition London: Fisher Unwin, 1907; A. Hochschild, *King Leopold's Ghost*, Boston: Houghton Mifflin, 1998, especially Chapters 7-15.

61   Ageron (note 41), pp. 36, 88-9.

62   J. Guy, *The Heretic: A Study of the Life of John William Colenso 1814-1883*, Pietermaritzburg: University of Natal Press, 1983, pp. 275-80.

What is the meaning—the spirit of this scramble for Africa? In whatever form it shows itself—as the lust for power domineering or the lust for gold in dividends—the Scylla of Chartered Companies, or the Charybdis of Imperialism—is the spirit of that scramble—is the spirit of that scramble anything but the spirit of unbelief—the worship of the lower self, of the only devil which is real?[63]

Arthur Shearley Cripps (1869-1952), an Anglican Franciscan missionary in Southern Rhodesia, defended Africans constantly, against churchmen's race prejudice as well as government ill-treatment, especially the unjust land allocation.[64]

The common missionary and humanitarian view was the one already indicated: that colonial rule should be accepted but must respect rules of decent treatment of the "natives", and the form of colonial rule most likely to do this must be preferred. That view was adopted by many politicians also.

Socialists in all Western countries, including those who formed the Labour Representation Committee (LRC)—nucleus of the Labour Party—in Britain in 1900, were generally unsympathetic to imperialism. Socialist parties emerged at the very time of the imperialist Scramble, which went ahead without regard for them; they could thus decide freely what attitude to take to it, while the Liberals in Britain and the Radicals in France, both often critical of imperialism before, came to power and accepted the colonial empires. But the question for left-wing parties was, what should their attitude be?

The common response was to accept colonial rule—not, that is, to demand immediate evacuation of the colonies—but insist that it really must be for the good of the "natives" or at least not highly oppressive towards them. This could mean strong condemnation of some imperialist actions. For Hobson and many others the Boer War of 1899-1902 was a particularly outrageous imperialist action. While that war aroused bellicose patriotic feelings seldom if ever seen before in Britain, it also aroused a strong moral protest movement involving clear condemna-

---

63   Quoted in J. Guy, *The View Across the River: Harriette Colenso and the Zulu Struggle against Imperialism*, Oxford: James Currey and Charlottesville: University Press of Virginia, 2001, p. 411. By "imperialism" Harriette Colenso meant imposition of colonial rule as opposed to Chartered Company rule. See ibid., chapters 18-29 on her campaign on behalf of the Zulu ruler Dinuzulu.

64   D.V. Steene, *God's Irregular: Arthur Shearley Cripps*, SPCK, 1973.

tion of aggression against independent states, and of the role of the Rand capitalists and imperialist politicians, above all Chamberlain.[65]

In view of all that happened in South Africa later, it seems amazing that the liberal, left-wing, anti-capitalist and moralistic condemnations of the Boer War, depicting the Boers solely as victims, showed so little concern for the Boers' treatment of Africans, for this was already well enough known; Africans of the South African elite community, and British missionaries such as Livingstone, had been denouncing it for a century. And there was more outrage over aggression against two white Afrikaner republics than over comparable aggression against black African kingdoms. But one who attacked imperial aggression generally was the Liberal MP and newspaper proprietor Henry Labouchere (1839-1911), who declared in 1887 that the British were "without exception the greatest robbers and marauders in regard to...annexations that ever existed," being "worse than other countries" because they plundered hypocritically and always pretended that it was "for other people's good". In 1893 he called for withdrawal from Uganda and said that the "Khedive and people of Egypt...have a laudable desire for national independence; they want Home Rule, precisely as the Irish want Home Rule, and...they ought to have it, just as the Irish ought to have it." He criticised the Ashanti expedition of 1896, and constantly attacked the South African business magnates and Rhodes' BSAC.[66]

In parliamentary discussions of the colonies Sir Charles Dilke, Herbert Samuel and other Liberals showed concern for years over the treatment of Africans in South Africa, Kenya and the Congo, but after the Liberals took power in 1906 African causes were increasingly taken up by Labour MPs; they put 300 parliamentary questions on India, 200 on South Africa, and several on Egypt and other colonial areas between 1906 and 1914.[67] The Independent Labour Party (ILP) founded in 1893, which remained a separate organisation even though its MPs belonged also to the larger Labour Party created in 1906, was for decades Britain' main left-wing force, with working-class roots and a militant

---

65 R. Price, *An Imperial War and the British Working Class*, London: Routledge & Kegan Paul, 1972, *passim*, e.g. pp. 16-17, 19-43, 46, 71, 130.

66 R.J. Hind, *Henry Labouchere and the Empire*, London: Athlone Press, 1972, pp. 15, 19, 34; B. Porter, *Critics of Empire*, London: Macmillan, 1968, p. 85.

67 Porter (note 66), pp. 299-303, 306-7.

outlook; for long it was the principal anti-imperialist party in Britain. In contrast the quiet intellectuals of the Fabian Society were divided on the Boer War; Beatrice Webb recalled later that Ramsay MacDonald and Sydney Olivier were opposed to the war, Bernard Shaw "almost in favour", and her husband Sidney Webb in the middle.[68]

Sidney Webb was to remain a cautious advocate of improved colonialism, while Olivier (1859-1943) was a colonial official who became Colonial Secretary of Jamaica in 1899 and later Governor of Jamaica from 1907 to 1913. Shaw was always to voice provocatively independent views on imperialism as on every subject, but a booklet he drafted for the 1900 elections, *Fabianism and the Empire*, set out the basic principles of what became accepted un-militant left-wing views on colonialism. These included "the fundamental principles of responsibility towards colonial peoples, defence of indigenous peoples against exploitation by settlers, accountability in some form to other world powers for administration of dependent territories, abstention from economic exploitation of other members of the colonial empire, and the confederation of empire being used as an instrument of world peace...".[69] Ramsay MacDonald, who was to become leader of the Labour Party for the first time from 1911 to 1914, said in a short essay on *Labour and the Empire*—giving his personal views—in 1907, "The Labour Party...no more thinks of discussing whether the Stuarts should be restored to the throne than it does of debating whether we should break the Empire to pieces."[70]

But Labour politicians could be sympathetic, if unable to promise much. Keir Hardie, founder of the ILP in 1893 and Chairman of the Parliamentary Labour Party (and as such, at that time, leader of the Labour Party) in 1906-8, wrote to Herbert Bankole-Bright, a Sierra Leonean medical student at Edinburgh, in 1906, "I hope the day will speedily come when your race will be able to defend itself against the barbarities being perpetrated against it by hypocritical whites, who re-

---

68   P. Pugh, *Educate, Agitate, Organize: 100 Years of Fabian Socialism*, London: Methuen, 1984, p. 77; M. Cole, *The Story of Fabian Socialism*, London: Heinemann, 1961, p. 100.

69   Pugh (note 68), p. 81; Porter (note 66), pp. 116-17.

70   J. Ramsay MacDonald, *Labour and the Empire*, London: George Allen, 1907, reprinted with introduction by P. Cain, London: Routledge/Thoemmes, 1998 ("The Empire and its Critics, 1899-1939" series).

gard the blackman as having been created in order that they might exploit him for their own advantages."[71]

Individual writers and journalists became noted critics of colonial rule over various specific countries. Wilfred Scawen Blunt (1840-1922), a lobbyist on behalf of Egypt against British rule and a friend of Abduh, wrote in 1907 the *Secret History of the British Occupation of Egypt*. The journalist E.D. Morel (1873-1924) achieved lasting fame in the ranks of campaigning journalists for bringing the nightmare regime of Leopold II in the Congo Free State to the world's attention. After several years of energetic campaigning, backed by missionaries' revelations and a report by the British Consul Roger Casement in 1903, Morel founded the Congo Reform Association (CRA) in 1904 and published his book *Red Rubber* in 1906, among other exposés of the atrocities. This single-issue campaigning organisation exposed the Congo Free State crimes in Britain and other countries; consciously following the tradition of the slave trade and slavery abolitionists, it was one of the most effective humanitarian lobbying organisations since them.[72]

However, Morel was not opposed to colonialism as such—he admired Lugard's government of Northern Nigeria in particular—and neither were the well-known public figures who backed the CRA, such as Johnston who wrote a Foreword to *Red Rubber*. The CRA sought to replace Leopold II's personal tyranny with a more conventional form of colonial rule by the Belgian state, and this was achieved in 1908.

Morel also campaigned against the French Congo's reproduction of the Leopoldian system, whereby forty concessionary companies were allocated in all nearly 80 per cent of the area of Middle Congo, Ubangi-Shari and Gabon, and were given monopolies over exploitation of wild rubber and ivory in particular, with unlimited powers to force Africans to find them; British firms trying to conduct normal trade with Africans were squeezed out and Morel took up their case.[73] Another campaign

71   Akintola J.G. Wyse, *H.C. Bankole-Bright and Politics in Colonial Sierra Leone, 1919-1958*, Cambridge University Press, 1990, p. 10.

72   Hochschild (note 60), pp. 177-224; C. Cline, *E.D. Morel 1873-1924: The Strategies of Protest*, Belfast: Blackstaff Press, 1980, pp. 21-79.

73   Félicien Challaye, *Le Congo français: La question internationale du Congo*, Paris: Félix Alcan, 1909, especially Part Two, pp. 162-239; R.A. Austen and R. Headrick, "Equatorial Africa under Colonial Rule," pp. 27-94 in D. Birmingham and P.M. Martin (eds), *History of Central Africa*, Volume Two (Long-

against extreme exploitation was waged in Britain over some years from 1906 to 1913, relating to the shipment of Angolan forced labourers by the Portuguese to São Tomé for work on cocoa plantations. This was exposed by Henry Nevinson (1856-1941), a journalist, writer, pacifist and early Labour Party stalwart, in his 1906 book *A Modern Slavery*, and by George and William Cadbury, whose firm bought large amounts of São Tomé cocoa but halted purchases during the campaign against what amounted to slavery on the island, which was the main world producer.[74]

Granted that campaigners on behalf of victims of colonialism did not question colonialism as such, it is still remarkable that their protests could strike a chord in Britain at the height of the imperialist era. One needs to recall the common mentality in Europe at that time. In Britain great numbers of people were swallowing and repeating racist ideas, imbibing Kipling, writing and reading boys' adventure stories starring "hostile tribesmen", sniggering about cannibals, discussing outlandish and offensive theories about different races, gaping at Africans displayed as exhibits at major exhibitions.[75] Indeed the Rev. John Harris (1874-1940), who after working in the Congo Free State and helping expose the crimes there became Secretary to the CRA and then Organising Secretary of the ASAPS in 1910, could well write in 1912, "Certainly the African, modelled upon a combination of the reports of travellers, officials and missionaries, is a creature the devil himself would disown."[76] And yet protest campaigns about colonial crimes against Africans could arouse support. The least one can say is that not everybody was influenced only by racist and superior attitudes the whole time.

---

man, 1983), pp. 46-54; R. Jaugeon, "Les sociétés d'exploitation au Congo et l'opinion française de 1890 à 1906", *Revue Française d'Histoire d'Outremer* vol. XLVIII, 3rd-4th quarter 1961, pp. 353-437.

74   J. Duffy, *A Question of Slavery*, OUP 1967, chapters VII and VIII; G. Wagner, *The Chocolate Conscience*, London: Chatto & Windus, 1987, pp. 90-102.

75   J. R. Mackenzie, *Propaganda and Empire: The Manipulation of British Opinion 1880-1960*, Manchester University Press, 1984, e.g. chapter 4, "The Imperial Exhibitions". Cf. B. Porter, *The Absent-Minded Imperialists: Empire, Society, and Culture in Britain*, OUP 2004, a more comprehensive work which covers antiimperialism (but has little on the inter-war period).

76   J.H. Harris, *Dawn in Darkest Africa*, 1912, p. 104.

Concern for proper treatment of Africans under colonial rule was much more widespread than doubts about the rightness of colonial aggression. The European powers did leave Ethiopia alone after its victory over the Italians at the Battle of Adowa in 1896 (until Italy attacked again in 1935), though there were imperialist struggles for influence there, especially between France and Britain over the building of the railway to Addis Ababa.[77] Occupation of Morocco—a kingdom that had lasted for centuries and had diplomatic relations with several European countries at the time France began encroaching on it—was considered a matter for international diplomatic attention. After Britain gave France a "free hand" in Morocco in the Entente Cordiale of 1904, France proceeded with its piecemeal occupation, but anti-colonial protests in France were particularly aroused over Morocco. The Socialist Gustave Hervé praised the Moroccans at the 1902 Congress of the Parti Socialiste Français and in 1907 told French troops that he hoped they would be welcomed as the Italians had been in Ethiopia in 1896.[78] Socialist and other criticisms of the creeping Morocco intervention continued until the final stage of the establishment of the French "Protectorate" (which did not, however, end Moroccan resistance) in 1912, and beyond. In that year, for example, the future Communist Marcel Cachin wrote of "eminently courageous people defending their independence".[79]

Such protests followed an honourable tradition going back to France's anti-slavery movement, which triumphed briefly during the first French Revolution and permanently in the 1848 revolution, when the work of France's Wilberforce, Victor Schoelcher, was crowned with the abolition of slavery in all French territories. Later in the 19th century Algeria was the main focus of disagreements over colonisation. Although Algeria (excluding the Saharan part occupied later on) was legally part of France from 1871, most of its inhabitants had no French citizenship; they were subjected to the Indigénat from 1881 and to special "Arab taxes" and other discriminatory measures, and not allowed to travel freely to France or on the Mecca pilgrimage, and there were only a few

---

77   L. Woolf, *Empire and Commerce in Africa: A Study in Economic Imperialism*, London: Allen & Unwin, 1920, chapter V.

78   Ageron (note 41), p. 79.

79   G. Oved, *La Gauche française et le nationalisme marocain 1905-1955*, Paris: Harmattan, 1984, vol. 1, p. 109.

elected representatives for whom only a few Muslims were allowed to vote. The settlers steadily expanded their holdings to own most of the best agricultural land and dominated the country in every way, and their representatives, notably Eugène Etienne, lobbied to ensure that they kept their privileges. Other French people opposed the settlers' power and favoured more rights for Muslim Algerians—within French Algeria, that was always understood.[80]

When French occupation of Tunisia, Black Africa, Madagascar, the Saharan territories south of Algeria, and Morocco got under way, there was condemnation from many quarters. It was very much linked with opposition to militarism, a sentiment also common in Britain but particularly strong in France because of Republican suspicion of the officer class, culminating in the Dreyfus case; the military, as in Algeria earlier, had an exceptional influence in French colonial expansion in sub-Saharan Africa.

Protests against the Morocco intervention sometimes emphasised the danger of international war; the "Morocco question" did indeed lead to crises in 1905-6 and 1911, and to many left-wing critics imperialism, militarism and the risk of war went together, with capitalism added. The writer Anatole France, aroused to political activism by the Dreyfus case, wrote in 1904 that "a syndicate of financiers and industrialists has made an alliance with the generals' party to drag us into Morocco."[81] Other writers also protested against imperialism, such as the journalist and novelist Pierre Mille who, typically of the time, criticised actual colonial practice but still dreamed of a humane and fraternal "France of 100 million inhabitants".[82] Paul-Etienne Vigné (1859-1943) served in Africa as a navy doctor in the 1880s and later wrote several strongly worded books, fiction and non-fiction, under the name Vigné d'Octon, in which he exposed crimes committed by the French in the occupation of the colonies. He also served as a deputy, and in that position did not take much interest in or show much concern about imperialism; but his

80   Jean-Pierre Biondi, *Les Anticolonialistes (1881-1962)*, Paris: Laffont, 1992, pp. 47-9, 85-7.

81   Ibid., p. 59.

82   Ibid., p. 73; A.G. Hargreaves, *The Colonial Experience in French Fiction: A Study of Pierre Loti, Ernest Psichari and Pierre Mille*, Basingstoke: Macmillan, 1981, chs. 5 and 6 on Mille.

books—*La Sueur du burnous, Biribi et la Légion étrangère* and others—had an impact.[83]

News of the brutalities committed by the concessionary companies and their inseparable partner the colonial state in French Equatorial Africa caused disquiet in France, with the press highlighting the crimes, until particular shock was aroused by the case of two colonial officials, Fernand Gaud and Georges Toqué, who killed a number of Africans; they were tried in Brazzaville, convicted, and given trifling sentences of five years' imprisonment each. The trial revealed that their crimes were only a part of a general pattern of oppression and extortion inherent in the whole system established in that colony. An investigative mission was despatched, headed by the original founder of French rule in the area, Pierre Savorgnan de Brazza; on its return—minus de Brazza, who died on the way back to France—its full report was never published, but measures were ordered in February 1906 to ease the impositions on the Africans. One who was not convinced that these measures would be enough was Félicien Challaye, a French traveller who had accompanied the investigation mission. In 1909 he published a book recording the crimes committed, while also recalling briefly the events in the Congo Free State and the campaign for reforms there.[84]

Challaye exposed the Congo crimes plainly, and called for drastic changes. But he did not reject colonisation entirely. He wrote,

Colonisation is a necessary social reality. It is inevitable that Europeans should go to the Centre of Africa to look for the rubber and ivory that they need. It is inevitable that they impose over the former native institutions a new society, where trade and exploitation of the wealth of the soil may be possible.

But justice requires that the white peoples' domination does not lead to the worst consequences for the black people—slavery, robbery, rape, torture, murder. Justice demands that the natives draw some advantage from our presence among them.[85]

---

83   Biondi (note 80), pp. 53-6; J. Suret-Canale, introduction to 1984 reprint (Paris: Quintette) of Paul Vigné d'Octon, *La gloire du sabre* (1900).

84   Challaye (note 73), pp. 108-144; Jaugeon (note 72); Biondi (note 79), pp. 71-3.

85   Challaye (note 73), p. 313.

That, with a few variations, was what most of the strongest critics of empire among the colonisers peoples said at that time. Challaye himself was to go further in later years, as will be shown in the coming chapters, but his earlier attitude came to be that adopted by most Socialists in France.

Some French Socialists came to accept colonialism at an early stage; exceptionally, the Socialist Millerand joined the empire-conquering government in 1899, and a Socialist politician (an independent Republican Socialist), Victor Augagneur, was Governor-General of Madagascar from 1905 to 1910. But many took a very different view. Two years after the merger of Socialist parties in the Section Française de l'Internationale Ouvrière (SFIO), the Nancy Congress of the SFIO in 1907 passed a strong resolution declaring that

Socialism is necessarily hostile to colonialism, which relies on violent conquest and institutionalises the subjection of Asiatic and African peoples...Colonialism contributes to the transformation of the world by exacerbating the antagonisms which constitute the very foundation of the capitalist system.[86]

The language of that resolution suggests the influence of Marxist theory of imperialism, then being developed by Rosa Luxemburg in Germany as well as Lenin; similarly, in his 1905 book *Le Colonialisme* one fierce critic of empire, Paul Louis, agreeing with or echoing Hobson, wrote that colonialism was "the last card of capitalism at bay, panic-stricken at the growing threat of overproduction which it cannot ward off."[87]

Jean Jaurès said in 1903 that he would support "peaceful and reasonable expansion of French interests and French civilisation"; however, he believed beneficent colonialism would only be possible under Socialism.[88] But in 1908 Eugène Fournière wrote in the *Revue Socialiste*, "If an area as big as France is occupied by twenty or five thousand

---

86   Biondi (note 80), p. 82.

87   R. Thomas, "La Politique socialiste et le problème colonial de 1905 à 1920", *Revue Française d'Histoire d'Outremer* Vol. XLVII, 2nd quarter, 1960, pp. 213-45.

88   Biondi (note 80), pp. 62-3, 90-93. See also "Jaurès, un engagement progressif" (interview with Madeleine Rébérioux), in Jean Lacouture and Dominique Chagnollaud, *Le Désempire: Figures et thèmes de l'anticolonisme*, Paris: Denoël, 1993, pp. 154-66.

Blacks who spend the best part of their time dancing and making war, should we bow before the occupancy rights of these idle landlords?"[89] Commonly Socialists came to adopt the views of humanitarian defenders of "natives" of the colonies, who condemned ill-treatment but not colonialism as such. These included the Ligue des Droits de l'Homme (LDH), which regularly took up cases of human rights abuse in the colonies,[90] and the Comité de Protection et de Défense des Indigènes, whose leading figure for several years at the turn of the century was Paul Viollet.[91]

In 1913 a number of those who were called *indigénophiles* formed an Alliance Franco-Indigène, headed by the economist Charles Gide, who was a member of the Comité de Protection et de Défense des Indigènes.[92] Earlier, in 1906, a *Revue Indigène* was founded, stating that its aim was "to lend our support to the people of good will who seek to improve the natives' situation".[93] The first issue, published in the midst of the outcry over the French Congo atrocities, referred to a conference on *"barbarie coloniale"* in Paris on 30 January 1906, with Anatole France in the chair. The *Revue* was, however, another expression of critical and qualified acceptance of colonialism, and it often echoed the French phobia about Islam.[94]

A peculiar feature of French attitudes to imperialism was the ideal or dream of extending French culture, and French citizenship, to other peoples. After 1848 Black inhabitants of the four "old colonies" (Guadeloupe, Martinique, French Guiana, Réunion) became full French citizens. But it was soon clear that the French authorities had no intention of extending citizenship to newly occupied colonies, or of making more than very limited attempts to spread French culture there; there was very little state education for Africans and missions were not much favoured officially. All colonial powers, includ-

89   Oved (note 79), Vol. 1, pp. 42-3.

90   C. Liauzu, *Aux Origines des Tiers-mondismes: colonisés et anticolonialistes en France 1919-1939*, Paris: Harmattan, 1982, pp. 88-90; Biondi (note 79), p. 97.

91   Ageron (note 41), pp. 35-6.

92   Koulakssis and Meynier (note 50), p. 74.

93   *Revue Indigène*, January 1906, p. 2 (Kraus reprint, 1977).

94   E.g. P. Bourdarie in *Revue Indigène* no. 54, October 1910, pp. 552-72 (Kraus reprint, 1977). On Anatole France's speech at that 1906 meeting, see Biondi (note 80), p. 74.

ing France, claimed to be spreading "civilisation", but the idea that France set out to turn Africans generally into "Black Frenchmen" was a myth. Africans could indeed become fully French by culture, but no more than many Sierra Leone Creoles became British by culture, and in each case it was not an aim of colonial policy. Colonial subjects could become French citizens, but—apart from the exceptional case of Senegal—only on conditions (including a considerable degree of French culture) which ensured that they were indeed "black Frenchmen" but few in number. Yet the idea of spreading French civilisation reconciled many left-wingers to colonisation.[95]

The Socialist International (the Second International, founded in 1889) passed anti-colonial resolutions at its congresses in Paris in 1900, Amsterdam in 1904, and Stuttgart in 1907.[96] Members of individual Socialist parties were constantly making criticisms in their national parliaments and elsewhere, but, as noted, not usually declaring unambiguous hostility to imperialism. Their attitude would later be derided as "reformism" by Communists, but should not be simply despised. Socialists and other critics were right to believe that specific evils in the colonial empires could be removed. They called for this consistently, braving constant colonialist attack, in parliamentary debates and questions in Britain, France, Belgium and Germany. The Belgian Socialist leader Emile Vandervelde, for example, exposed the Congo Free State crimes in the Belgian parliament (exchanging information with Morel);[97] but his solution, again, was beneficent colonialism, which he and MacDonald advocated at the 5th Congress of the International in 1900.[98]

In Germany there was constant critical intervention in colonial matters by the Reichstag, especially through control of colonial budgets and resolutions attached to these, and especially by the German Social Democratic Party (SPD), with some support from the Centre Party. There was continual criticism of colonial occupation and administration, highlighting forced labour, land expropriation, military operations, and individual crimes, in Cameroon and South-West Africa for

---

95   Oved (note 79), vol. 1, pp. 15-16.

96   Ageron (note 41), pp. 23-4.

97   J. Marchal, *E.D. Morel contre Léopold II: L'Histoire du Congo 1900-1910*, 2 vols., Paris: Harmattan, 1996, e.g. Vol. 1 pp. 116-24, 318-22.

98   Biondi (note 80), p. 64.

example.[99] Critics of German colonial rule agreed that it was improved after the reforming Colonial Secretary Bernhard Dernburg took office in 1907, but they continued their attacks in the Reichstag, possibly stronger than those in any other colonising country's parliament.[100] Resolutions attached to the 1914 budget by the Reichstag called for a complete end to forced labour and an imperial decree to assure the "natives" life, freedom and property, among many other reforms.[101] In the same year the Reichstag examined the land expropriation in Douala and the Duala people's protests; later Dualas believed that it had refused to approve the expropriation, but this turned out to be untrue— the German parliament did not go that far.[102] There were some Social Democrats who strongly supported German colonialism, while at the opposite extreme Rosa Luxemburg and Karl Kautsky vigorously condemned colonialism.

Who, then, were the anti-colonialists by the year 1914? What indeed does such a term as "anti-colonialist" mean, as applied to people active then? This is not an easy question to answer, which is why this work did not start with an attempt at a definition.

The case of some Africans who were still fighting then against the initial colonial occupation, as in Somalia, was fairly straightforward. But their numbers were dwindling. As for other Africans, the majority submitted to the situation as the majority always does everywhere. Among the Western-educated people whose views are known through African newspapers and other sources, one can clearly see widespread discontent with colonial rule—which, however, many of the Western-educated class served well, if only in the lower ranks of service.

Among Europeans, there were numerous condemnations of colonial crimes, some vehement, some involving prolonged campaigns. But it must be noted again that these could come from people strongly in favour of empire, or involved in governing it. Even among those who were more independent and critical, few opposed colonialism altogeth-

---

99   Rudin (note 57), pp. 142-52, 210-12, 316-37; Drechsler (note 2), pp. 134-5, 217.

100   Rudin (note 57), pp. 141-52.

101   Ibid., pp. 330-31.

102   J. Derrick, "Douala under the French Mandate, 1916 to 1936", PhD, London, 1979, pp. 261-5.

er. If "anti-colonialism" is taken to mean only the advocacy of early independence for the colonies, there was very little of it in 1914. However, in this work it is given a wider sense than that.

Discussing Vigné d'Octon, the French Communist historian Suret-Canale, in his introduction to Vigné's leading political book *La gloire du sabre*, quotes these words from another of Vigné's works:

I had this dream: there was at last on the earth a Justice for all the subjected races and conquered peoples. Tired of being robbed, pillaged, pushed around, massacred, the Arabs and Berbers drove their dominators from the north of Africa, the Black people did the same for the rest of that continent, and the Yellow people for the soil of Asia.

Quoting some further lines in this vein, this Marxist historian acknowledges that Vigné d'Octon's writings were those of a man of emotion rather than theory, but concludes,

To write that in 1911, one had to have unusual courage and lucidity. So can one refuse to describe Vigné d'Octon as an anticolonialist? That does not seem even worth considering![103]

The same can be said of others, such as Labouchere and the more critical Social Democratic deputies in the German Reichstag. People who constantly highlighted the violent and oppressive aspects of colonial occupation and rule, and condemned the aggression and economic exploitation involved, challenged the prevailing view that colonialism was beneficial, and raised fundamental doubts about it. Such people are considered as "anti-colonialist" in this work, together with those—for long very few in number—who called plainly for an early end to colonialism.

The First World War and Africa

The European colonial powers had scarcely completed their occupation of Africa when they went to war among themselves in 1914; they not even yet completed it in Libya, where the Muslim religious order of the Sanusiyya went on resisting for years in Cyrenaica and other Libyan leaders in Tripolitania, or in Morocco, Somalia or Angola. But from the start their new African subjects had to help them fight their

---

103 J. Suret-Canale, Introduction to 1984 reprint of *La gloire du sabre* (note 83), pp. 11-12.

European tribal war. Incredibly, they were expected to do so willingly, out of gratitude for the benefits of colonial rule. The declaration by the French Lieutenant-Governor of Senegal on the outbreak of war is a prize example of colonial self-delusion:

Formerly...the existence of our native subjects was precarious, they had hardly any choice except between two roles, to pillage or to be pillaged...Today, on the contrary, the native enjoys for his person and his property absolute security, he is certain to harvest himself the grain he has sown, to die a free person among his people in the corner of land he has chosen. Never has Africa, the classic land of pillage and slavery, known such a fate.

Obligatory recruitment by call-up, apart from any other moral and patriotic consideration, finds its justification there: it is in some way the recompense for the well-being that we have given to the native.[104]

The reality was that the previous quarter-century had been a time of exceptional disruption, violence, destruction and upheaval over most of Africa, and now the intra-European war was to add to all this considerably. First of all, there were the campaigns by the Allies to occupy the four German colonies. Togo was occupied in only three weeks, South-West Africa (by South African forces) in less than a year, but the "Cameroons campaign" lasted eighteen months and the campaign in German East Africa (Tanganyika) until the end of the entire war.

Thousands of Africans fought for both sides in these campaigns, including troops from British West Africa sent to Cameroon and Tanganyika. Tens of thousands were recruited or conscripted as porters in several countries bordering the German colonies, to accompany the campaigns. In response to the recruitment of soldiers and porters in Nyasaland there was a serious rebellion in early 1915, led by the American-trained clergyman John Chilembwe. Having headed an independent mission, he now seems to have aimed at an independent state, and had some contact with the Germans in their neighbouring colony. The rising lasted from 23 January to 4 February 1915; Chilembwe was killed in action.[105]

---

104   *Journal Officiel du Sénégal,* 13 August 1914, p. 29.

105   G. Shepperson and T. Price, *Independent African,* Edinburgh University Press, 1958, pp. 267-319.

The sufferings due to conscription of porters extended to Northern Rhodesia, Kenya—nearly 24,000 of the Kenyan porters died according to official figures, possibly twice as many in fact—and the Belgian Congo. The African soldiers fighting for Britain in those campaigns were supposed to be volunteers, but many of the Nigerian ones were not. Formal military conscription had been started in the French colonies before the war, and now France, unlike Britain, sent African conscripts to the main fighting front in France, and some to the Dardanelles and Salonika campaigns. In all, according to one estimate, 170,891 soldiers were drafted during the war from AOF, 17,910 from AEF and 41,355 from Madagascar.[106]

The French-African infantry, the Tirailleurs, suffered all the nightmare of troops on the Western Front; they were hit by the first German gas attack in 1915. They fought well even so, but there was considerable resistance in Africa to conscription. It was a major cause of a revolt in the Beledougou region north of Bamako in French Sudan in February-March 1915, a considerably bigger revolt in the western part of Upper Volta from November 1915 to July 1916, and another major one in the Atakora and Borgou regions of northern Dahomey from April 1916 to April 1917.[107] Thousands of Africans fled from French to British territory to escape conscription.

Conscription and war service for Africans added to the burdens the people suffered, sufficiently to cause concern among French officials, especially Governor-General Joost Van Vollenhoven of AOF, who secured a brief halt after his appointment in 1917; but they went on apart from that respite. At the same time Blaise Diagne took advantage of the war situation to have the Senegalese Originaires of the Four Communes first of all declared by law in 1915 to be liable to military service on the same terms as in metropolitan France—different from the terms of

---

106   See especially M. Michel, *L'Appel à l'Afrique: Contributions et réactions à l'effort de guerre en A.O.F. 1914-1919*, Paris: Publications de la Sorbonne, 1982 (figures for troops: p. 404).

107   Ibid., pp. 54-7, chapter V, pp. 118-20; Hélène d'Almeida-Topor, "Les populations dahoméennes et le recrutement militaire pendant la première guerre mondiale", *Revue Française d'Histoire d'Outremer* Vol. LX no. 219, 1973, pp. 196-241; and a thorough study of the main Upper Volta revolt, Mahir Saul and Patrick Royer, *West African Challenge to Empire: Culture and History in the Volta-Bani Anticolonial War*, Athens, OH: Ohio University Press and Oxford: James Currey, 2001.

compulsory military service for African *sujets* under a 1912 decree—and then, by another law, to be French citizens subject to French citizens' military service obligations. This second law was passed by the Senate on 29 September 1916. The colonial authorities in AOF were very much opposed to this concession to all the Originaires, but in the war situation the "man on the spot" was for once overruled.[108]

The loyalty of Diagne and the Originaires of Senegal to the colonial "mother country" at war was typical of African elites everywhere. Their declarations of loyalty could be quoted at great length. For example, an editorial in the *Gold Coast Leader* on 10 July 1915 said this was

not the time to ventilate grievances which might prejudice the cause of England or lead her enemies to impugn the solidarity and loyalty of the sons and subject races of the British Empire...We shall play the role of passive spectators with loyalty, determination and devotion in order to qualify for greater trust.[109]

Dr J.K. Randle, a medical doctor and leading Lagos elite figure, told a meeting in Lagos on 4 August 1916, "The people see that the Government is not carried out in their interest. But, however painfully true this is, let us not forget the wider principle that we are citizens of the British Empire."[110]

However, another leading Lagosian, James Bright-Davies, wrote in the 29 August 1916 issue of his *Times of Nigeria* that because of British firms' conduct in the produce trade during the war, "one frequently hears the wish and the most sanguine hopes expressed in the daily conversations of the people about trade, that Germany should win this war..."[111] For this he received a six-month prison sentence. Whether the feelings he mentioned were really widespread or not, generally Nigerians and other Africans remained quiescent when they did not actively help their colonial rulers, the Allied powers. They certainly felt the economic effects of the war even when they were not affected more directly, and huge numbers of them died in the great flu epidemic of

---

108   Conklin (note 52), pp. 155-6; Michel (note 106), pp. 61-4, 90-92.

109   Quoted in D. Killingray, "Repercussions of World War I in the Gold Coast," *Journal of African History* Vol. XIX no. 1, 1978, pp. 39-59 (p. 40n).

110   Quoted in M. Crowder, "West Africa and the 1914-18 War," *Bulletin de l'IFAN* (Dakar) Series B, Vol. XXX no. 1, January 1968, pp. 227ff. (p. 230).

111   Omu (note 9), p. 191; A. Osuntokun, *Nigeria in the First World War*, London: Longman, 1979, pp. 181-4.

1918; while the Nigerian elite's general strong hostility to Governor-General Lugard continued to be expressed throughout the war,[112] and was returned in full. But the elite's hostility was combined with general support for the Allied cause. There were some revolts in Nigeria during the war, but not directly linked to it.[113]

In South Africa the SANNC decided, in Plaatje's words, "to hang up native grievances against the South African Parliament till a better time and to tender the authorities every assistance."[114] Everywhere Western-educated Africans, like Indians, noted the Allies' propaganda about defending freedom, and constantly returned to the idea that the loyalty of colonial subjects in the hour of need should receive some reward from the colonial powers. *West Africa*, a weekly started in Liverpool in February 1917, said in an editorial on 17 March 1917, "Naturally, all sections of native society are asking what political changes, if any, the war will bring in West Africa. In almost every number of the native newspapers there are traces of the discussion."

Colonial subjects' calls for rewards for wartime loyalty of course implied criticism, and a few adopted a more critical attitude still. Among the Dualas of Cameroon—initially pleased at the expulsion of the Germans, who had followed the urban land expropriation with the execution of the paramount chief of the people affected, Rudolf Duala Manga Bell—there was a good deal of dissatisfaction when, after a short period of British military administration, France took over most of the area of occupied Kamerun in 1916. A number were calling for an independent state like Liberia, or at least for them to be consulted over the future of occupied Kamerun; some suggested that the 1884 treaty between the Duala rulers and Germany had been a genuine two-sided treaty and had either expired or become void.[115] In the following years Dualas were to go further than most Western-educated people in sub-Saharan Africa in anti-colonial protests against French rule, expressed in modern political language.

---

112   Osuntokun (note 111), pp. 64-99.

113   Ibid., pp. 100-38, 145-6.

114   S. Plaatje, *Native Life in South Africa*, 1916, reprint Longman, 1987, pp. 210-11.

115   Derrick (note 102), pp. 120-25.

In Madagascar, where Western education had been brought by British missionaries (of the London Missionary Society) and literacy in the Malagasy language had been spreading before the French occupation, an association of Western-educated Malagasy people, the Vy Vato Sakelika (VVS), was suspected of plotting against French rule during the First World War. Teachers, clerics, journalists and others joined this society which appears to have been a loosely organised discussion circle to promote "the progress civilisation of the country, by training good citizens for the moral, social, cultural and physical improvement of the Malagasy people, especially the youth." It seems to have had nationalist ideas of a sort, inspired by articles written by one of its presumed founders, Pastor Ravelojaona, expressing admiration for the example of Japan; and it was an oath-bound secret society, which was bound to arouse suspicion. In the latter part of 1915 there were rumours of the VVS planning an armed rebellion to start on the last day of 1915, to restore independence. The French authorities, who alleged that the plotters had German help, arrested about 500 people in December 1915, but found no arms and, it seems, no proof of a plan—though much seems to be still obscure about this episode. Eight people were sentenced to life imprisonment and twenty-six to prison terms of fifteen to twenty years; many Malagasy-language publications were banned.[116]

There may well have been no plot and no German intrigues in Madagascar, and no German efforts to encourage revolt against British or French rule in Black Africa, apart from some contact with Chilembwe; the revolts that occurred were spontaneous and unaided. The Afrikaner rising in South Africa in September-December 1914 was also a spontaneous revolt, against South Africa's entry into the war on the Allied side, with only slight German involvement;[117] it was suppressed by the Union government whose main Afrikaner leaders, Botha and Jan Christiaan Smuts, were now more heroes than ever to the British—Smuts joined the British War Cabinet in 1917.

---

116   S. Randrianja, *Société et luttes anticoloniales à Madagascar (1896 à 1946)*, Paris: Karthala, 2001, pp. 141-60; M. Adejunmobi, *J.J. Rabearivelo, Literature and Lingua Franca in Colonial Madagascar*, New York: Peter Long, 1996, pp. 27-9.

117   J. Meintjes, *General Louis Botha: A Biography*, London: Cassell, 1970.

In the Arab world and Asia the Germans and Turks encouraged uprisings in the Allied colonies on a large scale.[118] Particular attention was paid to "Britain's oldest colony", Ireland, and to India, where a revolt really would have caused trouble for Britain. Various Indian exiles joined in the plots, including several living in the USA at the outbreak of war, one of whom was to become famous later, M.N. Roy.

In North Africa it was hoped, or feared, that many would follow the *Jihad* proclaimed by the Ottoman Sultan on his entry into the war in 1914. In Egypt, which Britain formally annexed as a Protectorate when Turkey entered the war, there was no revolt in response to the *Jihad* proclamation, but the large British garrison in a country that was a major Allied base helped to ensure that. There was in fact sympathy for Turkey there, together with resentment at wartime hardships such as conscription of non-combatant labour. Muhammad Farid and Abbas Hilmi, the Khedive deposed by the British in 1914, were active in exile on the Turkish side;[119] propaganda against British imperialism in the Central Powers and neutral countries concerned especially Egypt, India and Ireland. In the Sudan, where the Turks were remembered as oppressors, the leader of the Mahdiyya proclaimed loyalty to the British. But Ali Dinar, Sultan of Darfur, who had been left virtually independent after the 1898 conquest of the Sudan, sympathised with the Sanusiyya of Libya and the Turks; however, he was defeated by a British expedition in early 1916.[120]

In Libya Italian control was only established over a small area in 1915, when Italy joined the Allies, and the Sanusiyya (Senussis) were able to drive the Italians further back until a truce was signed in 1917. Resistance continued in Tripolitania, aided by the Turks, the Germans and Abd al-Rahman Azzam, a young Egyptian, recently a politically active student in London, who played an important role.[121] There were

---

118   More needs to be published about these German-Turkish plans. They are covered very partially in some published works, most fully in Peter Hopkirk's *Setting the East Ablaze*, London: John Murray, 1984 and *On Secret Service East of Constantinople: the Plot to Bring Down the British Empire*, London: John Murray, 1994—which, however, still leave a large gap to fill.

119   Goldschmidt (note 45), pp. 328-33.

120   A.B. Theobald, *Ali Dinar: Last Sultan of Darfur, 1898-1916*, London: Longmans, Green & Co., 1965, pp. 162-207.

121   Ralph M. Coury, *The Making of an Egyptian Arab Nationalist: The Early Years of*

risings against the French in the Sahara, including the great Tuareg uprising in 1916-17 (separate from the Senussi rising). The Tuareg leader Ag Mohammed Kaocen led fighters in besieging the French post at Agadez in Niger from December 1916 to March 1917; British troops from Nigeria (Nigerian in the other ranks) helped the French to raise the siege.[122]

There was also a rising in 1915-16 in southern Tunisia, with a base in the area of Libya from which the Italians had withdrawn, but involving Tunisians under Khalifa Ben Asker, who was later disavowed by the Sanusiyya; French forces used poison gas and aircraft in operations against the dissidents, eventually defeating them and executing Khalifa.[123] Meanwhile the nationalist *Revue du Maghreb* was started in Geneva in May 1916, edited by Mohamed Bach-Hamba, brother of Ali Bach-Hamba, who had like him gone to Constantinople; this monthly magazine restated the Jeunes Tunisiens' demand for reforms, and aimed to influence pro-Arab (but not anti-colonial) French public figures, such as those who published the periodical *La France Musulmane*. Thus these exiles working with France's Turkish enemies simply called for reforms in Tunisia and Algeria, amounting to equality for all under French rule; but that involved strong criticisms of the existing colonial order, and copies of the magazine sent to people in Tunisia were confiscated. As the war went on, the *Revue*—in fact subsidised by Turkey—went further and called for self-determination according to the Allied governments' declarations. There was also a Comité pour l'Indépendance de la Tunisie et de l'Algérie, headed by the Tunisian Salah Chérif and based in Berlin.[124]

France's occupation of Morocco was very incomplete when war broke out, but Marshal Lyautey, the first Resident-General, sent most of his troops back to France. The French were not driven back in Morocco after this, but large areas were outside their effective control, and German

Azzam Pasha, 1893-1936, Reading: Ithaca Press, 1998, chs. 3 and 4.

122 A. Salifou, *Kaocen ou la Révolte Sénoussiste*, Niamey: Centre Nigérien de Recherches en Sciences Humaines, 1973; F. Fuglestad, "Les Révoltes des Touareg du Niger (1916-17)", *Cahiers d'Etudes Africaines* vol. XIII, 1973, 2me cahier, pp. 82-120; Osuntokun (note 111), pp. 155-61.

123 Goldstein (note 49), pp. 146-59. The world's first ever bombing from aircraft had taken place in the Italian occupation of Libya in 1911-12.

124 Ibid., pp. 265-79; Lejri (note 46), pp. 157-63.

agents helped widespread Moroccan resistance, including a campaign begun from Spanish Morocco in 1915 by the Algerian Abdelmalek, son of Emir Abdelkader and uncle of Emir Khaled (who, for his part, served in the French forces in the war).[125]

Except in Libya—whose colonial rulers were themselves in dire straits by the end of 1917—the resistance in some Muslim countries was fairly easily defeated or, in Morocco, at least contained. The main Muslim regions in sub-Saharan Africa, such as Northern Nigeria and Senegal, made no trouble for the colonial rulers. Nor, as noted, did the Western-educated communities, except for the possible Madagascar plot. But Europeans were aware that the war was affecting Africans' view of their colonial subjection. The very spectacle of Europeans fighting each other must have affected it; so did the Allies' constant talk of defending freedom and the rights of subject nations; so, undoubtedly, did the extra burden of suffering caused by the war; while imperialist propaganda about saving Africans from "tribal wars" must have rung more hollow than ever now. In February 1918 Dr Norman Leys, a British colonial medical officer in Kenya who was to be a prominent anti-colonialist, wrote to the Colonial Secretary, "The old claim of governments to be the protectors from inter-tribal warfare has been swept away for ever by the miseries and destruction of the present war".[126]

Fears about the possible effect of Africans' military service in the war proved groundless. South Africa recruited no black soldiers—none, in fact, for the next sixty years—and for the Western Front recruited only the non-combatant South African Native Labour Contingent sent to France in 1917.[127] But other rulers over Africans readily employed African soldiers, in war and peace, and found them useful and indeed indispensable; the African soldiers serving in the First World War, especially

125 Koulakssis and Meynier (note 50), pp. 102-113. The French operations against Moroccan fighters and their German helpers were described regularly, from an obvious viewpoint, in the colonialist periodical *L'Afrique Française* during the war.

126 Norman Leys to Secretary of State, 7 February 1918, quoted in J.W. Cell (ed.), *By Kenya Possessed: The Correspondence of Normal Leys and J.H. Oldham 1918-1926*, University of Chicago Press, 1976, p. 118.

127 A. Grundlingh, *Fighting their Own War: South African Blacks and the First World War*, Johannesburg: Ravan Press, 1987, pp. 42-77.

the Tirailleurs who had seen Europe, must have brought back to Africa a heightened awareness of Europe's technical and military superiority.

The dream of Europe's workers joining together to prevent a war by general strikes rather than turn their guns on fellow workers evaporated in 1914, and Socialist politicians joined the wartime governments in Britain, France and (in the government in exile) Belgium. In Britain, however, the ILP refused to back the war effort; so did Ramsay MacDonald himself, resigning as Leader of the Labour Party on the outbreak of war as a result. In Germany the SPD backed the war effort except for a few dissenters of whom Karl Liebknecht and Rosa Luxemburg were the most prominent. Some other Socialists, including the Socialist Party under Eugene Debs in the USA and the Bolshevik faction of the Russian Social Democratic Labour Party, opposed the "imperialist war"; the Bolshevik leader Lenin joined some anti-war dissenting Socialists from other countries at the Zimmerwald Conference in September 1915.

Among the left-wing dissenters and pacifists who held out against the prevailing war fever some were to be linked with anti-colonialism. Archibald Fenner Brockway (1888-1987), a young ILP activist who had become editor of the ILP organ *Labour Leader* in his 20s, went to prison for conscientious objection and opposition to conscription for twenty-eight months; later he was to be a leading British left-wing anti-colonial campaigner for half a century. Arthur Creech Jones (1891-1964), also of the ILP, active like Brockway in the No Conscription Fellowship and similarly gaoled, was to be one of the principal colonial experts in the Labour Party. The Suffragette and future champion of Ethiopia Sylvia Pankhurst (1882-1960) edited the *Women's Dreadnought*, later the *Workers' Dreadnought*, which in 1917 called on soldiers to refuse to continue fighting. In France the novelist Romain Rolland, who withdrew to Switzerland and vainly preached reconciliation during the war, was later to be prominent in anti-colonialist campaigns.

In Britain the Union of Democratic Control (UDC), formed at the beginning of the war, protested against the secret diplomacy that had led the countries of Europe into war, and opposed the idea of outright victory as the only way to peace; it was widely denounced as "pro-German". MacDonald was one of its leaders, but its Executive Secretary and dominant leader was E.D. Morel. In 1917 he was sentenced to six months' imprisonment for arranging for a pamphlet by him, on Tsarist Russia's role in the war, to be sent to Rolland in Switzerland.[128] The UDC was to continue after the war as a liberal-left pressure group, taking up colonial issues among others.

In wartime Britain colonial issues were very secondary, but there was concerted official propaganda about German colonial rule, to justify the Allies' desire not to return any of the conquered colonies to Germany. This propaganda did not need to exaggerate about the repression of the Hereros of South-West Africa by the proto-Nazi General von Trotha, but one Allied accusation, that Germany was planning to "militarise" Africans on a large scale, was outrageous in view of France's massive conscription in the colonies. And obviously those seeking to portray German colonial rule as particularly oppressive did not want people to remember the monstrous crimes of Leopold II, whose country was now "gallant little Belgium". Duse Mohammed Ali, in his magazine, suggested that German crimes in Belgium were God's punishment for the crimes in the Congo,[129] but he condemned German rule strongly, even though he had been a supporter of Turkey; the *African Times and Orient Review* however ceased publication between August 1914 and January 1917, resuming then until October 1918. Although other Africans must have wondered if the British and French had a right to adopt a morally superior tone on German colonialism, the Nigerian press joined in the demand that the German colonies should not be restored to Germany after the war.

Debates on the future of the German colonies were bound up with wider debates on a new international organisation to prevent further wars, involving proposals for international control of the occupied German colonies or even, as the British Labour Party recommended in 1917, of all colonies. Eventually agreement was reached in the peace settlement on the Mandates under the League of Nations created in 1919, which reflected some ideas on improved (but indefinitely continuing) colonial government in Africa. But Wilson's self-determination principle was not considered applicable to Africans, either by the President himself—for the colonial empires the Fourteen Points announced in January 1918 spoke only of a "free, open-minded and ab-

---

128   Cline (note 72), p. 111-12; *West Africa*, 8 Sept. 1917.

129   *African Times and Orient Review*, 11 August 1914.

solutely impartial adjustment of all colonial claims" —or by Du Bois, the most prominent leader of the NAACP as editor of its magazine *The Crisis*, and the leading African American spokesman after Washington's death in 1915.[130]

Nobody, in fact, was seriously challenging colonialism then except Africans fighting against it in their countries, the Germans and Turks who were encouraging rebellion for their own purposes, and the Russian Bolsheviks. Lenin's *Imperialism*, published in Switzerland in 1916, was a work of analysis, not a call to mount barricades. But in the same year Lenin praised the Easter Rising in Ireland, and when the Bolsheviks seized power in Russia the following year they turned their attention without delay, as they had promised, to the colonised areas of the world (of this much more later).

The main immediate effect of the October Revolution and the Treaty of Brest-Litovsk for Africa was the massive recruitment of yet more African soldiers for the French army, to help prepare for the concentrated German offensive in the West. Diagne was appointed by Prime Minister Clemenceau as Commissioner of the Republic, reporting directly to the minister of the Colonies, with the task of recruiting more troops in AOF, and succeeded in recruiting 63,378 there.[131]

Galandou Diouf, the leading politician of the Four Communes of Senegal after Diagne, and at the time a lieutenant in the army, wrote in his newspaper *L'Indépendant Sénégalais* (27 Sept. 1917) that there must be "equality in society as in the trenches facing death."[132] Whether he was referring to the Four Communes or to French Africa generally, he expressed a widespread African view, that loyalty in wartime must be rewarded. In France, besides the Black African troops 172,000 Algerians fought at the front, and 120,000 Algerian civilian workers gave indispensable help, together with workers from Indochina and China; in all 569,000 soldiers (of whom 78,000 were killed) and 239,000 workers from outside Europe helped the French war effort. There was also the burden borne by Africans within their home countries, and the great help that most of them gave by not revolting at a time of their colonial

---

130   Wolters (note 47), p. 125.

131   Michel (note 106), chapters XI, XII.

132   Ibid., p. 229.

masters' weakness. Many Europeans accepted the need to reward all this, and in 1918 Diagne made specific promises to soldiers.

Great expectations were aroused by the Allied victory, owing partly to British and French promises, but very much to the role of the United States and highly unrealistic hopes placed in Woodrow Wilson. In fact Wilson was a Southerner who had introduced new discriminatory measures; many of the African Americans conscripted into the US forces during the war (numbering about 368,000 in all) suffered discrimination and humiliation at the hands of other Americans while in France fighting or working for the Allies, as Du Bois found in an investigation soon after the Armistice;[133] and Wilson had sent Marines to occupy Haiti in 1915. Yet despite all this, there were hopes that the US President would promote great changes in the world order, for colonial subjects among others. For a few brief months, many people around the world believed that all sorts of things were possible.

133   Wolters (note 29), pp. 108-42.

2

CHALLENGING TRIUMPHANT EMPIRES, 1918-25

Africa in the aftermath

The British and French victory in the First World War meant that the colonial empires in Africa were more solidly established than ever, except for the one which had been ended by the victors. In North Africa the Egyptians revolted and obtained partial independence, but Britain retained a great deal of control; the Italians hardly controlled any of Libya in 1918, but were to impose their rule later; and some southern areas of French Morocco, and parts of the French territory of Mauritania (attached to the AOF), were only brought under control in 1934, but the most important areas of Morocco were under French control long before then. South of the Sahara only a few pockets of resistance remained to be overcome: in Angola for example, and in Somalia, where Abdille Hassan was finally defeated in 1920 in a campaign involving bombing by the RAF.

In the rest of Africa colonial or white settler rule was secure, it was part of the landscape, Europeans assumed it would last indefinitely and were proud of it. In Britain the Empire Exhibition at Wembley in 1924-25 was one spectacular expression of empire pride.[1] One of the anti-colonialist minority, Leonard Woolf, wrote later that in 1920

---

1   J.R. MacKenzie, *Propaganda and Empire: The Manipulation of British Public Opinion 1880-1960*, Manchester University Press, 1984, pp. 107-12; B. Porter, *The Abset-Minded Imperialists: Empire, Society, and Culture in Britain*, OUP 2004, pp. 260-1, 265-6.

The vast majority of Frenchmen and Britons were extremely proud of their empires and considered that it was self-evident that it was for the benefit of the world as well as in their own interests that they ruled directly or dominated indirectly the greater part of Asia and Africa.[2]

So this was a time to perfect systems of "native administration" and pursue some economic projects such as new railways and export crop expansion. For much of British-ruled Africa the doctrine of Indirect Rule was now applied and spread, as set out by Sir Frederick Lugard in his influential book *The Dual Mandate in Tropical Africa* (1922), where he also summarised what the majority of Westerners—one can safely assume—thought about empire in Africa:

…the civilised nations have at last recognised that while on the one hand the abounding wealth of the tropical regions of the earth must be developed and used for the benefit of mankind, on the other hand an obligation rests on the controlling power not only to safeguard the material rights of the natives, but to promote their moral and material and educational progress.[3]

Most Africans now really did have the "peace" which the colonial rulers constantly boasted of having brought them. But they also had, over most of the continent, flat-rate taxation (usually a poll tax) whose assessment and collection occupied much of a colonial official's time, while it was said for Kenya (but true of other parts of Africa too) that "the most overwhelming fact of life to Africans is the tax."[4] In French colonies there was also the hated Indigénat which allowed an official to impose fines and imprisonment within certain limits on any African, as he thought fit; this was a major cause of protests in French Africa. Forced labour and forcible crop cultivation continued and were to be extended. Settler occupation was soon expanding, with ex-servicemen seeking their shares, in Kenya and Southern Rhodesia; and they would all need to farm with African labour.

The armistice and the peace settlement brought immediate relief for all; extra burdens due to the war ended. But apart from that the peace brought no positive benefit for Africans. The British and French set about exploitation of their colonies' resources with quickly restored

---

2   L. Woolf, *Downhill All the Way*, London: Hogarth Press, 1967, p. 222.

3   F. Lugard, *The Dual Mandate in British Tropical Africa*, 1922, reprinted London: Frank Cass, 1965, p. 18.

4   N. Leys, *Kenya*, London: Hogarth Press, 1924, p. 317.

vigour; this meant yet more direction of the African economy to the needs of the industrial West, new railways and harbours, for example, being built for that purpose. The Treaty of Versailles divided the German colonies between Britain, France, Belgium and South Africa, who received their shares as Mandates under the League of Nations; while the League's Permanent Mandates Commission in Geneva scrutinised the Mandates Territories' administration, in most respects it was like ordinary colonial administration.

Apart from the exceptional developments in Egypt and Libya, Africans remained almost totally excluded from participation in government, with none of the expected increase in representation for several years after 1918. In Algeria, by the Loi Jonnart (4 February 1919), the franchise for Muslim men was considerably extended, though still very restricted, for elections to municipal councils, departmental councils (*conseils généraux*) and the Délégations Financières (a representative body, with limited powers, including Muslim Algerian representatives); this was without any obligation to give up Islamic customs and laws governing their personal lives. French citizenship, a separate matter, remained almost impossible for Muslim Algerians.

South of the Sahara, very little changed in the form of government for years. The wartime concession of full French citizenship to the Senegal Originaires stayed, but French citizenship remained out of reach for the vast majority in the other French territories, where there was also no increase in African representation. In British territories some increased representation was to come, but not for a few years. Africans did not however accept the situation, so contrary to what they had expected after their support for the victors in the war and many promises by the latter.

Discontent had always been there and the colonial rulers were used to handling it, tolerating the loyal but critical African press in some areas, suppressing even that in others, and watching constantly for any sign of serious subversion. In 1919 they had Africa in hand. But it would have been impossible for Africans not to be affected by the great convulsion of the previous years, bringing down the old European order and bringing in an entirely new force—Communism—in a major country, and affecting many colonial territories as well as Turkey, whose fate aroused the concern of Muslims everywhere. The South African educationist and political activist D.D.T. Jabavu (1885-1959, son of John Tengo Jabavu) wrote in 1922, "The aboriginal black people of South Africa have not remained unaffected by the general world movement of awakening race-consciousness that is stirring all coloured peoples in Japan, China, Egypt, the United States and the British West Indies."[5] Nor did other Africans, from north to south, in the turbulent years of what Churchill called the "Aftermath".

African unrest and protest, 1919-22

There were immediate moves in Egypt, as soon as the war was over, to try to get independence as part of the peace settlement. A permanent delegation to represent Egypt—al Wafd al Misri, "the Egyptian delegation"—was formed by Sa'ad Zaghlul Pasha (c.1860-1927) and others in November 1918. It aimed to seek independence by negotiation, but when the British authorities evinced clear hostility agitation developed in Egypt, and after the arrest of Zaghlul and others on 8 March 1919 demonstrations, strikes and riots began in Cairo and other cities, leading to clashes and many deaths and on 17 April a general strike. Afterwards Zaghlul and his colleagues were released and allowed to go to Europe. There were no concessions to the Egyptian nationalists at the Peace Conference, but later the British agreed to end the protectorate, and began negotiations in 1921 with Adli Yeken, the Prime Minister, excluding the Wafd. Zaghlul, who was highly popular in Egypt, was deported to Aden and then the Seychelles in late 1921. Britain unilaterally offered independence to Egypt, which was declared on 15 March 1922. It was far from being full independence, as Britain retained responsibility for imperial communications through Egypt, protection of foreign interests, defence (supposedly, the defence of Egypt) and the Anglo-Egyptian Sudan. But Zaghlul, who protested at this pseudo-independence, cooperated with it after returning in 1923, led the Wafd to victory in elections in January 1924, and then became Prime Minister.[6]

---

5   D.D.T. Jabavu, "Native Unrest in South Africa," *The International Review of Missions* vol. XI no. 42, April 1922, pp. 249-59 (p. 249).

6   J. Berque, *Egypt: Imperialism and Revolution*, London: Faber & Faber, 1972, pp. 282-4, 304-16.

In Libya the Italians negotiated with the Sanusiyya who controlled Cyrenaica and with the Arab leaders in Tripolitania, and offered both regions wide-ranging self-government by "Fundamental Laws" in 1919. In Tripolitania a National Reform Party was founded and started a newspaper, *Al Liwa al Tarabulsi*, but the factional quarrels among the leaders there continued, and when they eventually agreed that the Sanusiyya leader Idris should be Amir (king) of the whole country in late 1922, he was reluctant and left for Egypt. By then the Italians, for some years prostrated by the World War and obliged to leave the Libyans effectively in control of most of the country, had begun to recover and occupy more of Libya. A hard-fought and ruthless campaign was to follow.[7]

The examples of Egypt and Libya, and Mustafa Kemal's victories in Turkey from 1919 onwards, encouraged nationalists in Tunisia, and some of the Tunisian nationalists who had joined Germany and Turkey continued their struggle for a while. Salah Chérif, Mohamed Bach-Hamba, another Tunisian, and three Algerians signed a memorandum to the Peace Conference from a Comité Algéro-Tunisien. A "group of Tunisians" sent a separate memorandum to Wilson and the Peace Conference, calling for a return of Tunisia's "lost freedoms"; this may have been the work of Abdel-Aziz Tha'alibi (or Tha'albi, 1876-1944), a Jeunes Tunisiens activist and admirer of the Egyptian nationalist Kamil before the war.[8] In 1919 Tha'alibi was in Paris, to pursue efforts started in November 1918 in Tunis, together with Ahmed Sakka. Early in 1920 a 212-page pamphlet, *La Tunisie Martyre: ses Revendications*, was published, under Tha'alibi's name (though Sakka and others were involved also, as Tha'alibi spoke very little French). It rejected the French protectorate, condemning French rule particularly in its economic aspects, and calling for a return to Tunisia's 1861 Constitution—in effect, for independence. Tha'alibi was in contact with Bach Hamba in Berlin,

7   E.E. Evans-Pritchard, *The Sanusi of Cyrenaica*, OUP, 1949, pp. 147-56; R.M. Coury, *The Making of an Egyptian Arab Nationalist: The Early Years of Azzam Pasha, 1893-1936*, Reading: Ithaca Press, 1998, pp. 128-96.

8   D. Goldstein, *Libération ou annexion: aux chemins croisées de l'histoire tunisienne (1914-1922)*, Tunis: Maison Tunisienne de l'Edition, 1978, pp. 270-5.

who said there must be an unambiguous demand for independence; Bach Hamba and Chérif, however, both died in Berlin in 1920.[9]

Tha'alibi's demands were opposed by some Tunisian nationalists as going too far, but the Parti Libéral Tunisien, founded in Tunisia in February 1920, also called for a new constitution, and at its congress in June 1921 Tha'alibi was elected chairman; the party aimed at independence, though it advocated a cautious approach towards achieving it. Renamed the Parti Libéral Constitutionnel, it came to be popularly known as the Destour (the Arabic word for constitution).[10] Delegations went to Paris but did not come near getting approval for any of the Destour's demands, and there were rival political leaders in Tunisia; Tha'alibi stepped down as the party's chairman in November 1922 and—responding to heavy hints from the Resident-General, Lucien Saint—went into exile in July 1923, first spending some time in Italy. Some reforms in 1922 in representation of Tunisians in the Consultative Council, renamed a Grand Council, and at local level made little change to the state of domination by the settlers and France, and demonstrations in support of the Destour in Tunis in April 1922 achieved nothing.[11] But the Destour remained in being, and Tunisia had become the second African country (after Egypt) where a nationalist party campaigned for full independence. It did not use the term "nationalist" in its name, as Kamil's party had done in Egypt, but in retrospect it is considered a nationalist party.

The word "national" or "nationalist", or *watani* in Arabic, had been used by movements against colonial or settler rule before, for example by the SANNC in South Africa since 1912. It was used of some African movements in the 1920s, when nationalism was a powerful if not dominant force in the world, revealed in the emergence of (more or less) national states after the collapse of multi-national empires. That development clearly inspired Africans opposing colonialism, but how comparable were the movements they led with the Irish or the Polish national movement? That is a complex question relating to the whole very wide question of what nationalism means and, even more basically, what a "nation" is. In recent decades this has been the subject

9   Ibid., pp. 278-85.
10   Ibid., pp. 293-338.
11   Ibid., pp. 336-496.

of academic debate.[12] It was debated in the inter-war period too, but then arguments about whether a colonial territory could be called a "nation" or not had immediate political implications—Europeans saying it could not be so called were implying, or actually saying, that therefore it might as well stay under colonial rule.

Early in the 20th century, as mentioned in Chapter 1, Attoh Ahuma in the Gold Coast responded to that argument in his short booklet *The Gold Coast Nation and National Consciousness*, a collection of his newspaper articles, in which he wrote,

It is strenuously asserted by rash and irresponsible literalists that the Gold Coast, with its multiform composition of congeries of States or Provinces, independent of each other, divided by complex political institutions, laws and customs—could not be described as a nation in the eminent sense of the word…But the objection appears to us to be purely academic…we dare affirm, with sanctity of reason and with the emphasis of conviction, that—WE ARE A NATION.

He went on to mention the Akan group of languages which many Ghanaians (though not all) have in common. But then he added,

We are being welded together under one umbrageous Flag—a Flag that is the symbol of justice, freedom and fairplay; and we have ruling over us, as king of our kings and in the bond of peace, one paramount emperor—His Majesty King George V. The Gold Coast under the aegis of the Union Jack is the unanswerable argument to all who may incontinently withhold from us the common rights, privileges, and status of nationality.[13]

It was not an "unanswerable" point: the fact that most African colonial territories did not correspond at all with precolonial states, and were united only by boundaries fixed arbitrarily during the partition, was precisely what led some to argue that the terms "nation" and "nationalism" could not have any meaning there. Another Ghanaian, J.E. Casely Hayford, made in the 1920s nationalist arguments on behalf of all the four British West African colonies together. In modern times,

---

12   The abundant literature on the topic includes a useful summary of the arguments in Anthony Smith, *Nationalism: Theory, Ideology, History*, Cambridge: Polity, 2001.

13   S.R.B. Attoh Ahuma, *The Gold Coast Nation and National Consciousness*, Liverpool 1911, reprinted (with new Introduction by Prof. J.C. de Graft Johnson) London: Cass, 1971, pp. 1-2.

when colonialism is no longer an issue but the unity or disunity of post-colonial African states certainly is, scholars still emphasise the fact that those states were originally unified only by artificial colonial borders. Ernest Gellner wrote that African reaction to colonial rule

was simply the summation of all the blacks, the non-whites of a given historical accidental territory, now unified by the new administrative machinery. The adherents of the new nationalism did not necessarily share any positive traits.[14]

However, colonial rule was maintained and defended even in territories that were identical to or corresponded closely with pre-existing states—Morocco, Basutoland, Tunisia, Madagascar. What mattered to both colonisers and colonised was the fact of European rule. That is what matters for the present study, which will not examine further the question of what nationalism meant then or means now. For this is a study of *opposition*—the opposition which alien invasion, occupation and exploitation have always aroused among subjected peoples, with the important addition of moral opposition from within the dominating peoples. This story is part of the wider, age-old and worldwide story of all sorts of popular opposition and resistance, including everyday passive resistance—minimal working or malingering by the "lazy native" employee, moonshine, evasion of controls on movement, rude remarks about whites in languages they did not understand, etc.[15]—as well as more overt acts: armed uprisings (very rare in sub-Saharan Africa in the inter-war period), dissident religious movements, and modern forms of political activity—which were often called "nationalist" at the time and are often recalled as "early nationalism" today.

In Algeria no nationalist party like the Destour was formed in the immediate aftermath of the war, but the Emir Khaled became an unofficial leader of Muslim Algerians when elections were held in 1919-20 with the extended franchise. He headed one strand of the Jeunes Algériens movement, emphasising the people's Muslim and Arab character and heritage, in opposition to the other formed by naturalised French citizens, led by Dr Belkacem Bentami. On 23 May 1919 Khaled sent a petition to President Wilson denouncing continued land-grabbing by

14   E. Gellner, *Nations and Nationalism*, Oxford: Blackwell, 1983, p. 83.

15   An important study of this, relevant to colonial Africa though not quoting many examples from it, is James C. Scott, *Domination and the Arts of Resistance: Hidden Transcripts*, Yale University Press 1990.

settlers, the gap between *colon* prosperity and indigenous poverty, the special laws applied to Muslims only, military conscription, and other aspects of French misrule, and calling for freely chosen Algerian Muslim delegates to be sent to "decide our future fate, under the aegis of the LEAGUE OF NATIONS". He added,

Your fourteen conditions for world peace, Mr President, accepted by the Allies and the Central Powers, must serve as a basis for the emancipation of all oppressed small peoples, without distinction of race or religion.[16]

The wording of this appeal seemed to envisage reconsideration of Algeria's position as part of France, at least as a possibility, and was taken that way by many at the time;[17] but if Khaled was briefly carried away by the worldwide excitement Wilson had aroused, he did not cling to unrealistic hopes that were far from Wilson's mind, and he joined in the electoral politics of Algeria as three French departments, accepting the status quo. Elected in 1919-20 as a city councillor, an Algiers departmental councillor and a member of the Délégations Financières, Khaled won wide support among Muslims, drawing big crowds at his meetings, but ferocious hostility among the settlers and their press. On his side he was backed by his bilingual French-Arabic newspaper *Ikdam*, which covered events in Egypt and Turkey extensively.[18]

Although Khaled's main demand was representation of Muslim Algerians in the French National Assembly and increased (but not majority) representation for them in elective bodies in Algeria, and his other demands—for an end to the special laws, for compulsory education in French and Arabic, etc.—were similarly moderate and similarly implied acceptance of French rule, he was denounced as a dangerous firebrand; he was called a "nationalist" by his enemies, who meant it as an insult. The constant colonialist attacks and official suspicion that Khaled suffered, accompanied by annulment of elections, fines and administrative harassment, angered and discouraged him, while after he had briefly reunited the Jeunes Algériens movement behind him in 1920-21, divisions set in. In 1923 he agreed to go into exile in return for having his

16   A. Koulakssis and G. Meynier, *L'Emir Khaled premier Za'im? Identité algérienne et colonialisme français*, Paris: Harmattan, 1987, pp. 340-42.

17   Ibid., pp. 126-30.

18   Ibid., pp. 114-20, 184. See ibid., pp. 197-299 for a full examination of Khaled's political action and ideas.

debts paid by the Governor-General's office, and left for Egypt.[19] But despite this seemingly humiliating deal, he was to be back on the scene in 1924.

In most of French Africa south of the Sahara there was no major protest activity in the immediate post-war years, apart from a railway strike in Senegal in 1919, but there was some activity (of which more shortly) by some Africans in France. By then French Africa had an outstanding political leader in Blaise Diagne, whose efforts to raise more troops in 1918 made him more than ever a good Frenchman, while he remained popular in French Africa. He was re-elected in the French National Assembly elections of November 1919, and soon afterwards the party he had just founded, the Parti Socialiste Républicain, won control of all the Four Communes and the General Council of Senegal. He came to be seen by many as a representative of Africans under French rule generally; he often helped Africans in difficulty in France, for example. He suggested that there should be more African representatives in Paris, with the vote not confined to full French citizens, and proposed extension of the French Penal Code all over AOF. All this made many French officials and defenders of empire highly suspicious of Diagne and "Diagnism" for a time. But in 1923 Diagne signed a pact with the Bordeaux-based firms dominating the economy in Senegal, and became fully one of the French colonial "establishment".[20]

The example of the Senegalese French citizens, which the colonial rulers dreaded, was indeed the object of keen attention in Dahomey, where there was a small coastal elite community with no citizen's rights or elective representation but a fair amount of mission education and a fairly free press. An elite group called the Jeunes Dahoméens was active during the war years, and elite criticism of the French administration continued later. Early in 1923 strikes and riots broke out in Porto Novo after an increase in the head tax from 2.25 francs per person to 15 for a man, 10 for a woman and 5 for a child; the AOF government authorised a state of siege on 25 February, and reinforced troops quickly

---

19   Ibid., pp. 118-20, 167-91. He had earlier been surrounded by obsessive official suspicion during his war service: ibid., pp. 102-13, 154-66.

20   G. Wesley Johnson, *The Emergence of Black Politics in Senegal: The Struggle for Power in the Four Communes, 1900-1920*, Stanford University Press, 1971, pp. 198-216.

ended the unrest. Tension had been building up because of a dispute among the city's Muslims, but in addition the unrest was attributed to outside instigation, as colonial unrest commonly was then and later. A militant teacher, Louis Hunkanrin, who had been active before and after the War in Dahomey and France, and had later made contact with left-wing groups, was particularly suspected, and was arrested and banished.[21]

The elite of one West African coastal people, the Dualas of what became French Cameroun (handed to French administration in 1916, a Mandated Territory from 1920), produced protests going further than most others in sub-Saharan Africa at that time. Soon after the Armistice a meeting of Duala chiefs agreed on a joint message saying their people wanted to be heard by representatives of the Allies on the question of their future. Soon afterwards they sent another which, according to a summary sent in a telegram from the French Commissioner (governor), said, "We all await the Allied representatives and will receive them with pleasure." The Commissioner was well aware of plenty of anti-colonial feeling behind these messages.[22]

On 18 August 1919 a group of prominent Dualas including two paramount chiefs sent a petition to the French government for forwarding to the Peace Conference. Written in German, the petition mentioned the "world League which would be formed now and whose first task would be to back the interests of the natives and to deliver them from every arbitrary principle." Speaking on behalf of all Cameroonians, the petitioners asked the Allies to study "whether Cameroun cannot be considered a neutral territory"; clearly "neutral" meant "independent". They added that alternatively, they would agree to be ruled by an Allied power, but they wanted "the right to choose the power". There followed specific demands, for example for civil rights, security of office for chiefs, an end to summary justice, revision of the trial of Rudolf Duala Manga Bell, executed in 1914, and an end to expropria-

---

21   C. Harrison, *France and Islam in West Africa, 1860-1960*, CUP 1988, pp. 150-58; A.L. Conklin, *A Mission to Civilize: The Republican Idea of Empire in France and West Africa, 1895-1930*, Stanford University Press, 1997, pp. 160-3. See pp. 122-3 for more on Hunkanrin.

22   J. Derrick, "Douala under the French Mandate, 1916 to 1936," PhD, London, 1979, pp. 136-41.

tions like the Bonanjo expropriation in Douala in 1914.[23] The petition of August 1919 was inevitably ignored, but in French Cameroun and other Mandated Territories Africans noted that the mandates involved some idea of accountability for treatment of "natives", and a new way of getting grievances against French colonial rule heard—and before an international forum, too. Several petitioners in French Togo (then called Togoland in English) approached the League of Nations, in at least one case seeking support in Britain also.[24]

Other West African coastal elite communities, which had much in common with the Dualas, were also stirring at this time. The National Congress of British West Africa (NCBWA) held an inaugural conference in Accra on 11-29 March 1920, and then sent a delegation to Britain. Its leading members, who headed the delegation, were J.E. Casely Hayford and a young Sierra Leonean doctor, Herbert Bankole-Bright; the delegation also included the Nigerian surveyor Herbert Macaulay (1864-1946). The delegates tried to meet the Colonial Secretary, Lord Milner, but he refused to see them. London accepted the view of Governor Guggisberg of Gold Coast and Governor Clifford of Nigeria that these elite protesters were unrepresentative of the Africans. But they received a sympathetic reception in England from the League of Nations Union, a respected lobbying organisation founded in 1918; Bankole-Bright told that audience, "We do not believe in unconstitutional principles or the principles of Bolshevism", while adding that the Congress sought to calm "the present political unrest in West Africa", which otherwise could cause Britain greater difficulties than it had faced in Ireland, Egypt and Ceylon.[25]

This was in line with the NCBWA's Constitution agreed at its second full session, in Freetown in 1923, which declared

23   Ibid. pp. 141-7.

24   M. Callahan, *Mandates and Empire: The League of Nations and Africa, 1914-1931*, Portland, OR: Sussex Academic Press, 1999, pp. 117-20.

25   D. Kimble, *Politics in Ghana 1850-1928*, Oxford: Clarendon Press, 1963, pp. 381-9; J.S. Coleman, *Nigeria: Background to Nationalism*, Berkeley and London: University of California Press, 1958, pp. 192-5; J.A. Langley, *Pan-Africanism and Nationalism in West Africa 1900-1945*, OUP, 1973, pp. 110-94, 243-85; G.O. Olusanya, "The Lagos Branch of the National Congress of British West Africa," *Journal of the Historical Society of Nigeria* vol. IV no. 2, June 1968, pp. 321-33.

That the policy of the Congress shall be to maintain strictly and inviolate the connection of the British West African Dependencies with the British Empire, and to maintain unreservedly all and every right of free citizenship of the Empire and the fundamental principle that taxation goes with effective representation...to aid in the development of the political institutions of British West Africa under the Union Jack...and, in time, to ensure within her borders the Government of the people by the people for the people; to secure equal opportunity for all, to preserve the lands of the people for the people.[26]

This was not mere slavish submission to "the Union Jack"; all over Africa people were taxed without representation, and reforming that situation would totally transform a colonial system which could never resemble "Government of the people by the people for the people". However, the difference between groups like the NCBWA and those who followed "the principles of Bolshevism" or other radical principles was clearly seen at the time.

Perhaps because of the NCBWA's campaign, some election of African Legislative Council (LegCo) members was introduced in 1922 in Nigeria—three elected members for Lagos Colony and one for Calabar, in the Legislative Council for the Colony and the Southern Provinces of the Protectorate—and in 1926 in Gold Coast Colony and in 1924 in Sierra Leone Colony (essentially, Freetown). Thus leading Western-educated people could seek election in the small areas where they were numerous; in the greater part of those territories there was no question of any such representation then, and in Nigeria LegCo had no competence in the North.

The formation of the National Congress was one episode in the constant peaceful but impassioned battle between the West African coastal elites and the government. More than ever, the British with their Indirect Rule policy favoured chiefs against Western-educated Africans. In the Gold Coast they had a staunch chiefly ally in Nana Ofori Atta, paramount chief (with the title Okyenhene) of Akyem (or Akim) Abuakwa and a leading spokesman for traditional authority at that time when the Asante kingdom had been abolished; he too said the NCBWA delegation was unrepresentative.[27] However, Western-educated Africans did

---

26   Quoted in Langley (note 25), p. 117.
27   Kimble (note 25), pp. 389-96; B.M. Edsman, *Lawyers in Gold Coast Politics c. 1900-1945*, Uppsala, 1979, pp. 54-67. On Nana Ofori Atta (reigned 1912-43),

not generally oppose chieftaincy or other traditions. In the Gold Coast the elite and its newspapers called for the return of the former Ashanti King Prempeh from exile in the Seychelles, which eventually occurred in 1924, though they also criticised the role given to chiefs in the 1926 Constitution and refused for some time to cooperate in applying it.[28]

In London in 1920 Macaulay worked in London as secretary to Chief Amodu Oluwa, titular head of a Lagos chiefly family, and helped him in a land case against the government, which he won at the Judicial Committee of the Privy Council; after this the government withdrew recognition from the traditional king (the Oba of Lagos or Eleko) for backing Oluwa. Reactions to this in Lagos led to the foundation in 1922 of the Nigerian National Democratic Party (NNDP), with Macaulay as General Secretary, which won the 1923 elections of African elective members of LegCo. Its declared aim was "A Government of the People, by the People, for the People," but it proclaimed loyalty to the King-Emperor. Its specific demands included Africanisation of the civil service (a demand echoing a deeply-felt elite grievance) and universal compulsory education in Nigeria (not yet achieved today).[29]

The NCBWA was an organisation of the Western-educated elite, and more particularly of its upper stratum of lawyers, doctors, clergymen and newspaper proprietors. While they had grievances Western-educated communities in West Africa had considerable freedoms and privileges. They included the clerks and other junior staff indispensable to the work of the government and the firms, and although these suffered from racial discrimination in government service, combined with the appalling attitude of Europeans to "educated natives", they were able to make progress in many directions.[30] Many people of the Westernised communities of Freetown, Lagos, Accra and other coastal towns were able to do well in business, despite the dominance of European firms—notably those that were to be merged in 1929 into the United

---

see R. Rathbone, *Murder and Politics in Colonial Ghana*, Yale University Press, 1993, pp. 1-67.

28   Kimble (note 25), pp. 443-55, 479-85.

29   P.D. Cole, *Modern and Traditional Elites in the Politics of Lagos*, CUP 1975, pp. 109-139; Coleman (note 25), p. 198.

30   See J. Derrick, "The "Native Clerk" in Colonial West Africa", *African Affairs* vol. 82 no. 326, January 1983.

Africa Company (UAC)—in import-export trade; some Africans tried to challenge that dominance. A good look at the life of those West African communities[31] shows that these were definitely not people who had "nothing to lose but their chains". Nationalism arose among them, but a revolutionary movement never could.

In South Africa the SANNC, soon after the Armistice, sent a memorial to the King of England via the Governor-General calling on Britain to revise the South African Constitution "in such a way as to grant enfranchisement of natives throughout the Union".[32] This may have meant non-racial selective suffrage, but as worded it could have been a bold demand for one man, one vote—not to be granted for 75 years, and then not by Britain. Such a demand can be explained by the feeling, widely expressed in South Africa and elsewhere, that many great changes could and should come after the war and the Allied victory.

The Congress sent a delegation of five men to Britain and to the Paris Peace Conference (where an Afrikaner delegation also went, headed by J.B.M. Hertzog, to ask for the former independent Afrikaner republics to be restored). The SANNC delegates achieved nothing in Paris but aroused some sympathy and support in Britain and were able, on 21 November 1919, to meet the Prime Minister, David Lloyd George. He listened with genuine shock to their account of the land dispossession, lack of political rights, and obligation to carry passes, and promised to discuss the Africans' grievances with Smuts, now Prime Minister of South Africa following Botha's death in June 1919. Sol Plaatje, one of the delegation, recalled the Allies' claim to be "fighting for the protection of oppressed nations". Lloyd George did write to Smuts, who dismissed his concerns, saying that the SANNC was unrepresentative and its accusations exaggerated, and that Africans had avenues to express grievances within South Africa. After this private exchange of letters the British government did little or nothing more.[33] Some non-whites did

31   A fascinating and lifelike portrayal of them is to be found in A. MacMillan, *The Red Book of West Africa*, Collingridge, 1920, reprint London: Frank Cass, 1968. For a scholarly and vivid account of the Lagos elite, see K. Mann, *Marrying Well*, Cambridge University Press, 1985.

32   B. Willan, *Sol Plaatje: South African Nationalist 1876-1932*, London: Heinemann, 1984, pp. 228-9.

33   Ibid., pp. 241-6.

not even then abandon the hopes of getting help from Britain, but it was a more forlorn hope than ever.

The Black and Coloured[34] voters in Cape Province were organised, and had some influence on elections because they were numerous enough in certain constituencies to affect the result. However, they were too few to make a real difference. Politics was about rivalry among whites, with the Afrikaner National Party under Hertzog out to take revenge for the defeat of 1899-1902, against the British, the Rand mine owners, the English-speaking Cape politicians, and the hated turncoat Smuts—and to enforce ever greater subjugation of non-whites. The segregated white workers' labour movement defended the interests of those relatively privileged workers, and the Labour Party was a fierce defender of white supremacy.

Besides political protests, and at first separate from them, there was a good deal of industrial unrest in South Africa in the years following 1918. It was a worldwide phenomenon—other examples were the great Clydeside strike in Scotland in 1919, and massive strikes in that year in France and the USA—and there were plenty of economic reasons besides the others in colonial territories. There was considerable hardship in the immediate post-war period, when a railway strike and riots broke out in Sierra Leone in July 1919, provoked mainly by the high price of rice and grievances against Syrian traders.[35] In South Africa in 1920, 80,000 Black mine workers on the Rand staged a massive strike, not to be repeated on that scale by Africans in that country until 1946.

In 1918-19 a new African trade union was founded in South Africa, starting with Coloured dock workers, and formally constituted in 1920 as the Industrial and Commercial Union of Africa, abbreviated ICU; the following year it absorbed the rival Industrial and Commercial Workers' Union (ICWU). Clements Kadalie, a teacher who had migrated from Nyasaland to Cape Town in 1921, became National Secretary in 1921 and built the ICU up into a considerable force for a time, with its headquarters in Johannesburg. By 1923 there were seventeen registered

---

34   That is of the South African community of mixed descent called "coloured" in a sense confined to South Africa. At the time under review non-whites were also generally called "coloured" by Europeans outside South Africa.

35   Langley (note 25), pp. 205-13; L. Spitzer, *The Creoles of Sierra Leone*, Madison and London: University of Wisconsin Press, 1974, pp. 168-9; F.R. Anthony, *Sawpit Boy*, Freetown: published by author, 1980, pp. 31-3.

branches, and the ICU was an energetic champion of Africans' rights for a few years.[36] It was able to expand because there were still some liberties protected by the law in South Africa then; the police-state legislation had begun but had far to go. But there was regular state violence against non-whites, for example in the suppression of the miners' strike of 1920. The worst incidents of such violence in those years were the Bulhoek massacre of up to 190 members of an independent sect called the "Israelites" in Cape Province, on 24 May 1921; and a punitive expedition in late May and early June 1922 against an independent-minded segment of the Nama people of South-West Africa, the partly-European Bondelzwarts, of whom 115 were killed. The Bondelzwarts slaughter was discussed at the League of Nations, as South-West Africa was a Mandated Territory.[37]

In addition there was constant extension and reinforcement of control over Africans' lives, through the pass system, to control especially movement into towns. Among white South African politicians the arguments over "native affairs" were about how best to maintain white supremacy, and the outcome of the arguments, from the 1920s onwards for six decades, was more regimentation and more subjection. In this situation the SANNC, in the 1920s and 30s, had to fight a rearguard action against worsening tyranny, seeking any available allies to do so, rather than pressing for its long-term hopes. But the Congress, which was renamed the African National Congress (ANC) in 1925, did have those long-term hopes, set out in resolutions of the Annual Conference on 28-9 May 1923. These included a "declaration, statement or Bill of Rights" which said that "the Bantu" and the Coloureds had a right as British subjects to enjoyment of the British principles of the "liberty of the subject, justice and equality of all classes in the eyes of the law" (article 3) and the benefits of Rhodes' formula of "equal rights for all civilised men south of the Zambezi" (words often quoted, probably seen as meaning more that Rhodes had intended); they had a right to "the democratic principles of equality of treatment and equality of citizenship in the land, irrespective of race, class, creed or origin." (article 4) Then, in article 5, the declaration went on:

---

36   C. Kadalie, *My Life and the ICU*, reprinted with introduction by S. Trapido, London: Frank Cass, 1970.

37   W.K. Hancock, *Smuts: The Fields of Force*, CUP, 1968, pp. 89-110.

...the peoples of African descent have, as an integral and inseparable element in the population of the great Dominion of South Africa, and as undisputed contributors to the growth and development of the country, the constitutional right of an equal share in the management and direction of the affairs of this the land of their permanent abode, and to direct representation by members of their own race in all the legislative bodies of the land, otherwise, there can be 'no taxation without representation..'[38]

While this declaration did not actually mention African majority rule, that would have been the result of the application of its principles. Very few white politicians, if any, were ready to consider those principles even in the long term.

A few white South Africans opposed this white consensus. The International Socialist League (ISL), founded in 1915 by breakaway white members of the Labour Party, rejected that party's attitude to Black workers. Its leaders D. Ivon Jones and Sidney Percival Bunting took a lead in this respect, as when Bunting issued a leaflet urging white workers not to help break the 1920 strike.[39] In 1921 the ISL was to become the nucleus of the Communist Party of South Africa. But, as will be explained below, non-racial slogans were soon to be drowned in the reality of racial conflict.

In Southern Rhodesia there was some African protest activity in the post-1918 era. But the settlers were already almost in control, and they became completely so after their referendum of 1922, in which they voted for "Responsible Government" on their own rather than inclusion in South Africa. Some Southern Rhodesia Africans who had the vote as in Cape Province then formed a Rhodesian Bantu Voters Association (RBVA) on 20 January 1923, to negotiate a better deal for Africans with the settler leaders. This small reasonable group could achieve nothing, and settler self-government after 1923 was not far from total

---

38   Text in Document 48b, T. Karis and G.M. Carter (eds), *From Protest to Challenge: A Documentary History of African Politics in South Africa 1882-1964, Vol. I: Protest and Hope 1882-1934* (by Sheridan Johns III), Stanford, CA: Hoover Institution Press, 1972, pp. 297-8. The Congress reaffirmed these resolutions at its Annual Conference of 4-5 January 1926, but in the Bill of Rights changed "Bantu" to "African" (Karis and Carter, eds, p. 301). The word "Bantu" was later to be the official one used by the white supremacy regime, though not at the time under review, when "Native" was always used.

39   E. Roux, *Time Longer than Rope*, London: Gollancz, 1948, pp. 140-42.

independence; the British Crown had reserve powers but in practice was almost never to use them.[40]

In Kenya white settlers wanted similar control, but clashed with the larger Indian immigrant community, and as a by-product of this struggle, but primarily as a result of missionary and humanitarian pressure, a White Paper issued by the Colonial Secretary, the Duke of Devonshire, in July 1923 said that

Primarily Kenya is an African territory and His Majesty's Government think it necessary definitely to record their considered opinion that the interests of the African natives must be paramount, and that if and when those interests and the interests of the immigrant races should conflict, the former should prevail... in the administration of Kenya. His Majesty's Government regard themselves as exercising a trust, on behalf of the African population, themselves and they are unable to delegate or share this trust the object of which may be defined as the protection and advancement of the native races.

This expressed the basic principle on which proponents of better, beneficial colonial rule, such as missionaries, insisted. Ultimately its assertion on this occasion was to ensure that Kenya eventually passed from colonial rule from London to African majority rule. However, for three decades settler interests were "paramount" in practice.[41]

In Kenya Kikuyus were aroused by the loss of land, the settlers' labour demands which led to registration of Africans for direction of their labour, and multiple privations in the war years. First a Kikuyu Association held talks with the government over the land issue; then a more vigorous Young Kikuyu Association was formed in June 1921 under the leadership of Harry Thuku, a telephone operator. Soon renamed the East African Association, it campaigned for an end to the hut tax, suspension of the labour registration ordinance and other steps to lighten the oppression, and aroused wide support until Thuku was arrested on 14 March 1922 and banished to distant areas; police fired on a protest demonstration against his arrest in Nairobi, and over 20 people were

---

40   T.O. Ranger, "African Politics in Twentieth-Century Southern Rhodesia," Ch. 9 in T.O. Ranger (ed.), *Aspects of Central African History*, London: Heinemann, 1968, pp. 218-26.

41   J.D. Kamoche, *Imperial Trusteeship and Political Evolution in Kenya, 1923-1963*, Washington: University Press of America, 1981, pp. 28-80.

killed.[42] Although the Kikuyus were badly divided among themselves, they continued to seethe and were to be heard from again after a few years.

There was, then, a wave of unrest around Africa in the years after 1918. Protests could have considerable support, as in Egypt in 1919 especially, but sometimes the numbers involved were small. But they represented something fairly new. In place of the almost vanished "primary resistance" by people living in and defending tradition, now there was dissidence led by people influenced by Western education, Western-style employment, urban and industrial life, and mission teaching. This was a sign of things to come. All sorts of influences were there to encourage protests.

Several leaders of protest movements, notably of the SANNC, were Christians, and some were clergymen. The Rev. Sefako Makgatho was President of the SANNC from 1917 to 1924, and was succeeded by another clergyman, the Rev. Zaccheus Mahabane. Concerning them and the Rev. Walter Rubusana—co-author of the Congress' Constitution, the first African to be elected to the Cape Provincial Council (in 1910), and editor of the revised Xhosa Bible published in 1905—it has been rightly observed that "By rejecting white domination in terms of liberal and Christian doctrine, they were no less radical than socialists who rejected capitalist domination in Marxist terms."[43] The colonial and white settler regimes knew well that, however firmly missionaries preached obedience to authority, their basic Christian teaching, and the schooling that went with it, could encourage criticism of authority. Norman Leys wrote in 1918:

The real crux is the teaching of the doctrine that "there is no difference, Jew nor Gentile, slave nor free." That doctrine is the real root of the trouble. The fact to face is that it is of the essence of the religion.[44]

---

42   Harry Thuku with assistance from Kenneth King, *An Autobiography*, Nairobi: OUP, 1970, pp. 18-34; M.S. Clough, *Fighting Two Sides: Kenyan Chiefs and Politicians, 1918-1940*, Niwot, CO: University Press of Colorado, 1990, pp. 19-64; J. Murray-Brown, *Kenyatta*, London: Allen & Unwin, 1972, pp. 85-7, 100-3.

43   J. and R. Simons, *Class and Colour in South Africa 1850-1950*, London: IDAF, 1983, p. 251.

44   J.W. Cell (ed.), *By Kenya Possessed: The Correspondence of Norman Leys and J.H. Oldham 1918-1926*, University of Chicago Press, 1976, p. 108. The allusion is

While concerned about the results of white missionaries' work, those regimes were still more wary of the independent African churches which continued to emerge. Those churches preached faith and morals like other churches, often being as strict as mission churches on some moral matters, and they too commonly preached obedience to the authorities; but they were African initiatives sometimes attracting mass enthusiasm and outside white control. This meant repressive action against some of them, such as the church founded in the Belgian Congo in 1921 by Simon Kimbangu, who was actually sentenced to death, though the sentence was commuted to life imprisonment plus 120 strokes; he spent thirty years in prison, much of it in solitary confinement.[45] The colonial authorities feared that church dissidence encouraged general anti-colonial feeling, and they were not altogether wrong. In Douala some disciples of the Baptist mission broke away to join a Native Baptist Church (NBC) headed by Pastor Adolf Lotin Same, a minister of that mission and a noted writer of Duala-language hymns, and when the French Protestant Mission authorities suspended Lotin Same from his pastoral functions in March 1922 there was a strong movement of protest among the Dualas, though most of them did not join his church.[46] The French Chef de Circonscription (equivalent to District Officer) in charge of Douala wrote in 1920 of the NBC:

It is normal to preach on themes taken from Scripture, apparently innocent, but in which the initiated can recognise the French administration in the Roman praetor who sends Christians to the wild beasts, in the Beast of the Apocalypse, or in Nebuchadnezzar or King Herod.[47]

The offshoots of the Watch Tower Bible and Tract Society (the Jehovah's Witnesses) in Nyasaland, Northern Rhodesia and the Belgian Congo, called Kitawala in some African languages and attracting considerable numbers by the 1920s, openly preached that colonial authority was of Satan, or that it would be ended by the coming reign of Christ. One British official wrote to another in Northern Rhodesia in

---

to Colossians 3, 11.

45   M.-L. Martin, *Kimbangu*, first published in German 1971, English translation Oxford: Basil Blackwell, 1975.

46   Derrick (note 22), pp. 228-39.

47   Douala Circonscription Annual Report 1920, pp. 5-6, file APA 11873, Cameroon Archives, Yaounde.

1925, "Should you be able to prove that any Watch Tower preacher is saying that Europeans are rich and oppressive, and deliverance is coming next year, I would recommend prosecution..."; and a missionary said the movement was "African Bolchewism" (*sic*).[48]

Like Christianity, Islam taught about something higher than the colonial rulers' laws. This simple fact meant that they could encourage a critical attitude to colonial—or other—authority. In the case of Islam the Salafiyya reform movement—inspired by Abduh and his followers whose leader was Rashid Rida—did not usually call for resistance, but its moral rigorism could only encourage a critical view of "infidel" rule. In Morocco, where it spread in the 1920s and was active in founding new modern Islamic schools called "free schools", the reform movement condemned the Sufi brotherhoods (*turuq*, singular *tariqa*) which were widely popular and were used by the French to secure Muslims' loyalty; they were denounced for both false doctrine and collaboration.

In Black Africa there was less challenge to the leading *turuq* like the Tijaniyya, the main confraternity in Senegal, which was thoroughly loyal to France, and the new Mourides or Muridiyya founded in that country by Amadou Bamba (c. 1850-1927), which was not only loyal but very useful to the French by encouraging disciples to grow more groundnuts. In the Anglo-Egyptian Sudan Abd al-Rahman al-Mahdi (1885-1959), son of the famous Mahdi who had conquered the Sudan in the 1880s, steadily rebuilt the Mahdist movement on peaceful lines, telling his followers to obey the British.[49] But the French were initially highly suspicious of Bamba, deporting him twice, and as for Mahdism, it was still feared by the British and French despite Abd al-Rahman's attitude. There was panic among the British rulers of Nigeria when Sa'id ibn Hayatu, son of a former dissident Islamic leader, gathered a community around him at Dumbulwa in Fika emirate; he was suspected of plotting a rising, and despite lack of good proof, was deported without trial in 1923, and spent over twenty years in banishment.[50]

---

48   J.M. Assimeng, "Sectarian Allegiance and Political Authority: the Watch Tower Society in Zambia, 1907-35," *Journal of Modern African Studies* vol. 8 no. 1, 1970, pp. 97-112, pp. 104-5.

49   Awad al-Karsani, "The Establishment of Neo-Mahdism in the Western Sudan 1920-1934," *African Affairs* vol. 86 no. 344, July 1987, pp. 385-404.

50   C.N. Ubah, "British Measures against Mahdism at Dumbulwa in Northern Nigeria, 1923: A Case of Colonial Overreaction," *Islamic Culture* vol. L no.

Pan-Islamism was still a force for colonial rulers to reckon with. Solidarity with Turkey was shown again in the enthusiasm aroused in North Africa by Mustafa Kemal's victories in 1919-22, but this was followed by shock and disappointment when Kemal abolished the Caliphate and carried out frenzied secularisation. Feelings of Islamic solidarity continued to be widely aroused in support of the Libyan resistance and especially, for a few years, in support of the famous resistance leader in Spanish Morocco, Abd el-Krim (in full Sidi Mohammed ben Abd el-Krim el-Khettabi, 1882-1963). After working for the Spanish administration for some time, becoming a judge, in 1920-21 he toured the Rif mountains whose Berber people had never been fully subdued, and gathered forces to fight Spanish troops sent to enforce fuller control. The Rif fighters won a great victory at Anual in July 1921, and for five years Abd el-Krim effectively ruled most of the interior of Spanish Morocco. Early in 1923 he proclaimed a state, the Dawla Jumhuriya Rifiya, with himself as President. Under his government based at Ajdir, with six members besides Abd el-Krim, a National Assembly, local government based on tribes and clans, there was a regular army plus universal conscription for short periods each year, a flag and a national anthem. It established arms production and a telephone system, and raised Koranic taxes, besides earning good money from ransoms for prisoners taken at Anual. Abd el-Krim's success aroused romantic excitement around the world and particular enthusiasm among Muslims in many countries, as far as South Africa and India.[51]

The impact of Marcus Garvey

Whether they were fighting like the Rif Berbers, going on strike, or forming political organisations, Africans acted, obviously, on their own initiative and for their own local reasons. But of course the influence of

---

3, July 1976, pp. 169-83; P.B. Clarke, *West Africa and Islam*, Edward Arnold, 1982, pp. 120-1.

51   S. Balfour, *Deadly Embrace: Morocco and the Road to the Spanish Civil War*, OUP 2002, Chs. 2-3; A. Youssoufi, "Les institutions de la République du Rif," pp. 81-100 in *Abd el-Krim et la République du Rif: Actes du colloque international d'études historiques et sociologiques 18-20 janvier 1973* (no editor named; Charles-André Julien headed the committee sponsoring the seminar), Paris: Maspéro, 1976.

outside events was considerable. Recalling this period Ferhat Abbas, a later nationalist leader in Algeria, wrote:

President Wilson's Fourteen Points, the resurrection of Poland, of Czechoslovakia, the liberation of the Balkan peoples, the coming of the USSR and Communism, the creation of the League of Nations, the new Turkey and Mustapha Kemal's victory over European imperialists, the creation of the Destour in Tunisia, the Rif war and the epic of Emir Abd el-Krim, all these events were the theme of our conversation.[52]

Besides the Russian revolution—on which plenty more will be said later—and Kemal (until the disappointment and shock at his policies after victory), and Abd el-Krim and the Sanusiyya, Egypt was also an inspiration, for even though its independence declared in 1922 was very incomplete, it was more than most other Africans had. Keen interest and admiration were also aroused, around the colonial world, by the Irish political and guerrilla resistance that led to the Treaty creating the Irish Free State in 1921—a challenge to the greatest power in the world on its doorstep—and by the Indian National Congress campaigns in India. The INC was dissatisfied with the Montagu-Chelmsford reforms announced in 1918, providing for limited Indian participation in government at the provincial level only. Under Gandhi's leadership it launched a mass campaign against legislation to continue some wartime powers of arrest and detention; this led to the Amritsar massacre of 13 April 1919, in which 379 people were shot dead by Indian Army troops. There followed Gandhi's "non-cooperation" campaign in 1920, to back the Muslims' Khilafat movement protesting at the perceived threat to the Ottoman Empire and the Caliphate. After the killing of twenty-two policemen at Chauri Chaura in February 1922 Gandhi suspended the civil disobedience campaign he had launched, and he was sentenced to six years' imprisonment, but he was freed in 1924, and his campaign was just beginning.

There was also inspiration from the African Americans, especially from the new movement started among them by the Jamaican Marcus Aurelius Garvey (1887–1940). He founded the Universal Negro Improvement Association (UNIA) in Jamaica in 1914 and, after he moved to New York in 1916, it spread especially in the Northern cities of the

---

52   F. Abbas, *La nuit coloniale*, Paris: Julliard, 1962, p. 117.

United States—where the black population had been greatly increased by mass migration from the South during the war years—against the background of poverty and racism leading to the race riots of the "Red Summer" of 1919 in those cities. The riots, including thirteen days of rioting in Chicago and some in Washington, were in fact, in most cases, organised attacks on African Americans by white mobs.[53] Black Americans however often fought back, and to express that spirit of defiance Claude McKay, the Jamaican poet then living in New York, was moved to write his famous poem *If We Must Die*. Amid the hardships of African American life Garvey's UNIA made a special new sort of appeal, a "black pride" appeal. In New York it started the newspaper *The Negro World* in 1918 and opened Liberty Hall in Harlem in 1919. The theme of all this activity was that Black Americans should be proud of being Black and proud of their ancestral continent.

From the start Garvey was always evoking Africa. The UNIA Convention of 1-31 August 1920 at Liberty Hall adopted a Declaration of the Rights of the Negro Peoples of the World, parts of which read:

(13) We believe in the freedom of Africa for the Negro people of the world, and by the principle of Europe for the Europeans and Asia for the Asiatics; we also demand Africa for the Africans at home and abroad.

(14) We believe in the inherent right of the Negro to possess himself of Africa, and that his possession of same shall not be regarded as an infringement on any claim or purchase made by any race or nation.[54]

The UNIA paid attention to the African Americans' situation in the USA—the 1920 Declaration condemned discrimination, lynching and other ill treatment—but seeking to improve that situation was not its priority. It declared rather that the black people of the world must rule their homeland in Africa, and leave the white people to rule the United States where they would always be the majority and would never allow

---

53   E.D. Cronon, *Black Moses*, Madison: University of Wisconsin Press, 1955, pp. 31-2.

54   Amy Jacques Garvey (compiler), *The Philosophy and Opinions of Marcus Garvey*, 1923 and 1925, 2 vols. combined in new edition Dover, MA: The Majority Press, 1986, vol. II, pp. 135-43 (full text of the Declaration). Amy Jacques Garvey was Marcus Garvey's second wife, the first being Amy Ashwood Garvey.

equal rights for black people.[55] While in America Black people could be loyal citizens; Garvey wrote in 1923,

Fighting for the establishment of Palestine does not make the American Jew disloyal; fighting for the independence of Ireland does not make the Irish-American a bad citizen. Why should fighting for the freedom of Africa make the Afro-American disloyal or a bad citizen?[56]

And he went further to say, "To fight for African redemption does not mean that we must give up our domestic fights for political justice and industrial rights."[57] However, the UNIA disagreed strongly with the NAACP, its bitter rival for African Americans' support. Du Bois and many other African American leaders insisted that their people's home was now in America and they must seek full equality with other Americans, not be distracted by dreams of the ancestral continent.

Garvey was accused of wanting all Black Americans to move to Africa, and certain statements did suggest something like this. In a speech in New York in March 1924 he said,

The thoughtful and industrious of our race want to go back to Africa, because we realize it will be our only hope of permanent existence. We cannot all go in a day or a year, ten or twenty years. It will take time under the rule of modern economics, to entirely or largely depopulate a country of a people, who have been its residents for centuries, but we feel that, with proper help for fifty years, the problem can be solved.[58]

But he also said not all Black Americans were wanted in Africa, and he must have realised that the idea of any significant number going there was a pipedream. For those staying in the USA Garvey, an admirer of Booker T. Washington, called for self-help efforts, especially in business; he and his colleagues set up the Negro Factories Corporation, which had little success, and the Black Star Line, which won considerable publicity. It was not intended to transport Black Americans to Africa, as some suggested, but to be a successful Black business venture; there it failed utterly, its few decrepit ships making very few voyages.

---

55   See several statements in Garvey (compiler) (note 54), e.g. vol. II, p. 3, p. 39, pp. 97-8.

56   Ibid., vol. II, pp. 35-6.

57   Ibid.

58   Ibid., vol. II, p. 122.

Generally Garvey was an impractical dreamer and a showman, but that did not stop him winning huge popularity for a time. In fact the great parades the UNIA organised in Harlem, the creation of organisations like the African Legion with fancy uniforms, the adoption of a green-black-red flag, the creation of titles such as "Provisional President of Africa" (Garvey himself) and "Duke of the Nile", did not arouse only ridicule. Such things, and the UNIA's encouragement of "race pride and love", struck a chord among African American communities in Northern US cities. When Garvey extended "race pride" to crude racism, calling for maintenance of a "pure" black race and expressing sympathy with the Ku Klux Klan which talked similarly about the white race (and even meeting a Klan leader),[59] many people were shocked but not everyone. The parades and rhetoric of the UNIA offered a form of escapism; E.D. Cronon's biography said later, "When Garvey spoke of the greatness of the race, Negroes everywhere could forget for a moment the shame of discrimination and the horrors of lynching."[60]

Marcus Garvey aroused strong hostility from more serious Black American leaders who tried to persuade their people that he was a fraud, including the particularly venomous hostility of Du Bois, which Garvey returned in full.[61] Yet Garvey, an eccentric character contested among his own people, still sent shivers up the spines of the colonial rulers of Africa. It did not matter much that he was utterly vague about how to achieve his dream for Africa; what mattered was how the dream would sound to Africans, as when he declared in 1922:

As four hundred million men, women and children, worthy of the existence given us by the Divine Creator, we are determined to solve our own problem, by redeeming our Motherland Africa from the hands of alien exploitation and found there a government, a nation of our own, strong enough to lend protection to the members of our race scattered all over the world, and to compel the respect of the nations and races of the earth.[62]

---

59   Ibid. vol. I, p. 35, vol. II, pp. 71, 260-1.

60   Cronon (note 53), p. 4.

61   R. Wolters, *Du Bois and his Rivals*, Columbia, MO and London: Missouri University Press, 2002, ch. 5; Ras Makonnen, *Pan-Africanism from Within*, recorded and edited by K. King, Nairobi: OUP, 1973, chapter 4.

62   Garvey (compiler) (note 54), Vol. I, p. 52.

He said much more in this vein over the years, constantly evoking the idea of a free Africa aided (but not dominated, he urged) by Black Americans.

While Garvey suggested in 1923 that Europeans might voluntarily hand over parts of Africa,[63] on other occasions he talked of a struggle, as at the second UNIA Convention in August 1921: "If you want your liberty you yourselves must strike the blow".[64] In August 1920 Garvey sent a message to Eamonn de Valera as President of the Irish Republic, saying, "We believe Ireland should be free even as Africa shall be free for the Negroes of the world";[65] and in 1922 he declared,

...if for seven-hundred and fifty years Irishmen found perseverance enough to have carried the cause of freedom on and on until they won, then four hundred million Negroes are prepared to carry on the fight for African liberty even if it takes us to the seat of the Most High, yes if it takes us until judgment day, we shall fight on and on without relenting.[66]

Such words were more than enough to alarm the colonial powers. They were not followed by any open or secret preparations; Garvey was a speechmonger, not a conspirator. But they were bound to appeal to Africans, and so, above all, was the *Negro World*, which was commonly banned in British and French colonies.

Africans visiting the USA joined in UNIA activities; Plaatje spoke at some meetings, Duse Mohammed Ali worked on the *Negro World*. In Africa Casely Hayford said the UNIA had done more than anyone else to tell the world of the "disabilities of the African race", and a Lagos branch of the UNIA was founded in 1920.[67] That Lagos branch may have had little impact on local politics, but one young Nigerian read a copy of the *Negro World* with interest and was impressed particularly by the UNIA motto, "One God, One Aim, One Destiny." However, when the young man—Nnamdi Azikiwe, who was to become President of Nigeria—talked with his father about Garvey,

---

63   Ibid.. Vol. II, p. 61.

64   Ibid. vol. I, p. 94.

65   Cronon (note 53), p. 64.

66   Garvey (compiler) (note 54), vol. I, p. 41.

67   Kimble (note 25), p. 544; Coleman (note 25), p. 191.

he warned me that if I was found in possession of anything written by that man I would be arrested, because he was *persona non grata* with the authorities. Then I wanted to know why the mere possession of any newspaper containing the opinions of this remarkable West Indian should be a crime. Father explained to me that the colonial administration regarded his teachings as seditious, the crime for which Jesus of Nazareth was crucified. He refused to say more about this man and dismissed me with a warning to be careful not to be found with *The Negro World* in my possession.[68]

In 1920 Garvey's emissary Elie Garcia went to Liberia and, for a time, interested its government in a scheme for large-scale settlement of New World Black people. This scheme was based more on enthusiasm than on practical planning, like Garvey's other schemes; it never got under way and the Liberian government was probably suspicious of it from the start. The Liberian oligarchy, itself of American origin, suspected that the UNIA would encourage resistance by the indigenous people, called "Aborigines" by the oligarchy. Indeed the Liberian government saw a secret report by Garcia to Garvey, expressing contempt for the Americo-Liberians and saying the "Aborigines" were treated like slaves.[69] Garvey's speeches show that he did not want African Americans to act like the Americo-Liberians had done for a century after returning to Africa.

In February 1922 Garvey and three others were charged with fraud in connection with the Black Star Line's operations. The case was weak—Garvey was most probably not a fraudster, just an incompetent businessman—but Garvey alone was convicted the following year. While free on bail pending appeal he continued to organise the UNIA, now portraying himself as a martyr. But he lost the appeal and went to prison in Atlanta on 8 February 1925.[70] J. Edgar Hoover, Special Assistant to the US Attorney-General and head of the Justice Department's General Intelligence Division from 1920 to 1924 (when he was appointed head of what became the FBI), carried out investigations leading to Garvey's conviction;[71] his well known hostility to Black activism was thus shown

---

68   N. Azikiwe, *My Odyssey*, London: C. Hurst & Co., 1970, pp. 34-5.

69   M.B. Akpan, "Liberia and the Universal Negro Improvement Association: The Background to the Abortion of Garvey's Scheme for African Colonization", *Journal of African History* vol. XIV, no. 1, 1973, pp. 105-27.

70   Cronon (note 53), pp. 100-34.

71   R.G. Powers, *Secrecy and Power: The Life of J. Edgar Hoover*, Hutchinson, 1987,

at the start of his long career, but then it reflected the US government's general attitude. But the Justice Department, closely watching all sorts of Black activism, considered in 1919 that "by long odds the most dangerous of all the Negro publications" was the Harlem *Messenger*, the Socialist newspaper edited by Philip Randolph and Chandler Owen.[72] This was among Garvey's strongest critics, and Communists were generally against him also.

But if Garvey was strongly contested in America, far away in Africa he became a legend. Jabavu described in 1922 how, in South Africa, the payment of "unjust wages" had

rendered the Natives, in their disturbed state, easy victims to the belief in Marcus Garvey, whose Black Republic propaganda promises great things. It promises among other things: the expulsion of the white man and his yoke of misrule from their midst; Negro autonomy ('I Afrika mayi buye'=Let Africa be restored to us) with Garvey himself as Lord High Potentate; a black star fleet with powerful black armies bringing salvation, and bags of grain to relieve Africans from the economic pinch.

Even from "backwood hamlets", Jabavu said, one heard "*Ama Melika ayeza*", "the Americans are coming".[73] There were five UNIA branches in Cape Town in the 1920s, formed by resident West Indians and Africans and Coloureds; one leading organiser, Timothy Robertson, said Garvey was a "true Moses" who would "emancipate the children of Ethiopia from the fetters of bondage."[74] "Doctor" (self-styled) Wellington Butelezi led an "American" movement in the Transkei for some years, turning Garveyism into a sort of messianic movement proclaiming the coming arrival of Black American liberators—aboard aeroplanes, it was usually said. It was popular for a time in an area hit by drought, locusts, crop failures, and in 1925-26 new taxes, but eventually Butelezi was deported from Transkei in 1927.[75]

p. 128.

72 J. Anderson, *This Was Harlem: A Cultural Portrait, 1900-1950,* New York: Farrar Strauss Giroux, 1981, 1982, pp. 119-20.

73 Jabavu (note 5), p. 250.

74 R.J. Vinson, ""Sea Kaffirs": "American Negroes" and the Gospel of Garveyism in Early Twentieth-Century Cape Town", *Journal of African History* 47, 2006, pp. 281-303.

75 R. Edgar, "Garveyism in Africa", *Ufahamu* vol. VI no. 3, 1976, pp. 31-57.

By then Garvey had been gaoled, to the great relief of the colonial rulers, but he was freed later and those rulers continued to fear his influence. This was not because his followers set up any lasting political organisation in Africa, or devised any practical conspiracies. He was dangerous because he appealed to underlying feelings against colonial rule, as dissident Christian and Muslim movements also did (Butelezi's form of Garveyism was a sort of religious movement). Those feelings were always there, and even the fairly small numbers of activists described in these pages could appeal to them.

Black Americans' interest in the ancestors' homeland in Africa had started long before Garvey, and W.E.B. Du Bois expressed it continually, as in the pan-African movement which was very much his pet project. A meeting between Du Bois and Diagne in France led to the convening, with Prime Minister Clemenceau's blessing, of a second Pan-African Congress, in Paris on 19-21 February 1919. Diagne was in the chair, and the resolutions were in accordance with Diagne's approach: cautious advocacy of reforms. Du Bois himself shared the unmilitant outlook expressed in the Conference's resolutions, which were nonetheless unacceptable to the French and British rulers of Africa, as they called for international supervision of all African colonies by the League of Nations; they also called for improved living conditions for Africans and gradually increasing participation by them in the government of the colonies. There were fifty-seven people at the Conference in all.[76]

Two years later, again on Du Bois' initiative, forty-one Africans, twenty-four people of African descent living in Europe, and seven from the Caribbean attended the Third Pan-African Congress, which met in 1921 successively in London (28-9 August), Brussels (31 August-2 September) and Paris (4 September). Among the London delegates were the Nigerians Peter Thomas and L.B. Agusto and the Sierra Leoneans Eldred Taylor and the Rev. W.B. Mark. The London session was dominated by a highly critical spirit, unusually antagonistic for the time. The London manifesto included praise of France for granting full equal-

---

76   I. Geiss, *The Pan-African Movement*, tr. Ann Keep, London: Methuen, 1974, pp. 234-40; J.D. Hargreaves, "Maurice Delafosse in the Pan-African Congress of 1919", *International Journal of African Historical Studies*, vol. 1 no. 2, 1968, pp. 233-41.

ity to "her cultured black citizens", but called for sweeping changes in French colonial policy, saying for example that only men with the vote should be subject to military conscription. Generally it declared, "Local self-government with a minimum of help and oversight can be established tomorrow in Asia, Africa, America and the Isles of the Sea." It condemned "the outrageously unjust distribution of world income between the dominant and suppressed people" and blamed "white labour" for complicity in this; it was, said the manifesto, "shameful, irreligious, unscientific and undemocratic that the estimate that half the peoples of the earth put on the other half, depends mainly on their ability to squeeze money out of them."[77]

At Brussels the final declaration was a mild one, mainly through the influence of Diagne. Then Diagne was chairman of the Paris session, also attended by several Haitians and a young Senegalese lawyer and future politician, Amadou Lamine Gueye. Following the meeting Gratien Candace, deputy for Guadeloupe and a cautious advocate of reform like Diagne, founded an Association Panafricaine in December 1921, with another Guadeloupean, Isaac Béton, as General Secretary. Its declared aim was to "study and implement all that can contribute to the improvement of the fate of the Black race in all corners of the globe." But Candace soon resigned as chairman, left-wingers joined the association, and it quickly withered away.[78]

A Fourth Congress met in 1923 in London.[79] Some accounts suggest that there was another session in Lisbon, and it seems that some organisations of Africans of the Portuguese colonies planned such an event. For decades Western-educated communities in Mozambique and Angola had been actively producing newspapers and associations, still freely operating then; there was a Liga Africana, an umbrella body for African and *mestiço* organisations in the Portuguese colonies. However, there are doubts about whether any conference took place in Lis-

77   Geiss (note 76), pp. 240-8; Langley (note 25), pp. 375-9.
78   Langley (note 25), pp. 78-83; Amadou Lamine Gueye, *Itinéraire africain,* Paris: Présence Africaine, 1966, pp. 52-3; P. Dewitte, *Les mouvements nègres en France 1919-1939,* Paris: Harmattan, 1985, pp. 58-61.
79   Geiss (note 76), pp. 250-54; Richard B. Moore, "Du Bois and Pan-Africa", pp. 187-212 in J.H. Clarke *et al.* (eds), *Black Titan,* Boston: Beacon Press, 1970, pp. 204-5; A.M. Cromwell, *An African Victorian Feminist: The Life and Times of Adelaide Smith Casely Hayford 1868-1960,* London: Cass, 1986, pp. 109, 215.

bon, apart from meetings that Du Bois may have held when he visited there in November 1923.[80] Kamba Simango, a Mozambican trained in the USA who spent most of his life as a businessman in Gold Coast, attended the London Congress in 1923. Several of the British critics of colonialism were there, while Félicien Challaye attended the 1921 Paris session. But most of those attending all these conferences were African and African-Diaspora people living in Europe; people of the Diaspora, especially Williams in 1900 and DuBois from then until 1927, took much of the initiative in Pan-Africanism.

Africans in Europe

Africans and people from the New World African Diaspora living in Europe[81] played an important part in the anti-colonial activity described in this work. This was not because no such activity was possible in Africa; a good deal was possible, and in fact activists in Europe were sometimes representatives of organisations back in Africa. But there were severe restrictions on African collective action, even the most peaceful protests, in much of Africa; none at all was allowed in the Belgian Congo or much of French Africa, or in many British territories such as Northern Nigeria. In contrast, Africans in Europe were free to meet, write and organise as they liked—though in fact the majority just wanted to get on with their commonly difficult lives. They could write to the uncensored European press, meet European critics of colonialism, and, often with those critics' help, lobby the European governments and organise meetings and rallies. African and Caribbean students and professional people living in Britain and France were busy with such activity for decades.

The Black communities in Europe in the 1920s were small, and most were not students and professional people but seamen and former seamen, often living in great hardship and facing prejudice and hostility,

---

80 Geiss (note 76), pp. 254-5.

81 An interesting but inadequate study of Africans in Europe generally from the Middle Ages to 1918 is H.W. Debrunner, *Presence and Prestige: Africans in Europe* (Basel: Basler Afrika Bibliographen, 1918). There are several studies of the history of the Black presence in Britain in particular, including K. Little, *Negroes in Britain: A Study of Racial Relations in British Society*, Kegan Paul, Trench, Trubner & Co., 1947 (mainly on Cardiff); D. Killingray (ed.), *Africans in Britain*, London: Frank Cass, 1994; R. Lotz and O. Pegg (eds) *Under the Imperial Carpet: Essays in Black History 1780-1950*, Crawley: Rabbit Press, 1986.

which led in 1919 to "race riots" in several British seaports, especially in Liverpool, Barry, Newport and Cardiff in June.[82] France had similar black waterfront communities, but it also had a larger community of non-European proletarian immigrants by the 1920s: North Africans, mostly Algerians. Most of the North Africans recruited during the war returned home after the Armistice, but then more went to France and found work in a country busy rebuilding after losing more than a million of its own men of working age. They lived in the industrial outer Arrondissements of Paris (15e, 18e, 20e, etc.) and Paris suburbs such as Aubervilliers, Clichy and Saint-Denis, and in other industrial cities of France; one of their biggest communities developed in Lyons. Many lived deprived lives, often suffering from tuberculosis, but they had better pay than obtained in Algeria and greater freedom. Many of them were politically active, and in fact the early growth of Algerian nationalism was very much driven forward by the Algerian workers in France.[83] There were moves to restrict their migration to France after the war; a severely restrictive circular of 8 August 1924, which contravened a decree issued ten years earlier, was replaced by somewhat less stringent regulations on 4 August 1926, but the flow of migrants was slowed down.[84]

Students and professional people from Africa and the Caribbean generally came from the more privileged minorities in their home countries; commonly their families had to pay for their studies, as there were very few scholarships available in the inter-war period for Africans of the British or French colonies. Many, no doubt, were not politically active, but others formed political groups from the turn of the century or earlier, mainly to publicise and campaign about the situation

---

82   D. Frost, "Racism, Work and Unemployment: West African Seamen in Liverpool 1880s-1960s," *Immigrants and Minorities* vol. 13 nos. 2 & 3, July/November 1994, pp. 22-33; N. Evans, "Across the Universe: Racial Violence and the Post-War Crisis in Imperial Britain, 1919-25," *Immigrants and Minorities* vol. 13 nos. 2 & 3, July/November 1994, pp. 59-88; J. Jenkinson, "The 1919 Race Riots in Britain: A Survey," in R. Lotz and I. Pegg (eds) (note 81), pp. 182-207.

83   B. Stora, "Les Algériens dans le Paris de l'entre-deux-guerres," in A. Kaspi and A. Marès, *Le Paris des étrangers*, Paris: Imprimerie Nationale, 1989, pp. 141-55; G. Massard-Guilbaud, *Des Algériens à Lyon de la grande guerre au Front populaire*, CIEMI: Harmattan, 1995.

84   Massard-Guilbaud (note 83), pp. 67-109.

back home. Several student organisations in Britain were small-scale and short-lived.[85] In Britain the African Progress Union (APU) founded in December 1918 was more successful than most, but was not confined to students and was in fact dominated by businessmen; its first Chairman was John Archer, a former Mayor of Battersea in London, of "mixed" Barbadian and Irish parentage.[86] A prominent member was the Trinidadian doctor John Alcindor, who attended the 1900 Pan-African Conference. Duse Mohammed Ali was a member, but he went soon after the end of the war to the USA and later to Nigeria, where he settled. In 1920-21 Robert Broadhurst, President of the APU, lobbied for the NCBWA delegation and took part in the 1921 Pan-African Congress. J. Eldred Taylor, who had sponsored the *African Times and Orient Review*, was one of the leading Africans in Britain until his death in 1924; his activities included starting a newspaper, *The African Telegraph*, in London in 1918, and the Society of Peoples of African Origin (SPAO) in 1919.[87]

In Belgium there were a number of Congolese residents in the 1920s; they had an association whose leader was M'Fumu Paul Panda Farnana (1888-1930), an agricultural scientist trained in Belgium, who worked as an agricultural officer under the colonial government in the Congo but was in Belgium on the outbreak of war, when he fought with a corps of "Congolese" volunteers (nearly all Europeans) against the Germans. Back in Brussels after four years as a POW, he founded with other Congolese in Belgium a Union Congolaise which protested at forced labour and ill-treatment of prisoners and called for extension of education.[88]

---

85   See for example C. Fyfe and D. Killingray, "A Memorable Gathering of Sierra Leoneans in London, 1919," *African Affairs* vol. 88 no. 350, January 1989, pp. 41-6; I. Duffield, "John Eldred Taylor and West African Opposition to Indirect Rule," *African Affairs* vol. 70 no. 280, July 1971, pp. 252-68; H. Adi, "West African Students in Britain, 1900-1960: The Politics of Exile," pp. 107-28 in Killingray (ed.) (note 81).

86   See report of inaugural meeting on 18 December 1918, in *West Africa* 4 Jan., 11 Jan., 18 Jan. and 25 Jan. 1919.

87   Fyfe and Killingray (note 85), p. 44.

88   F. Bontinck, "Mfumu Paul Panda Farnana 1888-1930, premier (?) nationaliste congolais," pp. 591-610 in V.Y. Mudimbe (ed.), *La Dépendance de l'Afrique et les moyens d'y remédier*, Actes du Congrès International des Etudes Africaines de Kinshasa, Paris: Berger-Levrault and ACCT, 1980.

In Germany many of the Cameroonians who had gone there before 1914 stayed for several years, with some other Africans. On 19 June 1919 Martin Dibobe, a Duala working on the Berlin U-Bahn who was recognised as a leader or spokesman of Cameroonians in Germany, and a number of other Cameroonians sent a note to the National Assembly at Weimar, saying that he and other Cameroonians in Germany wanted to remain under German rule, but on certain conditions. These amounted in practice to an end to the normal colonial system. Not only should there be full application of the German legal code, with no more special laws, but Africans must be allowed to hold all public posts except that of Governor, and each Governor must be appointed for a six-month trial period, to be recalled if the Africans were not satisfied with him; there must be permanent representation of Kamerun in the Reichstag.[89] Dibobe was allowed to go home in 1921 and several other Cameroonians also went home, but others who stayed in Germany were seen as a source of subversion in French Cameroun.

Paris was already becoming the cosmopolitan city it now is.[90] In the mid-1920s there were, according to one estimate, about 10,000 people from the French Caribbean and 1-2,000 Africans—that is, sub-Saharan Africans.[91] Another estimate, by the ministry of the Colonies in 1926, was of 2,580 Africans including 255 servants and 800 seamen; probably the real figure was higher, up to 3-5,000.[92] The Black population of Paris was mainly from Guadeloupe, Martinique and French Guiana (Guyane); there was a Paris Caribbean elite including lawyers, doctors and those "old colonies'" deputies and senators in the National Assembly. The Africans included a still small number of students (75 recorded in 1926).

---

89   Part of the German text is reproduced, with an English translation, in Paulette Reed-Anderson, *Rewriting the Footnotes: Berlin and the African Diaspora*, Berlin: Die Ausländerbeauftragte des Senats, 2000, in German and English, pp. 46-9. A French translation of the letter is enclosed with Minister of Colonies to Commissioner for French Cameroun, Paris, 5 November 1920, file APA 10222, Cameroon Archives, Yaounde.

90   As is described in an excellent study edited by A. Kaspi and A. Marès, *Le Paris des étrangers*, Paris: Imprimerie Nationale, 1989.

91   P. Dewitte, "Le Paris noir de l'entre-deux-guerres," pp. 157-69 in Kaspi and Marès (eds) (note 90), p. 159.

92   Dewitte (note 78), pp. 25-6. Europeans had been bringing African servants to Europe since the 19th century.

An important element among the Africans in France was the military one, from which several anti-colonial activists were to emerge. The service of the Tirailleurs on the Western Front was admired and respected by French people. After the war conscription of Africans was made permanent by a law of 1919, and conscripts served in many parts of the French empire and France itself;[93] there were 20-30,000 African conscripts regularly stationed in France, and among French people the sentimental (patronising) affection for the Black soldiers continued.

When French African troops took part in the occupation of the German Rhineland, accusations of rape of German women by African soldiers spread around Europe. A professional press campaign was orchestrated by Dr Margarete Gärtner, then director of the Rheinische Frauenliga, and financed by Krupps. E.D. Morel in Britain backed this campaign with a book, *Horror on the Rhine*, and with much of the energy he had put into the campaign to expose Leopold II's crimes. The charges of rape were largely unproven, and it was shocking that Morel, the great campaigner against oppression of Africans two decades earlier, descended to join in a strident racist campaign; equally shocking that the Labour Party's *Daily Herald* and the ILP's *Labour Leader* backed the campaign. The purpose, to some extent, was to protest—in line with Morel's stance during the war—against the Treaty of Versailles which had sanctioned the occupation. But instead of sticking to reasonable criticisms of that Treaty, supposed champions of the oppressed incited racist feeling against conscripted African soldiers.[94] There had been similar exaggerated reports of rape by African American troops in France during the war, and an investigation by Du Bois found that there had been hardly any proven cases.[95] The outrage expressed then, and in the "Horror on the Rhine" episode, was due much less to normal shock at the crime of rape than to white people's obsessive and hysterical feelings

93   M. Echenberg, *Colonial Conscripts: The Tirailleurs Sénégalais in French West Africa, 1857-1960*, Portsmouth, NH: Heinemann and London: James Currey, 1991, chs. 4, 5; Dewitte (note 78), pp. 27-33, 47-54; P. Dewitte, "Regards blancs et colères noires", *Hommes et Migrations* no. 1132, May 1990, pp. 3-14.

94   C. Cline, *E.D. Morel 1873-1924: The Strategies of Protest*, Belfast: Blackstaff Press, 1980, pp. 126-8.

95   Wolters (note 61), pp. 126-31.

about all sexual relations between black and white, or more precisely between black men and white women.[96]

Claud McKay, in England at the time, protested in 1920 against Morel's campaign, in the *Workers' Dreadnought*, Sylvia Pankhurst's militant newspaper, for which he worked for some months.[97] Panda Farnana condemned the campaign at the 1921 Brussels Pan-African Conference. MacKay's novel *Banjo*, published in 1929 and set among a community of African and Caribbean seamen, beachcombers and other itinerant people in Marseilles, was written as fiction but seems to have been based on McKay's observations during his stay there, and has interesting contemporary allusions—for example to Marcus Garvey, about whom the little waterfront community's opinions are shown as divided. One character talks about the outcry over Black French troops in Germany: "The odd thing about that propaganda was that it said nothing about the exploitation of primitive and ignorant black conscripts to do the dirty work of one victorious civilization over another, but it was all about the sexuality of Negroes..."[98]

In response to this propaganda the French public took the side of the African soldiers.[99] It was generally observed at the time that there was little personal display of racism against Black people in France, especially by comparison with the USA, South Africa and Britain. There was considerable racist feeling in France against North Africans,[100] who were to remain the main target of French xenophobes until today. But where Black Africans and West Indians were concerned, there was a sharp contrast between French or French-descended people in Africa, who were often virulently racist, and French people in France itself. Racist theories about Africans were as prevalent in France (the home of

---

96   When discussing this subject Africans, and some white writers like John Harris (who was not free from other prejudice himself), reasonably referred to the common, even normal sexual relations between white men and black women in Africa.

97   Cline (note 94), p. 128.

98   C. McKay, *Banjo*, New York: Harvest, 1929, new edition New York: Harcourt Brace Jovanovich, 1957, p. 146. For a study of the book see B.H. Edwards, *The Practice of Diaspora: Literature, Translation, and the Rise of Black Internationalism*, Cambridge, MA: Harvard University Press, 2003, Ch. 4, especially pp. 198-229.

99   Dewitte (note 78), pp. 49-50.

100   Massard-Guilbaud (note 83), p. 82; Stora (note 83), p. 154.

Count Gobineau, the 19th-century pioneer of pseudo-scientific racism) as anywhere, and common racist colonial ideas, especially the belief in the "lazy native", influenced French colonial policy. Even so, where personal encounters and dealings were concerned Africans and people of the African Diaspora encountered little prejudice in France; their testimony to this is too persistent to be doubted.

Relatively speaking, the British also showed more racism in the colonies than at home. Jabavu wrote, "During my eleven years in England I constantly admired the Englishman's spirit of open-mindedness, justice and real goodness towards foreigners"; for example, English people could support black boxers against white ones; but, he added, when white people went to South Africa they changed.[101] In fact there was considerable racism in Britain itself, shown particularly in Black people being refused accommodation; one response was to propose a hostel for Africans in London, an idea constantly discussed for years without result.[102] Both there and in France there was also special police activity directed against political activists, including African and Asian ones as well as the main targets, white dissidents such as Bolsheviks and Sinn Feiners. In France the Ministry of the Colonies set up on 12 September 1923 a Service de Contrôle et d'Assistance en France des Indigènes des Colonies, normally abbreviated the SCAI or CAI; its surveillance work included recruiting of informers among activists. There was also a Service des Affaires Indigènes Nord-Africains under the Prefecture of the Seine, created on 21 October 1924.[103]

Friendly natives

By 1914 there was a recognisable group of missionary and humanitarian sympathisers with African causes in Europe, ready to take up cases of injustice and ill-treatment while not questioning colonial rule itself. The ASAPS under John Harris was prominent among them. Harris paid particular attention to African land issues, and visited Southern Rhodesia in 1914-15 to discuss the important land case in which the Privy

---

101   Jabavu (note 5), pp. 253-4.

102   Adi (note 85), pp. 110-13.

103   Dewitte (note 78), pp. 21-4; C. Liauzu, *Aux origines des tiers-mondismes: colonisés et anticolonialistes en France (1919-1939)*, Paris: L'Harmattan, 1982, pp. 179-83.

Council in London examined the BSAC's claim to commercial ownership of all land not ceded in full property or set aside as "reserves". After
consultations in London in 1914 the SANNC and the ASAPS agreed
that Africans' claim to land ownership should be considered in the case
as well. However, there were misunderstandings between the SANNC
and the white humanitarian campaigners, and a particular quarrel between Plaatje and Harris, who even attacked Plaatje's book *Native Life
in South Africa*, published in Britain in 1916; and Harris even came
round for a time to accepting the principle of land segregation in South
Africa. The Southern Rhodesia case ended in 1918 in a Privy Council
judgment declaring that the land did not belong to the BSAC but did
not belong to the Africans, either; it belonged to the British Crown.[104]

Harris, who published *Africa: Slave or Free?* (with a preface by Sydney
Olivier) in 1919, continued his campaigning for some years, joining in
the efforts to secure adequate land for the African "Reserves" in Southern
Rhodesia. The missionary Arthur Shearley Cripps was active in these efforts, and more vigorous than Harris who called him "quite a potential
John Brown of Harper's Ferry". But neither the cautious Harris nor the
fiery Cripps could make headway against the settler regime.[105]

Harris was reconciled with Plaatje when a new SANNC delegation
came to Britain in 1919-20; later, back in Britain after a visit to Canada
and the USA, Plaatje campaigned for Harris when he stood as a Liberal
candidate in the 1922 general election[106] (he was defeated then, but was
briefly Liberal MP for North Hackney in 1923-24). However, Harris'
paternalism was very common among Europeans with genuine sympathy for Africans. It was something Africans seeking European allies
against imperialism had to endure regularly. Their strongest white supporters could be ready to make trouble but incurably inclined to remain
in charge of the trouble-making.

But Africans still sought to exploit the fact which Harris wanted to
impress on the Southern Rhodesia chiefs in 1914-15: "There is in England a body of white people, who seek only to do good for the native

104   R. Whitehead, "The Aborigines' Protection Society and the Safeguarding of
       African Interests in Rhodesia, 1889-1930," DPhil, Oxford, 1975, pp. 88-95,
       chapter IV; Willan (note 33), pp. 176-203.
105   Whitehead (note 104), pp. 197-225.
106   Willan (note 32), pp. 246-7, 283.

races, and they are allowed to speak to the King and his counsellors all the words of their hearts upon matters which touch the welfare of the native tribes."[107] Africans under both British and French rule hoped to appeal to a better Britain, or a better France, against what British or French representatives were doing in the colonies. Various European individuals and organisations felt a corresponding moral obligation to uphold a better British or French tradition, to show the spirit of Wilberforce or the spirit of the Declaration of the Rights of Man.

The ILP expanded its activities greatly in the 1920s, and was the party most critical of colonialism, with the Communist Party (on which more below); Fenner Brockway, who had already begun his lifelong anti-imperialist career in the ILP, became its Secretary in 1923. Its Empire Policy Committee, founded in 1925, declared that the long-term aim should be a Socialist Commonwealth of self-governing states; it added that "for many races in tropical Africa, self-government, is an ideal which could not be realised for some years", but it did call for widespread reforms in Africa in the meantime, including League of Nations supervision,[108] which the Labour Party itself had considered advocating a few years earlier and the LDH in France proposed in April 1925.[109]

The Labour Party had a loose structure; the ILP and other bodies were affiliated to it and provided many of its MPs, but retained their own organisation; and there were various elements in the party and the affiliated bodies, including the trade unions and a number of intellectuals, few by comparison with the workers but influential. Many of these had been prominent in campaigning journalism, sometimes over colonial issues, or in the Fabian Society—which remained very active and influential in the Labour Party—or the Liberal Party, the UDC or the LNU. They gradually joined the Labour Party and provided it with informed critics of colonialism. Prominent among them were H.N. Brailsford, a journalist and supporter of liberation movements who had joined the ILP in 1907, finding the Liberals and Fabians too soft on British imperialism in Egypt, and edited the ILP's *New Leader* from 1922 to 1926; and E.D. Morel. Morel's career in the Labour Party was

---

107   Whitehead (note 104), p. 136.

108   S. Howe, *Anticolonialism in British Politics: The Left and the End of Empire*, Oxford: Clarendon Press, 1993, p. 68.

109   J.-P. Biondi, *Les Anticolonialistes (1881-1962)*, Paris: Laffont, 1992, p. 135.

thwarted not by his "Horror on the Rhine" campaign, but by his early death—elected to parliament in 1922 (defeating Winston Churchill at Dundee), and re-elected later, he died on 12 November 1924.

Most prominent was Leonard Woolf (1880-1969), who after working for some years as a British official in Ceylon (Sri Lanka) resigned in 1912; he wrote later, "I had been born in the age of imperialism and I disapproved of imperialism and felt sure its days were already numbered."[110] He founded the Hogarth Press with his wife Virginia Woolf in 1917. From 1919 to 1945 he was Secretary to the Labour Party Advisory Committees on Imperial and on International Questions set up after the party adopted its constitution in 1918.[111]

Woolf made his name as a critic of empire with his *Empire and Commerce in Africa,* begun under the auspices of the Fabian Society, and handed to the Labour Research Department in December 1919.[112] There he wrote,

The European state, if it remains in Africa, is necessarily an instrument of... exploitation; if it withdraws, it merely hands over the native to the more cruel exploitation of irresponsible white men. The question then is, how the European State can be changed from an instrument of economic exploitation into an instrument of good government and progress, not for a few hundred white men, but for the millions of Africans.[113]

Hence Woolf, whose book scathingly exposed business and political chicanery in the partition of Africa, believed even so that colonialism could be improved to make it beneficial. This was the view of others on the Committee, including the Fabian Sydney Olivier.

Although many imperialists believed that the Labour Party was out to wreck the empire, in fact neither the first MacDonald government in 1924 (which, as a minority government, had its hands tied anyway) nor

---

110   L. Woolf, *Growing: An Autobiography of the Years 1904 to 1911*, London: Hogarth Press, 1970, pp. 247-8.

111   Woolf (note 2), pp. 221-39. Some sources speak of a single committee on Imperial and International Affairs, but Woolf, who knew them better than anyone, said there were two, "each of which met in the House of Commons on alternate Wednesdays" (p. 221).

112   V. Glendinning, *Leonard Woolf,* London and New York: Simon & Schuster, 2006, pp. 209-10, 235, 436.

113   L. Woolf, *Empire and Commerce in Africa: A Study in Economic Imperialism,* London: Allen & Unwin, 1920, p. 358.

the second in 1929-31 made noticeable changes in imperial policy. The empire was in fact a low priority for the Labour Party. The LPACIIQ informed itself and the party thoroughly, but Woolf later wrote that it "did an immense amount of work, pouring out reports and memoranda which the Executive Committee accepted, which became "party policy", and were then never heard of again."[114] One reason for the Labour attitude was prevailing prejudice, shown by support for Morel's "Horror on the Rhine" campaign. Trade union leaders also feared undercutting at home by ill-paid white and non-white immigrants, as well as competition from cheap labour in the biggest and most industrialised colonial territory, India.[115] But besides such sentiments, which not everyone shared, there was a simple basic reason for the low priority: the number one concern for Socialist parties' rank and file, and for very many of their leaders, was the wretched situation of the underprivileged in Europe. Socialist leaders who inevitably devoted most attention to this often knew little and cared little about the colonies; David Kirkwood, one of the Clydeside MPs elected in 1922, said, "I know that all this interest in foreign affairs is a heritage from Liberalism."[116]

But some in the Labour Party were strong defenders of the colonised peoples. Colonel Josiah Wedgwood was one Labour MP noted for his persistent parliamentary questions on colonial affairs. India received special attention from the British Left, but Africans had their defenders such as Dr Norman Leys, who concentrated his highly critical attention on Kenya in the 1920s, making his surgery in Derbyshire the centre of a ceaseless campaign.[117] It followed and developed the themes of his long letter of 1918 to the Colonial Secretary,[118] and the criticisms were summed up in his book *Kenya*, published by the Hogarth Press in 1924. He wrote plainly about labour coercion for settlers' benefit, the virtual impunity of settlers even when they killed Africans, the severe and unjust taxation system, and other features of the regime which had been installed—and quite avoidably, as he rightly said—in Kenya. He wrote,

114   Woolf (note 2), p. 224.

115   P.S. Gupta, *Imperialism and the British Labour Movement, 1914-1964*, Macmillan, 1975, pp. 49-51, 62-71.

116   *New Leader*, 30 March 1923, quoted in Howe (note 105), p. 49.

117   Cell (note 44), p. 8.

118   Ibid., pp. 91-136.

"Indeed, in African opinion the Government has no redeeming feature. It is always interfering, they think, and it has an insatiable appetite for money."[119]

Leonard Woolf and others of the Labour Party, and Harris of the ASAPS, were contacted by Du Bois in 1921 about the organisation of the Pan-African conference.[120] Leys, Harris and Woolf were members of the League of Nations Union's Mandates Committee formed in 1920. Gilbert Murray of the LNU attended the 1923 London Pan-African Congress, as did Olivier (who was to be Secretary of State for India in the MacDonald government the following year), Leys, H.G. Wells and Harold Laski, who was to become Professor of Political Science at the London School of Economics from 1926 and a very influential figure. A group of Labour-Liberal colonial critics had thus emerged, committed to improving colonial rule in Africa but not ending it; the LNU Mandates Committee included the empire-builder Sir Harry Johnston.[121] Leys did not totally reject imperialism or cast off the prejudices of his time—while describing the expropriation of the Maasai people's land, for example, he said firmly that the old Maasai way of life had to be ended in the name of modern development. Even so, Leys' constant criticisms of the colonial-settler regime were a thorn in the side of the Colonial Office. Besides Leys another Scotsman who worked in Kenya became a vocal critic of the settler regime there: McGregor Ross, who was the Colony's Director of Public Works from 1905 to 1922. He opposed concessions to settlers, notably the measures to force Africans to work for Europeans, and the routing of the Uasin Gishu railway to help certain settlers' marketing of agricultural products. He too wrote a book denouncing the settler regime, *Kenya from Within*.[122]

Kenya was a special focus of protest in the post-1918 years, particularly because of the effects of the white settlement, the subject of a Labour policy pamphlet in 1925. Missionaries condemned the gov-

---

119   Leys (note 4), pp. 293-4.

120   Geiss (note 76), pp. 241-2.

121   Callahan (note 24), p. 53.

122   D. Wylie, "Norman Leys and McGregor Ross: A Case Study in the Conscience of African Empire 1900-39", *Journal of Imperial and Commonwealth History* vol. V no. 3, May 1977, pp. 294-309. *Kenya from Within* was published by Allen & Unwin (London) in 1927.

ernment encouragement of Africans to work for settlers in Kenya in 1919-20, in one of the biggest colonial protest campaigns in Britain in the immediate post-war years. It started after Governor Northey issued through the Chief Native Commissioner, John Ainsworth, circulars on the importance of "encouraging" young Africans to work on settlers' farms. Besides missionaries the press joined in the protest campaign in Britain, including the *New Statesman* founded a few years earlier (1913); the protests reached the House of Lords, and eventually the Colonial Secretary, Winston Churchill, forbade compulsion to work for private employers.[123] Many missionaries were not at all active in defending Africans, but Bishop Frank Weston of Zanzibar was vigorous in condemning forced labour, writing a pamphlet on it, *The Serfs of Great Britain*.[124]

Both missionary and secular critics of colonialism usually wanted to see it improved, not ended. This was true of *indigénophiles* in France, such as those in the LDH. However, the League included a more anti-colonial minority led by Challaye,[125] now one of the leading critics of French colonial rule, who had for example denounced the brutal French military repression in Ivory Coast during the First World War. The newspaper *L'Action Coloniale*, founded in 1918 by Maurice Boursaud and LDH *indigénophiles*, at first followed the humanitarian criticism line; however, in 1920 it became more radical under a new editor, Olivier Brémond. One contributor was a Martinican, Fernand Gouttenoire de Toury, a Socialist and LDH militant for years, with a special interest in Madagascar.[126]

By the early 1920s most French Socialists had accepted colonialism, while calling for reforms and an end to particular abuses, though they too included a more anti-colonial minority. The way French colonial rule was in fact applied aroused many criticisms, which some supported in the SFIO after 1920; the Socialist deputy Marius Moutet, for ex-

---

123   On this campaign see Lord Olivier, *White Capital & Coloured Labour*, London: Hogarth Press, 1929, pp. 225-53 (including the text of Ainsworth's circular of 23 October 1919); Leys (note 4), pp. 186-225; R.L. Buell, *The Native Problem in Africa*, New York: Macmillan, 1928, vol. 1, pp. 332-6; Cell (ed.) (note 44), pp. 144-94.

124   Olivier (note 123), pp. 230-3, 246-53.

125   Dewitte (note 78), p. 62.

126   Ibid., pp. 70-71.

ample, tried to introduce a bill for representation of Muslim Algerians in the Assembly. But activists commonly found the new Communist Party more sympathetic. SFIO leaders were reserved about calls for independence in Tunisia, as was the *Revue Indigène*, though Ahmed Safi's nationalist delegation in mid-1920, which toned down Tha'alibi's demands, was well received by the LDH and the *indigénophiles*.[127] The message from such sympathisers was the same in both France and Britain: We'll back you if you don't ask for too much. They would never agree with Africans making any real trouble, and urged colonial protestors to have nothing to do with "Bolshevism".

Communism and the colonial world

After the October Revolution the Bolsheviks turned their attention without delay to "the East" (*Vostok*), which in Russian usage then meant the Russian Asian territories, the rest of Asia, and (geography notwithstanding) Africa as well. From the beginning the Communist message to colonial subjects was twofold. It called for an end to imperialism, hence for liberation of subject peoples; it also called for liberation for the oppressed classes within colonial territories. Communists had to work out how to fit the "national question" into their vision or programme of the class struggle; this was examined extensively, before 1917, in writings by Lenin, Rosa Luxemburg, the Austrian Marxist Otto Bauer, Josif Djugashvili alias Koba alias Stalin,[128] and James Connolly, who said when he founded the Irish Socialist Republican Party in 1896: "The struggle for Irish freedom has two aspects; it is national and it is social". While despising the Home Rule politicians, Connolly campaigned for Ireland's independence, and died for it after taking part in the Easter Rising. Lenin disagreed with left-wing rigorists who disapproved of Connolly dying for Ireland rather than for socialism,[129] and this indicated the ideas he was to follow when in power soon afterwards.

127 Goldstein (note 8), pp. 286, 311, 386.

128 See Walker Connor, *The National Question in Marxist-Leninist Theory and Strategy*, Princeton University Press, 1984, chapters 1-3, pp. 172-9; M. Löwy, "Marxism and the National Question", pp. 136-60 in R. Blackburn (ed.) *Revolution and Class Struggle: A Reader in Marxist Politics*, Hassocks, Sussex: The Harvester Press, 1978, for this debate among early Marxists.

129 C.D. Greaves, *The Life and Times of James Connolly*, London: Lawrence & Wishart, 1961, pp. 60, 69, 340.

The Provisional Workers' and Peasants' Government in Petrograd issued on 2 (15) November 1917 a "Declaration of the Rights of the Peoples of Russia", proclaiming the equality and sovereignty of all peoples and the right to self-determination, including the formation of independent states. Then followed a manifesto to "all the toiling Moslems of Russia and the Orient" on 24 Nov./7 Dec.1917:

Moslems of Russia, Kirghiz and Sarts of Central Asia and Siberia, Turks and Tatars of Transcaucasia, Chechens and mountaineers of the Caucasus - all those whose mosques and prayer houses were destroyed, whose beliefs and customs were trampled under foot by the tsars and oppressors of Russia...from now on your customs and beliefs, your national and cultural institutions, are declared free and inviolable...Support this revolution, it is your government...Moslems of the Orient, Persians and Turks, Arabs and Hindus - all those whose lives, property, fatherlands, and liberties were the objects of speculation by the predatory robbers or Europe, whose lands were seized by the spoilers who started the present war...Our banners carry the liberation of all the oppressed people of the world.[130]

Among the Muslim nationalities subject to the Russian Empire, such as the various peoples of Central Asia (then commonly called Turkestan) who had just experienced brutal suppression of a major uprising in 1916, the events of 1917 were at first welcomed; not only the Tsarist monarchy, seen by Muslims for centuries as the greatest aggressor and oppressor, had been overthrown, but the whole Russian ruling class and the Russian Orthodox Church also. At first some of the nationalists in non-Russian areas had some sympathy for the Bolsheviks against the White armies, which aimed to restore the old Russian empire. But the Bolsheviks had that aim also, as became apparent within a few months of their takeover. In Central Asia, the Bolsheviks who held Tashkent and surrounding areas without a break from November 1917 came from the European settler community. They acted as violent oppressors of the Asians, and their campaigns against the Autonomous Provisional Government of Turkestan based at Kokand led to the slaughter of hundreds of thousands of Asians, directly and through famine.[131]

---

130   Reproduced in translation in S.A. Zenkovsky, *Pan-Turkism and Islam in Russia*, Harvard University Press, 1960, pp. 161-2.

131   E. Allworth (ed.), *Central Asia: A Century of Russian Rule*, Columbia University Press, 1967, pp. 225-45; Zenkovsky (note 130), chs. XIV-XVI; X.J. Eudin and R.C. North, *Soviet Russia and the East 1920-1927: A Documentary Survey* (Stan-

The Moscow leadership subsequently condemned the massacres by the settler Bolsheviks in Tashkent, and replaced their leaders. Central Asia was then largely occupied by 1920, though resistance by the Basmachi guerrillas went on until 1922; in Transcaucasia Azerbaijan and Armenia were occupied in 1920, Georgia (by then an internationally recognised independent state) in 1921, and the Union of Soviet Socialist Republics (USSR) created on 30 December 1922 included all the territory of the Tsarist Russian empire except Finland and some other areas in the west. The Soviet leaders' statements on "self-determination" for non-Russian portions of the former Russian Empire subjected it to conditions—e.g. that it must be for the "toiling masses", or compatible with Soviet state interests[132]—that meant in practice suppressing the independence of Georgia while calling for the independence of India. But Communists proclaimed that what had been established in Central Asia and Transcaucasia was not mere colonial rule, that the peoples of those areas were being liberated from local class and religious domination as well as imperialist political domination.

In the Asian Soviet republics, while Moscow was in full charge, from an early stage the Communist regime—in which a Georgian, Stalin, was prominent as Commissar of Nationalities—recruited and promoted non-Russians to govern their ethnic territories. In Central Asia in 1919-20 Moscow recruited local Asian leaders from the ranks of the Jadid movement, a widespread movement among Russian Muslim peoples for reformed, modern Islamic education and wider modernisation begun well before 1917. However, many of the people who collaborated with Moscow in this way were not convinced Communists, and were soon to be dismissed[133]—but replaced, increasingly, by other indigenous people.

Some Communists of the Muslim nationalities had their own ideas, involving more leeway for their peoples. Their leader was Sultangaliev, one of the Volga Tatar Muslim minority people, who wanted the Russian Muslim peoples, and his own people in particular, to lead a great worldwide movement of colonial revolt: "Deprived of the East and cut

ford University Press, 1957); M.D. Kennedy, *A Short History of Communism in Asia*, London: Weidenfeld & Nicolson, 1957.

132   Connor (note 128), Ch. 3.
133   Zenkovsky (note 130), pp. 242-52.

off from India, Afghanistan, Persia and other Asian and African colonies, Western European imperialism will collapse and will die a natural death," he wrote in 1919.[134] To achieve this he recommended backing nationalist movements, as Lenin also did, but unlike Lenin he said this should be a permanent policy, and he wanted the Revolution in Russia to tolerate a reformed Islam, such as the Jadid movement had advocated.

Such ideas were put forward by some who shared Sultangaliev's ideas, such as the Kazakh Communist Turar Ryskulov, at the First Congress of the Peoples of the East on 1-8 September 1920, held at Baku in newly-occupied Azerbaijan. This gathering, said to have been a very large one, was opened by Mikhail Pavlovich—a scholar (an expert on Africa in particular) who was one of the Bolsheviks' leading advisers on "the East"—with the call, "Arise, then, peoples of the East! The Third International calls you to a sacred war against the capitalist rabble."[135] But the ideas expressed by Ryskulov, which could have aroused more interest in a "sacred war", were rejected by the Bolshevik leaders at Baku, who firmly slapped down the Asian semi-Communists of the Jadid movement and declared that there must be simultaneous revolutions against colonial rule and against local exploiters. Ideas like Sultangaliev's were denounced as "pan-Islamism".[136]

For all their concern with "the East", the number one preoccupation of the Soviet leaders and the Third International—the Communist International, Comintern, established on 4 March 1919—was Europe and America. Communist parties were founded in the major countries there from 1918 onwards, eventually to be brought under the control of the Comintern—in some countries a complex process. In Britain Sylvia Pankhurst and her Workers' Suffrage Federation were involved in negotiations leading to the formation of the Communist Party of Great Britain (CPGB) in 1921, but she was quickly expelled from it; she remained a tireless independent campaigner, defending Africans among others in the *Workers' Dreadnought* (which however ceased publication

---

134   A. Bennigsen and C. Quelquejay, *Les mouvements nationaux chez les Musulmans de Russie: Le "Sultangalievisme" au Tatarstan*, Paris: Mouton, 1960, pp. 207-12.

135   Eudin and North (note 131), p. 80; E.T. Wilson, *Russia and Black Africa before World War II*, New York: Holmes & Meier, 1974, pp. 100-6, 124.

136   Bennigsen and Quelquejay (note 134), pp. 64-193, 212; Zenkovsky (note 130), pp. 250-1.

in 1924) and publishing a 638-page book on India in 1926.[137] In the
USA Communists emerged from Socialist parties, the Syndicalists of
the Industrial Workers of the World (IWW), and scattered groups of
"radicals" in New York, Chicago and other cities,[138] including John
Reed (1887-1920), whose glowing account of the October Revolution
became famous (*Ten Days that Shook the World*). For years the small
band of American Communists was divided into factions, and hit by
repression—the "Palmer Raids", ordered by Federal Attorney-General
Palmer, on 2 January 1920. Eventually the Workers' Party of America,
founded in 1921, became the Workers' (Communist) Party of America
in 1925 and later the Communist Party of the USA in 1929.[139] Despite
the internecine quarrels Reed went back to Russia in 1920 and played
an important role in the Second Comintern Congress (but died in Russia later that year); and other American Communists were to play international roles in the next few years, especially in connection with "the
Negro Question".[140]

In France the process of creating a Communist party was somewhat
exceptional. There, on 25-30 December 1920, a majority at the Tours
Congress of the SFIO voted for affiliation to the Comintern, calling
itself at first the Section Française de l'Internationale Communiste but
soon afterwards adopting its well known name of the Parti Communiste Français (PCF). One consequence was that the Communists in-
herited the daily newspaper of which Jaurès had been a co-founder in
1904, *L'Humanité*.[141] The rest of the SFIO which rejected the Tours

137   H. Pelling, *The British Communist Party*, 1958, reprint London: A. and C.
       Black, 1975, chs. I, II; P.W. Romero, *E. Sylvia Pankhurst: Portrait of a Radical*,
       New Haven: Yale University Press, 1987, pp. 133-54, 179-81; S. Harrison,
       Sylvia Pankhurst: A Crusading Life, London: Aurum Press, 2003, pp. 200-15,
       218, 243.

138   T. Draper, *American Communism and Soviet Russia*, New York: Viking Press and
       London: Macmillan, 1960, pp. 13-16. The life of these small American groups
       is recalled in Warren Beatty's (artistically mediocre) film *Reds* (1981), centred
       mainly on John Reed and his partner Louis Bryant, and continuing until Reed's
       stay in Russia and his attendance at the Baku Congress.

139   The complex story is told in Draper (note 138), pp. 16-310.

140   As Communists called it; the use of such a term grates today, but it could
       be used at the time even by sympathetic white people. It should be recalled
       that the word "Negro" was itself fully acceptable then and until Martin Luther
       King's time.

141   See E. Mortimer, *The Rise of the French Communist Party 1920-1947*, London:

decision continued the party as before, joining the Labour and Socialist International founded at a congress at Hamburg in 1923. Similarly, a revolutionary minority of France's central trade union body, the Confédération Générale du Travail (CGT), broke away in 1921 to form the Confédération Générale du Travail-Unitaire (CGTU), which was to be a close ally of the PCF.

The CGTU and other trade union groupings linked with Communist parties were affiliated in a Red International of Trade and Industrial Unions (or Red International of Labour Unions, RILU), also called the Profintern, founded in 1921. This was to be involved in anti-imperialist activity, as were some other international Communist bodies: the Krestintern, the peasant movements' international, based like the Comintern and Profintern in Moscow, and International Workers' Relief and International Red Aid. The history of the last two is somewhat difficult to unravel; they have been confused with each other and the second used many different names. International Workers' Relief (Internationale Arbeitshilfe, IAH) grew out of a committee established in Germany in 1921 for relief of victims of the 1921 Russian famine and, after aiding a very few of them, was involved in some economic ventures in the USSR. International Red Aid—also called International Labour Defence (in the USA) or International Class War Prisoners' Aid (in Britain, for a certain period) or in Russian Mezhdunarodnaia Organizatsia Pomoshchi Revolutsioneram (MOPR)—was founded in 1921 and helped with the legal defence of Communists and others in trouble with the law in many countries.[142]

The German Communist Party (Kommunistische Partei Deutschlands, KPD) was founded in the last days of 1918. Soon afterwards the government headed by the Social Democratic Party (SDP) leader Friedrich Ebert used the paramilitary Freikorps to suppress the Communist revolutionaries, whose foremost leaders, Karl Liebknecht and Rosa Luxemburg, were summarily executed. After the first chaotic years of the Weimar Republic the KPD became the leading Communist

---

Faber & Faber, 1984, which however has little on the party's work on colonial questions.

142   Sean McMeekin, *The Red Millionaire: A Political Biography of Willi Münzenberg, Moscow's Secret Propaganda Tsar in the West*, New Haven and London: Yale University Press, 2003, pp. 106-92.

party in western Europe for many years, but there was special bitterness between it and the SPD. However, all over western Europe there was a big gulf between Communists and democratic Socialists.[143] Western Socialists, including continental ones much influenced by Marxism as well as the British Labour Party, also including the very left-wing ILP, condemned the dictatorship and police-state brutality installed by the Soviet regime. Communists on their side accused the leading mainstream Socialist parties of compromising with capitalism, especially when they formed or joined governments—as they did during the 1920s in Britain, Germany and Belgium, though not yet in France, where the SFIO formed an alliance with the Radicals for the 1924 elections, the "Cartel des Gauches", but did not join the government formed after the alliance had won. In taking ministerial office British and Belgian Socialists helped to run colonial empires, and on colonial matters there was a great gulf between them and Communists.

Communist opposition to Western colonialism was never in doubt, least of all among the colonial rulers. There was comradely debate, however, about the attitude to take to "bourgeois nationalist" or "national democratic" movements in the colonies or the countries called "semi-colonies" by Moscow (China, Turkey and Persia). At the second Congress of the Comintern, held mainly in Moscow from 19 July to 7 August 1920, different approaches were proposed by Lenin and by the leading Communist from the Western colonial empires in Moscow at the time, M.N. Roy. This Indian revolutionary (real name Narendra Nath Bhattacharya) had been active in anti-British conspiracies in contact with the Germans early in the First World War, and had then lived in the USA for a time before being arrested and jumping bail to Mexico and founding the Communist Party of Mexico, and later travelling to Russia in 1920.[144]

Lenin's *Theses on the National and Colonial Question* were presented to the Congress, arguing that Communists must back the national lib-

---

143   See K. McDermott and J. Agnew, *The Comintern: A History of International Communism from Lenin to Stalin*, Basingstoke: Macmillan, 1996, pp. 27-40.

144   On Roy's activities in those years see (with caution) *M.N. Roy's Memoirs* (published posthumously in 1964, Bombay: Allied Publishers Private Ltd., with introduction by E.D. Parikh and epilogue by V.B. Karnik), pp. 3-216; see also J.P. Haithcox, *Communism and Nationalism in India: M.N. Roy and Comintern Policy 1920-1939*, Princeton University Press, 1971, pp. 4-12.

eration movements in the colonies. Roy, who spoke for India although he was present as a delegate of the Communist Party of Mexico, was more cautious about cooperation with nationalist leaders; he believed in a "revolution from below" and wanted only limited and cautious cooperation with bourgeois nationalists. In their discussions on "bourgeois nationalists" Communists always had the Indian National Congress very much in mind. The revolutionary movement in which Roy had been involved had long since parted company with the INC, and after Roy had been (apparently quite recently) converted to Socialism his "sympathies were with Left Communism", as he recalled later.[145]

The new militant direction of the INC under Gandhi did not make it more congenial to Communists. Although Gandhi sought support in the villages, encouraged the use of indigenous homespun cloth, and fought against centuries of prejudice by preaching equality for "Untouchables", the party was still led by high-caste Hindus and financed by Indian businessmen like the Tata family. According to Roy's recollection

The role of Gandhi was the crucial point of difference. Lenin believed that, as the inspirer and leader of a mass movement, he was a revolutionary. I maintained that, a religious and cultural revivalist, he was bound to be a reactionary socially, however revolutionary he might be politically.[146]

But his alternative thesis was studied at the Congress, and both it and Lenin's were adopted. In fact the differences were slight; basically Communists everywhere agreed that Western colonialism must be opposed.

Between its Congresses the Comintern headquarters in Moscow studied and helped anti-imperialist activist movements and individuals, in the Eastern Secretariat and the Anglo-American Secretariat for example. Individual Comintern leaders active in dealing with non-European affairs included Roy (who worked mainly from a base in Berlin for some years); the exiled Japanese Communist pioneer Sen Katayama, who after working for the Comintern in the USA went to Russia in 1921 and became a leading consultant on Asian and colonial affairs for the Comintern;[147] and Henk Sneevliet alias Maring, a Dutchman

---

145   *M.N. Roy's Memoirs* (note 144), p. 280.
146   Ibid., p. 379.
147   H. Kublin, *Asian Revolutionary: The Life of Sen Katayama*, Princeton University

who had started a Communist (at first "Social Democratic") movement in the Dutch East Indies (Indonesia). From an early stage some activists from the West's colonies attended courses at the new Communist University of the Toilers of the East (Kommunisticheskii Universitet Trudiashchikhsia Vostoka, abbreviated Kutvu) in Moscow, established for Soviet Asians and others by a decree of 21 April 1921.

The Fourth Comintern Congress, held in Moscow from 7 November to 3 December 1922, adopted "Theses on the Eastern Question" drafted by an Eastern Commission including Roy, declaring that Communist workers' parties of the colonial and semi-colonial countries must both "fight for the most radical possible solution of the tasks of the bourgeois-democratic revolution, which aims at the conquest of political independence" and "organise the working peasant masses for the struggle for their present class interests, and in doing so, exploit all the contradictions in the nationalist-democratic camp."[148]

In India, building on the activity of exiles in Russia for several years, small Communist groups were operating by 1922; the British were soon arresting their activists, but Communist activity developed steadily. In Egypt, small Communist groups had emerged by 1920, mainly formed by members of the cosmopolitan foreign community that was large and influential in Egypt for decades (recalled in Lawrence Durrell's novels). The main activist was Joseph Rosenthal, a Jewish Russian jeweller, also active in organising trade unions. Muslim Egyptian activists joined him in an Egyptian Socialist Party in August 1921, and Rosenthal also organised a General Union of Workers in the same year. The new party split in 1922 and one faction sent Al-Hosni al-'Arabi, one of the main founder members, to Moscow to discuss affiliation to the Comintern, which was accepted, after the party agreed to the conditions laid down, in December 1922.

In its initial declaration of 29 August 1921 the Egyptian Communist Party called for "The Liberation of Egypt from the tyranny of imperialism and the expulsion of imperialism from the entire Nile Valley" and "support for the freedom and self-determination of all people and brotherhood among all nations on the basis of equality and mutual interests". But it also promised to "Work for the abolition of exploitation of one

---

Press 1964, p. 319.

148   Haithcox (note 144), pp. 11-12, 33.

class by another, the elimination of class distinctions in society in natural rights, and the extinction of tyranny by exploiters and speculators". On 22 December 1921 it declared that it "will not renounce its struggle against the Egyptian capitalist tyrants and oppressors, accomplices and associates of the tyrannic foreign domination." The party was not only highly dissatisfied with the pseudo-independence granted in 1922—as were many other Egyptians—but also hostile to the Wafd, essentially a party of the landlord class. It had to face the hostility of the Egyptian government, before and after the Wafd took power in 1924, and the British. After major strikes in 1924 the government cracked down, and al-'Arabi and four other leaders were gaoled in October 1924.[149]

It must always be borne in mind that however firmly Moscow imposed its control over Communist parties outside Russia, people joined those parties out of genuine conviction, based especially on moral indignation at inequality and exploitation. As in Egypt, so in other colonial and "semi-colonial" countries early Communists revolted against the indigenous privileged classes as well as foreign imperialists, and were wary, at least, of the nationalist movements led by members of those privileged classes. Even so, movements for national independence were popular among all classes. Communists initially backed those movements, if only as a temporary expedient, regardless of their upper-class leadership. There is an air of unreality in the Communist debates about those movements. Reading the debates one might suppose that the Comintern was actually able to dictate what happened in colonial territories; but it was not. Generally Communists in Asia and Africa could only respond to situations not created by them, where the colonial rulers and the independence movements called the shots.

China was the only non-European country, for many years, where Moscow was able to influence events and Communists' policy on "the East" could be put properly to the test. The Chinese Communist Party was founded in 1919 and was soon involved in the complex civil strife started by the Chinese revolution of 1911. During the wars—which cannot be recounted in any detail here—between the Kuomintang (KMT), the nationalist party led by Sun Yat-sen, and numerous warlords ruling various fiefs, Moscow supplied arms and military advisers

149   Tareq Y. Ismael and Rifa'at El-Sa'id, *The Communist Movement in Egypt 1920-1988*, Syracuse University Press, 1990, pp. 12-29.

to the Kuomintang and the Soviet Communist leadership sent Mikhail Borodin (who had worked with Roy in Mexico in 1919) as a senior adviser to the KMT's base in Canton in 1923. He persuaded the Chinese Communists, against their will, to accept subordination to the KMT—while playing important roles in its ranks—as he saw that the KMT, a nationalist and anti-imperialist party, was the only force that could at least make a start at revolution in China. With Soviet aid the KMT in 1923-25 gradually extended more control over southern China and planned a Northern Expedition. It resisted Soviet calls for radical reforms to benefit peasants and workers, but Moscow continued to back it, before and after Sun died in Peking, where he had gone for talks with other factions, on 12 March 1925.[150] Meanwhile, in Outer Mongolia a Communist state was established from 1924—the only one outside the Soviet Union, until the 1940s.

Outside China the much dreaded "hand of Moscow" was unable to achieve anything in Asia or Africa at this time; where Communist parties were begun they could not influence events at all. They could only try to exploit situations created by others, as recommended in an article by Pavlovich in 1921:

The persistent struggle by the people of India and Egypt against the British yoke; the national-revolutionary movement in Morocco, Tunisia, and Algeria, directed at liberation from the French imperialists; the unending struggle by the Persian people for their complete liberation from British influence; the awakening of the dark tribes of the Sudan, South Africa, and South America— all these movements, in spite of the their narrow national character, undermine the very bases of the capitalist order, which cannot exist without the exploitation and enslavement of colonial and semi-colonial countries.[151]

At the Comintern's Fifth Congress, held in Moscow from 17 June to 8 July 1924, Roy—now a member of the Presidium of the Executive

---

150   Dan N. Jacobs' biography of Borodin, *Borodin: Stalin's Man in China*, Cambridge, MA: Harvard University Press 1981, gives a good readable outline of the complex events in China in those years. There was plenty of contemporary writing about those events, while modern studies include J.P. Harrison, *The Long March to Power: A History of the Chinese Communist Party, 1921-72*, New York: Praeger, 1972, and J. Guillermaz, *A History of the Chinese Communist Party*, New York: Random House, 1972.

151   *Zhizn Natsionalnostei* 14, 16-21 July 1921, quoted in translation in Eudin and North (note 131), p. 190.

different, lower-paid jobs, and white workers, however exploited they might be, had relative privileges which they wanted to keep. In this situation non-racial workers' solidarity was just a dream. This emerged clearly when the question of "job reservation" became acute in the mining industry. For several years after 1903 the reservation of certain skilled jobs to whites became entrenched, for about 7,000 of them by regulation, for about twice that number by a "status quo agreement". Then the employers, concerned to cut labour costs—in 1921, 21,455 white mine workers earned £10,640,521 and 179,987 black ones £5,964,428—decided to open more semi-skilled jobs to Africans; in January 1922 the Chamber of Mines gave one month's notice of an end of the "status quo agreement". White mine workers responded with a strike, starting on coal mines and extending to gold mines, that turned into open revolt on the Rand in March 1922, suppressed by government forces with heavy artillery and aircraft.[158]

The small Communist Party was heavily involved in the uprising. It believed that the employers were attacking white miners' livelihood and must be opposed, and that defeating them would ultimately benefit non-white workers also. Communists dreamed of guiding the strike in a class-conscious, revolutionary direction. It was an absurd ideological daydream which in fact led to the Communist Party, claiming to defend the oppressed, being involved in defence of the colour bar, intended to keep Africans in perpetual subordination. The "Commandos" who staged the rising had no interest in Communist ideas, and their members and supporters, or else common-law criminals joining in the mayhem, killed about thirty Africans; of the four men hanged after the rising one had killed two Africans. Yet Communists defended the rising for what they thought it should have been—even defending the slogan "Workers of the World, Fight and Unite for a White South Africa" on one banner—and continued to do so after the defeat of the strikers.

This was a case of ideological obsession blinding people to reality: the workers *must* be class-conscious defenders of all workers' rights in their hearts, even if they did not show it, and the mine bosses *must* be the evil ones to be combated, even if they were in fact, for once, defending the interests of the most oppressed. Continuing the daydreaming, Bunting

---

158   N. Herd, *1922: The Revolt on the Rand*, Johannesburg: Blue Crane Books, 1966; J. and R. Simons (note 43), pp. 281-99; Hancock (note 37), pp. 62-88.

(who became secretary of the CPSA after attending the 1922 Comintern Congress) said in his Communist Party pamphlet *Red Revolt and the Rand* that the strike was right and proper, but making the campaign racial was not.[159] But of course it was simply a racial campaign from the start. Africans saw the strike for what it was—there were furious protests from the ANC and ICU against it—but Communists claimed to have fought the bosses and the Smuts government, not the indigenous people of the country.[160]

The issues raised by this episode extended beyond South Africa and beyond the ranks of Communists. Other left-wingers, and trade unionists, easily fell or jumped into the same trap whenever industrial problems arose in a context of racial division. When employers recruited or promoted non-white workers—for their own business reasons, of course—and sought thus to lower white workers' wages, lay them off or weaken their unions, the unions and left-wing parties should have defended white workers against the bosses without attacking the other workers. In fact, they attacked the non-white workers. Generally, of course, in industrial disputes the "scab"—often a man desperately in need of work—was attacked, rather than the proper target, the boss who employed him. Things became even uglier when the strike-breaker, or undercutting employee, was black. In the USA employers took advantage of the great migration of black people from the South to the North to break white workers' unions; white workers' reaction against this was a major reason for the notorious East St Louis race riot on 2 July 1917, in which 100 to 200 Black people were killed. The US Socialist leader Eugene Debs declared that what happened there was "a foul blot on the American labor movement...Had the labor unions freely opened their door to the Negro instead of barring him...and, in alliance with the capitalist class, conspiring to make a pariah of him, and forcing him in spite of himself to become a scab...the atrocious crime at East St Louis would never have blackened the pages of American history."[161] In Britain, the National Seamen's and Firemen's Union

---

159   E. Roux, *S.P. Bunting, A Political Biography*, Cape Town: published by the author, 1944, p. 54.

160   "F." to D.I. Jones, 16-20 March 1922, and other documents in Davidson *et al.* (eds) (note 155).

161   E.R. Ellis, *Echoes of Distant Thunder*, New York: Coward, McCann and Geoghe-

(NSFU, later renamed the National Union of Seamen, NUS) fought fiercely against the employment of non-white-British seamen—Black, Chinese and Arab—before and after the 1914-18 war.[162]

Communists, thinking above all of Western workers, found it difficult to deal with this traditional attitude. In the USA, as elsewhere, their constant message was that the class struggle was what mattered and workers of all races were allies. But in reality white American workers did not see black workers as allies against the bosses at all.[163] Communists condemned this "white labour chauvinism" consistently; this was an honourable stance that made them more enemies, but it was accompanied by naïve hopes of success. In South Africa they did not face reality but, for some years, obstinately saw only a fight against the bosses, though Jones in Moscow saw the implications of what happened in 1922 at an early stage.[164]

In the two years after the Rand revolt the Labour Party, which had fiercely backed the revolt, formed an alliance with the Afrikaner National Party, on a programme including strengthening of the industrial colour bar. Still dreaming, the Communist Party sought affiliation to the Labour Party, following the "united front" principle then favoured by Moscow, and Jones thought that the CPSA could form an anti-imperialist front with the Labour Party and African nationalists. The Labour Party rejected its approach, yet the CPSA still backed the Labour-Nationalist Pact in the elections of 19 June 1924. However, it was not alone. Kadalie of the ICU made the same crass mistake and persuaded the SANNC, which had turned against Smuts the previous year, to do the same. All three had good reason to dislike Smuts and his South African Party and their capitalist allies, but the naivety of thinking that an alliance of resurgent Afrikaners and white workers devoted to the "colour bar" might be better was extraordinary; the African Political

gan, 1975, p. 419.

162   Evans (note 82); T. Lane, "The Political Imperatives of Bureaucracy and Empire: The Case of the Coloured Alien Seamen Order, 1925", *Immigrants and Minorities* vol. 13 nos. 2 & 3, July/November 1994, pp. 104-29.

163   E. Johanningsmeier, "Communists and the Black Freedom Movements in South Africa and the United States: 1919-1950", *Journal of Southern African Studies* vol. 30 no. 2, June 2004, pp. 155-80 (pp. 159-60).

164   D.I. Jones to O. Kuusinen, Moscow 22 March 1922, in Davidson *et al.* (eds) (note 157), pp. 97-9.

Organisation (APO), the Coloured party active since 1902, knew better. In fact the National Party-Labour coalition won the elections and took power under Hertzog, and then promptly strengthened the mining industry colour bar in the Mines and Works (Amendment) Act of 1926, and began moves—not to succeed for several years—to remove African voters from the common roll in Cape Province.[165]

Rebuffed by the white-supremacy Labour Party, the CPSA now became the Africans' champion. Bunting, who became Chairman of the CPSA in 1924, had in fact always paid more attention than other white comrades to Black South Africans, and under his direction the CPSA was soon recruiting and promoting black comrades. Some Africans soon joined it regardless of its disastrous earlier attitude. The Communists became genuine defenders of victims of the racist regime, but they did not shake off ideological obsessions. In Moscow the Comintern did not at first see a "national" question in South Africa, but only a racial question, a question of black-white relations which it called "the Negro Question"—and which it seemed somehow to regard as common to South Africa and the United States.

The Fourth Comintern Congress in 1922 appointed a Commission on the Negro Question, and proposed the holding of a special Negro Congress. After considerable correspondence involving the CPSA[166] the Congress idea was eventually dropped. American Communists were even more involved in discussions on the "Negro Question", having been given a special responsibility for it, though the leaders of the various factions were initially all white, like John Reed who spoke about the "question" at the Second Comintern Congress in 1920. He, however, then invited Claude McKay to visit Russia. The Jamaican-born literary man—a leading star of the "Harlem Renaissance" of the 1920s, by then author of the poetry volumes *Spring in New Hampshire* (1920) and *Harlem Shadows* (1922)—attended the Fourth Congress in November 1922, as a "Special Delegate".[167] The US Communist delegation there included an African American of Caribbean birth, Otto Huiswoud, originally from Dutch Guiana (Surinam); he and Lovett

165   Simons (note 43), pp. 310-52.
166   Davidson *et al.* (eds) (note 157), pp. 120-33.
167   C. McKay, *A Long Way from Home,* 1937, reprinted 1970 by Harcourt, Brace & World, Inc., pp. 159-225.

Fort-Whiteman, both of the group surrounding the Harlem *Messenger*, were among the first Black Americans to join the Communists. Leaders of the African Blood Brotherhood (ABB), which had been founded independently in 1919 by Caribbean immigrants in the USA—Cyril V. Briggs (from Nevis), Richard B. Moore (from Barbados) and W.A. Domingo (from Jamaica)—and published the newspaper *Crusader*, also joined the Communist ranks.[168]

Communists were generally against ideas of Black solidarity, and attacked the Garvey movement for most of its life; they agreed with the mainstream of African American thinking since the 19th century, represented especially by the NAACP, when they emphasised that the future of the Black Americans was in the USA.[169] To further the Communist campaign for full racial equality, an American Negro Labor Congress was founded in October 1925 in Chicago (a leading centre of African American political and artistic activity, and of socialism), with Fort-Whiteman, back from an extended stay in the Soviet Union, as National Organizer.

Communists were far from discouraging thinking about the African roots; in fact the 1922 "Theses on the Negro Question" said, "The history of the Negro in America fits him for an important role in the liberation struggle of the entire African race."[170] This was simply a slight variation on a very old theme: that African Americans, having through forced migration ended up with modern education and skills and familiarity with the West (and Christianity, it was traditionally added), had a duty to spread these back in the African homeland. In fact the influence of African American Communists on Africa, apart from the Comintern activity of some, was probably just a slight influence through African students in the USA. The wider influence of African Americans on Africa was a constant from the 19th century onwards, but African Americans or Caribbeans could never lead a movement back in Africa, and none

168 Draper (note 138), pp. 319-26; Cedric J. Robinson, *Black Marxism: The Making of the Black Radical Tradition*, Chapel Hill and London: University of North Carolina Press, 1983, pp. 215-16.

169 Draper (note 138), pp. 320-1.

170 Ibid., p. 327. See also K. Baldwin, "The Russian Routes of Claude McKay's Internationalism," ch. 4 in M. Matusevich (ed.), *Africa in Russia, Russia in Africa: Three Centuries of Encounters*, Trenton, NJ: Africa World Press, Inc., 2007.

tried, apart from the few Caribbean UNIA activists who campaigned briefly with African comrades in Cape Town.

Communists and Africans: activists in France

Three Africans who had fought for France in the war stayed on in France and launched militant anti-colonial activity soon after it ended: Louis Hunkanrin from Dahomey and Jean Ralaimongo and Samuel Stéfany from Madagascar, all teachers in earlier life. In Hunkanrin's case this was a resumption of activism begun before 1914. After teacher training in Senegal Louis Hunkanrin (1886-1964), from Porto Novo, worked for some years as a teacher in Ouidah before returning to Dakar, where he went into private business and also took part in Diagne's election campaign in 1913-14. In 1914 he returned to Dahomey and established a local branch of the LDH.

This initiative by Hunkanrin could not have pleased the French, but more followed to annoy them. In late 1914 an arrest warrant was issued for Louis Hunkanrin, who had been dismissed from another job as a teacher, and had been denouncing "abuses" by the Governor, Charles Noufflard; he escaped to Nigeria. But when Diagne's 1918 recruitment drive was extended to Dahomey, Hunkanrin returned and enlisted.[171] After the war Diagne got him a job in France on the military staff in charge of colonial troops, but in the next two years Hunkanrin broke with the Senegalese deputy and embarked on radical politics. Some details are obscure, but it appears that he asked to be demobilised in France to continue studies there; this was refused in February 1920, and he was ordered to be deported. Apparently he was deported to Senegal, returned to France, and then was deported to Dahomey.[172] Later, back in Cotonou, he was tried for evading the deportation order in December 1921, and sentenced to three years' imprisonment and five years' banishment. Meanwhile, in 1920-21 six issues appeared in France of a militant newpaper, Le Messager Dahoméen; a French citizen—Max Clainville-Bloncourt, a lawyer from Guadeloupe prominent in radical activity in the 1920s—was nominally in control (having a French citizen rather than a colonial "subject" in charge could avoid some trouble

171   M. Michel, L'Appel à l'Afrique: Contributions et réactions à l'effort de guerre en A.O.F. 1914-1919, Paris: Publications de la Sorbonne, 1982, p. 64.

172   Dewitte (note 78), pp. 66-8.

with the authorities), but the writing was by Africans using assumed names, headed by Hunkanrin. Bloncourt and Hunkanrin both supported ideals of French "civilisation", but they denounced France's failure to live up to them in practice; this was enough to make assumed names a sensible precaution. After the Porto-Novo riots of 1923, as mentioned earlier, Hunkanrin was accused of involvement—without direct evidence—and this "Bolshevik of Dahomey" (as the AOF Governor General called him) was banished to Mauritania.[173]

Jean Ralaimongo (1884-1943), a Betsileo, was kidnapped in childhood and held as a slave for some years, but later returned to his parents—"*grâce à la France libératrice*", he wrote later—and went to school, eventually qualifying as a teacher and working at government schools. In 1910, having got a job as a houseboy with a French family, he went with them to Paris; he soon parted company with that family, but had jobs in France and obtained a higher qualification. This did not mean any higher pay when he returned home, and he left teaching. In France he was helped by the *indigénophile* Charles Gide, an LDH member who was to be one of Ralaimongo's main French contacts a few years later, when after enlisting (as a volunteer) in the Tirailleurs Malgaches in 1916, and serving in the war, he requested to be demobilised in France, rather than being sent home first as was the general rule for colonial troops. This was refused six times, but eventually allowed in April 1920, through the intervention of a deputy. Gide, a leading figure in the French Cooperative movement, meanwhile found him a job in a wholesale cooperative store, while Ralaimongo, who had been married earlier in Madagascar, married a French wife.[174]

Ralaimongo joined with others in France to form in 1919-20 a new association, the Ligue Française pour l'Accession aux Droits de Citoyen des Indigènes de Madagascar (LFADCIM). As its name showed, it had a specific aim, to campaign for French citizenship for all Malagasys without distinction, and without the conditions imposed for granting of citizenship by the existing law. More generally, the League claimed

173 Conklin (note 21), pp. 160-3, 301; J. Spiegler, "Aspects of Nationalist Thought among French-Speaking West Africans 1921-1939", DPhil, Oxford, 1968, p. 25, pp. 41-2; Harrison (note 21), pp. 150-58.

174 J.-P. Domenichini, "Jean Ralaimongo (1884-1943), ou Madagascar au seuil du nationalisme," *Revue Française d'Histoire d'Outremer* vol. LVI, no. 204, 3rd quarter, 1969, pp. 236-87.

that its aim was to "appeal to all French people to fight against any illegality, any arbitrary act of which Malagasys may be victims, and to have the Malagasys receive the benefits of the Republic's motto: Liberty, Equality, Fraternity." It held a meeting on 21 December 1920 in the Latin Quarter of Paris, at 16 rue de la Sorbonne, attended by about thirty Malagasys, half of them in uniform; Anatole France was there, and Charles Gide was a patron.[175]

Among the African protest leaders of the immediate post-1918 years Ralaimongo's approach was unusual. It appears at first sight like taking submission to France, indeed love of France to extremes. But the French authorities did not see it that way, for granting French citizenship, with all the rights this involved, to all Malagasys without conditions would have ended the colonial order in Madagascar. A quarter of a century later, when France did grant citizenship (though it was a special category of citizenship) to all its African subjects, this turned out to be the prelude to independence. The colonial system could not continue unless the majority remained *sujets*.

The French idea of "assimilation"—a word that can easily cause confusion—had several meanings. One was allowing some colonial subjects, in practice a very limited number, to obtain French citizenship. This was an idea favoured mostly by those French people most devoted to the special ideals of the Republic; it was in a sense a non-racial ideal—an African could be a true Republican Frenchman. In Madagascar the left-wing Freemason Victor Augagneur, Governor-General from 1905 to 1910, actively encouraged the spread of French Republican *mores* including Freemasonry among some Malagasys of the elite. Stéfany and Ralaimongo were among the disciples recruited. LDH sections were founded at the instigation of the Freemasons, always closely linked with the Ligue, in Madagascar as early as 1903.[176] The League and the Masons were particularly devoted to the idea that France was liberating people from their traditions, their monarchies, religions, etc., and leading them to the superior French Republican way.

175   S. Randrianja, *Société et luttes anticoloniales à Madagascar (1896 à 1946)*, Paris: Karthala, 2001, pp. 89-90, 166-70; Domenichini (note 174), pp. 245-8.

176   Randrianja (note 175), pp. 120-30. Diagne's Masonic membership may have saved him from trouble when he was working in the Customs in Madagascar during Augagneur's governorship; see Johnson (note 21), p. 156.

However, such liberation or advancement for Africans required a degree of French education or culture which only a small number could acquire. For other "natives" the policy misleadingly called "assimilation" was purely negative, destroying Africans' traditions but not making them Frenchmen afterwards. Augagneur and almost everyone else in the government of the French empire rejected mass naturalisation. Not only would it effectively end French colonialism, it would devalue the gift of citizenship. The granting of citizenship to all the Originaires of Senegal was exceptional, and shocked some French people. With that exception Muslims were virtually prevented from becoming French citizens, and the few who did were—because of the conditions they accepted—seen as renegades by fellow Muslims, as in North Africa. For other Africans, too, the way the laws on citizenship were applied made it almost impossible to obtain. Ralaimongo applied for naturalisation for himself several times, and was refused—a good indication of what French ideas of "assimilation" actually meant.

In this context, Ralaimongo's demand was virtually revolutionary, and he was going far beyond what his French freethinker mentors could have taught. It is not surprising that a police spy was present at the inaugural meeting of Ralaimongo's Ligue. He was not really so far removed from nationalism, and at the LFADCIM inaugural meeting a picture of the last independent ruler of Madagascar, Queen Ranavalona III (who had died in 1917 in banishment in Algiers), was projected to cheers from the audience.[177] Demanding independence to give better rights and more freedoms to one's people, and demanding French citizenship for all for the same reason, were somewhat similar in 1920, and both equally daring. In later years Ralaimongo was remembered as a founder of Malagasy nationalism.

Samuel Stéfany, who worked closely with him, is less well remembered. Yet according to one account[178] it was he who founded the LFADCIM in 1919. Born in 1890 at Betafo, he went to France in 1915 and fought in the Dardanelles-Salonika theatre, ending up 35 per cent

---

177   Randrianja (note 175), pp. 89-90. Queen Ranavalona's remains were eventually
       reburied in Madagascar in 1938.

178   Domenichini (note 174), p. 245.

incapacitated.[179] After the war he worked for a time as a lecturer at the Paris Ecole des Langues Orientale Vivantes.

Most of the people who joined the LFADCIM—about 200 at the end of 1920, according to a police estimate—were Tirailleurs. But the Secretary General was Bloncourt, Hunkanrin's West Indian comrade, an activist in the SFIO who was shortly to join the PCF. The formation of the Ligue was encouraged by the LDH and an Association Républicaine des Anciens Combattants (ARAC), which had been founded in 1917 by the writer Henri Barbusse and some future founders of the PCF, and had befriended some African ex-soldiers.[180]

Whatever the respective roles of Ralaimongo, Stéfany and Bloncourt were, certainly Ralaimongo was a leading figure in the Ligue, and for years a vigorous advocate of mass naturalisation of his people as French citizens. In June 1921 he travelled back to Madagascar on behalf of the League, trying to get support for that idea; his fare was paid by *L'Action Coloniale*, in which he had written attacks on the then Governor of Madagascar, and to which Stéfany also contributed. Only a few hundred signed a petition calling for naturalisation.[181] Probably many Malagasys were unconvinced that seeking French citizenship for everyone was the right way forward, but in addition the French authorities were very hostile. Governor Hubert Garbit offered Ralaimongo 50,000 francs, later raised to 250,000 plus a government job and French citizenship, if he renounced his ideas, but he refused. He was allowed to travel around, but not to hold public meetings. On his tour he studied the VVS affair (see Chapter 1), and when he returned to France after six months, he sought to explain the facts about that affair, in particular, in his published report on the journey.[182]

A belief grew up later that Ralaimongo was present at the Tours Congress that led to the creation of the PCF, but a study of his career[183] concluded that he was not there. However, he and Stéfany were involved in anti-colonial activity close to the Communist Party in the early 1920s, centred around the Union Intercoloniale and its month-

179   Dewitte (note 78), p. 63.
180   Ibid.; Spiegler (note 173), p. 21.
181   Randrianja (note 175), p. 168; Dewitte (note 78), pp. 63-6.
182   Randrianja (note 175), pp. 168-9; Domenichini (note 174), pp. 246-50.
183   Domenichini (note 174), p. 246.

ly organ *Le Paria*, and involving the Vietnamese activist Nguyen Tat Thanh, alias Nguyen Ai Quoc, the future Ho Chi Minh. Nguyen Ai Quoc's years in Paris have been thoroughly studied, though there are still some obscure points despite constant police surveillance of him and other Vietnamese activists in France. Nguyen Tat Thanh apparently reached France some time before 1919, and used the name Nguyen Ai Quoc; this was also the signature placed on some articles not by him (a device to confuse the police, no doubt), but it became his *nom de guerre*. While working as a photo retoucher, Ai Quoc wrote for *L'Humanité* and contacted its editor Marcel Cachin, the prominent early Communist Paul Vaillant-Couturier, and others. He was already a noted Communist critic of colonialism before he addressed the Tours Congress in December 1920.[184]

During 1921 a small group of militants in Paris formed the Union Intercoloniale. The inaugural meeting was held in Paris in October 1921, but Stéfany mentioned its beginnings in a letter of 7 March 1921, and invited Nguyen Ai Quoc to join.[185] This suggests that he may have taken some of the initiative for the formation of the new body, and he became its first Secretary General.[186] He was replaced at the end of 1921 by Joseph de Monnerville, a Martinican who had served in the navy in the war.[187] Hunkanrin may have helped found the Union Intercoloniale before leaving Paris.[188] But at first the Union's leading figure was Nguyen Ai Quoc. He was a fully committed Marxist and Communist. How many of the other leaders of the Union Intercoloniale were similarly committed it is hard to say. At first they were mainly from the Caribbean, including Bloncourt, with one from Réunion, the lawyer Jean-Jacques Barquisseau.

---

184   Thu Trang-Gaspard, *Ho Chi Minh à Paris (1917-1923)*, Paris: Harmattan, 1992; S. Quinn-Judge, *Ho Chi Minh: The Missing Years*, London: Hurst & Co., 2003, pp. 11-42.

185   Thu Trang-Gaspard (note 184), p. 140; Quinn-Judge (note 184), who gives his name as Stéphany Oju Oti, p. 35.

186   Dewitte (note 78), p. 98.

187   Not to be confused with Gaston Monnerville, the politician from French Guiana who rose to become President of the French Senate in the Fifth Republic, and who was also in Paris in the 1920s.

188   Spiegler (note 173), p. 26.

The aims of the Union, according to its statutes—as quoted in a declaration by Nguyen Ai Quoc and de Monnerville—were:

...to group together and guide the colonials living in France; to enlighten those who are in the colonies on events in France, for the purpose of *solidarity*; to debate and study all questions of colonial policy and economics.[189]

In fact it was a strongly anti-colonial body linked with the PCF and using some Communist language. Several left-wing organisations, not all Communist, helped it with office space in Paris. The Union Intercoloniale organised a number of public meetings in the capital, but its principal activity was the publication of *Le Paria* from April 1922, from offices at no. 3, rue du Marché des Patriarches, Paris 5e.[190] On 1 February 1922 Stéfany wrote to friends urging them to support a proposed new anti-colonial newspaper, emphasising the importance of explaining the truth about the colonies to "our friends in metropolitan France" and also to the colonised people who thought that the French were all like "authoritarian and pitiless officials" or "settlers whose programme is exploitation of the assets and people of the Colonies."[191]

This was to be the basic theme of *Le Paria* and of all the activists in France close to the PCF at this time: the colonised peoples and the ordinary people of France were on the same side, they must join against the common enemy. This somewhat resembled the decades-old African hope of appealing to the French or British public over the heads of the local colonial representatives, but it reflected a basic Communist idea: capitalism was the common enemy of European workers and colonial subjects. But although *Le Paria* echoed that and other Communist themes, it is not obvious that it and the Union Intercoloniale were launched on the PCF leaders' initiative. They were however in line with Comintern instructions about the colonies; of the 21 conditions for membership of the Comintern, accepted by the PCF, the eighth stated that a party must

...support, not only in words but in deeds, all movements for emancipation in the colonies, demand the expulsion from the colonies of the imperialists of the

---

189   Thu Trang-Gaspard (note 184), pp. 142-3.

190   Quinn-Judge (note 184), p. 35; Liauzu (note 102), p.109n.

191   Thu Trang-Gaspard (note 184), pp. 204-5, quoting an archival reference (Série III, Carton 87); the authorities saw this letter.

metropolis, encourage in the hearts of the country's workers truly fraternal feelings towards the working people of the colonies and oppressed nationalities, and maintain among the troops of the metropolis continuous agitation against all oppression of the colonial peoples.[192]

The PCF set up its own Comité d'Etudes Coloniales in 1921.[193] The Union Intercoloniale was separate from the Comité d'Etudes (though the authorities sometimes confused the two), and it seems quite likely that the former, and *Le Paria*, were started by people from the colonies, probably all or mostly Communist Party members, on their own initiative, but with the approval of the party leaders.

This is suggested by Stéfany's letter quoted above, which gives the impression that the PCF did not provide funds to start *Le Paria*. On 3 October 1922, at a meeting of Union Intercoloniale and *Le Paria* activists reported to the police, Stéfany said the coffers were empty, though it had been possible to pay the printers; de Monnerville said he had got some more subscriptions, making 300 in all.[194] From April to December 1922 *Le Paria*'s income, calculated by Ai Quoc (presumably in a statement seen by a police spy), was 1,173 francs, its expenditure 3,745 francs.[195] It did not succeed in appearing regularly every month. The evident failure to provide an adequate share of "Moscow gold" for this venture at that stage—even though Stéfany, Nguyen Ai Quoc and Bloncourt were members of the Comité d'Etudes in 1922-23, together with a lawyer from Martinique, Georges Sarotte[196]—seems to fit in with regular complaints by militants interested in colonial matters that the PCF was not doing enough, a criticism also made by the bosses in Moscow. Many of the early PCF leaders had limited interest in colonial issues—the lawyer, writer and ex-officer Vaillant-Couturier, who visited Tunisia to promote the party, being a notable exception—while the party was also riven by disputes and purges in its first years.[197]

192 E. Sivan, *Communisme et Nationalisme en Algérie 1920-1962*, Paris: Presses de la FNSP, 1976, p. 14 (my translation).

193 Liauzu (note 102), pp. 15-16.

194 Report of meeting in note of 17 October 1922, Services Politiques, Government-General, Hanoi, quoted in Thu Trang-Gaspard (note 184), p. 213.

195 Liauzu (note 102), p. 109n.

196 Ibid., p. 229.

197 Mortimer (note 141), pp. 69-82.

Spiegler's pioneering study of the Francophone Africans' movements in inter-war France concluded that the Union Intercoloniale appeared as "a colonial organization for the most part run by members of the PCF, and linked with the PCF rather by conviction than by direct lines of hierarchic control."[198]

The impression given of the Union Intercoloniale and *Le Paria* is that of typical struggling ventures by small numbers of dedicated but penniless people. They were certainly few—a hard core of about fifteen. The Union had 98 paid-up members in October 1922, 150 in February 1925; the members tended to be minor clerks or factory and dock workers, many being West Indians.[199] *Le Paria* had a print run of 2,000 in March 1922, 3,000 in October 1924; but the hope of sales was mainly in the colonies, for which 2,000 of the October 1924 print run were intended, and bulk supplies for sale there were vulnerable to confiscation by the police (who also took out subscriptions); 800 copies of the April-May 1925 issue were seized in Indochina.[200]

Few though they were, the militants producing *Le Paria* greatly worried the French authorities. Because of their activities and others, from 1922 the Ministry of the Colonies sent monthly circulars on revolutionary activity to the governors of the colonies. These circulars (*"Notes sur la propagande révolutionnaire intéressant les pays d'outre-mer"*) are today a valuable source of information on anti-colonial activities, especially those in France. The reports included in them often came from police informers attending meetings in France, but public events that could inspire anti-colonial militants, such as those in India and China, were also covered.

One of the earliest circulars gave an intriguing glimpse of an African activist who has otherwise vanished from history. It quoted a report in *L'Humanité* on Prince Ibrahim Mengani Kachala from Bornu, who had ended up as a labourer at the port of Marseilles, and commented that this was a suspect who had lived in Berlin and Vienna before the war, and later in Egypt, Morocco and Spain, and had been suspected of pan-Islamic sympathies.[201] Having come to the authorities' attention,

198   Spiegler (note 173), p. 94.
199   Ibid., p. 83.
200   Liauzu (note 102), p. 110n.
201   Note on Revolutionary Propaganda, Paris, 1 July 1922, in file APA 10430,

he may have returned, voluntarily or by deportation, to his homeland, by then part of British Northern Cameroons (now in Nigeria).

Pan-Islamism was still feared by the French colonial authorities, as were German activities (in Cameroon especially), but the "Red Scare" was what most preoccupied them. In 1922 the minister of the Colonies expressed what had already become, and was to remain, a common colonial obsession:

At present, we need to consider that the movements displaying a so-called national character are bound to allow us, most often, to suppose prior preparation imputable to Communist manoeuvres...Any manifestation of separatist tendencies must from now on be considered a major element favouring the spread of maximalist [i.e. Bolshevik] ideas.[202]

Similarly, Governor Fourn of Dahomey, who banned the local LDH section in 1921, quoted a Colonies ministry circular the following year as saying that although the League was not revolutionary, "some of its adherents in the colonies often show towards authority feelings whose very existence implies a state of receptiveness favourable to Communist propaganda."[203]

The first issue of *Le Paria* in April 1922 carried an article on Hunkanrin, recently gaoled in Dahomey, and in 1922-23 400 copies of each issue were sent to Dahomey. *Le Paria* also reprinted an article by Ralaimongo in *L'Action Coloniale* of 10 March 1922, comparing Governor Garbit with Queen Ranavalona I, who had persecuted the early Christians in Madagascar.[204] *Le Paria* included some specifically Communist writing, but also plenty of exposure of crimes and abuses in the colonies, such as could come from many sorts of critic (this was fully in accordance with Comintern instructions). It published extracts

---

Cameroon Archives. In 1978 I appealed in a journal published in Nigeria for more information to be unearthed about this figure (J. Derrick, "A Militant 'Prince' from Borno", *Savanna*, Zaria, vol. 7 no. 2, 1978, pp. 178-9), but there was no response so far as I know.

202   "Notes sur la propagande révolutionnaire intéressant les pays d'outre-mer," 19 April 1922, quoted in G. Oved, *La gauche française et le nationalisme marocain 1905-1955*, Paris: Harmattan, 1984, vol. I, p. 181.

203   Quoted in E.D. Zinsou and Luc Zouménou, *Kojo Tovalou Houénou, Précurseur, 1887-1936: pannégrisme et modernité*, Paris: Maisonneuve et Larose, 2004, p. 116, referring to circular of 19 May 1922.

204   Spiegler (note 173), pp. 26, 85; Domenichini (note 174), p. 252.

from Vigné d'Octon's pre-war writings, for example, and constantly recalled non-Europeans' service in the war and the false promises used to recruit them. In its issue of 1 December 1922 Nguyen Ai Quoc wrote a long article on the *cause célèbre* of the Senegalese boxer "Battling Siki" (real name M'Barrick Fall), whose victory over Georges Carpentier at the Buffalo stadium in Paris was questioned.[205] Boxing matches regularly aroused racial feelings around the world, as with the Jackson-Jeffries fight in 1910 and later the Louis-Schmelling bout in 1937; the Siki fight was another such case, arousing strong reactions in the Black world. *Le Paria* must have highlighted this case because of its general (non-Marxist) interest for African and Caribbean readers.

There were probably no attempts to establish a Communist party organisation in French sub-Saharan Africa at this early stage, but it was possible in Algeria and Tunisia. There as elsewhere Communists were told to back "national-democratic" movements. A young French comrade living in Oran in Algeria (but not of French-Algerian birth), Charles-André Julien, who was on the French delegation to the Third Comintern Congress in Moscow in mid-1921, declared in a speech there on 12 July 1921:

Yes, we must spread Communism in the East, we must form Communist parties, we must back all Communist aspirations. But in doing so, we must not be deceived by false hopes: in the present economic situation, in the struggle against imperialism, it is inevitably national questions that will be in the forefront.[206]

He had earlier written, apparently referring to Algeria especially, that many "natives" came to Socialism "less by intellectual adherence to socialist principles than to find in Parliament and public opinion [in France] support against the settlers who exploit them." Confirming this predictable fact, in Tunisia the French Resident-General said some Tunisians were interested in Communism "because they see it as a means to start the struggle against the Infidel."[207]

But those who started out as anti-colonialists rather than Marxists could become active Communists; Abdelkader Hadj Ali, an Algerian

205   Thu Trang-Gaspard (note 184), pp. 210-12.

206   C.-A. Julien with M. Morsy, *Une pensée anticoloniale: positions 1914-1979*, Paris: Sindbad, 1979, pp. 53-64.

207   Goldstein (note 8), p. 391.

who said he joined the PCF "because of the eighth condition",[208] was one of several Algerians active in the party in the early 1920s. Born in 1883 at Sidi Saada in Constantine department, he was one of the small minority of Muslim Algerians who obtained French citizenship, in 1911; after going to France and working as an itinerant trader and shop assistant, he served in the war and was wounded. After the war he set up in business as an ironmonger at Brunoy in the Paris region, and joined the PCF.[209]

Other North Africans who did not join the Communists still found their sympathy and support welcome. In France the Communists and their allies defended and sought support from the Algerian migrant workers; the CGTU issued a leaflet calling them to meetings in Paris on 1 May 1924 to demand the eight-hour day and other improvements in working conditions.[210] In Algeria—where there was a local Communist periodical, *La Lutte Sociale*—the Jeunes Algériens backed the Communist candidate Mazoyer in a by-election in Algiers, "not because he is a Communist, but as a defender of the natives", as *Ikdam* expressed it (22 June 1922); Khaled's newspaper also said that Communists "treat us on a footing of equality". While it also said (8 April 1921), "The native question, being a race question, cannot be resolved by the means of class struggles," it and *La Lutte Sociale* were on the same side in 1922-23 in particular. Emir Khaled had a devoted supporter in the Algiers Communist Victor Spielman, through his *Trait d'Union* newspaper and publishing company; Spielman called him "our Zaghlul Pasha".[211] During the early Communist propaganda efforts in Tunisia in 1921-22, led by Robert Louzon who ran a press printing Communist material, there were attempts to show areas where Communism and Islam were in agreement, and some material was printed in Arabic; those efforts

208 Sivan (note 192), p. 43.

209 Liauzu (note 102), pp. 266-7; B. Stora, *Dictionnaire biographique de militants nationalistes algériens 1926-1954: E.N.A., P.P.A., M.T.L.D.*, Paris: Harmattan, 1985, entry on Hadj Ali, pp. 51-5.

210 Liauzu (note 102), p. 245. Liauzu says however (pp. 183-93) that the PCF was generally slow to take an interest in these workers, and affected by hesitations and prejudice. A resolution at the PCF Lyons Congress of January 1924, saying capitalism aimed to divide immigrant from French workers (ibid.), suggests one reason for prejudice.

211 Koulakssis and Meynier (note 16), p. 195.

were cut short when Louzon was gaoled briefly for "attacks against the rights and powers of the French Republic in Tunisia" and deported.[212] Louzon left the PCF later, as did Spielman and Julien.

Most early Communists in Algeria were French-Algerian *colons*, and some retained normal settler attitudes like early white Communists in South Africa and the settler Bolsheviks in Central Asia. When the Comintern Executive issued an "Appeal for the Liberation of Algeria and Tunisia" (24 May 1922) the PCF section at Sidi bel Abbès in Algeria criticised it, saying liberation must follow the revolution in France itself, while a Muslim rising before then would lead the country back "towards a regime close to feudalism". This view was condemned by Trotsky at the Fourth Comintern Congress in 1922.[213] Communists were sometimes to return to the idea that the colonies must wait for the revolution in Europe, after which their own liberation would follow automatically, but such views were almost always condemned. It was rather proclaimed that loss of the colonies would help bring about the ruin of Western imperialist countries; addressing the PCF National Council in June 1924, the Algerian comrade Abdelaziz Menouar alias El Djazaïri declared, "The day that India frees itself from the yoke of British capitalism, England—deprived of raw materials and the inestimable wealth from servile manpower—will be in a catastrophic situation and its entire economy will collapse."[214] By sticking to its line which some members disliked, the PCF was able to work with non-European anti-colonial activists.

It would be wrong to suppose that non-Communist left-wing organisations and personalities showed no sympathy for colonial demands and protests. In Tunisia the SFIO, after the 1920 split, supported the idea of gradual progress towards self-determination in which Tunisians would decide whether to remain under the French Protectorate, while the CGT admitted Muslim Tunisians as well as members of the European settler communities to membership, and showed sympathy for Tunisians. But after a major dock strike in Tunisia in 1924, in De-

---

212   Goldstein (note 8), pp. 387-94.

213   Sivan (note 192), pp. 16-51, gives the fullest account of the controversies and ensuing purge aroused by the Algerian settler Communists' views; see also Dewitte (note 78), p. 102; Biondi (note 108), pp. 124-5.

214   Liauzu (note 102), p. 54.

cember of that year a separate Confédération Générale du Travail Tunisien (CGTT) was created, on the initiative of M'hammed Ali (in full M'hammed Ali Ben Mokhtar El-Ghaffari), a chauffeur who had just returned from several eventful years abroad; he had gone to help the Libyan resistance in 1911, fought or worked with the Turks in the 1914-18 war, and then travelled to Germany. Like many other trade unionists to follow later in colonial territories, the CGTT leaders combined anticolonial protests with industrial ones, inevitably in a setting where the employers were mostly European. After more strikes the CGTT was quickly banned and M'hammed Ali arrested. At a trial in November 1925 he was accused of conspiracy with Communists and Germans; he was sentenced to ten years' banishment.[215]

One serious step that the Communists were prepared to take was encouraging dissidence and even mutiny among soldiers—crossing a red line firmly drawn by Western democracies. As part of its campaign against France's military occupation of the Ruhr in 1923 the PCF appealed directly to the North African troops of the French army. Leaflets were distributed to North African troops involved in the Ruhr occupation; one declared,

...the French imperialists recruit you by force into the army, lead you into the battlefield... The long war was not enough for them, because they have now taken you into the Ruhr...After stealing your land they are taking you to help them steal in Germany!

The German workers and peasants are suffering from the occupation just as the workers and peasants of the colonies have suffered and are still suffering from French imperialism.

...If you are ordered to beat and kill German workers, DON'T DO IT. Comrades of Algeria and Morocco, DON'T SHOOT. HOLD OUT A HAND TO THE GERMAN WORKERS WHO ARE YOUR FRIENDS.[216]

215   M-S. Lejri, *Evolution du Mouvement national tunisien,* Vol. 1, Tunis: Maison Tunisienne de l'Edition, 1974, pp. 220-39; E. Ahmed and S. Schaar, "M'hamed Ali: Tunisian Labor Organizer", pp. 191-204 in E. Burke III (ed.), *Struggle and Survival in the Modern Middle East,* London: Tauris, 1993.

216   Quoted in Sivan (note 192), p. 42 and B. Recham, *Les Musulmans algériens dans l'armée française (1919-1945),* Paris: Harmattan, 1996, p. 98.

The production of such leaflets, and of a bilingual French-Arabic newssheet to spread the same message, *Al Kazirna*, was organised by an early Algerian Communist activist, Mahmoud Lekhel alias Ben Lekhel (or Ben Lakhal). Born to a prominent Algiers family in 1894, he spent some years in Syria and later was one of the first students at Kutvu in Moscow, before joining in the campaign directed at Algerian troops in Germany. He was arrested at Mainz later in 1923 and sentenced to five years' imprisonment, but was amnestied after nine months.[217]

Jacques Doriot, one of the main organisers of the Ruhr protest campaign, became leader of the Jeunesses Communistes in 1923. For some years Doriot, who was elected to the National Assembly in the May 1924 elections while in prison for anti-militarist activity, was the leading advocate of colonial issues in the PCF. On those issues the Comintern's policy was, as noted earlier, reaffirmed at the Fifth Congress; there D.Z. Manuilsky declared on 1 June 1924:

There is no doubt whatsoever that the bourgeoisie cannot solve the national question within the framework of the capitalist state. But this does not mean that we must postpone the realization of the right of oppressed nationalities to separation until the social revolution has been victorious throughout the world.[218]

"Separation": that is, independence as at least a possibility. About the same time an article in *Le Paria* no 28 of August 1924, on "the tenth anniversary of the imperialist carnage", made this appeal:

Workers of the colonies! Slaves of imperialism! Wake up for the struggle and independence. The Communist International is with you![219]

Communists were almost alone in accepting the idea of colonial independence, and were ready to defy most of French public opinion in that way and by their encouragement to soldiers to disobey orders. The PCF further challenged French public opinion by putting forward the Communist Algerian Abdelkader Hadj Ali, who wrote for *Le Paria* and

---

217   Recham (note 216), pp. 98-9; Liauzu (note 102), p. 265; Koulakssis and Meynier (note 16), p. 290.

218   Quoted in English in Eudin and North (note 131), pp. 327-8.

219   Quoted in Dewitte (note 78), pp. 104-5. This was another example of the constant recalling of the Great War by these militants, many of whom had fought in the war, several being wounded.

Al Kazirna under the pseudonym of Ali Baba, as third on its list on the Seine department in the general election of 11 May 1924. He won 40,781 votes, an impressive score, and was only narrowly surpassed by another Communist on the list. His fellow countryman Menouar wrote (under his pseudonym El Djezaïri, "the Algerian") in *Le Paria* of June 1924, "40,781 Parisian workers condemn colonialism."[220]

Earlier Hadj Ali had joined the Union Intercoloniale committee in November 1922, at a time of several changes in the small band of militants. Some changes at least were due a breach between Communists and Freemasons. Anti-colonial activists had been ready to seek help from both Communists and the LDH-Freemasons colonial protest tradition, even to join the Masons as Nguyen Ai Quoc did. But in December 1922 the Comintern ordered that all Communists must sever ties with the Freemasons and the Ligue des Droits de l'Homme. This seems to have affected in particular Ralaimongo, who had relied on Freemason contacts such as Charles Gide.

A few months after returning to France Ralaimongo went back to Madagascar again in May 1922, this time to promote a new cooperative society he had set up for marketing of Malagasy products to assist growers, the Société Union France-Madagascar. The Governor-General threatened to banish him to Mayotte in the neighbouring Comoro Islands unless he agreed to return to France; he preferred to go back to France, at government expense, leaving his long-time comrade Jules Ranaivo to continue his work in Madagascar. Back in France his French *indigénophile* contacts raised the matter of the VVS case prisoners and they were released. Ralaimongo himself obtained an audience with the Minister of the Colonies, Sarraut, and the Madagascar banishment order was then cancelled. This was achieved through Ralaimongo's Freemason contacts.[221] A Communist deputy, Me. Berthon, also took action on Ralaimongo's behalf in France, but Ralaimongo assured Sarraut that he himself was not a Communist—although he was present, according to one source,[222] at the PCF's congress in September 1922. Ralaimongo now founded his own newspaper for his Malagasy campaign, *Le Libéré*, with Gouttenoire de Toury, who had been involved with *Le Paria* at

---

220   Liauzu (note 102), p. 266; Dewitte (note 78), p. 105.

221   Domenichini (note 174), p. 253.

222   Liauzu (note 102), p. 132.

the beginning, as manager; Charles Gide was also involved. The first issue of *Le Libéré* appeared on 15 May 1923; the second, appearing after six months in November 1923, declared that the new publication was above parties and none of its editorial team belonged to the PCF.

About the same time Stéfany was removed as editor of *Le Paria* in March 1923; he left the PCF and joined the SFIO.[223] There may have been other causes of disagreement, but at this time activists had to choose between the Party on the one hand and the Freemasons and the LDH on the other. Ai Quoc, who obediently left the Masons, and Bloncourt chose the Party; Bloncourt denounced his former LDH comrades in *Le Paria* of November 1923.[224] In June 1923 Nguyen Ai Quoc left France for Moscow; the French authorities heard from an informer that Bloncourt had paid for the journey with Union Intercoloniale funds.[225] Ai Quoc attended the founding Conference of the Krestintern in October 1923, addressed the fourth Comintern Congress in June 1924 (condemning French rule in Africa as well as Indochina, and criticising French and British Communists for neglecting the colonies), and then headed for China, where a number of Vietnamese exiles were gathered and their fortunes were to be linked for years to the Chinese civil wars.[226]

Ralaimongo went back to Madagascar again later in 1923, permanently as it turned out, while *Le Libéré* continued for a time in Paris. He arrived at Diego Suarez on 20 November 1923 and continued his political activity there, with supporters including Paul Dussac, a white Réunionnais (son of a Paris Communard). For the moment Ralaimongo no longer pursued the call for mass naturalisation as actively as before, but he took action to defend local people, against settlers for example, and soon faced trouble with the authorities for this.[227]

In 1924 more North Africans joined the Union Intercoloniale and Menouar, an Algerian Communist (born to a well-off family in Algiers in 1893) who had travelled to Soviet Russia, became editor of *Le Paria*. The newspaper's line continued as before, close to that of the PCF,

223   Ibid., pp. 132-3.
224   Dewitte (note 78), p. 104.
225   Quinn-Judge (note 184), pp. 40-42.
226   Ibid., pp. 43-68.
227   Randrianja (note 175), pp. 172-4.

and it and the Union were under Party supervision; from April 1923 the party's Colonial Commission provided a subsidy. But the subsidy, if it was continued, seems not to have been enough, for the newspaper continued to appear irregularly, producing ten issues in 1924 and five in 1925. *Le Paria* carried strong condemnations of local "lackeys" of colonialism, but admired non-Communist nationalists such as Sun Yat-sen (most of the issue of February-March 1925 was devoted to his death) and Gandhi.[228] It should be recalled again that this fitted in with the Comintern and PCF line.

In 1924 an African who was to become a leading anti-colonial campaigner from French Africa in the 1920s, Lamine Senghor, joined the Union Intercoloniale, the CGTU and the PCF. Born on 15 September 1889 at Joal in Senegal, son of a Serer farming family,[229] Senghor worked as a houseboy and an employee of the major colonial trading firm Maurel et Prom, before being called up in 1915 and sent to the Western Front. He won the Croix de Guerre and was wounded and gassed. Demobilised back in Senegal in 1919 with the rank of sergeant and a 30 per cent invalid ex-serviceman's pension, he returned to France in 1921 and got a job with the PTT in the Paris 19th Arrondissement, and at some point he became interested in left-wing politics.[230] He married a white Frenchwoman and they had two children.

France's colonial policy did not change when the Cartel des Gauches won the May 1924 elections and the Radical Edouard Herriot became Prime Minister. But after the elections Emir Khaled returned to France (though banned from revisiting Algeria) and sent an open letter to Herriot, calling for representation of Muslims ("in equal proportions with the Algerian Europeans") and other such reforms—though not for extension of citizenship for Algerians through relaxing of conditions to make them acceptable to Muslims. At the same time Khaled sought and obtained strong support from the Communists. *Le Paria* of July 1924 published the Herriot letter on its front page. In that month Khaled addressed two meetings in Paris, on 12 and 19 July; the second, at the Salle Blanqui, was under the auspices of the Union Intercoloniale,

---

228   Liauzu (note 102), pp. 109, 113-30.

229   He was possibly related to Léopold Senghor, who became President of Senegal; this seems to be uncertain.

230   Dewitte (note 78), p. 127; Spiegler (note 173), p. 91.

and attended by 12,000 people according to the booklet reproducing Khaled's speech, 6,000 according to the police. Ben Lekhal, then still in prison, was the honorary chairman of that meeting, and Khaled presided in reality along with Bloncourt, Louzon and a Vietnamese activist, Nguyen The Truyen; Hadj Ali was one of the other speakers.[231]

There was nothing strange about this collaboration between the aristocratic ex-officer Khaled and Communists, though it shocked Pierre Bourdarie, editor of the *Revue Indigène*, who broke with Khaled, and Communists on their side had misgivings about Khaled's approach. Despite disagreements Communists readily backed nationalist protests, and nationalists everywhere sought support wherever they could in Europe. In the two speeches[232] Khaled dealt at length with the oppression of Muslim Algerians and the power and privileges of the *colons*. He said, for example, "Consider...the situation of a European vine grower, making a million a year in profits from vines cultivated for 2 to 4 francs for a 14-hour day"; he spoke of continued application of special laws for Muslims (except for those who now had the vote), the spread of alcohol and prostitution, punishment of poor rural people under severe forestry laws, unequal treatment of settler and Muslim national servicemen, and the need for representation of Muslim Algerians in the French parliament: "How is it conceivable, in a democratic country, that four-fifths of the Algerian population is left without representatives, while the taxation and military laws affect them in the same way as the privileged minority?" The government paid no heed to such demands and Khaled was invited or persuaded to leave France again, and returned to Egypt.

As Communists supported a cautious protest leader like Khaled, it is not surprising that they supported another Maghrebian leader who not only called for independence but successfully achieved it, for several years, by force of arms. In the latter part of 1924 the PCF began a campaign of support for Abd el-Krim. Pierre Sémard, who had become General Secretary of the PCF in July, and Doriot sent a telegram to Abd el-Krim, published in *L'Humanité* of 11 September:

---

231   Liauzu (note 102), pp. 111, 128; Koulakssis and Meynier (note 16), pp. 120-21, 256-63.

232   Published together in a booklet at the time by Spielman's Editions du "Trait-d'Union" in Algiers, reprinted in 1987: Emir Khaled, *La situation des musulmans d'Algérie*, edited with introduction by Nadya Bouzar Kasbadji, Algiers: Office des Publications Universitaires.

Parliamentary group, steering committee of the Communist Party, national committee of the Young Communists greet the brilliant victory of the Moroccan people over the Spanish imperialists. They congratulate its valiant chief Abd el-Krim. Hope that after the definitive victory over Spanish imperialism it will continue, with the French and European proletariat, the struggle against all imperialists, the French ones included, until the complete liberation of Moroccan soil.[233]

When Abd el-Krim invaded French Morocco in 1925 and French troops were involved in a fierce new colonial war, there was to be an exceptionally vigorous campaign against the war, to be described in the next chapter.

In September 1924 the PCF set up a Colonial Commission to replace the Comité d'Etudes Coloniales. It was headed first by Henri Lozeray and then by Doriot. In February 1925 the three main Algerian Communist activists—Hadj Ali, Menouar and Ben Lakhal—all joined it, together with Lamine Senghor, Nguyen The Truyen and two other Vietnamese, Bloncourt, Stéphane Rosso (a West Indian who was to remain faithful to the PCF throughout the inter-war era), and a Haitian engineer born in France, Camille Saint-Jacques.[234] A new bureau of the Union Intercoloniale was elected in 1925 including that Algerian trio and Bloncourt (secretary general), Senghor (assistant secretary), Rosso, Saint-Jacques and The Truyen; indeed it almost replicated the Colonial Commission, but this only reaffirmed the ties to the PCF that were already obvious.[235] The Union may well have been started on an initiative from below, but it was subject to orders from above.

The first Black militant group in France

During the build-up to the Rif war protest campaign, separately some Black activists in Paris, African and Caribbean, started a new venture in 1924: an association, the Ligue Universelle de Défense de la Race Noire (LUDRN), and its newspaper, *Les Continents*. These were the initiative of another Dahomean (apparently not connected with Hunkanrin),

233   R. Blachère, "L'Insurrection rifaine, préfiguration des émancipations maghrébines," pp. 159-66 in *Abd el-Krim et la République du Rif* (note 51).
234   Dewitte (note 78), pp. 99-100, 106-7; Liauzu (note 102), p. 229. The Black community in Paris included numerous Haitians.
235   Dewitte (note 64), p. 107.

Marc Kodjo Tovalou Houénou. Born on 25 April 1887 at Porto Novo, he was the son of a prominent trader and a great-grandson of King Ghezo of Dahomey. He was sent to France for education at the age of 13, studied law and medicine, served in the medical corps in the war and became a French citizen in 1915. After being wounded and then discharged, he joined the Paris Bar in 1918.[236] A learned and cultivated man, in 1921 he published an erudite book far removed from political agitation: *L'involution des métamorphoses et métempsychoses de l'univers: Tome I – L'involution phonétique ou Méditations sur les métamorphoses et métempsychoses du langage.* This, according to Spiegler, was "a highly abstruse, diagrammatic discussion of phonetic theory; a collection or urbane, graceful epigrams—observations on life, friendship, religion, love; and seventy pages of a dictionary of French compared to Indo-European languages."[237]

In 1921 Tovalou Houénou revisited his home country. Back in Paris he began to produce a different sort of writing, on his country's affairs, and aroused suspicion even though he showed utter loyalty to France as chairman of an Amitié Franco-Dahoméenne association founded in January 1923, calling for closer ties and the development and modernisation of the colony. Then, on 29 June and 3/4 August 1923, there were two publicised incidents in Paris in which white American customers forced the management of a bar and then of a restaurant in Montmartre to throw Tovalou Houénou and his companions out. The French press generally backed the African and raised an outcry, and the restaurant owner received a two-week gaol sentence.[238] Tovalou wrote about the incident in *L'Action Coloniale*, to which he was now contributing; he was also on the editorial team of *Le Libéré*, which was called the *tribune du peuple malgache* but covered events in other colonies too.[239]

On 30 April 1924 Tovalou founded the LUDRN and became its chairman, with two vice-chairmen from the French Caribbean, René Maran and Camille Mortenol. The latter was a 70-year-old Guadelou-

---

236   Zinsou and Zouménou (note 203), chs. 2, 3.
237   Spiegler (note 173), p. 51. See Zinsou and Zouménou (note 203), ch. 6.
238   A detailed account in Zinsou and Zouménou (note 203) (pp. 131-6) describes fully these incidents not clarified in earlier accounts; see Dewitte (note 78), pp. 74-5 and Spiegler (note 173), p. 54.
239   Dewitte (note 78), pp. 72-3.

pean ex-naval officer who had commanded the Paris air defences in the Great War.[240] Maran (born in Martinique, but to parents from French Guiana) had joined the French colonial service like a number of other French Caribbean people, including notably his friend Félix Eboué, from French Guiana. These black French officials could rise high in the colonial service and Eboué was to become a famous governor; they reinforced the misleading impression of the French empire held by some non-French people at the time, who noted that black Frenchmen could reach high positions but forgot that life for the majority of Africans under French rule was very different. French rule was at its most vicious in French Equatorial Africa, where both Maran and Eboué served.[241]

In 1921, however, Maran described some of the colonial misrule that he had helped to enforce in a novel, *Batouala*, and added a damning introduction, saying for example:

After all, if they [the Africans] die in their thousands, like flies, their country is being made to produce value added. Only those who do not adapt to civilisation disappear.

Civilisation, civilisation, the pride of Europeans, and their charnel-house of the innocent...You build your pride on corpses. Whether you like it or not, you move in lies...[242]

This novel was awarded the Prix Goncourt for 1921. That was no doubt because of its literary merit, but it should be noted that Maran did not call for France to leave AEF, and declared faith in an ideal France of 1789. In fact, remarkably, he returned to Africa and a new posting for a time, leaving only in 1923; Eboué, who welcomed the prize awarded to *Batouala* while continuing his own loyal colonial service, advised him to leave the service, after reports of threats to his life; he was also criticised in the National Assembly (but defended by Candace).[243] The Black "establishment" in Paris in the 1920s was close-knit and links could be maintained despite political differences, while Maran retained

---

240   Zinsou and Zouménou (note 203), pp. 141-6.

241   See B. Weinstein, *Eboué*, New York: OUP, 1972, especially Chapters III and IV.

242   R. Maran, *Batouala*, 1921, quoted in Dewitte (note 78), p. 68-70. On *Batouala* see Edwards (note 97), Ch. 2, especially pp. 81-98.

243   Weinstein (note 241), p. 81.

his belief in the true ideals of France. So did Tovalou Houénou, as they with their colleagues (who included the young Gaston Monnerville, the future politician from French Guiana) showed in *Les Continents*. It produced its first issue on 15 May 1924, with a print run of 7,000; later issues were printed, roughly twice a month, in numbers not over 5,000. The newspaper was the LUDRN's main activity, though it organised cultural events also.

Tovalou Houénou was editor (*directeur*), while the editor-in-chief was a Frenchman, Jean Fangeat, who had worked for *L'Action Coloniale*. The editorial team also included Maran and Gouttenoire de Toury, who had left the Communist side and was working with the LDH to support the Malagasy campaigners. The world of militants from the colonies in early-1920s Paris was a small one, but not too small to be divided into the major tendencies described earlier; the LUDRN and *Les Continents* were definitely on the side of law-abiding protesters backed by the LDH and the Freemasons. This meant that they proclaimed their belief in French republican ideals, but condemned the French rulers of Africa strongly for going against those ideals. Tovalou denounced the Indigénat and other oppressive acts, and the lack of schools; Gouttenoire de Toury exposed injustice in Madagascar; Maran said the wartime conscription of colonial subjects had led to subsequent unrest; Tovalou asked Diagne in the issue of 31 May 1924, "Are you going to be a guide for us only on the sacred road leading to the hecatombs of Verdun? Get this clear, excessive prudence, equivocal diplomacy and reticence here verge on complicity and treachery." This attitude had already been shown in a lecture given by the Dahomean on 24 February 1924, where he said of the French in Africa,

If the monsters lost in vice, sodden with alcohol, sick with syphilis, which you send to us, have nothing else to offer than what they have already given, then keep them yourselves, and let us revert to our misery and our barbarity.[244]

Tovalou was ready to express naïve hope of change under the Cartel des Gauches, but he also made a most radical call for French citizenship

---

244   Zinsou and Zouménou (note 203), pp. 136-41, 157-81. Some Gabonese led
       by Laurent Anchouey expressed this idea—appealing to Frenchmen of France
       against those running the colonies—in a newspaper *L'Echo Gabonais* published
       in Dakar in 1922: B. Weinstein, *Gabon: Nation-Building on the Ogooue*, Cam-
       bridge, MA and London: MIT Press, 1966, pp. 41, 115.

for all Africans under French rule. Like Ralaimongo's similar call for citizenship for all Malagasys, it would have meant altering the colonial order beyond recognition. And Tovalou Houénou said in *Les Continents* in July 1924,

We ask to be citizens of some country or another. That is why, if France rejects us, we demand self-government (*autonomie*). If it accepts us, total, wholesale assimilation.[245]

This presumably was another call for citizenship for all Africans. As France would not contemplate that, and as *Les Continents* said the alternative was self-government, it was certainly not preaching abject submission to France. The authorities in fact considered it subversive and interfered with its sales in Africa. They also informed Tovalou Houénou's aged father, who had been remitting money to him for years but now cut him off.[246]

Tovalou Houénou visited the USA and attended the UNIA Convention in New York in August 1924; there were links between *Les Continents* and the *Negro World*, but Tovalou approved of the Garvey movement only partially, and he met its arch-enemy Du Bois. In his speech in New York he praised the lack of anti-Black racism in France, but used virulent language about the European rulers of Africa, without distinction.[247] The authorities' view of him was certainly confirmed.

In the 15 October 1924 issue of *Les Continents*, edited in Tovalou Houénou's absence by Fangeat, an unsigned article not only condemned Blaise Diagne for the 1918 AOF recruitment campaign, but said, "Mr Clemenceau, cunning as always, hastened to inform Mr Diagne by telephone that he would be paid a certain commission for every soldier recruited." Diagne sued for libel. Maran, supposed to be the author of the article, was co-defendant with Fangeat. When the case was heard on 24-5 November 1924, Challaye (who had contributed to the newspaper) and the former AOF Tirailleur Senghor gave evidence for the defence, but they could not affect the outcome; the court found against

245 Zinsou and Zouménou (note 203), p. 169.
246 Ibid., pp. 179-81, 187.
247 Ibid., pp. 146-56; (text of New York speech, translated from *Negro World* 13 Sept. 1924), Appendix 1. See also Edwards (note 97), pp. 99-104.

the defendants, and Fangeat received a six months' suspended gaol sentence plus a 1,500 francs fine, 2,000 francs damages, and costs.[248]

The damage caused by this case finished *Les Continents*. There were talks on a merger of *Les Continents* and *Le Libéré,* but neither newspaper seems to have appeared after January 1925. The LUDRN ceased activity about then or soon afterwards also. Tovalou Houénou returned to Dahomey just before his father's death in December 1925. He only got a fair share of the estate after a lawsuit, and did not succeed to the chieftaincy until 1927. Having resumed legal practice, he was arrested in court in Lome (French Togo) in April and held in custody for ten months on various charges; eventually he was cleared only after an appeal which was allowed in December 1927 in Dakar, where he went the same month.[249]

Agitators and petitioners

Radical anti-colonial activity was less developed in Britain than in France in the early 1920s, and it was very much concentrated on India. However, one prominent early Communist who was Indian and became an MP in Britain was interested in other parts of the empire besides his own. Shapurji Saklatvala (1874-1936), a Parsi Indian, was a nephew of Jamsetji Tata, founder of the Tata business empire. He went to England in 1905 to manage the London office of the Tata Iron and Steel Co. (TISCO), but joined the ILP at Manchester in 1909. The British police in India suspected him of links with the exiled Indian revolutionaries active at that time. In 1919 he voted for affiliation of the ILP to the Comintern, but the party voted against this. Saklatvala then joined the new CPGB. He attended the 1921 Pan-African Conference, where he was introduced by John Archer; Archer also worked

---

248   Ibid., pp. 182-5. According to an official document quoted here, Senghor was told by the Union Intercoloniale to testify. This was one of the documents based on police reports which must be taken with caution. But clearly Senghor felt free, at least, to defend people not in full agreement with the Communist anti-imperialists.

249   Ibid., pp. 186-93. This recent study corrects other accounts of Tovalou Houénou's return to Africa published in two unreliable works, by Roi Ottley (*No Green Pastures*) and Gustave Gautherot ("Le Bolchévisme en Afrique," *Renseignements Coloniaux* no. 7, 1930, supplement to *L'Afrique Française* vol. 40, no. 7, July 1930, pp. 418-29) (quoted in Langley (note 25), p. 300).

to secure adoption of Saklatvala as Labour candidate for the inner London constituency of Battersea North, and became his election agent. He was elected MP in the General Election of 1922, but defeated in the following year's General Election, although that produced Labour gains leading to the formation of the first Labour government. In the 1924 General Election Labour lost power but Saklatvala was elected as a Communist with Labour support, to remain an MP until 1929, strongly defending the Indian cause against Britain in the House of Commons and outside. The earlier, uneasy Labour-Communist coexistence ended when Labour expelled Communist members in 1925-26; the division that followed (in which Archer took the Labour side) ensured that Saklatvala was defeated by the Labour candidate in Battersea North in 1929.[250]

In Britain the Communist Party was never the dominant anti-colonial voice; the ILP came nearer to being that. But it did take part in open and secret anti-imperialist activity, in which, besides Saklatvala and others, the brothers Clemens Dutt and Rajani Palme Dutt, two intellectual comrades (of Indian and Swedish parentage) who had been among the early Communist students at Cambridge and Oxford respectively, were active. Opposition to imperialism was expressed for example in the *Labour Monthly*, founded in 1921 and edited by Rajani Palme Dutt, the more famous of the brothers.[251] The CPGB set up a colonial department in 1924. Although Communist anti-colonial activity was concentrated on India, and although the Comintern felt it necessary to push the British comrades into paying more attention to the colonies, any Africans and West Indians wanting to form an organisation like the Union Intercoloniale in Britain could have counted on the CPGB's help. Why were there no initiatives like that in Britain in the 1920s?

It may be partly because neither Britain nor any other European country had a large African migrant worker community like the North African community in France, from which several radical campaigners

---

250   Mike Squires, *Saklatvala: A Political Biography*, London: Lawrence & Wishart, 1990, e.g. Ch. 7, "Saklatvala the Anti-Imperialist"; R. Visram, *Ayahs, Lascars and Princes* (London: Pluto Press, 1986), pp. 144-58; S.K. Sen, *The House of Tata (1839-1939)*, Calcutta: Progressive Publishers, 1975, pp. 128-9.

251   J. Callaghan, *Rajani Palme Dutt: A Study in British Stalinism*, London: Lawrence & Wishart, 1993, Chs. 1-3, especially 3, "The Anti-Imperialist Struggle".

came; in addition there were probably fewer Black ex-servicemen in the postwar years in Britain than in France, though there were some, as well as other Black residents. However, the early radical anti-colonial activities were the work of very small groups of people. The reason why such people were even fewer or less successful in Britain could well lie in a difference in the British and French colonial situations in Africa. In the British Crown Colonies, and—despite the worsening repression—in South Africa, there was organised African political activity that was neither totally subservient nor revolutionary; this offered a non-radical way forward, whereas in French Africa, with the important exception of Tunisia, there was no middle way between total submission, as preached by Diagne, and advocacy of revolution. This could account for the creation of independent-minded but not radical African student groups in Britain, culminating in the West African Students' Union (WASU) in 1925 (of which more later); in France there was nothing like this then, but there was more "agitation".

Contemporaries saw an important difference between "Bolshevist agitators", on the one hand, and those Africans who in the 1920s were still continuing the established forms of protest activity developed by, for example, the Creoles of Sierra Leone, and well described by a leading Sierra Leonean historian:

...active citizens, in and out of the Legislative Council, endeavoured to articulate their grievances through ad hoc committees and associations, the Church (for instance, the Native Pastorate Crisis of the middle of the nineteenth century), mass petitions, memorials, memoranda, delegations in London, private visits of individuals to London to lobby friends and acquaintances to champion the colony's interests, and, of course, most important, the newspaper.[252]

The respectful Tunisian delegations sent to Paris in 1921-22 were in the same tradition, as well as the NCBWA delegation of 1920-21. The two groups of people were distinguished most clearly by the colonial authorities' treatment of them; the polite reform petitioners, who reassured everyone that they were not Bolsheviks, might be despised and their demands rejected, but they were not arrested and their newspapers were not banned; but the Communist "agitators" were harassed and trailed everywhere, taking up many Sûreté man-hours in France.

---

252   Akintola J.E. Wyse, *H.C. Bankole-Bright and Politics in Colonial Sierra Leone, 1919-1958*, CUP, 1990, p. 22.

Among the European sympathisers people like Woolf, Leys and Harris were officially seen as nuisances to be privately cursed, but Communists were seen as a menace to be watched constantly.

Anyway the efforts of all these people, agitators and petitioners, got almost nowhere. The years of unrest in Africa in the "Aftermath" had largely petered out by 1922, leaving the British, French, Belgian and Portuguese empires firmly in control.

3

NATIONALISTS AND COMMUNISTS, 1925-31

The Rif War protest campaign in France

The years from about 1925 to 1932 marked the peak of Communist involvement in anti-colonial activity in Europe and in one African country, South Africa. In France in 1925-26 there was the biggest campaign ever launched in Europe against a colonial war, a largely Communist campaign that backed Abd el-Krim. Support for the Rif insurgents was organised in France by the PCF, the Union Intercoloniale and *Le Paria* in 1924, at which point Abd el-Krim was yet to attack French Morocco and it seemed possible that he would be content with running his independent government over most of Spanish Morocco. But during 1924 French forces established control in the Ouergha (Wargha) valley, among a tribe living on both sides of the internationally recognised border, and this was a threat to Abd el-Krim. Already, at that time, there was a Comintern call for fraternisation with the Rif fighters. In Spain some Socialists favoured evacuation of the Rif and its independence, and there was an isolated general strike at Santander in 1923, organised by the UGT (the main trade union organisation), against the sending of troops to Morocco, while the small Communist Party joined in condemnation of the war against Abd el-Krim.[1]

---

1   M.-R. de Madariaga, "Le parti socialiste espagnol et le Parti communiste d'Espagne face à la revolution rifaine", *Abd el-Krim et la République du Rif: Actes du colloque international d'études historiques et sociologiques 18-20 janvier 1973* (no editor named; Charles-André Julien headed the committee sponsoring the seminar), Paris: Maspéro, 1976, pp. 308-66 (pp. 324-37, 343-65).

As recorded earlier, a telegram of support for Abd el-Krim from Sé-mard and Doriot was published in *L'Humanité* of 11 September. The Young Communist organisations of France and Spain proclaimed, "Soldiers of France and Spain, fraternise with Abd el-Krim!"[2] The French Communists went beyond support for the Spanish Morocco insurgents to call on France to leave its zone also; Doriot said in the Chamber of Deputies on 4 February 1925, "Yes, we want the evacuation of Morocco."[3]

At a meeting of about 400 people in Paris on 30 September 1924 Abdelkader Hadj Ali praised Abd el-Krim "who is fighting, like Abd el-Kader before, for the independence of his country."[4] North Africans in France rallied in support of Abd el-Krim, who was a hero all over the Arab world; a meeting of North African workers in the Paris region on 7 December 1924 ended with a telegram being sent to him.[5]

Abd el-Krim approached the French for talks in April 1925, only to be told that France would not make terms separately from Spain; the two countries' joint terms included submission to the Sultan of Morocco (who regarded Abd el-Krim as a rebel) and the Rif President's own exile.[6] Then Abd el-Krim attacked in force on 12 April 1925. In Paris the Herriot government had fallen two days earlier; the new government under Paul Painlevé, which held power only until 22 November 1925, and its successor under Aristide Briand had the support of most of the National Assembly and the public for the war against Abd el-Krim, but it faced the unprecedented Communist-led campaign against the war, and at first the war itself went badly for the French forces, who retreated steadily and lost 1,500 dead—including, it was said, 500

---

2   R. Gallisot, "Le parti communiste et la guerre du Rif", pp. 237-57 in *Abd el-Krim...*(note 1), pp. 238-9.

3   P. Isoart, "Le Mouvement ouvrier européen et l'Occident face à la guerre du Rif", pp. 173-217 in *Abd el-Krim...*(note 1), p. 177.

4   G. Oved, *La Gauche Française et le Nationalisme marocain 1905-1955*, Paris: Harmattan, 1984, vol. 1, pp. 240-1, quoting Ministry of the Colonies Circular on Revolutionary Propaganda, 30 September 1924.

5   Ibid., quoting Ministry of the Colonies Circular on Revolutionary Propaganda, 31 December 1924.

6   D. Rivet, "Le Commandement français et ses réactions vis-à-vis du mouvement rifain, 1924-1926", pp. 101-36 in *Abd el-Krim...*(note 1); R. Sanchez Diaz, "La Pacification espagnole", pp. 75-80 in ibid. (p. 78); Isoart (note 3), pp. 177-80.

who committed suicide rather than surrender—in the first weeks.[7] The command of operations was taken over by Marshal Pétain, and Lyautey resigned as Resident-General on 24 September 1925.

The initiative for a new, much extended anti-war campaign in France[8] was taken by the PCF, which organised a meeting at Luna Park in Paris on 16 May 1925 with the Young Communists, the CGTU, and the allied ARAC. For several months a Central Action Committee, backed by local Action Committees in many parts of France, campaigned against the Moroccan war. The four watchwords for the campaign were immediate peace with Abd el-Krim, withdrawal from Morocco, the independence of the Rif, and fraternisation between French soldiers and Abd el-Krim's fighters.[9] On 10 May 1925 Doriot declared,

The action of the French proletariat, more in solidarity than ever with the Rifis provoked in cowardly fashion into war, must be clear and rapid in face of the distressing danger. It must force French imperialism to accept immediate peace with the Rif, as requested and desired by the Rifis. It must demand that the Rif republic should be recognised and respected. It must back this young movement of liberation. It must demand and impose the immediate evacuation of Morocco, tomb of the children of the proletariat and of its billions [of tax money spent on the war, presumably].[10]

At least 105 meetings were held in the Paris region and 458 in the provinces between 15 May and 15 October 1925.[11] The Communists tried to get wider support, but many non-Communist left-wingers were unwilling to give it. In the National Assembly the Socialists abstained in the vote for military credits on 9 July 1925, rather than voting in favour, Léon Blum saying, "War colonialism which is established by occupation and conquest is something that we have always criticised

---

7   C.R. Pennell, *A Country with a Government and a Flag*, London: Menas Press, 1986, pp. 186-90.

8   The fullest description of this campaign are in Oved (note 4), vol. 1, chapters V-VII, and several papers in *Abd el-Krim....*(note 1).

9   9. Oved (note 4), pp. 228-35.

10   Gallisot (note 2), p. 240. The PCF also opposed the government strongly over Finance Minister Caillaux' economic measures, and in fact the Action Committee was called in full the Comité Central d'Action contre la Guerre du Rif et les Impôts Caillaux.

11   Oved's calculation (note 4), p. 235.

and will continue to reject".[12] Some Socialists supported the anti-war campaign, in Lyons for example, but many supported the government dominated by their semi-allies the Radicals and its war effort.[13]

The monthly magazine *Clarté*, founded by Henri Barbusse in 1919, joined in the Rif war protest campaign. On 11 July 1925 it published an "Appel aux travailleurs intellectuels", telling them to make their choice for or against the Moroccan war. Signed by Barbusse and then by the editorial board of the magazine and several other intellectuals including Rolland, Georges Duhamel and the novelist Victor Margueritte, as well as Breton and Eluard of the "Surrealist group", the appeal declared, "We proclaim once again the right of peoples, all peoples, to whatever race they belong, to decide their own fate"; it called on France to negotiate a "just armistice" and on the League of Nations to intervene in favour of peace.[14]

Eventually 170 intellectuals signed the Barbusse appeal, but others responded it to it by refusing to condemn France out of hand. Some, including Maran and Roger Martin du Gard, described Abd el-Krim as a "feudal adventurer", a "brigand chief", a "pirate", leader of "one of those ferocious little Sultanates" where "half-savage petty tyrants" reigned; Maran spoke of the danger of "Islamism" and expressed hope for a French victory; François Mauriac said the "Rif Republic" was an invention of the Communists.[15] French left-wingers, and many other orthodox French republicans, generally had a strong aversion to all religion, including Islam, and could only see Muslim resistance fighters as "backward" and "fanatical"; this was true of many critics of French colonialism.

So the anti-war campaign remained mainly a Communist effort; the secretary of the Comité Central d'Action was Maurice Thorez, a young and rapidly rising PCF activist. André Marty wrote in *L'Humanité* of

---

12   Oved (note 4), p. 212.

13   Ibid., pp. 259-61, 279-86; M. Kharchich, "Left Wing Politics in Lyons and the Rif War", *Journal of North African Studies* vol. 2 no. 3, winter 1997, pp. 34-45.

14   C. Liauzu, *Aux origines des tiers-mondismes: colonisés et anticolonialistes en France (1919-1939)*, Paris: L'Harmattan, 1982, p. 253 (reproducing the appeal); Gallissot (note 10), p. 244; J.-P. Biondi, *Les Anticolonialistes (1881-1962)*, Paris: Laffont, 1992, pp. 142-3. On the Surrealists see below, pp. 256, 271.

15   Liauzu (note 14), pp. 80-83.

27 May 1925, "Sailors, remember the Black Sea sailors! Raise the red flag, do not embark corpses-in-waiting for African shores...Mothers, women, isn't the blood of your sons an infinitely more precious treasure than the bankers' millions?"[16] Doriot spoke uncompromisingly in the Chamber of Deputies, infuriating non-Communist deputies. The Jeunesses Communistes led by Doriot were particularly active in the campaign, through their newspaper *L'Avant-garde*, anti-militarist plays and artistic evenings.[17] Pierre Sémard spread the message in his books *Contre la guerre du Maroc* (1925) and *La guerre du Rif* (1926).

The Rif War protests were extended to oppose also the suppression of a rising in Syria, which had begun when the Druze revolted in July 1925 and won a big initial victory on 3 August; it spread beyond the Druze homeland, and the French response, including a ruthless two-day bombardment of a part of Damascus, did not overcome resistance until the latter part of 1926, with some fighting going on until the middle of 1927.[18] The Action Committees called for a general strike on 12 October 1925 in protest against the Moroccan and Syrian colonial wars. About 50-100,000 people obeyed the summons, far fewer than the hundreds of thousands claimed by Communist leaders. In Lyons, for example, hardly anyone stayed away from work.[19] This was almost the only protest strike against a colonial war ever attempted in Europe; the poor response was revealing.

The Communist Party called openly for fraternisation with the Rifis.[20] Such calls were shocking to French people at a time when the army was more than usually sacred, and were unacceptable to the SFIO; the PCF, while continuing to encourage fraternisation, said at a national conference on 1 December that this should not be made an essential condition for the (imagined or hoped for) *front unique* against the war.[21] In fact it

16   Gallisot (note 10), p. 248.

17   Biondi (note 14), pp. 136-7.

18   Philip S. Khoury, *Syria and the French Mandate: The Politics of Arab Nationalism*, London: I.B. Tauris, 1987, Part III: "The Great Revolt, 1925-1927"; S.H. Longrigg, *Syria and Lebanon under French Mandate*, OUP, 1958, reprinted 1972, pp. 151-68.

19   Oved (note 4), pp. 261-73; Kharchich (note 13); Gallisot (note 10), pp. 244-6.

20   Isoart (note 3), p. 185.

21   Oved (note 4), pp. 257-8.

was difficult to induce French soldiers to go over to the enemy; Doriot admitted this, and it hardly ever happened. In all seven soldiers from France and 32 men of the Foreign Legion, mostly Germans, deserted to join Abd el-Krim. However, there was some discontent in the French forces; during the summer of 1925 there were protests among the crews of the warship *Strasbourg* (whose crew protested at orders to bombard the Rifis at Ajdir) and three other ships. This was not nearly enough to help Abd el-Krim much. As for Communist supplies of arms and fighters to Abd el-Krim, these were inevitably suspected, but not proved.[22]

The war effort was generally supported in France, but there was some non-Communist criticism, and the SFIO, though condemned out of hand by the Communists for its attitude, was not in fact uncritical. At an extraordinary National Congress on 18 August 1925, it resolved that the party's deputies could not support "the improvident Moroccan policy of the present government," but rejected calls for fraternisation and desertion and the idea of evacuating French Morocco. The French and Spanish Socialist parties and the British Labour Party called at a meeting in Paris on 28 July 1925 for an immediate cease-fire, publication of the Franco-Spanish peace terms and acceptance of the principle of independence for the Rif and its admission to the League of Nations; and this was endorsed by the second Congress of the Labour and Socialist International, which happened to take place in France, at Marseilles, soon afterwards (22-7 August).[23] These resolutions show that democratic Socialists' acceptance of imperialism was not 100 per cent. How could the French in North Africa have lived with a recognised independent Rif Republic in "Spanish" Morocco, a living inspiration to nationalists in the rest of the Maghreb and beyond?

After the initial retreat French forces counter-attacked, and Spanish forces launched their own offensive from September 1925. After a lull for the winter months French and Spanish forces pushed on into the Rif. Abd el-Krim surrendered to the French in May 1926 and was banished to Réunion. Fighting went on in Spanish Morocco for over a year but had ended by the middle of 1927.[24]

---

22   Ibid., pp. 288-96.

23   C.-R. Ageron, "Les socialistes français et la guerre du Rif", in *Abd el-Krim...* (note 1), pp. 273-301 (p. 283).

24   S. Balfour, *Deadly Embrace: Morocco and the Road to the Spanish Civil War*,

Many Communist organisers of the anti-war campaign were arrested and charged; Henri Lozeray, an active young Communist who worked with Doriot at Saint-Denis and was involved with him in the Ruhr anti-militarist efforts, was now gaoled for two years, Thorez for 14 months; in all 535 Communist organisers received prison sentences.[25] They had organised an exceptionally powerful campaign, but it had never had any prospect of success; everything was against them in France and around the world.

The Union Intercoloniale and *Le Paria*, which had played their part in the campaign against the Rif war, collapsed while it was going on. The Union seems to have been wound up at some point in 1926 or 1927. The PCF Colonial Commission discussed its critical situation in February and again in April 1926, but it did not continue for long under that name, though the last issue of *Le Paria*, dated April 1926—seven months after the last but one in September 1925—published a plan for creation of four sections out of the Union Intercoloniale.[26]

Abd el-Krim had been widely admired, but Moroccans in the French zone had not risen to help him, the Sultan had condemned him, and the alliance between the respected traditional monarch and the French "protecting" power continued after the departure of its main creator, Lyautey, keeping most Moroccans quiescent for the time being. Sultan Youssef died in November 1927 and was succeeded by Mohammed V. Things were to change under him, but not for some years. However, although there was little armed resistance after 1926, some southern areas remained outside effective French control and some occasional fighting occurred there. The French authorities in France and Morocco constantly received and examined reports of Communist subversion, even of plans for arms supplies, in Morocco, throughout the 1920s and 30s; Oved, in his study of the French left's attitudes to colonialism in Morocco, suggests that these reports, involving many spies of many nationalities, had little basis in fact.[27]

OUP 2002, pp. 106-20. This study gives details (Ch. 5) of the use of chemical weapons by Spain in the Rif campaign, ten years before the more notorious use of them by Italy in Ethiopia.

25   Biondi (note 14), pp. 140, 145-6.

26   Liauzu (note 14), pp. 129-30.

27   Oved (note 4), vol. I, pp. 162-85.

During the Rif war there was strong support for Abd el-Krim in Tunisia. Ahmad Tawfiq al-Madani, born in Tunis of an Algerian family, a nationalist follower of Tha'alibi who was interned during the 1914-18 war for pro-Turkish and anti-French sentiments, wrote in an Arabic-language Socialist newspaper, *Ifriqiya*, on 25 May 1925: "We want the heroic Rif to live happily under the flag of complete liberty and independence". After this *Ifriqiya* was suspended and Madani deported to Algeria. In Algeria there were several arrests for activity in support of Abd el-Krim, and there was continual concern about Communist "subversion". In Constantine on 22 April 1927 the French minister of the Interior, Sarraut, declared,

Rebellion in the colonies, the loss or abandonment by France of its colonies is one of the essential articles of the programme of France's decay whose methodical execution is being imperiously traced by a foreign influence with French affiliates in servile submission to its law...For the government and parliament, as for the working masses, the watchword must remain the same: Communism, there is the enemy.[28]

Agents crossing the Sahara?

By the mid-1920s suspicions of Communist instigation of unrest in the colonies were firmly entrenched in Paris and London, where some officials, at least, seemed unable to believe that Africans or Asians could have their own reasons for making trouble. Communist encouragement of protests and radical demands was of course open and beyond doubt, but instigation of armed revolts was imaginary. Painlevé suggested absurdly that the Comintern had told Abd el-Krim to invade French Morocco,[29] but in fact Communists were never proved to have actually organised and started any rebellion, however much they might approve uprisings started by Africans.

There was however one series of incidents in 1927-28 which was suspected to be the start of a Communist-connected plan for dissident action in Africa. They were isolated events in areas where nothing similar happened for decades afterwards, Northern Nigeria and the neighbouring French colony of Niger. The story of these almost forgotten inci-

---

28   *L'Afrique Française*, 37th year, no. 5, May 1927, pp. 185-6.
29   Ageron (note 23), p. 281.

dents, hardly noted at the time and never properly explained, remains intriguing.

On 5 June 1927, at the French post at Tessaoua about 40 miles north of the border, raiders killed one European and two African police-man. According to the French they were a small band of Mahdists from Northern Nigeria, acting with the tacit approval of some local chiefs. The attack was isolated in French Niger, but it caused a stir among the Africans there.[30] Some troops of the Royal West African Frontier Force were sent from the Nigerian side to the border near Maradi, to meet the French Commandant of Maradi and "demonstrate friendly relations and "show the flag"." A British District Officer who accompa-nied them, Bryan Sharwood Smith, was later carrying out liaison duties (in fact watching over forced labourers—contented forced labourers, in his account) with a construction team working on the extension of the railway to Kaura Namoda when F. Clements, an inspector on earth-works construction, was murdered in the area of Kaura Namoda (now in Zamfara State of Nigeria) on 3 March 1928. Investigations begun by Sharwood Smith led to the arrest of a common-law criminal; he was hanged, but Sharwood Smith, writing decades later, said that he had doubtless deserved this for other offences but "I do not, to this day, believe that he was Clements' murderer".[31]

Soon afterwards, there was an attempt on the life of a British Assist-ant District Officer, P.W.D. Thurley, near Minna (not mentioned by Sharwood Smith), and investigations into the incidents led the British authorities to suspect a political conspiracy.[32] In the Nigerian Legisla-tive Council it was officially stated that the attacker "suffered from a religious mania following a visit to the East."[33] But an editorial in *West Africa* in London, while saying that the recent incidents in Northern Nigeria might be unconnected, expressed the hope that "a close watch

30 Chief, SD Tahoua, 13 Nov. 1928, AP Maradi; speech by Governor General Carde, 1927, quoted in F. Fuglestad, *A History of Niger 1850-1960*, CUP 1983, pp. 126-31.

31 B. Sharwood Smith, *But Always as Friends: Northern Nigeria and the Cameroons, 1921-1957*, London: Allen & Unwin, 1969, pp. 57-67.

32 E.T. Wilson (*Russia and Black Africa before World War II*, New York: Holmes & Meier, 1974, pp. 222-3) has written the only account of these inquiries and suspicions in any published work so far, to my knowledge.

33 *West Africa*, 28 April and 12 May 1928.

is kept, especially in the direction of Egypt."[34] The editorial hinted at secret information received about possible Communist involvement, and official suspicions were in fact directed at a North African link.

An intelligence report spoke of a number of Tunisians or other Arabs entering Nigeria especially to carry out some conspiracy. One, named Abdul Turki, was said to have visited the Sultan of Sokoto—head of the traditional Hausa-Fulani empire and the senior of the Northern Nigerian emirs—and it was suspected that plotters sought to enlist him and the Emir of Katsina (whose emirate was close to the Tessaoua attack and to the Clements killing) to rise up against British rule, and when that failed, to get those rulers deposed on suspicion of involvement in the attacks. A police report suggested that two disgruntled members of the Fulani aristocracy had been involved. Many details were given in these top secret documents, including details of the movements of the Arab suspects. Some of these were arrested, and it seems fairly certain that this group of Arabs, generally described as Tunisians, did go to Nigeria at the time.[35]

Descriptions of the suspect Abdul Turki suggest a Mahdist, and Mahdists were likely to be seen as, and perhaps likely to be, promoters of dissidence in Muslim lands under colonial rule. British fears about Mahdism had been revived after the gathering of supporters around Sa'id ibn Hayatu, as noted earlier. After the latter's deportation in 1923 a British official in Nigeria, G.J. Lethem, was in late 1924 sent on "leave" on a special mission to travel from Nigeria to the Sudan and Egypt to inquire into "religious or political propaganda".[36] This followed a meeting of the Inter-Departmental Committee on Eastern Unrest in London, which considered that various forms of propaganda in Nigeria came almost certainly from Egypt, possibly connected with al-Azhar

34   *West Africa*, 19 May 1928.

35   Northern Provinces of Nigeria Political Intelligence Report for the quarter ending March 1930, enclosed with letter Governor of Nigeria (Sir Graeme Thomson) to Secretary of State, 5 May 1930, file CO 583/174/1, National Archives, London; reports by Lieutenant-Governor of Northern Provinces of Nigeria (Richmond Palmer), 5 March 1930 and 13 March 1930, with note by Captain J.T. Spender of Police Intelligence Bureau, enclosed with Governor of Nigeria to Secretary of State, 23 April 1930, same file. The Police Intelligence Bureau was set up following the 1927-28 incidents.

36   Governor of Nigeria to G.J. Lethem, two letters of 29 Nov. 1924, file CO 583/147/11, National Archives, London.

University in Cairo and including efforts to win over Nigerian students there.[37] His report was submitted in May 1927 and published.[38] Three years later Richmond Palmer, Lieutenant-Governor of the Northern Provinces, mentioned Lethem's report but said that since then the volume of "subversive propaganda" from the Sudan and Jeddah had not been great and had not caused "observable unrest".[39] But the authorities in Nigeria were concerned about influences from that direction.[40]

Links between Muslim dissidents and Bolsheviks were suspected. They were not an impossibility at that time; debates about Communism and Islam had begun years before in Egypt,[41] and at least some people on both sides accepted, for most of the 1920s, the possibility of a tactical alliance against colonialism. But there was plenty of the usual paranoia in official suspicions.

The Acting Director of Intelligence in the Sudan reported in 1926 that there were links between the USSR and "Egyptian Extreme Nationalists"; Abdel Rahman Bey Fahmi was the principal agent on the Egyptian side, according to the intelligence official, who found indications that the "Wafd-Bolshevik coalition" was taking a special interest in the Sudan.[42] This was after Zaghlul Pasha's Wafd government had lost power in November 1924, effectively driven from power by the British, who responded to the assassination in Cairo of Sir Lee Stack, Sirdar (C.-in-C.) of the Egyptian army and Governor-General of the Sudan, by arresting several people—including Abdel Rahman Fahmi, who had organised Wafdist trade unions—and forcing Egypt to accept demands including withdrawal of all its forces from the Sudan; over the next few years Egyptian civilian officials left also and the Sudan, while remain-

37   Colonial Secretary, London, to Governor of Nigeria, 11 Nov. 1924, file CO 583/147/11, National Archives, London.

38   It was published under the names of G.J.F. Tomlinson and J.F. Lethem in London in 1927, with the title *History of Islamic Political Propaganda in Nigeria*.

39   Report by Lieutenant-Governor of Northern Provinces of Nigeria, 5 March 1930 (note 35).

40   Northern Provinces of Nigeria Political Intelligence Report for the quarter ending March 1930, enclosed with letter Governor of Nigeria to Secretary of State, 5 May 1930, file CO 583/174/1, National Archives, London.

41   T.Y. Ismael and R. El-Sa'id, *The Communist Movement in Egypt 1920-1988*, Syracuse University Press, 1990, pp. 23-5.

42   Secret Intelligence report from Acting Director of Intelligence, Khartoum, 31 July 1926, file CO 583/147/11, National Archives, London.

ing "Anglo-Egyptian" in name, became a British colony for practical
purposes. Egyptians, not only Wafd supporters, resented this as well
as the continued British domination of Egypt itself. Sudanese were divided, but a number favoured independence from Britain in union with
Egypt, such as the White Flag League headed by Ali Abd al-Latif, which
held demonstrations in June 1924; later some Sudanese troops muti-
nied in sympathy with Egyptian troops being arrested and sent home.
On the subject of British domination of Egypt Wafdists, Communists
and many others could agree, Sudanese included, and British imagina-
tions no doubt built on this. In reality there was no "Wafd-Bolshevik
coalition"; the Wafd had begun the suppression of Communists which
was continued in 1925 by the government of Ahmed Ziwar Pasha.[43]

Regarding the 1927-28 incidents in Northern Nigeria, a Moscow
link was suggested in the Intelligence report mentioned earlier and another later in 1930, which quoted a recent report that

a person name Abdul Salami who came to Nigeria from Tunis told an informant that he knew about some conspiracy between "Muscobia" (Moscow) and
the "Sarkin Tunis, Mohammed Nasr Ibn Aliyu" and that the Sarikin Tunis,
Mohammed Nasr Ibn Aliyu was asked by "Muscobia" to send them five intel-
ligent and reliable men who would be willing to undertake a mission to Nigeria
for which purpose they would be entrusted with a large sum of money, and that
instructions would be given to them by "Muscobia" whose intention it was to
acquire Nigeria.[44]

This is a highly spurious account. *Sarki* or *sariki* means "ruler" in
Hausa, and the reference is presumably to the Bey of Tunis, but the
Bey named Nasr (or Naceur) had died in 1922. Obviously neither he
nor his successor, tightly supervised by the French, would have been
entrusted by Moscow with such a mission. Possibly these details were
invented by a Nigerian informant who knew that the British would be
interested in a tale of Communist intrigue. All the other details in the
various reports on this case, except for some that were verified in Nigeria, are suspect. Informants spoke of a letter from the Sultan of Con-

43   Ismael and Rifa'at El-Sa'id (note 41), pp. 30-1.
44   Northern Provinces of Nigeria Political Intelligence Report for Quarter Ending
     June 1930, enclosed with Governor of Nigeria to Secretary of State, 13 August
     1930, file CO 583/174/1, National Archives, London.

stantinople, though the Sultanate and Caliphate had been abolished years before by Kemal.

Some accounts of or by the suspects seemed to implicate the Italians in Libya; in fact there had been encouragement and some assistance to Tunisian nationalists from Fascist Italy, as an expression of the lasting Italian grievance against French rule in Tunisia.[45] But although some faint awareness of real events can be seen in these accounts, it is slight, and they cannot be trusted at all. Palmer—though he had gone so far as to suggest, very implausibly, that one of the Tunisian plotters was the trade unionist M'hammed Ali[46]—said he was not sure that "Bolshevik cells in Tunis or elsewhere in North Africa" had tried to cause trouble; however, he thought it "extremely probable" that they might try. He admitted that the 1927-28 incidents had "not yet been satisfactorily explained" and called for further investigations by "the organisation in England which deals with Bolshevik and other subversive propaganda."[47]

The archives give no clue as to any solid information that the inquiries revealed. A group of North Africans, some at least being quite possibly Tunisians from Gabes as reported, may well have been involved in the attacks, but who they were and why they acted remain mysterious. The alleged fomenting of a rising sounds fairly far-fetched, and maybe there was none. And the story of Soviet involvement cannot be credited.

There were probably no further attacks of this sort, and Mahdists aroused no serious dissidence from then on in British or French West Africa. One Muslim preacher did arouse support in AOF which led to French action against him; in Mauritania Hamallah, born in 1886 to a Moorish father and Fulani mother, claimed to be the Khalife of the Tijaniyya Confraternity, in place of the recognised Khalife who was a good friend of France; at first the French were not concerned about

---

45   Juliette Bessis, *La Méditerranée fasciste: L'Italie mussolinienne et la Tunisie*, Paris: Karthala, 1981, pp. 82-98.

46   Northern Provinces of Nigeria Political Intelligence Report for the quarter ending March 1930 note 40). In fact M'hammed Ali, after being banished, went to work in Egypt and then in Saudi Arabia, where he died in a road accident in 1928: M-S. Lejri, *Evolution du Mouvement national tunisien,* Vol. 1, Tunis: Maison Tunisienne de l'Edition, 1974, p. 238.

47   Report by Lieutenant-Governor of Northern Provinces of Nigeria, 5 March 1930 (note 35).

disciples joining him, but after some disturbances in 1924-25 he was banished for ten years. His followers were blamed for more sporadic disturbances in 1928-30, and he was moved to Ivory Coast, to be allowed to return to Nioro only in September 1936. The "Hamallists" were said to voice the feelings of the more deprived sections of society, as many Islamic militants have done until today.[48]

Except for this, and for the brief revolt of the Muslim preacher Haidara in Sierra Leone Protectorate in 1931 (see below, pp. 241-2), there was hardly any anti-colonial unrest in Muslim sub-Saharan Africa in the 1920s and 30s. But there was always official concern about the possibility. In Northern Nigeria the British worked with the Emirs to establish what seemed like a solid regime under the "Indirect Rule" doctrine, but they knew it was not really so solid, and the incidents in 1927-28 worried them.

This is an interesting case study of official colonial vigilance against "subversion". Several agencies in the various colonies, plus ordinary officials there, and agencies in London and Paris like the Special Branch, MI5 and the Sûreté, were all involved. They had Communist subversion particularly in mind. While there was plenty of legend-spinning and paranoia about Comintern agents in the 1920s, such agents did exist. The Comintern, and the Communists of various countries, did conduct a good deal of secret activity. From the early days Comintern couriers delivered funds (in jewellery as well as cash) to foreign Communists. A secretive Department of International Communication (OMS), under Osip Piatnitsky, ran such clandestine activity, including provision of fake passports; Berlin was a major centre of such operations from the early 1920s.[49] British Communists sent to India in the 1920s used classic devices such as cover names, ciphers and invisible ink (but were tracked down).[50] But Communist agents in the colonies did not

48   C. Harrison, *France and Islam in West Africa, 1860-1960*, CUP 1988, pp. 172-9.

49   K. McDermott and J. Agnew, *The Comintern: A History of International Communism from Lenin to Stalin*, Basingstoke: Macmillan, 1996, pp. 21-2. For examples of clandestine operations in the early years see Dan N. Jacobs, *Borodin: Stalin's Man in China*, Cambridge, MA: Harvard University Press 1981, pp. 59-107.

50   H. Pelling, *The British Communist Party*, 1958, reprint London: A. and C. Black, 1975, pp. 41-2.

create dissident movements, or armed revolts, where none existed. They could only encourage or finance colonial subjects' own efforts, and this only rarely.

The founding of the Etoile Nord-Africaine

Communist support for some legal, though "subversive", anti-colonial organisations was undisguised, though it is not always clear how much initiative for starting them, if any, came from the Communist hierarchy. French as well as North African Communists, and the Comintern, were closely involved in a radical North African nationalist party started among the North Africans in France: the Etoile Nord-Africaine (ENA).

Its leader for many years, one of the main pioneers of Algerian nationalism, was Messali Hadj (1898-1974). Born in Tlemcen, he went to France first as a soldier in 1918 and then as a worker in 1923; he was living in the Paris area and married to a Frenchwoman, Emilie *née* Busquand, when in 1925-26 he participated in talks leading to the formation of the ENA. A key figure in those early meetings was the energetic Algerian Communist Abdelkader Hadj Ali. He and Messali became friends and often met, with their French wives, at Hadj Ali's house at Brunoy at weekends. Hadj Ali won Messali over to Communism, or to faith in Communist support for anti-colonialism. It seems that Messali always retained faith in Islam—at a PCF meeting he spoke of the glories of the old Caliphate and said Muslims were suffering now "Because we have strayed far from Allah and Islamic principles"; but such views were not a problem for Communists (outside Russia) at that time. He wrote in his memoirs that he joined the PCF "as a sympathiser" after returning from a journey to Tlemcen in September 1925, and that "My countrymen and myself were won over to the Communist Party, but without understanding well what its ideology was."[51]

Those memoirs are an important source for the history of the ENA, which several scholars have studied also, but several points in the history remain uncertain. In his recent study Jacques Simon suggests that Messali's memoirs, a posthumous work based on his writings in old age

---

51 *Les Mémoires de Messali Hadj*, edited posthumous text, Paris: J.-C. Lattès, 1982, pp. 119-46; J. Simon, *L'Etoile Nord-Africaine (1926-1937)*, Paris: Harmattan, 2003, pp. 69-83.

in seventeen exercise books but considerably edited, are unreliable.[52] Messali's work does include inaccuracies, and what he records about the Communists may be coloured by his embittered separation from them in the 1930s. Simon's work, which in fact confirms much of what Messali recalled, adds details on Communist involvement with Algerian activists in France.

Messali recalled that Hadj Ali went to Moscow with other "colonials" in 1925, and on his return "appeared to us like a pilgrim returning from the Holy Places with the Philosopher's Stone in his pocket."[53] According to Simon's study Hadj Ali went to Moscow in November 1925 and on his return "told his friend of the plan, decided in Moscow, to create an organisation for North Africans"; Moscow ordered that it should be a mass organisation with PCF involvement, and the PCF then discussed details.[54] Messali recalled that the PCF had been involved, and had been helpful,[55] but his account does not suggest that the ENA started simply as a subsidiary of the Communist Party. The original idea of creating the ENA seems to have been discussed with Hadj Ali in Moscow, but in the absence of clear evidence, which might come from the Comintern archives, one cannot tell whether Hadj Ali or the Comintern developed the idea initially. It could well have been Hadj Ali, a Communist of some importance in the party but also, to judge from what is known of him, an Algerian nationalist. Stora suggests that the initiative for the meetings leading to the ENA came from Hadj Ali.[56] What is certain is that the PCF was closely involved in the establishment of the ENA for the first few years.

In later years a legend grew up that the "Emir" Khaled had been the original founder of the ENA. This has been disproved by studies of the ENA and by the biography of Khaled by Koulakssis and Meynier. Those authors examine carefully Khaled's comings and goings between

52   Simon (note 51), pp. 291-309.

53   *Les Mémoires de Messali Hadj* (hereafter Messali) (note 51), p. 146.

54   Simon (note 51), pp. 79-80.

55   Messali (note 51), pp. 151-3.

56   B. Stora, *Dictionnaire biographique de militants nationalistes algériens 1926-1954: E.N.A., P.P.A., M.T.L.D.,* Paris: Harmattan, 1985, entry on Hadj Ali, pp. 51-5.

Egypt and France, and finally to Syria, in 1924-26;[57] for most of that time French officials and agents watched him closely, suspecting him of links with the Rif rebels and the Soviet Union, even of planning to join Abd el-Krim. Neither the police reports on him nor any other sources have confirmed that he founded the ENA or any comparable body, or indeed that such a body existed, during that time. In fact he spent the rest of his life in Syria, then a French Mandated territory, where many of his family had lived since his grandfather went there in the previous century; and he dissociated himself from the ENA in 1929, when Messali annoyed him by announcing that he would appear at a meeting in Paris.

According to Messali the ENA was founded at a meeting of himself, Hadj Ali, Mohamed Si Djilani (a Communist very active in the Party and the CGTU) and others in Paris in March 1926, and he, Messali, was chairman from the start.[58] However, Simon says Hadj Ali was the first chairman.[59] According to Simon the ENA held a public meeting as a section of the Union Intercoloniale, on 12 June 1926, and then was formally established at a general meeting on 20 June held at the Union's address at 3 rue du Marché des Patriarches. This and other evidence suggests that the ENA was originally conceived, at least by some, as a branch of the Union Intercoloniale, perhaps one of four branches suggested in *Le Paria*. The 12 June meeting adopted the ENA's programme and elected an executive of 25 members; but in August, again according to Simon, Messali became secretary-general at Hadj Ali's request. In the meantime there was a big meeting at La Grange aux Belles on 14 July 1926, where Hadj Ali spoke.[60] About 350 people attended that meeting, but the first "public meeting" is said to have taken place at the Salle des Ingénieurs Civils in Paris on 7 October 1926.[61]

---

57   A. Koulakssis and G. Meynier, *L'Emir Khaled premier Za'im? Identité algérienne et colonialisme français*, Paris: Harmattan, 1987, pp. 192-5, 305-188.

58   Messali (note 51), p. 151.

59   Simon (note 51), p. 238.

60   Ibid., pp. 80-1, 83.

61   On the early years of the ENA see Messali, pp. 144-69; B. Stora, *Messali Hadj (1898-1974), Pionnier du nationalisme algérien*, Paris: Harmattan, 1986, pp. 49-83.

The agreed programme called for a struggle to end abuses in the colonial system and improve North Africans' situation, but Article 5, section 2 called for use of "the press, public meetings, posters, parliamentary action, petitions to public authorities, or any other action, so as to obtain the total emancipation of the North African Muslims."[62] This is what the ENA set out to do, the press being particularly the newspaper *Ikdam*, which developed themes that Hadj Ali also set out at the 14 July 1926 meeting: an end to the Indigénat, application of French social and work legislation, democratic freedoms, and free movement between Algeria and France. This last demand was important for Algerians especially; efforts to restrict the migration of workers continued, despite a scandal when Algerian stowaways were found dead in the hold of a ship on 29 April 1926.

In July 1926 the Paris Grand Mosque was opened by the Sultan of Morocco. *L'Humanité* wrote on that occasion that the "true Muslims" were at the ENA meeting at almost the same time and "declare that the only men worthy of representing them are: the Emir Khaled, Sheikh Thaalbi and Abd el-Krim."[63] This confirmed the Communists' continued search for common ground with Muslims of the French colonies. In fact many of the North African community in France rejected that officially sponsored mosque.[64]

Messali recalled[65] that he was chairman and secretary-general for a time, but was succeeded as chairman in 1927 by Chedly Khairallah—a Tunisian who had gone to Paris to study law and had become editor of *Ikdam*[66]—while he (Messali) remained secretary-general. Certainly Khairallah did become chairman, and in February 1927 he, Messali and Hadj Ali all attended the Brussels congress which founded the League Against Imperialism (see below, pp. 172-82). In his speech there Messali spoke particularly of Algerians' conscription into the French army, an issue which the ENA was to continue to highlight; not only did

<hr/>

62 Simon (note 51), p. 81.

63 Ibid., p. 102.

64 B. Stora, "Les Algériens dans le Paris de l'entre-deux-guerres", in A. Kaspi and A. Marès, *Le Paris des Etrangers*, Paris: Imprimerie Nationale, 1989, pp. 141-55 (p. 146).

65 Messali (note 51), p. 155.

66 Stora (note 56), entry on Khairallah, pp. 56-7.

they have to serve for six months longer than French conscripts, they were used, Messali said in Brussels, "to serve in imperialist wars and to suppress revolutionary movements in the colonies and in Metropolitan France."

Messali actively organised the ENA among the immigrants, holding meetings in the cafes, restaurants and hotels which were a centre of the North Africans' lives in the big French cities. Bases were established among the North African communities at Levallois-Perret, Colombes, Puteaux, Aubervilliers and other working-class suburbs of Paris. The ENA was organised on the basis of cells on the Communist model; by 1928 there were more than 4,000 members.[67] A North African migrant workers' organisation was bound to be as proletarian as any Communist could wish, and the PCF and the ENA worked together well for a time, Messali being able, for example, to use PCF and CGTU halls for meetings. In fact the PCF's Commission Coloniale and its Sous-Commission Nord-Africaine supervised the ENA's work and made decisions about it—at least until early 1927.[68] Communists did much of the work of organising the ENA, including Hadj Ali, Si Djilani, Ben Lekhal, Menouar, and another activist from Algeria, Mohamed Ben Kalidour Marouf, an active trade unionist.[69]

While the ENA was mainly a workers' organisation, in July 1926 it held a dinner party with North African students.[70] Students from the colonies were few in France in the 1920s, but although they aroused the authorities' concern because they were commonly anti-government (what did the authorities expect?), a number did go there, and some indeed had government scholarships, including several Tunisians until 1929. In 1927 an Association des Etudiants Musulmans Nord-Africains, AEMNA, was founded in Paris; of this more later.

During 1927 problems developed between the ENA and the Communists. This much is clear from the various accounts, though the true picture seems confused. At some point during the year Hadj Ali told Messali that the PCF was suspending aid it had been giving including payment of a salary to Messali, who was now told to get a job; he found

---

67   Simon (note 51), pp. 91-2, 114.

68   Ibid., p. 84.

69   Ibid., p. 82; Liauzu (note 14), pp. 267-8.

70   Liauzu (note 14), p. 163n.

work as a shop assistant and travelling salesman.[71] There may well have been policy disagreements, as Messali recalled, but the ENA's call for national independence was acceptable to Communists in principle. The issue may have been more the Communists' efforts to assert control after beginning to lose it.[72] Khairallah wrote in *Ikdam* after Brussels that there was "no need to cling to one political theory or to accept a tow from a political party, whichever one it may be."[73] Such words may have been enough to cause dissension, and the ENA drifted away, though slowly, from the PCF.

On 27 December 1927 Khairallah was deported from France. After that the ENA was almost entirely an Algerian organisation, but statutes presented to a general meeting of the ENA by Messali on 19 February 1928 declared (in Article 3) that the "fundamental aim" was "organising the struggle for the independence of the three countries of North Africa".[74] Messali eventually realised, apparently about the beginning of 1928, that the Communists did not want him at the head of the ENA, while his friend Hadj Ali remained on good terms with them. He recalled later, "The Communists had a plan which they sought to impose on us, but the majority among us did not agree", but "neither we nor the Communists wanted to put an end to our relations".[75] He and Hadj Ali both addressed a meeting of over 1,200 Maghrebian workers on 21 January 1929 at La Grange aux Belles. But the PCF's sixth Congress, in March-April 1929, resolved that Communists should infiltrate nationalist parties to direct them the right way.[76] This meant opposing Messali, if he and his colleagues thought then what he wrote much later:

The Algerians living in France had a way of life, struggle and liberating themselves that corresponded to their temperament and their religion and was not like that of other societies. The friction between us and the French Communists was therefore inevitable. We certainly wanted to be helped and to cooperate, but without being subjected. We wanted to remain sole masters of our destiny.[77]

---

71   Messali (note 51), pp. 100-1; Simon (note 51), p. 106.

72   Simon (note 51), p. 100.

73   Stora (note 56), entry on Khairallah, pp. 56-7.

74   Simon (note 51), p. 111.

75   Messali (note 51), pp. 161-2.

76   Simon (note 51), p. 117.

77   Messali (note 51), p. 162.

But there was still no complete break at this time when the government became more hostile than ever in 1929. In 1928 the ENA, so far organised only in France, had begun to spread the message in Algeria, distributing *Ikdam* and leaflets.[78] This made the ENA, calling for independence in what was supposed to be a part of France, even more of a menace to the authorities. On 20 November 1929 the Etoile Nord-Africaine was banned by court order.[79] It appears, from sources that are unclear on some points, that the ban was not applied effectively at this time, and Messali and his comrades were able to continue their activity without being arrested for reviving a banned organisation; later the ban was to be applied, but then overturned in court (see Chapter 4). But it also appears that in the immediate aftermath the ENA could not operate openly, though Messali and his comrades continued to meet in Paris cafes[80] and some sort of organisation continued; and that at this same time what remained of the ENA, under Messali, broke with the Communists. Of Messali's comrades Si Djilani took the ENA side while Marouf—who was arrested while in Algeria in 1929, and deported to the south of the country until the following year, as Ben Lekhal had been from 1926 to 1929—took the PCF side. Hadj Ali also stayed on the Communist side for while, but at some point was expelled from the PCF, for standing in local elections without the Party's authorisation.[81]

After that Abdelkader Hadj Ali apparently gave up political activism for some time, and became a prosperous businessman.[82] Plenty remains to be told about this little-remembered Algerian. There is a good deal to suggest that he was the real originator of the ENA. When he returned to nationalist activity for a time in the later 1930s, Messali described him, at a meeting on 17 May 1937, as "the founder of the Etoile".[83]

78   Simon (note 51), p. 115.

79   Stora (note 63), p. 79; Simon (note 51), pp. 118-19. Messali is wrong in recalling 24 April 1929 as the date of the ban (p. 163), but according to Simon the Prime Minister informed Messali of a coming ban on that day (p. 118).

80   Messali (note 53), p. 164.

81   Messali (note 53), p. 167; Stora (note 63), p. 80, who dates this expulsion in early 1930; Simon (note 53), p. 119n. Messali's account does not say when he himself left the PCF.

82   Stora (note 58).

83   C.-R. Ageron, "Emigration et politique: L'Etoile Nord-Africaine et le Parti du peuple algérien", appendix to Messali (note 53), pp. 273-97 (p. 284).

Considerably later he claimed this himself, in a letter to an Algerian nationalist newspaper in 1948;[84] however, he gave the date as 1924, and the ENA, as noted, was not started then. He certainly played a big role in its foundation, and although he was a Communist then and for a while afterwards, he seems to have had a mind of his own.

Messali and his followers, living "like nomads" and shunned by many of their own people in France, were still able to organise, in 1930, some protests against the lavish official celebrations of the centenary of the French occupation of Algeria, which, Messali said, made Algerians feel "scoffed at, humiliated, provoked, crushed in their dignity, their feelings and their religion." Then, after some months of planning, they launched a new newspaper, *El Ouma*, whose first issue appeared in October 1930.[85] The second issue, however, did not appear until September 1931. The supporters of the banned ENA had a difficult time for about four years, facing the hostility of the PCF—which launched a rival newspaper, *El Amel*, edited by Marouf, back from his banishment[86]—as well as the endless harassment by the authorities, whose Service de Surveillance et de Protection des Indigènes Nord-Africains had been set up in 1925 at 6 rue Lecomte, Paris 17e, to watch over the welfare of that community but in addition, especially, to order their lives around, keep tabs on them and spy on agitators among them.[87] And life for the North African community in Paris, always hard, became still harder when the Slump struck France from 1931.

The Brussels Congress and the League Against Imperialism

At a congress held in Brussels, at the Palais Egmont, from 10 to 15 February 1927 scores of anti-colonial campaigners—Africans, Asians and others including sympathetic Europeans—met and formed a League Against Imperialism (LAI). The organiser of the congress was the German Communist Willi Münzenberg (1887-1940), who after spending eight years (including the war years) in Switzerland had become active

84 A. Mahsas, *Le Mouvement Révolutionnaire en Algérie de la 1re guerre mondiale à 1954*, Paris: Harmattan, 1979, p. 52

85 Messali (note 53), pp. 167-9; Stora (note 61), pp. 82-4; Simon (note 51), pp. 134-6.

86 Liauzu (note 14), pp. 267-8; Stora (note 61), pp. 85-8.

87 Messali (note 51), pp. 172-3; Stora (note 64), pp. 152-4.

in the KPD and, after visiting Russia in 1920, a leading international Communist operator. He ran IAH (International Workers' Relief) which organised some relief efforts in Germany during the economic crisis in 1923-24, and distribution of Russian films and production of new films in Germany. He was elected to the Reichstag in 1924.[88]

Münzenberg began organising new anti-imperialist activity even before getting the Kremlin's approval. Some of it was concentrated on China; British intelligence reports spoke of protest activities on China, Syria and Morocco leading to the formation of a new League against Cruelties and Oppression in the Colonies, with F. Danzinger as chairman.[89] Another intelligence report said that a meeting organised in Berlin on 10 February 1926 by IAH and a protest organisation opposing French repression in Syria, the Committee Against Atrocities in Syria, led to the formation of a Liga gegen Kolonialgreuel und Unterdruckung.[90] The new organisation, sometimes referred to in English as the League Against Colonial Oppression (LACO), set about planning a big conference to which many anti-imperialist organisations and individuals, including (it was hoped) many from the colonies, would be invited. Münzenberg was assisted in this by Louis Gibarti, a Hungarian Communist.[91] The Indian revolutionary Virendranath Chattopadhyaya (1880-1937), although not then a Communist Party member, also helped in the planning. "Chatto", as he was always called, had after

88   S. McMeekin, *The Red Millionaire: A Political Biography of Willi Münzenberg, Moscow's Secret Propaganda Tsar in the West*, New Haven: Yale University Press, 2003, Chs. 1-10. See also R.N. Carew Hunt, "Willi Muenzenberg", pp. 72-87 in *St Antony's Papers* No. 9, International Communism, 1960, ed. D. Footman, London: Chatto & Windus.

89   Report enclosed with latter from New Scotland Yard to G.L.M. Clauson of Colonial Office, 17 December 1926; report dated 26 December 1926, enclosed with letter from Scotland Yard to Clauson, 30 December 1926; both in file CO 323/966/1, National Archives, London.

90   Secret document headed "The League against Imperialism", enclosed with letter of Secretary of State for India to Home Secretary, 27 February 1929, file HO 144/10693, National Archives, London. See also J. Saville, "Bridgeman, Reginald Francis Orlando (1884-1968)", *Dictionary of Labour Biography*, ed. J.M. Bellamy and J. Saville, Basingstoke: Macmillan, 1984, vol. VII, pp. 25-40 (p. 41); J.D. Hargreaves, "The Comintern and Anti-Colonialism: New Research Opportunities", *African Affairs* vol. 92, no. 367, April 1993, pp. 255-61. Prof. Hargreaves did some research into the LAI in the Comintern archives.

91   His real name was given as Ladislas or Wladislaus (presumably in fact Laszlo) Dobos: see documents in file KV2/1401, National Archives.

years of militant activity in Britain and France joined other Indian revolutionaries in Germany to cooperate with German and Turkish plans
for revolts against British rule in the First World War. Later he lived in
Sweden for some years, contacted the Bolsheviks, and went to Russia
in 1920-21. He and other Indian exiles who had been living in Germany quarrelled with Roy, who had the Comintern's favour then, and
returned to Germany without an important role in Moscow's plans for
India. But Chattopadhyaya was a well known exiled Indians' leader and
journalist in Berlin, where he shared his life for some years with Agnes
Smedley, the American left-wing journalist who later became noted for
her sympathetic reports on the Communists in the wars in China.[92]

The plan was to invite non-Communists and keep the Communist
organisers in the background, to present a united front against imperialism. In accordance with this, "Chatto" was able to interest another
Indian, Jawaharlal Nehru, in the coming congress. Nehru was a rising
leader of the more radical section of the Indian National Congress, calling for full independence or *Swaraj* and hence described as "Swarajists",
while Gandhi called for Dominion Status and the difference was still
seen as very important. While travelling in Europe, mainly because of
his wife's medical problems, Nehru got the INC's approval for him to
go to the anti-imperialist gathering as the INC representative.[93] Communist documents have now shown how hard Münzenberg pushed for
his congress, against serious hesitations in Moscow.[94] There were also
problems with the colonial governments; the British authorities were
well informed of the plans.[95] However, the Belgian government agreed
to let the congress meet in its country.

The number of delegates at Brussels seems to have been 174 or 175.
George Padmore, the Trinidadian whose revolutionary career will be
examined in the coming pages, wrote later that Münzenberg

92 Nirode K. Barooah, *Chatto: The Life and Times of an Indian Anti-Imperialist in
    Europe*, New Delhi: OUP, 2004, chs. 1-5 and pp. 246-50.

93 J. Nehru, *An Autobiography*, John Lane The Bodley Head, 1936, pp. 161-5;
    Barooah (note 92), pp. 249-50.

94 McMeekin (note 88), pp. 194-204. While thoroughly examining those docu-
    ments about the planning, unfortunately this source says almost nothing about
    the conference and the subsequent progress of the LAI, and that little is inac-
    curate.

95 See documents in file CO 323/966/1, National Archives, London (note 89).

had a flair for organization and showmanship. The Brussels Conference was a tremendous success. Herr Munzenberg gathered Colonial representatives from moderate bourgeois to extremist nationalist politicians from all over South-East Asia, the Middle East, Africa, Latin America and the West Indies. The people of Brussels had never seen such an exotic gathering in their city before. There were Muslims, Hindus, Chinese, Negroes, Koreans, Vietnamese, Burmese, Ceylonese, Egyptians, Senegalese, Indonesians, all promenading the streets of the Belgian capital in their different national attire.[96]

Padmore was not there, however, and he may have used his imagination a little in writing this.

From Africa Messali Hadj, Abdelkader Hadj Ali and Chedly Khairallah represented the ENA; Khairallah, often called Chedly Ben Mustapha at the time, also represented the Destour of Tunisia.[97] From Egypt came Hafiz Ramadan Bey, a Nationalist Party (i.e. the old Watani Party of Mustafa Kamil) member of the Egyptian parliament. He was no revolutionary,[98] but the organisers of the Congress had wanted precisely to get un-revolutionary nationalists to attend.

Lamine Senghor attended as representative of a new radical movement formed by Africans and West Indians in France, the Comité de Défense de la Race Nègre (CDRN), to be described more fully below (pp. 216-26). Narcisse Danaé, a Guadeloupean, was another CDRN delegate, while Max Bloncourt and Camille Saint-Jacques represented the Union Intercoloniale (still continuing then, on paper, but apparently not for long afterwards). In a speech Senghor denounced forced labour, settler oppression, and slavery which, he said, "has not been abolished, on the contrary it has been modernised"; he condemned Diagne and the 1918 recruitment drive, and the colonial expeditions in the Rif and elsewhere. He said, "When we are needed, to make us kill or make us work, we are French; but when it comes to give us rights, we are no longer French, we are *Nègres*." He declared, following the Communist line, that victims of imperialism in the West and in the colonies must stand together, and warned,

96   G. Padmore, *Pan-Africanism or Communism?* Dennis Dobson, 1956, p. 324.

97   Liauzu (note 14), pp. 31-5; Lejri (note 46), vol. 1, pp. 245-6.

98   In 1928 he privately proposed an Arab federation under the aegis of Britain: R.M. Coury, *The Making of an Egyptian Nationalist: The Early Years of Azzam Pasha, 1893-1936*, Reading: Ithaca Press, 1998, pp. 445-6.

Comrades, the Negroes have been asleep for too long, but watch out! He who has slept too well and has woken up will not go back to sleep.[99]

Three delegates came from South Africa. Josiah Tshangana Gumede (c.1870-1947), a Zulu who had toured Europe with a Zulu choir in the 1890s before helping to found the Natal Native Congress in 1901, and had been an organiser of the black mine workers' strike in 1920, represented the African National Congress (ANC). He was accompanied by a white trade unionist, Daniel Colraine, and the CPSA representative, James La Guma. One of the party's rising stars, La Guma was a "Coloured" in South African classification, born in 1894 in Bloemfontein of French and Malagasy descent. He had also risen high in the ICU until his sacking two months before the Brussels conference; Kadalie himself refused to attend that conference.

The three South African delegates at Brussels submitted a resolution in the name "of all workers and oppressed peoples of South Africa, irrespective of race, colour and creed," calling for unity to support the right of self-determination, the overthrow of capitalist and imperialist domination, and full freedom of organisation. In his address Gumede said, "We have nothing, and can only tell each other sad stories of our slavery. We have waited long for a liberator, but we do not know where to find him." He then suggested where he was looking: "I am happy to say that there are Communists also in South Africa. I myself am not one, but it is my experience that the Communist Party is the only party that stands behind us and from which we can expect something." [100]

After Brussels the South African delegates travelled to Moscow and had talks with Bukharin, then head of a "collective leadership" running the Comintern. As enthusiastic as ever, Gumede said in Cape Town on his return, "The only friends of oppressed people are the Communists". Later he said he had had his eyes opened to the "universal truth" that it was not the white man as such "but the capitalist class which grinds

99   P. Dewitte, *Les Mouvements Nègres en France 1919-1939*, Paris: L'Harmattan, 1985, pp. 146-8, citing *La Voix des Nègres*, March 1927. There is more of Senghor's speech (translated into English) in J. Ayo Langley, *Ideologies of Liberation in Black Africa 1856-1970*, London: Rex Collings, 1979, p. 256-60.

100   J. and R. Simons, *Class and Colour in South Africa 1850-1950*, London: IDAF, 1983, pp. 353-4. The quotation is those authors' translation from a German text.

176

the faces of white and black the world over".[101] Soon afterwards he was elected President-General of the ANC for three years; E.J. Khaile, a Communist recently expelled with La Guma from the ICU, became the Congress General Secretary. Gumede and La Guma returned to the USSR for celebrations of the tenth anniversary of the October Revolution and visited some non-Russian areas. On his return Gumede declared, "I have seen the new world to come, where it has already begun. I have been to the new Jerusalem." He added, "Others are persuaded to be Communists. The Bantu has been a Communist from time immemorial. We are disorganized, that's all."[102]

Nehru was on the Presidium of the congress, and drafted its resolution on India which included a call for full emancipation of the peasants and workers, "without which there can be no real freedom". This fitted in with the general outlook of the conference: radical anticolonialism not following Moscow dictation but agreeing in some respects with Communist ideas and seeing the Soviet Union as an ally. Later Jawaharlal Nehru and his father Motilal Nehru also attended the Moscow tenth anniversary celebrations.[103]

Among the other delegates at Brussels were Mohammed Hatta from the Dutch East Indies; the Dutch trade unionist Edo Fimmen, Secretary of the International Transport Workers; Barbusse, at the head of a French delegation; and several anti-imperialists from Britain, mostly of the ILP but attending as individuals. George Lansbury, MP, who was to be Leader of the Labour Party from 1931 to 1935, led the delegation, which also included notably Fenner Brockway, now a leading figure in the ILP, editor of the *New Leader* from 1926 to 1929; Arthur McManus, chairman of the CPGB; and Ellen Wilkinson, a left-wing Labour MP who had briefly joined the Communist Party and was to be most famous as leader of the Jarrow "Hunger March" of 1936. She wrote a glowing report on the Congress, declaring that it was not a purely Communist venture.[104] This was the impression that the organis-

---

101   Ibid., pp. 390-2.

102   Ibid., p. 404, quoting *South African Worker*, 2 March and 30 March 1928; Hargreaves (note 90), pp. 257-8.

103   S. Gopal, *Jawaharlal Nehru: A Biography: Vol. One: 1889-1947*, London: Jonathan Cape, 1975, pp. 100-9.

104   *Labour Weekly* 19 February 1927.

ers had wanted people to have. However, others saw the Congress as a Communist-dominated venture, and the League Against Imperialism (LAI), set up by a resolution of the Congress, was seen similarly, by the British Labour Party among others.

The LAI had an honorary presidium consisting of Barbusse, Soong Ching-Ling—Sun Yat-sen's widow, who chose the Communist side when the Kuomintang and the Communists parted company in 1927 (see below)—and Albert Einstein; and an Executive Committee including, as the first Chairman, George Lansbury. Other members included Münzenberg, Nehru, Fimmen, Senghor, and Liau Han Sin of China.[105] For some time in 1927 Gibarti and Liau were joint General Secretaries.

Following the congress a Brussels Manifesto was published, signed by members of the honorary presidium and the Executive Committee. It proclaimed that "The representatives of the oppressed nations and the working class of all peoples of the world" had "concluded a fraternal alliance among themselves." It recalled that

For hundreds of years, European capitalism has drawn its main source of nourishment from the ruthless, fierce, stop-at-nothing exploitation of transoceanic, Asiatic, African and American nations and tribes. Indescribable oppression, inhuman enslavement, and back-breaking labour, the complete extermination of whole nations and tribes, so that even their names have vanished, were necessary for the construction of the proud building of European, later Americo-European capitalism, and its mercenary material and spiritual civilization.

After this passage which even people far removed from Communism could readily have written, the Manifesto echoed Marxist theory when it declared, "The surpluses of capitalist accumulation, in the new form of financial capital, categorically demand the subjection of the whole non-capitalist world." The Great War, it went on, had followed from imperialist rivalry, but had not ended it, and had involved "the murder of millions of people, including hundreds of thousands of colonial slaves from India and the French African colonies who fell on all the fields of struggle for the interest of the slave-owners." The War had forced the imperialists to adopt the slogan of self-determination, and in answer to continued repression,

---

105   Secret document headed "The League against Imperialism" (note 90).

The powerful wave of the national-liberation movement has swept over immense, colossal regions of Asia, Africa, and America.

The banner of rebellion against enslavement and oppression was raised in China, India, Egypt, north-west Africa, Indochina, Mexico, and the Philippines.

And there was also the inspiration of the Russian Revolution, which "turned the old predatory Russian monarchy, which oppressed hundreds of nations, into a free federation of equal nationalities" and "like a torch, lights the path of the liberation struggle of the oppressed and enslaved nations."

The Manifesto spoke of the "new colonial wars in Morocco and Syria", the Amritsar massacre, resistance in Nicaragua (where one of many American interventions was then in progress), and the foreign intervention in China, where "Britain herself is to all intents and purposes in a state of open war with the forces of the Chinese national-liberation movement, represented by the Canton government and the Kuomintang." The Manifesto concluded,

Let him who has no interest in oppression, who does not live by the fruits of that oppression, who hates modern slavery and serfdom, and who strives for his own freedom and that of his neighbour join us and support us.[106]

The Manifesto may have been drafted by Communists, but by Communists anxious to seek allies from outside their party ranks, following the Comintern's policy—at that time—of working with "bourgeois nationalist" movements. But disagreements broke out at an early stage because of the Communist role, which was in fact important, in the new organisation. Lansbury resigned after two months on 6 June 1927, possibly because of this, though he said it was because of pressure of work.[107] Then Fenner Brockway became chairman, but he had to relinquish the post, because he was also the ILP representative on the executive of the Labour and Socialist International (LSI). According to Padmore, Münzenberg secured the election of Brockway so that the Communists could use him, a non-Communist, for their purposes, but

---

106   Text reproduced (in English) from *Novy Vostok* xvi-xvii, 1927, in J.A. Langley, *Pan-Africanism and Nationalism in West Africa 1900-1945*, OUP, 1973, pp. 383-8. *Novy Vostok* was a monthly publication of the All-Russian Association of Eastern Studies (Wilson (note 32), p. 101).

107   Saville (note 90), p. 42.

the German Communists used Brockway's name to attack the German Social Democrats (the SPD), who had forbidden their followers to join the German section of the LAI; the SPD protested to the LSI, and the ILP then advised him to resign from the LAI chair.[108] Brockway confirmed this account in its essentials.[109] A report by the British India Office later suggested that Brockway had not even taken up the post of LAI Chairman, because of the conflict of loyalties, but this was probably wrong; however, he certainly did not last long in the post.[110]

According to that British government report, a new Chairman of the LAI was elected in December 1927, at the third meeting, held in Brussels, of the Executive Committee. This was James Maxton, one of the Scottish Clydeside MPs elected in 1922, Chairman of the ILP in 1926, whose election was a clear sign that cooperation between Communists and non-Communists was still the aim. At some point both Joint General Secretaries left, and in April 1928 Münzenberg and Chattopadhyaya were chosen to replace them.[111] They were to hold the posts for several years and run the League from its international headquarters in Berlin, where an *Anti-Imperialist Review* was published by the League from 1928. Chattopadhyaya is said to have done much of the work of running the Berlin headquarters,[112] and this is likely as Münzenberg was very busy with German politics in the next few years.

National branches of the LAI were set up soon after the Brussels Congress. The first Executive Committee of the British section included Brockway, Lansbury and Saklatvala. Lansbury quickly withdrew because of the Labour and Socialist International's hostile attitude, fully endorsed by the Labour Party, which later sent out a circular quoting extensively from the official LAI report on Brussels—*The Beacon of the*

---

108 Padmore (note 96), pp. 325-6. Padmore (whose years of Communist activity are yet to be described in this chapter, below) wrote this after he had broken with Communism.

109 F. Brockway, *Inside the Left*, London: Allen & Unwin, 1942, pp. 167-9; F. Brockway, *The Colonial Revolution*, London and St Alban's: Hart-Davis, Mac-Gibbon, 1973, pp. 35-6. Unfortunately the latter book is sketchy and full of errors about that early period. Brockway's memory at the time I interviewed him (14 February 1984) was imprecise.

110 Secret document headed "The League against Imperialism" (note 90).

111 Ibid.

112 Barooah (note 92), p. 253.

Palais Egmont, published in Germany—and detailing the LAI's Communist links.[113] The fiery Maxton adopted a different attitude, and in January 1928 became chairman of the British section as well as international Chairman. Then an enlarged Committee was chosen, excluding Brockway but including Ellen Wilkinson and A.J. Cook, the miners' union leader who had headed the coal mines strike leading to the General Strike of 1926. The British section organised a general conference in London on 7 July 1928, with 343 delegates; Cook, Saklatvala and Brockway were among the speakers.[114]

The Secretary of the British section, for several years from its inception, was Reginald Bridgeman, who had been at the Brussels Congress. One of the leading radical anti-imperialists in Britain for many years, Bridgeman (1884-1968) had started a fairly conventional governing-class career, serving as a diplomat in Paris from 1908 to 1920 except for a break at the embassy in Athens, and acting as private secretary to the Ambassador to France during the 1919 Peace Conference, before experiencing a conversion. This seems to have happened gradually between 1919 and 1922; while working at the Legation in Tehran he annoyed his superiors by contacts with Soviet representatives there, and when passing through India he was struck by the country's poverty and illiteracy; but there seems to have been a gradual process, not a road to Damascus experience. He retired on a pension in 1923 and was soon active in the Labour Party in Pinner, a suburb of London. He also took part in the widespread left-wing campaign against Western intervention in China, which the ILP pursued actively ("Hands off China").[115]

The LAI's French section, the Ligue Anti-Impérialiste, was formed soon after Brussels and elected an Executive Committee including Gabrielle Duchêne, founder of the French section of the Women's International League for Peace and Freedom; Victor Basch, chairman of the LDH; Barbusse and Challaye; the SFIO deputy Moutet; the Africans Senghor and Khairallah, and the West Indian Bloncourt. It held a big meeting on 26 April 1927 to launch its action, with about 600 peo-

113 Circular of Labour Party Industrial Department, apparently dated early 1928, on the "League against Colonial Oppression", enclosed in file HO 144/10693, National Archives, London.

114 Ibid.

115 Saville (note 90).

ple present; speeches were delivered by Senghor, Khairallah, Challaye, Vaillant-Couturier and others.[116] At that stage the pursuit of a "united front", or the appearance of one, was taken quite far in France—Basch and Moutet had opposed the campaign against the Rif war. But it was soon to end. Difficulties had come from the democratic Socialist side first, but were soon to come from the other side.

The Comintern Congress of 1928 and anti-colonial militancy

The Brussels Congress was held as the civil war in China was reaching a climax. Chiang Kai-shek, emerging as the leading figure in the Kuomintang after Sun Yat-sen's death, continued the Soviet alliance, useful for arms supplies, while the Soviet leaders through Mikhail Borodin continued to back the KMT and forced a reluctant Chinese Communist Party (CCP) to do the same. Eventually Chiang captured Shanghai on 24 March 1927, but then he turned on his Communist allies and on 12-13 April his forces killed thousands of Communists, trade unionists and other left-wingers in that city and others. The CCP briefly held on to a base in Wuhan, a revolutionary centre visited by foreign Communists including Doriot from France, but then it was thoroughly defeated and Borodin returned to Russia.[117]

During 1927 the Soviet leaders, and the Comintern which was totally under their control, began telling Communists to rally against a threat of war against the USSR. There were in fact no plans for an attack on the Soviet Union then. The defeat in China may have reinforced the paranoia always present in the Soviet leadership, and about the same time Britain cut diplomatic relations with the USSR in May 1927, while relations were worsening with France also.[118] But it is hard to tell whether there were ever real fears of a Western attack. At any rate those fears were whipped up constantly for the next few years, and even though they could see no war preparations around them, Communists

---

116   "Report on the Activities of the League Against Imperialism in the different countries February to May 1927", signed by H.S. Liau and L. Gibarti, enclosed with Special Branch report received at Home Office, London on 9 June 1927, in file HO 144/10693, National Archives, London; Liauzu (note 14), pp. 35-7.

117   See Jacobs (note 49), chs. 10-17.

118   McDermott and Agnew, p. 71.

in France and Britain, and elsewhere, dutifully rallied to denounce the threat and "defend the Soviet Union".

Then the Sixth Comintern Congress was held, once again in Moscow, from 17 July to 1 September 1928. Its main outcome was a more critical attitude both to non-Communist left-wing parties in the West and to non-Communist nationalists in the colonies and "semi-colonies". Regarding the latter, a more suspicious attitude was to be expected after the disaster in China; why collaborate with "bourgeois nationalists" if they were going to turn out like Chiang Kai-shek? However, despite those events the "Theses on the Revolutionary Movement in the Colonies and Semi-colonies" adopted by the Congress, based on a draft submitted by the Finnish Communist Otto Kuusinen, did not call for total condemnation of "reformist" nationalists in the colonies such as the Swarajists in India and the Wafdists in Egypt.[119]

The Comintern—seemingly forgetting the possibilities of what would later be called "neo-colonialism"—still thought imperialism must inevitably, always oppose political independence for the colonies. This implied that independence, even under "bourgeois nationalists", was still a proper Communist aim. It was indeed still considered so, but now Communists were no longer encouraged to join forces with those non-revolutionary nationalists. The Sixth Congress itself merely ordered a very critical attitude to them, but the next year the Comintern made a new rigorist line explicit and obligatory: outright struggle against nationalists such as Gandhi and his INC. At the tenth Plenum of the ECCI in July 1929 Indian Communists were told to attack all sections of the INC, including Jawaharlal Nehru's left-wing section. The Comintern leadership had already turned against M.N. Roy by the time of the Congress (accusing him of the heresy of believing that industrialisation was possible under imperialist rule), and expelled him from the Comintern in September 1929. In 1930 he left Germany and returned to India; landing in disguise but caught later, he was sentenced

---

119   Text of the "Theses on the Revolutionary Movement in the Colonies and Semi-colonies", published in *Inprecorr* 8 (88), 12 December 1928, pp. 1665-66; quoted in S.D. Gupta, *Comintern, India and the Colonial Question, 1920-1937*, Calcutta, K.P. Bagchi & Co., 1980, chapter 4, p. 151. Gupta's earlier chapters describe the Communist arguments on colonial questions in earlier years.

to twelve years' transportation, a sentence later reduced to six years' rigorous imprisonment.[120]

The Sixth Congress made special decisions on South Africa and on the African Americans; of these more shortly. These were also put forward by Kuusinen, but in fact reflected the views of his master Stalin. By then Stalin was well on the way to complete victory in the power struggle in the Kremlin, defeating Trotsky and Zinoviev who in December 1927 were expelled from the Party.

For several years after the Sixth Congress Communists were ordered to treat Western democratic Socialist parties as enemies. There had in fact been strong antipathy between Communists and parties like the British Labour Party for years, and the use of the term "social fascist" to describe those parties had begun soon after the real Fascists took power in Rome in 1922; but after 1928 the gloves were off. Moscow ordered not only an end to cooperation with social democratic parties, but especially concentrated attacks on them. Reluctantly obeying the new instructions, the CPGB issued a manifesto plainly entitled *Class against Class* (the general term for the revised policy) for the 1929 elections that brought a Labour government under Ramsay MacDonald to power.[121] In France the Communists entered into headlong confrontation with the state, which they lost, in 1929, when the PCF led a semi-clandestine existence for some months; for some time PCF membership and voter support declined.[122] In Germany the new Comintern policy led to the KPD concentrating attacks on the SPD and thereby helping the Nazis gain power.

The Communists' new zeal for attacking people on the same side was extended to the League Against Imperialism and struck Jimmy Maxton, who had remained Chairman after other ILP-ers had left the League. Soon after MacDonald became Prime Minister again on 5 June 1929 Maxton attended the second congress of the LAI, held at Frankfurt-

---

120   J.P. Haithcox, *Communism and Nationalism in India: M.N. Roy and Comintern Policy 1920-1939*, Princeton University Press, 1971, pp. 80-88, 109-42, 164-98.

121   N. Branson, *History of the Communist Party of Great Britain 1927-1941*, London: Lawrence & Wishart 1985, pp. 21-9; S. Howe, *Anticolonialism in British Politics: The Left and the End of Empire*, Oxford: Clarendon Press, 1993, p. 61.

122   E. Mortimer, *The Rise of the French Communist Party 1920-1947*, London: Faber & Faber, 1984, pp. 144-9, 164, 199-200.

am-Main in Germany from 20 to 31 July 1929, and spoke against the "imperialist policy" of the new Labour government; but when he was ordered by the LAI leaders to republish this in the ILP organ, the *New Leader*, he refused, and was expelled from the League. After he was expelled from the LAI British section on 17 September 1929 several others resigned, including Cook.[123] The new Chairman then chosen for the British section was the Rev. Conrad Noel, a High Church Anglican minister who had founded a Church Socialist League and supported the Irish and Russian revolutions.[124] Bridgeman did not join the Communist Party then, if he ever did, for he was able to stand for election as a Labour candidate in the 1929 general election, calling during the campaign for self-determination for every British colony and mandated territory; but he was defeated, and in November 1929 the Labour Party excluded LAI members from joining it; when Bridgeman stood as a "workers' candidate" in 1931 he was heavily defeated.[125]

There were still non-Communists at the second LAI Congress at Frankfurt, and others could readily join in its condemnations of imperialism, as when it declared:

The revolt of the African peasantry and the struggle against the inhuman oppression of English, French, Belgian, Italian and Portuguese imperialism and its agents, as well as the recent peasant insurrection in French Equatorial Africa, are only the beginning of a new more extensive struggle against imperialist domination in Africa.[126]

But increasingly, those not considered acceptable to the Communists were driven out. In 1929 the French section was brought under closer control from the headquarters and Basch, Challaye and some others resigned.[127] Jawaharlal Nehru and other INC leaders, seeing the growing

---

123   G. Brown, *Maxton*, Edinburgh: Mainstream Publishing Co., 1986, p. 201; Mike Squires, *Saklatvala: A Political Biography*, London: Lawrence & Wishart, 1990, pp. 170-4.

124   R. Groves, "Noel, Conrad le Despenser Roden", *Dictionary of Labour Biography* (note 90), Vol. II pp. 276-86.

125   Saville (note 90).

126   *Inprecorr* (no. 68) report cited in Wilson, p. 180. On the rising in French Equatorial Africa, see below, pp. 239-40.

127   Liauzu (note 14), pp. 36-7.

Communist domination of the LAI, were gradually estranged from it, and formally expelled in 1931.[128]

While Communists attacked other anti-imperialists, they continued to attack imperialism as strongly as before, if not more. In fact, despite all their policy tergiversations, Communists' condemnation of Western colonial rule was a constant for about fifteen years. It appeared regularly in the Communist newspapers in particular: *L'Humanité* in France, *Rote Fahne* in Germany, *Drapeau Rouge* in Belgium, the *Daily Worker* (following some earlier publications) from 1 January 1930 in Britain, and the separate New York *Daily Worker*.

ANC, ICU and Communists in South Africa

For South Africa the Sixth Comintern Congress made a special decision: that the Communist Party of South Africa should declare its aim to be a "Native Republic". This was confirmation of what had been decided in previous discussions, following the Brussels conference and talks held by La Guma in Moscow. The slogan meant rule by the African majority. Bunting opposed it, but La Guma said majority rule should be sought first, with Socialism to follow; as in Egypt, he said, a struggle for independence was "objectively revolutionary" as it weakened imperialism. Majority rule in South Africa, which was already independent, was equivalent to independence for a colony.

Bunting, representing the CPSA at the Congress with his wife Rebecca and Edward Roux, tried to argue against the slogan, although he had already made the party a mainly African one in membership (1,600 Africans out of a total of 1,750 in 1928); he said white people would be alienated, and Roux recalled later, "Was it not similar, we said, to Marcus Garvey's "Africa for the Africans" which the C.P. had always opposed as the exact opposite of internationalism?"[129] The CPSA delegation therefore proposed an amendment on 28 August 1928.[130] But earlier Douglas Wolton had said,

---

128   Barooah (note 92), pp. 253-66.

129   E. Roux, *S.P. Bunting, A Political Biography*, published by the author, Cape Town, 1944, pp. 88-100.

130   Reproduced as document no. 63 in A. Davidson, I. Filatova, V. Gorodnov and S. Jones (eds), *South Africa and the Communist International: A Documentary History*, London: Frank Cass, 2003, Vol. 1, pp. 188-91.

Eventually blacks must predominate in this country, and a Black republic be realised...Slogan Workers of the World Unite is abstract in this country and in face of daily oppression at hands of white worker cannot be easily understood. Hence, the need for slogan reaching out to native masses especially.[131]

The Comintern insisted on its ruling, and Bunting and the rest of his party accepted the slogan, calling on white workers to back the demand for African power. The wording eventually agreed after long debate was "A South African Native Republic, as a stage towards a Workers' and Peasants' Government, with full protection and equal rights for all national minorities."[132]

Africans now advanced rapidly in the CPSA, notably Albert T. Nzula. Born on 16 November 1905 at Rouxville in Orange Free State, Nzula worked as a teacher and then became an activist first for the ICU and then for the CPSA; he was noted as an orator and pamphleteer, and rose rapidly. In 1929-30 Nzula was the first Black African General Secretary of the CPSA, and Editor of its newspaper, the *South African Worker*, which was renamed *Umsebenzi* ("worker") in 1930 and carried articles in the Xhosa, Zulu, Sotho and Tswana languages.[133] By then the CPSA was beset by internal feuds which were to last for several years; it seems they were not, generally, about the "Native Republic" slogan.

With that slogan the CPSA called, roughly, for what actually came about in 1994. The ANC, which was to take power at that remote future date, had implicitly called for such an outcome by demanding equality; equality for all would eventually mean majority rule. As already mentioned Josiah Gumede, very sympathetic to Communism, became President-General of the ANC in 1927. But the ANC was in a weak state then, while Gumede's enthusiasm for the Communists and the Soviet Union caused some dissension within it. For some years past the most active and formidable defender of the Africans had been not the ANC

---

131   Minutes of CPSA Executive Committee meeting on 15 March 1928, document 57 in A. Davidson *et al.* (eds) (note 130), vol. 1, pp. 177-9 (wording *sic*).

132   Roux (note 129), p. 103n.

133   R. Edgar, "Notes on the Life and Death of Albert Nzula", *International Journal of African Historical Studies* vol. 16 no. 4, 1983, pp. 675-79; Introduction by R. Cohen to A.T. Nzula, I.I. Potekhin and A.Z. Zusmanovich, *Forced Labour in Colonial Africa* (1933), English version London: Zed Press, 1979, pp. 2-16; Simons (note 100), p. 414.

but the Industrial and Commercial Union. By 1928 ICU membership was estimated at 70,000. Even if only half of these were fully paid up, as was estimated, it was a considerable figure in view of the persecution Africans joining the union had to face. The ICU, which had its newspaper *The Workers' Herald*, organised workers against heavy odds, even on white-owned farms where working conditions were particularly vile. By concentrating on pay and conditions—though it did not confine itself to those—the ICU had a special appeal that the SANNC/ANC lacked. Kadalie had some able lieutenants such as Henry Tyamzashe and A.W.G. Champion.[134]

Kadalie sought in April 1926 to strengthen its position by seeking affiliation to the British Trades Union Congress, which replied that the ICU should rather apply to join the non-Communist trade union international, the International Federation of Trade Unions (IFTU) based in Amsterdam. An application to the IFTU was accepted in January 1927, and meanwhile Kadalie consulted with a number of British trade unionists and socialists. He pleased them by sacking the Communists from the ICU in December 1926, and that can only have encouraged the decision to give him aid.

Within South Africa some white liberals backed Kadalie, but when the ICU applied to the South African TUC for affiliation in December 1927 this was refused. Earlier that year the Hertzog government refused to nominate him as the South African workers' delegate to the annual International Labour Office (ILO) assembly in Geneva. However, he attended as an unofficial delegate and made a good impression. He also made a lecture tour of England and Scotland under the auspices of the ILP, and visited some other European countries, returning to South Africa in November 1927. The following month a special ICU congress at Kimberley adopted a new constitution and agreed to accept a trade union adviser from Britain. The ILP and Walter Citrine, General Secretary of the TUC, sent William Ballinger, a Scotsman who was given a three-month entry permit after Scotland Yard reported that his job was to counteract Communism among African workers. He did more in

---

134   Clements Kadalie, *My Life and the ICU*, reprinted with introduction by S. Trapido, London: Frank Cass, 1970; H. Bradford, *A Taste of Freedom: The ICU in Rural South Africa 1924-1930*, Yale University Press, 1987 (chapter 2 describes farm working conditions); Simons (note 100), p. 356.

fact, but his efforts to reform the ICU may have been unhelpful in the South African situation, and Kadalie later said, "I asked for an adviser and received a dictator." Kadalie himself, however, was accused of being autocratic, among other things, during disputes which largely wrecked the ICU in 1927-29: in particular a power struggle between Champion and Kadalie, amid accusations of financial irregularities (which had indeed been widespread in the ICU).

Clements Kadalie was sacked, or given a twelve-month leave of absence, in January 1929, and formed a new Independent ICU in April. Champion now headed an ICU Yase Natal, while the ICU Johannesburg branch was run independently by Ballinger. Champion's organisation did well for a time, but before long little remained of the ICU's efforts to defend African workers.[135] Its internal disputes were very much to blame, but what really counted was the overall situation in South Africa. As the Hertzog government added to the impositions and disabilities facing Africans, those seeking to defend or extend Africans' rights came up against a brick wall.

Reading the recriminations among opponents of the South African system at that time, one needs to recall that anything any of them did would have been useless against a determined regime dominated by the aggressive National Party, which won new elections on 12 June 1929. The ANC called openly for a complete change of regime; Gumede said in Johannesburg in early 1929 that the people must demand the franchise, seats in parliament, and a republic representing all nationalities regardless of colour. To achieve this, he said, they should raise their voice "so that we fill all the gaols". Kadalie, speaking on the same platform, similarly said, "Prepare yourselves to go to gaol, prepare yourselves to be hung if you want freedom."[136] But what could they do to follow up such rhetoric? Resisting the white supremacy government was hopeless. However, many brave people tried it in the years following the new Nationalist election victory.

---

135 Kadalie (note 134), chapters VII-XIV; Simons (note 100), pp. 354-76; Bradford (note 134), pp. 167-80; P.S. Gupta, *Imperialism and the British Labour Movement, 1914-1964*, Macmillan, 1975, pp. 122-4; B. Bush, *Imperialism, Race and Resistance: Africa and Britain, 1919-1945*, London and New York: Routledge, 1999, pp. 164-5, 167-71, 183-6.

136 Simons (note 100), pp. 375.

Two months after the elections a League of African Rights (LAR) was formed by the ANC, the ICU, the Communist Party and the Federation of Non-European Trade Unions (FNETU) founded in 1928; Gumede was president, Bunting chairman and N.B. Tantsi of the Transvaal ANC vice-chairman. It planned to mark the next Dingaan's Day (16 December), a sacred day for Afrikaners commemorating a victory over the Zulus in 1838, with demonstrations against the hated pass laws, the basis of the system of control over Africans' lives.[137]

The League's leaders went around gathering signatures to a mammoth petition against the passes. The government published a bill to amend the Riotous Assemblies Act to curb the Communists in particular; a mass meeting in Johannesburg on 10 November 1929 condemned the bill, with the effigy of Oswald Pirow, the minister of Justice, being burned. Pirow claimed that the ANC, the ICU and the League were all in correspondence with the Comintern. But about that very time a telegram came from Moscow ordering the immediate dissolution of the LAR.[138] This was a doctrinaire application of the new Comintern policy that Communists should cut themselves off from people who were on the same side but not in total agreement with them; the CPSA obeyed the order slowly and unwillingly.

Several in the ANC were uneasy about the mass protest campaign, but Gumede called on 15 December 1929 for more mobilisation against the new legislation proposed; he said they looked to the League Against Imperialism for support, and hoped that the world would "once more wake up and speak out for the cause of freedom". The next day he, Kadalie and Bunting addressed a demonstration on the planned day in Johannesburg; although Gumede spoke there, the ANC as a body was not involved. There were demonstrations in other big towns on that day.

Repression was further reinforced by new legislation in 1930-32.[139] Protests continued during 1930 but achieved nothing. In April 1930 Gumede gave a rousing address to the annual ANC convention, refer-

---

137   The "pass laws" were a complex variety of laws and rules. George Padmore listed twelve principal sorts of pass in *The Life and Struggles of Negro Toilers* (on this see below), pp. 14-15, quoting "Tymzo-shi" (probably Henry Tyamzashe of the ICU). See D. Hindson, *Pass Controls and the Urban African Proletariat*, Johannesburg: Ravan Press, 1987.

138   Simons (note 100), pp. 417-21.

139   Ibid., pp. 423, 430, 452-3.

ring to the world Depression already raging, and to revolts by Chinese, Javanese and Indians against imperialism. He expressed continued faith in the Soviet Union as "the only real friend of all subjected races". He declared firmly that the ANC's appeals to the government, the Governor-General, and Britain had achieved nothing and MacDonald's government in Britain was then crushing the Indian revolt (a reference, no doubt, to Gandhi's "Salt March"). He said, "We have to demand our equal economic, social and political rights," a Native Republic with equal rights for all; "Let us go back from this conference, resolved to adopt the militant policy" in "the spirit which has been exhibited by oppressed peoples all over the world." But the more cautious and conservative figures in the ANC now voted Gumede out and elected as President Pixley ka Isaka Seme (c.1880-1951), a Zulu lawyer and founder of the newspaper *Abantu-Batho*.[140] Under him the ANC followed a mild, un-militant line.

Greater militancy did not get very far, either. The CPSA certainly remained very active; it established the Communist affiliates usual in the West, a trade union organisation and International Red Aid, which was set up in South Africa in 1931 under the name of Ikaka la Basebenzi. But all this activity was carried on by a very small number of dedicated people. At some point during 1930 Nzula was removed from the post of General Secretary. He was a talented young man who had risen high in the CPSA very fast and was shortly to go to the USSR and become co-author of a major book there, before dying a tragic early death in Moscow. Thus he is better remembered than other early Black South African Communists; but strangely, the various published accounts of him[141] do not mention exactly how he came to be sacked as General Secretary. There is just one brief reference in the collection of Comintern archival documents published in 2003, suggesting that the "Bunting leadership" drove Nzula to drink and then drove him out of the General Secretaryship.[142] Nzula did have a drink problem, but the facts about the internal squabbling are hard to unravel.

---

140   Ibid., pp. 427-9.

141   See note 133.

142   Report of E.S. Sachs to ECCI, 8 October 1930, document 89 in Davidson *et al.* (eds) (note 130), Vol. 1, pp. 247-9.

For the next Dingaan's Day, 16 December 1930, the CPSA planned mass burning of passes, but the ANC refused to join it and Kadalie opposed the idea. Many felt disinclined to risk trouble to no purpose, much as they might agree with the words of Nzula: "Whether educated or uneducated, rich or poor, we are all subject to these badges of slavery. We are slaves as long as we think we can only beg and pray to this cruel government." Nzula, like other educated Africans, had a "pass exemption certificate", but of course this was another sort of pass; he threw it into the bonfire on the day, when thousands of passes were burned in several cities.[143]

The following year Wolton took over the CPSA at the head of a new Central Committee which in September 1931 expelled W.F. Andrews, who had been the first Secretary of the CPSA in 1921-22 before concentrating on trade union work, and S.P. Bunting. Others were purged also, including La Guma. The new leadership denounced Bunting and "Buntingism" until his death in 1936. The CPSA was now turned, thanks in part to Comintern orders, into a small, isolated group of verbal extremists. Africans now dominated the leadership.[144]

The ANC, too, went through a period of decline. Some of the defeated left-wing faction tried to form an Independent African National Congress, but their leader, Brandley R. Ndobe, was deported to Basutoland. Gumede joined that group, and in a letter to Münzenberg and Chattopadhyaya of the LAI in 1931 said the ANC had left him with the newspaper *Abantu Batho* and large debts attached to it; he appealed for help "so as to be free to lead the militants".[145] The new party did not last, but the ANC was at a low ebb under its new mild leadership, unable to do much at a time when Africans faced not only increased repression but the combined effects of the Slump and one of South Africa's worst ever droughts. Thousands of white farmers were also ruined then and the "Poor Whites", camping in the cities, became a

---

143   Simons (note 100), pp. 433-5; Cohen (note 133), pp. 8-9.

144   This is a very brief summary of the CPSA's internal crises, described in Simons (note 100), pp. 439-53 and more fully in Roux (note 129), pp. 124-7, 130-3, 143. See also R. Cohen (note 133). On the wider South African events, see also P. Walshe, *The Rise of African Nationalism in South Africa*, pp. 135-222.

145   Letter to International Secretariat, League Against Imperialism from J. Gumede, Pietermaritzburg, 1931 (full date not given), document no. 2 in A. Davidson *et al.* (eds) (note 130), Vol. II, pp. 4-5.

new feature of the landscape. This did not bring about united action by the underprivileged of all races. Instead government relief efforts were directed at the "Poor Whites", and over time many were to be recruited into the Afrikaner Nationalist movement. For the Africans of South Africa, much harder hit by the economic distress, the early 1930s were a very low point.

Black militant leaders and the Comintern

In the black world in the 1920s, Communism played a part only in two places, South Africa and the USA, and in both it was only a small part of the protest movement. In the USA the NAACP was much the most important African American organisation. Its rival, Marcus Garvey, was deported at the end of 1927 on his release from prison, arriving in Jamaica to a hero's welcome. His wife Amy Jacques Garvey and others had kept the UNIA going, and back in Jamaica Marcus Garvey set out to revive it; but it never returned to its former strength and popularity, even though the British authorities watched his every move apprehensively. Garvey travelled in 1928 to London and Paris, where he attracted some support; he addressed a meeting at the Albert Hall in London on 6 June 1928. In Kingston the Sixth International Convention of the Negro Peoples of the World was held in August 1929; however, Garvey split from the remnants of the UNIA in the USA.[146]

Du Bois organised a new Pan African Congress in 1927, this time in New York.[147] A Circle for Peace and Foreign Relations, based in New York, sponsored the conference; its one African member was Adelaide Casely Hayford (1868-1960), a leading Freetown elite figure who had been briefly married to J.E. Casely Hayford.[148] Richard B. Moore, the African American civil rights champion and scholar (then a Communist), recalled later that 208 delegates from the USA and ten other countries attended this gathering from 21 to 24 August 1927; they included

146   E.D. Cronon, *Black Moses*, Madison: University of Wisconsin Press, 1955, pp. 142-56.

147   Langley (note 106), p. 87; I. Geiss, *The Pan-African Movement*, tr. Ann Keep, London: Methuen, 1974, pp. 234-40, pp. 256-8.

148   A.M. Cromwell, *An African Victorian Feminist: The Life and Times of Adelaide Smith Casely Hayford 1868-1960*, London: Cass, 1986, p. 134.

some from West Africa and the Surinam-born American Communist Otto Huiswoud, and the American scholar Melville J. Herskovits, well known for his studies of the link between the former Kingdom of Dahomey and African culture in Haiti. One paragraph of the resolution said, "We thank the Soviet Government of Russia for its liberal attitude toward the colored races and for the help which it has extended to them from time to time." But on Africa the Resolution called simply for "The development of Africa for the Africans and not merely for the profit of the Europeans," while it called in contrast for "freedom and real national independence in Egypt, in China and in India."[149] At the Conference Du Bois, who had visited the USSR in 1926, praised that country's treatment of nationalities; but many people said such things while not becoming Communists, and Du Bois rejected Communism, whose leadership was soon to be denouncing him and the NAACP.[150]

Some African Americans had joined the Communists, and in 1925 five Black students went from the USA to the Soviet Union to study at Kutvu (the Communist University of the Toilers of the East). They included an African who may well have been the first Black African to study at Kutvu and to spend a considerable time in the Soviet Union, Bankole Awoonor-Renner from the Gold Coast. Born to a Sierra Leonean family living in Gold Coast, he studied at the Tuskegee Institute and took a journalism course at the Carnegie Institute of Technology at Pittsburgh; he was in 1922-24 Secretary of the African Students' Union of America. In 1925 he may have gone to Britain,[151] but it seems he did not stay long there if so, because that year he joined the group selected by the US Communists to go to Kutvu. According to a study based on Soviet Communist Party archives he used the name Kweku Bankole in Russia, and argued with Zinoviev about the Comintern attitude to the "most oppressed people" in Africa.[152] Published sources give

149   R.B. Moore, "Du Bois and Pan-Africa", pp. 187-212 in J.H. Clarke *et al.* (eds), *Black Titan: W.E.B. Du Bois*, Boston: Beacon Press, 1970; pp. 205-6.

150   He was to join the CPUSA in 1961, at the age of 93.

151   S.K.B. Asante, entry on Awooner-Renner in *Dictionary of African Biography*, New York 1977, pp. 208-9.

152   W. McClellan, "Africans and Black Americans in the Comintern Schools, 1925-1934", *International Journal of African Historical Studies* Vol. 26 no. 2, 1993, pp. 371-90, pp. 373-4. See also W. McClellan's more recent "Black *Hajj* to "Red Mecca": Africans and Afro-Americans at KUTV, 1925-1938", Ch. 3

strangely varying lists of the people (most or all American) who went to the USSR at about the same time as Awooner-Renner, but it seems clear that Otto Hall, a black American Communist, was among them, and his brother Haywood Hall went the following year; Haywood Hall, who like his brother had served in the Great War, assumed the name of Harry Haywood.[153]

Stalin received several of these students and told them, "You [the Black Americans] are a national minority with some of the characteristics of a nation"; the students did not agree with this approach to their situation,[154] but Stalin apparently stuck to it. Katayama, similarly, said in 1928 that Lenin had "considered the American Negroes as a subject nation, placing them in the same category as Ireland".[155] This view apparently lay behind the decision at the Sixth Comintern Congress that Communists should advocate self-determination and a separate Negro state in the Southern USA. The Political Secretariat of the Comintern declared on 26 October 1928 that "the Party must come out openly and unreservedly for the right of Negroes to national self-determination in the southern states, where the Negroes form a majority of the population."[156]

This idea was not only absurdly impractical, it went against the general idea of African Americans that they belonged to America and must seek full equality with other Americans. Garvey had indeed struck a chord by emphasising difference, but the generally accepted aim was full

in M. Matusevich (ed.), *Africa in Russia, Russia in Africa: Three Centuries of Encounters*, Trenton, NJ: Africa World Press, 2007.

153 According to McClellan, "Black *Hajj*..." (note 152), the six who went with Awooner-Renner were Oliver Golden (an agricultural scientist, graduate of Tuskegee, who worked for several years in Central Asia), accompanied by his then wife Bessie "Jane" Golden"; Otto Hall; Aubrey Bailey, a Jamaican-American; Moses Coleman; and a Liberian tailor, Kolliseleh Tamba (p. 64). However, according to Harry Haywood the group that he joined in 1926 (who may have come at different times) comprised Otto Hall, Bankole, O. and J. Golden, Harold Williams, Roy Mahoney and Maude White: H. Haywood, *Black Bolshevik*, Chicago: Liberator Press, 1978, pp. 66-7, 217, quoted in Cedric J. Robinson, *Black Marxism: The Making of the Black Radical Tradition*, Chapel Hill and London: University of North Carolina Press, 1983, p. 223.

154 T. Draper, *American Communism and Soviet Russia*, New York: Viking Press and London (1960), pp. 332-5.

155 Ibid., p. 339.

156 Ibid., p. 351.

citizens' rights within the USA. Many African American Communists protested at the new slogan, though some strongly backed it, including especially Harry Haywood who was said to have been impressed by Garvey's success and sought to channel "black nationalism" in a direction more acceptable to Communists; he defended the new policy against other American Communists in an open debate in the periodical *Communist International* in 1928.[157] Haywood also helped draft the "Native Republic" programme for South Africa, and it seems that the Comintern thought the "Negro question" was similar there and in the United States; the decisions on both countries were explicitly linked in the same Sixth Congress resolutions.[158] But of course there was the vital difference that Black people were a minority in one country and the indigenous majority in the other.

At the Congress a 32-member Negro Commission was set up, with Kuusinen as chairman, also including Hall, Haywood and James P. Ford, two other African Americans, and Bunting of South Africa.[159] At the same time the Profintern started to play an important part in Communist activities in the black world, seeking as elsewhere to promote separate, Communist-affiliated trade unionism. The International Trade Union Committee of Negro Workers (ITUC-NW) was set up under the Profintern in 1928. According to information reaching the French Ministry of the Colonies, it was founded in Hamburg on 31 July 1928, and its newspaper the *Negro Worker* appeared that month in English, followed by a French edition, *L'Ouvrier Nègre*, in September 1928.[160] It seems the organisation may have been called originally the International Negro Workers' Information Bureau, in whose name the first issue of the *Negro Worker* appeared on 15 July 1928; it was headed by James W. Ford.[161]

---

157 Ibid., pp. 346-51; H. Haywood, *Negro Liberation*, New York: International Publishers, 1948, chapter VII, "The Negro Nation"; Robinson (note 153), pp. 223-8.

158 E. Johanningsmeier, "Communists and the Black Freedom Movements in South Africa and the United States: 1919-1950", *Journal of Southern African Studies* vol. 30 no. 2, June 2004, pp. 155-80 (p. 169).

159 Draper (note 154), p. 345.

160 Dewitte (note 99), p. 188, quoting note on "Comité syndical international des ouvriers nègres" in Slotfom III, 47, s/doss in Archives SOM.

161 Wilson (note 32), pp. 176-8.

The factional fighting among the American Communists was finally ended in talks in Moscow in 1929, with a new leadership imposed and its opponents expelled,[162] and the now united and obedient CPUSA had to follow the Comintern decision on the African Americans. Hall, Ford and Briggs fell into line, and Haywood became National Secretary of a new body formed in November 1930, the League for Struggle for Negro Rights, replacing the ANLC.[163] The poet and novelist Langston Hughes, drawing closer to Communism though he never actually joined the Party, became President of the League.[164]

Otto Huiswoud attended the Convention in Kingston in August 1929, as delegate of the ANLC, and debated with Garvey a motion he (Huiswoud) proposed that "The Negro problem can only be solved by International Labour co-operation between white and black labour"; he criticised ideas of "Back to Africa" and "Black Capitalism".[165] This debate summed up the basic disagreement between Communist ideas on the one hand and ideas of African or Black people's solidarity on the other. That disagreement was to remain, as Communists would always insist that class struggle overrode any racial questions, while what struck Africans and people of the Diaspora most was that they, as black people, were suffering oppression and exploitation *as a race*. They were aware that other people were oppressed also, and could feel sympathy with them. But they felt that they as a race were collectively despised and oppressed, and so felt special affinity with other black people everywhere, including those who were not suffering so much. The corrupt and oppressive Liberian regime was seen as one of the very few national governments run by black people, to be defended if white colonialists threatened it. A well-to-do African or African American businessman was likely to be admired as one of a disadvantaged race who had made good, not resented as a class enemy. When the Lagos Chief Oluwa returned home in 1921 after winning his land case in London he was greeted by 10,000 people at the quayside, congratulating a well-off traditional ruler on winning a sum eventually assessed at £22,500, a small

---

162   Draper (note 154), pp. 406-29.

163   Ibid., p. 353.

164   A. Rampersad, *The Life of Langston Hughes, Vol. I: 1902-1941, I, Too, Sing America*, OUP 1986, pp. 216-20.

165   K. Post, *Arise Ye Starvelings*, The Hague: Martinus Nijhoff, 1978, pp. 2-5.

fortune in the 1920s. The answer to European companies' profiteering and exploitation was seen as Africans competing successfully with them in business—or attacking regimes that prevented them from doing so; in West Africa there were several ventures by Africans to compete with the European firms in produce buying and export, shipping and other business, but their own mistakes, and the many obstacles put in their way, caused them to fail.[166]

Such attitudes were racial, but only defensively racial, and were bound to be popular. Communists sometimes understood this, but they still insisted that the class war was what mattered. Their attitude, not easy for those outside the party to accept, was nonetheless sincerely non-racial and anti-racist, and a number of Black Americans became convinced Communists, the most prominent in the late 20s and early 30s being James W. Ford. In 1928, the ranks of Black Communists in the USA were joined by the Trinidadian George Padmore.

Padmore, Wallace Johnson and Small

Malcolm Ivan Meredith Nurse, who was to become famous under his adopted name of George Padmore (1901/2-59), was born and brought up in Trinidad, and went in 1924 to study in the USA; after decades of emigration from the West Indies to the USA, quotas were imposed on immigrants from there and other countries by US laws in 1921 and 1924, but Nurse got onto a quota and was admitted to study at Fisk University, Tennessee. He was noted there as a speaker, especially on colonial issues, but did not take a degree there before going on to Howard University in Washington, another leading Black American university. By then he had joined the Communist Party. He defended its cause openly as a student activist, but by 1928 he had adopted his *nom de guerre* to cover up at least some of his tracks in his activity for the Party. He had some experience in journalism since his young days in Trinidad, and now began editing, with Moore, a Communist newspaper, called first the *Negro Champion* and then the *Liberator*.[167]

166   S.K.B. Asante, *Pan-African Protest: West Africa and the Italo-Ethiopian Crisis 1934-1941*, London: Longman, 1977, pp. 27-30.

167   J.R. Hooker, *Black Revolutionary: George Padmore's Path from Communism to Pan-Africanism*, New York: Praeger, 1970, pp. 1-9.

Padmore attended the second Congress of the LAI, at Frankfurt in July 1929, along with other delegates including Ford of the Trade Union Unity League, Tiemoko Garan Kouyate of the Ligue de Défense de la Race Nègre (possibly the only African present), and Katayama.[168] However, there was also William Pickens representing the NAACP; the full rigorist line of the Comintern, telling Communists to regard the NAACP and other non-Communist opponents of racial domination and imperialism as enemies, was imposed after that Congress.

After the Frankfurt Congress Padmore and Ford helped prepare for a black workers' conference, and Padmore returned to the USA and attended the Trade Union Unity League convention in Cleveland. He then travelled to Russia with the CPUSA leader William Z. Foster, to deliver a report on the Cleveland convention in December 1929. Padmore, who had been refused a re-entry permit to the USA, stayed on in Russia, working for the RILU and lecturing on colonialism at Kutvu. He also wrote for the *Moscow Daily News*, an English-language newspaper then edited by Borodin, now returned from China. He was also said to have been elected to the Moscow City Soviet.[169] He lived the privileged life of the Communist rulers, which contrasted starkly with the life of the majority; Margaret McCarthy, a British mill worker from Lancashire who spent some months as a working-student at the Profintern headquarters, recalled later, "I know of one chief of the Negro section of the Profintern who even had apartments at two hotels for his sole personal use at that time."[170] Later he did higher-level and more confidential work for the Comintern or Profintern. He joined a commission to investigate charges of "left-wing deviationism" against one of the Chinese Communist leaders, Li Li-san, who had been removed from the Chinese party's Politburo.[171]

The First International Congress of Negro Workers was held in Hamburg from 7 to 9 July 1930, after the British government had refused permission for it to be held in London. In Hamburg the German Communist Party, whose leader Ernst Thälmann lived there, had good

168   H. Kublin, *Asian Revolutionary: The Life of Sen Katayama*, Princeton University Press, 1964, pp. 319, 333; Hooker (note 167), pp. 12-13.

169   Hooker (note 167), pp. 14-16; Wilson (note 32), pp. 212-17.

170   M. McCarthy, *Generation in Revolt*, Heinemann 1953, p. 189.

171   Padmore (note 96), p. 297.

relations with the city administration. Most of those who wanted to go to the Congress from colonial territories were denied passports, and Communist archives have revealed some of the problems faced in organising the Hamburg gathering of "agitators". Some were shadowed by detectives in Britain or, it was reported, prevented from sailing with a German shipping line because of British pressure; some Africans were stranded in Berlin and Padmore had to seek help for them.[172]

Only seventeen delegates eventually attended the Hamburg conference, which set out guidelines for action by Black workers in many countries through independent working-class organisations[173] and elected a new ITUC-NW. The Committee established its headquarters in the waterfront district of Hamburg, at 8 Rothesoodstrasse. Communist maritime activity had been organised by the German Communist Albert Walter for some years from Rothesoodstrasse,[174] and Hamburg was a useful location for distribution of the newspaper through seamen, as well as local Communist support. In Hamburg the ITUC-NW published the *Negro Worker*, which had new serial numbers starting in January 1931; the first two issues had the title *International Negro Workers' Review*,[175] but then the former name was resumed. Ford was the first editor; a few months later he was succeeded by Padmore, who edited the *Negro Worker* from 1929 to 1933, and at some point became Secretary of the ITUC-NW.[176] Ford returned to the USA and contested the Presidential election of 1932 as the Communist vice-presidential candidate.

Some Africans managed to get to the Hamburg conference despite the obstacles: E.F. Small from Gambia: E.S. Sachs from South Afri-

172   Wolf-Peter Martin, "The 'Negro Question' and the Comintern", paper given at the "Africa in the World" conference, 50th Anniversary Civic Celebration at Manchester commemorating the 1945 Pan-African Congress, in October 1995.

173   Hooker (note 167), pp. 17-19.

174   J. Valtin, *Out of the Night*, Heinemann 1941, p. 92. There is plenty more about Walter and the Communist activity among seamen in this book, by a leading participant who later ceased working for the Comintern. The book is a good read but needs grains of salt.

175   Hooker (note 167), p. 18.

176   Wilson (note 32), pp. 212-20; Hooker (note 167), pp. 17-21. Valtin (note 174) gives a colourful but doubtful account of how Ford was replaced by Padmore (pp. 275-6).

ca; Joseph Ekwe Bile, a Cameroonian long resident in Germany; and from Nigeria Frank Macauley, son of Herbert Macauley, leader of the NNDP. Kouyate was not there; according to Dewitte[177] he was not invited, because the CGTU and the Profintern were annoyed at his initiatives to help Black seamen in France. However, as often he was forgiven, and joined the new ITUC-NW; he also went with Padmore to the Fifth Congress of the RILU in Moscow in August 1930.[178]

Edward F. Small (1890-1957) had recently been linked with a major strike, one of the few in sub-Saharan Africa (apart from South Africa) up to that time. He was one of the Aku community of The Gambia (an offshoot of the Creoles of Sierra Leone, and mainly of Yoruba descent), and worked as a clerk and a teacher. He founded the *Gambia Outlook and Senegambia Reporter* in 1922. He joined the NCBWA in 1920 and was on its delegation to London in that year; later he was abroad from 1922 to 1926. He was already known for radicalism and willingness to hold "mass meetings" before he organised the Bathurst Trade Union (BTU) in 1929. In October 1929 4-500 employees of the Seamen's Society, working on coastal steamers, went on strike over wage cuts, and the BTU, which the Seamen's Society now joined, backed the action. The strike went on for 62 days and was joined by many port and maritime workers, until the Chamber of Commerce agreed with the BTU, on 16 November, on union recognition, pay rises and no victimisation.[179]

There were some other strikes in colonial Africa in the inter-war era—besides the Sierra Leone rail strike of 1926 there were others in Senegal, including a well organised seamen's stoppage at Saint-Louis in 1928.[180] But the Gambian strike, though it took place in a very small

---

177   Dewitte (note 99), pp. 202-3.

178   Wilson (note 32), p. 185.

179   An account of the strike was given in the *Monthly Circular of the Labour Research Department* of January 1930, which also spoke of the "effects upon the workers of capitalist rationalisation", referring to the recent creation of UAC. This account was reproduced by Padmore in *The Life and Struggles of Negro Toilers*, pp. 91-5. See also A. Hughes and A. Perfect, "Trade Unionism in The Gambia", *African Affairs* vol. 88 no. 363, October 1989, pp. 549-72 (pp. 552-5). On Small, see Langley (note 147), pp. 136-9.

180   N. Bernard-Duquenet, *Le Sénégal et le Front populaire*, Paris: Harmattan, 1985, pp. 48-50.

colony, had more impact than most others. The BTU had support in Britain from the Labour Research Department, which had been loosely linked with the Labour Party but now worked closely with the LAI, both being repudiated by the Labour Party; the LRD probably helped Small set up the BTU.[181] However, police action against the strikers also led to protests from many in the Labour Party—by December 1929 five constituency Labour Parties, four local Cooperative Societies, ten trades councils, four national trade unions and seven trade union branches had demanded an inquiry. The Under-Secretary of State for the Colonies in the Labour government, Drummond Shiels, while sharing officials' hostile view of Small who was regarded as a dangerous dissident linked with Communism,[182] decided that it was best to encourage trade unionism in the colonies with a view to keeping it "on sound and constitutional lines", as he put it in a minute of 11 April 1930. The Colonial Secretary, Lord Passfield (Sidney Webb), then sent a circular in September 1930 calling for annulment of any law making the formation of trade unions a criminal offence, and for legislation to allow them to be legally registered.[183]

Frank Macaulay was one Hamburg delegate who was involved the following year in an effort to start a new trade union, perhaps hoping to follow the Hamburg recommendations, in Nigeria. This also involved one of the leading African anti-colonialist campaigners of the inter-war era, Isaac Theophilus Akunna Wallace Johnson (1894/5-1965) of Sierra Leone, who is stated by many studies to have been at Hamburg also. While Wallace Johnson contacted Padmore and the ITUC-NW about that time, research into Communist documents now suggests serious doubts about whether he attended the Hamburg Conference.[184] This is one of several unresolved questions about the life of a leading "agitator". Macaulay was certainly at Hamburg, but there is mystery about him also. The *Negro Worker* and the official report of the conference[185] state that he represented his father's party, the NNDP. That was an

181 Hughes and Perfect (note 179), p. 554n.

182 Langley (note 106), p. 138. Some of the reports of Small's Communist connections, mentioned here, are doubtful.

183 P.S. Gupta (note 135), pp. 143-4.

184 Personal information from Holger Weiss.

185 Quoted by Wilson (note 32), p. 184.

un-revolutionary party which Communists could well have considered "bourgeois-nationalist misleaders", and while it might have been approached even so—because of the extreme ignorance in Moscow about West African affairs—it would have been strange for Herbert Macaulay to annoy the British unnecessarily by sending his son to a conference that they were busy trying to thwart. No published sources give any clue as to how the younger Macaulay came to be at Hamburg. Many Nigerians could have known about Communist ideas and activities, but who did Macaulay contact, and where and how?[186]

Wallace Johnson was born in Wilberforce, a district of Freetown, to a poor Creole family (the Freetown Creoles were collectively a privileged group, but had considerable income/class differences among themselves). After limited education he took on various jobs; he became a clerk with the Customs in 1913 but was sacked for involvement in a strike, the start of a long career of resistance to authority. In the First World War he served as a clerk with the Carrier Corps in various campaigns. Then he returned to Sierra Leone, working in various jobs for Freetown City Council.[187]

For some years after 1926 there is some mystery about his activities, even after the thorough study of his life and work by LaRay Denzer, the major source of information on Wallace Johnson for other scholars. She writes of those years in his life,

Legend predominates, and it is a legend which Wallace-Johnson himself fostered. A natural-born story-teller, he used the mystery of this cloak-and-dagger episode in his life to enhance his image as a radical working against tremendous odds.[188]

The year 1926 saw a railway strike in Sierra Leone and financial scandals in Freetown City Council. The railway strike lasted for six weeks (12 January-26 February) and was backed by a Committee of Citizens

---

186 British Colonial Office and MI5 documents that I have seen do not give a clue; I have to urge others to find out more, probably by research in Nigeria.

187 LaRay Denzer, "I.T.A. Wallace-Johnson and the West African Youth League: A Case Study in West African Radicalism" PhD, Birmingham, 1973, pp. 1-16; L. Spitzer, *The Creoles of Sierra Leone: Responses to Colonialism, 1870-1945*, Wisconsin, 1974, pp. 181-2. Wallace Johnson's name can be spelt with or without a hyphen; he normally used a hyphen. His date of birth, normally given as 1895, was put as 6 February 1894 on his tombstone (Denzer, p. 1).

188 Denzer (note 187), p. 26.

including Bankole-Bright and the Mayor of Freetown, Cornelius May. The British government of Sierra Leone was appalled at the African elite backing a strike, and determined to win what it saw as a "trial of strength" against both; it did win, the strikers returning to work on the government's terms.[189] At that moment of official anger against the Creoles, the government ordered an inquiry into the City Council, an important arena for Creole political activity. As a result some malpractice was discovered, and the elected Council was dissolved in December 1926 and replaced by an appointed Municipal Board.[190]

The President of the Railway Workers' Union who led the strike was E.A. Richards, a fitter. In the Comintern archives it is recorded that Richards, President of the Sierra Leone Railway Workers' Union, was on a list of people invited to the Brussels conference. He did not go there, but he was mentioned as staying at a Moscow hotel during the tenth anniversary celebrations in November 1927. According to LAI documents in the Comintern archives studied by Professor Hargreaves, Richards declined at that time to attend a meeting of the LAI General Council in Brussels, but nominated Awooner-Renner to represent the Sierra Leone railwaymen.[191] Hargreaves comments that "This seems a bit mysterious" and it is "just possible" that Richards was Wallace Johnson. Wilson's study of Communist anti-colonialism in the inter-war era mentions him as attending the tenth anniversary celebrations, but not that he was or could have been Wallace Johnson.[192] In fact it was much more probably the real E.A. Richards, who had just led a strike which could have been considered well deserving of invitations to Brussels and Moscow. If so, there is an untold story to be unearthed about the Sierra Leonean railwaymen's leader going to Moscow in 1927. According to a report by Münzenberg in *International Press Correspondence of the Comintern* (abbreviated *Inprecorr*), an official bi-weekly Comintern

189   A.J.G. Wyse, "The 1926 Railway Strike and Anglo-Krio Relations: An Interpretation", *International Journal of African Historical Studies* vol. 14 no. 1, 1981, pp. 93-123; A.J.G. Wyse, *H.C. Bankole-Bright and Politics in Colonial Sierra Leone, 1919-1958*, CUP 1990, pp. 69-73; Denzer (note 187), pp. 18-21; R.L. Buell, *The Native Problem in Africa*, New York: Macmillan, 1928, vol. I, pp. 888-90.

190   Wyse, *H.C. Bankole-Bright* (note 189), pp. 76-9; Buell (note 189), pp. 882-7.

191   Hargreaves (note 90), pp. 258-9, quoting Comintern LAI archives.

192   Wilson (note 32), p. 153.

publication, about that time Richards joined Clara Zetkin, one of the leading German Communists, and Lenin's widow Nadezhda Krupskaya in presiding over a congress of the Friends of Soviet Russia.[193] Three years later, according to Denzer, Wallace Johnson attended the Hamburg conference in July 1930, using the name of E.A. Richards and representing the Railway Workers' Union.[194] As already noted, Wallace Johnson may well not have been there; the person using the name of E.A. Richards may have been the real E.A. Richards, or another delegate using the same alias.

I.T.A. Wallace Johnson may have worked as a seamen for some years after 1926, but this seems uncertain.[195] The mists lift to show Wallace Johnson toiling as a clerk (his earlier occupation) at Sekondi in Gold Coast in 1929, and moving with his wife—one of four that he had in the course of his life—to Lagos in 1930.

Communist eyes on colonial Africa

While Nzula said in South Africa a few months later that the Hamburg conference had "created a stir in this country",[196] there were limits to what the delegates could achieve back home. Small was never to repeat his brief moment of militant glory; the BTU split in 1933-35, with British encouragement.[197] But Wallace Johnson, who was in contact with the ITUC-NW, helped found the African Workers' Union (AWU) in Lagos in June 1931, at a meeting on the premises of Nigeria Press Ltd, a firm owned by T.A. Doherty, a leading Lagos elite figure and member of the Legislative Council; Frank Macaulay was among about 200 other people present.[198] It is difficult to tell what those founding the Union were planning or hoping for; in fact it made little impact. Doherty was no proletarian, and as Wallace Johnson had worked as a clerk, it is pos-

193   *Inprecorr,* 7 December 1927, quoted in Wilson (note 32), p. 153n (p. 334).

194   Denzer (note 187), pp. 18-19.

195   L. Spitzer and L. Denzer, "I.T.A. Wallace Johnson and the West African Youth League," *International Journal of African Historical Studies* vol. VI no. 3, 1973, pp. 413-52 and vol. VI no. 4, pp. 565-601; p. 418.

196   Minutes of 9th CPSA Conference, document no. 90 in Davidson *et al.* (eds) (note 130), Vol. 1, pp. 251-2.

197   Hughes and Perfect (note 179), pp. 556-7.

198   Denzer (note 187), pp. 43-4.

sible that any "workers" at that meeting came from that category of employee, a relatively privileged one among Africans. Wallace Johnson was probably very far from organising a militant workers' organisation such as Padmore and the RILU hoped for.

Later in 1931 Frank Macauley died in Lagos. The *Negro Worker* of October-November 1931 reported his death, saying that on his return he had set out to help the workers of Nigeria "free themselves from the reformist and petty bourgeois tendencies of the Democratic Party and other nonworking-class organizations"; it also reproduced a letter from him shortly before his death, expressing the wish to receive advice on a programme for "our struggle".[199] This adds to the mystery about him mentioned above, for the NNDP was headed by his own father and he was supposed to have represented the party at Hamburg.

Wallace Johnson was for a time acting editor of one of the African-owned daily newspapers of Lagos, the *Nigerian Daily Telegraph*, and this may have added to British suspicions of that paper, also aroused when it subscribed in 1930 to the Press Service of the LAI.[200] In that year the newspaper was bought by a company owned by T.A. Doherty—involved in Wallace Johnson's trade union venture—and two partners.[201] But the British were not seriously worried in Nigeria, despite the events in the North a few years before; in 1931 a senior police officer's view on "Communist and revolutionary movements" was, "It may be said that up the present these movements have not shown themselves to any great extent in Nigeria." [202]

The *Negro Worker* carried in September 1931 an article headed, "What the Workers of Sierra Leone Should Do. Open Letter from the ITUC-NW to the Workers of Sierra Leone", speaking of recruiting for

---

199   *Negro Worker* vol. I no. 10/11, October-November 1931, quoted in Wilson (note 32), p. 243n.

200   *Nigerian Daily Telegraph*, 22 July 1930, enclosed with Governor of Nigeria to Secretary of State, 15 August 1930, file CO 583/174/1, National Archives, London.

201   F.I. Omu, *Press and Politics in Nigeria 1880-1937*, Longman, 1978, pp. 66-7. In 1931 Duse Mohammed Ali, who had arrived to settle in Nigeria the year before, became editor of the *Nigerian Daily Telegraph* (ibid.).

202   Major G.N. Faux-Powell, Commissioner of Police, to Under-Secretary of State, "Memorandum on the Organisation of the Nigerian Police", sent to Under-Secretary of State 28 October 1931, pp. 22-3, file CO 323/1150/18, National Archives, London.

the railway workers' union, organisation of seamen's and dockworkers' unions and others, and the need to struggle particularly for the right to organise and to strike, improvements in labour conditions, and freedom of assembly, speech and the press; this may well have been the work of Wallace Johnson.[203]

Another contributor to the *Negro Worker* was a Kenyan who had not gone to the Hamburg conference—though he was incorrectly reported to have gone there—but was in contact with the militants working under Comintern direction. This was Johnstone Kenyatta, later known as Jomo Kenyatta, who had contacted the militants after going to Britain to pursue, through un-revolutionary means, the claims of the new Kikuyu Central Association (KCA).

Born probably in 1897-98, he was enrolled under the name Kamau wa Ngengi at the Church of Scotland mission school at Thogoto, but was coming to use the name Kenyatta in the 1920s, when he worked as a stores clerk and meter reader and slowly became interested in politics, joining the KCA in 1927.[204] He became General Secretary and editor of the KCA newspaper *Muigwithania* when it started publication in May 1928. In *Muigwithania* he expressed support and praise for the British government, the empire, chiefs and missionaries. But this did not make the colonial authorities feel sure of him as he rode around the Kikuyu country on a motor-cycle starting new KCA branches. At that time there was a growing rift between the Kikuyu Association (KA), dominated by Koinange wa Mbiyu and other chiefs and supported by missionaries, and the more critical KCA. The government was concerned to see the KCA winning more support; however, when the KCA decided to send Kenyatta to London in 1929 to deliver a petition to the Colonial Office, the authorities in Nairobi did not stop him leaving in February 1929.[205]

---

203   *Negro Worker* vol. I no. 9, 15 Sept. 1931, cited in Wilson (note 32), pp. 217-18.

204   J. Murray-Brown, *Kenyatta*, London: Allen & Unwin, 1972, pp. 33-113. Kenyatta's year of birth was often given as several years earlier; in fact it is not known. Murray-Brown notes that when young the future president wore Maasai ornaments called *kinyata*.

205   Ibid., M.S. Clough, *Fighting Two Sides: Kenyan Chiefs and Politicians, 1918-1940*, Niwot, CO: University Press of Colorado, 1990, pp. 19-64, pp. 91-134.

In England Kenyatta was welcomed and helped by West African students, and met Norman Leys, McGregor Ross, and Church of Scotland missionaries in Edinburgh. Soon after arrival he met the Governor of Kenya, Edward Grigg, who was in London then, and gave him the petition, also discussing the two main points he had been told to raise, the land question and the call for the release of Harry Thuku; the petition in fact also dealt with the compulsion on Africans to work for Europeans, the obligation to carry a *kipande*, and the ban on growing of Arabica coffee by Africans. The petition achieved nothing, unless, perhaps, it contributed to the decision to release Thuku at the end of 1930.

According to the Special Branch, which was told to follow his movements from an early stage, Kenyatta met Saklatvala and another leading anti-imperialist, Elinor Burns. He also met Bridgeman, and travelled to the Soviet Union. Ross found in August 1929 that Kenyatta had left for Moscow; on 4 October he returned to London.[206] Kenyatta probably went to Moscow with the idea of seeking a new source of support for his cause. But strangely little seems to be known about that 1929 journey. To Ross and others he said that an African American "commercial traveller of sorts" had offered to take him on a "business trip", all expenses paid, to Germany and Russia. This American may well have been a Communist agent. But there is no evidence that Kenyatta attended the Frankfurt Congress of the LAI on 22-31 July. In Moscow, if he saw any Comintern officials, they most probably encouraged him to work with the CPGB, which he did on his return, at least by contributing to its publications.

On 27 October 1929 a long article under the name of Johnstone Kenyatta appeared in the *Sunday Worker,* a British Communist paper. Written in the form of an interview, it was headed "Give us Back our Land", and declared, "The present situation means that once again the natives of the colony are showing their determination not to submit to the outrageous tyranny which has been their lot since the British robbers stole their land." Going further, Kenyatta said, "Discontent has always been rife among the natives and will be so until they govern themselves." In January two more articles under his name appeared

---

206   Murray-Brown (note 204), pp. 114-19; A. Beck, "Some Observations on Jomo Kenyatta in Britain, 1929-1930", *Cahiers d'Etudes Africaines* vol. VI, 2me cahier, 1966, pp. 308-29.

in the new *Daily Worker*, "An African People Rise in Revolt" and "A General Strike Drowned in Blood", describing the events surrounding Thuku's arrest in 1922.[207]

Despite such Communist writing calculated to shock the authorities, Kenyatta remained in contact with the "reformist" Ross, who was able to arrange for him to meet Shiels, the recently appointed Undersecretary of State at the Colonial Office, on 23 January 1930. He was apparently striving, at that stage, to get back into favour with the "colonial liberals". Shiels had some understanding of their views and wrote to Governor Grigg that the KCA should be tolerated as long as it continued to follow "constitutional lines":

..something of the nature of the Central Association is springing up in most colonies, and must be regarded more or less as a permanent feature which Governments have to reckon with. [208]

But Shiels and his Secretary of State, Lord Passfield, did nothing to meet the grievances of the KCA, which Kenyatta repeated in the *Manchester Guardian* of 18 March 1930. The Association's five aims, he wrote there, were recognition of the legal right to land held by the tribe before white occupation, and prevention of further encroachment on "reserves"; an end to the hut tax for women; African representation in the Legislative Council; practical educational facilities; and permission to keep good customs and, through education, lead people towards willing abandonment of bad ones. This was probably a reference to female genital mutilation (FGM, commonly though wrongly called female circumcision), which was a burning issue among the Kikuyus because the Church of Scotland mission strove hard to end it.[209] Many Kikuyus opposed the abolition of a custom they saw as fundamental to their traditions. Kenyatta thought the KCA should not mix this issue with others such as the number one question of land; this was reasonable as the tradition being defended was a cruel and odious one, bound to be seen as such in Britain, but Kenyatta himself thought FGM could only be ended by a patient process of education, and, in his explanation of its importance in Kikuyu tradition,

---

207   Murray-Brown (note 204), pp. 119-33.

208   Ibid., p. 124. See also P.S. Gupta (note 135), pp. 193-4.

209   Clough (note 205), chapter 7.

he seemed almost to defend it. And in Kikuyuland the stand taken by the KA and the missionaries against FGM aroused opposition which the KCA exploited to gain popularity.[210]

Passfield issued in June 1930 a *Memorandum on Native Policy in East Africa* which reaffirmed the 1923 statement of policy on Kenya, but no concrete action was promised to improve the Kenya Africans' situation. There were no promises to reduce settler power by, for example, the common franchise which Leys wanted to see.[211] In September 1930 Johnstone Kenyatta returned to Kenya. But he was back again in May 1931, having been included among African delegates from Kenya, Uganda and Tanganyika sent to London to testify before the Parliamentary Joint Committee on East Africa. He had been included, with Parmenas Mockerie, only after protests by the KCA and by Ross, the ASAPS and others in London.

Kenyatta had become like one of McGregor Ross' family, and Ross welcomed him on his return. He also met Ross' friend Charles Roden Buxton (Conrad Noel's cousin), a Labour MP from 1929 to 1931, chairman of the Imperial and International Advisory Committees for years, and a leading Labour colonial affairs spokesman who visited several African countries. Going for walks on Hampstead Heath with Ross or Buxton, studying at Buxton's expense at the Quaker College at Selly Oak in Birmingham, attending ILP summer schools, attending discussions by the UDC among other groups, Kenyatta was well integrated into the circles of colonial liberals in Britain. His biographer Murray-Brown speaks of Kenyatta's stay with the Rosses at Hampstead at Easter in 1932:

They were typical days in the life of a member of the Hampstead set, with visitors from Africa home for tea and visits out to left-wing intellectuals, long walks over the Heath and drafting Kenyatta's letters to the papers.[212]

But the colonial liberal community, without intending it, caught Kenyatta in a sort of trap. It welcomed him and helped him in legally cor-

---

210   J. Kenyatta, *Facing Mount Kenya*, London: Secker & Warburg, 1938, chapter VI and pp. 273-8; Murray-Brown (note 204), pp. 134-51.

211   J.D. Kamoche, *Imperial Trusteeship and Political Evolution in Kenya, 1923-1963*, Washington: University Press of America, 1981, ch. III; P.S. Gupta (note 135), pp. 174, 179-87.

212   Murray-Brown (note 204), p. 156.

rect and non-Bolshevik attempts to gain redress for his people, and tried to use its contacts with the government. But none of these efforts—the letters to the press, the meetings, Kenyatta's evidence before the Parliamentary Select Committee and then before the Morris Carter Commission on Kenya land questions in 1932—achieved anything for the KCA or the Kikuyu people. Neither the Labour government nor MacDonald's National Government formed after the crisis of August 1931 made any difference to the Africans' situation in Kenya. Their failure to do so angered the less militant KA also; Koinange, who was also invited to give evidence to the parliamentary committee in 1931, was given the official guided tour often provided for "loyal" African chiefs, but his evidence to the committee made many demands about land, education, and African representation, and now the KA's relations with the government worsened. The KCA and KA were now able to work together to defend their people's land rights before the Morris Carter commission.[213] But that commission was never likely to make much difference to the settler regime, and eventually it did not. If Kenyatta (who never published his own story) concluded then that his Hampstead friends' "reformist" approach was getting nowhere, he had some cause. At any rate he left for Germany and the Soviet Union in August 1932.[214]

In June 1931 Kenyatta had attended a conference on colonial child welfare in Geneva. Although the Soviet leaders and also their Communist disciples cared little for the League of Nations, Ford attended that conference organised by the ILO, an agency of the League; he represented the LAI and ITUC-NW but was able to address the assembly—only to denounce it, however, for failing to see that all the evils the delegates were discussing were the inevitable result of colonialism. His speech was reproduced as a CPUSA pamphlet, *Imperialism Destroys the People of Africa*.[215]

In 1931 Padmore achieved more fame among Communist anticolonialists, and those attracted by their message, when his book *The Life and Struggles of Negro Toilers* was published by the *RILU Magazine* for the ITUC-NW.[216] Surveying the situations in the USA, South Africa,

213   Clough (note 205), pp. 154-67.
214   Murray-Brown (note 204), pp. 152-71.
215   Hooker (note 167), p. 25.
216   The addresses given were 59 Cromer St., London WC1 for the *RILU Magazine*,

British, French, Belgian and Portuguese colonies in Africa, and the West Indies, it included vehement condemnations of all non-Communist leaders of Black peoples' labour and political movements, such as "the social-fascist labour bureaucrats of the *Amsterdam International*, the *II International*, and the black reformist trade union leaders (Kadalie and Champion in South Africa, Randolph and Croswaith in the United States), as well as the national reformist misleader, Marcus Garvey..." (p. 6). This was in line with Moscow's policy at the time, which Padmore loyally reflected throughout, speaking for example of French plans to use African troops to attack the Soviet Union (pp. 33, 112)—something that the Soviet leaders professed to fear greatly, responding by encouraging propaganda among those troops.[217] Mentioning the US occupation of Haiti and Santo Domingo, and the outside intervention in Liberia, Padmore suggested also that US imperialism was encroaching on Ethiopia (pp. 75-7).

The book's main concern was with labour questions, and the role of the RILU or Profintern, which, Padmore said, had "mapped out a correct line for solving the national-race problem." He condemned white chauvinism in the trade union movement, which the Profintern was combating. "The Negro workers are the most exploited, the most oppressed in the world," he wrote, but "The white worker, in many cases even today, still regards the Negro as a pariah, and scornfully refuses to stretch out a helping hand to his black brother." (p. 122) Like all Communists he was, or made himself out to be, totally deluded about the Soviet Union: imperialist reports about forced labour in that country were lies, he said; it was "the only country that knows no oppression, knows no exploitation," and it supported "the revolutionary liberation movements of the workers and toiling peasants of all countries as well as the emancipatory struggles of the Negro toiling masses for self-determination." (pp. 111) *The Life and Struggles*, which was of course banned by colonial governments, was a well-researched, well-written and forceful work. Padmore, a talented and thorough writer, also wrote five other of the ITUC-NW's twenty-five pamphlets: *What is the International Trade Union Committee of Negro Workers?*, *Negro Workers and the Im-*

---

and 8 Rothesoodstrasse, Hamburg for the ITUC-NW.

217   Wilson (note 32), pp. 138, 140, 207-10.

perialist War, Forced Labour in Africa, American Imperialism Enslaves Liberia, and *Labour Imperialism and East Africa.*[218]

Stories circulated later of secret trips to Africa by Padmore at this time. One story mentions interrogation by the police in Dakar; if Padmore went there he might have been on the way to nearby Gambia, where he was said to have gone in April 1930. This was just a few months after the great Gambian strike which he was to describe at some length in *The Life and Struggles of Negro Toilers* the following year. Padmore, an experienced journalist, did not add any personal observation to that account, or any words indicating that he had been in Gambia. However, his journey there has been established,[219] though other secret journeys may have been invented.

There is some doubt about Padmore's secret journeys, but the Comintern was certainly trying to find good agents for spreading the message in Africa, by secret means. On 20 May 1930 the Eastern Secretariat of the ECCI sent to the Political Commission proposals for sending of instructors to "the Negro colonies" and for training of such instructors in Moscow. The note said instructors should be initially recruited from the British, French, American and Belgian Communist Parties and from students finishing their courses at Kutvu and the International Lenin School (another training school in Moscow, set up in 1926 for Westerners, who included some black students); and some students selected for those Moscow schools should be sent on a course to be permanently set up for "the training of instructors for the Negro colonies." The note called for the Communist Parties of Britain, France and Belgium, and the USA and other New World countries with large black populations, to send black students immediately to Kutvu and the Lenin School.[220]

Several Africans did study at Kutvu. The first Black African, as already mentioned, was probably Bankole Awooner-Renner, who published *This Africa,* an anthology of poems, in Moscow in 1928; in 1931-32 he was back in the Gold Coast, as editor of the *Gold Coast Leader* in

218   Hooker (note 165), p. 22.

219   By B. H. Edwards, *The Practice of Diaspora: Literature, Translation, and the Rise of Black Internationalism,* Cambridge, MA: Harvard University Press, 2003, pp. 248-9, quoting a report from the French Consulate in Bathurst. See also Hooker (note 167), p. 16; Wilson (note 32), pp. 212-21.

220   Document no. 87 in A. Davidson *et al.* (eds) (note 130), Vol. 1, pp. 240-1.

Sekondi; other journalistic and political activity followed, and he continued to proclaim support for Communism.[221] Several dozen Black Africans and West Indians are estimated to have studied at Kutvu and the Lenin School from 1925 to 1938. Although it was not publicly acknowledged, the programme of study included lessons in conspiratorial and underground work including espionage, guerrilla warfare, codes, arrest and interrogation, etc.[222]

But the organisations linked to Moscow sought the support of Africans and people of the Diaspora through public, overt means above all. In that their task was aided by the crimes of the colonial powers and the white racists of South Africa and the USA. One in particular aroused horror that was genuine and justified, however much it was exploited by Communists, in 1931: the case of the Scottsboro Boys, nine Black boys arrested on 25 March 1931 in Alabama while riding the trains—as hundreds of thousands of Americans did in the Slump—and quickly charged at the town of Scottsboro with the rape of two white girls on the same train. Although there was no good evidence then or later that any rape had occurred, eight of them were quickly sentenced to death as a white mob bayed for blood outside, filled with the hideous white psychosis prevalent in the Southern USA—and elsewhere—about black men and white women. But then opponents of the Southern tyranny intervened. International Labour Defence (ILD) and its allies in the CPUSA acted decisively to arrange proper defence for the boys—all teenagers except one aged 20—in an appeal.[223] The NAACP also tried to help them, and for several months there was a bitter and shameful battle between two rival defenders of justice for Black Americans. The Communists won and the NAACP withdrew from the case in January 1932.

American Communists aroused objections by their aggressive propaganda against the NAACP, suggesting that only they, the Communists, really cared about the Scottsboro victims. But the fact was that the ILD did act most promptly in the case and deserved credit for saving the

221   Asante (note 149).

222   McClellan (note 150), pp. 375-6, citing an official Soviet document of 9 September 1930.

223   D.T. Carter, *Scottsboro: A Tragedy of the American South*, revised edition Baton Rouge and London: Louisiana State University Press, 1979, chapters I-III.

boys from the electric chair; many African Americans respected them for this. The case was to drag on for years, through all the complexities of the American legal process. Meanwhile protests and rallies multiplied in 1931-32, with mothers of the victims often speaking; there were protests in many countries. Naturally the case aroused horror among Africans and people of the Diaspora.

Another issue that aroused concern among Africans and African Americans in the early 1930s was the seeming threat to the independence of Liberia, after a League of Nations commission investigated in 1930 the sale of Liberian labourers for work on plantations in Fernando Po in Spanish Guinea. This trade had been going on for some time, with other Liberians being sold for work in French Gabon (which got less publicity). The investigation, which followed a protest note to Liberia by the US State Department in June 1929, exposed exploitation of labour at both ends of the trade. In Liberia the recruiting of labourers for export was part of the general oppression of the "Aborigines" or "Tribesmen" by the Americo-Liberian ruling class. The indigenous people were subjected to forced labour within Liberia also, and the American researcher R.L. Buell reported that after Liberia's 1926 agreement with the Firestone company of Akron, Ohio for establishment of rubber plantations, Firestone arranged to pay officials for supply of labourers via chiefs. Buell heavily criticised the agreement under which up to a million acres of land was leased to the company for 99 years, in return for a loan to the chronically insolvent Liberian state, and his book in 1928—*The Native Problem in Africa*—led to the US government intervention.[224]

Following the League of Nations inquiry report President C.D.B. King of Liberia decreed an end to export of labour, but was forced then to resign and replaced by Edwin Barclay, sworn in on 3 December 1930. Then there were more League of Nations investigations into Liberia's internal situation, and years of discussions about plans for international supervision of the country's highly defective administration, to secure

224   I.K. Sundiata, *Black Scandal: America and the Liberian Labor Crisis, 1929-1936*, Philadelphia: Institute for the Study of Human Issues, 1980, pp. 1-47. See below (pp. 240-1) on Buell's book.

reforms.[225] In the end the Americo-Liberian settler regime promised some reforms to benefit the indigenes, and retained its independence.

During these years the attention of Africans and people of the Diaspora was concentrated on Liberia as never before. Many saw the Liberian government as a victim of imperialist schemes, including the Firestone agreement already in force and the plans put forward by the League of Nations for improved government under foreign supervision. Defenders of Liberia pointed out, rightly, that the Western colonial powers also used forced labour extensively, and suggested that the affair indicated double standards used to demonstrate that Black people were incapable of self-government.[226] Communists, while also opposing any imperialist moves against Liberia, saw things from a different angle.

Lamine Senghor and African and Caribbean militants in France

Relations between Black left-wing militants in France and the PCF were not easy, because of the Communists' insistence on running the show themselves. This much is clear from the history of radical anti-colonial organisations in Paris in the late 1920s and early 30s. It should be recalled always that that history, outlined in two valuable works in France—the major history of the Black militant movements by Dewitte,[227] and the wide-ranging study by Liauzu of anti-colonial movements relating to all the French colonies in the inter-war years[228]—has to rely heavily on reports in the Ministry of the Colonies, which were based on police and intelligence reports. This meant, in fact, that they came from informers among the small bands of militants. Liauzu cautions, in connection with the far-left arguments about the Rif war, that, "The reports from informers leave these disagreements in confusion,"[229] and this applies more generally. But there is no doubt about the tension between Africans and West Indians wanting to do things their own way, on the one hand, and the domineering PCF on the other.

---

225   Sundiata (note 224), pp. 55-78.

226   Ibid., chapters 3, 4 and 5.

227   Dewitte (note 99).

228   Liauzu (note 14).

229   Ibid., p. 130n.

In 1926 Lamine Senghor and others founded a Comité de Défense de la Race Nègre, CDRN, which later began producing a newspaper, *La Voix des Nègres*. Senghor was chairman of the CDRN and Joseph Gothon-Lunion secretary-general; Masse Ndiaye, a Senegalese ex-serviceman, was treasurer-general. There were several West Indians on the executive, and one other African who was to become, with Lamine Senghor, the most prominent anti-colonialist militant in France in the 1920s and 30s: Tiemoko Garan Kouyate. Born at Segou in French Sudan (now Mali) on 27 April 1902, Kouyate was one of the Western-educated minority called by the French of that period *évolués*. He went to the Ecole William Ponty at Goree in Senegal, where teachers and other African junior staff of the colonial administration were trained for decades, and the worked as a teacher in Ivory Coast in 1921-23. When it was decided to provide government scholarships for some AOF African staff to go to France, to the Ecole Normale d'Aix-en-Provence, for further training (as announced by an AOF decree of 12 September 1923), Kouyate was among the first to make the trip. But the students at Aix seem to have turned quickly to political agitation, perhaps of a normal enough sort but intolerable to the French authorities, who expelled three of them. Probably Kouyate was one of these; at any rate he stayed in France and worked for a time as an accountant with the Hachette publishing company in Paris. In the non-European left-wing circles he joined he was distinguished by his good education; he also had an African hair style, and remained a Muslim, though never bringing Islam into his political writing.[230]

Kouyate's hour was soon to come in the small band of black activists, but in 1926-27 the leading figure was Senghor. He was an indefatigable fighter, forever battling against tuberculosis and the effects of a wartime gas attack—he had only one working lung and was eventually considered 100 per cent incapacitated—as well as against imperialism and the Communists' efforts to keep anti-imperialism under their control. Many people joined the Committee, mostly West Indians, and there were reported to be about 500 by the end of the year; many may have been attracted by the declared "social" aims, which were very over-ambitious. When the CDRN ran out of money in late 1926, Senghor,

---

230   Dewitte (note 99), pp. 34-5, 130, 174-7.

who had tried to get backing from a variety of sources before without success, decided to approach the Communist Party for backing; he had never ceased to be a Communist himself. According to an informer codenamed "Désiré", the PCF offered a subsidy of 2,000 francs per month and this was apparently accepted; soon afterwards a first issue of *La Voix des Nègres* was published in January 1927.[231] But there were internal quarrels which led to the expulsion of Gothon-Lunion and were still unresolved when Senghor went to the Brussels congress. An extraordinary general meeting of the CDRN on 27 February re-elected Senghor as chairman, but the rest of the executive was opposed to his ideas. So, in March 1927, Senghor, Kouyate and another of the more radical faction, Vilfort Poujol, left the CDRN and immediately started forming a new organisation. In the same month a new issue of *La Voix des Nègres*, also called no. 1, was published, and followed a more strictly Communist line than the other issue.

In these squabbles among activists personal factors doubtless came in, but there was also a fundamental disagreement, the one already described, between the Communist view of the colonial situation and the common African or African-Diaspora view. The latter approach was the one preferred by Senghor, Communist though he was, and emerged in the January 1927 issue of *La Voix des Nègres*, for example in an article signed by the CDRN collectively on the use of the term *nègre*;[232] it declared that Black solidarity extended from the peasant of the "Senegalese bush" to the intellectual with a qualification from "European institutions of higher education", from the "sugar cane cutter" to the skilled worker "who follows the same profession as a White man and adapts like White people to their life and their ways and customs"[233]— which did not fit in with the Communist message that class mattered more than race.

In that January 1927 issue Senghor denounced "imperial brigandage" but did not call for independence, instead calling for an end to abuses of colonial rule, racism and inequality. All sorts of concerned people could make such calls, and there was no inconsistency in calling

---

231   Ibid., pp. 130-46.

232   While that term was used by racists, it was also adopted by black militants, as in this case; they preferred it to *noir*, which suggested a "black Frenchman".

233   Dewitte (note 99), p. 144.

for reforms or improvements in the colonised people's situation, while aiming one day to end that situation altogether. But the open call for independence in the March issue of *La Voix des Nègres*[234] indicated following of the Communist line.

During the CDRN episode—which coincided with the founding of the ENA among North Africans—the Communists' role was one of meddling but not effective control. But the new organisation founded by Senghor and his left-wing comrades was to be, of all the Black militant groups in inter-war France, both the longest-lasting and the one most under Communist control. This was the Ligue de Défense de la Race Nègre (LDRN). It too went through a phase of asserting Black and African solidarity as opposed to Communist class analysis, but failed; once again small numbers of enthusiasts, mostly with low-paid jobs or no jobs at all, found it impossible to raise enough funds, and the PCF was there offering money in return for following the party line. The LDRN was started in May 1927 in close alliance with the PCF, and with its financial support.

Senghor was elected chairman; Kouyate was secretary general, Stéphane Rosso treasurer-general. In June the first issue of the LDRN's newspaper, *La Race Nègre*, appeared. For years the leading "seditious" newspaper in the eyes of the French rulers of Africa, it adopted a defiant tone from the first issue. This included an article by Kouyate, under the pseudonym Dorarlie, on the question of naturalisation, making an important point: individual naturalisation was an "instrument of division" for the French rulers, but mass naturalisation would be beneficial to Africans and would pave the way for nationalism.[235] This was close to the ideas of Ralaimongo, who was then arousing the anger of the local colonial administration back in Madagascar by taking up local grievances in the Diego-Suarez area and had not abandoned his mass naturalisation idea. Kouyate's article is a reminder that calls for French citizens' rights for all Africans challenged the whole colonial order and were quite consistent with basic opposition to colonialism. In that vein, an article in *La Race Nègre* of March 1929 said mass naturalisation would involve access to education, full civil liberties, and local self-government.[236]

---

234   Quoted in ibid., p. 151.
235   Ibid., pp. 156-7.
236   J. Spiegler, "Aspects of Nationalist Thought among French-Speaking West Afri-

In June 1927 also, Senghor published a booklet, *La violation d'un pays*, with a preface by Vaillant-Couturier. It described the French colonisation of Africa as an allegorical tale, again recalling African soldiers' war service, with an allusion to Diagne; and it ended with the revolution of the oppressed:

The slaves became free! The citizens of each country headed the government of their state. They formed the brotherly alliance of free countries. VIVE LA REVOLUTION![237]

But Senghor, the life and soul of the LDRN, was an increasingly sick man, and spent long periods in the south of France, while he was also accused of misappropriating the Communist Party's subsidy to the LDRN (in fact he had largely handled the Ligue's business and funds himself). Lamine Senghor died at Fréjus on 25 November 1927. The arguments over the funds were forgotten and the fifth issue of *La Race Nègre*, not published until May 1928, included a tribute, emphasising Senghor's courage amid adversity. He was one of the half-dozen outstanding anti-colonial campaigners from Africa in the Western world in the 1920s and 30s, and was to be commemorated decades later in independent Senegal.

Meanwhile some Caribbean activists in France, led by Maurice Satineau and Georges Forgues, continued the CDRN and renamed it the Comité de Défense des Intérêts de la Race Noire (CDIRN), which paved the way for a new newspaper started by Satineau in February 1928, the *Dépêche Africaine*. This called for French citizenship to be granted selectively, an indication of its general ideas which were close to those of the SFIO, with Maran and other contributors calling for reforms within a continuing French empire.[238] West Indians may have been more inclined to adopt that approach—they were already French citizens, and to this day the movement for independence in the French West Indies is confined to a minority—though some supported the Communists and the idea of independence. Cautious as it was, the *Dépêche Africaine* evidently included enough criticism to be banned in Madagascar, where

cans 1921-1939", DPhil, Oxford, 1968, pp. 147-8.

237   Dewitte (note 99), pp. 160-61; Edwards (note 219), pp. 229-33.

238   Dewitte (note 99), pp. 224-40.

15 parcels of 1,300 copies of the third issue, smuggled in, were seized in the house of a Malagasy dentist at Diego Suarez in August 1928.[239]

Tiemoko Garan Kouyate and the LDRN

Kouyate remained secretary-general of the LDRN and was now its effective leader, though Emile Faure, an engineer and activist of French and African birth from Saint-Louis in Senegal, became chairman. Taken as a whole, Kouyate's political activity over fifteen years suggests that he probably saw independence as the right aim but preferred the African way of opposing imperialism to the Communist way. The two approaches had much in common, and that, as well as the PCF's money, could have persuaded Kouyate to surrender to the party line. But he did not surrender easily. For much of 1928 he struggled to continue the LDRN as an independent organisation; whether it was the cause or the effect of that, the PCF for a time halted its direct subsidies. According to a police informer's report (which can be believed in this case) Kouyate sought support from Gibarti of the LAI, but also from Garvey, who was now travelling to various countries; Henri Junod, chairman of the Bureau International de Défense des Indigènes in Geneva, and John Harris of the British ASAPS, two leading humanitarian and most un-revolutionary defenders of "natives"; some Haitian politicians; William Rappard, member of the Permanent Mandates Commission (which quite often criticised mandatory governments but wholly accepted colonialism); "James Weldon" (obviously James Weldon Johnson) of the NAACP; and Laurent Sambe, of the Union Congolaise in Belgium. Little money if any came in as a result, and Garvey ignored Kouyate when he visited Paris in October 1928; instead Garvey established his "headquarters for Europe", maybe briefly, at the offices of *La Dépêche Africaine*, although its ideas did not correspond with his own, as Maran said.[240]

The LDRN was inactive for much of 1928. *La Race Nègre* however produced a fifth issue in May and a sixth in October 1928. The May issue carried a proposal for a *Banque Nègre*—a Garvey-style proposal—by the Guadeloupean lawyer André Béton; this idea aroused interest

---

239   S. Randrianja, *Société et luttes anticoloniales à Madagascar (1896 à 1946)*, Paris: Karthala, 2001, p. 200.

240   Dewitte (note 99), pp. 178, 182, 238; Edwards (note 219), pp. 293-6.

but did not get off the ground. Kouyate was clearly pursuing a pan-African, broad-church approach including promotion of "Black business" and support for the democratic opponent of Diagne in Senegal in the elections of 1928: Galandou Diouf, who went to France to accuse Diagne of rigging the elections which he won. Diouf was accompanied by Lamine Gueye and by the former leader of the LUDRN, Tovalou Houénou, now based in Senegal and helping Diouf's campaign; they all joined the LDRN.[241] Diouf and his delegation failed to get any satisfaction about Diagne's election victory, and the efforts to continue the LDRN as an independent Black militant movement failed.

The LDRN's inclusive approach did not mean rejecting Communist ideas. In the October 1928 issue of *La Race Nègre* Stéphane Rosso supported the Comintern line while adding, referring to Black people's attitudes,

Probably they do not accept the Communist programme in its entirety, but they accept without reservations, as being in perfect agreement with their concept and their ideal, the part of that programme relating to the colonial question.

That Comintern policy, he said, was to support "the complete and absolute independence of colonial peoples."[242] Many non-Communists might indeed agree with this without wanting to come under direct Communist Party control, but the Communists wanted to assert control over radical anti-colonial movements. Kouyate succumbed to them in early 1929. In October 1928 Faure had put up money to make it possible for issue no. 6 of *La Race Nègre* to appear; he then became the owner of the newspaper's title, but he presumably could not go on subsidising it. At any rate, in January Kouyate and Rosso held talks with the PCF leading, so an informer reported, to agreement on subsidies, starting with 800 francs on 2 February 1929, in return for submission to the Communist line.[243]

241 Dewitte (note 99), pp. 178-86; E.D. Zinsou and Luc Zouménou, *Kojo Tovalou Houénou, Précurseur, 1887-1936: pannégrisme et modernité*, Paris: Maisonneuve et Larose, 2004, pp. 193-205. Tovalou Houénou afterwards spent some years in Paris, married an African American of Martinican origin, and then went back to Senegal where he died in obscure circumstances in 1936, possibly after falling ill in prison: Zinsou and Zouménou, pp. 206-10.

242 Dewitte (note 99), p. 186; Spiegler (note 236), p. 166.

243 Dewitte (note 99), pp. 186-90; Edwards (note 219), pp. 250-6.

Faure, as chairman of the LDRN, opposed the new line, as others did, but the subsidy was increased and *La Race Nègre* appeared again in March 1929. Kouyate's submission, however, was not total; the PCF was to find him an obstinately independent comrade, within limits. On 29 April 1929 he wrote a letter to Du Bois that came to the attention of the CAI, asking him for financial support from the NAACP.[244] However his organisation depended on Communist money, and he was himself a Communist anyway.

In July 1929 Kouyate attended the Frankfurt LAI conference and gave a strong speech against French colonialism. Then he visited Berlin and founded the German branch of the LDRN, headed by the Cameroonian Joseph Ekwe Bile (of this more later). He went on to visit the Soviet Union. Despite his good relations with Communists in Moscow and elsewhere, his organisation still remained fairly inactive for the rest of 1929; only at the end of the year did *La Race Nègre* appear again. But the LDRN held a protest meeting about Haiti in Paris on 20 December 1929, where Kouyate also spoke about the Congo Ocean Railway construction and 25,000 dead labourers; *La Race Nègre* of January 1930 wrote of the suppression of the AEF rising.[245] It had organised a protest meeting on 13 February 1929 where Kouyate said France had reduced the AEF's population from 15 million in 1880 to 2,850,000.[246]

Emile Faure was an important figure in the Ligue, sometimes taking charge when Kouyate travelled. The son of a manager of Maurel et Prom, a leading Bordeaux firm operating in Senegal, and a mother who was said to be a descendant of Samory, he had been educated in France, and with his engineering diploma had apparently prospered more than most of the Africans in France.[247] Having become the legal owner of the

244 Letter preserved in Mali archives, cited by Dewitte (note 99), pp. 191-2.

245 Circular on revolutionary activity, Paris, 31 Dec. 1929, file APA 10367, Cameroon Archives, Yaounde. Suspicions of actual involvement by the LDRN in France in the Kongo-Wara rising (see below, pp. 239-40) were however very improbable, as there was almost no way in which it could have made contact with almost wholly illiterate people in a remote area. Wilson (note 32) (p. 231) appears to believe that there was such involvement, but giving no source except the rather predictable suspicions of the AEF Governor-General.

246 Circular on revolutionary activity, Paris, 31 Dec. 1929, file APA 10367, Cameroon Archives, Yaounde.

247 Dewitte (note 99), p. 196; Edwards (note 219), pp. 255-6, 259.

newspaper's title in late 1928, as well as being chairman of the LDRN, he remained so despite his apparent opposition to Kouyate's acceptance of Communist direction. In fact, in the first months of 1930 Kouyate showed his independence and initiative again by establishing separate Black seamen's trade unions in Marseilles and Bordeaux. This was a challenge to both the Communist CGTU and the main trade union body, the CGT. Kouyate negotiated directly with shipping lines about inclusion of certain numbers of black seamen in their crews; at a time of stiff competition for berths this could have helped the African and Caribbean seamen, but Kouyate's initiative angered the Communists who denounced it in May 1930 as "counter-revolutionary". However, Communist leaders tolerated a good deal of rebellion on Kouyate's part. As noted earlier he seems not to have attended the Hamburg conference in July 1930,[248] though a British Colonial Office report placed him there, but in August 1930 he represented the LDRN at the Fifth Congress of the RILU (Profintern) in Moscow, which recommended new Communist initiatives among Black workers including seamen.

He spent three months in Russia and came back a more loyal Communist, to judge by the LDRN's newspaper, which now had a larger print-run (6,000 in February-March 1930) and became more Communist in its content.[249] During 1930 the Ligue was denounced frequently by a prominent right-wing writer, François Coty, in the daily *L'Ami du Peuple*. Coty, who collected his articles in a 1931 book entitled *Sauvons nos Colonies: le Péril rouge en pays noir*,[250] and another writer, Gustave Gautherot, who published a book and a long magazine article on the subject in the same year,[251] made a speciality of "exposing" and denouncing the Bolshevik threat to France's colonial empire. Many others had been doing this for years, in the colonialist monthly *L'Afrique Française* for example, but those two propagandists went all out to depict a vast and dangerous conspiracy centred on Moscow. Coty made the LDRN

---

248   Dewitte (note 99), pp. 202-3.

249   Ibid., pp. 197-210.

250   Spiegler (note 236), p. 174.

251   G. Gautherot, *Le bolchévisme aux colonies et l'impérialisme rouge*, Paris: Editions de la Vague, 1930; G. Gauthérot, "Le Bolchevisme en Afrique", *Renseignements Coloniaux* no. 7, 1930, supplement to *L'Afrique Française* vol. 40, no. 7, July 1930, pp. 418-29.

out to be much more formidable than the small band of campaigners actually was. Kouyate thought of legal action but then told Georges Sarotte, the LDRN's West Indian lawyer, not to proceed.

In late 1930 Faure and Abou Koite, secretary of the LDRN during Kouyate's absence in the USSR, rebelled against Kouyate's leadership. In the ensuing crisis the authorities backed Faure, owner of the title; the police raided the rue du Simplon offices and the homes of Kouyate and two of his comrades, and the archives of the LDRN were sealed up. There was now a clear breach in the Black activists' ranks, between Communists and those following a pan-African or Black solidarity approach. The LDRN was divided into two bitterly rival factions and each produced a new edition of *La Race Nègre*, insulting the other, in April 1931.[252]

While the legal ownership of the title was being decided in court, the Communist faction complied with the law by ceasing to use it, and published a new newspaper, *Le Cri des Nègres*, from July 1931. It appeared with the aid of the Profintern, and in June 1931 Kouyate, travelling to Berlin to attend the LAI Congress as representative of the LDRN, met the head of the ITUC-NW, George Padmore. Kouyate resumed work among the black seamen and port workers of France, but this time on behalf of the CGTU, which sought to recruit those workers into its own ranks.[253]

Le Cri des Nègres carried articles on themes which concerned Black and African people of varied political sympathies—the Colonial Exhibition of 1931, French rule in Madagascar, the US occupation of Haiti, the Scottsboro Boys—but it followed the Communist line closely, for example in denouncing the SFIO and LDH and talking of the threat of war against the USSR. Kouyate, Danaé and Rosso contributed a good deal of the copy. They highlighted the call for independence—"*Libérons nos Patries!*"—and drew from Padmore's recent publications which had been translated into French. The LAI as well as the ITUC-NW subsidised the newspaper.[254] Apart from the newspaper the LDRN was fairly inactive in the latter months of 1931, and in February 1932 a judge

252   Dewitte (note 99), pp. 210-16.

253   Ibid., pp. 283-8.

254   Ibid., pp. 288-94.

declared that Faure was the legal owner of the name of the LDRN and Kouyate had to hand over the files of the Ligue.

French authorities were particularly worried for years about the radical newspapers reaching Africa, through subscriptions or smuggling; African government employees in French Sudan, for example, were receiving "revolutionary propaganda" from Kouyate in 1931-32.[255] The Colonies Ministry heard in early 1932, apparently from an informer as usual, of people in Cameroon, Togo, AOF, Guadeloupe and French Guiana receiving Padmore brochures and SRI literature, apparently sent by the LRDN, and of correspondents of the LDRN in Cameroon being asked to choose two people to go to the USSR for studies.[256] This report, if correct, clearly referred to the Kouyate faction of the Ligue, and to the known Comintern instruction to recruit Africans for training as instructors about that time.[257]

West African 'constitutional' politics

An article in *La Race Nègre* in September 1927 said,

A Mahatma Gandhi could never stay out of prison in a French colony. In the English colonies of Africa, the Africans hold congresses, have outspoken and native newspapers, are in intellectual relations with the outside world.[258]

This difference between British and French rule in Africa was often noted at the time. It should not be overstated, because the public freedoms found in the Crown Colonies like Lagos and Freetown were not present in the Protectorate which covered the bulk of Nigeria, and were less in Eastern and Southern Africa, while they were found in one French territory, the Four Communes of Senegal, and Madagascar also had a flourishing press. But apart from those exceptions French Black

255 C.H. Cutter, "The Genesis of a Nationalist Elite: The Role of the Popular Front in the French Soudan (1936-1939)", in G. Wesley Johnson (ed.), *Double Impact: France and Africa in the Age of Imperialism, Westport*, CT: Greenwood Press, 1985, pp. 107-39 (p. 118). Cutter's brief account of the African and Caribbean militants' organisations in France has been superseded by Dewitte's work.

256 Typed notes headed "Rapport de Victor", 14 Feb. and 19 Feb. 1932, in File on Communist Propaganda in Box Cameroon AP II 29 & 30, Archives SOM, Paris/Aix.

257 See note 220 above.

258 Quoted in Spiegler (note 236), p. 159.

Africa had nothing like the higher education, the newspapers or the political organisations of the British West African Crown Colonies. The dominant politician of French Black Africa was Blaise Diagne, who was now such a complete French politician that he defended France's forced labour policies in Africa before the ILO, at a conference in 1930 which, despite his stance, adopted a Forced Labour Convention that France refused for years to ratify. Diagne was challenged only by the vigorous democratic opposition (fully accepting the French connection) led by Diouf and the *Périscope Africain* newspaper in the Four Communes.

In British West Africa, in contrast, there was the National Congress of British West Africa (NCBWA), typical of the respectful, cultivated elite nationalists of the inter-war era. Following the advice of Casely Hayford to "be constitutional", they sought by reasoning and persuasion to get a greater role for Africans, under the leadership of people such as themselves, in the running of the four British West African territories. The NCBWA met in full session in Freetown in January-February 1923, and in Bathurst in December 1925-January 1926, and its national sections organised their own activities for several years. The full Congress met again in Lagos in 1930. But on 11 August 1930 Casely Hayford died, and after 1930 the Congress continued only in Sierra Leone.

Besides the NCBWA there were two other nationalist bodies in British West Africa, the older ARPS in Gold Coast and the recently formed NNDP in Nigeria. But although they had many supporters, in those areas, where colonial rule was relaxed, it was not always the main focus of attention. Indeed, it sometimes seems to have mattered less than local political issues, especially those relating to chieftaincy which aroused strong feelings for years. In Lagos Colony, after the government recognition of the Eleko Eshugbayi in 1920, he was deposed by traditional procedures in 1925, and then an intense battle followed over his restoration, until this took place in 1931, with both traditional and "modern" (Western-educated) elite groups split.[259] In Gold Coast a long-running dispute between Nana Ofori Atta, Paramount Chief of Akyem Abuakwa, and two lesser traditional states, fought out in the courts up to the Privy Council in London, involved leading lawyers on

---

259   P.D. Cole, *Modern and Traditional Elites in the Politics of Lagos*, CUP 1975, chs. 5, 6.

one side or the other, and the government.[260] In such cases the colonial government was very much involved, but it was not a straight colonisers vs. colonised issue. However, besides the Akyem Abuakwa case there was a general division in the ARPS between the head chiefs and the more politically minded section, over the Native Administration Ordinance of 1927. This was an extension of "Indirect Rule", which Western-educated Africans generally opposed.[261]

Only limited numbers of Africans benefited from the lighter-handed form of British colonial rule. Far more, even in West Africa where there was not the aggravating factor of white settlers, suffered many impositions and restrictions and injustices, which occasionally aroused resistance. In one well remembered incident in 1929, women led mass protests among the Igbos of Nigeria, provoked by a census and fears that women would have to pay tax. While this was not in fact planned by the British, the rumour led to riots by women, starting in the Bende area in November 1929. Women led attacks on the new artificial chiefs created by the British ("Warrant Chiefs") and on European trading posts in many Igbo areas, in what came to be remembered as the "Aba riots" but in fact extended well beyond the town of Aba; Igbos recall them as the *Ogu Umunwanye*, the "women's war". They went on sporadically well into 1930, and led to shooting of protestors in several places, 32 being killed at Opobo.[262]

Among the more privileged groups of West Africans under British rule the nationalist movements that were to win independence took root. In 1925 sons of the British West African elite founded the West African Students' Union (WASU) in Britain, in the same spirit of peaceful criticism and campaigning as the older generation's NCBWA and ARPS. It was founded at a meeting in London on 7 August 1925, mainly through the initiative of Ladipo Solanke (c. 1880-1958), from Abeokuta in Nigeria, and Dr Herbert Bankole-Bright. Solanke qualified as a lawyer but devoted the rest of his life to WASU, which soon

---

260 B.M. Edsman, *Lawyers in Gold Coast Politics c. 1900-1945*, Uppsala, 1979, pp. 134-47. For more on this case see Chapter 4, p. 275.

261 D. Kimble, *Politics in Ghana 1850-1928*, Oxford: Clarendon Press, pp. 491-505.

262 A.E. Afigbo, *The Warrant Chiefs*, Harlow: Longman, 1972, chapters 6, 7; H.A. Gailey, *The Road to Aba*, University of London Press, 1971, chs. IV-VI; E. Isichei, *A History of the Igbo People*, Macmillan 1976, pp. 151-5.

eclipsed the African student bodies founded earlier, and for many decades provided a place for students to meet, debate and seek help, while its magazine *Wasu* was a forum for African ideas. The Union was where many future African politicians cut their political teeth.[263]

WASU's aims as stated at its foundation included acting as an information bureau and centre of research on Africa; promoting a spirit of self-help, unity and cooperation among members; presenting to the world a "true picture of African life and philosophy" and so making a definitively African contribution to the progress of civilisation; promoting a spirit of goodwill, better understanding and brotherhood between all people of African descent and other races; and "to foster a spirit of national consciousness and racial pride among its members." It was particularly concerned to oppose racism and the special colonial prejudice against educated Africans, but it was not a left-wing body at all, though Solanke spoke of a "united states of West Africa" and even a "United Africa" as a long-term aim.[264] The first president was Joseph Danquah of the Gold Coast (1895-1965), brother of Nana Ofori Atta; after law studies he was awarded a PhD for a thesis in Philosophy at University College, London in 1927 and then went home, practising as a lawyer and in 1931 founding the *West African Times*, later renamed the *Times of West Africa*. WASU's first secretary-general was Solanke, who in 1927 published *United West Africa at the Bar of the Family of Nations;* the first patron was J.E. Casely Hayford.

WASU devoted considerable attention to the problems faced by West Africans in Britain, including racism on the part of landladies and hotels. This was not ended by the court victory of Oluwole Ayodele Alakija, a Nigerian student who was then President of WASU, who successfully sued when a London hotel where he had booked a room by letter refused to lodge him when he turned out to be an African.[265] It had led to calls over many years for an African students' hostel

---

263   P. Garigue, "The West African Students' Union", *Africa* vol. XXIII no. 1, January 1952, pp. 53-69; H. Adi, "West African Students in Britain, 1900-60: The Politics of Exile", pp. 107-28 in D. Killingray (ed.), *Africans in Britain*, London: Frank Cass, 1994, pp. 114-16; G.O. Olusanya, *The West African Students' Union and the Politics of Decolonisation, 1925-1958*, Ibadan: Daystar, 1982.

264   Olusanya (note 263), pp. 9-10, quoting *West Africa* 15 August 1925; Asante (note 166), p. 49.

265   *West Africa* 5 March 1932; Adi (note 263), p. 116.

in London, which WASU took up when it was founded. But WASU aimed to create an independent hostel, for which Solanke went on a fund-raising tour to West Africa in 1929-32, while the Colonial Office thought of a hostel under its control. Eventually two hostels were opened in 1933-34.[266]

Challenges to colonialism in Africa: the Dualas and Madagascar

In two French territories of Africa groups of Western-educated Africans, while not forming parties, were beginning to call openly for self-government or independence—as the parties in British West Africa were not yet doing—by the late 1920s and early 30s. One group was among the Duala community of French Cameroun. The Dualas' position was ambiguous; they provided most of the vital junior administrative staff of the colonial regime at that time, but were the leading African critics of that regime in all French Africa except for Senegal and Madagascar. By no means all were critics; some, not only those employed by the French regime, backed that regime strongly. Robert Ebolo Bile, a trader who became a member of the Administrative Council of French Cameroun and a pillar of French rule who went at government expense to the Colonial Exhibition of 1931, was the brother of Joseph Ekwe Bile, the Communist in Germany. But generally the Dualas showed an independent spirit that constantly annoyed the French.

To resolve one problem with them, in 1926 the French government sought to end the long dispute over the land seized by the Germans from the Bonadoo (Bell) section of the Dualas in 1914. They initially persuaded the Bell chiefs and elders to accept a deal under which the government kept one area, Joss, where government offices were situated, but the expropriated Bonadoo were given plots in another area close by, Bali. But the chiefs and elders had second thoughts about the deal and the Bell paramount chief Richard Din Manga Bell (brother of the martyred Rudolf Duala Manga Bell) resigned in March 1927 and left later that year for France. He tried to get satisfaction over the land issue through Blaise Diagne, who had links with Douala;[267] but Diagne

---

266   Adi (note 263), pp. 115-17; Olusanya (note 263), pp. 23-7.

267   J. Derrick, "Douala under the French Mandate, 1916 to 1936", PhD, London,

gave no help, as many Africans in Paris could have warned the Dualas to expect.

On 11 August 1929 the chiefs and elders of all the four sections of the Dualas (Bell, Akwa, Deido and Bonaberi) sent a petition to the League of Nations on the land case. It followed a telegram to Geneva beginning, "Relative our petition 18 August 1919." Written in German, the new petition went over the land case and concluded, "The League of Nations should order at a high level, and proclaim publicly, that our property over our land holdings in Douala and elsewhere in Cameroun must return to its previous state."[268]

A few months later, on 19 December 1929, another petition was sent to Geneva by the four Duala sections paramount chiefs, calling plainly for self-government. Written, again, in German, it said it was "the petition of the Camerounians before the League of Nations concerning the absolute reform of the political system and administration of Cameroun." It asked the League to end the French mandate and proclaim Cameroun a "neutral" country; if this was agreed, said the paramount chiefs, "We transfer" the "protectorate over Cameroun" to the League of Nations Assembly. Then it detailed many criticisms of French rule. The petitioners said, "Absolute independence must be the reward for our state and its development," and for the time being proposed a sort of international self-governing colony, with League representatives running the administration together with Cameroonians and training them to take over fully.[269]

While the Dualas' paramount chiefs signed this petition, which mentioned the one of August, the initiative for the second one probably came from a group of activists based mainly in the Akwa section, while Richard Bell concentrated on the land case, for which a Guadeloupean lawyer, Maître Henri Jean-Louis, was engaged and drew up a memorandum, completed on 30 July 1930; Richard Bell sent this, with a small covering letter, to the French Prime Minister for forwarding to the League of Nations.[270] Apart from that Richard Bell was not

---

1979, pp. 250-83.

268   French translation in file 1, Box Cameroun AP 615, Archives Section Outremer (SOM), Paris/Aix-en-Provence.

269   French translation in file Cameroun AP 10890, Cameroon Archives, Yaounde.

270   Richard Bell to French Prime Minister, 5 Sept. 1930, Box Cameroun AP 615,

very active in Paris. But he helped start a newspaper edited by Dualas living there, Joseph Ebele and Gaston Kingue Jong, written in Duala and called *Mbale* ("Truth"), which was banned in French Cameroun in March 1929 after its first issue, but was allowed to circulate there later; generally it had little to offend the French, though one issue included a criticism of Diagne for his defence of forced labour. *Mbale* ceased publication in 1930.[271]

The more radical Duala activists apparently behind the Self-Government petition had talks with Vincent Ganty, a former colonial official originally from French Guiana, living at Kribi, another town of Cameroon, where he formed, or constituted on his own, a branch of the LDRN.[272] He was deported in March 1930, but the activists made agreements with him, appointing him their representative in Europe, on 31 August 1930 and 25 January 1931. He contacted the non-Communist faction of the LDRN under Faure, which was as strongly anti-imperialist as Kouyate's faction, and Faure wrote about Cameroun in *La Race Nègre* of September 1930 and then in his version of *La Race Nègre* published in April 1931, where he wrote:

Cameroon, a free country, means to be free effectively. *La Race Nègre* will give its support to the Cameroonians as it has done for the Haitians, without fail, until the immediate evacuation of the country by foreigners.[273]

After some delay Vincent Ganty, who called himself the "Delegate in Europe of the Cameroun Negro Citizens", sent a petition to the League of Nations on 18 or 19 May 1931, and then another on 19 June. The 19 June 1931 petition was briefly examined by the PMC the following year; Ganty spoke of forced labour and of low pay and ill-treatment on Europeans' plantations, and called for an inquiry.[274]

Archives SOM, Paris/Aix.

271   Interview, Gaston Kingue Jong, Douala 1972; information from Joseph Ebele in René Douala Manga Bell papers, Douala; issues of *Mbale* enclosed, with translations, in file APA 10889, Cameroon Archives, Yaounde.

272   On Vincent Ganty see Derrick (note 267), pp. 306-8, 213-17, 325-6, 333-6; A. Owona, "La Curieuse Figure de Vincent Ganty," *Revue Française d'Histoire d'Outremer* vol. LVI no. 204, 1969, pp. 199-235; E. Ghomsi, "Résistance africaine à l'impérialisme européen: le cas des Doualas du Cameroun," *Afrika-Zamani*, no. 4, July 1975; Dewitte (note 99), pp. 322-6.

273   Quoted in Dewitte (note 99), pp. 323-4.

274   Owona (note 272), pp. 214-19.

In Douala, on 21-22 July 1931, there were big demonstrations by women against the head-tax, following a recent decision to end the exemption of mothers of children under twelve from payment; and on the second day gendarmes fired on the women, injuring some.[275] Protests at this incident reached the League of Nations, one being sent by the LDRN on 5 August and one by Ganty on 14 August.[276] But at some point the Duala activists must have realised Ganty was an eccentric who would not do much for them; anyway he eventually sued them for fees allegedly promised.

The dissidence had wide support in Douala.[277] The leading Duala critics of French rule included a number of people who had received Western education and held jobs under the Germans. Later a belief grew up[278] that they turned against French rule because similar jobs were not made available to them. However, many of the German-trained Dualas did find employment with the French administration; so those who did not probably gave the French a special reason for refusing them, such as overt anti-French sentiments, or else refused to seek employment with the new rulers for a similar reason. But for years the French had suspected German incitement and intrigues behind the dissidence among some German-educated Dualas.[279] In view of the Dualas' normal attitudes and their bad memories of the Germans it is unlikely that most of them wanted a return to German rule, but it is not impossible that some Cameroonians did; in French Togo some German-educated Africans founded a Bund der Deutscher Togoländer, which announced its existence in 1925 and petitioned Geneva calling plainly for a restoration of German rule. The French government, annoyed by the Bund's criticisms of French ill-treatment, including heavy taxation, said its

---

275   Derrick (note 266), pp. 326-33; Chef de Circonscription, Douala to Commissioner, 27 July 1931, and related correspondence, APA 11217/B, Cameroon Archives.

276   Permanent Mandates Commission, Geneva, report of 22nd session 3 Nov.-6 Dec. 1932, pp. 350-1.

277   Derrick (note 266), pp. 317-25.

278   expressed by I. Kala-Lobe, "The Greatness and Decline of Mun'a Moto," *Présence Africaine* no. 37, 2nd quarter 1971, English version, pp. 69 ff.

279   J. Derrick, "The 'Germanophone' Elite of Douala under French Administration", *Journal of African History* vol. 21 no. 3, 1980; R.A. Joseph, "The German Question in French Cameroun, 1919-1939", *Comparative Studies in Society and History* vol. 17 no. 1, January 1975, pp. 65-90.

leaders were unemployed former clerks of the German government and it "probably" received help from Germany.[280]

The Douala dissidence achieved nothing in the short term, but while it lasted it annoyed the French considerably. In no other part of Black Africa, at that time, were there such organised and sustained efforts, directed from within Africa, to seek an early end to colonial rule. Why did this happen only in Douala? West African elites gained both awareness and power through their Western education, power because they were useful to the colonial rulers who commonly loathed "educated natives" but had to employ and tolerate them. The Dualas had an exceptionally independent position because of their widespread ownership of plantations producing cocoa and palm products for export.[281] But most of all, they had their particular attitude to the colonial rulers, believing that the original 1884 treaty with Germany was a two-sided bargain, and that after the expulsion of the Germans a new agreement had been required, not simple transfer to France; they also understood that there were some differences between mandated territories and colonies. The French, of course, emphasised that the Dualas were just one small tribe who could not speak for Cameroonians generally—the standard colonial response to protests by "educated natives". But the Dualas seem to have argued that as their chiefs' treaty with Germany had been the start of German annexation of the whole territory—which in fact took its name from the Dualas' town on the shore of what had been called the "Cameroons river" by earlier navigators—they could legitimately speak about what later happened to the whole territory.

As the West and its culture and ideas so much mattered both to the colonial rulers and to their African subjects, Africans who came under Western and "modernising" influence from non-French sources may have been, for that reason, less submissive to France than others. Events in the inter-war period seem to suggest this for both the Dualas of Cameroon and the Malagasys, with the difference that in Madagascar there were many newspapers and periodicals, in French or Malagasy.

---

280   M. Callahan, *Mandates and Empire: the League of Nations and Africa, 1914-1931*, Sussex Atlantic Press, 1999, pp. 149-52.

281   R. Austen and J. Derrick, *Middlemen of the Cameroons Rivers*, Cambridge University Press, 1999, pp. 116-20, 164-8.

A few years after his return Jean Ralaimongo started a new French-language newspaper in Madagascar, *L'Opinion*, first appearing on 27 May 1927. His main associates in the new venture were Joseph Ravoahangy, a former VVS convict, and Paul Dussac. The newspaper soon incurred the wrath of the colonial administration, which it attacked over forced labour (called SMOTIG) and its land tenure policy. Governor-General Olivier issued a decree on 15 September 1927 against writings or illustrations "likely to damage respect for French authority", and soon afterwards Ralaimongo and Dussac were imprisoned. Ralaimongo was in gaol from October 1927 to October 1928, but contributed to *L'Opinion*, which continued to appear, from his cell.[282] Soon afterwards Ralaimongo, Ravoahangy and Dussac drew up a *Pétition des Indigènes de Madagascar*, published in *L'Opinion* and calling for recognition of French citizenship for all Malagasys and full equal rights. This explicitly continued the ideas held by Ralaimongo for years, and they remained shocking to the French authorities.

On 19 May 1929 there followed an event celebrated in the annals of early nationalism in the French empire: a great demonstration in Tananarive, the Malagasy capital. Dussac, after arriving on 12 May, greeted by a big crowd, with a petition calling for collective admission to French citizenship and the choice of himself and Ravoahangy as deputies for Madagascar, planned a meeting for 19 May with Jules Ranaivo and Abraham Razafy and with two European Communists, Planque and Vittori. Their involvement was the first open involvement of known Communists in protests in sub-Saharan Africa, except for South Africa. On 19 May the planned meeting in a cinema in Tananarive was banned, and there was a demonstration of about 3,000 people, followed by several arrests.[283]

After the arrests the French SRI (Secours Rouge International, i.e. International Red Aid) sent a lawyer, Maître Foissin, to Madagascar to defend Planque and Vittori; they, however, were the only defendants convicted on 18 January 1930, which suggests that the court was somehow convinced of Communist instigation. Foissin then set up a

---

282 J.-P. Domenichini, "Jean Ralaimongo (1884-1943), ou Madagascar au seuil du nationalisme," *Revue Française d'Histoire d'Outremer* vol. LVI, no. 204, 3rd quarter, 1969, pp. 236-87 (pp. 261-3).

283 Ibid., p. 264.

Madagascar committee with Ravoahangy as secretary, even though Ra-voahangy—writing in a new newspaper founded by Dussac and Razafy, *Le Réveil Malgache*—had recently rejected both Communism and inde-pendence. Ravoahangy drew up a "memorandum for economic action to take in the struggle against imperialism" about May 1930, for Foissin to take back to France,[284] and Foissin said Ravoahangy's support for as-similation was purely tactical and the general aim was independence.[285] It was probably true that many nationalists now agreed on the aim of independence, and as has already been suggested, the call for mass French naturalisation had never really been support for "assimilation". Ralaimongo, who had first made that call, wrote to the SRI on 5 Octo-ber 1931 saying he had never belonged to the PCF or the SFIO, but was now a member of the SRI because "its programme is ours".

Ralaimongo was banished for five years to Port-Bergé after a new petition drawn up by Ralaimongo, Ravoahangy and Dussac, which re-ceived thousands of signatures, had been published in *Le Réveil Mal-gache* on 2 May 1930 and *L'Opinion* ten days later. Ravoahangy, who sought an audience with the new Governor-General, Léon Cayla, to present the petition, was also banished, to Maintirano. They were ac-cused of creating "a state of mind hostile to French action and influence in native circles". In Port-Bergé Ralaimongo was not detained, and was able to work as a public letter writer helping people make complaints, and contribute to yet another newspaper started by Dussac, *L'Aurore Malgache*. He was harassed by the administration but not effectively stopped. In his letter to the SRI on 5 October 1931 he wrote:

Since the Malagasys annoy the French government in demanding the full ap-plication of the Annexation law of 6 August 1896, according to which the Malagasys must be considered French citizens, they demand freedom to make themselves a free and independent people.[286]

This shows how he simply called for two alternative ways to end his people's colonial subjection.

---

284   Randrianja (note 239), pp. 174-87, 226-8.

285   Ibid., p. 232.

286   Domenichini (note 282), pp. 264-71; Randrianja (note 239), pp. 243-4, 257-8.

The SRI Madagascar section was banned in August 1932, and many members were arrested the following October (400 according to SRI of France).[287] But although the colonial repression in Madagascar was unpleasant enough, and Cayla was particularly criticised as a harsh authoritarian, what is noteworthy about Madagascar at that time was the extent to which opponents of French rule could operate there. Generally, anti-colonial campaigners had more freedom to operate in Europe than in Africa in the 1920s and 30s, but in several colonial territories repression was within limits, and hence the political action was in Africa, as well as Europe.

The Congo-Ocean Railway and the Gbaya revolt

In French Equatorial Africa, from 1921 to 1934 tens of thousands of Africans were conscripted by force to build the Congo-Ocean Railway from Pointe-Noire to Brazzaville, and huge numbers died in one of the worst forced labour atrocities since those carried out by the Concessionary Companies in the same AEF (which were still operating) and the similar atrocities in the former Congo Free State. The contractor, the Société des Batignolles, used little machinery until 1930; labourers dug tunnels with mining rods, hammers and their own hands. The 300 million francs loan provided for the project in 1924 was not needed to pay labourers, who were supplied free by the colonial government. Massive recruiting operations extended from Middle Congo, where the construction took place, over sparsely-populated colonies of Ubangi-Shari and Chad, to round up labourers by force with the help of chiefs or pseudo-chiefs working for the French, who could choose which men should go. Very many of the workers died before they reached the construction site, many died there; poor food, clothing and lodging, overworking, forced removal of men from savanna to forest areas, and respiratory diseases contributed to a horrific death toll, and ever more intense man-hunts were needed to find workers.[288]

The Congo-Ocean railway cost even more lives than the railway from Edea to Yaounde in French Cameroun, begun about the same time and

---

287   Randrianja (note 239), p. 245.

288   G. Sautter, "Notes sur la construction du chemin de fer Congo-Océan (1921-1934)", *Cahiers d'Etudes Africaines* vol. VII, 1967, 2me cahier, pp. 219-99.

completed in 1927; that killed many thousands also, and led to strong criticisms at the Permanent Mandates Commission.[289] The number who died building the Congo-Ocean Railway was at least 16,000.[290] There were strong protests in France by 1926, when Maran wrote about the railway horrors in *Le Journal du Peuple* of 24 April; Robert Poulaine joined in the protests in *Le Temps,* and Georges Anquetil in *La Rumeur;* Albert Londres, who estimated that 17,000 workers had died well before the end of the construction, made the facts better known when his articles in *Le Petit Parisien* in October and November 1928 were published together in 1929 as a book, *Terre d'Ebène (La Traite des Noirs),* making a comparison with the old slave trade. There were protests in the National Assembly where the matter was raised several times between 1927 and 1929; the deputy Georges Nouelle said on 14 June 1929 that 20,000 had died and 40,000 more would die.[291] The often repeated estimate that a worker died for every sleeper laid was fairly wild (there were over half a million sleepers), but it indicated proper outrage at what was going on.

André Gide was, with Albert Londres, the most prominent writer to expose French rule in the AEF. Unlike Londres, Gide did not say much about the railway construction. But after he had travelled to French Equatorial Africa in 1925, at the height of his literary fame after the publication of *Les Faux-Monnayeurs,* he recorded in *La Nouvelle Revue Française* in 1926-27, and then in his books *Voyage au Congo* and *Le Retour du Tchad,* shocking details of oppression by the Concessionary Companies. In AEF Gide was received by colonial officials, such as Eboué in the Bas Mbomou region of Ubangi-Shari in 1925; Eboué told another official to go with Gide to "try to put some blinders on his eyes because they don't know what he has come to do here. It would be a good idea to make sure everything is in order at the post and along the roads."[292] But Gide learned a good deal. He gave brief but appalling accounts of forced labour of women, for road repairs, and of children

---

289   Permanent Mandates Commission, reports for 9th session (June 1926), 11th session (July 1927) and 13th session (June 1928). See also H. Manga Mado, *Complaintes d'un Forçat,* Yaounde: CLE, 1970.

290   Sautter's conclusion (note 288), p. 269.

291   Ibid., p. 267.

292   B. Weinstein, *Eboué,* New York: OUP, 1972, pp. 99-100.

between the ages of nine and eleven, who "were said to have been taken from their village with ropes round their necks; they were made to work for six days, without pay and without being given anything to eat."[293] He did not come out plainly for an end to French rule, but his revelations—in magazines, and in meetings with ministers and parliamentarians, as well as the books—caused considerable shock.[294]

The conscription of workers for the railway led to a revolt of the Gbaya (Baya) people of Ubangi-Shari, on the border with French Cameroon, in 1928. They had already suffered from the rubber tyranny of the Compagnie Forestière Sangha-Oubangui (CFSO), and the combined impositions drove them and several other peoples to revolt in a large area of Ubangi-Shari and the adjoining territories. A prophet or traditional healer born in the Bouar area, whose real name was Barka Ngainoumbey but who came to be known as Karnu (or Karinou), spent some years gathering disciples, preaching against French rule, and telling people not to pay taxes to the white man or work for him, without being discovered by the French. In May-June 1928 he and his followers started attacks that initially had some success; the town of Bouar was evacuated by the French, and burned. Karnu was killed in action on 11 December 1928, but the war went on and spread. It came to be known as the "Kongo-Wara war" after a traditional hoe called *kongo-wara*. The insurgents spread over the western areas of Ubangi-Shari and into the neighbouring colonies of Chad, Middle Congo and French Cameroon; people of several other tribes joined the Gbayas. French forces drove the insurgents back only slowly, but by 1931-32 last-ditch fighters in the Bocaranga, Paoua and Baibokoum regions had been largely defeated; some who retreated into caves were smoked out or forced out in the "war of the caves". There was brutal punishment after their defeat, including forced resettlement, while press-ganging for the railway building went on until completion of the work, which was followed by a grand ceremonial opening in 1934.[295]

---

293   A. Gide, *Voyage au Congo*, quoted in C. Hodeir and M. Pierre, *L'Exposition Coloniale*, Brussels: Complexe, 1991, p. 123. (I was not able to find a copy of *Voyage au Congo*.)

294   Jean Lacouture and Dominique Chagnollaud, *Le Désempire: Figures et thèmes de l'anticolonisme*, Paris: Denoël, 1993, pp. 186-7.

295   R. Nzabakomada-Yakoma, *L'Afrique centrale insurgée: La Guerre du Kongo-Wara 1928-1931*, Paris: Harmattan, 1986, pp. 19-140; Y. Zoctizoum, *Histoire de la*

The French authorities at first tried to conceal the AEF uprising, but soon the true facts were publicised, not only by the left-wing press but by other newspapers, including some normally pro-colonial ones. *L'Humanité* dealt with the modern-day slavery in AEF and the revolt at length during 1929, and the LDRN made public protests. A Communist deputy, speaking in the National Assembly on 15 June 1929, condemned the way in which the involvement of witchcraft, fetishism, etc. in the rising was emphasised:

If fetishists have led the tribes into following them, it is because the tribes found in them people to inspire them, but above all because they had serious reasons for discontent.[296]

Obviously it was to evade that basic fact, and to depict rebels as frightening hordes of savages, that the involvement of occult beliefs and practices was emphasised. Karnu was indeed a "medicine man" or traditional healer; he was also a fighter against alien misrule.

In the new Congo scandal of the 1920s, as in the others twenty years earlier, ordinary newspapers and magazines, and ordinary journalists, helped expose colonial crimes. In addition, all sorts of Europeans were travelling to various parts of Africa and writing about them in 1920s and 30s, and some travelled to find out what was going on, sometimes objectively—though colonial governments kept an eye on white visitors and were quick to suspect some of them.[297] One exceptional traveller was a researcher who annoyed the colonial rulers considerably but benefited future historians: the American scholar Raymond Leslie Buell, whose research produced the two-volume *The Native Problem in Africa* in 1928. The title reflected the peculiar outlook of the time (regarding people as a "problem" in their own homeland) but the book was the most thorough survey of colonialist treatment of Africans, including the worst aspects, in the 1920s. Buell was no Communist or radical, but his careful scholarly exposés of forced labour in many parts

---

Centrafrique, Vol. I, 1879-1959, Paris: Harmattan, 1983, pp. 138-58; P. Burnham, *The Politics of Cultural Difference in Northern Cameroon*, Edinburgh University Press for International African Institute, 1996, pp. 34, 76-7.

296   Nzabakomada-Yakoma (note 295), pp. 140-54.

297   Bush (note 135), pp. 78-9.

of Africa were as telling as any. He examined the forced labour in AEF at some length.[298]

In French Equatorial Africa an African protest movement, separate from the Gbaya rising, was headed for a few years by André Matsoua (1899-1942). Born at Manzakala-Kinkala in Middle Congo, he went to Paris where, on 17 July 1926, he founded with others an Association Amicale des Originaires de l'Afrique Equatoriale Française, to help people from that region in France and contribute to improving conditions back home; he was the chairman. Matsoua also wrote two letters to the French prime minister in 1928, protesting against the Concessionary Companies' exploitation and the Indigénat. Back in the Congo their association, at first approved and aided by Governor-General Antonetti, held meetings and gathered thousands of supporters. Then they were arrested in November 1929, and Matsoua was arrested in France and sent back. Amid mounting racial tension, Africans in Brazzaville rallied in support of Matsoua and three others who were brought to trial in April 1930; they received three-year gaol sentences plus years of banishment (ten for Matsoua), and the Amicale was banned in the Congo, though it was authorised to restart in Paris in July 1930.[299]

Apart from the Gbaya revolt there were very few armed uprisings in Sub-Saharan Africa after about 1920. In the Belgian Congo there was a rising from May to September 1931 among the Pende (Bapende) people in the Kwango region in the west, provoked by pressure to pay taxes and supply palm fruit for big companies (the Huileries du Congo Belge (HBC) and Compagnie du Kasaï) and labourers for cutting the fruit and other forced tasks; hundreds of Africans, possibly as many as 5,000 according to later research, were killed during the suppression of the revolt.[300] In the Sierra Leone Protectorate in February 1931, followers of Haidara Kontorfilli, a popular Muslim preacher from French West Africa who proclaimed that British rule was coming to an end, fought British forces at Kambia and were quickly defeated, Haidara be-

---

298   Buell (note 189), vol. 2, pp. 258ff.

299   Georges Balandier, *Sociologie des Brazzavilles noires*, Cahiers de la NFSP, Paris: Armand Colin, 1955, pp. 171-3; M. Sinda, *André Matsoua: Fondateur du Mouvement de Libération du Congo*, Paris: ABC, 1978.

300   L.-F. Vanderstraeten, *La Répression de la révolte des Pende au Kwango en 1931*, Brussels: Académie Royale des Sciences d'Outremer, 2000.

ing killed.[301] In these risings, too, traditional occult beliefs played a part, combined with Islam in the Sierra Leone case. Communists in Belgium took up the Congo Africans' cause and protested at the repression of the Pende rising, arousing some public concern; they had declared support in principle for the Congo's independence in 1929.[302] Such risings were rare in that heyday of colonialism; neither "native doctors" nor Communists inspired much armed resistance in Africa during those two decades.

Anti-Colonialists, Socialists and Communists

Communists often liked to suggest that their party alone was the true friend of colonial subjects. This was unjust to many sincere critics of colonialism, who may have been "reformist" but still angered colonialists by their calls for reforms. They included two international bodies. One, the Bureau International de Défense des Indigènes, was set up in 1913 by René Claparède in Geneva. A Protestant-inspired organisation linked to the French Protestant missionary society, the SME (Société des Missions Evangéliques), it denounced the LAI as a Communist venture, but annoyed the French Colonies Ministry by its own criticisms. The Women's International League for Peace and Freedom (WILPF, founded in 1915 and still continuing) also criticised colonialism. Its 5th Congress at Dublin and Geneva on 8-15 July 1926 had as its theme "Economic imperialism and colonial imperialism"; it opposed the Moroccan and Syrian wars in that year and its magazine *Pax International* was banned in France; in the USA it was involved, like the NAACP, in protests against the occupation of Haiti.[303]

In Britain there was a recognisable group of "colonial liberals". Kenya and South Africa were their main areas of concern in Africa; in South Africa they were allied with the "white liberals". They were linked with the ASAPS and with the Society of Friends (Quakers), always involved

---

301   B.M. Jusu, "The Haidara Rebellion of 1931," *Sierra Leone Studies* New Series no. 3, December 1954, pp. 147-53; F.R. Anthony, *Sawpit Boy*, Freetown: published by author, 1980, pp. 55-9.

302   A. Nzula *et al.* (note 133), pp. 108-13; Wilson (note 32), p. 252n.

303   Liauzu (note 14), p. 64; on the occupation of Haiti and reactions to it, see M.W. Shannon, *Jean Price-Mars, the Haitian Elite and the American Occupation, 1915-35*, Basingstoke: Macmillan, 1996.

in humanitarian activity; the ASAPS backed initiatives of white liberals and Christians in South Africa—the Joint Councils set up in 1921 to promote cooperation between black and white and take up Africans' grievances, and the South African Institute of Race Relations (SAIRR) established in 1929.[304] In much the same spirit the South African novelist Etheldreda Lewis and the British novelist and poet Winifred Holtby, who stayed with her during a speaking tour of South Africa for the League of Nations Union in 1926, later helped arrange Ballinger's attachment to the ICU.[305] The arrangements were actually made by Arthur Creech Jones, National Secretary of the Administrative, Clerical and Supervisory Section of the Transport and General Workers' Union (TGWU), who already took a close interest in colonial affairs which he was to develop later as a Labour MP. Kadalie spoke at weekend meetings of the ILP Imperialism Committee and attended one of the ILP's well known Summer Schools, and met Dr Leys as well as Labour MPs, on his tour in 1927.

Winifred Holtby had become a "Negrophile" (her word) on her visit to South Africa, and in the following years was a close friend of Brockway, Maxton, Charles Roden Buxton, H.N. Brailsford and Creech Jones, and especially Norman Leys. The activities of this circle included help for Ballinger's continuing work on behalf of Africans in South Africa after the decline of the ICU and his departure from it, while Holtby herself was a "friend and adviser" to African students in London, helping to finance the studies of some of them.[306]

These well-meaning liberals were members of or close to the Labour Party. That party had not promised much change where Africa was concerned before gaining power in 1929. A Labour Party manifesto of 1928, *Labour and the Nation*, said that all dependencies "ought, as soon as possible, to become self-governing States"; imperial responsibility would continue during a gradual transition to "the establishment

---

304   Bush (note 135), pp. 181-90.

305   V. Brittain, *Testament of Friendship: The Story of Winifred Holtby*, London: The Book Club, 1941, pp. 198-209.

306   Ibid., Chapters XIII-XV. Vera Brittain's account of the British supporters of African causes at that time is rare and useful, but on events within South Africa her work has inaccuracies. Bush (note 135) has given a good account of that circle of supporters of African causes (Chapter 7).

of democratic institutions".[307] The ILP, at its Conference in 1929, went further and called for colonial self-government as and when the colonised people demanded it, and at the Congress of the International called for more support for "the growing movement among the coloured peoples of Africa to claim equality."[308] But even the ILP did not demand independence for African colonies as it had done for India since 1926.[309]

India was the prime colonial issue facing the MacDonald government in 1929. The Indian National Congress leaders were divided for some years in the 1920s on the question of whether to call for full independence or *Swaraj* (advocated by Jawaharlal Nehru) or for Dominion Status. There was in fact no real difference; after the Imperial Conference of 1926 Hertzog, who had called for an end to the link with the British crown, accepted and told his fellow Afrikaners that South Africa, as a Dominion, was in fact already independent. But there was some uncertainty about the point until the Statute of Westminster in 1931, and even afterwards there were some doubts about whether Dominions' independence was 100 per cent.[310] When the Labour government elected in 1929 declared that Dominion Status for India was an acceptable aim, Congress insisted on independence as its immediate aim, Gandhi organised a civil disobedience campaign, and "Eleven Demands" were made, including an end to the salt tax for peasants and the poor; Gandhi then launched his famous march to the sea at Dandi to collect salt (April 1930). Two Round Table Conferences, the second attended by Gandhi in 1931, ended without agreement, and early in 1932, Gandhi and many other INC leaders, and up to about 35,000 other people in all at one point, were arrested in India.[311]

307 John E. Flint, "Macmillan as a Critic of Empire: The Impact of an Historian on Colonial Policy", Ch. 10 in H. Macmillan and S. Marks (eds), *W.M. Macmillan, Historian and Social Critic*, Temple Smith for the Institute of Commonwealth Studies, 1989; p. 217.

308 Howe (note 121), p. 70.

309 P.S. Gupta (note 135), p. 112.

310 The legal and constitutional issues are examined at length in W.K. Hancock, *Survey of British Commonwealth Affairs, Vol. I, Problems of Nationality 1918-1936*, OUP 1937 (pp. 275-6 on the Statute of Westminster).

311 For a summary of these events see P. Moon, *Gandhi and Modern India*, English Universities Press, 1968, pp. 126-71; P.S. Gupta (note 135), chapter 7.

These events were followed with keen interest around the colonial world, while support for the Indian National Congress in Britain had been organised steadily since before 1914. The India League worked very actively in the 1930s to "support the claim of India to Swaraj" among the British public; its main moving spirit for years, after his studies at the LSE, was Krishna Menon, while speakers at its meetings included Harold Laski of the LSE, the Communist Rajani Palme Dutt, Ellen Wilkinson, and Reginald Sorensen, a Labour politician and Unitarian clergyman who also became a leading backer of African protests.[312]

The "colonial liberals" quickly lost confidence, if they ever had any, in those who headed the Colonial Office in the Labour government, the Fabian Sidney Webb (Lord Passfield) and his Undersecretary Drummond Shiels. Webb in particular exuded a superior attitude with little real empathy for humbler people. A historian of the Fabian Society considers that although Webb at the Colonial Office was "extremely gentle and patient with pressure groups while there, he could never understand why they became so worked up about colonial and Mandatory affairs", and he was irritated

at Fabians declaiming against his own policies at the Colonial Office. Leonard Woolf, Leonard Barnes, Charles Roden Buxton, McGregor Ross and Norman Leys had had no qualms about censuring his restraint in an office which they considered the stronghold of reaction.[313]

It was the facts of the situation, not Webb's attitude, that obliged the Labour government to continue running the empire much as before. However, the Labour Party had come out strongly against white settler domination in parts of Africa, and on that it was reasonably accused of not living up to expectations, for example regarding Southern Rhodesia. Two years after self-government under settler control, the Morris Carter Commission was appointed to inquire into land ownership in Southern Rhodesia in 1925, but in response to Africans' testimony protesting against the unjust land allocation it recommended only a small addition to the African "Reserves", plus an inadequate Native Purchase area. African associations held a Congress in 1929 which condemned

---

312   T.J.S. George, *Krishna Menon,* Jonathan Cape, 1964, pp. 53-69.

313   P. Pugh, *Educate, Agitate, Organize: 100 Years of Fabian Socialism* (London: Methuen, 1984), p. 77, pp. 157, 159. For more on Leonard Barnes see Chapter 4.

the Land Apportionment Bill following the recommendations, but they could not sway the settler regime. The British Labour government, which could have used its reserve powers to disallow the legislation, failed to do so, ignoring a campaign by the ASAPS and critics such as Cripps, Leys and Olivier;[314] and the Land Apportionment Act became law in 1930, enshrining robbery of land and laying up plenty of trouble for the future.

When it became clear that the settlers were similarly to have their way in Kenya, Leys wrote in his new book *A Last Chance in Kenya* (1931), "All over East Africa the news has gone out that the Labour Government has recanted."[315] The Labour government made hardly any changes to colonial rule anywhere, except for the directive to allow African trade unions (described above) and the Colonial Development and Welfare Act of 1930, which introduced (in a limited way) the idea of Europe aiding the colonies rather than the other way round. Nothing more should have been expected. Continuity is a very powerful force; the empire was too strong, too profitable and too popular a going concern for a democratic government, which had many other problems to handle as the Depression set in, to challenge.

Nor was there any change in relations with the supposedly independent Egypt. New talks with Egypt were held in March-May 1930, after the Wafd, now led by Mustafa Nahhas following Zaghlul's death in August 1927, had been elected to power. As an illustration of continuity under Labour, the British were still unwilling to accept Egyptian demands on the four reserved points that had greatly limited independence since 1922. The talks broke down over the Sudan, and on that point the Egyptians were being imperialist themselves, insisting that they had rights in that country and hence should have a greater role in the Condominium. Some Sudanese nationalists supported the Egyptian view, but many did not. In the 1930s a nationalist movement among Sudanese graduates of Gordon College, the leading government secondary school, emerged; the Intelligence department in Khartoum

314 T.O. Ranger, "African Politics in Twentieth-Century Southern Rhodesia", Ch. 9 in T.O. Ranger (ed.), *Aspects of Central African History*, London: Heinemann, 1968, pp. 224-8; R. Whitehead, "The Aborigines' Protection Society and the Safeguarding of African Interests in Rhodesia, 1889-1930", DPhil, Oxford, 1975, pp. 275, 286-9; P.S. Gupta (note 135), pp. 176-8.

315 N. Leys, *A Last Chance in Kenya*, London: Hogarth Press, 1931, p. 141.

detected the influence of Gandhi, for whom "especially the younger element of the intelligentsia have a great admiration and sympathy."[316]

Some Labour leaders positively liked the empire, and all had been resolutely opposed to Communism for years. The party had, for example, opposed the LAI from the start. Early in 1930 the Labour Home Secretary, J.R. Clynes, was at first ready to allow Münzenberg to visit Britain, but following protests from a shocked Colonial Office an order was sent that Münzenberg "should on no account be allowed to land in the United Kingdom."[317]

The colonial liberals who condemned the Labour government's policies shared its attitude to Communism fully, and one reason for their concern over Africans was fear of the influence of Communism. The ideas of these essentially paternalist British people corresponded little at all with those of the Africans they met or cared about.[318] The former were commonly ready to see colonial rule continue for a long time, though with many changes for Africans' benefit, like Olivier in his books *Anatomy of African Misery* (1927) and *White Capital & Coloured Labour* (1929). On South Africa Olivier was influenced by an analysis of the destruction of African peasant communities by William Macmillan, a "liberal" South African scholar who had considerable influence in both South Africa and Britain through his studies of the South African situation and particularly the position of Africans, notably *Bantu, Boer and Briton* (1929) and *Complex South Africa* (1930).[319] W.M. Macmillan was one of many colonial liberals who wrote for the *New Statesman and Nation*, whose famous editor from 1931, Kingsley Martin, was a prominent critic of colonial policy. In articles in that weekly in 1928-29[320] Macmillan expressed the common paternalism; but his

316   M. Abd al-Rahim, *Imperialism and Nationalism in the Sudan*, OUP 1969, pp. 115, 118-19, 125n.

317   Chief Inspector, Aliens Branch, Home Office to Immigration Officer, letter sent to all ports and Scotland Yard, 27 March 1930, file KV2/772; handwritten note by G. Clauson, Colonial Office, 12 March 1930, CO 323/1113/15; National Archives, London.

318   Bush (note 135), pp. 196-9.

319   P. Rich, "W.M. Macmillan, South African Segregation and Commonwealth Race Relations, 1919-1938", ch. 9 in Macmillan and Marks (eds) (note 308), p. 200.

320   Ibid., p. 201; *New Statesman and Nation* 9 June 1928 and 13 July 1929.

quietly academic but scathing criticisms were to have wide influence in
the 1930s, which he spent largely in Britain after 1933.

Democratic Socialists were not uncritical of colonialism and were
well aware (it was not just a Marxist dogma) that economic motives had
governed the occupation and running of the empire. Olivier however
believed, like Woolf and unlike Marxists, that the state had power of its
own and was not the puppet of vested class interests, and thought the
imperial power could play a role to improve conditions of life for Africans.[321] The Labour and Socialist International condemned many sorts
of labour coercion and exploitation in Africa strongly, as at its Congress
in Brussels in August 1928, which recommended that there should be
an ILO code for protection of "native" workers, to be supervised by the
Permanent Mandates Commission.[322]

The previous year that International, in a statement warning constituent party supporters against the LAI, said:

The Labour and Socialist International is filled with the warmest sympathy for
the people who are urging the fight against imperialist and colonial oppression;
it will continue now as before to lend the most urgent support to their struggle
and will do all that lies in its power to have the closest contact with the movements towards liberation of those peoples.

However it added:

But what the International views as its chief task is to rally the working-class
elements of these nations under the banner of international Socialism, and
not to create a new international organisation having for its aim the blending
of these elements into a pan-national element, nor to subordinate their interests and those of the whole nationalist movement to the political interests
of any Power.[323]

This statement seemed to be condemning the LAI and Communism
("any Power" obviously meant Russia) for favouring nationalism rather

---

321 F. Lee, *Fabianism and Colonialism: The Life and Political Thought of Lord Sydney Olivier*, London: Defiant Books, 1988, pp. 180-3.

322 The Congress' statement on *The Colonial Problem* was published by the Labour Party in London. See Sydney Olivier, *White Capital and Coloured Labour*, London: Hogarth Press, 1929, pp. 320-6.

323 Labour and Socialist International Executive resolution, 12 Sept. 1927, quoted in Circular of Labour Party Industrial Department on League against Colonial Oppression (apparently about February 1928), in file HO 144/10693, National Archives, London.

than the cause of the workers. Similarly, in an editorial praising the Brussels Congress, the ILP weekly *New Leader* had said that "some Nationalists are as capitalist as the Imperialism which they oppose; all they seek is the right freely to exploit their own peoples", while adding that a conference like the one at Brussels could influence nationalist movements to be concerned about "economic liberty" too.[324] These doubts about colonial nationalists resembled Communist views; they were inherent in left-wing thinking about imperialism, which was bound to be concerned, with or without instructions from Moscow, about indigenous exploitation and inequality in colonial territories.

In France the SFIO was particularly unfriendly to nationalists of the colonies, even though it was nowhere near taking power. In France and in Tunisia Socialists said there was no Tunisian nation[325]—though the Protectorate corresponded to a state that had governed itself, in much the same area with a common language and religion, for centuries. French Socialists were dazzled by the idea of "assimilation". One of the leading Black politicians in France, the former Martinique deputy Joseph Lagrosillière, said at the SFIO Congress in May 1926 that the party must call for "assimilation" which must mean full equality of rights and "the same numerical representation".[326] But he probably meant this to be combined with continued selective granting of citizenship, rather than full equal rights and universal suffrage for all the people of the colonies, for he also called for "the admission of native elements to direct management of public affairs", which implied a continuation of the colonial order with reforms.

What the party's leadership thought is not clear from the various statements by Léon Blum, who was the effective leader of the SFIO from 1920 onwards though he had no official position in the party except that of secretary and later president of its parliamentary group and political director of the party newspaper, *Le Populaire*. During the Rif war he said Socialists were "opponents of colonialism", but also said in the Chamber on 9 July 1925, "We love our country too much to repudiate the expansion of French thought and civilisation." Two years later, however, he told the Chamber, "*Nous désirons que la législation*

---

324   *New Leader*, 18 February 1927.

325   Lejri (note 46), Vol. II, pp. 10-12.

326   Biondi (note 14), pp. 131-2.

coloniale s'achemine de plus en plus vers l'indépendance, vers le self-government, comme les dominions."[327] This was an intriguing statement, using two English terms to suggest that France might follow the example of the British Empire. But Britain had at that time given "Dominion status" or self-government only to countries under the rule of locally settled Europeans, and there were no such countries in the French empire except (in a sense) Algeria, which was legally a part of France. So it is not clear what Blum meant by that idea.

In France, as in Britain, there were left-wingers more committed than others to opposition to colonialism. In France there were Yves Farge—who had worked in Morocco, and wrote in December 1926 that the colonies did not benefit France but only "a capitalist minority"—and Jean Zyromski and a husband and wife team of militants, Maurice and Magdeleine Paz.[328] Notably, there were Jean Longuet (1876-1938), a grandson of Karl Marx and one of the leading French Socialists, and his son Robert-Jean Longuet, who with the young activist Daniel Guérin gave useful help to the young Moroccan nationalists in Paris, in the protest actions against the "Berber Dahir" of 1930 (on which see pp. 264-8 below). Guérin had had his anti-colonial feelings aroused by a visit to Damascus: "For the first time, I saw colonialists—military, civilian, ecclesiastical—at work, their racism, their brutality, their cynicism, their fatuity, their idiocy."[329]

Guérin recalled later that the militants surrounding the independent far-left publications *Le Cri du Peuple* and *La Révolution Prolétarienne* were the first to support the Moroccan protest leaders. The independent left-wing groups were indeed consistently anti-colonialist, notably the Révolution Prolétarienne group founded by Pierre Monatte in 1925, surrounding the periodical of that name and including several ex-Communists such as Monatte himself and Robert Louzon.[330] But regarding the Moroccan protests of 1930, directed at the attempt to remove Ber-

---

327   Ibid., pp. 132-4.

328   Ibid., pp. 132, 166, 175-6.

329   D. Guérin, *Ci-gît le colonialisme*, Paris and The Hague: Mouton, 1973, pp. 9-13.

330   B. Stora, "La Gauche socialiste, révolutionnaire, et la question du Maghreb au moment du Front populaire (1935-1938)", *Revue Française d'Histoire d'Outremer* vol. LXX, 1983, no. 258-9, 1st-2nd quarters, pp. 57-79 (pp. 60-62); Biondi (note 14), p. 147; Liauzu (note 14), pp. 58-68.

ber areas from Islamic justice, Guérin recalled, "While separated from them by a gulf of social and philosophical concepts, anti-imperialism drew us together and we were not without influence on them which perhaps left traces."[331] Indeed the alliance between French left-wingers, anti-religion by definition, and Moroccan militants defending Islamic law could only be a limited one in the face of a common enemy. In reply to two French-Algerian deputies indignant at seeing Muslim Algerians marching behind the red flag in Algeria, Marius Moutet said, "I prefer to see them with French people behind the red flag than to see them behind the green flag of Islam."[332]

In both Britain and France criticisms, even strong ones, of extreme forms of oppression in Africa could come from defenders of empire and indeed from those who had been governing it. Johnston (who died in 1927) and Olivier were examples in Britain. In France the public must have been startled when a book entitled *Erreurs et Brutalités Coloniales* was published in 1927, not by a Communist, but by Victor Augagneur, former Governor-General of Madagascar and of AEF.[333] Such people simply professed the idea of responsibility or trusteeship strongly, in a way that invited attack from both ultra-colonialists and anti-colonialists. While Augagneur's book was almost entirely about events in Madagascar before his governorship, he alluded to use of the "*manière forte*" in AEF before and after his tenure of office—but in fact France's appalling misgovernment there had continued on his watch.

A similar sort of governor was Maurice Viollette, a Radical deputy who became Governor-General of Algeria from 1925 to 1927; he took firm action against supporters of the Communist Rif war campaign in Algeria, but he was opposed by the settlers for some limited measures to benefit the Muslim Algerians, such as the elementary one of banning wheat exports at a time of food shortage in 1927; he was called by some "Viollette l'Arabe". In reply he warned the settlers: "The natives of Algeria, through your fault, do not yet have a country. They are looking for one. They ask you to give them France as a country. Give it to them quickly, or without that they will make another." Later, as a senator, he

---

331   Guérin (p. 330), p. 13.
332   Biondi (note 14), p. 133. As Biondi says, this is "revealing".
333   V. Augagneur, *Erreurs et brutalités coloniales*, Paris: Editions Montaigne, 1927.

wrote a criticism of French policy entitled *L'Algérie vivra-t-elle?* (meaning French Algeria, of course).[334]

Critics of colonialism like Pierre Bourdarie of the *Revue Indigène* agreed with such proconsuls' ideas of trusteeship, and rejected the views of the committed anti-colonialists. By 1930 Bourdarie, the editor who wrote a good deal of the journal, was in fact hardly uttering any criticisms; in the *Revue* of May-June 1930[335] he replied angrily to criticisms of French forced labour in Africa and reproduced an article by Diagne, repeating the shameful defence of France the Senegalese deputy made about that time before the ILO. The general attitude of the Ligue des Droits de l'Homme was typified by its Chairman for many years in the 1920s, Victor Basch: he criticised the idea of withdrawal from the colonies in reply to Barbusse's appeal in 1925, but joined the LAI French executive in 1927, only to be driven out with other non-Communists later, after which he expressed admiration for Lyautey at the LDH Congress in Algiers in 1930.[336]

There was an anticolonialist minority in the LDH, of which Challaye was the leading figure; he drew up a motion that won 20 per cent of the votes at the Vichy congress of the League on 23-5 May 1931, and read there a statement by Habib Bourguiba, whom the LDH executive had refused to invite, about the situation in Tunisia.[337] The LDH generally rejected the views of that minority, but it did make criticisms and did have influence—aided by its close links with Freemasonry, which was very powerful in the Third Republic generally and particularly so in the ministry of the Colonies. Niger, a country that is prone to droughts and has suffered several famines, was hit by an exceptionally severe famine in western areas in 1931, due very much to French actions—such as grain requisitioning and continued tax collection from starving people—and negligence. The LDH protested at the government's dereliction in letters of 9 April and 29 September 1932; the AOF Governor-General

---

334   F. Gaspard, "'Viollette l'Arabe'", *L'Histoire* no. 140, January 1991, special issue, "Le temps de l'Algérie Française", pp. 68-72.

335   *Revue Indigène*, 25th year, Nos 256-7, May-June 1930, pp. 95-109.

336   Biondi (note 14), p. 143; Liauzu (note 14), p. 90n.

337   Liauzu (note 14), pp. 88-90, 249-50; Biondi (note 14), p. 167.

rejected the League's allegations, but then several French officials involved were quietly sacked.[338]

Some leaders of the SFIO and LDH could only lend colour to Communist claims that "reformists" would achieve nothing for Africans or others under colonial rule. Where Communists erred was in suggesting that their alternative could bring results; it could not and did not, uncompromising militancy was a blind alley. The PCF pursued its militancy despite its weakened state after 1929; its Commission Coloniale, later renamed the Section Spéciale Coloniale, collected material to inform deputies raising colonial issues in the National Assembly, and for press campaigns and meetings; it also printed leaflets and brochures, some in Arabic, at presses in Paris, Lille and Marseilles. But this commission or section had limited means and few active members, while its head was replaced frequently. Comrades from the colonies complained that the centralisation of the party meant a very limited, minor role for them.[339] André Ferrat was appointed Secretary of the Colonial Section on 12 May 1931, but because of a stay in Moscow and some time in custody, he only took charge of the PCF's colonial work effectively in October 1933.[340]

In Britain the CPGB, as already mentioned, sent agents to India, notably Philip Spratt and Ben Bradley. They helped established Communist control over the All-India Trades Union Congress, but in 1929 they and Lester Hutchinson (a future Labour MP), and most of the leading Marxists in the AITUC—33 people in all—were arrested along with many leaders of the Communist Party of India (CPI) and all the major ones of the Workers' and Peasants' Party (WPP). Their trial became a left-wing *cause célèbre*, the Meerut Conspiracy Case, which lasted for four years and occupied much of Bridgeman's energy among others', and most of the LAI British Section's resources.[341] Saklatvala, who lost his parliamentary seat in 1929, remained until his death in 1936 a

---

338 Fuglestad (note 30), pp. 132-6; F. Fuglestad, "La grande famine de 1931 dans l'Ouest nigérien: Réflexions autour d'une catastrophe naturelle", *Revue Française d'Histoire d'Outremer* LXI, 1974, pp. 18-33.

339 Liauzu (note 14), pp. 21-5.

340 Ibid., p. 41n.

341 Howe (note 121), pp. 64-5; Branson (note 121), pp. 59-60; Haithcox (note 120), pp. 156-60; Saville (note 90), p. 44.

leading Communist anti-colonial activist in Britain, Rajani Palme Dutt being another. The CPGB called for "Down with Empire" demonstrations on 24 May, Empire Day (an official holiday since 1916); more seriously for the government, it issued leaflets on several occasions in 1930-31 calling on British troops to refuse to fight against Indians opposing British rule.[342]

For some Westerners colonial issues helped to turn them towards Communism. Richard Krebs alias Jan Valtin, explaining the cause to his fiancée whom he married after she joined the party, told her about the Congo and its copper mine and cotton farm labourers—"It is against this inhumanity that we are fighting"—and Indochina, as well as the Communists in Mussolini's gaols.[343] Douglas Hyde, describing his journey to Communism and the staff of the *Daily Worker*, and then to disillusion and reception into the Catholic Church, recalled that in his young days in Bristol in the 1920s he was influenced by the Indian independence movement and anti-imperialist pamphlets about conditions on tea plantations and in cotton mills in India—"I became rebellious and angry about Indian conditions just as I had been about those in Britain."[344] But intellectuals' conversion to Communism was due more to the Slump and its hideous by-product, Nazism in Germany.

The Great Depression turned many minds towards Communism in the West, though not because Communist parties could save people from its effects—in fact they spent the worst Depression years fighting against other parties on the side of the workers and the unemployed, especially in Germany—and not because it brought the collapse of capitalism or workers' revolution nearer, whatever some hoped or feared. Rather, the Slump concentrated millions of people's minds on day-to-day survival. This was true in Europe and America and also in Africa, where there was great hardship—with earnings from export crops falling, many planters and other white employers ruined and forced to lay off staff, and governments also forced to lay off employees[345]—but

342   Branson (note 121), pp. 61-8, 71-2.
343   Valtin (note 174), p. 193.
344   D. Hyde, *I Believed*, London: Pan Books, 1953, p. 22.
345   Some chapters in I. Brown (ed.), *The Economies of Africa and Asia in the Inter-War Depression*, Routledge 1989, tell something of the Slump's effects in Africa; histories of individual countries should be read for more information.

no unrest such as to threaten the authorities, who did not hesitate to increase taxes at that time in South Africa. Africans in Europe—North Africans workers in France, and African seamen there and in Britain—suffered the hardships of their host countries, or more; many lost their jobs, some of these were then deported, and trade unions and the PCF in France for long feared that non-European workers could be used by capitalists or Fascists for their own purposes.[346] Like millions of others those African workers endured their fate. Revolution was nowhere near; there were of course political crises, like the one in Britain that led to the resignation of the Labour government and the formation of MacDonald's National Government in 1931, but the capitalist system stood up well.

But outrage at the effects of the Depression led a number of sensitive educated people in the West to believe that Soviet Russia had found a better alternative to the capitalist system. However, at that very time Communism in Russia was plumbing the depths. Farmers were coerced with extreme violence by a campaign against the larger farmers called "kulaks", started in early 1930, and then by forcible establishment of collective farms. Millions were killed in the process, many of them in 1932-33 when the independent farmers of the Ukraine were forced into submission by the systematic confiscation of every last ounce of produce from their farms and homes, creating a nightmare man-made famine.[347] This Soviet mass crime extended to the Asian republics; in Kazakhstan it was ordered that all nomadic and semi-nomadic herdsmen should be forced to settle, and that imposition, together with collectivisation, led to resistance, mass emigration to China, and a major famine in 1931-32, at least a million Kazakhs being killed.[348] But many Westerners, refusing to face the known facts, still came at this time to believe that Soviet Communism was better than the Western capitalist order, and many who were interested in colonial affairs praised developments in the Soviet Asian republics in particular.

---

346   Dewitte (note 99), pp. 277-83 (on seamen in France); Liauzu (note 14), pp. 185-98.

347   R. Conquest, *The Harvest of Sorrow: Soviet Collectivization and the Terror-Famine*, Hutchinson, 1986.

348   M.B. Olcott, *The Kazakhs*, Stanford, CA: Hoover Institution Press, 1987, pp. 179-87; Conquest (note 347), pp. 189-98.

In France many intellectuals and artists had joined the PCF or were close to it, such as Barbusse and some of the group of French artists and writers who adopted the name "Surrealist" from 1924, headed by André Breton, Louis Aragon and Paul Eluard. The Surrealists expressed revulsion against everything in the established order, and much else besides, and this naturally included colonialism. Their anti-colonialism was simply part of their general attitude of all-round revolt involving respect for the irrational, the unconscious, the instinctive.[349] An article on *La Révolution Surréaliste* of 15 October 1925, reproduced in *Clarté*, was entitled "La Révolution d'abord et toujours" and declared,

Well aware of the nature of the forces that are currently disturbing the world, we wish, even before counting ourselves and setting ourselves to work, to proclaim our absolute detachment, and in a way our cleansing, from the ideas that are at the basis of European civilisation which is still very near, and even of all civilisation based on the unendurable principles of necessity and duty...

It is our rejection of any consent-based law, our hope in new forces, underground forces capable of turning history upside down, of breaking the ridiculous fetters of facts, that makes us turn our eyes to Asia...It is the Mongols' turn to camp in our squares.[350]

Abd el-Krim would have been baffled by such ideas if he heard of them, but in their own way the Surrealists joined the critics of the Rif war. In later years several of them were drawn to Communism, though its emphasis on discipline, applied most fully by the OGPU in Russia, was alien to their ideas, which were nearer to Anarchism. While Breton was expelled from the party after a few years, Aragon remained a stalwart member for decades.

Others besides the Surrealists thought that Western civilisation had been discredited by the Great War and looked around for something better. Such sentiments encouraged interest in Asian cultures (on which Challaye wrote some books) and African cultures, and doubts about Western superiority.[351] In the 1920s there was some interest in Afri-

---

349   R. Brandon, *Surreal Lives: The Surrealists 1917-1945*, Macmillan, 2000, p. 217, quoting Aragon's *Une Vague de rêves* (1924); Mortimer (note 122), pp. 182-8; P. Archer-Straw, *Negrophilia: Avant-Garde Paris and Black Culture in the 1920s*, Thames & Hudson, 2000, pp. 81-8.

350   Quoted in Liauzu (note 14), pp. 254-6.

351   Ibid., pp. 79-80, 249-50; Biondi (note 14), pp. 153-4.

can sculpture, a number of anthropological studies were published, and there was a sentimental craving for the "spiritual" values Africa was thought to offer to mechanised, materialist Europe.[352]

But what interested the general Western public most was the African Diaspora's music, dance and theatre. White people had previously patronised the stereotyping and degrading "blacking-up" shows in the USA and other countries (which still continued), but now many were excited by jazz, various modern African American dances such as the Charleston, and Black singers and musicals. Much of this was centred on Harlem in particular, where some dancing venues were open to all races. There was close musical collaboration between white and black Americans, but the musical *Shuffle Along* (1921), starring Florence Mills, was written by Black people for Black people. Later Florence Mills starred in Lew Leslie's *Black Birds* show, originally from Harlem, on its Paris tour in 1927, before dying at a young age soon afterwards. In the 1920s jazz bands—both black and white—and other black bands began to play often in Britain and other countries of Europe.[353]

Black American artists and entertainers became popular in Paris in the 1920s. There was Le Grand Duc, a centre for Black musicians in Montmartre; there was the singer and dancer Ada Smith, a light-skinned African American commonly known as Bricktop; there were visiting jazzmen like Sidney Bechet. Above all, there was the celebrated Josephine Baker, who arrived in Paris in 1925 with a New York song and dance show that became the Revue Nègre and made her fame in a short time; many years of success as a singer, dancer and film actress followed.[354]

---

352   Archer-Straw (note 349), p. 78. Some Black literary people were to express this idea themselves in the "Negritude" movement in the 1930s.

353   L.F. Emery, *Black Dance from 1619 to Today*, Dance Books, 1972, 1988, pp. 215, 223-4; J. Anderson, *This was Harlem: A Cultural Portrait, 1900-1950*, New York: Farrar, Strauss and Giroux, 1981, 1982; Archer-Straw (note 345), pp. 147-8; Paul Oliver (ed.), *Black Music in Britain*, Open University Press, 1990, especially ch. 3: H. Rye, "Fearsome Means of Discord: Early Encounters with Jazz".

354   P. Rose, *Jazz Cleopatra: Josephine Baker in Her Time*, Chatto & Windus, 1989; W. Wiser, *The Crazy Years: Paris in the Twenties*, Thames & Hudson, 1983, pp. 157-65; Archer-Straw (note 349), pp. 94-5, 116-18, 132-3; Edwards (note 219), pp. 63-8.

Some African American writers also spent long periods in France at this time, including Claude McKay and Langston Hughes, two leading figures in the "Harlem Renaissance".[355] Although both were close to Communism, for many years they had little contact with the Black Communists of the LDRN in France. Their writings however aroused interest among Black people in France, such as Paulette and Jane Nardal, Martinican sisters who with two other sisters were at the centre of a Black literary group in Paris, mainly composed of West Indians, for some years. They and others in their circle developed, for example in the *Dépêche Africaine* magazine, ideas of special cultural features of the Black world generally. Black intellectuals of that school believed firmly that "assimilation" as Frenchmen could and should be made complete, but could be combined with recognition and respect for Black cultural difference.[356]

Black American travellers particularly enjoyed the freedom from racialism in personal relations and daily life in France, but the literary travellers can be seen as part of a wider migration of American, British and Irish writers and artists to Paris at that time. One of that group of migrants, the English poet Nancy Cunard (1896-1965), became a champion of Black causes and a Communist "fellow traveller". The wealthy great-granddaughter of the shipping tycoon Samuel Cunard, she rebelled against her highly privileged upbringing and became as well known for the string of men in her life (including Aragon) as well as for her writing. Her campaigning zeal for the Black world developed during a long affair with the Black American jazz pianist Henry Crowder.[357] It was to lead eventually to publication of her famous work *Negro: An Anthology*, of which more later.

Nancy Cunard said of white New Yorkers going to Harlem for fun, "This desire to get close to the other race has often nothing honest about it...it doesn't affect their conception of the Negroes' social status."[358] Of

---

355   On the links between black writers in the USA and France in this period see Edwards (note 219), e.g. Ch. 1, pp. 98-118, pp. 120-47.

356   Dewitte (note 99), pp. 222-45; Edwards (note 219), especially Ch. 3 (on Paulette Nardal (1896-1985)) and pp. 152-8, 167-71, 178-86.

357   A. Chisholm, *Nancy Cunard*, New York: Knopf, 1979, Harmondsworth: Penguin, 1981, chapters 1-14.

358   Ibid., p. 241.

course people of any race could patronise Black Diaspora entertainment because they liked it, but the vogue for Black music, dance and theatre certainly had nothing to do with racism or non-racism, or attitudes to colonialism. Most fans of Josephine Baker, who blatantly appealed to white men's fantasies, were probably in favour of colonial rule over other black people. She herself apparently shared the usual Francophilia of Black Americans; she took part in a show (*Paris qui Remue*) depicting the empire as exotic in a way satisfying to white audiences, at the Casino de Paris theatre in 1930-31, at the time of the Colonial Exhibition, and starred in films with a similar exotic colonial setting she was a special guest at the Exhibition itself.[359]

Germany as an anti-colonial centre

The Weimar Republic was an important base for radical anti-colonial activity. It seems likely that many Germans, including the government, tolerated activities directed against the British and French empires, out of resentment at the 1918 defeat and the loss of Germany's own colonies.[360] That resentment was felt by former colonial officials and supporters of empire who had no sympathy with Communism; German colonialist publications could, without intending it, join Communist ones to condemn French rule in Cameroun/Kamerun and other ex-German territories.

Leaders of the Committee of Union and Progress regime of wartime Turkey escaped to Germany in 1918 and had their main base there for a time, until Armenians killed several of them and support for their cause collapsed with Kemal's victory. Arab activists who had sided with Turkey and Germany also lived in Germany for a while after 1918: some Tunisians, and notably the Lebanese Shakib Arslan, who was based in Germany for much of the time until 1924, and was always welcome in Germany later, when based in Geneva and campaigning for the cause of Syria and Palestine.[361] Indian activists who had worked with the Germans remained in Germany after 1918, and Berlin was M.N. Roy's

359   Archer-Straw (note 349), pp. 132-3; Edwards (note 219), pp. 162-3.

360   That was Nehru's impression, following his visit in 1926: Nehru (note 93), p. 161.

361   W.L. Cleveland, *Islam against the West*, University of Texas Press and London: Al Saqi, 1985, pp. 40-3. On Arslan's later activity see below, pp. 265-8.

main base for several years; Chattopadhyaya was also based there. Chinese Communist students were active in Germany, where Madame Sun Yat-sen (Soong Ching-ling) also lived for a time in the late 1920s.

Then Germany became the base of the League Against Imperialism, operating from headquarters in Berlin, and for the ITUC-NW at Hamburg and its leading activist George Padmore (who spent some time at Vienna and travelled more widely also). The LAI international executive met in Berlin in May-June 1931; then or soon afterwards Clemens Dutt, Palme Dutt's elder brother and former head of the CPGB Colonial Committee, replaced Chattopadhyaya,[362] who had joined the KPD and now went to Russia.[363] Münzenberg was apparently elected or re-elected International Secretary.[364] Later in 1931 police raided the offices of the LAI in Berlin and the ITUC-NW in Hamburg, and 10,000 pamphlets were confiscated at 8 Rothesoodstrasse.[365] This may well have been a response to pressure from Britain and France, always annoyed by the tolerance shown to anti-colonial radicals in Weimar Germany. But on 20-24 May 1932 Padmore helped organise, and attended, a dockers' and seamen's conference in Hamburg which led to the formation of an International of Seamen and Harbour Workers (ISH), also based at 8 Rothesoodstrasse.[366] Krebs alias Valtin, a German Communist seaman and party worker involved in the creation of the ISH, recalled later that "Its chief task was the mobilization of seamen for the protection of the Soviet Union in case of war, by tying up the shipping of nations antagonistic to Russia."[367]

Radical anti-colonial activity attracted some of the African community in Germany. The latter consisted mostly of people who had gone there before 1914, mainly from Kamerun/Cameroon, and had stayed, sometimes marrying German wives. A number worked in Germany, at least initially, as entertainers or musicians. The worldwide Black music,

362 Government of India, Home Department, *Communism in India*, 1935, p. 172, quoted in Haithcox (note 120), p. 152n.

363 Barooah (note 92), pp. 283-5.

364 X-Reference document dated 13 July 1931 in file KV2/773, National Archives, London.

365 Carew Hunt (note 88), p. 77; Hooker (note 167), pp. 25-6, quoting *Negro Worker*, December 1931.

366 Hooker (note 167), p. 26; Dewitte (note 99), p. 298.

367 Valtin (note 174), p. 184.

dance and arts trends extended to Weimar Germany, where Josephine Baker made a very successful tour in 1926. In the late 20s one jazz band in Berlin included as singer Gladys Casely Hayford, daughter of J.E. Casely Hayford and a poet; she was one of several Africans who joined jazz bands in Europe in the 1920s. The history of these Black residents of Germany has been unearthed in recent years, notably in a book published in Berlin in 2000 by the Senate Representative for Foreigners.[368]

A Duala from Cameroon, Joseph Ekwe Bile, was secretary of the LDRN German section, the Liga zur Verteidigung der Negerrasse, founded on 17 September 1929. Victor Bell, another Duala, was chairman. Other founders of the section have been named[369] as Thomas Manga Akwa, Thomas ul Kuo Ngambi, Richard E. Dinn and M. Kotto Priso (all Duala names).[370] Ekwe Bile lived in Germany from 1912 and qualified as an architect. He attended the ITUC-NW Hamburg conference of 1930 as a representative of the LDRN German section, and then went to Moscow for three months later that year; then he joined the Communist Party and returned to the USSR to attend, it was later reported, the "Lenin School", or some other political school, for 18 months.[371]

Thomas Manga Akwa had been a signatory of the letter to the Weimar Assembly on 27 June 1919. According to a letter he wrote on 15 June 1929, he had lived in Germany since 1910 and had learned the trades of mechanical engineer, mechanic and chauffeur, and worked in munitions factories before the War. Then, he recalled, he returned to Cameroon in 1921 and made pro-German speeches; these, he said, were "heard with great enthusiasm by the people", but the French government "regarded me as a German spy and wanted to execute me. On

---

368 Paulette Reed-Anderson, *Rewriting the Footnotes: Berlin and the African Diaspora*, Berlin: Die Ausländerbeauftragte des Senats, 2000, in German and English. Reed-Anderson, an African American historian living in Germany, has also publicised this forgotten history in exhibitions and documentary films, and other books. On Gladys Casely Hayford see A. Cromwell (note 148), ch. X.

369 in Landesarchiv Berlin, Rep 42, Acc, 1743, No. 9054, Sheet 5, quoted in Reed-Anderson (note 368), p. 46

370 Circular on revolutionary activity, Paris, 31 Dec. 1929, file APA 10367, Cameroon Archives, Yaounde.

371 Notes of 30 Nov. and 5 Dec. 1938, and letter from Minister to Commissioner, 27 March 1935, in file on J.E. Bile, Box Cameroun AP II 28, Archives SOM, Paris/Aix.

the day before, however, I was saved by the population and helped to return to Germany." One must suspect this account, given in a letter asking for a job in Germany and saying he would help Germany regain its colonies,[372] about the same time as he joined a Communist organisation. In fact he was said to have left Cameroon after returning there in 1921 on suspicion of embezzlement from some of his clansmen.[373] However, the French rulers of Cameroun regarded him with deep suspicion. In 1930 the Commissioner for French Cameroun ordered that Manga Akwa could not be allowed to enter the territory.[374] Normally one would expect a governor to want an "agitator" under surveillance or detention in his home colony rather than roaming freely in Europe, but this was a time of strong anti-French feeling among the Dualas, and a politically active Duala exile returning from Germany was obviously seen as an extra danger. In fact Manga Akwa have been returning home simply because he was broke and had got no help in Germany.[375]

North African challenges and Shakib Arslan

In the early 1930s Communist action against Western imperialism was taken very seriously by the colonial powers, but was in fact losing what little strength it had had. The PCF was busy fighting the leaders of the ENA, the only radical nationalist party produced by any part of Africa until then, during the very year, 1930, when Algerians were angered by the centenary celebrations. Within Algeria the local Communists, numbering 280 in 1929 and 130 in 1932, were hardly able to organise any protests.[376] The celebrations, culminating on the exact centenary day on 5 July, included a visit from the President, publication of 1.2 million

---

372 Reed-Anderson (note 368), p. 52.

373 Joseph (note 279), p. 83.

374 Commissioner for French Cameroun to Chef de Circonscription, Douala, 8 October 1930, file APA 11908, Cameroon Archives, Yaounde.

375 There is no space here to examine the colonial governments' sweeping powers over Africans' movement and residence, which varied—in British territories they were less stringent in Crown Colonies than in Protectorates—but were always considerable.

376 E. Sivan, *Communisme et Nationalisme en Algérie 1920-1962,* Paris: Presses de la FNSP, 1976, pp. 55-6.

Cahiers du centenaire for schools and libraries, and visits by 80,000 people from France including 306 members of the National Assembly.[377]

Socialists, not Communists lent support when in 1930 massive new anti-colonial protests broke out in French North Africa, in Morocco. Those protests, which were to find an echo over many countries, were taken up also by the Lebanese campaigner for Arab causes Shakib Arslan (1869-1946), who represented a revival of Islamic anti-colonialism, as formidable as the left-wing variety.

Islamic anti-colonialism, still often called "pan-Islamism" at this time, had never faded away. It was aroused in the 1920s, in particular, by the Italian war against the Sanusiyya in Libya and by the Zionist immigration into Palestine. In Libya the Sanusiyya waged for years a classic guerrilla campaign, with probably no more than a thousand fighters most of the time, but taking advantage of the terrain they knew—woodland and mountains as well as desert—and above all of the support of the population. People who had apparently submitted to the Italians continued to help the fighters; General Graziani, who became Deputy Governor of Cyrenaica during the campaign, wrote, "The entire population thus took part directly or indirectly in the rebellion." Like many counter-insurgency officers, he responded by treating the entire population as rebels. The resistance was ably led by 'Umar al-Mukhtar, who had the title of al-Naib al-'Amm, Representative-General.[378]

After several years the Italians made more progress in 1927-28, and more again after a few months' truce agreed with Mukhtar in 1929; in that year Italian forces with tanks crossed a large area of desert to capture the Kufra oasis. The last phase of the Italian suppression was marked by great brutality, with tens of thousands of people put in concentration camps, a long barbed-wire barrier erected along the Egyptian border, and fleeing caravans bombed by Graziani's order. 'Umar al-Mukhtar was captured on 11 September 1931, and hanged before a crowd of 20,000 at Suluq on 16 September. On 24 January 1932 the Italians declared the war at an end.[379]

---

377   M. Thomas, *The French Empire between the Wars: Imperialism, Politics and Society*, Manchester University Press, 2005, pp. 197-8.

378   He and his resistance war are commemorated in the film *The Lion of the Desert* (1981).

379   E.E. Evans-Pritchard, *The Sanusi of Cyrenaica*, OUP, 1949, pp. 159-90; R. Da-

In Morocco, while some mountain-dwellers in the south still resisted French rule, other people manifested opposition by peaceful means. Muslims following the Salafiyya teachings founded "free schools", which have been described as the "cradle of Moroccan nationalism", and in the late 1920s some students formed secret societies. In Fez there was an Islamic one founded by Allal al-Fassi and some others, mostly students at Qarawiyin, and another by students at French secondary schools, several of whom went on to study in France. In August 1926 the nucleus of a secret society was started in Rabat, and its leading members became prominent nationalists—Ahmed Balafrej, Moham-med Hassan al-Ouazzani, Omar Abdeljalil, Mohammed Lyazidi and others attending French schools, Mekki Naciri and others who were receiving a Muslim education. These groups made contact with each other, and the Islamic and Western-educated strands were not separate; nationalism, Islam, and respect for the Sultan's throne—even though he was forced to collaborate with the French—went together in Moroc-can nationalism from the start. Respect for the Sultan always contin-ued in Spanish Morocco and the International Zone in Tangier also; a Khalifa represented the Sultan in Spanish Morocco, with the agreement of the two colonial powers, and nationalists also saw the country as one despite the partition.[380]

Moroccan nationalists were spurred into action by a French enact-ment of 16 May 1930 creating a separate system of justice in Berber areas, with French courts and some others supposed to be based on Berber tradition, to reduce the traditional jurisdiction of the Sultan's government (the Makhzen) in those areas. Like other French decrees in Morocco this was issued as a *dahir* (decree) of the Sultan, Moham-med V. The Berber Dahir, as it came to be called, was a typical colonial divide-and-rule measure, and was based on a division far less impor-tant than the French professed to believe. In both Algeria and Morocco most of the population is probably descended from the pre-Arab Berber population, whether or not they speak Berber, while the Berber-speak-

---

vico, "La guérilla libyenne, 1911-1932", pp. 402-39 in *Abd el-Krim...* (note 1).

380   J.P. Halstead, *Rebirth of a Nation: The Origins and Rise of Moroccan National-ism, 1912-1944,* Cambridge, MA: Harvard Univerity Press, 1967, pp. 166-70; Oved (note 4), vol. 2, pp. 22-5.

ers (about 40 per cent of Morocco's population in 1930) are Muslims like the rest. They had their separate traditions, but were increasingly adopting Islamic law. The Algerians in France, who backed the ENA in large numbers, were mainly Berber. Muslims and Arabs around the world protested against the Berber Dahir, just as they had backed the Berber Rif rebels shortly before. The French were sometimes accused of wanting to prepare the way for Christian evangelisation among the Berbers, usually of attacking Islam at least, and of using a supposed ethnic division to reinforce their own rule.

Besides protests led by nationalist leaders, and an attempted boycott of French goods, in Morocco itself, Moroccan student leaders in France were able to mobilise support around the world against French policy in Morocco. They cooperated with several left-wing activists including Pierre Renaudel, the Longuets father and son, and Daniel Guérin, who were not backed by their leaders in the SFIO. For its part the PCF saw the protests against the Berber Dahir as bourgeois and was no longer accommodating towards Islam.[381]

A book entitled *La tempête sur le Maroc* was published in Paris early in 1931, under a pseudonym (Mouslim Barbari) but in fact produced by student leaders in Paris including Naciri, who was studying at the Sorbonne and the Institut des Etudes Islamiques, and Balafrej, with Abdeljalil possibly playing an important role also; Guérin was also involved in its production. It called on the French authorities to change their policy, which the nationalists declared to be in contravention of the Protectorate Treaty of 1912. *La tempête sur le Maroc* said, "France has succeeded in arousing the Muslims of the whole world against it".[382] Indignation was aroused in Egypt—where the *ulama* of al-Azhar petitioned King Fuad to intervene with the French government and a "committee for the defence of Moroccan Muslims" was formed—and all over the Muslim world as far as Java.[383]

Shakib Arslan, in Geneva, was contacted by the Moroccan protest leaders in Paris and became a powerful defender of their cause, especially in his periodical which he started at just that time, *La Nation Arabe*. Arslan, a Druze born in Lebanon in 1869, was one of the Arab

---

381   Liauzu (note 14), pp. 55-6.
382   Oved (note 4), vol. 2, p. 33; Biondi (note 14), pp. 174-5.
383   Halstead (note 380), pp. 52-3, 70-74, 181-6.

elite of the Ottoman empire, and a strong believer in Ottoman pan-Islamism. In the 1914-18 war years he was a member of the Ottoman parliament and believed in Turkey's cause until the end, after which he escaped to Berlin. He plotted with Turkish leaders in exile and continued to believe in the Ottoman cause for a while, but from 1921, when he was secretary to the Syro-Palestinian Congress in Geneva, he concentrated on the cause of Syria and Palestine, heading a permanent delegation of the Congress in Europe.[384] He was also a vocal supporter of the Libyan resistance, writing after the execution of Mukhtar, "His blood will always cry for vengeance and that cry will be heard by all the Muslim world."[385]

Arslan was widely known in the Arab world. Like many Muslims he was not reconciled to the abolition of the Caliphate by Kemal and thought Islam should still have a Caliph.[386] Those ideas came to nothing in the end, but Arslan, influenced by Rashid Rida and the Salafi-yya school, strongly emphasised Islam in his nationalist message. As an anti-imperialist campaigner Arslan attracted wide attention, from the colonial rulers among others. He visited Soviet Russia in 1921 and 1927. Arslan had been writing for other newspapers for decades before launching *La Nation Arabe* as a monthly in Geneva in 1930, and in the 1930s was producing 80-100 articles per year in Arabic alone. He and his Syrian co-editor Ihsan al-Jabiri dominated *La Nation Arabe*'s pages, making it an organ of Islamic anti-imperialism. The journal was beset by financial problems, but struggled on until 1938, though it was an irregular quarterly by 1936; 38 issues appeared in all.[387]

La Nation Arabe reflected and spread Arab-Muslim indignation over French Morocco. Just as the protests were growing Arslan visited Spanish Morocco and Tangier in August 1930. In Tetuan he gave speeches and received visitors from several Moroccan cities; he met people such as Abd al-Khaliq Torres who were to become prominent nationalists in the Spanish Zone.[388] Those nationalists drew up a "Charter of De-

---

384   Cleveland (note 361), pp. 1-62.

385   Ibid., pp. 100-1.

386   Ibid., pp. 71-3.

387   Ibid., pp. 68-9.

388   Ibid., pp. 94-7; J. Wolf, *Les secrets du Maroc Espagnol: l'épopée d'Abd-el-Khaleq Torres,* Paris: Balland, 1994, pp. 154-8, 167-70.

mands" on 1 May 1931, soon after the declaration of a Republic in Spain, and presented it to President Zamora; in September nationalists won most seats in local elections in Spanish Morocco. The Spanish government then turned hostile to the nationalists, but talks were held in April-May 1932. The nationalists in Spanish Morocco, operating more freely than their French zone equivalents, remained like them in regular contact with Arslan, who had become their mentor.[389]

Moroccans respected Arslan particularly because he was a famous polemical writer from the Arab East (the Mashreq). Maghrebians had for long followed the intellectual lead of the East. Egypt had great influence in the Arab world, because of its renowned al-Azhar mosque-university, its newspapers and, from the 1920s, its films. The East was also much nearer to independence than the West of the Arab world; Egypt was nominally independent, Syria under French Mandate had its own indigenous government, and the British Mandate over Iraq ended in 1930.

Arslan helped Moroccan protesters get publicity in the Eastern Arab press besides giving them good coverage in *La Nation Arabe*. He worked closely with Muhammad al-Fassi, Ahmed Balafrej and Mekki Naciri; Ouazzani was his secretary in 1932-33.[390] To increase Arab and Muslim support for the Moroccan protests, *La tempête sur le Maroc* was translated into Arabic and published in Cairo, and was available to delegates at the Jerusalem Islamic Conference held on 7-16 December 1931.[391] That conference was attended, among others, by the exiled Tunisian nationalist leader Tha'alibi, and by an Egyptian representative, Abd al-Rahman Azzam, who was deported from Palestine by the British after condemning the Italians' actions in Libya.[392] It heard a report on Morocco prepared in Geneva by Naciri with Arslan and Ihsan al-Jabiri, and agreed to send a protest to the Secretary General of the League of Nations. That report was published soon afterwards in Cairo in Arabic, as a booklet whose title translated as "France and its Berber Policy in

389   Wolf (note 388), pp. 176-84.

390   Cleveland (note 361), pp. 94, 97-100.

391   Halstead (note 380), pp. 184-6.

392   See T. Mayer, "Egypt and the General Islamic Conference of Jerusalem in 1931", *Middle Eastern Studies* 18, 3, July 1982, pp. 311-22; Coury (note 98), pp. 299-313.

Morocco"; it said plainly that the Protectorate regime should help Morocco regain independence.

The upsurge in Muslim feeling manifest in the Berber Dahir protests and in Arslan's writings was widespread. The ENA in France was more Islamic as it slowly revived from 1931. In France, too, the AEMNA, officially declared to the authorities on 28 December 1927, after some years without much overt political activity became more political from 1930, and its politics showed Islamic commitment.[393]

In Algeria a new, strongly Islamic element in nationalism appeared with the foundation in 1931 of the Association des Oulémas Musulmans Algériens. It was founded by Abdelhamid Ben Badis (1889-1940), a scholar of Constantine influenced by Abduh of Egypt, as a movement for purified and reformed Islam and reform in society, establishing new Islamic schools which rapidly became popular. Earlier he had started a Muslim newspaper, *El Mountaqid*, quickly banned, and then another, *Ech Chihab*. Although at first it avoided standard political activity the new association of Islamic scholars (*ulama*), with its slogan "Algeria is my country, Arabic is my language, Islam is my religion," was implicitly nationalist. It encouraged a different approach from that of the remnants of the Jeunes Algériens movement which still continued and still had influence, as a grouping of French-educated people calling for assimilation. As noted earlier, the meaning of "assimilation" was variable and often imprecise, but for those elite Algerians it meant making Algeria fully a part of France, with all its people becoming French citizens. Among those who wanted this the pharmacist Ferhat Abbas (1899-1985) was becoming prominent by 1931, when he published a volume written by some of his group entitled *De la colonie vers la province: le jeune Algérien*. Their ideas may seem today to be the contrary of nationalism, but calls for "assimilation" like those made by Abbas—who wanted Muslims to retain their Islamic "personal status"—in fact

393   C.-R. Ageron, "L'Association des Etudiants Musulmans Nord-Africains en France durant l'entre-deux-guerres: contribution à l'Etude du nationalisme maghrébin", *Revue Française d'Histoire d'Outremer* vol. LXX, nos. 258-9, 1983, pp. 25-56; Liauzu (note 14), pp. 151-2, 156; M. Chenoufi, "Le rôle des mouvements d'étudiants tunisiens de 1900 à 1975," pp. 147-64 in *Le rôle des mouvements d'étudiants africains dans l'évolution politique et sociale de l'Afrique de 1900 à 1975* (no editor), Paris: Editions UNESCO/Harmattan, 1993, p. 152.

implied such sweeping changes, especially at the expense of the *colons,* that they never came near to being considered.

In Tunisia Muslim feelings were inflamed when the Catholic Church organised a Eucharistic Congress at Carthage in May 1930, and celebrations of fifty years of the French protectorate were held in May 1931. By then some younger activists educated in France were coming to oppose French rule more strongly and accuse the Destour leaders of timidity. They included Chedly Khairallah, the former Chairman of the ENA, who after his deportation back to Tunisia edited *L'Etendard Tunisien*; and Habib Bourguiba (1902-2000), who after studies in France spread the message of militant nationalism, from 1929 to 1933, especially through that newspaper and others, *La Voix du Tunisien* (founded by Khairallah in 1930) and *L'Action Tunisienne* (founded on 1 November 1932).[394]

Triumphant colonialism: France's Expo 1931

From 6 May to 15 November 1931 a Colonial Exhibition in Paris, at the Parc de Vincennes, attracted 8 million visitors. It was elaborately prepared over four years by a team headed by Marshal Lyautey as Special Commissioner. While there were stands exhibiting the Portuguese, Italian and Dutch empires (but not the British), the Expo was above all a grandiose display of the greatness and glory of the French empire, its propagandist message being reinforced by a special information bureau and by congresses held at the same time. The stands devoted to various parts of the French empire, illustrating the Angkor temples of Cambodia, the traditional buildings of Djenne in French Sudan and other features old and new, were designed to impress.[395] Blaise Diagne, who had been appointed Under Secretary of State for the Colonies in January 1931, joined the Minister, Paul Reynaud, and President Doumergue and Prime Minister Laval at the inauguration of the Expo on 6 May 1931. Reynaud proclaimed in his speech, "France now has 100 million inhabitants, an area of 11 million square kilometres, 35,000

---

394   Lejri (note 46), Vol. II, pp. 6-36.

395   See C. Hodeir and M. Pierre, *L'Exposition Coloniale*, Brussels: Complexe, 1991.

kilometres of coast, 700,000 kilometres of roads and 70,000 kilometres of railways."[396]

Some Africans and Asians cooperating with the French colonial regime had sponsored trips to France and the Exhibition, for example the Sultan of Morocco. Some other Africans were brought in to perform various roles in the African stands, to add to the general impression of an exotic other world being civilised by France. They were present as waiters in African and Tunisian restaurants, brassware dealers in souks recreated in the Morocco pavilion, a Sudanese (i.e. from French Sudan) family cooking mutton on a fire, Malagasy canoeists on the park lake, etc. Of course colonial troops were part of the spectacle also.[397] Those "native" participants would, no doubt, have reasonably enjoyed their trip to Paris and the pay and other benefits, whatever their private thoughts. But the Algerian band from Tlemcen, Messali's home town, gave a recital at a meeting organised by Messali outside the Expo, followed by a speech from him saying what he and his comrades thought of the Expo—not part of the authorities' plans.[398]

The Exhibition, whose buildings remained standing for decades afterwards, was popular and made a profit (unlike the Wembley exhibition of 1924). The anti-colonialists responded, but their efforts showed how small a minority they were.

The LAI, helped by the LDRN, produced a Counter-Exhibition, officially called *La Vérité sur les Colonies*. It was originally reported that this would be held in Germany, but eventually it was held in Paris. A good deal of the Contre-Expo was devoted to African, Oceanian and Native American sculpture. There was a display devoted to the USSR and the "republics formerly oppressed as colonies by the Tsarist regime", and a display of the evils of French colonial rule, recalling crimes committed in the occupation of Africa and the ordeal of colonial soldiers in the trenches in the Great War, and the Congo-Ocean Railway horrors. There was a room devoted to anti-colonial movements, with a reference to SRI aid to militants in Madagascar, Syria and Indochina. Everything, of course, was geared to the Communist anti-colonial message. The propaganda in the Contre-Expo about Soviet Asia showed

---

396   Biondi (note 14), p. 169.
397   Hodeir and Pierre (note 395), pp. 88-93.
398   Messali (note 51), p. 171.

women being freed from the veil, and the display on nationalist movements highlighted Kemal's revolution in Turkey, which had some features in common with Soviet rule in the Asian republics. The Counter-Exhibition ran from 19 September to 2 December 1931, and attracted precisely 4,226 visitors.[399]

A brochure, *Le véritable guide de l'Exposition Coloniale*, subtitled "*L'Oeuvre civilisatrice de la France magnifiée dans quelques pages*," was published by the SRI and distributed surreptitiously within the main Expo. Briefly, in a few pages—it was professionally poor and clearly produced on the cheap—it attacked French rule in Madagascar, AEF, Syria, North Africa, Indochina and the West Indies and Guyane. On Madagascar it mentioned the VVS imprisonments and the 1929 demonstration; on AEF it spoke of the mass deaths on the railway construction. It spoke of "ferocious repression" in Tunisia, and in Algeria of the massive seizure of land by settlers, the Indigénat, and punishments such as the banishment of Ben Lekhal ("by the good pleasure of Viollette, governor, member of the Ligue des Droits de l'Homme": it was necessary for a Communist publication to add such details). On Morocco it mentioned the profits of the Banque de Paris et des Pays-Bas, highlighted during the campaign against the Rif war.[400]

There was a separate pamphlet issued on 30 April 1931 by Surrealists, entitled *Ne visitez pas l'Exposition Coloniale*. It declared,

The presence on the inaugural rostrum of the Colonial Exhibition of the President of the Republic, the Emperor of Annam, the Cardinal Archbishop of Paris and several governors and old troopers, opposite the missionaries' pavilion and those of Citroën and Renault, clearly expresses the complicity of the entire bourgeoisie in the birth of a new and particularly intolerable idea: "Greater France".

The twelve signatories of the pamphlet, who called plainly for "immediate evacuation of the colonies", included Aragon, Eluard, Sadoul and Tanguy.[401]

But these voices were drowned in the festivities. The 1931 Paris exhibition was triumphal, as one would expect at a time when colonialism

---

399   Hodeir and Pierre (note 395), pp. 125-34; Dewitte (note 99), pp. 291-2.

400   Brochure reproduced in Liauzu (note 14), pp. 239-44.

401   Dewitte (note 99), p. 253-4.

was triumphant. In an editorial in *Le Populaire* on 7 May 1931 Blum said the Expo "would probably be a fine spectacle" but suggested that "one should not forget what reality is hidden behind this decor of art and joy. One should not forget that in the whole world conquered or subjected peoples are beginning to reclaim their freedom."[402] But nationalist movements were still very far from attaining their goal, especially in Africa. The colonial empires were going concerns, and therefore would go on until something was able to stop them.

---

402   Hodeir and Pierre (note 395), p. 103.

4

STRUGGLES IN THE THIRTIES, 1932–39

Red and Black in the early thirties

Communist party activity in Africa in the early 1930s was confined to South Africa, apart from limited activity in Algeria, and was not progressing well. But among African communities in Europe Communist activity against Western imperialism seemed to be having some success between 1931 and 1933, where Black Africans—though not North Africans—were concerned. In France, while the ENA was both struggling and outside Communist control, the quarrels in the militant African and Caribbean organisation, the LDRN, ended with Kouyate heading the Moscow-oriented faction which seemed to do well for a time. Kouyate, the Comintern's top African for a time, was placed in 1931 at the head of the Communist (CGTU) seamen's union, the Fédération des Gens de Mer, and headed the French delegation to the founding conference of the ISH in Hamburg in May 1932. He was removed from his position at the head of the union in August 1932, but continued to work under PCF and Comintern direction on a new organisation for the Black population in France.

After Kouyate lost the legal tussle with Faure over the LDRN and its newspaper, it was decided to replace Kouyate's LDRN faction with a new body with a distinct name. The Union des Travailleurs Nègres (UTN) was launched in September 1932, by Kouyate, Rosso and Thomas Ramananjato, a Malagasy, as a mutual benefit society. It was soon organising meetings, planning social events and arousing interest, while *Le Cri des Nègres*, now the UTN's organ, resumed publication after several months. In late 1932 it seemed for a moment that Faure's LDRN faction had won an empty court victory; *La Race Nègre* was now the organ of the recognised LDRN, but it ceased publication in February 1932—for over two years as it turned out—while the UTN's newspaper was subsidised.[1]

George Padmore, Secretary of the ITUC-NW and the world's leading Black Communist at that time, was in France in late 1932, watching over the creation of the UTN and also meeting Nancy Cunard, who had been corresponding with him about her book eventually published as *Negro: An Anthology*, and who about the same time took out a subscription to *Le Cri des Nègres*.[2] Padmore, whose main base was still in Germany, may also have visited Britain in September 1932, but this is very uncertain.[3]

During 1932 Padmore corresponded with the Gold Coast lawyer and nationalist William Essuman Gyira Sekyi, commonly known as Kobina Sekyi (1892-1956). One of the founders of the NCBWA, Sekyi was particularly concerned to defend African culture, and published a series of articles in the *West Africa* weekly in 1917-18 entitled "The Anglo-Fanti", to ridicule the imitation of European ways by Africans. He wrote a play in the same vein, *The Blinkards*, which was only published after his death.[4] He was a leader of the ARPS and a leading protester against the Native Authority Ordinance of 1927 which set out the role of chiefs as agents of British rule. In the course of the prolonged

1   1. P. Dewitte, *Les Mouvements Nègres en France 1919-1939*, Paris: L'Harmattan, 1985, pp. 283-302.

2   Ibid., pp. 300-2.

3   J.R. Hooker, *Black Revolutionary: George Padmore's Path from Communism to Pan-Africanism*, New York: Praeger, 1970 mentions briefly (pp. 26-7) an encounter in Britain between Padmore and C.L.R. James—a fellow Trinidadian who went to England in 1932 and was to be one of the leading anti-colonial activists there, as the coming pages will describe—and C.A. Smith of the ILP. However, James himself recalled different, later dates for that meeting. He said it was in 1933 that he heard about a meeting where George Padmore was speaking and went and saw "my boyhood friend Malcolm Nurse" (C.L.R. James, *At the Rendezvous of Victory*, selected writings and speeches, Allison & Busby, 1984, p. 240); but, he added, Padmore said he had been in Britain in 1932 recruiting people to go to Moscow for training. Elsewhere, however, he said Padmore had mentioned a recruiting visit to London in March 1933 (ibid., p. 254).

4   It was reprinted in 1974 (London: Heinemann), with an introduction by J. Ayo Langley on Sekyi's life.

legal battle between Nana Ofori Atta, Okyenhene of Akyem Abuakwa and the main chiefly ally of the British, and the subordinate chiefs of Akwatia and Asamankese, over a portion the Paramount Chief claimed on land concession fees for diamond mining, Sekyi defended the Asamankese ruler. The case went to the Privy Council in London and Sekyi travelled there to represent him, backed by the ARPS. Sekyi also contacted British, French and American financiers for a new cocoa-buying group planned by the Gold Coast Farmers' Association, which had organised a briefly successful Cocoa Hold-Up in 1930-31, and the ARPS, and went to Britain to conclude a deal.[5]

Kobina Sekyi—who ordered fancy waistcoats and suits from England, used silk handkerchiefs, and enjoyed wine, cigars and literature—lived in a world far removed from that of Communist agitation and clandestine activity. But before travelling he wrote to Padmore, who sent a friendly reply speaking of "the interest which you, as a professional man, are taking on behalf of the oppressed people...and the help you are rendering to the working class in your country." Later Padmore wrote to Sekyi, "We are certain...that you have the ambition to see your country a free independent nation from the yoke of alien domination." Sekyi did have that ambition, but he wanted to pursue it in the now established West African elite way. Padmore asked him for help in sending Gold Coast workers to Europe for study "to help the toiling masses of the Gold Coast in organising themselves for better economic and social conditions." However, Sekyi asked the West Indian revolutionary for help for engineering studies for his brother, and R.B. Wuta-Ofei, editor of the Gold Coast *Spectator*, wrote to Sekyi and Padmore, urging Sekyi to raise with Padmore the question of living costs during studies for himself, and future employment.

Maybe Padmore realised the gulf between his ideas and the outlook of educated West Africans, including those highly critical of colonialism. On 9 July 1932 he wrote to Sekyi,

...we cannot understand why there is no organized national movement... for independence...You lack the sustained organized movement, as in India, China...I think the trouble is that the Africans still have great illusions about Britain...they think...'The King is good, but the Governor is bad. Therefore all

---

5   S. Rohdie, "The Gold Coast Aborigines Abroad, "*Journal of African History* vol. VI no. 3, 1965, pp. 389-411.

you have to do is ask the King to remove the bad Governor.' All this is stupidity...What you must hit at is the *system* of imperialism.[6]

Sekyi replied that the case between the chiefs involved an attack on colonialism: an attack on Ofori Atta threatened the plans of his British allies. But he did not renounce the traditional approach which had been followed since the 19th century, and was more or less as Padmore described: appealing to the colonial power's better nature. He missed the point: expensive legal actions between chiefs had no relation to the seething spirit of revolution that Padmore and his comrades expected to see.[7]

This exchange illustrates how far the ideas of the Comintern and the Black activists working with it were from the realities in Africa—their efforts had very little impact. In South Africa the Communist Party and its sister organisations were active, but very few people were involved. On 16 July 1932 E. Dennis, an emissary sent to South Africa by the ECCI, reported that CPSA membership had risen to about 3,000 in 1928 but had fallen to about 1,500 in 1929; there was a further decline in 1930, and by April 1931 there were only about 100 members.[8] Dennis said his 1929 figure was for "those who held cards and still attended mass meetings"; Nzula must have followed other criteria in a report on 5 August 1931, where he gave details of the CPSA's organisation and activity and membership figures amounting to nearly 2,000.[9]

The small band of South African Communists continued to squabble among themselves for several years, but several of its leading lights were summoned to Moscow for training. Albert Nzula left soon after writing the report just mentioned. Edwin Mofutsanyana, Nzula's classmate and later party comrade, recalled fifty years later that Nzula, Moses Kotane and another person had tried to stow away on a ship at Durban

---

6   Ibid., p. 394.

7   R. Rathbone, *Murder and Politics in Colonial Ghana*, New Haven: Yale University Press, 1993, comments (p. 61n.) that Sekyi and the other main lawyer in the case, Thomas Hutton-Mills, "cleverly used their connections with the coastal politicians to portray Ofori Atta as an uncompromising feudalist but clearly had more than just radical politics on their minds."

8   Report by E. Dennis to ECCI, 16 July 1932, document 13 in A. Davidson, I. Filatova, V. Gorodnov and S. Jones (eds), *South Africa and the Communist International: A Documentary History*, London: Frank Cass, 2003, Vol. 2, p. 29.

9   Report by A. Nzula, 5 August 1931, Document 5 in ibid., Vol. 2, pp. 15-17.

and had been caught; then Nzula boarded a ship at Cape Town with a passport in the name of Conan Doyle Modiakgotla, posing as one of Griffiths Motsieloa's singing group going to London for recording.[10] Another account says Modiakgotla was a former ICU leader[11] (but does not explain why he risked trouble by lending his passport to a leader of a party that denounced the ICU constantly). In London the CPGB arranged for Nzula to go on to Russia under the name of Tom Jackson, the alias he used from then on.[12] He arrived in Moscow on 25 August 1931. Kotane also reached London, with false papers, and then stowed away from Tilbury on a ship to Russia.[13] He was followed to the USSR by Edwin Mofutsanyana in 1932, and by some other South African comrades including J.B. Marks, who had a European-sounding name but was a Sotho (Basuto).

An unusually large number of Africans spent quite long periods in Moscow in 1931-32. Besides Nzula, Kotane and Mofutsanyana, there were Joseph Ekwe Bile and Johnstone Kenyatta. The Cameroonian later suggested he had been in the USSR for eighteen months in or about 1931-32, before returning to Germany.[14] The Kenyan seems to have travelled to Russia in August 1932 or soon afterwards, and stayed for up to a year.[15] I.T.A. Wallace Johnson also travelled to Moscow at that time, to attend the Congress of International Red Aid/MOPR in November 1932, which Padmore and Nzula attended and addressed. The Sierra Leonean was involved in Lagos with a little known independent church organisation, the Koppeng African Universal Church Society, and travelled to London under the auspices of that society, before going—so he later recalled—to several other European countries besides

---

10   R. Edgar, "Notes on the Life and Death of Albert Nzula", *International Journal of African Historical Studies* vol. 16 no. 4, 1983, pp. 675-79. Motsieloa was a leading South African music promoter in the 1930s.

11   Introduction by R. Cohen to A.T. Nzula, I.I. Potekhin and A.Z. Zusmanovich, *Forced Labour in Colonial Africa* (1933, reprint London: Zed Press, 1979), pp. 2-16; p. 10. On this book see below.

12   Edgar (note 10).

13   Brian Bunting, *Moses Kotane, South African Revolutionary*, London: Inkululeko Publications, 1975, p. 58.

14   Notes of 30 November and 5 December 1938, and letter from Minister of Colonies to Commissioner for French Cameroun, 27 March 1935, in file on J.E. Bile, Box Cameroun AP II 28, Archives SOM, Paris/Aix-en-rovence.

15   J. Murray-Brown, *Kenyatta*, London: Allen & Unwin, 1972, pp. 163-71.

the USSR. As already indicated, a good deal of what Wallace Johnson recalled about his life at that time is doubtful. He claimed to have studied at Kutvu for eighteen months,[16] but it was apparently less than four months in fact.

The Africans who went to Russia for longer periods in those years probably all went to Kutvu, which in some reports is confused with the separate Lenin School. Kenyatta was there under the alias "James Joken", and Mofutsanyana under the alias "Greenwood", in January 1933.[17] Kotane left Russia at the end of 1932 to return to South Africa, where he became General Secretary of the CPSA, and at some point Ekwe Bile also departed, apparently (but it is not clear) to return to Germany. "Wallace Daniels", who was at Kutvu in January 1933, was almost certainly I.T.A. Wallace Johnson, who used the alias "Wal. Daniels" for several years; however, he left Moscow soon afterwards, returning to West Africa via London in February 1933.

The Africans at Kutvu led privileged lives, but research into the Comintern archives has shown that they had their grievances. By September 1932, after some complaints, the ECCI launched an investigation which found that there was "white chauvinism" and "political hooliganism" in the Anglo-American sector of Kutvu, where black students were commonly placed; there were racial problems involving Americans and other white foreigners, fuelled by drink and tension over women. On 19 January 1933 the head of the Comintern, Dmitri Manuilsky, went to Kutvu to listen to complaints from thirteen African and African American students, including Kenyatta and Mofutsanyana, about portrayal of black people in the Soviet theatre, racism among Soviet people, and other things.[18] Manuilsky's personal intervention shows that the Soviet leaders were anxious that promising young revolutionaries at Kutvu should leave Russia with a good impression. The trainees also complained about the poor food, unreliable heating and the high cost of living; they added, "We recognize the difficulties of socialist con-

---

16   LaRay Denzer, "I.T.A. Wallace-Johnson and the West African Youth League: A Case Study in West African Radicalism", PhD, Birmingham, 1973, pp. 46-8.

17   W. McClellan, "Africans and Black Americans in the Comintern Schools, 1925-1934", *International Journal of African Historical Studies* Vol. 26 no. 2, 1993, pp. 371-90.

18   Ibid.

struction in the Soviet Union", which may indicate that they knew how much worse off ordinary Soviet workers were.

Albert Nzula was attached mainly to the Research Association for National and Colonial Problems (Russian initials NIANKP), which was founded in 1927 as a research body linked to Kutvu, then reconstituted in 1929 to emphasise national and colonial questions. It had an African Bureau, set up after Endre Shiik (or Sik)—a Hungarian who lived in Russia from 1915 to 1945 and was considered the principal founder of Marxist African studies—had proposed a Soviet programme of African studies in April 1929.[19] Two Soviet Africanists at the NIANKP African Bureau, Ivan Izosimovich Potekhin (later to become head of the Africa Institute of the Soviet Academy of Sciences) and A.Z. Zusmanovich, worked with Albert Nzula on a joint book published in Moscow in 1933, in Russian, with the title *The Working Class Movement and Forced Labour in Negro Africa*. An English translation was published in 1979 as *Forced Labour in Colonial Africa*.[20]

The book deals not only with forced labour, but also with other economic exploitation in Africa. The first chapter emphasises the importance of Black Africa as a source of raw materials—"It is, of course, for this very reason the greatest source of conflict between capitalists" (p. 23)—but also describes, correctly, how it was also seen as a market: there had always been an important difference between capitalist interests seeing the African as a customer and those seeing him as a labourer or serf. The second chapter studies exploitation of peasants, noting the different colonial policies in various regions such as West Africa. In the third chapter the authors deal with forced labour itself, mentioning the Congo-Ocean railway, and give various facts about the Belgian Congo and South Africa. Other chapters deal, among other topics, with the effects of the Slump, peasant revolts in Africa, and the trade union movement, especially in South Africa.

---

19   Cohen (note 11), p. 11; E.T. Wilson, *Russia and Black Africa before World War II*, New York: Holmes & Meier, 1974, pp. 186-90; A. Davidson and I. Filatova, "African History: A View from Behind the Kremlin Wall", Ch. 5 in M. Matusevich (ed.), *Africa in Russia, Russia in Africa: Three Centuries of Encounters*, Trenton, NJ: Africa World Press, 2007 (pp. 113-17).

20   A.T. Nzula, I.I. Potekhin and A.Z. Zusmanovich, *Forced Labour in Colonial Africa*, London: Zed Books, 1979, p. 12.

Nzula presumably wrote a good deal of the sections on South Africa; the statistics could have come from literature which he brought with him or which had been gathered from CPSA or other sources in Moscow. Potekhin had a special interest in West Africa and probably wrote the parts of the book dealing with that region, while Zusmanovich had a similar interest in the Belgian Congo. The sections on that country are well researched, making use of the Belgian Communist newspaper *Drapeau Rouge*; they include a description of the Bapende rising of 1931 and Belgian protests that it aroused (pp. 110-13).[21]

While these authors said the Watch Tower movement in the Rhodesias and other countries "has a clearly anti-imperialist character", they repeated the Party line on African "reformists" including the ANC in South Africa. But it was a factual as well as a polemical work. It was written in 1932 and early 1933; meanwhile Nzula alias Jackson, besides working on the book, addressed the MOPR Congress in November 1932. He spoke about the campaigns against the passes and a garment workers' strike in late 1931 (after he left), and about repression of peasants unable to pay their taxes in South-West Africa. Another theme he addressed was colonial "terror" in Africa, probably thinking mostly of his own country, where the police state was certainly becoming steadily harsher at that time.[22]

The Working Class Movement and Forced Labour in Negro Africa was printed between 4 August and 28 September 1933.[23] This study of forced labour was published, and officially sponsored, by a country where millions were already being subjected to the same thing by Stalin's regime and many more millions were shortly to suffer the same fate. The Soviet book on oppression in Africa, including that of peasants, was completed at the very time when Stalin was busy turning the Ukrainian farm belt into something resembling Leopold II's Congo Free State. Even outside the area of the hideous man-made famine of 1932-33 ordinary Soviet citizens suffered for many years, after the end of the New Economic Policy, from poverty, shortages of almost everything,

---

21   Cohen (note 11), pp. 12-13.

22   Speech of A. Nzula at World Congress of International Red Aid (MOPR), 18 November 1932, document 20 in Davidson *et al.* (eds) (note 8), vol. 2, pp. 63-5.

23   Nzula *et al.* (note 20), p. vii.

and police terror. Nzula, Potekhin and Zusmanovich must have known about all this; what were their private thoughts? About Albert Nzula a clue was provided by Mofutsanyana in an interview published half a century later.

According to that interview Nzula drank heavily in Russia, and when drunk expressed anti-Stalinist and Trotskyist views.[24] There had been open support for Lev Trotsky within the Soviet Communist Party before he was banished from the country in 1929; then, in exile in Turkey for the next four years, he denounced Stalin's methods, and his views were expressed in a *Bulletin of the Opposition* published in Paris and then in Berlin.[25] Nzula could have heard about Trotsky's ideas in various ways, or he could simply have made his own similar criticisms of Stalin.

According to Padmore's biographer the Trinidadian revolutionary told, many years later, "of his shock when a young woman he had invited to share a meal with him in his Moscow flat asked if she might take the table scraps to her family."[26] But the radical anti-colonialists who became Communists or were close to Communism generally kept quiet about the horrible reality of what was going on under Stalin's rule—as countless Westerners, including many politicians and intellectuals, did in the 1930s. Langston Hughes travelled around the Soviet Union in the very worst period in 1932-33, and had a great time in Central Asia and then Moscow, where he published a small book, *A Negro Looks at Soviet Central Asia*; there he wrote that after seeing the progress made by Soviet Asian workers, "Now I know why the near-by Indian Empire trembles and Africa stirs in a wretched sleep."[27] This at the very time when millions of people, including many Asians, had just been sent to the sleep of death by Stalin's regime.

Kouyate, Padmore and the Comintern

In Germany, the main stronghold of Communism outside Russia and the main base for anti-colonial activity linked with Communism, Nazi

---

24 Edgar (note 10).

25 I.D. Thatcher, *Trotsky*, London: Routledge, 2003, p. 166.

26 Hooker (note 3), p. 15.

27 A. Rampersad, *The Life of Langston Hughes, vol. 1: 1902-1941, I, Too, Sing America*, OUP, 1986, pp. 242-75.

stormtroopers and Communists fought each other often in the street thuggery of 1930-33, but the KPD also kept up ceaseless propaganda against the Social Democrats, preventing any possibility of an alliance to stop the Nazis. When Hitler was appointed Chancellor on 30 January 1933 many people failed to foresee how quickly he would install a total and violent dictatorship, and when that process began, hastened after the Reichstag Fire of 27 February 1933, the Comintern still stuck obstinately to its line and the self-delusion on which it was based—it declared on 1 April 1933 that the new dictatorship "is accelerating the tempo of Germany's development towards a proletarian revolution"[28]—even though the KPD was banned at an early stage, on 6 March 1933. The strongest Communist party outside Russia crumbled in a few weeks, and thousands of Communists as well as Social Democrats were killed or locked up in prisons or concentration camps or driven into exile.

Hitler's demented racism was directed principally against the Jews, but black people were not far behind. An editorial in *Wasu* of April-June 1933 (vol. II no. 2) declared:

Nationalism on the lines of Hitlerism or Nazism is nothing less than fanaticism...Germany under the rule of Hitler is now following the wake of the blood-hunting savage whites of the Southern States of the United States of America, by murdering and torturing Jews, and ill-treating Negroes and Indians, or rather people who have been unfortunate enough to be non-Aryan.[29]

Mein Kampf included anti-black racist passages, and Hitler had joined in the hysteria about black French soldiers and German women in the Rhineland. Following the "Sterilisation Law" published in September 1933 and a call in the new Nazi journal *Neues Volk* in February 1934, hundreds of young people born to those black soldiers and German women were to be forcibly sterilised in 1937.[30] Africans living in Germany did not suffer this, nor did their German wives and their children. But in July 1933 they began to lose their jobs, and German passports

28   Richard J. Evans, *The Coming of the Third Reich*, Allen Lane, 2003, pp. 326-7.

29   Quoted in Roderick J. MacDonald, "'The Wisers who are Far away': The Role of London's Black Press in the 1930s and 1940s", pp. 150-72 in J.S. Gundara and I. Duffield (eds), *Essays on the History of Blacks in Britain from Roman Times to the Mid-Twentieth Century*, Aldershot: Avebury, 1992; p. 153.

30   Paulette Reed-Anderson, *Rewriting the Footnotes: Berlin and the African Diaspora*, Berlin: Die Ausländerbeauftragte des Senats, 2000, in German and English, pp. 54-6.

which had been issued to some were withdrawn, to be replaced by Alien Passports, and steadily increasing persecution followed, forcing many to leave Germany.[31]

Anti-colonialists linked with the Communists lost their good base in Germany and had to move out fast. The LAI moved its international headquarters initially to France, and then to Britain in November 1933; it was run from there by Reginald Bridgeman who was already managing the British section. The reason for the choice of Britain is unclear, but there was already well established anti-imperialist activity linked to Communism there. The LAI British section had held its second annual conference in London in May 1932, where statements were issued on India, Ireland and Cyprus and the CPGB leader Harry Pollitt made a closing statement calling for the "complete national independence" of the colonial and semi-colonial peoples, the full rights of self-determination for "all oppressed nationalities", and the removal of "imperialist armed forces" from all colonies and semi-colonies.[32]

The new LAI British section executive elected then included Bridgeman, Percy Glading, Clemens Dutt, Saklatvala and the "red vicar" Conrad Noel. Another member was Arnold Ward, a Barbadian-born Communist who was secretary of a Negro Welfare Association (NWA) founded in 1931. This body was to be active in the coming years; Bridgeman was its chairman at least originally, but Ward's name is the one associated with the NWA. It was mentioned at the LAI 1932 conference as being active in the Scottsboro protest campaign, and it was a campaigning body as much as a welfare organisation. According to an MI5 report Ward, born at Bridgetown in 1886, lived in Germany from 1907 to 1915, when he was sent to England after being released from internment; in 1932 Padmore arranged for him to go to the MOPR congress in Moscow, but he (Ward) was refused a passport.[33] Chris Jones, another Barbadian, and Nancy Cunard were on the committee of the NWA for a time, but in 1933 Cunard and, apparently, Jones resigned after a

---

31   Ibid., pp. 54-81.

32   J. Saville, "Bridgeman, Reginald Francis Orlando (1884-1968)", *Dictionary of Labour Biography*, ed. J.M. Bellamy and J. Saville, Basingstoke: Macmillan, 1984, vol. VII, pp. 25-40: p. 44.

33   "Communism and the West Indian Labour Disturbances", note enclosed with [Col. Sir] Vernon Kell [head of MI5] to F.J. Howard, Colonial Office, 8 June 1938, file CO 295/606, National Archives, London, appendix p. 3.

disagreement with Bridgeman.[34] Ward and Bridgeman met Sekyi on his visit to Britain in 1932, and Wallace Johnson contacted the NWA on his way back from Russia to Nigeria early in 1933.[35]

Bridgeman recalled, "All that was handed over to me on my appointment as the International Secretary of the League was a list of addresses which was not up to date and so of little value. It was necessary to reconstitute the work of the League from the beginning."[36] But a new international executive was formed by Ben Bradley, who now became secretary of the British section, and Saklatvala, Glading, Pollitt and Bridgeman, who remained the dominant figure. The London activity of the LAI included publication of *Colonial News* and monthly duplicated bulletins such as *Indian Front*.[37] In June 1933 it was agreed, at a meeting in Nancy Cunard's house in London, to found an International Labour Defence London Coloured Committee, with Jones as chairman.[38] Jones, who according to some sources was really named Braithwaite, was one of the leading black activists in Britain in the 1930s; he worked for some time as a docker, and lived in Stepney with a white wife.[39]

As a black Communist, running the ITUC-NW and editing the *Negro Worker* in Hamburg in conjunction with the other Communist waterfront activity there, George Padmore was a prime target for the Nazis. He was quickly arrested, and then deported as a British subject, while all the ITUC-NW's activity in Germany was closed down. There was later some confusion about exactly what happened to him; he was said to have been detained for three to six months,[40] but it was not so long. The ITUC-NW established new offices in Copenhagen, and the *Negro Worker* appeared again; its issue of April-May 1933 (Vol. 3, no.

34   Metropolitan Police Special Branch letters on Negro Welfare Association, 13 December 1932 and 9 June 1933, file MEPO 38/9, National Archives, London.

35   Denzer (note 16), p. 49.

36   Quoted in S. Howe, *Anticolonialism in British Politics: The Left and the End of Empire*, Oxford: Clarendon Press, 1993, p. 75.

37   Saville (note 32), pp. 45-6.

38   Special Branch letters 9 June and 19 June 1933, file MEPO 38/9, National Archives, London.

39   B. Bush, *Imperialism, Race and Resistance: Africa and Britain, 1919-1945*, London and New York: Routledge, 1999, p. 222.

40   Hooker (note 3), p. 30.

4-5), had an editorial entitled "Fascist Terror against Negroes in Germany", which stated:

Shortly after the infamous Captain Goering, the right hand man of Hitler and dictator of Prussia assumed office, he ordered his men to round up all Negroes and deport them from Germany. Among the first ones to be arrested was comrade Padmore, the militant Negro leader and Secretary of the International Trade Union Committee of Negro workers of Hamburg. Padmore was dragged out of his bed by Nazi police and imprisoned for about two weeks, during which time the Nazi raided the offices of the Negro workers' Union and destroyed all their property. Padmore was afterwards deported.[41]

There was not in fact an order to deport all black people, but the editorial may have been referring to black people visiting Germany; it mentioned some black British students being deported. Padmore was deported to Britain and spent some time there before going to France.

Meanwhile Kouyate's relations with the French Communists, always strained, were heading at this very time for a complete break. He quarrelled increasingly with André Ferrat, head of the PCF Colonial Section for most of the period 1931-36, and Eva Neumann alias Henriette Carlier, a German then working with the PCF to help enforce its control over black militants. The PCF's weak state at the time—just 12 deputies after the 1932 elections, membership down to 30,000 in 1933—did not stop it asserting its control rigorously. It called on Kouyate to give an account of funds he had received, but he refused. The basic issue was Communist direction versus efforts to attract wider black support; Kouyate chose the second. He resumed contacts with non-Communist black militants and discussed plans for a "*maison des Nègres*". A new editorial board for *Le Cri des Nègres* was formed in July without Kouyate. He contacted Maran, Faure and Satineau, all of whom had rejected the Communist line for years, and talk began of a World Negro Congress.[42]

L'Humanité of 31 October 1933 announced Kouyate's expulsion, declaring:

1. Kouyate has deceived the Party, he has never wanted to give an account of the management.

---

41   Quoted in Reed-Anderson (note 30), p. 62.

42   Dewitte (note 1), pp. 304-7; J. Spiegler, "Aspects of Nationalist Thought among French-Speaking West Africans 1921-1939", DPhil, Oxford, 1968, pp. 188-91.

2. He has tried to disrupt the Union des Travailleurs Nègres;

3. He maintains contact with expelled members and opponents of the Communist Party and the trade union movement;

4. Having been summoned on two separate occasions, he has not replied to the summonses.

Then, on 4 November, he was expelled from the UTN at a general meeting, accused of embezzlement. In a defiant but useless letter to the meeting Kouyate spoke of the universal desire of white men to dominate black men, and said,

A saying goes that nobody is more dangerous than a friend who declares that he loves us better than we love ourselves, and embraces us so as to strangle us and give us the kiss of Judas.[43]

Whatever the truth about the embezzlement charge—it is possible that Kouyate, like Senghor before him, handled the funds of his organisation himself—the cause of the breach was what Kouyate mentioned, the question of control, plus the fundamental difference between the Communist approach to anti-colonial activity and the one commonly preferred by Africans and people of the African Diaspora, including, very clearly, Kouyate from the start.

The UTN continued, and *Le Cri des Nègres* continued to appear as an orthodox Communist publication; it supported popular causes among black people like that of the Scottsboro Boys, and had a print run of 3,000 in early 1934. It must be recalled again that despite the fundamental disagreement between the Communist approach and the pan-African one (as it can be called), they could find plenty of common ground, especially in negative denunciation. That was certainly why Kouyate worked with the Communists for several years. It seems that he wanted to use them and they to use him; inevitably the parting of the ways had to come.

That parting of the ways had nothing to do with any change in the basic Communist commitment to opposing Western imperialism. There was no such change at that time, even though the Soviet Union and

---

43   Dewitte (note 1), pp. 307-9.

France signed, on 29 November 1932, a Non-Aggression Pact whose article 5 stated:

Each of the High Contracting Parties undertakes to respect in every connection the sovereignty or authority of the other Party over the whole of that Party's territories as defined in Article I of the present Treaty (i.e. including territories which it represents in external relations and the administration of which it controls), not to interfere in any way in its internal affairs, and to abstain more particularly from action of any kind calculated to promote or encourage agitation, propaganda or attempted intervention designed to prejudice its territorial integrity or to transform by force the political or social régime of all or part of its territories.[44]

This wording seems to have been designed to cover the French colonial empire (also, no doubt, to cover exiles campaigning for independence for Ukraine or Georgia in France). Applying that clause would have meant curbing Comintern and PCF anti-colonial propaganda. No such thing happened then or for some years; in 1933, for example, the French Communists strongly denounced a new military campaign in Morocco to subdue mountainous areas never brought under French control, speaking out in a National Assembly debate on 30 June 1933[45] (while on its side the French government gave asylum to Trotsky in 1933). Probably the French government never expected anything to change. A similar clause, specifying the British empire and British interests in Asia, had been written into the Anglo-Soviet trade agreement of 1921, and ignored by Moscow.

However, in 1933-34 George Padmore also broke with the Comintern, soon after Kouyate, in one of the more celebrated episodes in the history of early radical anti-colonialism, and he later said this was because Moscow sent out an order to curb anti-imperialist activity. Padmore's biographer, James Hooker, says he resigned his offices on 13 August 1933, immediately after hearing of a Comintern decision to "disband the ITUC-NW". Hooker quotes what Padmore later recalled in 1946 in the *New Leader*, organ of the ILP with which the

---

44   Max Beloff, *The Foreign Policy of Soviet Russia 1929-1941*, OUP, 1947, vol. 1, pp. 23-4.

45   G. Oved, *La gauche française et le nationalisme marocain 1905-1955*, Paris: Harmattan, 1984, vol. 1, p. 326; vol. 2, p. 43.

Trinidadian was linked after breaking with Communism: Padmore
had been holding

a responsible position in the higher councils of the Communist International,
which was called upon not only to endorse the new diplomatic policy of the
Soviet Government, but to put a brake upon the anti-imperialist work of its
affiliate sections and thereby sacrifice the young national liberation movements
in Asia and Africa. This I considered to be a betrayal of the fundamental interests of my people, with which I could not identify myself. I therefore had no
choice but to sever my connection with the Communist International.[46]

The story that Padmore broke with Moscow because Stalin wanted
to reduce support for anti-colonial agitation, in order to improve relations with Britain and France in the face of the Nazi menace, has been
repeated by many authors. But on closer examination it is clear things
did not happen in the way he recalled.

The ITUC-NW was not disbanded in August 1933. The *Negro
Worker* did have serious financial problems in Copenhagen, and in the
issue of August-September 1933 Padmore said it was bankrupt;[47] in
fact it ceased publication, but it resumed later, within a few months
at the most, which presumably meant that Moscow provided funds
and approved its policy. The latter was still militantly anti-colonialist
and Communist; Ivan Potekhin, for example, wrote for it from 1932
to 1935, sometimes under the pen-name John Izolta. In France, *Le
Cri des Nègres* remained equally militant. For example, in the issues of
November-December 1933, January 1934 and April-May 1934 *Le Cri
des Nègres* published a manifesto of a "Ligue des Peuples du Sénégal
et du Soudan". It was sponsored by the Ligue Anti-Impérialiste—the
French branch of the LAI, now enjoying a new lease of life—and clearly
drawn up by French Communists, using worldwide Communist language with little African adaptation.[48] There was no toning down of
Communist anti-colonialism at that time.

A change in Moscow's policy towards the Western democracies did
begin in 1934. It took until then for Stalin to see Nazi Germany as
the main enemy, though some Communists in the West saw it as such
from the start. The 6 February 1934 riots in Paris by right-wing par-

---

46   *New Leader*, 9 January 1946, quoted in Hooker (note 3), pp. 31-2.

47   Wilson (note 19), p. 260.

48   Dewitte (note 1), pp. 310-11.

ties and groups over the "Stavisky Scandal" shocked left-wing parties and led Communists to realise that there was a greater danger than the SFIO. The rank and file seem to have led in the change of attitude, and the PCF seems to have urged it on the leaders in Moscow. An article by the PCF leader Thorez in *Pravda* on 23 May approved an approach to the SFIO and the CGT for joint opposition to fascism, and on 2 July *L'Humanité* published a Comintern proposal for a "pact of struggle against fascism".[49] The Communists' decision to stop treating democratic Socialists as the enemy was pushed in Moscow by some non-Soviet comrades including notably Georgi Dimitrov, the Bulgarian who after being in charge of the Comintern's West European Bureau in Berlin from 1929 had been arrested by the Nazis and put on trial for organising the Reichstag fire; he went to Moscow in February 1934 after his acquittal in the show trial at Leipzig, and became General Secretary of the Comintern later that year. He urged an end to the "class against class" policy, and Stalin reluctantly accepted this.

On 27 July 1934 the PCF and SFIO signed an agreement which was to lead to the Popular Front in France. The change in attitudes to democratic Socialist parties coincided with a shift in Stalin's foreign policy towards Western governments, in which an important public step was the admission of the USSR to the League of Nations, and its Council, in September 1934. The two processes were quite distinct, since the Soviet state had been ready to sign agreements with capitalist and imperialist states from the beginning, regardless of Comintern views on any parties within those states. But in fact the two processes now went in step in response to the Nazi menace, and both had implications for Moscow's attitude to anti-colonialism.

This change in Moscow's policy did not emerge in 1933, nor did it cause the breach with Padmore in that year in the way he suggested. However, Padmore may have heard some talk of possible curbing of Comintern activity relating to the United States in particular. That issue did arise in discussions in 1932-33 about US recognition of the Soviet

49   E. Mortimer, *The Rise of the French Communist Party 1920-1947*, London: Faber & Faber, 1984, pp. 208-26; K. McDermott and J. Agnew, *The Comintern: A History of International Communism from Lenin to Stalin*, Basingstoke: Macmillan, 1996, pp. 123-35. But J. Jackson, *The Popular Front in France: Defending Democracy, 1934-38*, CUP 1988, suggests that the "decisive impulse" for the change came from Moscow (pp. 31-6). This question cannot be pursued here.

government, which Moscow wanted even though lack of recognition had been no obstacle for a number of American businessmen working in Russia to help achieve the Five-Year Plan targets.

In 1932 the Meschradpom film company, an affiliate of the IAH, planned a film to be made in the USSR, called *Black and White*, about striking black workers in Alabama calling for help from white American fellow workers. It paid for Langston Hughes and twenty-one other African Americans to travel to Russia in June 1932 to take part, but the plan did not proceed; there was hopeless muddle in its planning, and Hughes thought the scenario showed ignorance of the United States and "was not even plausible fantasy". Then it was announced that the filming was postponed, because of the quality of the script. Several of the African American group angrily suggested hidden reasons for the decision, some even accusing Stalin of wanting to curry favour with capitalist countries. It was reported that Colonel Hugh Cooper, the American chief engineer of the Dnieprostroi Dam, had criticised the proposed film, and at the time (August 1932) the American press suggested that it had been cancelled by Moscow's order to avoid annoying (white) America.[50]

When Manuilsky met the protest group of Kutvu students in January 1933 they expressed outrage at the cancellation of the film, and he admitted that white American engineers working in Russia had urged its cancellation and added:

If the Soviet Union were to be confronted by the danger of a major war, and... in the interests of preserving the dictatorship of the proletariat, were to be interested in at least the benevolent neutrality of America, would it have the right to maneuver occasionally on this or that issue?[51]

The scare talk of an attack on the Soviet Union had been going on for years, but now Japan really had occupied Manchuria in 1931, and Stalin was worried about this and anxious to get US recognition. The striking point is that there were sound ordinary reasons for dropping a botched plan—and yet Manuilsky half-admitted that Soviet foreign policy reasons were involved.

---

50   Rampersad (note 27), pp. 235, 242-51.

51   McClellan (note 17), pp. 384-5.

In the next few months the new Roosevelt administration which took office in March 1933 decided to recognise the Soviet regime, after prolonged talks in which one major sticking point was Communist propaganda relating to the United States. When agreement was reached on recognition in November 1933, the Americans obtained what they thought was a promise to curb Comintern activity directed at the USA. The Soviet side denied making such a promise,[52] and in fact Communist activity within and concerning the USA continued as before. But it seems that the idea of curbing the agitation had been in the air in 1932-33; this would have concerned the ITUC-NW very much, and Padmore must have known about the episode of the film project. If he heard about the mere idea of toning down Communist militancy on African American and other US affairs, he would probably have objected. He may also have thought the anti-propaganda clause of the Non-Aggression Treaty with France was another part of a new agenda, though his visit to France should have given him evidence to the contrary. When the *Negro Worker* ran out of money, Padmore would have expected the Profintern or some other agency in Moscow to provide funds promptly to save it, and may have suspected it was refusing to do so for ulterior reasons. In fact an ulterior reason may have been to undermine Padmore.[53] If Padmore's suspicions led to any protest, however private, that alone, in Stalin's time, would have been enough to start or reinforce suspicion against him in his turn.

Probably something happened to arouse suspicions against Padmore in Moscow about the middle of 1933, but he did not resign his Communist positions then as he wrote later, or else he did but withdrew his resignation. What happened behind the scenes in the next few months is obscure, but there was probably steadily mounting disagreement. He spent some time in France during 1933; at one point the Comintern summoned him, through Ferrat—presumably because Padmore was then in France—to go to Moscow, but he refused to go. Kouyate was said to have advised him to refuse, and it seems that the two black militants' friendship was growing.[54]

52   T.R. Maddox, *Years of Estrangement: American Relations with the Soviet Union, 1933-1941*, Tallahassee: University Presses of Florida, 1980, pp. 11-22.

53   As suggested by Wilson (note 19), p. 260.

54   Dewitte (note 1), pp. 312-13; B.H. Edwards, *The Practice of Diaspora: Lit-*

Meanwhile Nancy Cunard spent much of 1933 in London, meeting Jones and other black radicals, organising efforts to show support
for the Scottsboro Boys, and finishing her great collection of writings
by and about black people around the world. Padmore was in contact
with her about contributions to this book; some were reprints, mainly
from *The Life and Struggles of Negro Toilers*, but he also sent an original
entry about an African incident that hit the world's press in September
1933. In Bechuanaland Tshekedi Khama, regent of the Bangwato (or
Bamangwato) kingdom, was suspended from office by the British on 13
September after a white man, Phinehas McIntosh, had been summoned
before his chiefly court on an assault charge and, apparently, flogged or
beaten. A naval detachment was summoned from the Simonstown base
near Cape Town to reinforce this action against an African ruler who
had dared to punish a white man. There were strong protests in Britain
by Harris and the ASAPS, missionaries of the London Missionary Society who often defended their Bamangwato converts, the *Daily Herald*,
the MPs Josiah Wedgwood, William Lunn and Charles Roden Buxton,
and the London Group on African Affairs (LGAA). That group had
been founded in 1930 to help South African white liberals' efforts, with
John Fletcher, of the Society of Friends and the ASAPS, as chairman;
its delegation to the Dominions Secretary on the Tshekedi Khama affair
included Harold Moody and W.M. Macmillan. For a short while, this
was one of the most publicised colonial scandals in the 1930s; Tshekedi
was quickly reinstated, promising never again to try a white man.[55]

Johnstone Kenyatta returned to London about this time; he tele-
phoned the Rosses on 30 August 1933, not talking about his time in
Russia (an example of his usual secretiveness).[56] Soon afterwards the
book by Nzula, Potekhin and Zusmanovich appeared in the Soviet
Union, with two strange references. The Kikuyu Central Association
was described[57] as "ultra-reformist": it had sent delegations to the LAI,

erature, *Translation, and the Rise of Black Internationalism*, Cambridge, MA:
Harvard University Press, 2003, pp. 263-70.

55   See a full account of the case in M. Crowder, *The Flogging of Phinehas McIntosh:
A Tale of Colonial Folly and Injustice*, Bechuanaland 1933, Yale University Press,
1988. On the LGAA see Bush (note 39), pp. 183, 186-7, 232-3; on Moody see
below.

56   Murray-Brown (note 15), p. 174.

57   Nzula *et al.* (note 20), pp. 174, 177.

the Profintern, and the ITUC-NW, said the authors, but "at the same time has grovelled for the most minor concessions before the British King, Parliament and Lords". But the KCA delegate at revolutionary gatherings had been Kenyatta, who had also just been in Moscow with Nzula; he had also had an article, "An African Looks at British Imperialism", published in the *Negro Worker* of January 1933, calling for "complete self-rule".[58]

As Kenyatta was always very reticent about his time in Russia, one has to guess what may have lain behind that criticism of the body he had represented, until the Comintern archives, perhaps, reveal the reason.[59] The KCA had not authorised his journey to Russia.[59] During 1932 Harry Thuku was elected president of the KCA, and wanted to cut the remittance of funds to Kenyatta;[60] the book's authors, or censors who read proofs, may have wanted to separate Kenyatta from the organisation back in Kenya. But the indications are that Kenyatta was never a convinced Communist or Marxist, and the Comintern authorities probably guessed that he simply wanted to use both them and British "colonial liberals" to advance his people's cause. That was indeed his idea, and it did not please everyone. A letter from Ward to Padmore on 13 September 1933, read by MI5, said,

Kenyatta is here [apparently London] playing his old game again trying to enlist support from who he can this fellow game is played out He wants to know all about you and you are suppose to send him funds to live on did they throw Him out let us know.[61]

But the Communists did not repudiate him then. In November 1933 he wrote in Palme Dutt's *Labour Monthly* an article on Kenya whose wording and tone would gladden any Communist's heart, saying:

...the only way out is the mass organisation of workers and peasants of various tribes, and by having this unity we shall be in a position to put up a strong protest against this robbery and exploitation...

---

58   Murray-Brown (note 15), pp. 175-6.

59   Ibid., p. 172.

60   M.S. Clough, *Fighting Two Sides: Kenyan Chiefs and Politicians, 1918-1940*, Niwot, CO: University Press of Colorado, 1990, p. 170.

61   Wording *sic*; P.F.40174, file KV2/1787, National Archives, London.

In this fight we shall have the support of all who are oppressed by the British Slave Empire – the Indians, the Irish, the South Africans – all these people are revolting against this damnable Empire whose days are numbered.

With the support of all revolutionary workers and peasants we must redouble our efforts to break the bonds that bind us... [62]

The Nzula-Potekhin-Zusmanovich book also referred[63] to "a West African reformist, I.T.A. Wallace-Johnson". This is also baffling, as Wallace Johnson too had just been an honoured guest in Moscow. In this case of a brief reference, a simple error is a possible explanation; it was risky in Stalin's Russia to make such an error in labelling of a person, but it could happen. Wallace Johnson spent a strangely short time at Kutvu, and it is possible that he was considered an unsatisfactory pupil; but calling him a "reformist" in a book would be a strange punishment unless he was to be formally repudiated like Kouyate and Padmore, and this did not happen. He returned to West Africa in February 1933 and spent some months in Lagos, working with the AWU and distributing the *Negro Worker*, which was banned by the British, besides some journalistic work. Then the police raided his house at 22 Layeni Street in Lagos in October 1933 and seized many of his papers, but he had already left for the Gold Coast; he contacted Bridgeman about the police action, questions were asked in the House of Commons, and the papers were eventually returned.[64] In Gold Coast he was soon to launch a new and more radical nationalist party; he was not a "reformist", and for some years he remained a Marxist.

A few months after the appearance of the book of which he was co-author, Albert Nzula died in Moscow on 14 January 1934. It seems almost certain that he died a pathetic death due to his drinking; he fell

---

62   Quoted in Murray-Brown (note 15), p. 178. In referring to the Irish Kenyatta was no doubt thinking of the campaign begun in 1932 by de Valera's newly elected Free State government to end the oath to the King of England and the payment of sums owed for buying out of rural landlords before creation of the Free State.

63   Nzula *et al.* (note 20), p. 172.

64   Bridgeman to Under Secretary of State for the Colonies, 8 January 1934; note by Mr Fiddian of Colonial Office, London, 20 January 1934; A.C. Burns, Acting Chief Secretary to the Government, Lagos, to I.T.A. Wallace-Johnson, 29 March 1934, in file CO583/195/4, National Archives; Denzer (note 16), pp. 49-51.

down in a Moscow street and lay there for some hours, and died of pneumonia. Mofutsanyana and other South Africans, returning from a holiday by the Black Sea soon afterwards, were told that this had happened after Nzula had gone out with a British drinking companion. Later there were allegations that he had been murdered on official Soviet orders; one story was that he had been arrested in the middle of a meeting. But that story was told by C.L.R. James whose source was Kenyatta,[65] and Kenyatta had left Moscow well before Nzula died. Mofutsanyana—who on his return to South Africa was asked about Nzula's death by the police there—rejected the story in his interview long afterwards. He said Nzula had in fact been in trouble, and had been told at some sort of disciplinary hearing that he would not be allowed to return to South Africa with the ideas he had; there was talk of sending him to the USA, and he favoured this. So the Comintern authorities were annoyed with Nzula; however, Mofutsanyana never believed the stories of his being murdered.[66]

In fact those stories can safely be rejected. The time when great numbers of foreign Communists in the USSR were murdered in Stalin's Great Purge had not come then. Sen Katayama died peacefully in Russia on 5 November 1933—and Nzula, one can assume, died because of drink and the Russian winter.

Padmore would not have had to fear a violent death when summoned to Moscow in late 1933. However, he would have faced a lot of unpleasantness, and he might have thought the decision to expel him was already inevitable. Exactly what happened will no doubt be learned from the Comintern archives. By December 1933 MI5 in London knew that Padmore was in trouble; a letter said,

PADMORE is in disfavour with the Communists and the U.S.A., British and French Parties are intent on expelling him: the ostensible reason being that as Chairman of the Negro Committee in Hamburg and Paris he claimed too close a relationship with the R.I.L.U. In fact he was a loyal subordinate who failed to observe the subtleties of the Communist connection. This sounds like a garbled report coming from informers, but it is possible that Padmore had pulled rank over local Communist parties in dealing with matters concerning black people,

---

65   Cohen (note 11), p. 15.
66   Edgar (note 10).

and had made enemies that way. [67] That letter was mainly about Kenyatta, suggesting he might just possibly be in the running to take Padmore's place "as a comrade of International Status". At that time post delivered to 95 Cambridge Street, London SW was watched, several letters to Kenyatta and others being seen, including one to Kenyatta from Kouyate.[68]

Padmore was probably still Secretary of the ITUC-NW when the final proofs of Nancy Cunard's *Negro: An Anthology*, including his contributions, were passed, for when the book was published in London on 15 February 1934, by the small radical publishing firm Wishart & Co., he was described as holding that position.

The original edition of this work aimed at "the recording of the struggles and achievements, the persecutions and the revolts against them of the Negro peoples" was a monumental work of 855 pages. The contributions dealt with music, art and traditions of Black people in Africa, the Caribbean and the USA, but especially with their current situation.[69] Of the shorter version (still very long) published in 1970[70] more than half is devoted to aspects of African Americans' life and situation. Cunard had a special interest in art, poetry, music and other culture, and combined this with her commitment to the cause of oppressed Black people in the book. She had a good journalistic style and wrote readable entries herself on life in Harlem and on the Scottsboro case. Josephine Herbst and Theodore Dreiser also wrote on that case, and there were articles on lynch law, the history of slavery, Georgia chain gangs, and the question of black-white marriage and sexual relations among other such topics.

---

67   H.M.M. [*sic* – apparently MI5] to McSweeney of CO and others, 16 Dec. 1933, referring to police report on Kenyatta; file KV2/1787, National Archives. Padmore had indeed ordered the CGTU to use Kouyate's services for various purposes in mid-1931: Dewitte (note 1), pp. 285-6; Edwards (note 54), pp. 263-4.

68   MI5 [apparently] to GPO, 27 Nov. 1933; "Result of postal observation on 95 Cambridge Street", 29 November to 12 December 1933; document PF.40714/89, file KV2/1787.

69   A. Chisholm, *Nancy Cunard*, New York: Knopf, 1979, Harmondsworth: Penguin, 1981, pp. 283-95. Only a few of the 1,000 copies originally printed survived, many being lost in an air raid on London.

70   *Negro: An Anthology*, collected and edited by Nancy Cunard, 1970 edition edited and abridged with introduction by Hugh Ford, New York: Frederick Ungar, 1970.

Du Bois and Walter White, a leading NAACP figure, wrote contributions, but a number of others were devoted to the American Communist message for African Americans, which included denunciations of most of their well known leaders, Du Bois among them. Will Herberg, in "Marxism and the American negro" (pp. 131-5), summed up the Party line:

The racial emancipation of the Negro cannot come as the result of a "purely racial" movement – of a movement deliberately aiming to subordinate, in the name of an unreal "racial unity," the masses of the Negro people to the narrow interests of the Negro bourgeoisie (who work hand in glove with their white paymasters), of a movement consciously striving to divorce the liberation struggle of the Negro people from the chief social movement of our time, the class war of labor against capital. The racial emancipation of the American Negro, in the present historical situation, is possible only as an integral aspect and an inevitable consequence of the revolutionary overthrow of the capitalist system, of the victory of the proletariat. (p. 135)

This was supplemented by James W. Ford in "Communism and the Negro" (pp. 146-51). But the book also included an admiring article on Booker T. Washington—another sign of the extraordinary respect for him among people generally not at all sympathetic to his ideas of patient submission.

Nancy Cunard herself wrote in her Foreword (p.xxxi):

There are certain sections of the Negro bourgeoisie which hold that justice will come to them from some eventual liberality in the white man. But the more vital of the Negro race have realised that it is Communism alone which throws down the barriers of race as it finally wipes out class distinctions. The Communist world order is the solution of the race problem for the Negro.

But she was not a Communist in the fullest sense herself. Hugh Ford, editor of the re-edition who knew her, wrote (pp. 130-1), "Nancy herself did not understand what Marxism was or is, and of course she did not really mind."

Cunard probably felt obliged to allocate space to some of her literary friends; the book included light-weight inanities by Norman Douglas and the Surrealist group. But these were untypical of a generally serious work. Contributions included Black American stories and articles on black literature, black people in American and European literature, the Black American poet Sterling Brown, jazz orchestras (with a poem about Louis Armstrong), Florence Mills, dancing in Harlem, the Ku Klux Klan, racism in Britain (by Cunard) and lack of racism in France (by Henry Crowder). There was a contribution by George Antheil on "The Negro on the Spiral, or A Method of Negro Music", and a good entry by Lawrence Gellert on "Negro Songs of Protest". On the West Indies, Cunard wrote on Jamaica and Langston Hughes on Haiti, having in each case recently visited the country concerned. There were entries on African survivals in Latin America.

On Africa *Negro* included an article on Ewe proverbs in West Africa, entries on the history of pre-colonial empires by Raymond Michelet (one of Nancy Cunard's boyfriends), a number of illustrated entries on African art, especially sculpture, and extracts from "The Anglo-Fanti" by Kobina Sekyi (pp. 442-7). Ben N. Azikiwe, a young Nigerian student in the USA, wrote an entry on Liberia, "Liberia: Slave or Free?" (pp. 448-51), pointing out that forced labour was practised very widely in other parts of Africa as well as Liberia; he turned to the question "Is Negro Government Feasible?" before saying that Liberia was a sovereign country with full sovereign rights. Nnamdi Azikiwe—as he was called when he became famous later—was an active campaigner for Liberia; summing up the main point of the campaign, he wrote in 1932 that several authors had contributed to "a systematically organized propaganda that Liberia, Haiti and Abyssinia are failures, and that they furnish evidence to prove the incapacity of the Negro for self-government in the tropical regions."[71] In 1934 he published a book, *Liberia in World Politics*.

In *Negro* Kenyatta, who met Cunard often in the months following his return from Moscow,[72] wrote (pp. 452-60) on settler privileges, land seizure and forced labour— "That forced labor has no limits under the rule of British imperialism can be seen by the increased use of women and child labor by forcibly sending them on to the alienated plantations of the invading white imperialists." (p. 454)—and concluded: "let us unite and demand our birthright" (p. 456)

---

71   B.N. Azikiwe, "In Defense of Liberia", *Journal of Negro History* vol. XVII no. 1, January 1932, pp. 30-50.

72   As the police and MI5 noted in the careful watch they kept on him at this time: Vernon Kell to McSweeney of Colonial Office, 12 Dec. 1933, document PF.40714/89, file KV2/1787, National Archives, London.

Padmore wrote about the McIntosh case in Bechuanaland ("White Man's Justice in Africa," pp. 457-60) and contributed an entry (pp. 386-92) on Ethiopia—"Ethiopia Today: The Making of a Modern State"—which suggested that Emperor Haile Selassie was gradually making "progressive" changes in the feudal order. This was quite a common view in the West about Haile Selassie then and for some time afterwards, and permissible for a Communist. But James Ford, after publication of the book, criticised Padmore in the *Afro-American* newspaper for describing Haile Selassie as "progressive"; Cunard protested at this criticism.[73] Ford was reflecting the Communist condemnation of Padmore, which by coincidence was pronounced officially soon after *Negro: An Anthology* was published, on 23 February 1934.

The International Control Commission of the Comintern condemned Padmore for keeping up contact with the "provocateur" Kouyate, staying in the flat of another "provocateur" named Jacques (presumably a comrade of Kouyate in Paris), working openly for national bourgeois organisations on behalf of Liberia, arguing for black unity on the lines of race rather than class, and generally showing an incorrect attitude to the nationalities question. These accusations, published in the *Negro Worker* of June 1934,[74] show that Padmore, like his friend Kouyate, was rejected because he opposed imperialism in a Pan-Africanist way, rather than the Communist one.

The controversies about Liberia brought out the difference between the two approaches clearly. For Du Bois and other black American leaders the priority was preserving Liberia's sovereignty, as Azikiwe also emphasised in *Negro*. Because African Americans admitted even so that Liberia's internal situation needed a great deal of improvement, some drew up in 1933-34 a plan for economic aid and investment in Liberia.[75] It came to nothing, but Harry Haywood denounced Padmore for backing the plan, in the same June 1934 issue of the *Negro Worker*, saying Padmore failed

---

73   Note by Hugh Ford in *Negro*, pp. 456-7; Hooker (note 3), pp. 36-7; Chisholm (note 69), pp. 294, 298.

74   Hooker (note 3), p. 33; Edwards (note 54), pp. 268-9, 274-5. According to Edwards "Jacques" was Camille Saint-Jacques.

75   I.K. Sundiata, *Black Scandal: America and the Liberian Labor Crisis, 1929-1936*, Philadelphia: Institute for the Study of Human Issues, 1980, pp. 82-99, 122.

to recognise the fact that the condition of the two million natives in Liberia is not the same as the condition of the ruling stratum of the Americo-Liberians and that the natives must also fight against those black oppressors and imperialist lackeys.[76]

That issue of the *Negro Worker* (vol. IV no. 2) followed one dated May 1934, which apologised for a halt in publication, saying it was due to "serious technical difficulties, editorial shortcomings and the necessity to change our location."[77] The reference to a change of location is puzzling as the May 1934 and June 1934 issues were both published, again, in Copenhagen. And even though "editorial shortcomings" may have been an oblique allusion to Padmore, why did that issue not report the expulsion of Padmore, pronounced in February? Some obscure goings-on seem to have continued for several months. At any rate Charles Woodson, an African American, succeeded Padmore as Secretary of the ITUC-NW.

During those months, maybe even earlier, Padmore probably did support the unsuccessful development plan for Liberia, though he had no money to contribute and was not in the USA. On 17 February 1934 he wrote to DuBois, "Liberia has her faults, but since white politicians are no better than black ones, it is our duty to save the "black baby from the white wolves"."[78] Padmore protested later that his last writing on Liberia had been in January 1932, when he was still very much in favour with the Comintern. Orthodox Communists could certainly condemn imperialist threats to Liberia, as Padmore did in *The Life and Struggles* and *American Imperialism Enslaves Liberia*, regardless of the nature of the Americo-Liberian regime. But in fact reflexes of pan-African solidarity may never have left George Padmore in his Communist years. In 1927 Nurse/Padmore, as a student in the USA, wrote to Azikiwe that he and a Liberian student named Davies were "trying to establish a political organization among foreign Negro students in American colleges and universities." He went on, "The primary object will be to foster racial consciousness and a spirit of nationalism aiming at the protection of the sovereignty of Liberia."[79] In 1934 he and Azikiwe were both defend-

---

76   Quoted in Ibid., p. 122.

77   Hooker (note 3), p. 32.

78   Quoted in ibid., p. 33.

79   N. Azikiwe, *My Odyssey*, London: C. Hurst & Co., 1970, p. 138.

ing Liberia as an independent state. C.L.R. James, much later, recalled Padmore saying: "I stayed there [with the Communists] because there was a means of doing work for the black emancipation and there was no other place that I could think of."[80]

Communists may have concluded by 1933, or even earlier, what they said openly later: that Padmore backed Liberia's struggle to maintain independence, as a black solidarity cause. Woodson wrote in the June 1934 *Negro Worker* that Padmore's actions would serve to

undermine the unity of Liberian workers in their struggles against exploitation and oppression by the Imperialists and the Americo-Liberian ruling class; to weaken the working class movement under the slogan of race unity instead of class unity, thereby strengthening the hands of the Imperialist oppressors and their Negro allies.[81]

Woodson was uttering orthodox Communist slogans; but he and Haywood made justified criticisms of the black-solidarity campaign in favour of Liberia. The treatment of the indigenous people by the Americo-Liberians was shocking, and the concern that led to the League of Nations discussions on supervised reforms was in itself justified. The indigenous Liberians defended themselves, too, some by armed resistance—there was a Kru insurgency, which Britain was suspected of encouraging, from 1930 to 1936—and others by campaigning; a delegate of the "Aborigines", F.W.M. Morais, travelled to Europe, including Geneva, to present their case in 1931-32. They too could reasonably appeal to pan-African feeling, and Kobina Sekyi for one did criticise the Liberian elite.[82] But Azikiwe criticised Morais' action and Du Bois glossed over the treatment of the indigenous people.[83] Such campaigners were reluctant to recognise what Communists had the merit of recognising: that Africans could also oppress Africans. The main consideration for them was the one expressed with reference to African Americans by Du Bois, disagreeing with the Communist class-oriented view, in his *Black Reconstruction in America*, published in 1935:

80   C.L.R. James, *At the Rendezvous of Victory*, selected writings and speeches, London: Allison & Busby, 1984, p. 255.

81   Quoted in Sundiata (note 74), p. 122.

82   S.K.B. Asante, *Pan-African Protest: West Africa and the Italo-Ethiopian Crisis 1934-1941*, London: Longman, 1977, p. 16.

83   Sundiata (note 74), pp. 127-55.

American race prejudice has so pounded the mass of Negroes together that they have not separated into such economic classes; but on the other hand they undoubtedly have had the ideology and if they had been free we would have had within our race the same exploiting set-up that we see around about us.[84]

But he regarded the "exploiting set-up" in the independent black state of Liberia as a minor issue.

The efforts to persuade Liberia to accept a programme of reforms involving a considerable loss of control over its affairs, strongly resisted by the Liberian government, were eventually dropped by the League of Nations Council on 18 May 1934. Under Roosevelt the US government had ceased to press hard for acceptance, and in 1934 a State Department official told the bosses of Firestone that the period when the United States "intervened in small countries bending governments to their will, particularly on behalf of commercial interests, was definitely over."[85] Of course it was not over, but at that time the Roosevelt administration also withdrew US occupation forces from Haiti in 1934.

It should be stressed again that the ideas of black people's solidarity condemned by Communists were racial only in a defensive sense, opposed to the way black people were subjugated and exploited as a race. True racism directed against white people as a whole was rare, and was absent from Padmore, who worked closely with white people before and after his breach with Communism and—like Kenyatta, Ralaimongo and Lamine Senghor—had a white partner (in his case Dorothy Pizer, an Englishwoman).[86] A few people did express anti-white racism, however, as will be shown later.

There is no reason to doubt that the reasons given for the Communist excommunication of Padmore were the real ones. In the crucial months of 1933-34 the hidden agenda he alleged later—a decision by

84   Quoted in Cedric J. Robinson, *Black Marxism: The Making of the Black Radical Tradition*, Chapel Hill and London: University of North Carolina Press, 1983, p. 197.

85   Sundiata (note 74), pp. 75, 77.

86   Hooker (note 3), pp. 48-9. They met during Padmore's years in London in the later 1930s, to be described below. The others mentioned were married to white wives, but C.L.R. James recalled that Padmore had previously married a wife, Julia Semper, in 1924, and had a son and daughter by her, while Dorothy Pfizer (the spelling he gives) "became known as Padmore's wife": James, *At the Rendezvous of Victory* (note 79), pp. 227-8.

Moscow to soften opposition to Western imperialism—did not exist. Padmore was condemned for believing in the black peoples' struggle against white imperialism, rather than the struggle of all the oppressed against all (capitalist) oppressors. The key indicator of the distinction was the attitude taken to established black protest leaders like the NAACP and the ANC, and Padmore's friendly approach to W.E.B. Du Bois, whom he had been denouncing for years, was a sufficient sign of which side he had chosen. In his letter of 16 February 1934 he told the NAACP leader about a recent meeting of "French Negroes" under the leadership of Kouyate, which had decided to take the initiative for a "Negro World Unity Congress"; he went on, "They decided to invite your organization to participate in the Congress which has been fixed for the summer of 1935—providing the war-makers give us so much time". Despite considerable activity about it in Paris in 1933-34, the Congress never met. In planning it Kouyate and Padmore showed the broad, non-sectarian approach which had caused them to be rejected by the Communists, though it was for a venture that did not arouse enough interest in the Diaspora or Africa. [87]

Joseph Ekwe Bile, having returned to Germany from Russia, was driven from there by the Nazis and went to France, or so it seems from the French archives, where a document refers confusingly to him going to Paris "in April 1934 at the moment of Hitler's accession to power". A year later he said he wanted to return to Cameroon.[88] At some point, in or before November 1938, he did so; he claimed, then or earlier, to have rejected his Communist convictions "because of the crude errors committed in the USSR, notably by the Stalinist regime".[89] It is not clear when he rejected Communism, but it seems possible that after going to France he joined the non-Communist militants led by Kouyate and including Padmore, who spent a good deal of 1933-34 in France. One cannot be sure, because little was remembered afterwards about Ekwe

---

87 Hooker (note 3), pp. 39-40; Edwards (note 54), pp. 275-82.

88 Minister of Colonies to Commissioner for French Cameroun, 27 March 1935, in file on Joseph Bile in Box Cameroun AP (Affaires Politiques) II 28, Archives SOM, Paris/Aix.

89 Notes of 30 November 1938 and 5 December 1938, Paris, file on Joseph Bile in Box Cameroun AP II 28, Archives SOM, Paris/Aix.

Bile.[90] One brief mention of him is in Roi Ottley's *No Green Pastures*, but this book about Black people and their organisations in Europe, which could have been a good contribution to history, is filled with major errors throughout (e.g. calling Kenyatta a Tanganyikan). However, it could well be correct in saying that Ekwe Bile, in Paris, appealed to African Americans to help Black people in Germany.[91] This would have fitted in with Kouyate's initiative in calling a meeting where, in Padmore's words, "The Negro problem was discussed relative to the present economic and social crisis the world over, and the fascist danger which threatens our racial extermination."[92] And had Ekwe Bile, too, perhaps worked with the Communists without ever really accepting their view that class mattered more than race?

Many Black militants remained loyal to Communism, despite Stalin and despite Padmore, in South Africa and the USA. Some African American intellectuals, such as a group at Howard University including Alain Locke and Ralph Bunche, felt unable to join the Communists but maintained the view that class exploitation was the basic evil from which racism grew. Bunche and John P. Davis were leaders of the National Negro Congress founded in 1936, in which there was strong Communist influence though its President was the anti-communist Black trade unionist A. Philip Randolph.[93] The Communists made a constant stand against racism in the USA, as was emphasised in Cunard's *Negro*, and their ILD had saved the Scottsboro Boys from execution. The ITUC-NW continued for several more years as an organisation of black Communist militancy, with Huiswoud soon replacing Woodson as Secretary. But it was forced to leave Denmark in August 1934, and soon after moving to Belgium was expelled from there also. This may well have been connected with the arrest of Huiswoud in Antwerp in September 1934. Working then as a journalist for the Crusader News Agency, a

90   During my research in Douala in 1972 I learned that he had died some years before.

91   Roi Ottley, *No Green Pastures,* John Murray, 1952, p. 154.

92   Hooker (note 3), p. 39.

93   Robert R. Edgar, "Prologue" in R.R. Edgar (ed.), *The Travel Notes of Ralph J. Bunche, 28 September 1937-1 January 1938,* Athens, OH: Ohio University Press, pp. 6-8; E. Johanningsmeier, "Communists and the Black Freedom Movements in South Africa and the United States: 1919-1950", *Journal of Southern African Studies* vol. 30 no. 2, June 2004, pp. 155-80 (p. 175).

radical African American agency started by Cyril Briggs, Huiswood also published articles about the Belgian Congo in the *Negro Worker*.[94] The October-November 1934 issue of the *Negro Worker* was published from the offices of the Harlem *Liberator*, but the US authorities, according to a State Department document of 19 December 1934,[95] decided not to allow Huiswoud and his wife back into the USA. Maybe because of this (as Communist publications were not banned in the USA), the ITUC-NW and its newspaper moved back to Denmark and then, in March 1936, to Paris.[96] It went on until 1937 (see below, pp. 375-7) but is thought to have ceased publication that year.[97]

Among the black comrades who remained loyal to Communism, and in Moscow, Padmore was reviled as a Judas. This was shown when Nancy Cunard was refused a visa to visit the USSR in 1935 and later found, after getting a visa through intervention by Louis Aragon and the African American journalist Homer Smith and travelling to Russia, that it had been refused initially because of her links with Padmore.[98] In fact Padmore spent some time in 1934 as the guest of Nancy Cunard, who had returned to France, at her house at Réanville in Normandy, where he completed the book later published as *How Britain Rules Africa*.

Radical talk in Accra and London

While Africa was almost wholly at peace under colonial rule in the 1930s, changes were going on all the time, including one that many people recognised as a key change, the spread of Western education, institutions, commerce and influence. By the 1930s large numbers of Africans were living lives much affected by these changes—employees of the government, the firms and the churches, business men and women, some farmers (cocoa growers notably), and others, many with at least some Western schooling, all a little different in their livelihoods from the traditional agricultural majority in the villages (but not cut off from it; the word "detribalised" was in use by this time, but was always

---

94   Cedric J. Robinson, "Black Intellectuals at the British Core: 1920s-1940s", pp. 173-201 in Gundara and Duffield (eds) (note 29), pp. 197-8 (fn. 37).

95   Ibid.

96   Hooker (note 3), pp. 32-3.

97   R.J. MacDonald (note 29), pp. 153-4.

98   Chisholm (note 69), pp. 305-6; Hooker (note 3), p. 37.

misleading). These communities could not be called "elites"; but within them there was in many colonies a true elite of well-off lawyers, other professional people and newspaper proprietors and editors. These had controlled the political activity open to Africans, but now they were being challenged by the wider Western-influenced communities. This change became noticeable in the 1930s in the Gold Coast Colony, consisting largely of Fante traditional states plus the Ga state of Accra.

The true elite had for decades voiced criticisms of colonial rule, especially through African-owned newspapers which were as vigorous as ever in the 1930s. The ARPS, which despite the division between Western-educated leaders and senior chiefs continued after the NCBWA faded away, remained an organisation of elite protest. It concentrated criticism on the British Indirect Rule policies, and the prolonged legal dispute between Ofori Atta and the Asamankese and Akwatia chiefdoms was used by Kobina Sekyi and the ARPS to attack the leading chiefly ally of the British. The Western-educated leaders were not hostile to chieftaincy, but argued that they were the proper leaders of the Gold Coast people generally, and opposed British plans to give chiefs untraditional powers. Both elite politicians and chiefs were equally aristocratic in outlook, and the British accused anti-government lawyers of fomenting lawsuits like the Asamankese case to enrich themselves. But they also saw the ARPS campaign as a threat to their arrangements for governing the colony, as Sekyi explained to Padmore. In fact the campaign failed and the Privy Council rejected the appeal Sekyi went to defend in 1932.[99]

In Accra, Cape Coast and Sekondi-Takoradi there was active electoral politics surrounding the voting for LegCo municipal seats. Kojo Thompson was for long a leading figure in the Mambii Party, based in Accra and in fact more of a pressure group than a normal party. It was opposed in Accra by the Ratepayers' Association, whose candidate Dr F.V. Nanka-Bruce defeated Thompson in 1931 in the elections to the Accra municipal seat in LegCo. While he was himself a London-trained lawyer, Thompson was opposed to the Accra elite of which Nanka-Bruce was a prominent member.[100] In 1931 Thompson organised opposition to an Income Taxation Bill. Gold Coast Colony did not have the general

99   B. Edsman, *Lawyers in Gold Coast Politics, c. 1900-1945*, Uppsala 1979, pp. 82-92, 102-47.

100   Ibid., pp. 92-101.

direct taxation that most of Africa had, and the bill proposing to introduce it met strong opposition and was dropped. Rich and poor, chiefs and commoners joined in this opposition.[101] It should not be thought that political activity led by well-off lawyers was irrelevant to ordinary people or unpopular, even though the turnout of the limited electorate in the LegCo elections was low. However, some distinction between the top elite and a wider constituency was apparent by the 1930s.

Gold Coast Colony was one of the freest parts of Africa; but besides the basic fact of alien rule, there were many causes of discontent. 1934 was the worst year of the Depression for Gold Coast and cocoa farmers and wage earners were hard hit. The very fact that hardship was combined with a wide degree of liberty meant that any new impositions would be resisted. That happened in 1934 when the British introduced a Waterworks Bill and a Criminal Code Amendment Bill, commonly called the Sedition Bill and including severe restrictions on the press. The former introduced water rates, and although poor people were to be exempted this was seen as a new way of bringing in direct taxation. The second was introduced to deal with anti-colonial dissidence.

While allowing a very broad freedom of the press, the colonial government confiscated "seditious" literature from abroad: 940 items in 1932 and 1,750, including 1,100 copies of the *Negro Worker*, in 1933. It drew up lists of people receiving such literature, including Kobina Sekyi, the businessman A.J. Ocansey, and the editor R.B. Wuta-Ofei. Sekyi, Ocansey and Thompson had been involved in the cocoa marketing scheme already mentioned in 1932—one expression of this group's determination to resist European control, economic and political.[102] They and others formed a distinct group of more nationalist-minded people. Some such people met in a study group at the house of John Joseph Ocquaye, manager of the *Vox Populi* newspaper and founder of St John's School at Nsawam, discussing new political action through the ARPS or a new organisation.[103]

That group was joined by I.T.A. Wallace Johnson, who went to Gold Coast in late 1933. An energetic organiser and campaigner, he rapidly organised an agitation against the two bills presented in February 1934

---

101   Ibid., pp. 151-3.

102   Denzer (note 16), pp. 64-5.

103   Asante (note 82), pp. 109-10.

and, as representative of the London NWA, a campaign on behalf of the Scottsboro Boys. On 6 February 1934 Wallace Johnson and Joseph Danquah addressed a meeting on Scottsboro in Accra. Danquah was a well known lawyer and editor by then, founding the *Times of West Africa* (on which Bankole Awooner-Renner worked for a time) in 1931, and was a nationalist suspect in British eyes. But he had a basic aristocratic outlook sympathetic to the chiefs of whom the most important was his own brother, Nana Ofori Atta, and this separated him from the more anti-government group already mentioned, belonging mainly to the ARPS.[104]

The existence of two camps among African leaders of opinion became clear when both reacted angrily against the Waterworks and Sedition Bills. Although there was agreement that the Bills should be stopped, when a Committee of twelve was formed to oppose them, dominated by the more conservative element, the ARPS refused to join it. As a result two separate Gold Coast delegations went to London to protest at the two measures. The main delegation, which left for England in June 1934, was the Gold Coast and Ashanti Delegation headed by Nana Ofori Atta with Danquah as its secretary, while Dr Nanka-Bruce was another member. The separate ARPS delegates were Samuel R. Wood and George E. Moore. The two delegations' petitions were similar; both opposed the two bills, both proposed an elected Unofficial majority in LegCo, with property qualifications for members and voters.[105]

Wallace Johnson organised early protest action against the Bills with Awooner-Renner and B.E.A. Tamakloe, General Secretary of the Gold Coast Ex-Servicemen's Union, and later claimed to have helped draft the ARPS petition. He asked Bridgeman and Ward to help the ARPS delegates, though Ward advised against sending a delegation.[106] But the Sierra Leonean remained in Gold Coast himself, busy in various directions. He was very much concerned with working people's situation and grievances. West Africa, though not industrialised anywhere near the extent of South Africa, did have many thousands of wage workers who had plenty of cause for complaint. Nonetheless trade union-

104 L.H. Ofosu-Appiah, *The Life and Times of Dr J.B. Danquah*, Accra: Waterville Publishing House, 1974, pp. 18-29.

105 Rohdie (note 5), pp. 398-401.

106 Asante (note 82), p. 109; Denzer (note 16), pp. 78-9.

ism took time to become popular, even after the order to legalise it in British colonies in 1930. Wallace Johnson worked with—and, he claimed later, helped to establish—a Gold Coast Workers' Protective Union, a mutual benefit organisation which also expressed grievances; he also worked with the Motor Drivers' Union, composed mainly of lorry drivers complaining of police behaviour. In June 1934, 41 miners were killed when a tunnel collapsed at the gold mine at Prestea; Wallace Johnson set out to expose the mine owners' practices, revealing hazardous working conditions and very limited compensation rights; he later claimed to have gone down the mine in disguise.[107]

In London, the two delegations achieved nothing except the sympathy of critics of Empire. The Colonial Office did not listen to any of the protests, even from the loyal chiefly ally Nana Ofori Atta. Both the Sedition Bill and the Waterworks Bill were passed by Legco. The petition of the Gold Coast and Ashanti Delegation was rejected by the Colonial Office in September 1934, the ARPS petition in January 1935. The ARPS delegates however stayed in Britain for some time and continued efforts, already begun, to enlist support from MPs and others.

Besides the LAI and NWA, two other organisations were ready to help African anti-colonial protesters in Britain by this time. One, the League of Coloured Peoples (LCP), was founded in 1931 and headed by Dr Harold Arundel Moody, a Jamaican doctor who opened a practice in Peckham in South London in 1922 and ran it for many years, making his surgery a centre for the London Black community. An active Christian who became Chairman of the Board of Directors of the London Missionary Society, Moody built up the LCP as a Christian body working for harmony and good relations, and this spirit filled its newspaper, *The Keys*, launched in July 1933; its title recalled the words of Aggrey, whose memory was revered by Africans, about both black and white keys on a piano being needed for harmony.[108] The LCP was run mainly by West Indians, but with some African involvement. In early years a Jamaican girl who became a successful playwright and broadcaster, Una Marson, stayed with the Moodys and was the League's unpaid secretary.[109]

---

107   Asante (note 82), p. 110; Denzer (note 16), pp. 86-8.
108   David A. Vaughan, *Negro Victory*, Independent Press Ltd, 1950.
109   Delia Jarrett-Macauley, *The Life of Una Marson 1905-65*, Manchester Univer-

The League organised social events, for the visiting West Indies cricket team in 1933 for example, and was concerned with issues of Black people's welfare in Britain; LCP investigators and Moody himself went to examine the plight of the black waterfront community in Cardiff in 1935.[110] But Moody and the LCP were interested in political and worldwide racial issues also. Moody wrote in 1932 about Liberia, "It is better to do wrong in liberty than to do right in chains."[111] The first issue of *The Keys* had an editorial referring to the Scottsboro case and racial injustice in parts of the British Empire and "on our very doorsteps in Cardiff, Liverpool, London and elsewhere." It was the Nana Ofori Atta delegation from Gold Coast, not the ARPS one backed by Ward and other left-wingers, that the LCP worked with in London; Ofori Atta and Moody spoke at a conference organised by the LCP at the Albert Hall on 14-15 July 1934 on the theme "The Negro in the World Today". Some black activists criticised Moody's emphasis on harmony and cooperation, but the eirenic LCP and the left-wing militants had much in common and often worked together in London; Ward proposed a resolution on Scottsboro at an LCP meeting on 8 December 1933.[112]

Rather different from the LCP was the National Council for Civil Liberties (NCCL), founded in February 1934 by Ronald Kidd, a freelance journalist, and his girlfriend Sylvia Crowther-Smith, later Sylvia Scaffardi. Kidd was inspired to take this initiative particularly by police misconduct during a Hunger March in 1932, and this strongly left-wing body concentrated mainly on internal British issues. But it was interested in colonial questions from the start, and helped the Gold Coast ARPS delegation.[113]

---

sity Press, 1998, pp. 52-4.

110 Vaughan (note 108), pp. 30-81; R.J. MacDonald, "Dr. Harold Arundel Moody and the League of Coloured Peoples, 1931-1941: A Retrospective View," *Race* (London), vol. XIV no. 3, January 1973, pp. 291-319 (pp. 297-8).

111 *Manchester Guardian*, 30 October 1932, quoted in Peter O. Esedebe, *Pan-Africanism: The Idea and the Movement, 1776-1991*, 2nd ed. Washington: Howard University Press, 1994, pp. 122-3.

112 Macdonald (note 110), p. 293.

113 M. Lilly, *The National Council for Civil Liberties: The First Fifty Years*, Macmillan, 1984, pp. 1-42; Obituary of Sylvia Scaffardi, *The Guardian*, 30 January 2001; G. Bing, *Reap the Whirlwind*, MacGibbon & Kee, 1968, p. 43.

By 1935, with the help of the LAI and the NCCL, Moore and Wood had contacted several Labour MPs, including Maxton, Lansbury, Dingle Foot, and Clement Attlee, who was to take over as the leader of the party a few months later; Eleanor Rathbone, Independent MP for the Universities, was a prominent supporter. Articles dealing with the Gold Coast protest appeared in the *Daily Herald*, the *Labour Monthly*, the *Manchester Guardian*, the *New Age*, and the weekly *West Africa*, whose Editor, Albert Cartwright, was a friend of Sekyi and had publicised the lawsuit against Ofori Atta in 1932. Moore and Wood met Foot and some Liberal MPs in March 1935 and Woolf the following month. There was a meeting on 20 March where the NCCL and WASU were represented, and more meetings in April and May 1935. A petition was presented to parliament on behalf of the ARPS on 29 May 1935, and was referred to the Colonial Office, which finally gave an interview to the petitioners on 8 August, but made no concessions.[114]

The efforts on behalf of the ARPS delegation in Britain were among the biggest anti-colonial lobbying efforts in the 1930s. They aroused support from a fairly wide spectrum of opinion critical of colonial rule. On a lesser scale such widespread support was sometimes aroused over other African issues, such as the action against Tshekedi Khama in Bechuanaland in 1933 and the question of a hostel for WASU in London. WASU, with funds raised on a long tour of West Africa by Solanke, opened its hostel in leased premises at 62 Camden Road, London NW on 9 March 1933, but the following year the Colonial Office opened its own hostel, Aggrey House, which WASU boycotted. An African Hostel Defence Committee was set up in 1934 to support WASU's campaign in favour of its independent hostel; many leading left-wing, "colonial liberal" and anti-colonial personalities were linked with it, including the Countess of Warwick, who was President, and Norman Leys, W.M. Macmillan, Kingsley Martin and Julian Huxley; a meeting was held and invitations were sent to the LAI, the NWA, International Labour Defence and several other bodies. However, in 1935 all Gold Coast students but one broke away from WASU and accepted lodging at Aggrey House. WASU's hostel went into decline, but in 1936 it reached an agreement with the Colonial Office, whereby both hostels would

---

114   Rohdie (note 5), p. 410.

continue and both would receive subsidies from colonial governments in West Africa. Later WASU set up a new hostel, Africa House, opened on 9 July 1938 at 15th Villas, Camden Square, London NW1.[115]

The Gold Coast delegations' protests against the Sedition Bill aroused support because the Bill's provisions were very severe; when enacted, it punished not only the publication, but the mere possession of a newspaper, book or document, "or any part thereof or extract from", containing "seditious words or writing", unless the person in possession could prove he did not know "the nature of its contents".[116] But neither the two ARPS representatives nor their European backers did anything more than call for reforms and an end of abuses. Bridgeman, for years a rabid Bolshevik in the eyes of the Colonial Office, now helped organise a definitely "reformist" campaign. The LAI's and NWA's backing for Wallace Johnson's protests against mine workers' conditions in Gold Coast can be seen in the same way (there was a long tradition of protest in Britain against South African mine working conditions). G.E. Moore and S.R. Wood wrote in 1935, describing the role of the ARPS (which they called in this case the Aborigines' Protection Society), that these included the inculcation of "continued loyalty to the British connection" and the promotion of "sound National educational policy with particular attention to agricultural, scientific and industrial training"—which was close to common colonial ideas about education for Africans.[117]

The petitioners did indeed say in the same article that the Gold Coast "was never a conquered or ceded country", but that simply expressed the common Gold Coast view about an agreement that chiefs had signed with the British back in 1844, called the "Bond". This had provided for introduction of British magistrates' courts and "the general principles of British jurisdiction", and Fantes often argued that it precluded any further imposition of British jurisdiction or control. The British official view was of course quite different; the Chief Justice of the Gold Coast ruled in 1936 that the Bond was a dead letter and LegCo could pass

---

115   G.O. Olusanya, *The West African Students' Union and the Politics of Decolonisation, 1925-1958*, Ibadan: Daystar, 1982, pp. 26-35; P. Garigue, "The West African Students' Union", *Africa* vol. XXIII no. 1, January 1952, pp. 53-69 (pp. 60-1).

116   Quoted in Azikiwe (note 79), p. 263.

117   G.E. Moore and S.R. Wood, "A Plea for an Enquiry", *West African Review*, Liverpool, October 1935, pp. 9-12.

any laws that it liked.[118] But Danquah declared that "the Gold Coast was never conquered, ceded, or given over to the British in any shape or form".[119] This suggested that the entire basis of British rule was illegal. This sort of legal argument, similar to that made by the Dualas of French Cameroon, might seem an obvious one for Africans to make, since Europeans had commonly made treaties and then done far more than what African chiefs had thought they were agreeing to. But such an argument was made in the name of chiefs, for it was they who had signed those treaties, and nationalists did not generally want self-government under chiefly rule.

In the Gold Coast protests in 1934-35 the more militant anti-imperialism came from the African end, not from left-wingers in Britain. It came especially from Wallace Johnson, who was probably still a convinced Communist then and certainly had a poem praising the Soviet Union published in the *Negro Worker* of October-November 1934, under his usual alias of Wal. Daniels; another contribution appeared in the issue of February-March 1935.[120] When Wallace Johnson wrote to ask him to support opposition to the restoration of the Ashanti Confederacy Bridgeman replied that he would not help, as Asante had a strong tradition of resistance and could generate resistance again. Wallace Johnson accepted this advice, unlike Awooner-Renner, who was against the restoration of the historic Asante kingdom and founded a Friends of Ashanti Freedom Society to oppose it (it was however carried out at a big ceremony at Kumasi in 1935).[121]

The nationalist group surrounding Wallace Johnson and Awooner Renner was joined in late 1934 by a Nigerian already mentioned, Nnamdi Azikiwe (1904-96). The son of an Igbo government clerk, Azikiwe studied in the USA from 1925 to 1934, latterly at Lincoln University, Pennsylvania. After leaving the United States and stopping in England for three months he reached Accra on 31 October, to start a new newspaper for the businessman A.J. Ocansey. One of the first people he met

---

118   Edsman (note 99), p. 144.

119   Dr. J.B. Danquah, "The Next Phase in the Gold Coast Constitution," *West African Review*, October 1934, pp. 44-5.

120   Denzer (note 16), p. 68.

121   Ibid., pp. 93-4.

was Wallace Johnson, who defended what Azikiwe called "an extremist or leftist point of view", pointing to the example of Russia:

He told me point blank that if Africans depended upon intellectuals or leaders of thought they would not get beyond the stage of producing orators and resolution-passers. It was necessary for doers or leaders of action to step on the scene and prove that the African has a revolutionary spirit in him.[122]

Azikiwe disagreed, but the two were to work together for the next year and a half. When Azikiwe started his newspaper, the *African Morning Post*, he called there not only for repeal of the Sedition Ordinance, which was now in force, but for "Dominion status for the Gold Coast". He recalled later, "It was my view that our editorials should punch hard at all elements which sought to slow down the progress of the Gold Coast to freedom." There were worries about the Sedition Ordinance, which declared that it was a "seditious intention" to "bring about a change in the sovereignty of the Gold Coast"; but Azikiwe said this could not apply to a call for Dominion Status, as under the 1931 Statute of Westminster that status meant (so Azikiwe said, writing later) "self-government within the Commonwealth, of which the King was head".[123] The *African Morning Post* attacked the Ratepayers Association of Accra as well as the colonial government. Azikiwe, or "Zik" as he was commonly known then and for the next sixty years, brought in American journalistic ways and made the *Morning Post* the most successful West African newspaper to date in terms of circulation: 2,000 daily in 1934, 10,000 in 1936.[124]

After working at first with leaders of the ARPS Wallace Johnson went on to found a new organisation, the West African Youth League (WAYL), in February 1935. He was its organising secretary and in effect ran the new organisation. Bankole Awooner-Renner and R.B. Wu-ta-Ofei joined the executive of the WAYL, while supporters included

---

122   Azikiwe (note 79), pp. 218-19.

123   Ibid., pp. 254, 256, 263, 279. In South Africa, even after two new laws following the Statute of Westminster were passed in 1934, Smuts still said the country had no right to leave the British Commonwealth or be neutral in a future war: W.K. Hancock, *Survey of British Commonwealth Affairs, Vol. I, Problems of Nationality 1918-1936*, OUP 1937, pp. 279-80. But in fact the Statute laid down that the dominions had equal status with Britain, and Britain was independent.

124   Azikiwe (note 79), pp. 258-9.

Sekyi, Thompson and Azikiwe.[125] In Legco elections in 1935 Nanka-Bruce of the Ratepayers' Association and Thompson of the Mambii Party again contested the Accra municipal constituency, Thompson being supported by Ocansey, the *Morning Post*, the *Gold Coast Spectator*, Azikiwe, Sekyi and Wallace Johnson. They brought in anti-imperialist and socialist slogans, and Azikiwe and Wallace Johnson poured invective on Nanka-Bruce, whose followers replied in kind. Thompson won by 1,030 votes to 926, but there was a successful election petition, and a new poll had to be held; there, on 16 April 1936, Thompson won by an even bigger margin, 1,022 to 867.[126]

Under Wallace Johnson the WAYL rallied popular feeling in a way not seen on that scale in the Gold Coast before. Was this a new phase of nationalism? Wallace Johnson thought so, or had such a hope. He said the aim of the WAYL was to champion the cause of the people and particularly the "less favoured and down-trodden", and to defend the "natural and constitutional rights of the inhabitants of West Africa". He clearly aimed at something different from the old style of a small elite making loyal protests through newspapers and petitions. He said the League aimed to bring together "the high and the low, the rich and the poor, the learned and the unlearned," but he was out to supplant the high, the rich and the learned. West Africa, he said, "needs new ideas and new vision; new determination and will" and these were far more the "virtue of the youth—the youth in age and the youth in mind—than of the old and decrepit".[127] He wrote of Nana Ofori Atta's delegation:

They went to England with somebody else's ideas. The idea and conception of what they went to prosecute was not theirs. They were, as it were, stolen. The *Boys* of the *Old School* wanted to play a game with the tactics of those of the *New School*.[128]

But there was not really a break with the past. While Wallace Johnson was a Communist, and Awooner-Renner kept pictures of Lenin and Sta-

---

125 Asante (note 82), p. 110; Wilson (note 19), p. 248; S.K.B. Asante, entry on Awooner-Renner in *Dictionary of African Biography*, New York 1977, pp. 208-9.

126 Edsman (note 99), pp. 181-4.

127 Wallace Johnson Papers, quoted in Asante (note 82), p. 111.

128 Quoted in Rohdie (note 5), p. 408.

lin on a wall, the delegation they helped used the most un-revolutionary language, as has been shown. Although Thompson made, within limits, a popular, anti-elite appeal in Accra, and Azikiwe said Mambii became "a mass movement", there was a good deal of continuity rather than change.[129] Anyway the WAYL was to decline rapidly after a peak of activity during the Ethiopia protests in 1935-36, to be described shortly.

In Nigeria a similar movement founded in 1933 as the Lagos Youth Movement, then renamed the Nigerian Youth Movement, proved more effective than the WAYL in Gold Coast. It too was a conscious initiative of younger educated people to make protests against and demands on the colonial power, challenging the role of older politicial leaders—Macaulay's NNDP in this case—who were seen as too cautious. The NYM was headed by Dr James Churchill Vaughan, a medical doctor, and after his death by another doctor, Kofo Abayomi. The NYM had support outside Lagos and beyond the Yoruba provinces; Azikiwe and the editor Ernest Ikoli became prominent members. In Sierra Leone, similarly, a younger group of Freetown Creoles, including the nationalist lawyer C.D. Hobotah During, challenged the Creole "establishment" headed by Herbert Bankole-Bright of the NCBWA. None of this shook the empire, but Zik's open call for "Dominion Status" did break new ground for British-ruled Africa.

Paris, Moscow and African nationalists, 1934-35

A more radical party challenging colonial rule developed in these years in one African country, north of the Sahara. In Tunisia a group of younger activists in the Destour party broke away at a congress at Ksar Hellal on 2 March 1934 to form a new party which they claimed to be really a continuation of the Destour. Called the Neo-Destour, it was led by Habib Bourguiba and his comrades who based their campaign on the newspaper *L'Action Tunisienne*. They sought modern change combined with respect for Muslim teaching, and conducted a successful campaign in 1933 against burial of Muslims naturalised as French citizens in Muslim cemeteries. They made many demands falling short of independence, but they challenged French rule more than the older Destour leaders, though these had declared the aim of independence

---

129   Edsman (note 99), pp. 184-7; Rohdie (note 5), p. 408.

some time before. The gap between the impatient young campaigners and the older leaders widened until the breach came in March 1934. Bourguiba gathered support around the country and the Neo-Destour rapidly became a new sort of party—well organised, appealing to people of both Islamic and French education and to all classes and regions, and determined and vocal in calls for change. This meant that it could survive when the French Resident, Marcel Peyrouton, ordered a severe clampdown which aroused protests in France—it included, for example, a ban on 292 publications. Bourguiba was banished to the south of the country in September 1934 but was left free to gather support there; similar action was taken against the leaders who replaced him and his colleagues early in 1935.[130]

Morocco had no organised party like the old and new Destour, but an organisation called first the Jama'a al-Wataniyya (National Group) and later the Kutlat al-'Amal al-Watani (National Action Bloc) led campaigning directed, at first, especially against the "Berber Dahir", aided by the student leaders in Paris.[131] Balafrej, Ouazzani and Abdeld-jalil called on the Longuet father and son team at their law chambers in Paris, and they, encouraged by Shakib Arslan who was a friend of the elder Longuet and of Renaudel of the SFIO, helped launch a monthly magazine, *Maghreb*, in July 1932. The younger Longuet was editor-in-chief; he worked with other members of the magazine's patronage committee (including several left-wing figures), left-wing journalists, and Jeunes Marocains leaders, Balafrej being responsible initially for contact with Morocco.[132] The magazine highlighted the poor living conditions of Moroccans, contrasted with the settlers who received most benefits of French rule, and everyday administrative and police repression, but it also emphasised the sovereignty of the Sultan and the temporary nature of the French Protectorate; in the first issue Balafrej said the Protectorate "must have an end". Ouazzani started a new publication, *L'Action*

---

130   M.-S. Lejri, *Evolution du mouvement national tunisien des origines à la deuxième guerre mondiale*, Tunis: Maison Tunisienne de l'Edition, Vol. II, pp. 23-137; J.M. Abun-Nasr, *A History of the Maghrib*, CUP 1971, 1975, pp. 346-8.

131   Abun-Nasr (note 130), pp. 369-70.

132   Oved (note 45), vol. 2, pp. 33-6; J. P. Halstead, *Rebirth of a Nation: The Origins and Rise of Moroccan Nationalism 1912-1944*, Cambridge, MA: Harvard University Press, 1967, pp. 56, 146-7; J.-P. Biondi, *Les Anticolonialistes (1881-1962)*, Paris: Laffont, 1992, pp. 190-91.

du Peuple, in Fez in August 1933. Both periodicals were banned in Morocco after demonstrations of loyalty to the Sultan in Fez on 10 May 1934, but *Maghreb*, published in Paris, continued to appear until October 1935. Robert-Jean Longuet conducted a public ideological debate with his allies the Jeunes Marocains; he said capitalism was the root of colonial evil, but the Jeunes Marocains rejected class analysis and saw Frenchmen of all political persuasions in Morocco as oppressors.[133]

On 8 April 1934 the Berber Dahir's provisions were modified when traditional authorities had their judicial powers restored in Berber areas of Morocco.[134] Clearly the protests had had some effect, but the nationalists were not mollified. On 1 December 1934 their leaders, having formed a Comité d'Action Marocaine (not replacing the wider Kutlat al-'Amal al-Watani), presented to the Sultan a Plan of Reforms. It called for safeguarding of the country's unity and the Sultan's sovereignty, representative institutions, free movement and freedom of the press, recognition of Arabic as an official language, and ordering of respect for Islam. It did not call overtly for independence; rather, it treated Morocco as a state already (in fact it was, nominally, ruled through decrees of the Sultan).

By now the Moroccan nationalists were winning more sympathy on the French left. This did not come easily, but with changes in the French political scene, during 1934 support for the nationalists grew in the Socialist, the Communist and even the Radical party. The greater sympathy also extended to some Catholic writers, notably Emile Dermenghem; there was growing debate about the purposes of colonial rule among French Catholics in the 1930s, especially in the magazine *Esprit*.[135] Longuet *père et fils* set up a Patronage Committee for the Plan of Reforms, including themselves and some other Socialists, the journalist Andrée Viollis (close to the PCF), and Félicien Challaye.

French Socialists and Communists started cooperating over Morocco in 1934-35, with Longuet *fils* and Moroccan nationalists meeting Carlier, Lozeray, and Léonie Berger alias Léo Wanner, a Communist with a particular interest in North Africa. She was active in the Ligue

133   Oved (note 45), vol. 2, pp. 36-42.

134   Halstead (note 130), p. 187.

135   C. Liauzu, *Aux origines des tiers-mondismes: colonisés et anticolonialistes en France (1919-1939)*, Paris: Harmattan, 1982, pp. 84, 91.

Anti-Impérialiste which had a new active phase from 1933, publishing thirteen issues of a *Journal des Peuples Opprimés*. The March 1934 issue of that journal had an editorial encouraging rapprochement among opponents of imperialism. Francis Jourdain, Georges Valensi and Ramananjato were among other leading activists of the French LAI, which set up a number of committees dealing with Morocco, Tunisia and other colonial territories. On 18 September 1934 the LAI organised with the PCF, the CGTU, the ENA, the LDH, and the Tunisia Socialist federation a meeting at the Mutualité hall in Paris to protest against repression in Tunisia.[136]

The rapprochement between Communists, Socialists and colonial nationalists in France was of particular importance to the Etoile Nord-Africaine, as a largely proletarian party of Algerian workers in France. Those workers had every reason to fear the French far-right groups which voiced and encouraged the widespread racism in France, whose targets were Jews, East European immigrants, and North Africans; Messali took part in the great left-wing demonstrations against those far-right groups on 12 February 1934. After that the ice melted between French left-wingers and the ENA, as well as between the two main left-wing parties, and there was increasing contact and cooperation. But the ENA stuck firmly to its principles as a nationalist party, whose leader saw Islam as very important. Revival of the party in the industrial cities of France, after several hard years, was marked by the adoption of a new programme at a general meeting on 28 May 1933. It called plainly for "the total independence of Algeria", and went further to say that this must be under a "revolutionary national government" chosen by a constituent assembly elected by universal suffrage, and there must be large-scale land redistribution. The ENA also repeated its more immediate demands, for freedom of movement between Algeria and France, application of French social and labour legislation to Muslim Algerians, and so on.

Under a new executive elected on 30 May 1933, still dominated by Messali, the ENA had an elaborate organisation in districts and factories;[137] for a period Messali and Amar Imache were employed by

---

136   Oved (note 45), pp. 44-56, 80-92, 96; Liauzu (note 133), pp. 41-5.

137   J. Simon, *L'Etoile Nord-Africaine (1926-1937)*, Paris: Harmattan, 2003, pp. 145-50.

the party full-time. The ENA was still supposed to be banned, but it set up new offices in Paris (19 rue Daguerre, 14e). Its capacity for organisation was shown when a meeting in Paris on 26 May 1934 was banned but Algerian taxi drivers then took all the people who had gathered for it, over 600, to another hall.[138]

As this episode showed, the ENA was still harassed by the authorities. But strangely, there was no severe enforcement of the ban on the party for some years, even though the ENA continued to appeal to Algerian soldiers not to fight for France. The ENA programme of 28 May 1933 said the Koran forbade Muslims to kill other Muslims on pain of hell, and in November 1933 Messali called on Algerian soldiers not to fight fellow Muslims in Morocco; there were other such appeals, at meetings where Algerian soldiers in uniform sometimes went.[139] Despite this no severe action against the party followed immediately in France. However, Algerians back in their home country were suffering repression, as well as the effects of drought and the Slump; Oulémas preachers, for example, were excluded from official mosques in February 1933.[140] The crackdown was to culminate in a stringent new decree by the French Interior Minister, Régnier, on 30 March 1935 against incitement of Algerians to disorder or demonstrations against French rule.

The ENA feared more repression in France, and it was apparently to forestall this that the party was transformed into the Glorieuse Etoile Nord Africaine (GENA) in July 1934.[141] It held a general meeting in the Salle des Syndicats at Levallois-Perret on 5 August 1934; Messali there presented a new flag for Algeria, green and white with a red crescent.[142]

At the same time as that meeting, on 3-5 August 1934, there was an isolated but shocking incident in Algeria: riots at Constantine in which twenty-three Jews were killed by Muslims angered by some acts

---

138   Ibid., p. 155. On the ENA's organisation, membership and activity in the early 1930s see especially B. Stora, *Messali Hadj (1898-1974), Pionnier du nationalisme algérien*, Paris: Harmattan, 1986, pp. 95-116.

139   B. Recham, *Les Musulmans algériens dans l'Armée Française (1919-1945)*, Paris: Harmattan, 1996, pp. 114-17.

140   Stora (note 138), p. 108.

141   Ibid., p. 120; Simon (note 137), p. 154-5.

142   *Les Mémoires de Messali Hadj*, edited posthumous text, Paris: J.-C. Lattès, 1982 (hereafter Messali), pp. 177-8.

thought offensive to Islam.[143] Jean Longuet, who was Messali's lawyer at the time, organised his own inquiry into the incident, in which the GENA joined. The GENA, indicating its new Islamic orientation, approved of the rioters' original reflex in defence of Islam, though not of the killing and destruction, while blaming the French administration. The PCF spoke of popular feeling among the Muslim masses that had turned on the wrong target.[144] The ENA's and the PCF's ideas were still not very close, but they were now no longer as far apart as they had been as recently as 1933, when at a meeting on 30 June Marouf accused Messali of "appealing as much to the workers as to the bourgeoisie" and Messali said, "Algerians desire their country's independence and not Communist guardianship."[145] A year later André Ferrat, head of the PCF Colonial Section, was preaching cooperation to form a united anti-imperialist front. Messali recalled that it was Ferrat who approached him.[146] On 19 August 1934 those two men addressed a meeting attended by about 3,500 Algerians; the GENA agreed with the PCF, the LAI and Secours Rouge on united action; the agreed resolution included "*Vive l'Indépendance de l'Afrique du Nord! Vive l'Islam!*".[147] In October 1934 *El Amel*, which under its editor Marouf had continued fierce polemics with *El Ouma*, ceased publication. A new Algerian Communist publication, *Saout El Amel* ("the worker's voice"), began appearing in April 1935, showing sympathy for nationalists and calling for a "vast people's liberation front".[148] Meanwhile *El Ouma*'s circulation shot up from 12,000 in 1932 to 40,000 in 1934.[149]

Messali was arrested on 1 November 1934; Ferrat and Léo Wanner of the LAI addressed a meeting on 10 November to protest. Amar Imache and Belkacem Radjef ran the GENA for a time, but were then arrested themselves. Messali and two others were given six-month gaol sentences

143   A. Nouschi, *La naissance du nationalisme algérien*, 1914-1954, Paris: Minuit, 1962, pp. 74-6; Simon (note 137), p. 158.

144   E. Sivan, *Communisme et Nationalisme en Algérie 1920-1962*, Paris: Presses de la FNSP, 1976, pp. 78-81.

145   B. Stora, *Dictionnaire biographique de militants nationalistes algériens 1926-1954: E.N.A., P.P.A., M.T.L.D.*, Paris: Harmattan, 1985, entry on Marouf, pp. 57-9.

146   Messali (note 142), pp. 178-9. See also Stora (note 138), pp. 131-2.

147   Simon (note 137), pp. 157-9.

148   Liauzu (note 135), pp. 43n, 44n.

149   Simon (note 137), p. 161.

for reconstituting a banned organisation, and then, on 28 March, Messali was given a one-year sentence on a separate charge of inciting insubordination in the armed forces. On the advice of his lawyer, Messali declared the GENA dissolved and re-formed it as the Union Nationale des Musulmans Nord-Africains. Messali was freed on 1 May, and on 3 July 1935 the Appeal Court at Amiens ruled that the ban on the ENA in 1929 had been null and void because the provisions of the law had not been followed. So, after all that it had been through, the ENA could now resume work openly under its original name.[150]

Among the Black community in France and its activist and intellectual members the two main militant organisations by 1933, as noted, were the UTN, which continued after expelling Kouyate and published *Le Cri des Nègres*, and the LDRN. Mention must also be made of a group of writers, poets, students and others who in the late 1920s and early 30s examined and debated the culture of Black peoples and how they related or should relate to French culture. The debate was carried on particularly in the columns of *La Dépêche Africaine* and then in another magazine, *La Revue du Monde Noir*, published from October 1931 to April 1932, and particularly by Caribbeans such as the Nardal sisters and Maran. West Indians in France, already very assimilated, had pursued total assimilation for many years, but now began to take more interest in their African origins. While Haitians, including the famous writer Jean Price-Mars whose *Ainsi Parla L'Oncle* was published in 1928, took an interest in the African culture still flourishing in Haiti, and others were influenced by anthropology in Africa, Jane Nardal and others developed ideas of special common cultural and lifestyle features of Black people around the world.[151] These ideas were developed into the literary and artistic movement called Négritude, whose outstanding figure was the Martinican poet Aimé Césaire (1913-2008). One African who joined and furthered this largely Diasporan movement was Léopold Senghor, a young Senegalese student who arrived in France in 1928.

Partly because of Senghor (1906-2001), who was to become President of Senegal, the Black literary circles in Paris of the 1930s, and their ideas, are better remembered and studied than the Black anti-colonial activists of the same period. The two groups were fairly distinct. The

---

150   Messali (note 140), pp. 184-91.
151   Dewitte (note 1), pp. 229-67; Edwards (note 54), Ch. 3.

literary people were reacting in their own way against racism and the colonial situation—though their ideas (black people's spontaneity, relaxed view of life, dancing, laughter etc. contrasted with white people's cold rational, scientific, domineering spirit, etc.) echoed racist stereotypes and could reinforce them. But in the inter-war era people (both white and black) whose interest was concentrated on African or Diasporan culture commonly accepted or even applauded colonial rule. This was true of René Maran, for all the shock he had momentarily caused colonialists by *Batouala* in 1921 and the *Les Continents* libel action in 1924. The *Revue du Monde Noir* published paternalist colonial ideas, welcomed the Colonial Exhibition, and carried articles by Candace and Eboué. However, among those who founded that magazine, besides Paulette Nardal, there were Dr Léo Sajous, the Haitian dentist active for some time in the LDRN, and Me Henri Jean-Louis, the Guadeloupean lawyer who had acted for the Bonadoo Dualas of Cameroon in their land case; while Senghor, as head of the Association des Etudiants Ouest-Africains, had contact with the left-wing radicals in 1933-34. The magazine had articles on Scottsboro, Liberia and Ethiopia. In June 1932 Etienne Léro (who joined the UTN for a time) and some other Caribbean students published what turned out to be a one-issue magazine, *Légitime Défense*, with a more militant tone, influenced by Marxism and the Surrealists; it concentrated attacks on the Caribbean *bourgeoisie de couleur* and slavish imitation of whites.[152] This last theme had a long history in West Africa—it was Kobina Sekyi's main theme—and other ideas of these Paris literary people were also heard among African Americans; the *Revue du Monde Noir* published work by Langston Hughes and Claude McKay.

In September 1934 Maran and Gaston Monnerville agreed to work with the LAI Scottsboro committee.[153] This was a clear sign of the "thaw" going on between Communist and non-Communist opponents of imperialism and racism, extending to black as well as North African movements. Some UTN leaders resisted this more conciliatory approach, but they were brought into line when a new executive was elected in January 1935, with Joseph Ebele, a Duala Cameroo-

---

152   Dewitte (note 1), pp. 267-75; Edwards (note 54), pp. 191-8, 265-6.
153   Dewitte (note 1), p. 314.

nian who had edited the Duala-language *Mbale* in Paris in 1929-30, as general secretary.[154]

Meanwhile the LDRN carried on a sort of existence from February 1932 to November 1934, but without its newspaper. Emile Faure was more interested for a time in a small association called Sénégal Amical, set up in April 1933 and subsidised by the leaders of the opposition to Diagne in Senegal, Galandou Diouf and Lamine Gueye. But things changed after 11 May 1934, when Blaise Diagne died in France. Diouf was elected deputy for Senegal in the subsequent by-election in September 1934, and provided funds that allowed *La Race Nègre* to resume publication in November. Faure had always adopted a militant line, and before *La Race Nègre* halted publication in 1932 it had begun to preach pride in the black race and African culture, more forcefully than the literary circle mentioned earlier. Now Faure went further, not only denouncing the deportations of immigrants and other signs of anti-Black racism in France, but expressing disgust with France generally:

Faced with the irremediable social rot of France, Europe's endemic state of war, the monstrous political and social doctrines which are making their way ahead there, we can only have one watchword: LET'S GET OUT OF THERE.[155]

Obviously, *La Race Nègre* called for independence; in July 1935 it declared, "We want a single Negro State, encompassing all of Black Africa, and the West Indies...which the North Africans, if they wish it, could join."[156] Its reporting and comments could not have pleased Galandou Diouf, and he probably provided no more money. At any rate *La Race Nègre* only published two more issues, in July 1935 and February 1936, after the one in November-December 1934. It is curious that Emile Faure, the editor responsible for *La Race Nègre*'s unusually bitter and virulent tone at that time—answering racism with racism as Garvey had done, and verging on Fascism—was himself half-French.

Kouyate, after his expulsion from the UTN, spent some time in extreme difficulty; in May 1934 he was reported as selling North African perfumes and jewellery from door to door, and could not go to his

---

154   Ibid., pp. 316-17.

155   Ibid., p. 334.

156   Spiegler (note 42), p. 219.

home because of rent arrears.[157] But he probably kept up some contacts to pursue the idea that was spreading during those years, of unity among black people, or all colonised people, joined by European allies. In this spirit he contacted other activists including Faure. And in 1935 a cause came to unite African and Black people everywhere, among themselves and with many others as allies: the cause of Ethiopia against Italian aggression. After Italian troops in Somalia clashed with Ethiopian forces in the Wal Wal incident in the Ogaden on 5 December 1934, Mussolini went ahead gradually with plans to invade Ethiopia that had been under consideration since 1932. Two Italian divisions were mobilised and sent to Eritrea and Somalia in February 1935. As the crisis mounted in the following months, anti-colonial and left-wing organisations were now ready to respond with near unanimity.

This unanimity over Ethiopia extended to European left-wingers, but the better feeling between them and activists from the colonies in France had its definite limits. It was easier to agree about denouncing Mussolini's aggressive plans than about independence for French colonies. In October 1934 Galandou Diouf, Lagrosillière and Nguyen The Truyen launched a Fédération des Peuples Colonisés, with André Berthon, the lawyer and former Communist deputy who had now left the PCF, as chairman. It was supported by several other SFIO politicians including the Longuets and the lawyer and deputy Marius Moutet, who had long taken an interest in colonial matters, and several North Africans including Hedi Nouira of Tunisia, a Neo-Destour student activist. But there were disagreements over the question of independence and the ENA, the Neo-Destour and the Jeunes Marocains pulled out. The Federation issued an appeal to "native elites" on 11 March 1935, but only for removal of "misunderstandings" between France and the subject peoples and "getting their voice heard".[158]

In both France and Britain (in backing for the Gold Coast delegations), Communists and democratic left-wingers showed greater readiness to work together on colonial issues in 1934-35. This meant agreeing to support "reformist" demands, and it was to go further and lead to agreement by Communists to tone down demands for colonial independence, which would get them nearer the normal Socialist position as

---

157   Dewitte (note 1), p. 382.
158   Liauzu (note 135), pp. 202-3.

well as the government's and the general public's. This change, wrongly backdated to 1933 by Padmore, came about two years later, when the Franco-Soviet Pact of Mutual Assistance was signed, on the French side by the Foreign minister Pierre Laval, on 2 May 1935, and ratified on 27 February 1936. When Laval visited Moscow on 13-15 May 1935, the communiqué stated that Stalin "understands and fully approves the policy of national defence followed by France, in order to maintain her armed forces at the level required by her security."[159] This was taken to mean that the PCF must stop opposing the recent lengthening of national service to two years, and it did. That implicitly affected Communist opposition to French imperialism also. Supporting French rearmament to face the German threat was incompatible with encouraging disaffection among Africans in the French forces. More generally, it was hard to reconcile with inciting revolt in the French empire. And a "Popular Front" with democratic left-wing parties meant avoiding arguments over colonialism, which the SFIO accepted.

By October 1934 Thorez in France was urging left-wing parties to join a Rassemblement Populaire;[160] this term was used at first, but later the new alliance was called the Popular Front. It extended to the Radical Party which was not very left-wing and had been the major government party for over thirty years, and was still so in 1935. On 14 July 1935 half a million people attended a great demonstration of the Rassemblement Populaire in Paris. The emerging Popular Front movement received full Communist approval at the Seventh Comintern Congress which was held in Moscow soon after the great 14 July rally in Paris, from 25 July to 21 August 1935.

That Congress also passed a resolution on "The Anti-Imperialist Peoples' Front in the Colonial Areas", declaring that Communists in those areas must participate actively in the "mass anti-imperialist movements headed by the nationalists-reformists" and seek joint action with them on the basis of an "anti-imperialist platform".[161] This was in effect a return to the line followed before 1928. Its wording appeared to endorse cooperation with, for example, the ENA in France, and as worded

---

159   Beloff (note 44), pp. 138-61.

160   McDermott and Agnew (note 49), pp. 124-7.

161   J.P. Haithcox, *Communism and Nationalism in India: M.N. Roy and Comintern Policy 1920-1939*, Princeton University Press, 1971, pp. 212-13.

could have allowed the possibility of a "front" within a colonial territory to demand independence. But in fact Popular Fronts among European left-wing parties, including Labour and Socialist International parties that accepted colonialism, would probably mean Communists having to accept colonialism in the same way. And it seems the Comintern expected this and accepted it readily.

That is suggested by the Comintern's attitude to South Africa. In that country the economic crisis had led to the ruling National Party and the South African Party forming a coalition on 31 March 1933 and then formally merging to form the United South African National Party in December 1934. Hertzog remained Prime Minister with Smuts as minister of Justice; they had some disagreements about the "native question",[162] but the united whites' government worked well for the whites and showed how little disagreement there really was, among them, about their supremacy. Whatever little Smuts had done to oppose the fuller enforcement of white supremacy now ended. He himself admitted in December 1934, "The Natives are getting more and more suspicious and they think that Fusion [of the parties] means that they are now without champions and that the Nationalist viewpoint has won."[163]

Others who had been real champions of Africans were able to do very little now. The ICU was in serious decline, the ANC somnolent, the CPSA reduced to a bickering little club. Kotane said in 1934, "The once formidable African National Congress and ICU have disappeared".[164] But he also wrote to the ECCI in early 1935, "The [South African Communist] Party is disintegrating and the work is practically at standstill."[165] By 1935 the CPSA had just a few dozen members, but they still squabbled. Kotane was removed as Party Secretary by the end of 1934. To resolve the quarrel between the new leaders—Marks and Mofutsanyana (who had both returned from the USSR in 1934) and the Latvian-born Lazar Bach—and Kotane's group, both Kotane and Bach

---

162   W. K. Hancock, *Smuts: The Fields of Force*, CUP, 1968, pp. 251, 257.

163   Quoted in Ibid., p. 259.

164   *Umsebenzi* 27 January 1934, quoted in J. and R. Simons, *Class and Colour in South Africa 1850-1950*, London: IDAF, 1983, p. 468.

165   Kotane to Executive Committee of the Communist International (ECCI), 20 Feb. 1935, document 40 in Davidson *et al.* (eds) (note 8), p. 123.

were summoned to Moscow, but Kotane did not go then. Bach was present at the Comintern Congress but with only a "consultative" vote. The only CPSA delegate with full voting rights was Josephine (Josie) Mpama, Mofutsanyana's wife and a Communist activist then studying at Kutvu.[166]

Before the Congress the South African Communists had been debating again their official slogan of a "Native Republic", and now the Congress declared that the slogan was "sectarian" and should be dropped. The Communist policy of opposition to colonial nationalists and to Western democratic Socialists was also now rejected as "sectarian"— meaning narrow and rigorist, unable to win support except among a dedicated few. But Kotane had argued that the "Native Republic" was intended to mean first majority rule and only later a "Workers' and Peasants' Government", and could have wide appeal because of "the desire of every black man to be free from imperialist oppression and exploitation."[167] Josephine Mpama also said in her address to the Congress that a "popular front" was a step on the way to a "native republic". This was contrary to the new party line and she was questioned about it, and said the address had been written for her by Bach and Zusmanovich. They may have been confused about the change of party line, but they may also have agreed with Kotane's view, which within the parameters of Communist thinking was a reasonable one.

Soon after the Congress in Moscow there was a new purge in the CPSA, and the Comintern decided to sort that party's problems out. It summoned Kotane, Roux—who saw the "Native Republic" idea in the same way as Kotane and said it should be retained[168]—and two of the new leaders, Marks and Nikin Sobia, to Moscow; only Kotane went there. A Comintern commission examined the CPSA's situation; the "Native Republic" slogan was not the only issue, but Kotane had to

---

166   Davidson *et al.* (note 8), Introduction, pp. 15-18. Josephine Mpama said she was the daughter of a Coloured mother and a "Dutch" (probably meaning Afrikaner) father, and had four children, one by Moses Kotane: Autobiography of J. Mpama, 1936, document 57 in Davidson *et al.* (note 8), vol. 2, pp. 160-70.

167   Kotane to ECCI, 31 October 1934, document 38 in Davidson *et al.* (note 8), pp. 117-21.

168   E. Roux to ECCI, November 1935, document 53 in Davidson *et al.* (note 8), pp. 149-53.

submit to an order to drop it.[169] Kotane and Mpama did not suffer for their heretical declarations, but Zusmanovich was dismissed from his Comintern position, and Bach was told to stay in Moscow until the end of the investigation. Worse was to follow, including a concentration camp for Zusmanovich, for the Great Purge was getting under way.

The Comintern paid no attention to Kotane's and Roux' argument that the call for majority rule could itself be popular—among non-white South Africans, the majority. It was obviously thinking of white South Africans in assuming that that call was an unpopular minority call, a "sectarian" one; and it clung to the absurd hope that the Afrikaner chauvinist movement (now headed by the new Purified National Party of Daniel Malan, which denounced Hertzog as a compromiser) could listen to the Communist message. But it also encouraged united action among opponents of racism, and an All African Convention met at Bloemfontein on 15 December 1935, including the ANC and CPSA, to oppose Hertzog's new racist legislation, and received a message of encouragement from Moscow.[170]

The events concerning the Communist Party of South Africa are recorded because they revealed the Comintern's new line, not because they had the slightest effect on events in South Africa. In Britain and the USA, too, the Communists were so few that their party line had little significance for the majority. In Britain the ILP, which quarrelled with the true Labour Party continuing after the 1931 crisis as well as being a bitter opponent of the National Government including its National Labour component, split from the Labour Party in 1932, while Fenner Brockway was Chairman (1931-33); and it then held talks with the Communist Party, but these were eventually broken off. Later the CPGB, in the new spirit, decided not to contest most seats in the general election of November 1935, but to tell people to vote Labour; but the Labour Party and the TUC saw no need to soften their hostility to the Communists. In the USA the new line meant an end to the unseemly bickering over defence of the Scottsboro Boys, still not out of danger

---

169   His seemingly half-hearted grovelling is recorded in document 64 in David-son *et al.* (note 8), "M. Kotane's Statement to the South African Commission, 19 March 1936", pp. 188-92. See also Bunting (note 13), pp. 70-4; W. Mc-CLellan, "Black *Hadj* to "Red Mecca": Africans and Afro-Americans at KUTV, 1925-1938", Ch. 3 in Matusevich (ed.) (note 19) (p. 70).

170   Simons (note 164), pp. 475, 480-1.

at that time; in December 1935 the NAACP and ILD, and three other bodies, reached agreement to create a new Scottsboro Defense Committee.[171] But the CPUSA was unimportant in the overall American scene, where the underprivileged were more interested in Huey Long and Father Coughlin.

The German KPD and SPD were now able to stop sniping at each other, and Münzenberg took part in "Popular Front" talks among the German political exiles in Paris, though he was caught up in divisions within the exiled KPD that ended in his expulsion from the party in May 1938.[172] But the "Popular Front" programme was important mainly in France and Spain. In France the PCF, besides dropping its opposition to defence preparations, gave up its unpopular stance on Alsace-Lorraine also (it had called for self-determination); it was aiming to reduce areas of disagreement with democratic Socialists and with the French public at large—in fact, to become patriotic.[173] This meant softening its anti-colonialism, which would please both the Socialists and the government in power.

In January 1936 the PCF held its 8th Congress at Villeurbanne (Lyons), where Thorez formally became Secretary General after in fact heading the PCF for some years. Ferrat was not reelected to the political bureau at the congress, and was replaced by Lozeray as head of the PCF Colonial Section; the following July Ferrat was expelled from the party.[174] The Socialist-Communist rapprochement led to the CGTU being merged with the CGT in March 1936. It also led to a joint Radical-Socialist-Communist Popular Front programme for the coming elections, published on 11 January 1936, which made only one pledge regarding the colonies (Part 1, section 7): "Formation of a Parliamentary com-

---

171   Dan T. Carter, *Scottsboro: A Tragedy of the American South*, rev. ed. Baton Rouge and London: Louisiana State University Press, 1979, pp. 334-5. In 1937-38 four of the Scottsboro accused were finally acquitted but others, facing the same pseudo-evidence, were found guilty, and one sentenced to death; he was reprieved, but five men were gaoled for years for an offence that had not even happened: Carter, pp. 338-415.

172   S. McMeekin, *The Red Millionaire: A Political Biography of Willi Münzenberg, Moscow's Secret Propaganda Tsar in the West*, Yale University Press, 2003, pp. 279-94.

173   Mortimer (note 49), pp. 256-9.

174   Biondi (note 132), pp. 198-9.

mittee of inquiry into the political, economic and cultural situation in France's overseas territories, especially French North Africa and Indo-China."[175]

In January 1936 a book on Algeria sponsored by the LAI, and written under an assumed name by the exiled Palestine Communist leader Nachman List who was then secretary of the French LAI, was published under the title *La question algérienne*. It was a well documented condemnation of French rule, calling for "agrarian anti-imperialist revolution which will give independence to Algeria and will give it the possibility of developing its productive forces held in chains by colonisation." This was in line with Communist ideas for the past fifteen years, and the book had a preface by Francis Jourdain, a painter who had been active in Communist anti-colonial campaigns; it was well publicised by *L'Humanité*. But a few weeks later, the book was withdrawn from sale on orders from higher up in the party.[176]

By the time of the April 1936 elections the PCF had adopted the view of other French parties, that independence was not on the agenda for any part of the French Empire, except Syria and Lebanon. There progress towards self-government, required under the "A" Mandate provisions, continued very uneasily in the early 1930s, with constant clashes and crises between the French government and nationalists led in Syria by the National Bloc; but it did continue, the two countries had their constitutions, presidents and prime ministers, and talks on a new Syrian treaty were held in 1932-33, without success, and then begun again in Paris shortly before the French elections.[177]

In March 1936 Léo Wanner, after a tour of Algeria, met Messali, then in exile in Geneva (see below, pp. 343-4), and suggested "a little flexibility", which Messali took to mean abandoning the call for independence. Messali however urged his followers to back the Popular Front, as the elections approached, while sticking to the call for independence—or so he recalled later.[178] In an "open letter" in *El*

175   Jackson (note 49), p. 301.
176   Sivan (note 144), pp. 92-3. As Sivan comments, this gives a good idea of when the change of policy became effective.
177   Philip S. Khoury, *Syria and the French Mandate: The Politics of Arab Nationalism*, London: I.B. Tauris, 1987, Parts IV, V and VI.
178   Messali (note 142), pp. 208, 212.

Ouma of January-February 1936 Messali called for reforms in North Africa—the end of special legislation affecting Muslims, extension of French social laws, etc.—and for a representative assembly elected by universal suffrage.[179] While such an assembly could have led quickly to independence, this call may suggest that, as Stora argues,[180] Messali agreed in 1935 to suspend the demand for independence provisionally, for the sake of cooperation with Popular Front parties. His own memoirs suggest the contrary, and Stora also says that in April 1936 the PCF offered a subsidy to the ENA, then in serious financial trouble, in return for toning down the independence call, but Messali ordered his party to break off all discussions on the idea.[181] Messali did not record this, but it fits well with what he did record about Wanner's visit to him. However, he and other militants who had called for independence must have approached the elections knowing very well that the Popular Front parties promised nothing for the colonies except a commission of inquiry.

Ethiopia, Africa, France and Britain, 1935-36

However much British and French people accepted empire as a part of life, the invasion of Ethiopia, a member of the League of Nations, was another matter. In the spring and summer of 1935 Westerners of many parties or none joined to oppose and condemn Mussolini's war preparations. But Africans and people of the African Diaspora, while often respecting the Western opposition to Mussolini, widely regarded the cause of Ethiopia as their own in a special way. There was a remarkable surge of feeling in three continents in support of the independent African state under attack, which had always aroused sympathetic feelings in the Black world. There is no space here to recall all the meetings, demonstrations, newspapers and organisations in Africa, Europe and the New World involved in support for Ethiopia (which was often called by that name by Africans and Black Diasporans, and others, though others used the name Abyssinia which was commonly used then).[182]

---

179   Simon (note 137), pp. 179-80.
180   Stora (note 138), p. 134.
181   Ibid., pp. 141-2.
182   The best account of the pan-African support for Ethiopia is S.K.B. Asante (note 82). See also J.A. Langley, *Pan-Africanism and Nationalism in West Africa*

The protests began during the months when Mussolini's preparations for war became known. In Nigeria, for example, the *Nigerian Daily Telegraph*, now edited by Ernest Ikoli, called in July 1935 for protest demonstrations, urging that in all working organisations, trade unions, workers' clubs, churches and other places "work must at once be started to organise and build up "Hands of Abyssinia Committees"." A mass meeting was held at Glover Memorial Hall in Lagos on 20 September 1935, attended by over 2,000 people, with Eric Olawu Moore, Vice-President of the NNDP, in the chair, and Vaughan and Peter J.C. Thomas—a businessman who had attended the 1921 Pan African Congress—among the speakers. A resolution expressed support for Britain's stand at that time. Committees to raise funds to help the Ethiopians were formed in Nigeria, Gold Coast and Sierra Leone. After the war began, the Lagos Ethiopia Defence Committee, established by leading NYM figures, was formally launched at a mass meeting at the Glover Memorial Hall on 10 December 1935; there were others in several other parts of Nigeria. In April 1936 the Ethiopian minister in London, Dr Workneh Martin, sent out a special Abyssinian Appeal, already circulated in Britain and Ireland, to Duse Mohamed in Nigeria, aimed at raising a loan to buy equipment for the Ethiopians. Duse Mohamed's *Comet* published the Appeal in full and called on Africans everywhere to contribute, urging his fellow Muslims in particular to help.[183]

In Gold Coast the Ethiopian crisis boosted the WAYL in the Gold Coast, and there were over twenty branches by the end of 1935. The League held its first Annual Conference in Accra from 21 to 28 March 1936; it condemned the Italians and called for oil sanctions in resolutions sent to the Secretary-General of the League of Nations and the British Colonial Secretary. Wallace Johnson and Tamakloe signed an appeal concluding, "Ethiopia is calling. Mother Africa is shedding bitter tears against European aggression and she is appealing to you. Will you sit still?"[184]

There were strong protests among Black South Africans, with dock workers refusing to handle Italian goods at Cape Town and Durban.[185]

1900-1945, OUP, 1973, pp. 326-37.
183 Asante (note 82), pp. 148-53.
184 Ibid., p. 153.
185 Bunting (note 13), p. 96.

On 7 December 1935 a conference of chiefs, headmen and teachers of Natal and Zululand passed resolutions expressing sympathy with Ethiopia and also calling on the South African government not to end the Cape Native franchise, which, it said, was a symbol of a British tradition also expressed in defence of Ethiopia.[186] But a few months later both Mussolini and Hertzog had won.

African Americans rallied in support of Ethiopia. The NAACP magazine *The Crisis* carried an article by Padmore in May 1935, calling for support for Ethiopia.[187] There were demonstrations in New York, in Harlem in August 1935 and in Madison Square Garden the following month. Du Bois, James W. Ford, and Adam Clayton Powell Jr were among the campaigners for Ethiopia.[188] The Italian conquest of Ethiopia aroused similar feelings in the West Indies; the St Lucian economist W. Arthur (later Sir Arthur) Lewis wrote afterwards:

West Indians felt that in that issue the British Government betrayed a nation because it was black, and this has tended to destroy their faith in white government, and to make them more willing to take their fate in their own hands.[189]

African and Caribbean people in Britain and France joined in the protests. In London the International African Friends of Abyssinia (IAFA) was formed. Padmore, who settled in England in 1935, later recalled that he had headed an *ad hoc* committee to assist the Gold Coast ARPS delegation, and "When Mussolini declared war against Abyssinia, the Gold Coast *ad hoc* Committee was reconstituted to become the International African Friends of Abyssinia."[190] Padmore's memory was fallible, and it is clear that the IAFA was formed before the war began. And the founder, it seems, was his fellow countryman C.L.R. James.

Cyril Lionel Robert James (1901-89) went to England from Trinidad in 1932, on the invitation of another Trinidadian, Learie Constantine,

186   Hancock (note 123), p. 314.

187   Hooker (note 3), p. 44.

188   James H. Meriwether, *Proudly We Can be Africans: Black Americans and Africa, 1935-1961*, Chapel Hill: University of North Carolina Press, 2002, pp. 27-53.

189   W. Arthur Lewis, *Labour in the West Indies*, London: Fabian Society, 1938, reprinted London: Beacon Books, 1977 (with afterword by Susan Craig), p. 19.

190   G. Padmore, *Pan-Africanism or Communism?* Dennis Dobson, 1956, pp. 144-5.

and stayed with the famous cricketer initially at Nelson in Lancashire. He shared Constantine's love of cricket and it was always to remain one of his passions, but for James politics was another, starting in Lancashire and with the ILP. He published in 1932, with financial help from Constantine, *The Life of Captain Cipriani: An Account of British Government in the West Indies.* Arthur Cipriani was a white Trinidadian (of Corsican parentage) who led a longshoremen's strike in 1919 and then headed the Trinidad Workingmen's Association in the 1920s and made it a successful political organisation, later affiliated to the Labour Party in Britain and renamed the Trinidad Labour Party.[191] In 1933 James' book *The Case for West Indian Self-Government* was published by Leonard and Virginia Woolf's Hogarth Press; he wrote there:

Britain will hold us down as long as she wishes. Her cruisers and aeroplanes ensure it. But a people like ours should be free to make its own failures and successes, free to gain that political wisdom and political experience which come only from the practice of political affairs.[192]

James, who had experience of journalism in Trinidad, was cricket reporter for the *Manchester Guardian* for the 1933, 1934 and 1935 seasons, while also getting more involved in left-wing politics.

James said he founded the IAFA.[193] Padmore recorded that James was Chairman, Peter Milliard (from British Guiana) and T. Albert Marryshaw (from Grenada) vice-chairmen, and Kenyatta secretary, while the treasurer was Marcus Garvey's divorced first wife, Amy Ashwood Garvey. "They, together with Mr Sam Manning of Trinidad, Mr Mohammed Said of Somaliland, and the author formed the executive committee," Padmore recalled. A letter from Kenyatta to Sylvia Pankhurst on 14 August 1935 gave the names of several organisers or leading members of the IAFA, including himself, Amy Ashwood Garvey, Milliard (a doctor in Manchester), Samuel Manning, Marryshaw (a trade unionist who had attended the 1921 Pan African Congress), John Payne from

191   Lewis (note 189), pp. 26-7.

192   Paul Buhle, *C.L.R. James: The Artist as Revolutionary,* London and New York: Verso, 1988, pp. 7-42; Farrukh Dhondy, *CLR James: Cricket, the Caribbean, and World Revolution,* London, Weidenfeld and Nicolson, 2001, pp. 1-41. The second book was a shortened version of the first; Dhondy says both were based on an earlier work.

193   Interview, C.L.R. James, London, 4 June 1984.

the USA, Moore and Wood of the Gold Coast ARPS, and Danquah, who had stayed in Britain after the 1934 delegations' visit to do further studies.[194] The IAFA had headquarters at 62 New Oxford Street, where Amy Ashwood Garvey ran a restaurant. Meanwhile her former husband moved his base to London in 1934-35; the *Negro World* had ceased publication in 1933, but Garvey launched a new monthly magazine, *The Black Man*, in December of that year, and from November 1934 it was published in London.[195] It appeared until 1939 and Garvey was active as a Hyde Park speaker and campaigner, but he played only a minor part in the black militant activity organised in London in the later 1930s.[196]

The Ethiopian cause brought together a small group of militants who were to be active in London in the coming years, led by Padmore, James and Kenyatta. Probably Kenyatta agreed with Padmore's pan-Africanist approach and had no more connections with Communism by 1935, but the British secret service was suspicious that he might be working for Moscow still. The authorities, including MI5, kept a close watch on Kenyatta, recording his public activities including newspaper articles and speaking at meetings (such as a UDC meeting in Westminster on 19 November 1935). After a while Kenyatta's relations with the Rosses became strained and ended with a breach. After that the Kenyan lived a penniless life at 95 Cambridge Street, accumulating rent arrears, walking to save bus fares, getting girlfriends to pay for an evening's outing.[197]

Kenyatta earned a little money for a time as an extra in Zoltan Korda's film *Sanders of the River*, whose production began at Shepperton Studios in London in 1934.[198] A number of other Black people in Britain acted as extras in this film, and Edgar Wallace's story was altered to build up parts for Paul Robeson, the great African American actor and singer who had spent a considerable time in Britain since 1930, and

194   Esedebe (note 111), p. 127.
195   E.D. Cronon, *Black Moses*, Madison: University of Wisconsin Press, 1955, pp. 154-61.
196   Bush (note 39), pp. 219-20.
197   Accounts of Kenyatta's stay in England regularly recalled his popularity with girls there (e.g. Fenner Brockway, interview). One English girl became one of his wives; there were three other wives, one married before his journeys to Britain.
198   Murray-Brown (note 15), 180-7.

Nina Mae McKinney, the first African American girl to pass a film test for MGM at Hollywood, later a dancer with Lew Leslie's *Black Birds*. Robeson agreed to pay the part of Bosambo; later further scenes were written in that glorified imperialism, and Robeson objected strongly, but in vain.[199] Paul Robeson was to have many more contacts with Africans in London in the coming years, when he was a patron of WASU and studied African languages at the School of Oriental Studies, renamed in 1938 the School of Oriental and African Studies, of London University.[200]

The IAFA Executive Committee issued a manifesto and an appeal at a public meeting at Farringdon Hall in London on 28 July 1935, demanding action by the League of Nations and Britain; James addressed another IAFA meeting on 16 August.[201] James recalled that the IAFA passed a resolution supporting or demanding action by the League against Italy, but "most of us who were in the organisation and who were supporting it, had a conception of politics very remote from debates and resolutions of the League. We wanted to form a military organisation which would go to fight with the Abyssinians against the Italians." He added that Dr Workneh Martin dissuaded them, saying it would be more useful for them to stay in Britain and do propagandist work. At the time James mentioned all this in a letter published by the *New Leader* on 3 June 1936.[202]

It appears that a Pan-African Federation was also formed by the same and other activists. The Colonial Secretary in London, Sir Philip Cunliffe-Lister, wrote to West African governors on 3 June 1935 to warn about a "Pan-African Brotherhood" formed by Kouyate, "a prominent French Negro communist", and Padmore, and issuing a manifesto on Ethiopia.[203] Mentioning Kouyate as still being a Communist showed great ignorance, but it is possible that this organisation was created to

199   R. van Gogh, "Sanders...of the River", *West African Review* pp. 12-14; Edwin P. Hoyt, *Paul Robeson*, Cassell 1967, pp. 74-7.

200   Bush (note 39), p. 216.

201   Asante (note 82), pp. 45-6.

202   C.L.R. James, "Black Intellectuals in Britain", pp. 154-63 in B. Parekh (ed.), *Colour, Culture and Consciousness,* London: Allen & Unwin, 1974.

203   C.S.O. 1/36, Nigerian Archives, Ibadan, Secretary of State to Officers Administering British Colonies in West Africa, 3 June 1935, quoted in Asante (note 82), p. 52.

pursue Padmore's and Kouyate's ideas of a world conference of black people. MI5 later said Padmore's organisation had become the Pan-African Brotherhood in 1935.[204] The Federation was mentioned in a Special Branch note of 16 September 1935 which dealt with Nancy Cunard, mentioning how she had returned from Russia and met Kenyatta and Padmore at Bogey's Bar at the Royal Hotel to compare notes on the USSR, and was interested in "a young coloured student named HARRISON", born in Boston of Jamaican parents.[205]

Among others who championed Ethiopia's cause, WASU said the dispute between Italy and Ethiopia was the "age-old conflict between Right and Wrong", and set up an all-women Ethiopia Defence Committee.[206] Una Marson of the LCP had a temporary job with the League of Nations in Geneva at the time when it was trying to avert the war in September 1935, and then became English-speaking secretary at the Ethiopian Legation in London, handling the entire correspondence of the Legation as the war went ahead. [207]

Sylvia Pankhurst, the former Suffragette and former Communist, now dedicated herself to the cause of Ethiopia. She had never ceased militant activity in the previous few years while she and her Italian émigré partner Silvio Corio settled down in Woodford, in the Essex suburbs of London, and bore their son Richard Pankhurst. Now she leapt into prominence again, starting a new newspaper, the *New Times and Ethiopia News*. The first issue appeared on 5 May 1936, the very day Addis Ababa fell. It circulated in Africa and the West Indies and among African Americans; there were exchange arrangements with the *Chicago Defender* and other African American newspapers.[208] Many articles in the *New Times and Ethiopia News* were reprinted in full in the West African newspapers.

Black defenders of Ethiopia sometimes learned with unease about Haile Selassie's attitude of superiority to black people (a common at-

---

204   "Communism and the West Indian Labour Disturbances" (note 33).

205   Note of 16 Sept. 1935 in file KV2/1787, National Archives, London.

206   Asante (note 82), p. 48.

207   Jarrett-Macauley (note 109), ch. 10.

208   Richard Pankhurst, *Sylvia Pankhurst, Artist and Crusader*, London: Virago, 1979, pp. 192-6; S. Harrison, *Sylvia Pankhurst*, London: Arum Press, 2003, p. 239.

titude of the Amhara ruling people), but this could not reduce the anger against Italy, which was easily turned against France and Britain also. There were suspicions about those countries' policies, not unreasonably as they had shown a clear desire for good relations with Mussolini at the very time when the Italian military build-up in the Horn of Africa was proceeding. France and Italy signed an agreement on African questions on 7 January 1935, under which France agreed to cede a part of northern Chad to add to Italian Libya. It was rumoured that France promised not to interfere with Italian plans for Ethiopia, in return for Italian concessions over Tunisia; and in April France, Britain and Italy held a summit meeting at Stresa, Mussolini being on bad terms with Hitler at that moment. Tensions between France and Italy within and concerning Tunisia did in fact subside greatly—so much that Peyrouton, besides deporting two Italian Communists in Tunisia to Italy, also secured Italy's help in getting rid of one of the Neo-Destour leaders, Khairallah. The former ENA chairman became in January 1935 the head of a third Political Bureau of the Neo-Destour, after the other two had been locked up, but in April the Resident-General told the Italian Consul General in Tunis that having made use of Khairallah to calm the situation down, bringing him under Tunisians' suspicion, he (Peyrouton) now wanted to send him to Italy. This was agreed; although Khairallah spent only a few months in Rome and was closely watched there, he only played a minor role in the nationalist movement after this episode.[209]

Mussolini may have felt reassured that Britain and France would do nothing against him if he attacked Ethiopia, but in fact those powers decided that they had to follow their obligations under the League of Nations Covenant after Italy attacked on 3 October 1935. The National Government, now headed by Stanley Baldwin, after winning the General Election of 14 November 1935 declared support for sanctions, and they were imposed on 18 November 1935—despite the widespread

---

209   Juliette Bessis, *La Méditerranée fasciste: L'Italie mussolinienne et la Tunisie*, Paris: Karthala, 1981, pp. 158-60. The area of Chad which would have been ceded was the Aouzou Strip which independent Libya later occupied in 1973 under the terms of that 1935 Rome agreement. Libya withdrew after the International Court of Justice ruled that the territory had remained under French sovereignty then and passed to independent Chad later, as the Rome agreement had never come into force; it was ratified but ratifications were not exchanged.

support for Italy in Baldwin's Conservative Party and among some other British people. However, the following month it was decided not to extend sanctions to oil supplies, and a secret agreement between the British and French Foreign ministers, Samuel Hoare and Pierre Laval, which involved offering to let Italy have a large part of Ethiopia, was leaked; Hoare had to resign, but Africans and others were widely shocked that the idea should even have been considered.[210]

The British Left, strongly criticised by George Padmore later,[211] was confused about whether its principles could accept sanctions applied by a government it distrusted. The ILP could not, and decided to oppose the League of Nations sanctions. The Labour Party similarly distrusted the National Government, but because of its belief in "Collective Security" did back League sanctions, under Attlee who replaced the pacifist Lansbury as party leader at almost the same moment as the Italian invasion. Brockway and others of the ILP called on workers to apply their own sanctions against trade with Italy; James, then active in the ILP, wrote in the *New Leader* of 4 October 1935 that the League of Nations' Committee of Five's proposals to avert war, and British policy, did not genuinely support Ethiopian independence, and urged,

Workers of Britain, peasants and workers of Africa, get closer together for this and for other fights. But keep far from the Imperialists and their leagues and covenants.[212]

It appears that James may have had divided loyalties as an international Socialist and a black man.[213]

In France, leading anti-colonialists and other intellectuals took up the Ethiopian cause. After a "Manifesto for Defence of the West" by intellectuals supporting Italy was published in *Le Temps* on 4 October 1935, a reply was signed by scores of people including Rolland, André Gide, Jules Romains, Henri de Montherlant, Langevin, Vaillant-Couturier, Viollis, Roger Martin du Gard, and one African, Auguste Azango from

---

210   See G. Padmore, *Africa and World Peace*, 1937, reprint London: Frank Cass, 1972, chapters IV and V.

211   Ibid., p. 155.

212   Third extract in James (note 80).

213   As suggested by Robinson (note 94), pp. 188-9.

Dahomey,[214] who during the Italo-Ethiopian war started a small news service, the Agence Métromer.[215] Other Africans too, and West Indians, backed Ethiopia's cause in France as in Britain. *La Race Nègre* of July 1935 published the names of Africans declaring themselves ready to fight for Ethiopia, and toned down its anti-white message by recognising that white Muslims and other white people were backing Ethiopia: "This is the first time that a dispute among Europeans has the aim of respecting one of our freedoms."[216] The ENA offered the use of its headquarters and the columns of *El Ouma* "to our Black friends", as Messali recalled,[217] and Algerians in France condemned the Italian invasion.[218]

On 22 August the LDRN and ENA organised a big rally in Paris where Imache presided and Kouyate, Faure, Paulette Nardal, and Nouira were among the speakers; *El Ouma* said 2,000 "Muslims, Black and Coloured" attended.[219] Then, in September, an International Conference for the Defence of Ethiopia was held at the Mutualité hall, including the PCF and the ENA, and a delegation was chosen to go to Geneva, including Messali.[220] In Geneva Messali met Shakib Arslan[221] and there was an instant meeting of minds, with long conversations about the Arab world and other countries. Soon afterwards Messali attended the Islam-Europe Congress in Geneva on 12 September, attended by representatives of nearly seventy countries; it elected a permanent committee headed by Arslan and including Messali.[222]

At the time when the League of Nations was getting ready to condemn Italy, and the French delegation went to Geneva to encourage

---

214 Liauzu (note 135), pp. 257-62.

215 Spiegler (note 42), pp. 246.

216 E. Faure, "Abyssinie. L'agression italienne', *La Race Nègre,* 8th year, no. 1, July 1935, quoted in Dewitte (note 1), p. 344.

217 Messali (note 142), p. 193.

218 G. Massard-Guilbaud, *Des Algériens à Lyon de la grande guerre au Front populaire,* CIEMI: Harmattan, 1995, p. 397.

219 Spiegler (note 42), p. 248. Paulette Nardal was secretary of a Comité de Défense d'Ethiopie: Edwards (note 54), p. 298.

220 Ibid. Messali (note 142), p. 195 recalls it as a "Popular Front meeting".

221 They may not have met before, but according to a Sûreté report in 1933 Arslan was funding the ENA by then: W.L. Cleveland, *Islam against the West,* University of Texas Press and London: Al Saqi, 1985, p. 107.

222 Messali (note 142), pp. 196-9; Simon (note 137), pp. 168-9.

it to do so, Shakib Arslan had already begun the contacts with Mussolini's regime that were to lead to him declaring support for Italy and Germany as allies of the Arab cause. This was an extraordinary about-turn for one who had condemned the Italian reconquest of Libya so strongly. He apparently rationalised it by saying that Italy had decided to adopt a less repressive policy towards the Libyans after its victory. To some extent Mussolini did put on a show of benevolence towards Libyans, so as to revive and extend Italian plans to seek other Arabs' support. Italian denunciations of other Europeans' actions in North Africa came strangely from the ruthless oppressors of the Libyans, yet in Tunisia, besides regularly raising the question of the Italian settlers with France, and extending fairly complete Fascist control over that settler community (which outnumbered the French settlers), the Fascist regime sought support from Muslims. And in 1934 the regime, dreaming of a new Roman Empire, began to encourage Egyptian feelings against the British and Syrian feelings against the French in the Arabic language broadcasts of Radio Bari, which also covered Tunisia extensively and was easily heard there.[223]

Arslan decided to cooperate with this Fascist Italian approach to the Arab world. In February 1934 he visited Italy and had two meetings with Mussolini.[224] He angrily denied suggestions that he supported Italy and later Germany for money, and may always have simply followed the old principle of "the enemy of my enemy is my friend". Others had such ideas also. More will be said later about the Italian and German efforts to enlist Arab support against France and Britain, efforts that met some response. As early as 1934 Messali's lieutenant Radjef said at a big meeting in Paris (on 15 September), "If France had to defend its borders, it could not keep order in North Africa, the Muslims would revolt and helped by the Germans would throw the French into the sea."[225] Such words could however be seen as a provocative warning to the French to heed North Africans' demands, rather than a serious proposal to seek Hitler's help against France. At any rate Messali was

---

223   C.A. MacDonald, "Radio Bari: Italian Wireless Propaganda In the Middle East and British Countermeasures 1934-38," *Middle Eastern Studies* vol. 13, no. 2, pp. 195-207; Bessis (note 209), ch. III and pp. 138-54.

224   Cleveland (note 221), pp. 144-51; Bessis (note 209), p. 145.

225   Recham (note 139), p. 116.

an outspoken anti-Fascist, supporter of the Popular Front moves, and comrade of French left-wing leaders. But like some of those leaders, he admired Arslan—and yet Arslan defended Italy over Ethiopia.[226] In his memoirs, written long after Arslan had gone even further, Messali says not a word about it.

Besides helping the Black activists, after his visit to Geneva Messali visited Lyons and other provincial cities, held meetings in Paris, and continued contacts with Ferrat and others on the French left. But the problems with the law were not over for Messali and his party. On 19 October 1935 Messali, Imache and Radjef lost their appeals against the sentences passed in March. This meant that they could soon be rearrested, but Messali went into hiding in Paris for a time and then went back to Switzerland on 18 January 1936. There he continued to spread and publish his ideas, met other Arab nationalists there, and was in close contact with Arslan. Tunisian students helped run the ENA during Messali's exile.[227]

In December 1935 Kouyate founded a new magazine, *Africa*, with the help of the ENA; it was published from the offices of *El Ouma*, unaffected, it seems, by the ENA leaders' problems with the authorities at that time. Information reaching the Colonies Ministry suggested that Gaston Bergery—who had left the Radical Party to form a "Common Front against fascism" (separate from the main Popular Front moves, and largely unsuccessful) in March 1933—had, with some colleagues, provided financial aid. Bergery published his own newspaper with some influence, *La Flèche*, and took an active interest in colonial affairs. He was in contact with Habib Bourguiba for some years, and, so the latter recalled,[228] approached him as early as 1931 with the idea of a federa-

---

226   Cleveland (note 221), pp. 145-6; Bessis (note 207), pp. 177-8, 205. These sources do not quote words uttered by Arslan during the war, but Bessis notes that Arslan wrote a preface to a 1937 propaganda book by Tayssir Zabian Kaylani, editor of *El Dzaziret* of Damascus, entitled *Ce que j'ai vu dans les pays musulmans. L'Ethiopie musulmane.* This justified the Italian invasion on the grounds of Haile Selassie's oppression of Muslims.

227   C.-R. Ageron, "L'Association des étudiants musulmans nord-africains en France durant l'entre-deux-guerre: Contribution à l'étude du nationalisme maghrébin", *Revue Française d'Histoire d'Outremer* LXX, 1983, nos. 258/9, pp. 25-56 (p. 40).

228   *9 April 1938: Le "Procès" Bourguiba*, Tunis: Editions SAEP, 1967, p. 128 (see note 285).

tion of France and some or all colonies. Bergery pursued this idea when his group was turned into the Parti Frontiste in 1936. A piece by him in the first issue of *Africa* said nationalism in the colonies was only justified for the sake of "resistance to oppression". Kouyate wrote about the attack on Ethiopia and called for all black organisations to unite; but now he no longer called for early independence.[229]

Africa, which declared itself to be "the most independent African monthly journal for defence of the African peoples' interests", was to be the major Black political periodical in France for the next two years; *La Race Nègre* published its last issue in January-February 1936, and *Le Cri des Nègres* had ceased publication by the time of the April-May elections in France, while *L'Etudiant Noir*, a magazine devoted to cultural and racial themes and including contributions by Senghor, Paulette Nardal and other literary people, avoided politics.[230]

All the protests and sanctions failed to save Ethiopia, and Haile Selassie went into exile in Britain, where he was welcomed in early June 1936. Although it did not achieve its object, the wave of support for Ethiopia it aroused is considered to have greatly encouraged the growth of general anti-colonial and nationalist sentiment. At the start of the war G.E. Moore wrote to Malcolm MacDonald—Ramsay MacDonald's son, just appointed Colonial Secretary—that Gold Coasters hoped he would "make a clear pronouncement on Liberty for Africans, whether in the Gold Coast or Abyssinia."[231] At a general meeting on 4 September 1935 the LCP, besides condemning Mussolini, declared that Europe should cease to "look upon Africa and the Africans as a country and people merely to be exploited" and urged the colonial powers and the League of Nations to "consider a plan for the future of Africa which plan should be nothing less than the ultimate and complete freedom of Africa from any external domination whatsoever."[232]

---

229   Dewitte (note 1), pp. 362, 367; Spiegler (note 42), pp. 266-83.

230   Dewitte (note 1), pp. 363, 367, 349-60; J.L. Hymans, *Leopold Sedar Senghor*, Edinburgh University Press, 1971, pp. 96-7. According to Hymans *L'Etudiant Noir* appeared from 1934 to 1936.

231   G.E. Moore to MacDonald, 9 November 1935, CO96/723/31135/2, quoted in Asante (note 82), p. 32.

232   *The Keys* iii, 3, Jan.-March 1936, quoted in Asante (note 82), p. 47.

Democratic left-wingers in Europe were far from accepting such ideas. In Britain, even where India was concerned Maxton went against the Labour leadership, as well as the National Government, in calling for Britain simply to get out.[233] Labour's Imperial Advisory Committee issued a statement in July 1933 saying that there was no reason not to grant immediately a "large measure of self-government" for territories "like Ceylon and the West Indies", while a Labour government would arrange to find ways to prepare other colonies for self-government over ten years.[234] But this did not represent party policy.

Where independence was not under consideration, left-wingers and "colonial liberals" could still call for reforms in the colonies, including constitutional reforms, and protest about abuses. There was for example the lobbying on behalf of the Gold Coast ARPS delegation; during the 1935 general election campaign Kidd and Geoffrey Bing of the NCCL went with the two ARPS delegates, still in Britain, to the Bassetlaw constituency being defended by Malcolm MacDonald, to put questions at meetings (MacDonald was defeated but remained in the government and became Dominions Secretary, returning to the Commons a few months later).[235] Economic hardships, daily poverty and poor living conditions in African and other colonies could lead to widespread concern mixed with a sense of duty or even guilt. This happened irregularly, and often when the victims rioted or went on strike. In 1935 this occurred in the Copperbelt of Northern Rhodesia and the British West Indies. There were stoppages at several of the Northern Rhodesia copper mines from 21 to 31 May 1935; the grievances included a reported tax increase which sparked off the strikes, and long-standing complaints over accident compensation, food rations, conditions in the miners' compounds, violence by European staff, and inequality of pay between black and white employees.[236] There were other strikes in Africa in the later 1930s, in Sierra Leone in 1938-39 for example. The peak of unrest

---

233   G. Brown, *Maxton*, Edinburgh: Mainstream Publishing Co., 1986, p. 253.

234   N.R. Malmsten, "The British Labour Party and the West Indies, 1918-39", *Journal of Imperial and Commonwealth History* vol. V no. 2, 1977, pp. 177-205 (p. 188 & n.).

235   Bing (note 113), p. 45.

236   J.L. Parpart, *Labor and Capital on the African Copperbelt*, Philadelphia: Temple University Press, 1983, ch. 3.

in the West Indies was to come in 1937-38, but at various times during 1935 there were a sugar plantation workers' strike in St Kitts, a short oil field workers' strike and a hunger march in Trinidad, widespread strikes by sugar plantation workers in British Guiana, riots in St Vincent, and a strike in St Lucia. In response to such outbreaks of discontent and its causes, in both Britain and France the later 1930s was a period of increasing concern for the welfare of the "natives"—under continued colonial rule.

Stirrings in North Africa, 1936-39

In the French elections of 26 April and 3 May 1936 the Socialists (SFIO) won 197 seats in the Chamber of Deputies, the Radicals 116 and the Communists 72. The Socialists and Radicals formed the Popular Front government under Léon Blum, while the Communists did not join it but supported it. This democratic left-wing government, like the one elected in Britain in 1929, aroused hopes that could not be realised. Within France the limits of its power were shown by both the workers, who staged the legendary strikes of mid-1936, and the capitalist bosses, whose export of capital led to devaluation of the franc in November 1936. Internationally, its ability to act was limited by the growing European crisis: the Nazi regime had sent troops into the Rhineland in a successful defiance of Britain and France in March 1936, while the Spanish Civil War broke out in July.

In colonial affairs the parties composing or backing the new government had promised very little, and it only made minor changes, much fewer than those called for by the SFIO Congress in May 1936 (extension of democratic freedoms, equal pay for equal work, general compulsory education for "natives", etc.).[237] Marius Moutet, who became minister of the Colonies, was responsible for colonial policy with Pierre Viénot, an independent Socialist who served as Undersecretary of State at the Foreign Ministry with responsibility for Morocco, Tunisia, Syria and Lebanon, and Charles-André Julien, Secretary-General of the Haut Comité Méditerranéen et de l'Afrique du Nord, which had been set up the previous year to coordinate French policy towards the Maghreb and

---

237 Liauzu (note 135), pp. 206-7. See T. Chafer and A. Sackur (eds), *French Colonial Empire and the Popular Front: Hope and Disllusion*, Basingstoke: Macmillan, 1999.

the Middle East Mandates. Moutet told the Chamber of Deputies on 15 December 1936, "Colonisation, for us, is the very development of the masses who live in the colonies, through the raising of their material, social, economic, intellectual and cultural level."[238] This summed up the Popular Front's policy: a vague commitment to improved conditions for the colonised people.

The promised Commission of Inquiry into the living conditions of "The Natives of the Colonies, Protectorates and Mandated Territories" was approved by the National Assembly on 30 January 1937. It was headed by Henri Guernut, a former Radical Minister of Education, in the top ranks of the LDH; other members included Théodore Steeg, former Governor-General of Algeria, and Professor Paul Rivet, Julien and André Gide.[239] Some useful research was carried out for the inquiry in some parts of Africa,[240] but it never completed its work—in 1938 the Senate refused to approve a budget allocation for it, and its members resigned en bloc. By then the limited will for colonial reform had petered out. This was partly because the Popular Front government itself fell in June 1937. In addition, the forces of continuity were strong. Some French people working in the colonies sympathised with the Popular Front; technical staff, especially schoolteachers, in French Sudan formed in 1937 Les Amis du Rassemblement Populaire (ARP) which took up Africans' problems and demands, to the annoyance of colonial administrators who were concerned about the effect of "new ideas" circulating in Bamako especially.[241] But many officials were probably as obstructive in the colonies as in France itself. At the top level in the Colonies Ministry Gaston Joseph, the powerful Director of Political Affairs, was retained by Moutet and kept his post until 1943; after each

---

238   Biondi (note 132), p. 210.

239   M. Thomas, *The French Empire between the Wars: Imperialism, Politics and Society*, Manchester University Press, 2005, p. 287; Liauzu (note 135), pp. 209-10.

240   Such as a food and nutrition survey of the Wouri region of Cameroon (including the city of Douala) (file seen at the ORSTOM Library in Yaounde, 1972; summary in J. Derrick, "Douala under the French Mandate, 1916 to 1936", PhD, London, 1979, pp. 436-47).

241   C.H. Cutter, "The Genesis of a Nationalist Elite: The Role of the Popular Front in the French Soudan (1936-1939)", in G. Wesley Johnson (ed.), *Double Impact: France and Africa in the Age of Imperialism, Westport*, CT: Greenwood Press, 1985, pp. 107-39 (pp. 110-14, 119).

meeting of Moutet's *cabinet* he and the minister would revise decisions taken by the Minister's Socialist collaborators.[242]

In 1937 the new National Assembly ratified the 1930 Forced Labour Convention, and trade unions were legalised in AOF. However, forced labour continued in many areas regardless. The "man on the spot" was often unable, even if he so wished, to impose changes on powerful colonial interests, who resisted vigorously in French Cameroon, for example.

In the early optimistic days the Blum government ordered many measures of relaxation in the colonies, such as amnesties and easing of restrictions on the press. This happened in Madagascar. There the repression under Governor-General Cayla in the early 1930s was, as noted earlier, severe but within limits; a new newspaper called *La Patrie Malgache*, and then another called *L'Opinion* (started by Ranaivo, now free, with regular contributions by Ralaimongo), were launched; Ralaimongo continued writing after the end of his banishment, and in October 1935 he, Ravoahangy and Dussac replaced *L'Opinion* by *La Nation Malgache*, "Organ for the defence of the vital interests and national aspirations of the Malagasy people." Ralaimongo was gaoled again in February 1936, for six months, but following the election of the Popular Front he was released after a telegram from Moutet ordering broad political "clemency measures". Cayla left, a period of greater press freedom followed, Ralaimongo, Ranaivo and Dussac made a triumphal entry into Tananarive on 31 July 1936; a Popular Front Committee was set up, and a few months later made demands for many reforms including the end of the Indigénat and, notably, granting of French citizenship to the Malagasy people en masse.[243]

A Parti Communiste de la Région de Madagascar (PRCM) was established on 12 August 1936, or possibly in secret earlier. The Secretary General was Dussac; Ralaimongo was a member but seems to have been unsure at first whether to support independence or mass French citizenship, until he eventually came out against independence.[244] Dussac

---

242   Jackson (note 49), pp. 157-8.

243   J.-P. Domenichini, "Jean Ralaimongo (1884-1943), ou Madagascar au seuil du nationalisme", *Revue Française d'Histoire d'Outremer* vol. LVI, no. 204, 3rd quarter, 1969, pp. 236-87 (pp. 275-9); S. Randrianja, *Société et luttes anticoloniales à Madagascar (1896 à 1946)*, Paris: Karthala, 2001, pp. 257-99.

244   Domenichini (note 243), p. 282.

called for independence in August 1936, but the PCRM called for mass naturalisation.[245] That party may not really have been Communist at all, and it eventually broke with the PCF; when Dussac travelled to France and appeared before the PCF Colonial Commission (June 1937) he failed in his efforts to defend the Malagasy party,[246] and it was decided to wind up the PCRM early in 1938. Cayla returned to his post, and there were few concessions to the Malagasys, though trade unions and cooperatives spread. This was typical of what happened in French Sub-Saharan Africa after May 1936: some reforms carried out or promised, and no questioning of France remaining in charge, whatever the absurd propaganda of the right-wing press suggested.

In Senegal politics and the press were already free in the Four Communes and did not need the relaxation measures of the Popular Front. Galandou Diouf, re-elected as Senegal's deputy in 1936, was no supporter of the Front and was on bad terms with the new Governor General of AOF, Marcel de Coppet. Amadou Lamine Gueye, returning to Senegal in 1935 after working for some years in Réunion, became chairman of a new Parti Socialiste Sénégalais. After the 1936 elections a Senegal section of the SFIO was created and a merger between it and the PSS was discussed, but not fully carried out.[247]

In French West Africa generally, including Senegal outside the Four Communes, de Coppet was one of the more reform-minded of the governors appointed by Moutet. He had been considered too favourable towards Africans in his earlier career in the colonial service, and as Governor of Chad had opposed massive recruitment for the Congo-Ocean Railway; he was suspected of leaking information to André Gide, but he went on to be governor of Dahomey, French Somaliland and Mauritania.[248] As Governor-General he ordered severe restrictions on the use of forced labour, with some effect, and introduced new labour legislation to benefit Africans, though again within limits. However, there was a wave of strikes in late 1936 and early 1937, and more in 1938. A big railway strike led to intervention by the army and six people being shot

245   Randrianja (note 243), pp. 293-4, 299, 304, 307-59.

246   Ibid,, pp. 348, 351, 357-9.

247   N. Bernard-Duquenet, Le Sénégal et le front populaire, Paris: Harmattan, 1985, pp. 22-31, 106-13.

248   Ibid., pp. 81-3.

dead on 27 September 1938. De Coppet had been attacked by French business, by Charles de Breteuil's newspaper *Paris-Dakar*, and by the right-wing gutter press in France (*L'Action Francaise* and *Gringoire*); in October 1938 he was recalled.[249]

Apart from Senegal, where it did not question the French connection, almost no party political activity developed in French sub-Saharan Africa in the Popular Front era; there was nothing like the WAYL and NYM in British West Africa, and still nothing like the African-owned press there. At this time, too, African students in France still had nothing like WASU. There were still the radical campaigners in France, of whom Emile Faure was the most militant and active at this time; more will be said shortly about their activity. In contrast Kouyate's *Africa* expressed support for the Popular Front and did not attack French rule. It covered the activities of local organisations in AOF, and trade union activity there (two articles in July 1937), but its criticisms were mild ones, about racial discrimination in French Sudan for example; that colony, Kouyate's home country, was well covered in the magazine. In June 1937 Kouyate advocated a federal system linking France and its colonies, with some African self-government; if followed up, this would have meant enormous changes in French Africa, but it never had any chance of being considered.[250]

French rule was not seriously challenged in Black Africa, but in North Africa it was. The Popular Front victory had an immediate impact in Algeria. Messali was allowed to return to France, held many meetings and went with Robert-Jean Longuet and others to present demands to the new government on behalf of Muslim Algerians in France and in their homeland.[251] On 25 June 1936 a meeting was held at the Mutualité by the ENA and, apparently, the new organisation founded the previous month to replace the French LAI and like it closely linked to the PCF, the Association pour la Défense et l'Emancipation des Peuples Colonisés;[252] Challaye, Viollis and Langevin were in the chair and Mes-

---

249   Ibid., pp. 91-104, 123-212.

250   Spiegler (note 42), 266-83; Dewitte (note 1), pp. 367-70.

251   Messali (note 142), pp. 212-16.

252   Liauzu (note 135), pp. 45, 251. It can be presumed that this was the body which Messali (note 142) recalled as the Association de Défense des Peuples Colonisés (p. 217).

sali, Bourguiba, and Lozeray of the PCF were among the speakers. Algerians demonstrated in thousands in Paris and several provincial cities on 14 July 1936.[253] There was a brief period of good feeling, based on confidence that big things would come from the Popular Front. And then the Etoile Nord Africaine, after organising for ten years among the North Africans in France, went home. It had carried on some activity back in Algeria before, but now Messali Hadj was able to land in Algiers on 2 August 1936 for a triumphal tour including Tlemcen, his home town, and many other towns. The ENA set up branches and aroused support around the country.

At a meeting on 4 November in Algiers, Messali again called for an Algerian parliament elected by universal suffrage.[254] This call might seem to confirm a retreat from the call for independence, but Messali— so he recalled later—declared in France in mid-1936 that such universal suffrage was "a starting point for economic emancipation and political independence",[255] and that probably was his aim all the time. At Tlemcen on 11 November he said,

We are anti-Fascists, for peace, freedom and democracy. But also anti-colonialists, for democratic freedoms, in the perspective of total emancipation.[256]

The ENA faced strong opposition, however, from the Congrès Musulman Algérien (CMA), formed on 7 June, at a "States-General of Algeria", by the Fédération des Elus, the Oulémas and the Algerian Communists. The Federation, founded in 1927 by Muslim Algerians occupying elective positions open to their people, was led by Ferhat Abbas and Dr Mohamed Bendjelloul. They and the Muslim reform leaders and the PCA agreed on a "Charter of Demands" including French citizenship with acceptance of Muslim personal status, Arabic as an official language, repeal of the special legislation for Muslims, and complete attachment of Algeria to France. This last demand would mean, for example, the abolition of the post of Governor-General and other institutions which showed that, although supposed to be a "part of France", Algeria was in fact run as a colony. Thus Muslim Algerians would be

---

253   Simon (note 137), pp. 189-91; Messali (note 142), pp. 217-18.

254   Messali (note 142), pp. 221-35; Simon (note 137), pp. 201-10.

255   Simon (note 137), p. 194.

256   Ibid., p. 207.

treated exactly like French people in France—and their country would be more closely tied to France than ever.[257]

This was in line with the constant position taken by Bendjelloul and others of the elite, but the Oulémas' support for it was more surprising. They followed the Salafiyya reform movement which had for long been an implicit threat to Western rule from Egypt to Morocco, and the French in Algeria had at first taken measures against it. When Abbas published his famous article saying he had found no evidence of an "Algerian nation" on 23 February 1936, Ben Badis published a strongly-worded retort in *Ech Chihab* of April-June 1936.[258] But now the Oulémas joined the Abbas-Bendjelloul group to call for closer union with France, on the understanding that Islam would be fully respected. As for the Algerian Communists, for them to be on the same platform as Muslims did not mean the same thing as it did in 1924. Now it meant that, following the new Moscow and PCF line, they accepted Algeria as part of France. Their numbers rose in 1936 and in October of that year a separate Parti Communiste Algérien (PCA) was founded, on paper directly subject to the Comintern,[259] but in fact subordinate to the PCF.

The CMA sent a delegation to Paris in July, received by Blum. Messali, who had corresponded with Abbas in the past few years,[260] met the delegates then and found that they were completely against any talk of independence. On its side the new government proposed only a limited increase in the number of Muslim Algerians able to vote, already proposed the previous year by Senator Maurice Viollette, former Governor-General of Algeria. Viollette was now appointed a Minister of State and entrusted by Blum with an initiative for Algeria, which produced the bill called the "Blum-Viollette bill"; about 20,000 people would be enfranchised, essentially an extended elite of teachers, local chiefs, retired serviceman and other leading figures in communities across the country.[261] The CMA supported the proposals eventually set out in the Blum-Viollette bill when it was published on 30 December 1936, but Messali declared on 25 July, shortly before leaving for Algeria,

---

257   Ibid., pp. 193-5.

258   Nouschi (note 141), p. 89.

259   Sivan (note 144), p. 89.

260   Stora (note 138), p. 105.

261   Messali (note 142), p. 239.

We refuse attachment of Algeria to France and reject it with all our strength. We declare that instead of parliamentary representation in Paris which cannot be effective, there should be the constitution of a parliament in Algeria which should be elected by universal suffrage without distinction of race or religion.[262]

At the same time the *colons* in Algeria, and their powerful lobby in the Senate in Paris, thought the Blum-Viollette bill was a major threat and vehemently opposed it.

The impression that Messali never gave up the aim of independence is supported by his address to a meeting in Paris, to report on his Algerian tour, on 27 November 1936; he said, "If you want to be free like your brothers in Egypt who are standing up to British machine guns, or like those in Syria, gather around the Etoile Nord-Africaine, the only organisation that will save the Algerian people."[263] His audience would have known that those countries were on the way to independence. In the latter part of 1936 France signed treaties with Syria and Lebanon on transition to independence; and by coincidence Britain signed a treaty with Egypt about the same time, on 26 August 1936. After years of a three-cornered political tussle in Egypt between the King, the Wafd and the British, all three agreed on new negotiations; the Egyptian government, a newly elected Wafd government headed by Nahhas Pasha again, did not get all it wanted, but Egypt did become more truly independent than it had been since 1922—independent enough to join the League of Nations, and get rid of foreign consular jurisdiction under the Capitulations, in 1937. Egyptian forces were now allowed to return to the Sudan, but in Egypt itself a large British garrison and British military bases remained. Many Egyptians were unsatisfied with the Treaty—the National Party voted against ratification, which was however passed—while the French treaties with Syria and Lebanon were followed by years of footdragging until war came without either being independent or having a date for independence.[264] But those countries' situation was, in late 1936, a clear contrast to that in the Maghreb.

---

262   Simon (note 135), p. 195.

263   Stora (note 138), p. 150.

264   Khoury (note 177), Part VII, especially pp. 483-93; S. Morewood, *The British Defence of Egypt 1935-1940: Conflict and Crisis in the Eastern Mediterranean*, London: Frank Cass, 2005, especially Ch. 5.

On 26 January 1937 the Blum government banned the Etoile Nord-Africaine. The PCF approved of the ban on the ENA, which followed attacks on it by Ben Ali Boukhort, secretary general of the PCA, as well as the CMA. The PCF now fully agreed with other French parties in defending French rule in Algeria especially. Indeed it went further on this occasion than the SFIO, whose Colonial Commission condemned the ban.[265]

In December 1937 Thorez declared at the PCF's Ninth Congress, at Arles,

The fundamental demand of our Communist Party regarding the colonial peoples remains free disposal of their fate (*libre disposition*), the right to independence. Recalling a formula uttered by Lenin, we have already told the Tunisian comrades, who agreed with us, that the right to divorce does not mean an obligation to divorce. If the decisive question of the moment is the victorious struggle against fascism, the colonial peoples' interest lies in their union with the people of France and not in an attitude that could favour the schemes of fascism.[266]

The Algerian Communist newspaper *La Lutte Sociale* expressed the official Communist view strongly in early 1938:

To conceive Algeria's independence without the Franco-Algerian alliance, in the face of aggressive international Fascism thirsting for colonial conquests, is mad and criminal…It is playing the game of international Fascism to go in for provocation by calling for independence.[267]

In the same vein, on a visit to Algeria in February 1939 Thorez declared that Algeria had a "duty to unite even more closely with French democracy" at that time; Algerians would be worse off under Hitler, and Tunisians would suffer like the Libyans under Mussolini.[268]

The PCF was rewarded for its new-found patriotism by a rapid rise in membership. It and other left-wing parties still criticised the actual daily government of the colonies, even during the Popular Front's year in power. They called for reforms, and like others who had called for colonial reforms, warned of the danger of unrest if there were no im-

---

265   Messali (note 142), pp. 240-1; Stora (note 138), pp. 155-61.
266   Sivan (note 144), p. 97.
267   *La Lutte Sociale,* 15 January and 19 March 1938, quoted in ibid., p. 97.
268   Mortimer (note 49), p. 277.

provement in "natives'" situation. *L'Humanité* gave a new twist to this warning on 3 July 1936:

If we do not want Hitler and Mussolini to establish themselves as masters in French Morocco, French social laws, freedom of the press, assembly and association must be applied in Morocco without delay. Schools must be provided...[269]

A brochure published by the Comité de Vigilance des Intellectuels Antifascistes (CVIA) in August 1936, *La France en face du problème colonial*, was on similar lines.[270]

After the ban on the ENA, at a protest meeting in Paris on 14 February 1937, Messali and Bourguiba spoke, and the Tunisian called for the "complete emancipation" of the three north African countries and a federation of them to follow.[271] Messali remained free, as did his lieutenants such as Si Djilani, and soon afterwards they formed a new party, the Parti du Peuple Algérien, PPA, on 11 March 1937. Messali headed an executive of four.

The ENA had been a largely Algerian party in fact, but the new party was Algerian in name also. Messali recalled that in the PPA's declaration of 10 April 1937 it called for democratic freedoms, and said that if these were granted, it would seek gradual progress to emancipation; if they were not, it would struggle for all its objectives, including independence. But according to Stora[272] the slogan put forward by Messali was "Neither assimilation, nor separation, but emancipation", and *El Ouma* no. 49 of April 1937 declared, "The Parti du Peuple Algérien will work for the total emancipation of Algeria, without that meaning separation from France," while Messali, writing in *Az Zohra* of Tunisia on 5 June 1937, spoke of a "dominion" as the aim. There was clearly still an idea that this term taken from the British empire, but probably ill understood, meant something short of full independence. So Messali may have moderated some of his ideas—the PPA economic programme did not include the ENA's plan for sweeping expropriation, for example. Communists and others denounced the new party, but it was allowed

269   Oved (note 45), p. 124.

270   Liauzu (note 135), pp. 92-3.

271   Simon (note 137), p. 222; Lejri (note 130), vol. II, p. 161.

272   Stora (note 138), pp. 164-9.

to continue in Algeria, where Messali returned on 20 June 1937, and France. It held rallies and gathered support, and its aim was made clear when its followers, at the 14 July parade in Algiers, carried the Algerian flag.[273] In 1937-38 Messali briefly worked with his old friend Abdelkader Hadj Ali again. He had become in 1935 the political editor of *Le Peuple Algérien*, published by the Ligue de Défense des Musulmans Nord-Africains, which was now affiliated to the PPA.[274]

Messali and the PPA continued the propaganda directed at North African soldiers, which had continued for years and had landed him in prison. After a lull in this "anti-militarist" propaganda in the Popular Front period, it revived, the main theme being the same as always— Algerians must not agree to fight for their French rulers, at least until the current colonial regime was totally transformed. Messali said in April 1937,

We want to tell the world that if France refuses us the crust of bread to which we have a right, it must not count on us to defend the Maginot line.

More efforts to spread the nationalist message among the troops were reported in 1938, in Algeria and France, despite efforts by the authorities to stop them.[275]

As usual, the authorities could get weird ideas from supposed intelligence sources; the minister of Defence wrote on 24 December 1936 to the minister of the Interior (responsible for Algeria) that the Oulémas, the ENA and the Communists were working together to spread disaffection among the troops. This was absurd, but the minister of Defence's reasons for concern were intelligible enough:

The defence of Metropolitan France is based on the despatch to France, in case of political tension, of African divisions. It is to be feared that extremist activities may succeed in threatening Algeria's internal security to such a point that it becomes necessary to maintain these large units on the spot.[276]

---

273 Messali (note 142), pp. 245-53; Stora (note 138), pp. 161-76.
274 C.-R. Ageron, "Emigration et politique: L'Etoile Nord-Africaine et le Parti du peuple algérien", appendix to Messali (note 142), pp. 273-97 (pp. 279-80). Ageron also mentions other relatively small North African organisations in France; the ENA had never been the only one.
275 Recham (note 139), pp. 119-22.
276 Quoted in ibid., p. 124. In French military usage "African" commonly meant North African.

The importance of North Africa—its territory, its Mediterranean coast-line and its sons of military age—for France's defence preparations was a key factor at that time. On 6 November 1937 Mussolini said Italy intended to stay in the Balearics (occupied during the Spanish civil war) so that "not one negro will be able to cross from Africa to France".[277] For both France and Britain the military necessities of the expected world war were an extra reason for maintaining their positions every-where, especially in the Mediterranean area. Egypt, for example, was vital for British defence planning, and the Egyptian government had to accept the continued presence of British troops.[278]

On 27 August 1937 Messali was arrested in Algiers. Despite massive support organised by his wife and other loyal supporters he was charged with reviving a banned organisation and incitement to disobedience and disorder, among other charges. He and the comrades arrested with him secured through a hunger strike the privileges of political prisoners. At their trial their counsel—again Maître Berthon, who also defended Bourguiba in the following two years—declared,

He [Messali] is criticised for holding meetings during which he called for the independence of his country. But today it is a common thing (*chose courante*) to call for the emancipation of colonised peoples.[279]

Possibly Messali, if he stopped calling for independence after founding the PPA, did so on legal advice to avoid trouble, but then, when he was arrested and charged anyway, saw no point in hiding his real aim. According to the book about the trial published—with a preface by Fé-licien Challaye—in 1938, Messali told the court that his party called for an Algerian parliament, but then added, "Is it because we even demand *independence* that we are anti-French?"[280]

Messali and three others were sentenced to prison terms, Messali to two years, on 4 November 1937. In prison Messali stood as a candidate

277   Michael Alpert, *A New International History of the Spanish Civil War*, Basing-stoke: Macmillan, 1994, p. 151.

278   Morewood (note 264). In the Second World War the British—in the good cause of defeating Nazi Germany—were to treat Egypt as if it belonged to them.

279   Messali (note 142), pp. 255–63.

280   *Le Procès de Messali*, Editions El Ouma, 1938, cited in Stora (note 138), p. 181.

in local elections in Algeria and won, though the result was declared null and void. In 1938 Messali's enemies in the CMA quarrelled among themselves and Abbas left to set up a new Union Populaire Algeriénne (UPA). Meanwhile the Blum-Viollette bill was rejected by the Senate and then withdrawn in September 1938.

In Tunisia, where Armand Guillon had been appointed Resident-General shortly before the Popular Front victory, Bourguiba and other Neo-Destour leaders were freed after that event and the party's National Council expressed confidence that the new government would establish in the colonies and protectorates "a new regime of freedom and justice helping the moral and material revival of the subjected peoples and leading them gradually towards their emancipation."[281] Restrictions on public liberties were quickly relaxed. The CGTT, banned back in 1925, was revived. Bourguiba and his comrades built up the Neo-Destour as an elaborate organisation with mass member-ship, estimated at about 100,000 in 1937, drawn from all regions and classes. There was no other indigenous nationalist party organised on this scale in any part of the continent at that time, outside Egypt. Bourguiba declared in *L'Action Tunisienne* of 23 December 1936 that emancipation was on its way and it should preferably be in coopera-tion with France, but would go ahead anyway.[282]

To counteract the Neo-Destour's influence the French allowed Tha'alibi to return in 1937 after fifteen years in exile and revive the fortunes of the original or "Old" Destour. This did not succeed. At the Neo-Destour Congress in October 1937 Bourguiba called for "gradual emancipation" under French auspices, the first stage to be "a return to the spirit of the treaties".[283] Later he explained that he and his party had not called for full independence:

Tunisia, a small country situated at a crossroads in the Mediterranean that is particularly sought after—I cannot bring myself to think of it as completely in-dependent. Our action has always been in the direction of gradually transform-ing the links that unite us with France, in such a way as to base them on freely

---

281   Lejri (note 130), Vol. II, p. 146.
282   Ibid., vol. II, p. 150.
283   Ibid., vol. II, pp. 175-86.

consented adherence, indeed adherence desired by the Tunisian people because of the necessity, a pressing necessity for us, to live under her protection.[284]

But the nationalists ordered a general strike on 20 November 1937 in support of the Moroccan and Algerian nationalists; then more confrontation with the French followed, including a refusal to pay taxes and a boycott of French goods in December. Some of Bourguiba's colleagues disagreed with his more aggressive stance, but he continued it until April 1938, when following demonstrations and arrests, a general strike was staged in Tunis on 8 April. Riots the following day led to the arrest of a neo-Destour activist, and when demonstrators tried to release him on his way to court the next day, the police fired, killing 112 people and wounding 62. The same day Bourguiba was arrested and a state of siege declared; later in 1938 he was moved with other political prisoners to France. He was investigated for attacking "the rights and power of the French republic", among other charges,[285] but never put on trial.

In North Africa it would be wrong to suggest that the Popular Front government made no difference. Without intending such a thing, it hastened a new phase in resistance to colonialism: large, organised nationalist parties with wide indigenous local support. This was different from the earlier phase when activity in exile—by students, for example, or in the case of the ENA among migrant workers—was relatively more important. That phase had ended in Tunisia, where the new phase actually began before 1936 but was hastened after then, and in Algeria, where the ENA, the migrant workers' party which had boldly called for independence since the 1920s, went home and took root there after 1936. In both countries repression soon followed, but the nationalist movement had taken root and was eventually to lead to independence, however distant that must have seemed in 1938.

This new nationalist phase did not start until years later in sub-Saharan Africa, French and British. No party dominated the scene in any colony then as the neo-Destour did in Tunisia in the late 1930s, not even in Madagascar where there had been plenty of political activity. The Duala militants in Cameroon never formed a party, the WAYL in the Gold Coast faded away quite soon, the NYM in Nigeria had a fairly

---

284   Le "Procès" (note 285), p. 112.

285   The full transcript of the interrogation of Bourguiba was published in 1967 as *9 April 1938: Le "Procès" Bourguiba*, Tunis: Editions SAEP.

narrow support base and impact, the Kikuyu activists in Kenya were divided and largely tribal in outlook. For colonial black Africa—as distinct from South Africa, where the action had always been at home—the activities of exiled dissidents was still important, though as has been shown in these pages, a lot was going on back in Africa also. Anyway none of this opposition shook the British and French rulers then. Their calm assumption that they must stay and would stay in Africa was as strong as ever, in North Africa as much as elsewhere. It was reinforced in France by the change of policy by a major party that had backed colonies' independence, and by the worsening European crisis, particularly important where Morocco was concerned.

Peyrouton, much criticised for his authoritarian regime in Tunisia, was transferred to Morocco in 1936, before the elections, but recalled a few months later, and then General Charles Noguès was appointed Resident-General. At first there was relaxation, with more freedom of the press and some Arabic language education, and the need for judicial reforms and more government service openings for Muslim Moroccans was accepted; but trade unions were authorised for Europeans only.[286] In November 1936 there were clashes in Casablanca following a ban on a meeting, and al-Fassi, Lyazidi and Ouazzani were arrested. There followed some days of unrest, a march to the Sultan's palace in Rabat, and a Comité d'Action Marocaine (CAM) protest to Blum. The imprisoned leaders were soon freed but the mutual distrust between the Resident General and the nationalists continued.

While there was a split in the CAM about this time, with most leaders following al-Fassi while Ouazzani headed another faction, the movement won wide support in the early months of 1937, until on 18 March 1937 the Kutlat al-'Amal al-Watani was banned, on the grounds that it was not legally constituted and demanded an oath of loyalty considered improper by the French. The nationalists had not formed a party on the scale of the ENA or the Neo-Destour, but they were numerous and active in Morocco also. They continued to organise despite the ban, distributing aid for the needy among other activities; there was considerable distress at the time, greatly worsened by very poor harvests, a frequent occurrence in Morocco but worse than usual then. In September 1937,

---

286   Oved (note 45), Vol. 2, pp. 125-37.

riots broke out in Meknés, provoked by a decision to cut water supply to some areas, but blamed by the French on the nationalists. Thirteen people were officially reported killed when troops opened fire.

After an extraordinary congress of the nationalists on 13 October, there was an incident at Khemisset, a Berber town, and Noguès—who according to Dermenghem based his policy on Arab-Berber division— used this pretext to crack down harder. Al-Fassi, Abdeljalil, Lyazidi and Ahmed Mekouar were arrested, followed by Ouazzani and others as protest riots spread. Several of the leaders were deported to the south of Morocco, but then al Fassi was moved to Gabon where he was to spend nine years. Jean Longuet organised a petition calling for him to be moved to a less unhealthy place, signed also by André Gide, Paul Rivet and other intellectuals including the eminent Catholics Jacques Maritain and François Mauriac.[287] There were many other protests against the repression in Morocco; Louzon and Magdeleine Paz went there, but the latter, sent by *Le Populaire*, was arrested on arrival at Meknès.[288] By that time the situation in Morocco was greatly complicated by the Spanish Civil War, in which Spanish Morocco played a decisive part.

Europe's hostile camps and Africa, 1936-39

From the beginning of the Spanish Civil War the rebel junta not only occupied Spanish Morocco but recruited thousands of Moroccans to fight in its forces. The world soon knew of "Franco's Moors", who contributed greatly to the Nationalists' eventual victory. To left-wing and liberal supporters of the Republic, the Moors were brutal and vicious mercenaries. Indeed that war saw innumerable war crimes on both sides, and the Moors committed their share. But how many Europeans backing the Republic stopped to wonder why colonial subjects of Spain were enlisting in such numbers to fight for the very army officers who had fought against their resistance under Abd el-Krim, had maintained a generally brutal occupation regime, and were proud heirs to the old monarchical, crusading Castile that had driven the Moors out of Spain centuries before? It is a good question.

---

287   Ibid., Vol. 2, pp. 104-21; William A. Hoisington, Jr, *The Casablanca Connection: French Colonial Policy, 1936-1943*, Chapel Hill and London: University of North Carolina Press, pp. 44-5, 56-68.

288   Oved (note 45), vol. 2, p. 115.

Muslims of Spanish Morocco had been cowed by harsh Spanish rule and the rebels, dominated by officers of the Army of Africa, occupied Spanish Morocco immediately in July 1936; and Moroccans had good cause to fear those officers. In addition, it was common in the colonial empires for European officers to have a good rapport with indigenous soldiers who often thought and reacted as soldiers first and foremost, and this was one factor in Spanish Morocco.[289] However, many of the thousands of Moroccans who went to fight for Franco—75 per cent according to one account[290]—came from French territory. Poverty was probably the reason for them—like so many soldiers throughout history—deciding to enlist (Northern Morocco is still a destitute region); the pay was good.[291] But the recruitment was made easier, and Franco's control of Morocco perhaps more secure, by the attitude taken by the Moroccan nationalists.

The youthful Abd el Khaleq Torres was the main nationalist leader by 1936, and on 1 March 1936 established a National Action Committee, Kutlat al-'Amal al-Watani (the same name as was adopted by nationalists in the French zone). At first the Kutlat declared that Moroccans should be neutral in the conflict among Spaniards. But soon Torres was moving towards the Franco side. He wrote in a new newspaper, *Er Rif,* in August 1936:

The ultimate objective of the Moroccan nationalist movement consists of preparing the whole country to gain independence...The real problem concerns France, which is seeking to establish itself permanently in the country, even with the Popular Front in power. There is no hope of seeing it change its colonial policy. It is the true enemy of Moroccan nationalism. As for Spain, it must understand that its interest lies in the friendship of Moroccans, who are always ready either for cooperation or for opposition, as the situation demands.[292]

Encouraged by this attitude, the Franco leadership's Director of Native Affairs in Morocco, Juan Beigbeder (who became High Commissioner in Spanish Morocco in 1937-38 and then the Burgos regime's

---

289   S. Balfour, *Deadly Embrace: Morocco and the Road to the Spanish Civil War,* OUP 2002, p. 275.

290   J. Wolf, *Les secrets du Maroc Espagnol: l'épopée d'Abd-el-Khaleq Torres,* Paris: Balland, 1994, p. 202.

291   Balfour (note 289), pp. 271-86.

292   Wolf (note 290), p. 201.

Foreign minister) arranged an apparent *modus vivendi* under which Torres and his followers were left alone while troops were recruited unhindered for the Franco forces.

Efforts were made by anti-colonialists to win the Moroccans of the Spanish zone over to the Republican side. It was an obvious idea as depriving Franco of his base and source of recruitment there would have been a severe blow, and the cause of the Spanish generals and their Italian and German allies was totally contrary to all that anti-colonialists had ever stood for. Those efforts merit further study, but some facts have emerged scattered in published works by Georges Oved and Jean Wolf.[293]

At the start of the war the ENA denounced the Non-Intervention policy followed by the French and British governments; on 31 July 1936 a resolution organised by the ENA in Paris declared that those present

send their fraternal greetings to their Muslim brothers of Morocco, who are suffering under the boot of Fascism, and call on them to place themselves on the side of the Republicans of the Spanish Popular Front, against the rebel generals.

El Ouma in September-October said the way to detach the Rif Moroccans from Franco was to "proclaim the independence of Spanish Morocco"; the ENA corresponded with the President of Spain.[294] Some of the Moroccan nationalists in the French zone agreed with this view, and were involved in active negotiations. Also involved were the French Socialist anti-colonialists Jean and Robert-Jean Longuet and the CGT leader Léon Jouhaux, and two French activists of the Trotskyist Parti Ouvrier Internationaliste (POI), David Rousset and Jean Rous. Wolf's account mentions only the two Trotskyists, but both accounts probably refer to one plan.

According to Oved the two Longuets and Jouhaux had talks at the Spanish embassy in Paris in August 1936, and it was agreed that the younger Longuet would travel to French Morocco to discuss with the nationalist leaders there the possibilities of winning the Rifis of Spanish Morocco over to the Republican side. Pierre Cot, the Radical Popular

---

293   Ibid., pp. 210-13; Oved (note 45), vol. 2, pp. 176-7.

294   Simon (note 137), p. 212.

Front minister who had worked hard to get aircraft delivered to the Spanish government, was aware of this other plan. Longuet and Léo Wanner flew to Fez and met Rifi people and Abdeljalil and Ouazzani; they were told that the Rifis wanted arms and money and political concessions by the Republican government, and Abdeljalil and Ouazzani were encouraged to go to Madrid. As Robert-Jean Longuet recalled it, the Madrid government was ready to grant genuine self-government to the Spanish zone if the French government agreed, but the French did not. The two nationalists later said Rousset had gone with them to Spain, and according to Wolf's account Rousset and Rous arranged for talks leading in September 1936 to an agreement on Spanish Morocco with the autonomous government of Catalonia, the Generalitat. But the agreement in Barcelona was useless unless the Madrid government accepted it.

In fact only a promise of independence, as the ENA suggested, would have had a chance of persuading the Moroccans of the Spanish zone to change sides. As Morocco was treated as one single sultanate by everyone concerned, especially the nationalists, it would have been impossible to give independence to the Spanish zone only without Moroccans demanding it for the French zone also. It is quite clear that the French vetoed any such idea. The Soviet Union and the Spanish Communists, helping the Republicans and increasingly asserting control over them, wanted to avoid trouble with the French government, including colonial trouble, as the PCF did within France. So nothing substantial could be offered to the Moroccans of the Spanish zone.

It is quite probable that some supporters of the Spanish Republic thought of releasing Abd el-Krim from his banishment in Réunion so that he could lead his Rif people over to the Republican side, but it seems that the French government was never ready to consider this; when a parliamentary committee discussed Abd el-Krim Socialists opposed the idea of release and Communists did not intervene, and the committee simply called on 30 December 1936 for him to be moved to another place of detention and better treated.[295] If the French government feared that more self-government for the Spanish zone would

---

295   Oved (note 45), vol. 2, pp. 176, 4354.

STRUGGLES IN THE THIRTIES, 1932-39

force them to give as much to the French zone, it would dread the impact in the French zone of the return of the Rif hero of the 1920s.

George Padmore wrote in 1937,

...had the People's Front Government made a gesture to the Moors by pointing out to them that the new régime was the defender of their economic political and social interests, then we feel certain that Franco would never have been able to have deceived these African tribesmen into supporting his cause.[296]

He criticised the French Popular Front also, mentioning that Abd el-Krim was still in exile "with not one voice raised on his behalf", and put his finger on the basic problem: "a colonial revolt in North Africa to-day would be a tremendous blow to French Imperialism."[297] Similarly an article in *International African Opinion*, published in London by Padmore's International African Service Bureau (of which more below, pp. 388-95), said that while Franco made lying promises to the Moors, "the Spanish Government does not even make these lying promises. It has nothing to offer the Moors. Not by promising, but by definitely proclaiming the independence of Spanish Morocco, it could have turned the Blacks (*sic*) against Franco."[298]

The Spanish insurgents' promises to Moroccans indeed did not amount to much—Franco's close colleague General Queipó de Llano declared in October 1936 that self-government was under study—but after a meeting with Franco in December 1936 Torres was formally allowed to form his party, and a decree of January 1937 allowed teaching in Arabic in Spanish Morocco's schools, a longstanding nationalist demand.

Shakib Arslan is said to have been involved in, or at least informed closely about, the talks with the Spanish Republicans. This seems strange as his links with Italy must have been known to everyone concerned, but it could be explained by the great respect he enjoyed among Moroccans. However, on 16 November Arslan wrote to Torres,

I am satisfied with the policy you are conducting towards Spain...The Madrid government will probably not emerge as the victor in this war. Muslims would not want the Madrid government to win...Nobody is unaware that the Com-

---

296   G. Padmore, *Africa and World Peace*, 1937, new edition London: Frank Cass, 1972, p. 266.

297   Ibid.,p. 270.

298   "Politics and the Negro: By the Watchman", *International African Opinion* vol. 1 no. 1, July 1938.

munist government is on the side of disorder. If the Republic is the stronger side, its harmful ideas risk spreading in the Northern zone. The Republic has done nothing for the Northern zone... If Spain had already given autonomy to the Rif, there would have been no regrets over the enlistment of more than 25,000 Moroccans...I mourn the death of those soldiers...What interests us on the part of Spain is that the Moroccan nationalists' aspirations would be realised, without concerning ourselves with right or left.[299]

What Arslan said about Communism was what most Muslims have always thought. While he did express caution, as well he might, about what Franco might offer, on the whole that letter was an encouragement to follow the path Torres had already chosen: to seek help from Italy, Germany and their allies for Arab nationalist causes. The Spanish Nationalist junta did not fully trust Torres and his party but it used them, giving them some freedom to operate and encouraging hopes of more. Torres said on a visit to Egypt in 1938:

The Spanish Zone enjoys a certain liberty, unknown in the French zone. However, it is not enough to leave us some liberties and respond to some of our demands for us to be automatically satisfied with Spain's work. We are fighting with all our strength to achieve our demands in full and attain self-government for the zone. We are not letting ourselves be deceived by their promises, we must have recognition of our rights, decisive acts, reforms...[300]

Events in the two zones of Morocco were closely intertwined. The AEMNA, after holding congresses in Paris in 1933, Tunis in 1934 and Tlemcen in 1935, planned to hold one in Rabat in September 1936, but recoiled at the prospect that Peyrouton, then still Resident-General, would be expected to open the congress. Then Torres decided to hold a congress of the Association at Tetuan in Spanish Morocco. Tunisians were at that time dominant in the AEMNA; some refused to go to a gathering in Franco-held territory, while others went and reported back to the French about Franco's efforts to win over Moroccan nationalists; some people from French Morocco and Algeria were refused passports to attend, and the congress in October 1936 was attended mainly by people of Spanish Morocco.[301]

---

299   Wolf (note 290), pp. 202-3.

300   Ibid., p. 213. See also Hoisington (note 287), pp. 138-49.

301   Ageron (note 227), pp. 39-44, 54.

Torres devoted much of his time to denouncing French rule in the other part of Morocco, and there were widespread suspicions among the French authorities and the left-wing parties that Franco and his German and Italian allies were aiming to stir up revolt in French Morocco, or were even in contact with the nationalists there. Some of the conspiracy stories were as doubtful as the earlier Red conspiracy stories, but now Communists and other left-wingers in France were ready to believe some reports. It was thought necessary to warn North Africans not to listen to Fascist-Nazi propaganda. On 1 December 1936 Wanner, speaking at the Mutualité in presence of Messali, Abdeljalil and Nouira among others, urged them to take the side of the democracies and encourage their people to do so. She and others on the left also continued to urge French reforms to reduce the appeal of hostile propaganda. Many nationalists readily agreed with such sentiments, but French left-wingers' suspicion of North African nationalists—which had a long history—was revived by the suspicions of intrigues by the Axis powers. Magdeleine Paz wrote after the Meknès riots, in *Le Populaire* of 11 September 1937, "There is in the agitation a shady and persistent work in favour of Franco." Louzon said agents of Franco, Germany and Italy had nothing to do with the disturbances, but added, "What is true is that the Moroccans do not intend to be prohibited from seeking support, when the moment comes, from Germany and Italy, to throw their oppressors out."[302]

Suspicions of contacts between Moroccan nationalists of the two zones were unproven, and were denied by the CAM; the Morocco SFIO Federation accepted its assurances in October 1936. A year later Abdeljelil wrote in *L'Action* on 2 October 1937,

Can it be seriously held against us that some of our compatriots in the neighbouring zone have let themselves be led into a trap and given their collaboration to the Fascists? We on our side have never been supporters of that cooperation and we have declared out loud that we expect nothing from the totalitarian regimes.[303]

But some Arabs at that time did expect something from Nazi Germany and Fascist Italy. There were several Arab grievances against Brit-

---

302　Oved (note 45), vol. 2, pp. 168-71.
303　Ibid., p. 433 (note 264 to p. 175).

ain and France, including, notably, the grievance against Britain over Palestine; the Palestinian revolt begun in 1936 attracted support and sympathy in many countries. What Louzon thought about Moroccans' sentiments was, one can be certain, true of many people in all the Arab world. Hitler, Mussolini and Franco seemed like possible allies, and their regimes encouraged such sentiments, starting with the Italian. For the Italian Fascists Tunisia remained particularly important, and from 1937 their Consulate-general in Tunis became the centre of vigorous Fascist activity, some of this being directed at winning Tunisian Muslim support, backed by Radio Bari, by other propaganda such as an interview with Arslan ("Champion of Arab Independence") in the Tunisia Italian newspaper (*L'Unione*, 5 January 1938), and possibly by some covert financial assistance.[304] Italian backing for the nationalists, however far it may or may not have gone, was overt enough to provoke reactions. The Neo-Destour's own newspaper, *L'Action Tunisienne*, published an anti-Fascist article by Challaye on 18 February 1937,[305] and the party probably always hedged its bets about Italy, not rejecting what might be useful offers of support, but not relying on them either.

Mussolini visited Libya in March 1937, inaugurating a coastal road from Tunisia to Egypt and posing as the "protector of Islam", receiving loud flattery from Libyan Muslim leaders and replying,

...Fascist Italy means to ensure peace, justice, well-being and respect for the laws of the Prophet to the Muslim peoples of Libya, and in addition, to demonstrate its sympathy for Islam and Muslims of the whole world.[306]

Amazingly, the Fascist regime used its rule in Libya as a basis for propaganda to win over Muslims elsewhere. But apart from the brutal repression of the Sanusiyya, Muslims and Arabs could not overlook the strenuous efforts to boost Italians' agricultural settlement in the small area of Libya suitable for cultivation.[307] Yet some were ready to listen to propaganda making out Fascism to be the champion of Islam. Franco

---

304   Bessis (note 209), chapter VII. A letter from Rome to Bourguiba, mentioning such assistance, may or may not have been a forgery (ibid., pp. 234-7).

305   Ibid., p. 217.

306   Ibid., pp. 203-4.

307   C.C. Segrè, *Fourth Shore: The Italian Colonization of Libya*, University of Chicago Press 1974, pp. 58-110.

backed this up with a propaganda line of Catholics and Muslims being on the same side against the anti-religious Republicans.[308]

Many Maghrebian nationalists refused to have anything to do with the Nazis and Fascists, like Messali. Their people in France were victims of racism and most probably felt no affinity with racist regimes and parties. But from 1934 some Muslim Algerians joined far-right French groups. When Jacques Doriot, who had for years been the most active anti-colonial leader in the PCF, founded the Parti Populaire Français (PPF) in June 1936, two years after breaking with the Communists, a few Algerians in France joined it. Many other Algerians would have remembered him from his Communist days, but few were attracted by the PPF, a new far-right party that was to embrace full ideological collaboration—as opposed to pragmatic collaboration—with the Nazis a few years later. In their virulent attacks on the PPA in 1937 Communists tried to link the PPA and PPF, playing on the similar names, but there was no link, and few Algerians joined such very alien French organisations.[309]

Some North Africans formed a Comité d'Action Révolutionnaire Nord-Africain (CARNA), on the initiative of Yassine Abderrahman of Tunisia, and made contact with Germany. Messali, from his prison cell, ordered expulsion of PPA members most involved in German contacts. But six leading PPA activists went to Germany in the spring of 1939 and received a small amount of training.[310]

In the years of increasing confrontation with the Axis powers these were now seen, by the French in particular, as sources of colonial subversion, more than the Communists.[311] Particular suspicion was directed at Shakib Arslan—while he said that it was French policies, not he, who aroused discontent. Arslan was contacted by the Nazis through Max von Oppenheim, an aristocratic diplomat and archaeologist who had helped organise the attempts by Germany and Turkey to stir up Islamic resistance against the Allies in 1914-18. When Arslan tried to return to Syria in 1939 he was banned from going there; after returning to Geneva in

---

308   Balfour (note 289), pp. 271-81.

309   Ageron (note 274), pp. 280-1, 294-5; Stora (note 138), pp. 161-2.

310   Ageron (note 274), pp. 296-7; Recham (note 139), p. 144.

311   Oved (note 45), vol. 2, pp. 166-72.

July, he visited Germany, and although he stayed in Switzerland, his support for the Axis became complete and vocal in the war.[312]

It is hard to guess how much real sympathy for Fascism and Nazism existed among Arabs at a time—the later 1930s—when all too many people around the world expressed such sympathy. The Arabic translation of *Mein Kampf* had insulting comments on Orientals and Muslims deleted,[313] but any member of a subjected people facing the facts would have doubts about ideologies based on the right of the strong to dominate and conquer the weak. However, in several Arab countries there was positive admiration for one feature of Nazism and Fascism—paramilitary formations, like the Brownshirts and Blackshirts. In Egypt the Wafd had its Blueshirts, and a small but noisy patriotic society called Young Egypt, Misr al-Fatat—founded in 1933 and turned into a political party at the end of 1936, calling for the restoration of Egypt's former greatness as "a mighty empire composed of Egypt and the Sudan, allied with the Arab states, and leading Islam"—had its Greenshirts. Its leader, Ahmad Husayn, visited Germany and Italy in 1938 and enthused over their regimes for a time;[314] but then it adopted an Islamist ideology similar to that of the Muslim Brothers, founded in 1928 and spreading rapidly in the late 1930s. Islamic sentiment could be combined after a fashion with support for Fascism and Nazism, as it was by Arslan. But probably what influenced Arabs more was the simple observable fact that Germany and Italy were winning all the time for several years after 1935, and France and Britain were caving in to them. In Morocco people could see a left-wing French government suppressing nationalists and Fascists in nearby Spain supporting them.

An independent government could develop commercial and other relations with Germany to gain greater freedom from Britain. Following the Treaty of 1936 Egypt was independent enough for this, and governments in power after the fall of the Wafd ministry in 1937 had the inclination. In South Africa, the Hertzog government sought like the Egyptian government to assert independence from Britain, and its close ties with Germany in the 1930s had that motive in part. But there

---

312   Cleveland (note 221), pp. 105-12, 133, 155-6.

313   Recham (note 139), p. 140.

314   J.P. Jankowski, *Egypt's Young Rebels: "Young Egypt": 1933-1952*, Stanford: Hoover Institution Press, 1975, pp. 1-43, 58-60.

was more. There was an obvious affinity of ideas between the Afrikaner movement and Nazism—a *Volk* with a special mission or destiny of domination over others considered as inferior. Within the Hertzog government itself, sympathy for Nazism was expressed most strongly by Oswald Pirow, an Afrikaner of German origin, who visited Germany in 1933, 1936 and 1938 and on the first occasion met Hitler and came away filled with enthusiasm.[315] Among other Afrikaners anti-Semitism increased in the 1930s,[316] there were Afrikaner demonstrations against German Jewish refugees arriving in South Africa, and Dr Malan, the strongly anti-Semitic leader of the Purified National Party, said organised Jewry was behind the doctrine of equality;[317] the Greyshirt movement expressed Nazi sentiments most strongly.

While Malan's party denounced it as not racist enough, in fact the Hertzog government was steadily enforcing its racist doctrines, especially by removing Africans from the common electoral register in Cape Province. This was done under the Natives Parliamentary Representation Act, passed overwhelmingly by the white supremacy parliament in May 1936. By what Hertzog saw as a generous concession, in response to African protests, those few African voters would now vote separately for three white members to represent them in the House of Assembly; at the same time Africans in all four provinces would indirectly elect four representatives to the Senate and twelve to a Native Representative Council (NRC). Another piece of legislation seen as a concession, to make the two "Hertzog Bills", added a little to the area of permitted African land ownership. The All African Convention—which was made permanent at a meeting in June 1936, with D.D.T. Jabavu as President, and representing the ANC, the ICU, the CPSA, the APO and other bodies—continued protests.[318] But African leaders agreed to contest election to the NRC, although it was totally powerless.

While Hertzog spoke in 1935 in favour of Germany returning to colonial rule in Africa, his government firmly rejected any idea of hand-

---

315 R. Citino, *Germany and the Union of South Africa in the Nazi Period*, New York, Westport, CT and London: Greenwood Press, 1991, pp. 39-42, 46-8, 50-4, 111-12.

316 Ibid., pp. 72, 86-7, 125, 143, 153.

317 Simons (note 164), p. 525.

318 Ibid., pp. 496-7.

ing South-West Africa back. The German demand for restoration of the lost colonies, rejected even by good friends in Pretoria, was eventually unsuccessful, but it was widely discussed in the international arena between 1933 and 1939. In those years the most worrying colonial issue in Paris and London was not between colonised and colonisers, but between the established colonial empires and the so-called "have-not" powers which demanded more territory, sometimes saying they needed it for raw materials—Germany, Italy and Japan. Where Africa was concerned only Italy was really keen on expansion; in November-December 1938 Italy denounced the 7 January 1935 agreement with France, which had never been put into effect, after big staged demonstrations calling for Italy to have Corsica, Tunisia and French Somaliland.[319] But for the Nazis Africa did not really matter. Expansion in Europe was what interested them, and the colonial claim was always secondary. The many politicians and others who thought of appeasing Hitler with a few colonies were as deluded as other advocates of "appeasement".

In Cameroun and Togo the French authorities had always suspected that some German-educated Africans were ready to respond sympathetically to the German demand to have those territories back. In reality several of the Germanophones in Douala were active nationalists behind the self-government petition of 1929 and other activities. But in 1934 a group of older-generation Dualas formed an organisation called the Kamerun Eingeboren (or Farbigen) Deutsch Gesinnten Verein (KEDGV)—meaning, in ungrammatical or "pidgin" German, the "Cameroon Natives' (or Coloured People's) German Thinking Union". Hunted by the police, most of them fled to British Cameroons. But it seems that they were a sentimental nostalgic group, for they swore oaths of allegiance to the Kaiser; and one of their leaders, Ferdinand Edinguele Meetom, was a leading nationalist activist.[320]

The French suspicions did not abate and Hitler's successes may have encouraged some Africans to think that German rule might return after all. Of course many Dualas knew first-hand, or from near relatives, about Nazi racism and brutality. The French authorities had sections

---

319   Bessis (note 209), pp. 239-44.

320   Derrick (note 240), pp. 418-19; R.A. Joseph, "The German Question in French Cameroon, 1919-1939", *Comparative Studies in Society and History* vol. 17 no. 1, January 1975, pp. 65-90 (pp. 84-5).

of *Mein Kampf* about Black people translated and told a Duala clerk-interpreter to visit people with German sympathies and read out those excerpts; however, they answered that this was a French forgery.[321]

Very few Africans who accepted the known facts about Nazism or Fascism could have had any sympathy for them. The Italian occupation of Ethiopia had been publicised all over Africa, and many people knew about crimes such as the three-day massacres in Addis Ababa in February 1937, in reprisal for an attempt on the Governor's life, and continued to oppose recognition of the conquest—which Britain, however, granted in 1938. There was less publicity about millions in sub-Saharan Africa who now lived under Fascist rule in the Portuguese colonies. The Portuguese dictatorship established after the coup of 1926, and dominated by Antonio Salazar from 1932, by luck or skill avoided international publicity; in the 1930s there was nothing like the outcry about Portuguese mistreatment of Africans that there had been earlier in the century, though there was still plenty of cause.[322]

But Portugal did not join the Axis and did not threaten or claim other countries. For Africans the German colonial restoration claim was or seemed a real threat. In France Gottfried Chan, a Cameroonian (of the Bassa people) who had served in the Foreign Legion, formed a Comité (or Comité National, in some sources) de Défense des Intérêts du Cameroun in 1936. Then two young Duala students sent by their elite families to study in France, Léopold Moume Etia and Jean Mandessi Bell, replaced it with a Union Camerounaise to defend the interests of Cameroonians in France and those living in Germany or expelled from there, and lobbied against any idea of handing the country back to Germany. They went further and called for French Cameroun to be made an "A" Mandate" like Syria or Iraq, which would mean guaranteed progress to independence; and for reunification with British Cameroons.[323]

---

321   Interview, Jacques Kuoh Moukouri, Douala, 1972.

322   A.H. de Oliveira Marques, *History of Portugal, Vol. II: From Empire to Corporate State*, New York and London: Columbia University Press, 1972, pp. 227-8; for an example of Africans' situation under the Salazar regime, see L. Vail and L. White, *Capitalism and Colonialism in Mozambique: A Study of Quelimane District*, Heinemann 1980, pp. 248-53, 272-82.

323   L. Moume Etia, *Les Années Ardentes*, Paris: Jalivres, 1991, pp. 46-8, 97-110; and interviews in 1972.

Back in Douala, in the months following the Munich pact (September 1938) Africans formed a new organisation, the Jeunesse Camerounaise Française (Jeucafra), to protest against the idea of coming under Hitler's rule. The French administration and French business community encouraged this, and were said to have sponsored it, but the young leader, Paul Soppo Priso (1913-96), said it was his own idea. On 8 January 1939 Soppo Priso addressed a great rally in Douala in support of French rather than Geramn rule. It seems he even called, as many French people did, for the Mandated territory to be turned into an ordinary French colony: an appeal signed by him and the paramount chiefs of Douala said, "Already French at heart, we want to be so definitively like our brothers of the French colonies."[324]

Communists opposed any restoration of colonies to Germany, and as has been shown, they urged nationalists in the French colonies to forget about independence in the current situation. However, the full picture of Soviet and Communist attitudes to the West's colonies in the years from 1936 to 1939 still needs to be clarified. George Padmore's recollection, as already noted, is unreliable about details such as dates. Writing twenty years later about Britain in the later 30s, he said in his most famous book, *Pan-Africanism or Communism?* that the "Communist hypocrites" in Britain had "soft-pedalled the demand of Africans for immediate self-government, while paying lip-service to Indian independence."[325] He said the LAI had gone into decline when the USSR joined the League of Nations, and

A hastener of its demise was the shock caused to its non-Communist members by the revelation in the British press that Stalin had sold oil to Mussolini during the fascist invasion of Abyssinia in 1935. This Soviet stab in the back made the League Against Imperialism exceedingly unpopular among non-Communist British anti-imperialists whose sympathies were with Abyssinia. The few Africans in London who were associated with the League through affiliated membership of the Negro Improvement Association (*sic*), headed by Arnold Ward, a West Indian, severed their association with the Communists and helped to form the International African Friends of Abyssinia, with the object of rallying support for Emperor Haile Selassie against Sawdust Caesar Mussolini. About

---

324   *L'Eveil du Cameroun*, Douala, 1 January, 8 January and 15 January 1939; interview, Soppo Priso, 1972.

325   Padmore (note 190), p. 148.

the same time, the International Trade Union Committee of Negro Workers, with which I was associated as secretary, was liquidated...[326]

There are many inaccuracies here.[327] The LAI went on until 1937 at least, and both it and the NWA retained their Communist links. The ITUC-NW went on for more than three years after Padmore was sacked from it. After Padmore published his *How Britain Rules Africa* in 1936, the *Negro Worker* of December 1936 and January and February 1937 published a very hostile review by William L. Patterson, saying (in the February issue), "Mr Padmore gives objective support to the imperialist oppressors". Criticising Padmore for supporting the slogan "Africa for the Africans" (essentially what he had been excommunicated for), Patterson stressed again that a non-racial class struggle was the right course, and echoed the preposterous Communist idea that the Afrikaners in South Africa should be seen "as an anti-imperialist force—a force against the common enemy"; this was still official Communist policy for South Africa then, seemingly based on an extraordinary interpretation of Afrikaners' rhetoric against British hegemony and big business. Patterson's whole review was preposterous, but at the same time it does not support Padmore's recollection of that period. Here was a Communist publication accusing him of not being anti-imperialist enough.[328]

A glance at the *Negro Worker* in 1937 shows that it was still totally Communist and loyal to Moscow and, at the same time, opposed to imperialism—most strongly to British imperialism. It was published in Paris, and the March 1937 issue had a remarkably sympathetic article on "Some Results of the French People's Front Government in Favour of the Colonies". It looks as though the Communist orders on colonial propaganda were interpreted differently for the French and the British

---

326 Ibid., p. 330. The USSR fully backed the proposal for oil sanctions against Italy at the League of Nations, but would not apply them if others did not, and when no agreement was reached on oil sanctions it exported large amounts of oil to Italy: Beloff (note 44), pp. 200-4. Between 1934 and 1939 Italy built a destroyer and patrol boats for the Red Navy.

327 Brockway's recollection (*Inside the Left*, London: Allen & Unwin, 1942, p. 261) was even briefer and vaguer.

328 *Negro Worker*, Paris, vol. 7 no. 1, January 1937, vol. 7 no. 2, February 1937, vol. 7 no. 3, March 1937, vol. 7 no. 4, April 1937 and vol. 7 no. 5, May 1937. Copies of these issues are enclosed in file CO 323/1518/9, National Archives, London.

empires. In the March 1937 issue C. Alexander said that the masses of the West Indies were now "forcing concessions from the imperialist rulers not by bowing down to their agents in England, but by taking to the streets, by massing on the plantations, by militant battles right here in the various islands." Wallace Johnson wrote in the May 1937 issue about the West African Youth League. There were reports and articles that could have an appeal going beyond the Communist faithful, condemning, for example, the idea of "colonial appeasement". The February 1937 issue published an appeal of the ITUC-NW, by Woodson, its Secretary: "No Colonies to Hitler! Keep the Nazi Scourge out of Africa! For a Free Africa!" In the April 1937 issue Wallace Johnson wrote, "... we, the Colonial peoples, are not the goods and chattels of the Western European nations, to be sold, bartered or given away as a means of pacification, whenever it suits their purpose." Condemning Nazi attitudes, as shown at the Berlin Olympic Games a few months earlier, he said,

The fact must be realised that the dawn of the period of the emancipation of the Colonial peoples all over the world has arrived.

But continued Communist dogma unchanged from the 1928-33 "sectarian" period was seen in 1937: "Our Aims", as stated in the issue of May 1937, included fighting not only for "the full independence of the Negro toilers in Africa and the West Indies" but also for "their right to self-determination in the Black Belt of the U.S.A."; the reference to "the reactionary programmes of the Negro misleaders and agents of imperialism in the colonies" also recalled that period. However, most of the aims were or could be widely supported: abolition of forced labour, the eight-hour day, government relief for the unemployed, freedom to form trade unions, and struggling against the colour bar in industry and white chauvinism. Besides regular praise of the Soviet Union the monthly devoted considerable attention to Spain, mentioning in the March and May 1937 issues two Ethiopians fighting for the Republic. Woodson was the editor-in-chief in May 1937; the editor was Paul Theanor and contributing editors were "W. Daniel" (Wallace Johnson), Ward, Cyril Briggs, J.W. Ford, Mofutsanyana and J. Gomas of South Africa, H. Critchlow of British Guiana, and C. Alexander.

A few months later the *Negro Worker* appears to have ceased publication, though the Governor of the Gold Coast signed an order banning it on 28 December 1937. The ITUC-NW's parent body, the Profintern, was dissolved in 1937. And it seems the LAI did not last much longer.

The sixth conference of the LAI British section was held on 27-8 February 1937 and passed resolutions calling for the right to self-determination, compulsory free universal education, repeal of pass laws and poll tax laws, universal adult suffrage and other major changes.[329] A circular letter on the LAI's new Bureau on 11 May 1937 said:

Since its foundation in 1927 the League Against Imperialism has done consistent work in connection with the different aspects of the colonial struggle. But it is essential that we should advance from the position of a small group of people interested in the colonial struggle, seriously restricted in their actions because of their association with a 'banned organisation', and activise the working class organisations and peace societies, especially their youth sections of whose growing interest in colonial questions we are aware, in the confident hope that they be brought into co-operation with the colonial peoples in the struggle against exploitation, war preparations and for democratic rights and freedoms.[330]

This summed up the post-1935 Moscow line on democratic left-wing parties and anti-colonial movements. It did not mention colonial independence as an aim to support. But neither did it exclude strong condemnations of colonialism. Until then, at least, there was evidently less desire to tone down anti-colonialism in Britain than in France, though the PCF did not say colonial government must never be criticised. No doubt this was partly because Communists had enough strength to make a difference in France but did not in Britain; many prominent intellectuals were Communist at that time in both countries, but France had seventy-two Communist members of parliament and Britain just one (William Gallagher). But the main reason for the difference was that the USSR had signed a pact with France, not with Britain. Moscow hoped to help France to be a bulwark against the German threat, but had fewer such hopes for Britain.

It has been suggested[331] that the LAI was closed down in 1937 and replaced by the CPGB's Colonial Information Bureau, which was run by Ben Bradley and published a fortnightly *Colonial Information Bul-*

---

329   *Negro Worker*, April 1937 (note 328).
330   Saville (note 32), pp. 46-7.
331   Saville (note 32), p. 37.

letin.[332] This was apparently the "Colonial Section" which was reorganised in 1936 and had taken over most of the functions of the LAI by 1938, according to an MI5 report in June that year (which did not say that the League had actually closed down).[333] At any rate Communist criticism of Western colonialism continued in Britain; Palme Dutt's *Labour Monthly* still carried plenty of material on the colonies, still very much concentrated on India but looking at Africa also, in the later 1930s.[334] However, it seems that Western colonialism and settler regimes in Africa were of even less importance than before for Moscow by the late 1930s. The CPSA was placed under the supervision of the CPGB; nobody in London or Moscow could have expected much of a party that was reduced at that time to a small insignificant band,[335] though it was to have a new lease of life later and Kotane, elected General Secretary at the end of 1938, was to hold the post until his death forty years later. The Comintern presumably kept in touch with colonial affairs, but it had other tasks including channelling aid to Spain, and it was hard hit by the Great Purge in Russia, which was at its peak from 1936 to 1939.

All over the Soviet Union millions of Communist leaders, ordinary Communist Party members, professional people, army officers and others were arrested for all sorts of reasons or none, tortured, forced into confessing anything they were told to confess, and sentenced to death or deportation to concentration camps (Gulag) after a rigged trial or no trial at all. The Comintern came under Stalin's particular suspicion and some of its prominent officials, including Osip Piatnitsky, were shot. Foreign Communists who had gone to the Soviet Union to seek refuge from persecuting governments, expecting to be sheltered and honoured there, were among those carried off to be shot.[336] Virendranath Chattopadhyaya, former joint Secretary of the LAI, was shot on 2 September 1937; two other Indians who had joined in the wartime German

---

332 Howe (note 36), pp. 105, 117.

333 "Communism and the West Indian Labour Disturbances" (note 33), pp. 1-2.

334 J. Callaghan, *Rajani Palme Dutt: A Study in British Stalinism*, London: Lawrence & Wishart, 1993, pp. 155-6.

335 See documents on it in Davidson *et al.* (note 8), Vol. 2, documents 67 to 93.

336 McDermott and Agnew (note 49), pp. 145-57; Davidson *et al.* (note 8), Intro, p. 22.

plans for revolution in India and gone to Soviet Russia later were also executed.[337]

The South African Communists did not escape. Lazar Bach and two other Latvians who had been among several East European migrants joining the CPSA, Paul and Maurice Richter, were arrested back in Russia in March 1937, convicted of counter-revolutionary agitation, etc. and sent to the Gulag. Then, in March 1938, the Richter brothers were executed; Bach died in a concentration camp in February 1941.[338]

The country described by some as "the hope of the world" was brought down by Stalin to depraved depths of mass slaughter for the second time in ten years, and this time a part of the killing was not concealed from outsiders. But the highly publicised trials like those of Zinoviev, Kamenev and others in August 1936 and Bukharin, Rykov, the Uzbek Communist Khodjaev and others in 1938 were only a minute part of the Great Purge, and those who wrote about "the Moscow trials" were only facing part of the truth. Those appalling faked trials were however enough to shock many people in the West who had been sympathetic to the Soviet "experiment". Others, notoriously, excused or whitewashed or defended Stalin, as the Webbs had done—before the Great Purge, but after collectivisation—in a massive book of praise in 1935, *Soviet Communism: A New Civilisation*. Those who remembered Sidney Webb's attitude to Africans as Colonial Secretary may not have been too surprised at his demonstrated lack of feeling for Stalin's victims. In contrast, some who had shown sympathy for colonial subjects joined in the condemnations of Stalin: André Gide travelled to the USSR and returned having realised at least some of the awful truth; Magdeleine Paz, who ran the colonial section of *Le Populaire* about that time, spoke out against the "Moscow trials"; Fenner Brockway always rejected Stalinism; Woolf criticised it in his book *Barbarians at the Gates* (1939).

But Moses Kotane, who said,

---

337   Nirode K. Barooah, *Chatto: The Life and Times of an Indian Anti-Imperialist in Europe*, New Delhi: OUP, 2004, pp. 320-5.

338   Davidson *et al.* (note 8), Introduction, pp. 20-21. Lovett Fort-Whiteman, a prominent African American Communist who spent most of the inter-war years in the USSR, died there in a Gulag in 1939: A. Blakely, "African Imprints on Russia: An Historical Overview", Ch. 2 in Matusevich (ed.) (note 19) (p. 51).

I am first an African and then a Communist. I came to the Communist Party because I saw in it the way out and the salvation for the African people[339]

remained loyal to Communism in spite of everything. Similarly, some African Americans rebelling against their people's situation retained blind faith in Soviet Communism as something better. William L. Patterson, a Black lawyer from Harlem and a leading figure in the ILD involved in the Scottsboro defence, said, "The Soviet Union is the only country in the world where there is no discrimination, the only country in the world where there is equality for all races and nationalities."[340] He had spent three years in the USSR before the worst of Stalinism, but he continued to defend the Soviet regime later. So did Langston Hughes; it was enough for him that "The greatest American opponents of the Soviet Union were also the greatest opponents of basic rights for blacks."[341]

And then there was Paul Robeson. Travelling between Europe and the USA in the early 1930s, he was popular in British fashionable society, but he began to take political stances when he played in a benefit performance of Eugene O'Neill's *All God's Chillun Got Wings* (originally performed in 1924) for Jewish refugees in 1933. He took the common, but not at all necessary, step from loathing of Nazism to admiration for Stalinism. He visited the USSR in December 1934, in connection with a planned Eisenstein film on Toussaint L'Ouverture, and in time became a Communist sympathiser as his wife Eslanda, who studied at the LSE in the early 1930s, already was.[342] He visited the Soviet Union again in December 1936 and January 1937, including Asian areas. He constantly referred to the respect shown to him and the lack of racism in Russia,[343] and sent his son Paul Jr to school in Moscow for two years. His admiration for Stalin's Russia no doubt arose from that contrast with the extreme diseased racism of the United States. But at the height of the Great Purge, it was a startling lapse for a great artist who was normally a man of enormous

339 Simons (note 164), p. 492; Bunting (note 13), pp. 90-2.
340 Carter (note 172), pp. 147-8.
341 Rampersad (note 27), vol. 1, p. 338. See McClellan (note 170) and Blakely (note 338) on Patterson (McClellan, pp. 67-8) and several other African Americans who spent many years in the USSR in the 1920s and 30s.
342 Hoyt (note 199), pp. 54, 58-61, 64-9.
343 Ibid., pp. 79, 85, 87-8, 101, 105-6.

sensitivity—expressed in support of the Spanish Republic (which he visited) and China, and also Africa.

Robeson later praised the progress of the Yakuts (a small Turkic people of Siberia) and other Soviet minority peoples and said, "I came to believe that the experiences of the many peoples and races in the Soviet Union... would be of great value for other peoples of the east in catching up with the modern world."[344] Such uncritical admiration for Soviet Asians' supposed progress was common, as already noted. But many of the Asian Communists who had directed the mass literacy campaigns in local languages, and other achievements, died in Stalin's crazed but systematic campaign of murder; some who had tried to defend their people's interests within the Soviet system were now put to death, including Turar Ryskulov, party leader in Kazakhstan for a time in the 1920s (executed in 1939).

Padmore wrote in *Africa and World Peace* that the Moscow trials

have deeply disturbed the confidence of the workers in Western Europe, America and the colonies in the Soviet bureaucracy, especially Stalin. But the point we want to emphasize is, that however indignant the workers may feel over these trials, they must still remain loyal and devoted to the October Revolution, and the 200 million Soviet toilers who stand guard over the first victorious workers' state.[345]

There were many Western intellectuals and politicians who thought similarly. With Europe polarised into hostile camps, already fighting each other in Spain, many on the left thought Stalin's crimes should be overlooked, when they admitted the crimes were even happening. Many intellectuals in Britain turned to Communism in what was called for that reason—not because of the CPGB's membership, still very small—the "Red Decade". That spirit was typified by Victor Gollancz' Left Book Club; he never joined the Party, but he and the Club's books praised Stalin uncritically—it was an unusual, reluctant concession to publish Woolf's book which contained suggestions that the Soviet Union could do wrong.[346]

---

344   Paul Robeson, *Here I Stand*, London: Cassell, 1958, p. 37.

345   Padmore (note 210), p. 258.

346   V. Glendinning, *Leonard Woolf: A Life*, London and New York: Simon & Schuster, 2006, pp. 340-1, 346-7.

No Popular Front was formed in Britain by the left-wing parties, though there were efforts by Gollancz and others to promote one; but Communists and other left-wingers in practice worked together on Spain (the recruiters of the International Brigades were Communist but most of the volunteers were not[347]) and other international issues, such as the growing Nazi threat and the new Japanese aggression against China from mid-1937. Sometimes Communists and others took similar positions on colonial issues also.

A new radical group in London

The small group of African and Caribbean militants in London, who formed the almost forgotten Pan-African Federation for a time, was joined in 1937 by I.T.A. Wallace Johnson, after the colonial government in the Gold Coast had taken action against his "agitation" there. He and Padmore, James and Kenyatta then led this activist group. The West African Youth League had taken advantage of the widespread civic rights and liberties prevailing in British Crown Colonies in West Africa, but Governor Arnold Hodson thought by early 1936 that things had gone too far. He wrote to London that Wallace Johnson "is in the employ of the Bolsheviks and is doing a certain amount of harm by getting hold of the young men for his Youth League"; he added that the Sierra Leonean "just keeps within the law, but only just", and declared, "There is something wrong in our Constitution which allows these sort of people to be at large." He added—rightly, where Black Africa was concerned at least—"The French would not tolerate this for one second."[348]

The authorities felt able to pounce on both Wallace Johnson and Azikiwe when the *African Morning Post* published on 15 May 1936 an article entitled "Has the African a God?", written by "Effective", who turned out to be Wallace Johnson. It was a vehement denunciation of colonial administration, and part of it was considered to contravene the Sedition Ordinance. That part began

---

347 They included a number of African Americans—between 80 and 100, according to one estimate (Robinson (note 94), pp. 189, 200)—and some of the Malagasy community in France (Randrianja (note 241), p. 196).

348 Hodson to Sir Cecil Bottomley, Colonial Office, 14 January 1936, CO 96/731/31230, quoted in Asante (note 82), p. 161.

Personally, I believe the European has a God in whom he believes and whom he is representing in his churches all over Africa. He believes in the god whose name is spelt *deceit*. He believes in the god whose law is Ye strong, you must weaken the weak. Ye "Civilised" Europeans, you must "civilise" the "barbarous" Africans with machine guns. Ye "Christian" Europeans, you must "christianise" the "pagan" Africans with bombs, poison gases, etc.

Wallace Johnson and the editor, Nnamdi Azikiwe, were arrested. According to Denzer Wallace Johnson was identified from correspondence with the LAI and NWA, but Azikiwe says the police found a signed duplicate of the article at his (Wallace Johnson's) home.[349]

Wallace Johnson was found guilty on two counts of sedition in October 1936 and sentenced to a fine of £50 or three months' imprisonment; he paid the fine, but appealed to the West African Court of Appeal, which upheld the conviction on 1 December 1936. Then he decided to go to Britain and appeal to the Privy Council. The case had already aroused protests in Britain, including an NCCL leaflet signed by Henry Nevinson, President of the NCCL, and A.D. Belden (NCCL Vice-President), Kidd, Leys, Moody, Paul Robeson, Eleanor Rathbone and Lord Olivier, and two Labour critics of colonialism now prominent, Arthur Creech Jones and Leonard Barnes.[350]

Without Wallace Johnson the WAYL in the Gold Coast declined rapidly; a new newspaper that it had started soon folded. But he took up some Gold Coast grievances in Britain with the help of the anti-colonial campaigners.[351] Azikiwe was also convicted over the offending article, but the conviction was quashed on appeal on the grounds that the prosecution had not proved that Azikiwe had been editor on the day the article appeared (though he had).[352] Azikiwe stayed in the Gold Coast until July 1937 and then left for Nigeria, where he started his own newspaper, the *West African Pilot*, whose first issue appeared on 22 November 1937. Its political standpoint as expressed then was not revolutionary:

Our programme is based on the quest for social justice. Politically, we look forward to a better Nigeria and a more glorious future for West Africa. Socially,

349   Azikiwe (note 79), pp. 260-72; Denzer (note 16), pp. 137-9.
350   Leaflet in file CO 323/1610/2, National Archives, London.
351   Denzer (note 16), pp. 145-6, 154-6.
352   Azikiwe (note 79), pp. 260-72.

we hope that tribal prejudice and social stratifications are gone for ever and they must be swept away if they dare raise their horrid heads. Economically, we aim at the eradication of such forces of profit motive which overlook the African producer as a human being, and which lay unnecessary emphasis on material values.[353]

On leaving Gold Coast in 1937 Wallace Johnson originally planned to create a Central Bureau for non-white peoples in Europe, based in Paris, and before going to London he visited Paris, but he apparently found little encouragement there.[354] Anyway his activity was to be concentrated in London. He was later remembered as still being a Marxist at that time, and in London he was at first in contact with Bridgeman and Ward, who if they followed the Communist view of Padmore regarded him, officially at least, as an evil renegade. A secret Colonial Office note in January 1938 said that when he arrived the British Communists were developing the CPGB Colonial Section and "Wallace Johnson, who is in any case known to be personally rather unreliable, was not encouraged by them." Then he turned to Padmore, "Secretary of the Pan-African Brotherhood" for assistance. Padmore's relations with the LAI and Bridgeman "have for long a time, been extremely acrimonious", the note added, but Wallace Johnson kept up contact with Bridgeman and Bradley.[355]

It is not surprising that Wallace Johnson, still contributing to the *Negro Worker*, tried at first to contact the Communist anti-colonial activists in London, but despite what Governor Hodson said, quite probably he had not worked directly under Communist direction since 1933; he could simply have been one of the anti-colonial activists who wanted to use the Communists for their own ends. Kenyatta had had that idea, but the Communists in Moscow and Britain must have given up on him by 1935—when he worked with the outcast Padmore and the Trotskyist James in the IAFA—if not before. However, the official obsession with Moscow manipulation, shared by many others besides Hodson, was shown when Kenyatta travelled to Denmark in 1936 and there were sus-

---

353   Ibid., pp. 286-96.

354   Denzer (note 16), pp. 152-3.

355   Secret Colonial Office note circulated 27 January 1938, "Wallace Johnson and the International African Service Bureau", CO 323/1610/2, National Archives.

picions that he was going to Russia also; on his return the police at Harwich found no sign in his passport that he had been there.[356]

Kenyatta lived for three years as the tenant of a Mr S. Hocken of Pimlico in London, apparently at 95 Cambridge Street, but had stopped paying rent for a long time when Hocken wrote to Jesse Kariuki in Kenya to complain in 1936 (the police intercepted the letter and then allowed it to proceed). The authorities in Kenya gathered that the KCA was trying to raise funds for Kenyatta to return.[357] In fact he stayed in London, and in 1937 he, Wallace Johnson, Padmore and James joined with others to form a new militant black anti-colonial organisation, quite separate from the LAI and other Communist activities.

The leader of this group was George Padmore. Like his comrades he lived a hard life in London in the later 30s. Padmore took rooms in London, first in Vauxhall Bridge Road, later in Guildford Street, with other hard-up West Indians. Padmore came to know several prominent left-wingers and in 1937 spoke at one of the ILP's Summer Schools; he attended others later. He was introduced by F.A. Ridley, author of a pamphlet entitled *Mussolini over Africa*, to the ILP leaders, and wrote for *The New Leader* and also for C.A. Smith's *Controversy*, but did not join the party. He also met K.D. Kumria, an Indian militant, founder of Swaraj House which was used for meetings of African protest groups.[358] From 1937 Padmore lived with Dorothy Pizer, an English typist, as his wife in all but name.

Padmore's *How Britain Rules Africa* was published in 1936, as already noted.[359] It has a chapter on the "Conquest and Partition" and then chapters on various parts of British-ruled Africa. It quotes from "reformists" (Leys, Ballinger) and speaks of some MPs interested in colonial issues, such as Lunn and Maxton. Padmore expressed an opinion which recalls his separation from the Communists: Africans did not have class or religious divisions as Asians had, and there was plenty of

---

356   Police reports of 3 August 1936 and 7 October 1936, Harwich, in file KV2/1787, National Archives, London.

357   Extract from "Events of Interest in Kenya" from Kenya Police, 13 Aug. 1936; J.E.W. Flood of Colonial Office to A. de V. Wade, Secretariat, Nairobi, 8 Sept. 1936; Wade to Flood, 5 Nov. 1936; file KV2/1787, National Archives, London.

358   Hooker (note 3), pp. 42-9.

359   G. Padmore, *How Britain Rules Africa*, London: Wishart Books, 1936.

"feeling of racial solidarity", shown in response to the invasion of Ethiopia (pp. 362-3). In 1937 Padmore published *Africa and World Peace*, with an introduction by Sir Stafford Cripps, MP, who said, "The problem of imperialism has never been fully understood within the Labour movement of Great Britain."[360] Dealing with a number of international issues relating to colonies, especially the Italian occupation of Ethiopia, Padmore spoke of the rivalry over colonies between the "Have-Nots" and the "Haves" and declared, "Empire and peace are incompatible" (p. 210). He examined the idea of extending the mandate system to all Crown Colonies and Protectorates in Africa, advocated by Roden Buxton among others, and the related idea of allowing Fascist countries to share in the mandates on certain conditions; he rejected those ideas, especially the second, and said, "It is the economic system that has to be changed"—after which, he went on, "The political and social emancipation of the subject peoples will automatically follow, as was the case in Russia" (pp. 240-2). He reiterated his admiration for Soviet achievements in the Asian republics, in education and literacy for example, by saying, "Whereas the Africans are still being ruthlessly exploited and oppressed in order to provide super-profits for rentiers and alien landlords, the Asiatic races under Soviet rule have moved forward by leaps and bounds." (pp. 201-2)

The band of activists was joined by a Guyanese, George Thomas Nathaniel Griffith, alias Ras Makonnen. He recalled that he took this Ethiopian name before the Second World War, and it must have been a gesture of support for the Ethiopians, but he also said one of his grandfathers had been an Ethiopian, met by a Scots miner in Eritrea and taken by him to British Guiana. Griffith/Makonnen spent some years in the USA, studied agriculture at Cornell University from 1932 to 1934, and then did further agricultural studies at Copenhagen, before going to live in England.[361] He claimed that he had been deported from Denmark (incidentally meeting Paul Robeson on the boat) after protesting at Danish exports of mustard, which could have been used for the mustard gas used in Ethiopia, to Italy. British police and secret service documents mention Griffith in England in 1936; it is not clear

---

360   Padmore (note 210), p. xi.
361   Ras Makonnen, *Pan-Africanism from Within*, as told to Kenneth King, Nairobi: OUP, 1973, pp. ix-xi, pp. 111-12.

when he went to live there, as his memoirs dictated decades later, while lively and interesting, are unreliable for details.[362]

A letter of 27 April 1936 in the MI5 file on Kenyatta spoke of Padmore, Griffith (so named) and Kenyatta living at 4 Calthorpe Street or 238b Grays Inn Road, London WC ("these premises are situated at the corner of those two streets, but the former is the recognised postal address"); they occupied rooms in the basement and were tenants of the ground floor occupiers, African Church Stores Ltd., "an organisation which has been formed ostensibly to act as a Co-operative selling agent for native wares from the Gold Coast." Surveillance of the place spotted only Padmore and Griffith, who were indoors most of the time but spoke at an IAFA meeting on 19 April 1936 and visited 47 Doughty Street, W1, the offices of the LCP.[363] Makonnen recalled that a Gold Coast "independent African orthodox church" leader named Bresiando, who was in Britain making another attempt at African direct marketing of cocoa, rented a building in London next door to the *Daily Sketch* offices; the basement was rented to Padmore and Griffith/Makonnen.[364]

The Pan-African Federation was clearly active in 1936; the MI5 file on Kenyatta mentioned him speaking at a Trafalgar Square meeting organised by the Federation on 14 June 1936,[365] and attending with "Tomasa Rawaki Griffith" and Robert Broadhurst a meeting of the Federation on 29 June 1936.[366] A Special Branch note on Kenyatta on 3 March 1938 mentioned a bulletin, *Voice of Africa*, published by the "Pan-African Congress (British section)" of 2 Calthorpe Street and edited by Padmore and Kenyatta, but it added that this had ceased to exist from about nine months before; "the departure from 2, Calthorpe

---

362   For example, they include a very inaccurate recollection of a Rassemblement Colonial conference in Paris in 1938, saying Félix Houphouet-Boigny of Ivory Coast was there (pp. 155-6). But the Rassemblement Colonial did exist (see below, pp. 411-12).

363   Letter 27 April 1936 in file KV2/1787, National Archives, London. Other police and intelligence reports give the address as 2 Calthorpe Street, which is more probable.

364   Makonnen (note 361), pp. 118.

365   P.F.40714 document 14 June 1936, file KV2/1787, National Archives, London.

366   P.F.40714 document, 3 July 1936, file KV2/1787, National Archives, London.

Street, W.C. 1 took place overnight, and the Congress left debts for rent, light etc."[367]

At any rate a new radical anti-colonial group was founded in 1937, the International African Service Bureau (IASB). It later recalled being founded in March 1937, which is about the time Wallace Johnson arrived in London, and this fits fairly well with information summarised in a note in the MI5 Kenyatta file in 1937. This said that on 6 April of that year "the Pan African Federation, known as the Pan Afro Group" met at 42 Alderney Street, London SW and set up a temporary committee of "radical Colonial elements": Wallace Johnson, "J. James", Padmore, Kenyatta, C. Jones and "N.O. Bungo, a student from Oxford, who hails from east Africa." A further meeting on 18 April was attended among others by Ralph Bunche, a young African American academic on his way to South Africa for part of a two-year anthropology research project. Bunche had belonged to a left-wing group of Howard University teaching staff (mentioned above) and his movements were watched by the British secret service; about this time tapping of the LAI's telephone line recorded a call from "Ralph Budge" to Bridgeman.[368] Bunche disagreed with Padmore's Pan-Africanist group, sharing Communist views about them.[369]

Makonnen later recalled that the IASB had been started "in an informal way" by Padmore, James, and others including Babalola Wilkie, a Nigerian formerly working for the Customs and Lagos Town Council. The British intelligence service thought Wallace Johnson was the main inspiration behind the IASB, and although the Sierra Leonean had only just arrived in London, Denzer suggests that he played a bigger role than that suggested in retrospect by Padmore and Makonnen, both of whom suspected his links with the Communists.[370] James recalled later that while some Africans were primarily African in outlook and only secondarily Marxist, this was not true of Wallace Johnson.[371] But such

---

367 Special Branch note, 3 March 1938, file KV2/1787, National Archives, London.

368 Note P.F. 41407, 24 April 1937, file KV2/1787, National Archives, London.

369 Edgar (note 93), pp. 14-15.

370 Denzer (note 16), 159-61.

371 Interview, C.L.R. James, 4 June 1984.

differences did not stop this small group from working together and with a wider range of supporters.

Makonnen recalled the IASB as a group of about thirty meeting for long discussions around a hot stove. It came to be fairly well documented, by its organisers and by the watchful police and secret service. According to information received by MI5, the officials of the IASB were: Chairman, George Padmore; Vice-Chairmen, Amy Ashwood Garvey, Jomo Kenyatta; Treasurer, Robert Broadhurst; Executive and Publicity Secretary, T.R. Makonnen; General Secretary, I.T.A. Wallace Johnson; Executive Committee, Chris Jones, H.O. Cendrecourt, C.L.R. James, J.J. Ocquaye, L. Mbanefo, Elsie Duncan, F.A. Bruce, K. Sallie Tamba, G. Kouyate, N. Azikiwe, O. Mandoh, Gilbert Coka, Aida Bastian, E. Damanya. Details given were fairly accurate, though Kouyate was called "G. Koyatte, Sudan" and Bastian, described as Ethiopian, was in fact Jamaican. Coka was South African, Makonnen and Cendrecourt were from British Guiana, and the rest were West Africans except for Kenyatta and the West Indians Padmore, Garvey, James and Jones.[372]

The IASB found offices at 94 Gray's Inn Road, and published the *African Sentinel*, which seems to have continued for four or five bi-monthly issues between the autumn of 1937 and the late spring of 1938. The March-April 1938 issue covered the Gold Coast, Trinidad, Ethiopia, Kenya and Nigeria, and had contributions from Wallace Johnson, Kenyatta, Maxton and Cunard among others.[373] Then the *Sentinel* was replaced by the monthly *International African Opinion* from July 1938. It was edited at first, for three months, by James, assisted by William Harrison, an African American research student at the LSE.[374] In addition, the IASB published a monthly duplicated newssheet called *Africa and the World*, for a time in 1937 at least.

The first issue of *International African Opinion* had an editorial recording the founding of the IASB in March 1937:

---

372   [Col. Sir Vernon] Kell to F.J. Howard, Colonial Office, 21 June 1937, file CO 323/1517/2, National Archives, London. Louis Mbanefo, then a Nigerian (Igbo) student in London, was to become Chief Justice of the Eastern Region of Nigeria.

373   Macdonald (note 29), pp. 158-9.

374   Esedebe (note 111), p. 134. This Harrison may have been the same one mentioned by MI5 as a friend of Nancy Cunard in 1935 (see above, p. 338).

No people, race or nationality has been oppressed, exploited and humiliated as the black people for centuries past up to the present day, and the Bureau was formed to assist by all means in our power the un-coordinated struggle of Africans and people of African descent against the oppression from which they suffer in every country... Our people are becoming alive to the nature of the struggle ahead. That struggle we shall pursue to the end, until economically, politically and socially, the Negro is everywhere as free as other men are.

As an intermediate stage, however, the editorial said black colonial subjects should be given what the Chartists had demanded in Britain a century before. It said, "Our organisation is AFRICAN. But we repudiate hostility to any other race as a race". They backed the causes of India, China and Spain.[375]

In a release entitled, "What is the International African Service Bureau?" Wallace Johnson said it was an independent "non-party" organisation, representing "progressive and enlightened public opinion" among Africans and people of African descent. Europeans and other non-Africans who sympathised with the Bureau's aspirations and wanted to show support in a practical way could become associate members. It aimed to agitate for constitutional reforms such as freedom of the press, assembly, speech and movement, and other democratic rights; to enlighten public opinion on conditions in the colonies; and to expose and combat "child labour, forced labour, colour bar acts" and other such legislation from which black people suffered.[376]

The IASB stood out by its determination to remain independent of all European parties and its call for self-government. James recalled later that he and his IASB comrades definitely wanted self-government, but that after an argument Padmore said they need not use the word.[377] The word may not have been used often, but Brockway recalled of Padmore, Kenyatta, Wallace Johnson and others, "So far as I can recall, they called for absolute independence";[378] he knew them over a long period

---

375 Enclosed in file CO 323/1610/2, National Archives, London, with letters V. Kell to F.J. Howard of Colonial Office, 8 Sept. 1938, and from Colonial Office, 31 Oct. 1938.

376 Asante (note 82), p. 204.

377 Interview, C.L.R. James, 4 June 1984.

378 Interview, Fenner Brockway, 14 Feb. 1984. Robinson suggests (note 84, pp. 273-4) that the IASB initially favoured armed rebellion, but bases this only on James' recollections, which seem mistaken in this case; other evidence does not

and may have been thinking of a more recent date, but it seems to have been probably true of the 1930s. In 1938 Makonnen wrote on behalf of the IASB to President Barclay of Liberia saying that the Bureau had criticised the conditions of the Liberian people and some aspects of the government, but those criticisms were

in the interests of the Liberian people and of the Negro race as a whole. Whereas we stand for the complete emancipation of every part of Africa from European domination, we stand firmly for the national independence of the State of Liberia. Liberia is not an Imperialist State. We unhesitatingly condemn all whose criticisms have as their aim, direct or indirect, the bringing of Liberia into the orbit of the European domination of Africa. [379]

This stance was not surprising as talk of independence or self-government was widespread in the colonies themselves, at least in West Africa. In Nigeria the 1938 Youth Charter of the NYM, which in that year won the three Lagos Colony elected seats for Africans in Legco, declared plainly, "The goal of our political activities is a complete taking-over of the Government into the hands of the people of our country." It accepted British trusteeship for the time being, but pledged itself "to make that period of trusteeship as brief as possible."[380]

Colonial liberals, Radicals and African issues in Britain, 1936-8

James recalled,

We allowed no opportunity of putting our case to pass us by. We had a lot of assistance from the Independent Labour Party, but whenever there was a meeting held by the Labour Party or a conference organised by the Communist Party or some trade union group, or a meeting of Liberals who were interested in the 'Colonial Question' we were there.

Only a few dozen people came to meetings, "often more whites than blacks".[381] But such activists had influence going beyond the small attendance at their meetings, especially through their efforts to stir promi-

---

support it.

379   Quoted in Sundiata (note 75), pp. 109-10.
380   Asante (note 82), pp. 186-7.
381   James (note 200), p. 161.

nent sympathisers, especially politicians, into action—supplementing the efforts made for some time by WASU, the LCP and the NCCL.

According to an MI5 report the patrons of the IASB included Nancy Cunard, who was said to have provided money to help the IASB.[382] They also included Sylvia Pankhurst, a leading figure in anti-colonialist circles in the later 1930s, often visited by Padmore, Wallace Johnson, Kenyatta and Makonnen. Others included the novelist Ethel Mannin; Dorothy Woodman, Kingsley Martin's partner, actively involved in African affairs as Secretary of the UDC from 1931; Victor Gollancz; and the MPs Reginald Sorensen, Ellen Wilkinson, George Daggar, D.N. Pritt, Morgan Jones, Philip Noel Baker, Arthur Creech Jones and E.L. Mallalieu. Curiously, this list did not include Fenner Brockway, who was in close contact with the activists. He and Sorensen were among the leading supporters of African causes in the ILP, where Mannin was another supporter. Pritt and Sir Stafford Cripps—two famous left-wing lawyers and politicians—and Norman Wiggins acted for Wallace Johnson in his appeal to the Privy Council; on 28 July 1938 he was given leave to appeal *in forma pauperis*, which meant that the Gold Coast government had to pay costs.[383]

Creech Jones, after his election to parliament in 1935, was one of the most active critics of colonialism in the House of Commons. In its efforts to explain the situation in the colonies the Bureau contacted Labour Party branches and various sympathetic bodies, supplying speakers for meetings. On 29 November 1937 Wallace Johnson and Makonnen met the Labour Party Commonwealth Group of the House of Commons; they mentioned the German colonial claim, linking it to the occupation of Ethiopia by the other member of the Rome-Berlin Axis.[384]

In opposition to the German demand for colonies staunch defenders of Empire agreed with left-wingers, just as many Conservatives were as strongly opposed to Nazism and Japanese imperialism as anyone else. Imperialists could also join in the opposition to the South African pressure for absorption of the three British Protectorates of Bechuanaland, Basutoland and Swaziland, which was much discussed during the

382   "Communism and the West Indian Labour Disturbances" (note 33), p. 6.
383   Denzer (note 16), pp. 148-9. He eventually lost the appeal in late 1939.
384   Asante (note 82), p. 206.

1930s and highlighted by the IASB. The Bureau published a pamphlet *Hands off the Protectorates*, published in London in 1938 (the press release by Wallace Johnson mentioned earlier was on its inside cover),[385] and the second issue of *International African Opinion* mentioned that "for the past few months the main energies of members of the Bureau have been devoted to presenting the case of the natives of the protectorates".[386] The IASB held a demonstration in Trafalgar Square on 8 May 1938 against transfer of those territories to what would have been Afrikaner rule.

Except for those two—important—issues, protests on behalf of Africans remained, as they always had been, mainly the preserve of left-wing parties. Besides Labour MPs there were new advisers to the Labour Party, critical writers on colonial Africa coming to attention in the 1930s: W.M. Macmillan, Julius Lewin and Leonard Barnes, all with South African connections. Barnes, who became the most radical and was for years a leading anti-colonialist, started off, after his Oxford degree, as a cotton farmer in South Africa, but he gradually turned against imperialism while there, encouraged by Norman Leys. In 1930 he published *Caliban in Africa*. Back in England later, he joined the Labour Party Advisory Committee and published *The Duty of Empire* (1935), The *Future of Colonies* (1936) and *Empire or Democracy* (published by the Left Book Club in 1939). In June 1938 he, Leys, Frank Horrabin and Lewin started a critical monthly called simply *Empire*; Barnes was the effective editor. Later it was handed over to the Fabian Colonial Bureau.[387]

Macmillan, based in England for most of the 1930s, became known particularly for his book *Africa Emergent* (1938). He condemned South Africa's segregation policies as "of the same genus as the racial decrees of Nazi Germany", and opposed the transfer of Basutoland, Bechuanaland and Swaziland. On the colonies generally, he called for a new approach aiming at economic development and progress towards

---

385   Esedebe (note 111), p. 136.

386   Enclosed in file CO 323/1610/2, with letters with letters V. Kell to F.J. Howard of Colonial Office, 8 Sept. 1938, and from Colonial Office, 31 Oct. 1938.

387   J. Saville, "Barnes, Leonard John", *Dictionary of Labour Biography* (note 32), vol. VIII pp. 4-9.

self-government.[388] From 1937 he began to attend meetings of the Labour Party Advisory Committee regularly, and he, Creech Jones, Ross, Drummond Shiels and Roden Buxton joined a Trades Union Congress Colonial Advisory Committee formed in December 1937.[389]

The ILP was fast declining at this time, but was if anything more strongly anti-imperialist than ever. Its organ the *New Leader*, edited by Brockway, devoted its May Day issue for 1938 to imperialism; the "Empire Special" supplement included an article by Kenyatta, "Their Land was Stolen: Slave Conditions in Kenya".[390] Although Padmore did not join the ILP, the IASB worked closely with it, for example when a new Empire Exhibition was held in Glasgow in August 1938.[391] To respond to the glorifying of the Empire there, a "Workers' Empire Exhibition" was opened in Glasgow on 13 August 1938 by Ethel Mannin. This followed soon after another ILP Summer School, addressed by Kenyatta, a Sri Lankan speaker, and a West Indian (apparently Padmore).[392]

African colonial causes and the causes of India, China and the Spanish Republic overlapped, with many of the same people becoming involved in them. Nehru, President of the Indian National Congress in 1936 and 1937, visited Britain in 1935, 1936 and 1938; he met Padmore and had friendly links and contacts with many Labour politicians and intellectuals such as Cripps, the Webbs, Brailsford and Wilkinson. He visited Republican Spain and spoke out about the Japanese aggression against China, also condemned by the National Congress generally.[393] Many INC leaders including Nehru had favoured a boycott of elections held under the reforms of the 1935 Government of India Act, giving

---

388   P. Rich, "W.M. Macmillan, South African Segregation and Commonwealth Race Relations, 1919-1938", ch. 9 (pp. 209-11); M. Macmillan, "Macmillan, Indirect Rule and *Africa Emergent*", ch. 11 (p. 233); John E. Flint, "Macmillan as a Critic of Empire: The Impact of an Historian on Colonial Policy", Ch. 10, in H. Macmillan and S. Marks (eds), *W.M. Macmillan, Historian and Social Critic*, Temple Smith for the Institute of Commonwealth Studies, 1989 (pp. 224-8).

389   Howe (note 36), pp. 134-5.

390   *New Leader*, 29 April 1938.

391   J.R. MacKenzie, *Propaganda and Empire: The Manipulation of British Public Opinion 1880-1960*, Manchester University Press, 1984, pp. 112-13.

392   James Maxton, "So this is Empire!" *New Leader* 19 August 1938.

393   S. Gopal, *Jawaharlal Nehru: A Biography: Vol. One: 1889-1947*, London: Jonathan Cape, 1975, pp. 201, 233-8.

wider self-government in the provinces but not much in the centre, but eventually Congress did contest elections in 1937 and won a clear majority in six out of eleven provinces, and took office in provincial governments.[394]

The colonial events that aroused most publicity and concern in Britain in the later 1930s, except perhaps for the Palestine events, took place in the Caribbean. The famous strike in the Trinidad oilfields in June-July 1937, whose leader was Uriah Butler, was followed by riots in late July 1937 in Barbados and other union activity, including strikes, in British Guiana.[395] The major strikes in Trinidad and Barbados were severely suppressed with several people killed. Then, in 1938, there was a sugar workers' strike in Trinidad in April, which failed, while in Jamaica the famous trade unionist Alexander Bustamante organised workers' meetings and became the hero of a wave of stoppages that hit the island in late May 1938.[396]

After the Jamaican disturbances two inquiries were ordered in London, one to inquire into the disturbances themselves, the other, under Lord Moyne, to examine the underlying economic and social conditions. Those conditions were widely agreed to be appalling, sugar plantation workers' conditions in particular,[397] and had aroused concern in the Labour Party, and some action from the 1929-31 Labour government, even before the outbreaks.[398] Now many in the party were stirred to action, including Lunn, Maxton, Creech Jones, Wilkinson, Aneurin Bevan and other MPs, and *the Daily Herald, Reynold's News* (which published on 5 June 1938 an article by the veteran Brailsford, "The Slavery that is Jamaica") and the recently started *Tribune*.[399] A Committee for West Indian Affairs was created by MPs on 8 November 1938, with Creech Jones as Chairman and Peter Blackman, a Barbadian who was editor of *The Keys*, as secretary. Besides Blackman other

---

394   Ibid., pp. 200, 210-22.

395   Lewis (note 189), pp. 22-33.

396   Ibid., pp. 33-8; K. Post, *Arise Ye Starvelings*, The Hague: Martinus Nijhoff, 1978, pp. 276-424 (a full account of the Jamaica rebellion and the subsequent inquiries).

397   Lewis (note 189), pp. 15-17.

398   Malmsten (note 234), pp. 177-88.

399   Howe (note 36), pp. 90-104.

anti-colonial campaigners joined in protests about the West Indies. A meeting in London in June 1938, with Moody in the chair and speakers including Bridgeman, Kidd, Lewis and Blackman, called for a protected market for West Indian exports (a widespread demand for years), land redistribution, universal free education, and, for all West Indians, "the same civil liberties as are enjoyed by the people of Britain, including universal adult suffrage and the removal of the property qualification for members of the Legislature; also Federation of the West Indies with complete self-government."[400]

A range of critics of empire joined in protests. The aged Lord Olivier was the first witness to testify before the Moyne Commission on its return from the West Indies.[401] The West Indian situation was examined by two academics, W.M. Macmillan—whose *Warning from the West Indies* (1936) proved prophetic—and W. Arthur Lewis, in *Labour in the West Indies*, published in 1938 as a pamphlet by the Fabian Society. Lewis, when a lecturer at the LSE, had been editor of *The Keys* from June 1935 to October 1936. On the more militant side, the IASB and NWA joined the basically more pacific LCP to present a petition to the Moyne Commission; the IASB's West Indian chairman naturally spoke out;[402] *Africa and the World*'s vol. 1 no. 4 (1 September 1937) was a "Special West-Indian Edition";[403] and Cripps attended a meeting in Jamaica where Norman Manley, Bustamante's cousin, launched the People's National Party in September 1938.

The critics of imperialism, of all shades, who had reacted to the West Indies disturbances also responded to a number of African issues about the same time. One was the Cocoa Hold-up in Gold Coast, starting in November 1937. Cocoa farmers halted bean deliveries on a large scale to protest against an agreement (commonly though not officially called a "pool") allocating fixed shares of the cocoa crop among almost all the major exporters. This was seen as a price-fixing arrangement to swindle farmers, and the Hold-Up was very effective. It was called off after the

---

400   Macdonald (note 110), p. 299, quoting *The Keys* 6, 1, July-Sept. 1938.

401   F. Lee, *Fabianism and Colonialism: The Life and Political Thought of Lord Sydney Olivier*, London: Defiant Books, 1988, pp. 213-14.

402   e.g. "Colonial Fascism in the West Indies", *New Leader*, 29 April 1938.

403   This issue and Vol. 1 no. 2 (27 July 1937) and Vol. 1 no. 3 (14 August 1937) are enclosed in file CO 847/11/16, National Archives, London.

announcement of a Royal Commission and the subsequent cancellation of the firms' agreement in April 1938.[404] WASU organised a meeting in support of the Cocoa Hold-up on 8 April 1938,[405] attended by Sorensen, who had denounced the colonial government's record in the Gold Coast at length in the Commons a few months earlier,[406] and Creech Jones. However, a secret Colonial Office note gave the reassuring news that there was "no direct evidence" of the Gold Coast Cocoa Hold-up's organisers being "in contact with the negro community in London led by Wallace Johnson".[407]

Kenya remained a major focus of British anti-colonial protest. The Morris Carter report in 1934, accepted by the government, proposed extinguishing of African land rights in areas of European farms in the "White Highlands", and only a small addition to the African "reserves".[408] Kikuyu organisations continued their protests; the KA was renamed the Kikuyu Loyal Patriots, but its leader Koinange wa Mbiyu drew closer to the KCA, eventually joining it; he was influenced in a more critical direction by his son Mbiyu Koinange, returning from studies in the USA, but probably also by the government's intransigent attitude to Africans' land rights.[409] The KCA, however, went through years of bitter internal division after 1932; Harry Thuku, KCA president for a time, broke away in 1935. But the KCA revived under other leaders, and voiced increasing anger over the land issue, especially against evictions in the Tigoni area of Kikuyuland. The KCA was renamed KCA (1938) and cooperated with associations formed by other ethnic groups increasingly angry at land and agricultural policies affecting Africans. All this protest activity was backed by Kenyatta in Britain, writing letters to the

---

404   D.K. Fieldhouse, *Merchant Capital and Economic Decolonization: The United Africa Company, 1929-1987,* Oxford: Clarendon Press, 1994, pp. 146-75, 230-1.

405   Olusanya (note 115), p. 41.

406   Speech reproduced in *Africa and the World*, vol. 1 no. 2, 27 July 1937 (see note 403).

407   Secret Colonial Office note circulated 27 January 1938, "Wallace Johnson and the International African Service Bureau", CO 323/1610/2, National Archives, London.

408   J.D. Kamoche, *Imperial Trusteeship and Political Evolution in Kenya, 1923-1963,* Washington: University Press of America, 1981, pp. 158-75.

409   Clough (note 60), pp. 163-6.

Manchester Guardian and supplying information, to add to that sent by the KCA and Koinange, to Creech Jones.[410] Kenyatta wrote in *International African Opinion*'s second issue about the Tigoni evictions and the culling of Kamba cattle herds.[411]

In late 1934 Johnstone Kenyatta met Bronislaw Malinowski, University of London Professor of Social Anthropology since 1927, and in the following academic year he studied under Malinowski at the LSE, reading for a three-year postgraduate diploma in Social Anthropology, designed for students lacking qualifications for the full PhD programme. While studying the traditions of his people, with the help of a studentship from the International African Institute, Kenyatta befriended Dinah Stock, who had been the first woman to chair the Oxford University Labour Club before going into far-left politics, and went to live in her London flat in Camden Town. She helped him put his essays for Malinowski's seminars together, and in 1938 he presented his diploma thesis and published it as *Facing Mount Kenya*.[412]

Kenyatta's book[413] is a study of the traditions of the Gikuyu people (that was the spelling he and many others have used). More than a study, it was a defence of traditions. His dedication was

To Moigoi and Wamboi and all the dispossessed youth of Africa: for perpetuation of communion with ancestral spirits through the fight for African Freedom, and in the firm faith that the dead, the living, and the unborn will unite to rebuild the destroyed shrines.

Kenyatta deals at length with land tenure, condemning the European view that much Gikuyu land was traditionally unoccupied: "every inch of the Gikuyu territory had its owner." (p. 25) Chapter VI on "Initiation" has a good deal on FGM; Kenyatta's explanation of it, as having a vital role in society, reads like a defence.

The book voices his anger at British rule:

410   Ibid., pp. 168-77; Murray-Brown (note 15), pp. 200-2. See also Harry Thuku (with assistance from K. King), *An Autobiography*, Nairobi: OUP, 1970, pp. 47-56.

411   Enclosed in file CO 323/1610/2 (note 375).

412   B. Berman, "Ethnography as Politics, Politics as Ethnography: Kenyatta, Malinowski, and the Making of *Facing Mount Kenya*", *Canadian Journal of African Studies* vol. 30 no. 3, 1996, pp. 313-44; Murray-Brown (note 15), pp.199-200.

413   J. Kenyatta, *Facing Mount Kenya*, London: Secker & Warburg, 1938.

Instead of advancing "towards a higher intellectual, moral, and economic level," the African has been reduced to a state of serfdom; his initiative in social, economic and political structure has been denied, his spirit of manhood has been killed and he has been subjected to the most inferior position in human society. If he dares to express his opinion on any point, other than what is dictated to him, he is shouted at and blacklisted as an "agitator." (p. 197)

Referring to the First World War and the Italian occupation of Ethiopia, he says:

With these glaring facts in view can the Europeans boast of having stopped the "tribal warfare" and having established "perpetual peace" in Africa? It would have been much better for the Africans to continue with their tribal warfare, which they fought with pride and with the loss of a few warriors, rather than receiving the so-called civilising missions which means the subjugation of the African races to a perpetual state of serfdom. (p. 212)

The daily headlines at that period were certainly not such as to support ideas of a superior European civilisation; an editorial in *Wasu* (vi, 1) of January 1937 said it was time for "Africans to start thinking of sending missionaries to Europe to humanise the natives."[414] But Kenyatta's pride in African tradition raised issues on which not all Africans agreed. Many readily accepted some change in accordance with Western ideas, calling in particular for more Western-type education, and criticised anthropologists for being interested only in traditional cultures; while European officials were often the keenest advocates of preserving African tradition—or what they saw as African tradition. But Africans asked, should the Western viewpoint be adopted on everything? FGM was one matter for such debate.

To reinforce his own message, Kenyatta was pictured on the cover like a tribal elder. Peter Mbiyu Koinange was now in Britain, studying for a year at Cambridge after his US studies, and helped Kenyatta by lending him his hyrax and blue monkey cloak for the photograph; they sharpened a piece of wood into the shape of a spear. They agreed that Johnstone Kenyatta should rename himself Jomo Kenyatta, which he did from then on. The book sold only 517 copies.[415]

---

414   Quoted in Garigue (note 115), p. 62.
415   Murray-Brown (note 15), pp. 195-6.

The British authorities continued to keep a suspicious watch on Kenyatta,[416] and on his comrades in the IASB. Inevitably they were suspected of involvement in the West Indies troubles. But the authorities were not blinded by Red-phobia, though it was still strong. In the West Indies case colonial business firms offered their own amateur intelligence services to the government, implicating both the CPGB and IASB,[417] but MI5 politely dismissed much of this "information", pointing out that Padmore was against the Comintern, and said, "In the case of the West Indies we have no direct evidence of Comintern instigation". It added, "Since 1935 it has not been the policy of the Comintern to creat [sic] labour troubles merely for their own sake."[418] MI5 concluded that, "There is no direct evidence to show that the Moscow Comintern has been deliberately fostering labour unrest in the West Indies".[419] This agreed with the view of St. Orde Browne, special adviser to the Secretary of State for the Colonies (who since May of that year was Malcolm MacDonald); in a letter of 9 December 1938 Browne predicted a new outbreak in the Caribbean in 1939, and said:

I have been able to discover no evidence to justify any suspicion of provocative influences from outside and in my opinion any disorder which may arise will be mainly attributable to that oldest and ablest of agitators, hunger.[420]

In another island colony of Britain dependent on sugar and employing workers for abysmally low pay, Mauritius, strikes and riots also broke out, in August 1937, and a week-long dock strike in September 1938; and as in the Caribbean, "agitators" were blamed. The Governor said that statements by Emmanuel Anquetil, a labour leader who had been deported from Britain in 1936, were concerned with "international Bolshevism"; an inquiry into the unrest found however that most of the workers' complaints were justified.[421]

---

416   Special Branch note, 3 March 1938 (note 367).

417   R. Beaumont of Trinidad Leaseholds, letter to CO 6 May 1938, enclosing documents; R.L.M. Kirkwood of The West Indies Sugar Co. Ltd. to Lord Dufferin, 17 May 1938; file CO 295/606, National Archives, London.

418   D.G. White of Box no. 500, Parliament Street, P.O., London SW1 [MI5], to F.J. Howard, Colonial Office, 26 May 1938, ibid.

419   "Communism and the West Indian Labour Disturbances" (note 33), pp. 1, 5.

420   Cited in Post (note 396), p. 114.

421   A. Simmons, *Modern Mauritius: The Politics of Decolonisation*, Indiana Univer-

MI5 confirmed its conclusion about Communist involvement in a detailed note on black activist organisations and their leaders. It noted that real Communist anti-colonialist activity still continued, and considered the Negro Welfare Association to be "the most important link for communist propaganda among negroes"; Ward had been expelled from the NWA and CPGB in 1936 for refusal to carry out orders on reorganisation of the NWA, and it was now headed by a Sierra Leonean seaman, Roland Sawyer, who had taken LAI and ITUC-NW literature to Jamaica in 1932 when working on an Elder Dempster ship. In 1937 he joined the Executive Committee of the Colonial Seamen's Association; as Secretary of the NWA he "receives his orders from Ben BRADLEY." According to MI5 Peter Blackman, aged about 25 in 1938, had gone to Nigeria as a missionary but renounced that work and returned to Britain after two months; "Since April, 1937, he has been entrusted by the Colonial Department of the C.P.G.B. with the work of organising Colonial and negro workers in the U.K." Yet Blackman, editor of the *Keys*, was secretary of the Committee for West Indian Affairs created by MPs in November 1938 with Creech Jones (not a fellow traveller) as Chairman. MI5's information may have been correct even so, as clearly anti-colonial activists of different groups and beliefs worked together a great deal.[422]

If Ward was indeed expelled from the NWA in 1936, he may have gone over to Padmore, as the latter recalled. But there may not have been a total ban on contacts between Communists and Padmore, despite the venom that certainly existed, as shown in Patterson's review. At a Trafalgar Square meeting on 8 August 1937 on the Trinidad and Barbados strikes, where Padmore presided, the speakers included Bridgeman, Jones, Ward, Wallace Johnson, James and Kenyatta; and Bridgeman was still Secretary of the LAI.[423] Bridgeman may now have left the Communist Party if he had ever formally joined it, for in 1937, despite his long and overt Communist links, he was readmitted to the Labour Party (only to be expelled again a few years later);[424] but as his Communist links had been so close for ten years, how could he share a

---

sity Press, 1982, pp. 58-76.

422   See note 33.

423   *Africa and the World*, vol. 1 no. 3, 14 August 1937 (see note 403).

424   Saville (note 32), p. 36.

platform with Padmore? In fact the anti-colonial and pan-African activists worked together, usually well, despite ideological differences, and this might even have extended sometimes to Padmore and his former Communist comrades. When Makonnen recalled later that

We were out to create a movement that was free from any entanglement; and any black man coming into our camp who had one foot in the communist camp, we would deal with ruthlessly.[425]

he was probably referring to membership of their own inner circle, not suggesting that others such as Communists could not share platforms with them at public meetings. It can be presumed that Chris Jones, active in Communist organisations before, had broken with the Communists before becoming Padmore's close comrade in the later 1930s.

As an example of the general collaboration, when the Colonial Seamen's Association, founded—according to the MI5 report—in 1935 as an offshoot of the LAI, held its first annual conference in London on 29 November 1936, the Christian-oriented LCP was represented as well as the LAI and NWA.[426] It seems that, as Makonnen recalled, it was a welfare and publicity association whose aims included urging Black seamen to join the white seamen's union.[427] The plight of the Black and Arab seamen and waterfront dwellers in seaports such as Cardiff and Liverpool—on which Chris Jones, head of the Colonial Seamen's Association for some time, wrote in *International African Opinion* (vol. 1 no. 1)—had for long interested those concerned with colonial issues, including the LCP.

Like the similar communities at Marseilles and Bordeaux in France, those waterfront peoples led a hard and deprived life, worsened by the Slump and, for an even longer period, by official and trade union discrimination in employment aboard ship. The Communists saw the Black seamen as greatly exploited workers, while sailors were often recruited to carry banned literature from France to the colonies; for Madagascar, for example, there were two secret distribution networks, one Communist and the other Malagasy and non-Communist.[428] In Britain

---

425   Makonnen (note 361), p. 117.

426   *Negro Worker*, February 1937 (see note 328).

427   Makonnen (note 361), p. 129.

428   Randrianja (note 243), pp. 198-205.

the CPGB and the LAI made contact with seamen from colonial territories in Britain; a police report in 1930 said many seamen had agreed to smuggle literature aboard ship.[429]

The non-white seaport communities needed the help and attention which they got both from Communists and the LCP. A Special Restriction (Coloured Alien Seamen) Order in 1925 ordered that all "coloured" seamen must register with the police, and be issued with identity cards, unless they could prove that they were British subjects, which was not always easy.[430] Ten years later the Black and Arab seamen were hit by a government measure to rescue the British shipping industry after the Depression: the British Shipping (Assistance) Act of 1935, under which there was a government subsidy available on condition that preference was given to seamen and firemen of British nationality. In practice many non-white men had no proof of their British nationality, because of the application of the 1925 Order, and were refused jobs. Hundreds were thus deprived of work and destitution followed in the "Coloured" community of Cardiff. The LCP investigated the situation at its worst in 1935 (it improved later) and was always concerned about these proletarian non-white communities.

In Liverpool the African Churches Mission and Training Home, opened in 1931 by the Nigerian pastor G. Daniels Ekarte (who was a patron of the IASB[431]), did excellent work among the non-white community in the city.[432] In great contrast, some others who showed concern about Black waterfront communities did so under the influence of a widespread pathological prejudice against African-European children. A survey commissioned by the Liverpool Association for the Welfare of Half-Caste Children produced a report in 1930 depicting such children

---

429   Howe (note 36), p. 66.

430   *Immigrants and Minorities* vol. 13 nos. 2 & 3, July/November 1994, special issue on "Ethnic Labour and British Imperial Trade: A History of Ethnic Seafarers in the UK", ed. D. Frost, especially T. Lane, "The Political Imperatives of Bureaucracy and Empire: The Case of the Coloured Alien Seamen Order, 1925", pp. 104-29; K. Little, *Negroes in Britain: A Study of Racial Relations in British Society*, Kegan Paul, Trench, Trubner & Co., 1947 (pp. 64-81).

431   Assuming that he was the "Rev. Daniel Escarte" named in Kell to Howard, CO, 21 June 1937, CO 323/1517/2.

432   See correspondence about the Mission's appeal for funds on 8 February 1937, in file CO 847/8/11; Marika Sherwood, *Pastor Daniels Ekarte and the African Churches Mission, Liverpool, 1931-1964,* London: Savannah Press, 1994.

as a problem contributing to moral decline. This report was condemned by the LCP, but its attitudes were widespread. Lamentably they were shared by Sir John Harris (knighted in 1933), head of the Anti-Slavery and Aborigines Protection Society. The excellent work he and his Society had done for decades to expose enslavement and oppression of Africans was in contrast (but he apparently did not see the contrast) with his actions as a member of a deputation to the Home Office in July 1936, which deplored sexual relations between Black and white and suggested gradual repatriation of Black seamen; for the half-caste children, Harris urged that "steps might be found for raising the standard of these children nearer to that of the white races rather than leave them to drift down to that of the black."[433] This sounds very like what was being done at that time, and for decades before and after, to children of Aboriginal mothers and white fathers in Australia—the "stolen children" forcibly removed from their mothers and given to white families. In 1929 the Chief Constable of Cardiff advocated legislation like "the recently passed 1927 Immorality Act in South Africa." Fortunately this idea was not pursued, and a few years later, in Cardiff, the Nigerian seaman Henry Bassey married a white English wife and had five children with her, including the singer Shirley Bassey. There was always resistance in Britain to the more extreme racist proposals, but it is as well to remember how recently those were considered respectable in Britain.

Others besides seamen and their children also suffered from racism in Britain; African students wrote about it frequently at this time in the *West African Review* of Liverpool. The LCP campaigned actively against racism, and Moody was a member of a Joint Council to Promote Understanding between White and Coloured People in Great Britain, founded in 1931; among other members were Winifred Holtby and her friend Vera Brittain. Holtby was a leading English friend of Africans until her early death in 1935; she joined other colonial liberals in founding the Friends of Africa in 1934,[434] to aid Ballinger's co-operative work in South Africa. The "race problem" was a constant preoccupation of the British colonial liberal group in the 1930s, but—unlike the LCP, which favoured independence for the colonies—its members com-

---

433   C. Holmes, *John Bull's Island*, Basingstoke: Macmillan, 1988, pp. 156-7.
434   Bush (note 39), p. 194.

monly accepted colonial rule.[435] They concentrated attention on settler domination in Kenya and the worsening racist regime in South Africa; the attention was certainly justified, but some went on to over-praise British rule in West Africa where there were no settlers. However, some of them, notably Creech Jones, were ready to listen to West Africans' protests and back them in the later 1930s.

West Africans' protests were directed constantly against Indirect Rule, which for Britain was the very basis of a colonial system supposed to continue indefinitely. The alternative to rigid application of that policy was increased elective representation of Africans in legislative councils given increased powers—as nationalists demanded, like the Nigerian Youth Movement whose Youth Charter declared, "We shall strive for the complete abolition of the Indirect Rule system".[436] Africans saw clearly what Norman Leys had written back in 1924: "In the end the franchise is the only weapon by which a subject race or class can win emancipation".[437] In the Gold Coast a widespread demand for progress towards representative parliamentary government was noted by Professor Macmillan on a visit.[438] Macmillan also studied the complexities of society in the cocoa growing areas of the Gold Coast—an intricate land tenure pattern including landlords and tenants, virtual buying and selling of land, employment of proletarians from the Northern Territories, growth of a class of African buying agents, investment of cocoa earnings in house building, etc.—and commented that much of this was "still unknown and unknowable" (to the British rulers, that is) and the simplistic notions of Indirect Rule did not fit such a region at all.[439]

Malcolm MacDonald told a summer school for colonial administrators on leave, at Oxford in June 1938, "The trend is towards the ultimate establishment of the various colonial communities as self-supporting and self-reliant members of a great commonwealth of free peoples and

435   Ibid., pp. 196-201, 228-36.

436   Youth Charter of the NYM, quoted in Asante (note 82), p. 178.

437   N. Leys, *Kenya*, London: Hogarth Press, 1924, p. 363.

438   C.K. Meek, W.M. Macmillan and E.R.J. Hussey, *Europe and West Africa: Some Problems and Adjustments*, OUP 1940 (University of London Heath Clark lectures, 1939), p. 106.

439   Ibid., pp. 80-93, 94-109.

nations." Long afterwards he recalled, "I made it clear that my policy, and the British Government's policy, in all the African colonies was eventually national independence with democratic majority rule."[440] Under MacDonald—who told his Whitehall officials, "I want a seething of ideas"—gradual erosion of the ideas of Indirect Rule, minimal government, and leaving everything to the man on the spot began behind office doors; William Macmillan is said to have been an influence behind this change.[441]

But in the late 1930s those calling for African self-government believed they had a hard struggle ahead. The small band of African and Caribbean radicals went to it with a will, organising and addressing meetings, writing to British dailies and weeklies like the *Manchester Guardian* and *New Statesman*, producing their own periodicals and occasional publications, meeting other activists like the leaders of the LCP, constantly lobbying and making contacts. Makonnen recalled,

Despite the suffering of our people, there was never a gloomy moment, particularly when we realized how much we could do in England: write any tract we wanted to; make terrible speeches; all this when you knew very well that back in the colonies even to say 'God is love' might get the authorities after you![442]

Their life was in fact fairly hard. The IASB's funds may have barely sufficed to pay for the office rent and produce publications on a shoestring, but the organisers lived on very little. Makonnen was a businessman unlike his comrades, and was to establish a number of restaurants in the coming years, and James, Kenyatta and Padmore earned some money from journalism and their books, including James' well known books published in 1938-39 (of which more shortly); James wrote about cricket as well as colonialism and revolution, and Padmore was a correspondent of the *Chicago Defender*.[443] But such income probably did

---

440 Clyde Sanger, *Malcolm MacDonald: Bringing an End to Empire*, Liverpool University Press, 1995, p. 147.

441 Flint (note 388), pp. 213.

442 Makonnen (note 361), p. 123.

443 Hooker (note 3), p. 54. A report from him datelined Berlin, published on 12 November 1938, was most probably written in London from news agency reports; although Hooker suggests that Padmore went back to Germany to report, it is most unlikely that he would have got a visa. Apart from much else, he had dedicated *Africa and World Peace* to Edgar André, a Communist executed by the Nazis.

not go far and generally, for these activists, stimulating talk and activity were combined with a spartan personal life.

They shared the life of the wider Black community in Britain, a generally hard life but with its compensations. Before Makonnen succeeded there was already the restaurant run by Amy Ashwood Garvey, one of the IASB executive. James recalled that Mrs Garvey was "a wonderful cook", while British food, he thought, was awful.[444] In June 1936 Mrs Garvey branched out further; with Sam Manning, who headed the West Indian Rhythm Boys band, and the Guyanese clarinettist Rudolph Dunbar she founded the Florence Mills Social Parlour in Carnaby Street in London, offering food and live music.[445] This was no doubt the "Florence Mill Club" recalled by Makonnen.[446] Black musicians were increasingly popular in Britain in the 1930s, with some "all-coloured" orchestras. There was a flourishing little world of Black entertainment in London,[447] as there was in Paris, where Langston Hughes, revisiting Paris before going to Spain, found that Montmartre in 1937 was "a little Harlem" and Bricktop "the reigning star of the Parisian night",[448] and the French West Indian biguine was a fashionable dance.[449]

The IASB activists in London were recalled much later by a Sierra Leonean who, as a young girl then called Constance Horton, went to England for studies in 1935. She recalled that Major Hanns Vischer, Secretary of the Colonial Office Educational Advisory Committee from 1929 to 1939, refused to give her a recommendation to go to the USA

---

444   Interview, C.L.R. James, 4 June 1984.

445   H. Rye, "Fearsome Means of Discord: Early Encounters with Black Jazz", ch. 3 of P. Oliver (ed.), *Black Music in Britain*, Open University Press, 1990, p. 63.

446   Makonnen (note 361), p. 130. "Mills" was correct as the name of the African American artiste who had died young in 1927.

447   J. Green, "Afro-American Symphony: Popular Black Concert Hall Performers 1900-1940", Ch. 2 (pp. 39-41), H. Rye (note 445) (pp. 53-7) and C. Stapleton, "African Connections: London's Hidden Music Scene", Ch. 5 (pp. 91-3), in P. Oliver (ed.) (note 445); R.E. Lotz, "Will Garland's Negro Operetta Company" (ch. 10), R. Funk, "Three Afro-American Singing Groups" (ch. 11), H. Rye, "The Southern Syncopated Orchestra" (ch. 15) and J. Cowley, "West Indian Gramophone Recordings in Britain, 1927-1950" (ch. 17) in R. Lotz and O. Pegg (eds), *Under the Imperial Carpet: Essays in Black History 1786-1950*, Crawley: Rabbit Press, 1986.

448   Rampersad (note 27), p. 342.

449   See the reminiscences of the Senegalese veterinarian and writer Birago Diop, *La plume rabutée*, Paris: Présence Africaine 1978, vol. 1.

for further studies, saying, "Do you want to be a Wallace-Johnson or an Azikiwe in Africa? Do you want to go and be the Governor of Sierra Leone?" However, she did go to the USA for a few months in 1936-37. Back in London for a time in 1937, she married Ethnan Cummings-John, a fellow countryman, and became involved in politics. Besides joining the Executive Committee of the LCP,

After my return [to Britain], I became very involved with the International African Service Bureau (IASB) organised by I.T.A. Wallace-Johnson. I met him one Sunday afternoon in Hyde Park...Because of what Major Vischer had said about Wallace-Johnson, I was very eager to hear what he had to say, so I went near his platform and listed to his speech. What he said impressed me very much, given my new outlook. All that I had thought of the white man's country, he confirmed. When he finished, I left my companions and went to talk with him. I just let off steam. Then he invited me to join the IASB, so afterwards I often went to the tiny office in Gray's Inn Road where they planned strategy, talked about colonial problems, discussed plans for demonstrations and other action. There I met George Padmore, Sylvia Pankhurst and Jomo Kenyatta.[450]

Constance Cummnings-John returned to Freetown later in 1937, became a very young principal of a girls' school, and founded a Freetown branch of the LCP, before becoming a leading activist in Wallace-Johnson's West African Youth League.

London, Paris and Freetown, 1938-39

The menacing international situation was the backdrop to the anti-colonial campaigning in Africa and Europe in the later 1930s, and the activists were of course constantly aware of it. They were all, naturally, horrified by Fascism and Nazism. They spoke out against the German colonial restoration claim, for example, and in *International African Opinion* criticised Africans who saw Japan, which joined Germany and Italy in the Anti-Comintern Pact in December 1937, as a possible ally;[451] some Africans did have such ideas in South Africa,[452] but the Jap-

---

450   C.A. Cummings-John, *Constance Agatha Cummings-John: Memoirs of a Krio Leader*, with introduction and annotation by LaRay Denzer, Sam Bookman for Humanities Research Centre, Ibadan, 1995, pp. x-xi, xxvi, 18-23, 37-8.

451   *International African Opinion* vol. 1 no. 2, August 1938, enclosed in file CO 323/1610/2 (note 375).

452   Bunting (note 13), p. 111.

anese, who had aroused other non-Europeans' admiration for decades by their skill in emulating the West's industrial and military strength while retaining their independence and traditions, were now using their strength to kill vast numbers of fellow Asians in China.

However, Padmore, Kenyatta and their comrades refused to consider that the menace of Germany, Italy and Japan should stop them concentrating on British imperialism. They continued to see this as their number one enemy. They probably had doubts, as many did at the time, whether the Chamberlain government was ever likely to fight Nazi Germany. Such doubts were reinforced, for a time, by the Munich pact of September 1938, and were felt in both Moscow and Berlin. At the time of the crisis leading up to Munich the IASB produced a manifesto entitled "Europe's Difficulty is Africa's Opportunity",[453] reflecting the view that Africans had nothing to do with Europe's conflicts and must defend their own interests.

The IASB's views were close to those of the ILP, whose weekly newspaper expressed concern in April 1938 that "there is a great danger at the present time that our hatred of the tyranny of Fascism may cause us to forget the tyranny of Imperialism."[454] Padmore and Kenyatta suggested that British imperialism was not very different from Nazism and Fascism. Kenyatta, in the course of lecturing around Britain in 1938-39,[455] told a meeting of the Manchester Fabian Society in October 1938,

I not only say there is British fascism in the colonies but can give you examples and facts for you to judge whether the Jews in Germany are treated worse than we are in the colonies. The natives have no freedom of speech, freedom of association, or freedom of movement.[456]

This echoed Padmore's views expressed in *How Britain Rules Africa*: "If the British people silently condone racial injustice within their Empire, we fail to see what moral right they have to criticise the Nazis for their inhuman treatment of the Jews."[457] Similarly Diana Stock wrote,

---

453   Hooker (note 3), p. 53.

454   *New Leader*, 29 April 1938.

455   D.C. Savage, "Jomo Kenyatta, Malcolm MacDonald and the Colonial Office 1938-39: Some Documents from the P.R.O.", *Canadian Journal of African Studies*, 3, 3, 1969, pp. 615-32.

456   Murray-Brown (note 15), p. 203.

457   Padmore (note 359), p. 103.

"Even Hitler's anti-Semitism is trivial compared with the indignities which Africans suffer on British African soil."[458]

It was fair enough to remind Europeans that controls over people's movements, often resembling those now being imposed in the European totalitarian states, had been imposed for some time in Africa, especially in South Africa, Southern Rhodesia (which imposed laws similar to South Africa's pass laws) and the Belgian Congo, a country of exceptionally tight police controls. However, comparisons with Hitler's Germany were excessive even in view of what was known of the Nazis in 1938. They were no doubt intended to provoke, but also to reinforce the anti-colonial radicals' main point: that the German threat must not affect the struggle against British and French imperialism. This view, directly contrary to that of the French Communist Party, was held by many anti-colonialists in France also.

A number of people were shocked by the PCF's change of colonial policy and rejected it, such as Gouttenoire de Toury, a militant of the early 1920s, who in 1939 published a pamphlet, *Le Front populaire ruiné par ses chefs*.[459] The Gauche Révolutionnaire, the left faction within the SFIO, had called from its foundation in October 1935 for the "liberation of the colonial peoples", though also saying socialism must be upheld "against native feudal, capitalist and petty-bourgeois elements".[460] In fact its leaders, who broke away to form Parti Socialiste Ouvrier et Paysan (PSOP) in 1938, gave priority to anti-imperialist agitation. The main leaders were Guérin, Marceau Pivert and Colette Audry; they declared that the colonies had a right to independence.[461]

On 6 March 1937 Africans and other people from the colonies in France formed a Rassemblement Colonial, as a grouping of organisations, including militantly anti-colonial ones but others too. The list of these, published in the *Journal Officiel* of 16 June 1937, included the LDRN, the PPA and the UTN. There were also two organisations of

458   *New Leader*, 6 May 1938.
459   Randrianja (note 243), p. 358n.
460   Liauzu (note 135), p. 66; Biondi (note 132), pp. 217-18.
461   B. Stora, "La Gauche Socialiste, Révolutionnaire, et la Question du Maghreb au moment du Front populaire (1935-1938)", *Revue Française d'Histoire d'Outremer* vol. LXX, 1983, no. 258-9, 1st-2nd quarters, pp. 57-79 (pp. 63, 68).

Cameroonians in France, the Association France-Cameroun of Joseph Ebele and the Comité (National) de Défense des Intérêts du Cameroun; and the Comité d'Entente Malgache, a former LAI affiliate headed by Ramananjato. The Malagasy militant Dussac, who had quarrelled with the PCF, also took part in the Rassemblement's activities, speaking for example at a meeting on 21 November 1937 with Balafrej, Radjef and Bourguiba.[462] The provisional executive consisted of Messali, Faure, Nguyen The Truyen, Ramananjato and two West Indians; Faure became secretary general. There was also an honorary committee including leading French anti-colonial figures: Challaye, Berthon, Jean and Robert-Jean Longuet, Rolland, Viollis, Spielman, Joseph Lagrosillière.

The Rassemblement sought a special position as colonial representative with the Front Populaire, and declared that it would work "within the framework of republican institutions".[463] The groups joining it differed on many points, but it was able to send petitions and delegations to the ministry of the Colonies, calling for political and trade union freedom and protesting at the idea of colonial appeasement of Germany for example. But this broad unity attempt did not last. On 10 December 1937 Faure adopted a much more critical tone, saying, "the Rassemblement Colonial believes that emancipation of the colonies is the primordial condition for peace".[464] The Communist-affiliated UTN left in November 1937, doubtless because of the Rassemblement's increasingly critical attitude; the Comité d'Entente Malgache also left.[465]

The French Communist view, that Nazism was such an extreme danger that opposing it must for the time being have priority over ending colonialism, helped wreck the plans to make the Moroccans of the Spanish zone change sides in the Civil War, as recorded above, while the non-Communist activists involved were trying to strike a serious blow against Franco and hence against Hitler. Even so, that PCF view could strike even non-party members as reasonable. Garan Kouyate, who had been expelled by the Communists years before and whose magazine

---

462   Liauzu (note 135), pp. 66-7. Dussac however died in France on 12 March 1938; according to Biondi (note 132; p. 220) he collapsed and died of starvation in a Paris street.

463   Liauzu (note 135), pp. 203-4; Dewitte (note 1), pp. 370-5.

464   Dewitte (note 1), pp. 373-4, quoting ANSOM source.

465   Dewitte (note 1), pp. 374.

Africa was backed by Gaston Bergery and his Parti Frontiste, also saw resisting Nazism as a priority. The magazine ceased to appear after the August-September 1938 issue, which called for a firm stance against Germany over the Sudeten crisis, going against the views of Bergery, an "appeaser". Dewitte's research found records, covering ten months between August 1938 and August 1939, of regular payments from a secret fund of the Ministry of Colonies to Kouyate, but he considers that the sums paid, 1,500 francs per month, were not nearly enough to run the magazine.[466] Kouyate also published *Le Jeune Sénégal* which became *La Jeune Afrique* in January 1939.[467]

In contrast to Padmore's old friend Kouyate, Emile Faure had ideas similar to those of the IASB, whose periodical reported his speech to a Conference on Peace and Empire, with Nehru in the chair, at Friends' House in London in 1938, as President of the LDRN and Secretary of the Rassemblement Colonial. He said illusions aroused by the Popular Front had been destroyed, people of the colonies did not trust the democracies or "anti-Fascist" slogans, and they must struggle for independence.[468] This was the theme of the new groups of anti-colonialists in Britain and France: European left-wingers were abandoning support for African and other colonised people's demands, and concern over the Nazi menace, however justified, was not a sufficient reason for doing so. Others thought it was a sufficient reason; anyway the fact—that many left-wingers considered the Nazi-Fascist menace a more urgent problem than colonialism or white supremacy—was certain. In South Africa, while there was plenty of anti-Nazi press coverage and activity throughout the 1930s—an all-white People's Front against Fascism was formed, including the CPSA—some anti-Nazis condemned the Greyshirts but did not back Africans against the pass laws and other disabilities.[469] Communists could still call for reforms in the colonial or white supremacy order in Africa, even though they had to oppose colonial independence in France for reasons of Soviet foreign policy, as suggested above; in Britain, with the *Colonial Information Bulletin*, they

---

466   Ibid., pp. 382-3.

467   Liauzu (note 135), p. 167n. This ephemeral publication had nothing to do with the *Jeune Afrique* founded in 1960.

468   *International African Opinion*, vol. 1 no. 2, Aug. 1938 (see note 375).

469   Simons (note 164), p. 481.

still put themselves forward as an anti-imperialist party. However, an editorial in the *New Leader*—echoing like-minded French criticisms of the PCF—condemned a new Communist statement of colonial policy; this called for a "Charter of Rights" for colonial peoples, involving very sweeping reforms, but the editorial said the colonial peoples would not be satisfied: "They want national independence."[470]

Fenner Brockway, editor of the *New Leader*, was a veteran anti-militarist, an example of the close links between anticolonialism and antimilitarism that were still apparent. Challaye was another clear illustration; after publishing *Pour la paix sans aucune réserve* in 1932, he reaffirmed his pacifist principles after Hitler's assumption of power, and published in 1934 *Pour la paix désarmé, même en face d'Hitler*. On both sides of the English Channel there were prominent individuals and groups determined to oppose imperialism regardless of the looming danger of war; in any case, while totally rejecting Nazism, they did not support the idea of, or preparations for, war against it. They were far from being alone in opposing such preparations in Britain, where the influence of pacifists like the Peace Pledge Union was considerable.

The IASB leaders were close to the ILP but kept out of British left-wing politics, except for James, a strong supporter of Trotsky's new Fourth International founded in September 1938; eventually he broke with the ILP, which refused to affiliate to that International.[471] He and his comrades in the IASB had some differences of outlook but still worked together well in the Bureau. In 1938 James' book *World Revolution: The Rise and Fall of the Communist International*, an early anti-Stalinist Communist work describing Stalin as a betrayer of the revolution, was published in 1938 by Secker & Warburg, a firm established in 1936 by Martin Secker and Brockway's friend Frederick Warburg. James also translated a similar condemnation of Stalin by Boris Souvarine, one of the earliest French Communist leaders who had broken with the PCF.[472]

Earlier James had written a play, *Toussaint L'Ouverture*, which opened at London's Westminster Theatre in 1936, with Paul Robeson in the title role, and in 1938 he published his most famous book, *The*

---

470   *New Leader*, 3 June 1938.

471   Buhle (note 192), pp. 48-51; Robinson (note 94), pp. 180-94.

472   *Stalin*, published in 1939; see Buhle (note 192), pp. 51-3.

Black Jacobins, a study of the Haitian revolution. About the same time he also published *A History of Negro Revolt*, covering revolts in the USA as well as in Haiti.[473] His general theme was to emphasise what Africans and their transported descendants had done for themselves; like his fellow Trinidadian Eric Williams, he sought to minimise the role of white philanthropists in the abolition of slavery and the slave trade. Williams did research, about the same time as James, for an Oxford DPhil thesis, "The Economic Aspect of the Abolition of the West Indian Slave Trade and Slavery". His downgrading of the role of Wilberforce and other abolitionists went against received ideas, and when he tried to get his thesis published,

> Britain's most revolutionary publisher, Warburg, who would publish all of Stalin and Trotsky, told me, 'Mr Williams, are you trying to tell me that the slave trade and slavery were abolished for economic and not for humanitarian reasons? I would never publish such a book, for it would be contrary to British tradition'.[474]

Eventually he did publish *Capitalism and Slavery* in the USA in 1944.

The Black Jacobins, based on research in French archives, is a very readable history in which James' analysis of the links between the French Revolution and developments in Saint Domingue (Haiti), making comparisons with the Russian Revolution, eschews unreadable Marxist jargon. But James, while a good journalist, was a Marxist thinker too. Of course it was the historical facts, not Marxist analysis that led James to emphasise the differences and conflicts between the "Mulattoes" and the black majority in Saint-Domingue (Haiti); but he saw class or similar distinctions as generally important in anti-colonial struggles, as at the end of the book where he made comparisons with contemporary Africa: after quoting one of the Northern Rhodesia strikers of 1935, he wrote,

---

473   Ibid., pp. 56-7, 59-62; Robinson (note 94), pp. 192-4. A new edition of *The Black Jacobins* was published by Penguin in 2001.

474   Eric Williams, *Inward Hunger: The Education of a Prime Minister*, Andre Deutsch, 1969, p. 53. Arguments like those of Williams and James were heard again in the recent bicentennial commemorations of the abolition of the slave trade by Britain. They are overstated: slave trading was still very big business in 1807, there was a belated but genuine moral revolt against it in Britain. But of course nothing can detract from the huge impact the successful slave revolution in Haiti had on Europe and its Caribbean slave colonies.

From the people heaving in action will come the leaders; not the isolated blacks at Guy's Hospital or the Sorbonne, the dabblers in *surréalisme* or the lawyers, but the quiet recruits in a black police force, the sergeant in the French native army or British police, familiarizing himself with military tacts and strategy, reading a stray pamphlet of Lenin or Trotsky as Toussaint read the Abbé Raynal.[475]

As has been emphasised in this work, the idea that independence for colonies either should, or inevitably would, mean power for the masses and not for privileged indigenous minorities was a general and constant left-wing idea, not confined to Communists but maintained by them and by Trotskyists, whose ideology was essentially Communism minus Stalin. James made an early formulation of Trotskyist views on imperialism, and he, as well as Du Bois and later the African American novelist Richard Wright, sought to separate the history of Black peoples' revolts and resistance from Western-centred theory and emphasise their importance in their own right.[476] But class-based ideas, whether uttered by Stalinists, Trotskyists or democratic Socialists, did not take root in Africa. In the nationalist movements developing from the 1940s graduates of Western universities and medical schools played an important part, however decisive was the role of the wider Western-influenced communities to which James referred, and to which Wallace Johnson had already appealed in the 1930s.

I.T.A. Wallace Johnson, James' colleague in the IASB leadership, left Britain in April 1938 to return to Sierra Leone, where he landed on 20 April. Customs confiscated 2,000 copies of the March-April issue of the *African Sentinel* in his luggage; this led to protests in London, in which the NCCL, Creech Jones and Sorensen took part, and gave Wallace Johnson a good start in his new campaign against the colonial government. He quickly set up, on 12 May 1938, a Sierra Leone branch of the West African Youth League, which was immediately popular. A rousing and popular speaker, he attracted hundreds of people to meetings, many at the Wilberforce Memorial Hall.[477]

---

475 James, *The Black Jacobins* (note 473), p. 304.

476 Robinson (note 84), pp. 251-7, 265-86, 313-16; A. Callinicos, *Trotskyism*, Milton Keynes: Open University Press, 1990, pp. 62-3.

477 For Wallace Johnson's activities in 1938-39 see especially Denzer (note 16), pp. 170ff; L. Spitzer, *The Creoles of Sierra Leone*, Madison and London: University of Wisconsin Press, 1974, pp. 183-216; Leo Spitzer and La Ray Denzer, "I.T.A.

The WAYL's demands, as submitted to the Governor on 16 June 1938, were fairly modest for an organisation whose motto was "Liberty or Death". It called for increased African representation in government and a commission of inquiry into the situation in Sierra Leone, attacked the censorship, criticised four recent Ordinances (on education, rural areas, "Native Administration" and minerals), and attacked poor work conditions.[478] But the WAYL wanted to see universal suffrage without property qualifications, which if applied to both the Colony and the Protectorate would have meant the end of colonial rule as it was known,[479] and the formal demands do not indicate the mood Wallace Johnson succeeded in arousing in Freetown. He spoke for the common man and woman, not only against the British but also against the Creole upper class. Wallace Johnson contrasted himself, "a man of the people", with one eminent Creole leader in particular: Dr Herbert Bankole Bright of the NCBWA, member of LegCo, the leading politician in Sierra Leone until Wallace Johnson came back. The two became sworn enemies. There was similar hostility in Nigeria between the older NNDP under Macaulay and the NYM at this time; in each case, by attacking the older generation of politicians, seen as too weak, the "young" faction was really attacking the British.

The extent and popularity of the popular campaign led by Wallace Johnson had no precedent in colonial Africa, even in his earlier WAYL activities in the Gold Coast. It was largely confined to Freetown; efforts to get support in the Protectorate had little success, but in the capital he was the hero of the streets. As Constance Cummings-John, one of the WAYL Central Committee, recalled,

Wallace-Johnson exposed the British, he was fearless, he became our idol. Our people crowded into the meetings, often gathering at the venue hours before the scheduled time. Sometimes the crowd grew so large that many people had to stand outside the hall....[480]

Wallace Johnson and the West African Youth League", *International Journal of African Historical Studies* vol. VI no. 3, 1973, pp. 413-52 and vol. VI no. 4, pp. 565-601; A.J. Wyse, *H.C. Bankole-Bright and Politics in Colonial Sierra Leone, 1919-1958*, CUP 1990, pp. 118-32; Cummings-John (note 450), pp. 42-55; Farid Anthony, *Sawpit Boy*, Freetown: published by author, 1980, pp. 93-115.

478   Denzer (note 16), p. 202.
479   Spitzer and Denzer (note 477), pp. 582-3.
480   Cummings-John (note 450), p. 49.

Despite its leader's class propaganda many of the top Creole elite also supported the WAYL. In elections for four of the twelve elective African seats in the Freetown Municipal Council in November 1938 all the list of candidates put up by the WAYL were elected.[481]

The party attracted clerks in particular. Government office workers were not allowed to join, but many did (the WAYL refused to submit a list of members as the authorities demanded); some gave further help by leaking information.[482] Sydney Boyle, who resigned as a senior customs clerk with UAC and worked actively for the WAYL, estimated its paid-up membership at 4-5,000; the number of supporters was certainly much higher. Generally the WAYL in Sierra Leone appealed to groups of people—clerks, railwaymen, teachers, clergymen, posts and telegraphs staff, etc.—that were to form much of the rank and file of nationalist parties from the 1940s, joined by market women and other business people who were also among the WAYL's supporters in Freetown in 1938-39. Six new trade unions were founded as a by-product of the WAYL's activity, and a Sierra Leone Trade Union Congress.[483]

What Wallace Johnson appealed to was a general desire for a better deal: "Now is the time and now is the hour. There is only one way out of our difficulties, and that is to organize and move."[484] He did not need to spell out a detailed programme to get support for what was essentially an "anti" movement. What he did was to *attack*, in the press as well as at meetings; while much of the press soon turned against him, in January 1939 he started the WAYL's own newspaper, the *African Standard*.[485]

While Wallace Johnson was rousing Freetown, back in London the IASB was in decline. The Colonial Office received information suggesting that Wallace Johnson left England following an audit of the IASB's books, which showed "that he had been mixing up the funds of the Bureau with his own—to his advantage";[486] and according to MI5 Wallace

481   Denzer (note 16), pp. 2354-43; Anthony (note 477), pp. 97-8.

482   Denzer (note 16), p. 221-2.

483   Ibid., p. 215.

484   Spitzer and Denzer (note 477), p. 567.

485   Anthony (note 477), p. 111.

486   M.M. Milne-Thomson, Sierra Leone Battalion, Royal West African Fontier Force, to Major W.H.A. Bishop, Colonial Office, secret, 14 April 1938, CO 323/1610/2, National Archives, London.

Johnson was dismissed for misappropriation.[487] If there was any truth in this, his comrades kept quiet about it, and it might not have done him much harm in Freetown anyway. Wallace Johnson was replaced as secretary of the IASB by Wilkey. The Colonial Office note recording this said of that Nigerian,

He is known to hold communist opinions, but his activities have not been registered with any concern in Nigeria, and he is unlikely to carry much weight as secretary of the Bureau. It seems possible, therefore, that the policy of the International African Service Bureau will remain in the hands of the Trotskyist, George Padmore.[488]

At some point in 1938-39 the IASB left its offices at 94 Grays Inn Road and established new ones at 12a Westbourne Grove. In October 1938 C.L.R. James left for the United States, where he was to live for many years. Among the remaining leaders of the IASB there was more internal dissension, to judge by reports reaching the authorities. The Special Branch reported on 27 February 1939 that Wilkey had been expelled from the IASB and Makonnen was no longer active in it, but still lived at 12a Westbourne Grove, with Harrison, and was trying to form a West Indian Co-operative Alliance; the Bureau was carried on by Padmore, Jones, Harrison and Kenyatta, though "most of the subscriptions in the past few months have gone into the pockets of WILKEY and MAKONNEN." Meetings were held at Padmore's home at 42 Alderney Street, SW.[489] In April 1939 the Colonial Office informed the Governor of Nigeria and other governors that "Edward Sigismund, alias Babalola Wilkey" had started a Negro Cultural Association at 41 Grafton Way, London W1, and added,

Wilkey is regarded as little more than a rather ineffective crook, but his organisation is affiliated to the National Council of Civil Liberties and is, therefore, of some interest.

By then the IASB's former headquarters at 12a Westbourne Grove was being used by the West Indian Co-operative Alliance being set up

---

487   "Communism and the West Indian Labour Disturbances" (note 33), Appendix pp. 2-3.

488   E.B. Boyd of Colonial Office, letter of 28 June 1938, CO 323/1610/2, National Archives, London.

489   Cross-Ref. 28 February 1939, enclosing Special branch report 27 February 1939, file KV2/1787, National Archives, London.

by Harrison, and the IASB had moved to 35 St Bride Street, London EC, headquarters of the ILP, with Padmore in charge, assisted by Kenyatta and "Chris Braithwaite, alias Jones".[490]

Wilkie (representing the Negro Cultural Association) and Kenyatta attended a conference on 21 January 1939 at Friends' House in London, where Fenner Brockway presided and it was decided to set up a British Centre Against Imperialism. This was to be headed by a council of nineteen members, ten from the colonial peoples and nine from British anti-imperialists;[491] Dinah Stock became its secretary. Guérin, who attended this meeting, joined in founding in France a Bureau de Défense des Peuples Colonisés, set up in March 1939 and joined by the PSOP, the Trotskyists, revolutionary trade unionists and pacifists. Its secretariat consisted of Robert-Jean Longuet (whose father had died the previous year), Marc Casati and Colette Audry; major participants were Challaye, Berthon, Louzon and Guérin.[492] A separate body, the Centre (de Liaison) Anti-Impérialiste, held its constituent general meeting on 29 April 1939 and drew up an Anti-Imperialist Charter. The PPA, the Neo-Destour, Faure's LDRN and the Rassemblement Colonial adhered to the Centre, and Faure was its secretary for black Africa.[493] This Centre was clearly modelled by Guérin on the British one. For some reason it apparently did not replace the Bureau de Défense, whose ideas were similar or identical. As war approached charges were brought against the Bureau de Défense following articles in the periodical *Solidarité Internationale Antifasciste*; on 31 July 1939 Louzon and three others were convicted.[494]

In Britain the anti-colonialists who stated clearly that colonial peoples must not support Britain in any new international war remained free to publish their views as war approached; Padmore spoke at a conference of coloured peoples at Memorial Hall, Farringdon Street, London,

490   O.G.R. Williams of Colonial Office to governors, 11 April 1939, CO 323/1690/5, National Archives, London.

491   *New Leader*, 20 and 27 January 1939; Hooker (note 3), p. 55.

492   Liauzu (note 135), p. 67.

493   Dewitte (note 1), pp. 379-80; Liauzu (note 135), pp. 67-8; Biondi (note 132), pp. 226; Stora (note 461), pp. 69-72. Stora suggests that the Bureau de Défense was founded in November 1938.

494   Liauzu (note 135), p. 68.

on 7-9 July 1939.[495] But things were different in Sierra Leone, where the approach of war, in which Freetown would be a vital naval base, was an extra reason for the British authorities to feel exasperated that the laws existing in Freetown since the liberal Victorian era were insufficient to stop Wallace Johnson's agitation—which Governor Jardine inevitably thought to be "inspired and probably partially financed by London Communists".[496] The government introduced six bills before the Legislative Council to rectify the situation from its viewpoint: the Undesirable British Subjects Control Bill, Sedition Bill, Undesirable Publications Bill, Incitement to Disaffection Bill, Trade Union Bill and Trade Disputes (Arbitration and Inquiry) Bill. There were strong protests against these measures by the WAYL, including a great demonstration on 16 May 1939, when markets were empty and children missed school as thousands marched on LegCo. There were also protests in Britain; Creech Jones, Bridgeman and Pankhurst protested against the Undesirable Literature Bill. But Bankole-Bright supported the bills in Legco and they were passed by June 1939.[497]

As war with Germany drew near, the problems of utterly sincere people confronted by utterly evil ones became acute. Charles Roden Buxton, a leading Labour critic of colonialism and a passionate peace campaigner, ended up pleading with the Nazis to accept African colonies as a price for peace. Challaye had favoured revision of the peace treaties in the cause of his pacifism, which was soon to lead him to favour surrender to Germany and collaboration. Many other people's strongly felt ideas were thrown into disarray at that time, including especially French and British Communists, who had to defend the Nazi-Soviet pact of 23 August 1939 and soon afterwards to condemn the war as an "imperialist war" in which neither side was better than the other. In doing so, ironically, they shared the views of the groups led by Padmore, Brockway and others, their bitter opponents on imperial issues in recent years (as recently as the London meeting in July, where Padmore had clashed with Communists).

---

495   Hooker (note 3), p. 55.
496   Spitzer and Denzer (note 477), p. 584.
497   Cummings-John (note 450), pp. 53-4; Spitzer and Denzer (note 477), pp. 589-94; Wyse (note 477), pp. 124-9; Asante (note 82), pp.192-8.

On 29 August 1939 the IASB and the British Centre Against Imperialism issued "A Warning to the Colonial Peoples". It poured scorn on the idea that the imminent war would be for Poland; the real reason was to stop Hitler overrunning Europe and stealing colonies from other powers; if democratic nations were so concerned with defending smaller nations, why had Mussolini been allowed to occupy Ethiopia? "What do you know of democracy in the Empire?" it went on, before calling openly for opposition to the coming Western war effort:

The colonial masses in war, as in peace, can have only one aim, one goal—INDEPENDANCE (sic). And we summon you in whatever country—India, Ceylon, Burma, Palestine, Africa—all people who fight for this end, to unite against the warmongers, both Democratic and Fascist, and all those who at this hour pledge in your name your living in defence of the Imperialists...

We denounce the whole gang of European robbers and enslavers of the colonial peoples—German Nazis, Italian Fascists, French, British, Belgian and Dutch democrats—all are the same IMPERIALIST BANDITS whose common aim is the enslavement of humanity throughout the world.[498]

The MI5 chief said this probably was mainly the work of Padmore, and contravened DR (Defence Regulations) 39B.

Padmore was not arrested, and the war did not halt all the activity of the black organisations in Britain; its continuation is another story that cannot be told here. But in Sierra Leone Wallace Johnson was arrested soon after the outbreak of war, and charged with criminal libel over an article in the *African Standard* of 11 August 1939, suggesting that a British District Commissioner had ordered the killing of an African. He received a one-year sentence, but was to remain in prison or detention until near the end of the war.[499]

In France, on the eve of the outbreak of war Faure and Guérin made a bold plan to rescue Allal al-Fassi from Gabon. They got a promise of help from a senior official of Air France, but the plan was dropped when war began.[500] It may not have had much chance of success anyway; the Air France official or an accomplice might perhaps have smuggled al-

---

498   Enclosed with [Col. Sir Vernon] Kell to Police Commissioner R.C.A. Cavendish, Kenya, 10 Oct. 1939, in file KV2/1787, National Archives, London.

499   Anthony (note 477), pp. 114-15.

500   Biondi (note 132), p. 226.

Fassi onto an aeroplane, but with the slow flights of the time, it would have been difficult to get him as far as Morocco or France before his escape was discovered. Emile Faure was arrested on 9 December 1939 because of letters he had sent to correspondents in Ivory Coast on behalf of the Centre Anti-Impérialiste, and sent to detention in Ivory Coast and then French Sudan.[501]

Many Africans in Germany were put in concentration camps, mostly after the outbreak of war, and a number died there.[502] Africans living in France, however, generally suffered no special ill-treatment after the German occupation in 1940. But Tiemoko Garan Kouyate was shot by the Nazis in 1942; there still seems to be some mystery about this, but one explanation is that he was executed for embezzling money given for propaganda among Black people.[503] The Nazis probably did hope to enlist Black people's support, extraordinary as it seems, though they concentrated more on North Africans in France, with some success.[504] But the wretched story about Kouyate is not proved; the Nazis had many things against him from his past activity. Also mysterious, to this day, is the murder of Willi Münzenberg in France in 1940, though the likely culprits were the NKVD, the Soviet secret police.[505]

The Germans did not occupy any part of Africa in the war except to reinforce their Italian allies, and both were driven out of Ethiopia, Eritrea, Italian Somalia and North Africa. Any consideration of ending colonial rule was put off for the duration in Britain, and by both Vichy and Free French leaders; in the short term, the British and French empires won. But in the longer run, there is no doubt that, for many reasons, the empires that the people described in this book had been opposing for many years with little prospect of success were undermined by the war and had to end.

---

501   Dewitte (note 1), p. 380.
502   Reed-Anderson (note 30), pp. 70-81.
503   Dewitte (note 1), pp. 383-5.
504   Recham (note 139), pp. 144-278.
505   McMeekin (note 172), pp. 304-7.

CONCLUSIONS

The period between the World Wars was the peak of colonial rule in Africa. Almost the whole continent was at peace under colonial or white settler control. The people described in this book, who actively opposed imperialism in one way or another, were always very few in number. Most Africans accepted the situation and tried to get on with normal life, as the majority always does everywhere. Among Europeans the great majority accepted the colonial empires as part of life and saw them as largely beneficial to everyone. And many always had a genuine sense of trusteeship and responsibility towards the colonial subjects. But in the last resort, colonialism was established by armed aggression, imposed and maintained for economic gain, and upheld by racial arrogance. That there was opposition to colonialism does not need explanation.

After the defeat of armed resistance—which had largely ended early in the period under study with two important exceptions, Libya and Spanish Morocco—Africans submitted to the new situation, while desiring improvements in it. But their submission, even when accompanied by obsequious declarations of loyalty that startle their descendants today, was not incompatible with a deep-seated desire to end foreign rule altogether. There were plenty of indications of lasting discontent, shown in some Christian and Muslim movements for example. This book has sought to confirm something that is fairly obvious but that colonialists sometimes professed not to see at the time: discontent was spontaneous, and the people called "agitators", though few in number, expressed wider feelings among their people, while white anti-imperialists provided support but not instigation.

This work has been a study of opposition to alien rule among Africans, and moral objection to colonialism among Europeans. It has only been able to deal far too briefly with either. The history of negative reactions to colonialism all over a great continent is a gigantic subject, if it includes all sorts of underlying discontent as well as organised activity and revolts. Inevitably events in any particular part of Africa have been given only summary attention in these pages, compared with what could be and to some extent has been written about them. But in this summary way, the present work has sought to show that opposition came from below, from among Africans, and that Western critics of colonialism, who provided valuable support and encouragement for Africans, were basically expressing genuine moral objections.

European critics focused attention on forced labour, heavy flat-rate taxation, control over everyday life as applied by the South African pass laws, and occupation of large areas of the best land for settlers. Often they were ready to accept colonial rule if these "abuses" were corrected, and in paternalist style accepted a need for trusteeship provided that the "wards" were better treated. Some were imbued with some of the prejudices of the time, as E.D. Morel and Sir John Harris illustrated. But much of their work of advocacy must still be respected, for they stood up for African victims when almost nobody else was ready to do so.

Missionaries were among those who championed African victims of oppression most consistently. In addition, the Christian evangelisation and education they provided were in the long term to enable and encourage Africans to reject alien rule, and the colonial rulers and propagandists knew this well. While most missionaries favoured colonial rule and, like almost all churchmen everywhere, told their flocks to obey authority, relations between them and the colonial governments were never easy. Still less easy were relations between those governments and the Western-educated Africans. *Africa's 'Agitators'* has not been a study of colonial administration, but it has recalled the extreme prejudice colonial officials commonly had against the "educated native", contrasting with a sentimental paternalism towards the "raw Kaffir". In fact Western-educated people provided loyal and indispensable service to the colonial state. But when they were allowed to do so, as in the British West African Crown Colonies, they also founded newspapers whose regular critical tone added to the officials' hostility to them as a class. So, even more, did organised movements to demand greater African representation.

This demand was at the core of African protest movements. There were demands for unrestricted access to the highest posts in government service—from which Africans had been excluded—and for elective representation. Later movements headed by Africans with Western education called for full self-government or independence or, in South Africa, for rule by the African majority. The earlier, more cautious, demands might seem at first sight like accepting colonial rule and demanding a better share in it. But the colonial or white minority rulers saw them—correctly, as it turned out—as the beginning of a process that would end in self-government and independence, or the abolition of white supremacy. In response they regularly dismissed the claims of "educated natives" forming parties and sending delegations to Europe, saying that they represented only themselves and wanted power only for themselves.

There was much self-delusion in this colonial attitude. By the 1930s, while the majority of Africans were still illiterate farmers, those who were influenced by modern changes—schooling, the growth of towns, international trade, Western culture—were fairly numerous; they were no longer small "elites", though there were true elites within them. The growth of these communities has been illustrated briefly in Chapter Four from the case of the Gold Coast; it was they who backed anti-colonial protests there in the 1930s, and were to form the rank and file of nationalist parties from the 1940s onwards. And while those with Western education, even just a few years of it as many people had, were still a minority, Africans did not want that situation to continue. A consistent, vocal African demand was for more education, which must be Western-style education—British proposals for more "adapted" education were regarded with extreme suspicion as an effort to keep Africans down. And the colonial governments created their own schools, which may have been geared to producing subordinate government staff—like Gordon College in the Sudan and the Ecole William Ponty at Goree in Senegal—but in fact bred many nationalists. However, as always, education did not turn out uniform products: many well-educated Africans were vocally loyal to the colonial rulers.

The record shows little sign of Africans generally preferring the white rulers over their own brothers who had "made good" through Western schooling. The normal attitude to them was to try to follow their example, or urge one's children to do so. When Lugard wrote, "The Europeanised African is indeed separated from the rest of the people by a gulf which no racial affinity can bridge", he was expressing widespread assumptions about psychology and culture that underlay views of Africans—it was thought that an African leaving his tribal background, or still more an African going to university, was bound to be disoriented because of cultural clash or confusion. Such ideas were simplistic at least and the term "detribalised", often used, was misleading. An African graduate's criticisms of European rule most probably reflected what people of his home village thought. Western-educated people did not reject all tradition, least of all chieftaincy, though they did oppose British Indirect Rule policies that were officially supposed to preserve tradition but in fact gave chiefs untraditional powers. On the question of land ownership, a very vital one, well-educated people and ordinary farmers were as one.

At any rate the Western-influenced communities in Africa grew, and led or supported demands for greater representation and power, which eventually came. That was Africa's way forward. The active opponents of imperialism described in this book could encourage and influence the process of change, but it was bound to continue anyway after colonial occupation had disrupted the old order and modernisation of all sorts proceeded.

Among those active opponents, a distinction is made here between those who made modest demands in loyal language, like the National Congress of British West Africa, and those who uttered and encouraged outright condemnations of imperialism. The latter, commonly called "agitators" by the authorities, have been the main theme of this study, which has however recalled that the distinction was not hard and fast: in South Africa the ANC, then a very polite law-abiding organisation, made demands which would have meant the end of white supremacy. But the colonial rulers clearly distinguished the Casely Hayfords from the Wallace Johnsons, the Roden Buxtons from the Bridgemans.

Towards the "agitators" the policies of the British and French were more or less identical. In other respects there were differences in colonial administration, but there was much in common also. In the French empire, the much discussed "assimilation" was not meant in the inter-war era to apply to more than a very small number of Africans, in either its cultural or its legal (French citizenship) sense, and Western-educated Africans generally had no better positions and possibilities than in the British colonies. And of course the privileged few followed their own different ways as individuals: Diagne became a true Black Frenchman, a true Third Republic Freemason politician, while Kouyate became a Communist.

Africans reacted above all to their own situation, but keenly followed events in other parts of the world and were influenced by them (there is of course no contradiction). There was, for example, the influence of the African Diaspora on African anti-colonialism. African American influence was passed through students in the USA, especially from South Africa, and missionaries working in Africa for many decades. The programmes and activities of African American leaders were known to Africans through those channels and through the press, and through contacts in Europe, which extended to African American artists also. None of the leaders had more impact, even if its peak lasted only for a few years, than Marcus Garvey. The admiration he aroused was widespread and lasting—it was expressed by Kwame Nkrumah in a later generation, for example. However, no Garveyite party, nor any lasting Garveyite organisation, was founded in Africa. What came from the Diaspora was inspiration, not any detailed organisation of activity in Africa. The influence was sometimes in a radical direction, as in the case of Garvey, but not always. Azikiwe, returning from the USA, found the ideas of Wallace Johnson, already active in the Gold Coast, too extreme. And there was the strange phenomenon of widespread admiration of Booker T. Washington and James Kwegyir Aggrey (who was African but spent much of his career in the United States) despite their preaching of peaceful cooperation with and submission to white rule. John L. Dube, a leading disciple of Washington, became the first President of the South African Native National Congress.

C.L.R. James, in a later appendix to *The Black Jacobins*, wrote, "Between the wars when [African] emancipation was being prepared, the unquestioned leaders of the movement in every public sphere, in Africa itself, in Europe and in the United States, were not Africans but West Indians." (Penguin edition 2001, p. 309) He mentioned Garvey and Padmore, and of course there was also James himself, but this was an overstatement about activities in the West, and quite wrong about activities within Africa, where Caribbean people played only small roles—for example Ganty's role as a representative of the Duala activists of French Cameroon. In Europe the outstanding role of Padmore is unquestioned, and so is the equally influential but rather different role—emphasising peace and goodwill—of the Jamaican Harold Moody in London. But Wallace Johnson and Kenyatta were prominent activists from the mother continent, and in France, while many West Indians were active in the anti-colonial militant movements, their most prominent activists were North Africans such as Messali and the black Africans Lamine Senghor, Garan Kouyate and Emile Faure. And the major role of Africans everywhere in the Ethiopia protests of 1935-36 must be recalled.

This whole book is the study of a fairly small number of individuals with their own ideas, not of parties and movements. Opposing imperialism in an active way could only be a matter of individual choice, and not an easy one. Nothing drove people to it in the way that unendurable oppression drove people to revolt in French Equatorial Africa in 1928. The First World War was a traumatic experience for African soldiers as well as others, but while a number of former Tirailleurs of the French army who had served in the war became anti-colonial activists, most of them returned home and were noted as pillars of French authority in their villages. Senghor could reasonably have drawn his invalidity pension and lived a quiet life, but he chose another course. Racism has been recalled in these pages as part of the background of Africans' life in Britain, but while the British people who condemned it had good intentions, their suggestion that it drove people into opposition to British rule was dubious—it suggested that calling for independence was a mere emotional reaction to personal humiliations, not a thought-out choice.

As for European anti-colonialists, what did they have to gain by their stance? There were no votes in it for politicians, Dr Leys could have concentrated on his surgery, Bridgeman could have continued his diplomatic career. There was nothing to be gained by becoming a Communist anti-colonialist or any sort of Communist. Outside Russia people became Communists out of conviction, which often involved risk; while intellectuals could join the Party without any cost when it was a fashion in the 1930s, for a worker being known as a "Red" often meant trouble, and an African student attending a Communist meeting could face some trouble also.

Communism occupies a large part of this book, not because it created opposition to Western colonialism, but because African and other opponents of that colonialism saw Communism as a new source of support, and in the view of some a particularly promising one whose ideas some of them accepted fully. Other non-African support had been sought since the 19ᵗʰ century, from politicians, the press, and churches and various organisations in the West. Many others besides Communists offered support for African protests and demands in the inter-war era, such as Labour Party politicians in Britain and individual writers and campaigners such as Norman Leys and Félicien Challaye. But Communists seemed to offer more, and often derided those others as "reformists".

That jibe was often unjustified, especially when coming from people whose alternative, militant campaigning and outright denunciation, did not produce any better results for Africans. "Reformist" attacks on the policy of giving land and power to settlers in Algeria or Southern Rhodesia, or forced labour conscription, or the regimentation of people's lives were not only proper, but could potentially benefit many Africans immediately. Those "abuses" were all avoidable, it was wrong to say that they were inherent in "the system". But in fact many continued, and despite their continuation democratic Socialists still commonly accepted colonialism as likely to be part of the landscape for a long time in Africa, if not in India. This attitude, shown in many studies before this one, was common for many reasons, including two very simple ones: democratic Socialists were preoccupied with the urgent needs of the underprivileged in Europe or America, and they sought or obtained political power within the existing capitalist order. Even out of power the ranks of critics condemning abuses overlapped at times with those of the more thoughtful and responsible governors of empire. Those who wanted to challenge the whole colonial order had to seek support elsewhere, from left-wing parties not prepared for the compromises that had to go with power in the existing order. In Britain the Independent Labour Party (ILP) was such a party, and sympathised with radical anti-colonialists, especially those who formed the International African Service Bureau (IASB) in the later 1930s. In France the Parti Socialiste

Ouvrier et Paysan (PSOP) was a similar sympathiser at the same period. But above all there were the Comintern, the Soviet Union, and Western Communist parties.

Communists made uncompromising condemnations of Western imperialism and supported colonial independence from an early stage; they were backed by a leading power that was on more or less permanent bad terms with Britain and France, the dominant colonial powers. This made the USSR and the Communist parties seem a good tactical ally. But some Africans and people of the Diaspora did not see them simply as that. Some were convinced by the analysis set out in Lenin's *Imperialism*, which of course did not discover the fact of economic gain being the basis of imperialism—a very obvious fact already—but did offer an explanation that seemed good to many, though it was in fact flawed. More important, the conviction that led people outside the Soviet Union to join the Communists was based commonly on moral revulsion against inequality, poverty and oppression; Africans joining them would expect to find active fellow feeling, not just a tactical ally. Some Africans who became Communist remained loyal to the cause, like Moses Kotane.

But about Kouyate, Messali, Padmore and Kenyatta it is safe to say that they saw Communism as a useful ally, even when they became Party members and activists. Their separation from the ranks of Communism was predictable. The two main reasons for it have been studied in these pages. One was the important question of control: whatever ideals, beliefs or principles a person had must be subordinated to Party discipline. The other was the question that led to the expulsion of Kouyate and Padmore, and to constant struggles in the Ligue de Défense de la Race Nègre: the Communist insistence on class as the most important consideration, rather than race or nationality. Was there to be a struggle of African people or all Black people against white colonialism and racial domination, or a struggle of all the victims of Western imperialism against all oppressors, indigenous and European? That was the question.

It is easy to see why Africans commonly preferred the first idea. For them the outstanding fact was common subjection to colonial or white settler rule, not any inequalities among themselves. There always were such inequalities, no human society has been without them, but a vital fact in sub-Saharan Africa—excluding Ethiopia, which remained independent except for the five-year Italian occupation—was the absence of agricultural landlordism of the sort found in Egypt, much of Asia and much of Latin America, and often provoking spontaneous class conflict. In the absence of rural landlord classes, who were the local oppressors and class enemies that Communists could urge Africans to attack? Two were identified, chiefs and the Western-educated elites. But in white-ruled Africa there was no spontaneous anger against either, least of all in a country like South Africa, where a well-educated professional Black person had to carry a sort of pass like other people (even though it was described as a pass exemption certificate). In West Africa in the 1930s there was some opposition between the upper elite and wider Western-educated communities, and Wallace Johnson made this explicit in his campaign as a "man of the people"; but many of the Creole upper crust in Sierra Leone in fact joined him, and earlier, in the Gold Coast, his comrade Kojo Thompson belonged to one of the prestige professions, as much as their adversary Dr Nanka-Bruce. In Nigerian the "Youth Movement" opposing established political leaders was led by doctors, not proletarians.

Padmore wrote in *How Britain Rules Africa* (pp. 362-3) that Africans did not have class or religious divisions like Asians, and had a strong "feeling of racial solidarity", shown in support of Ethiopia. Unity against the foreign rulers, unity stretching from the graduate to the farmer—that was the way Africa in fact chose. There was never complete unity or unanimity, of course. Widespread underlying feelings of resentment against alien rule certainly existed, as in many parts of the world, but such things can never be measured exactly. In Africa there were soldiers who served the colonial masters to the end. But this book has argued that the underlying anti-colonial sentiments were general, and specific expressions of them by some literate people reflected this. Seeing those literate people's activity in this way makes the debate about whether they were truly "nationalists" largely irrelevant. They sought a better deal for their people—that was what counted. Thus Ralaimongo, in calling for full French citizenship for all his people, with all the rights that would entail, was essentially seeking the same thing as those who demanded independence.

In some colonial and "semi-colonial" countries indigenous people including Communists did rebel against local inequalities and exploitation, especially where oppressive landlordism existed. In China Moscow had to force the early Chinese Communists to collaborate with the Kuomintang Nationalists headed by the landlord class. The idea that national independence would be unsatisfactory if it meant rule by local privileged minorities, with no benefit for ordinary people, was not an idea invented or imposed by the Comintern. It was an essential part of left-wing anti-imperialist ideology, expressed by the ILP for example, and there were Africans and Asians who agreed with it. Yet the nationalist parties led by people from the privileged classes, like Zaghlul Pasha—the well-off hero of the Cairo streets in 1919—or the Brahmins Gandhi and Nehru, were popular. Western left-wingers could do nothing about that, and had to decide whether to support or oppose movements headed by people of the indigenous upper classes and likely to bring those classes to power.

In *The Black Jacobins* James, drawing another parallel between the Haitian war of independence and modern anti-colonialism, wrote,

The race question is subsidiary to the class question in politics, and to think of imperialism in terms of race is disastrous. But to neglect the racial factor as incidental is an error only less grave than to make it fundamental. (p. 230)

This was a classic statement of the left-wing anti-imperialist view, but it also came near accepting that nationalist movements were in fact calling for self-government on behalf of a whole colonised people, regardless of classes, and that one might as well support them. In that spirit many democratic left-wingers were to lend support, with misgivings, to nationalists, an example being Guérin, whose Moroccan nationalist friends rejected his class-based criticisms and said indigenous class considerations did not matter when dealing with alien domination. Communists, by Moscow's order, called for opposition to nationalist movements between 1928 and 1935, but this simply divided the opposition to colonialism or white supremacy; the order to close down South Africa's League of African Rights was a blatant example—the South African Communists obeyed it reluctantly, thinking that collaboration with the ANC and other non-white leaders was a good idea in the current situation.

Communists made a valid point about Liberia, where an oppressive Black upper class was misruling other Africans but pan-Africanists felt obliged to defend it. One may ask what right Communists ever had to accuse others of oppression, but negatively, they could make justified comments, for example that Africans could also oppress Africans. Communist views about the developing local elites in the rest of Africa were strikingly similar to the colonial rulers' views. And they have been to some extent vindicated. The post-war nationalist movements brought to power privileged minorities which have been as selfish as any such minorities anywhere in the world. But while they predicted this, what did either colonialists or Communists offer as an alternative? Nothing that was possible and acceptable. And Communists were ready to reduce support for anti-colonial movements when they thought it necessary, as in 1935-39. Padmore may have remembered the details of this incorrectly, as has been shown, but he correctly noted how Communists subordinated everything to blind obedience to orders from Moscow.

The Communist role in anti-colonialism must be seen in proportion. The obsessive British and French assumption was that subversion flowed in only one direction, from the European or American master schemer through the African errand-boy to the African dupe. In fact it is likely that Africans and other people of the colonies took the initiative in forming groups that were under Communist control in France in the 1920s; they may have been Communists themselves, but acting on their own initiative. This seems probably true of the Union Intercoloniale and the LDRN; possibly of the Etoile Nord-Africaine also, but that has had to be left in doubt in this study. Some organisations were however created on orders from the Communist hierarchy—the League Against Imperialism certainly, the International Trade Union Committee of Negro Workers possibly, though its origins are among many topics examined in these pages that require more research.

Much of the Communist propaganda for the West's colonies was based on rigid ideology and ignorance of local conditions. Anyway Africans reading it could consider it, try to make sense of it, and decide carefully whether to follow it. The colonial powers' fear of "Bolshevist subversion", obvious throughout the previous pages, was based on an irrational fear that it would easily disturb the minds of "natives". An article in L'Afrique Française of May 1927, after quoting some Com-

munist leaflets addressed to North Africans, said, "These tracts are being distributed in French and Arabic. What effect can they have in the
minds of Arabs and Kabyles, in those feeble brains unable to accept
without perturbation that the guardianship authority should be so derided and revolt tolerated!"

It is interesting to note that the colonialist magazine made this comment after publishing the Communist document at length! It did so on
other occasions too, thus actually helping spread the Red message. Even
where this did not happen, Africans could often know about Communism and about world events in general. *La Race Nègre*, the *Negro
Worker* or Garvey's *Negro World* could be banned, but sailors smuggled
them in; European newspapers were on sale in many African cities, and
independent local newspapers in British West Africa published international news. Of course students and others in Europe could learn far
more and pass it on back home.

Those surveying the world situation could see other possible allies against the colonial masters besides the Soviet Union. In the later
1930s Nazi Germany and Fascist Italy seemed to be winning every time
against the British and French. As potential allies for opponents of British and French colonialism, they were not in the same category as Russia, for Communist ideas did suggest support for the underprivileged
of the world (whatever the actual practice was under Stalin), whereas
Fascists and Nazis proclaimed the right of the strong. So Shakib Arslan and other Arabs who thought Germany and Italy could be allies
were probably just following the principle of "My enemy's enemy is
my friend". About them, and about the many British, Arab, American
and other people who positively admired Fascism and Nazism in the
1930s, it is fair to recall that nobody then foresaw the depths to which
Nazism would sink. But already, by the late 1930s, the Nazis had done
enough to disgust decent people all over the world. When Padmore and
Kenyatta suggested to British audiences that their country's colonial
rule was much the same as Nazism, they were—provocatively—joining
the ranks of British and French people who detested Nazism but shrank
from the idea of backing a new world war, especially a war waged by
Chamberlain and Daladier. Fortunately for the world, the hesitations of
such people did not affect the course of events.

For anti-colonial campaigning the importance of activity carried out in Europe by people like Padmore, and others earlier, is very obvious. Africans and others could meet freely, hold their meetings, produce their newspapers and say within limits—as long as they did not incite African soldiers to disobey orders—whatever they liked about their colonial rulers, in the capitals of those rulers. But it should not be supposed that no anti-government activity at all was possible in Africa. A good deal was possible there, because Western-educated people in practice had greater freedom than the majority. This is ironic in view of what Europeans often said about "educated natives", but it is a fact. It was the humble general population who suffered from impositions like forced labour, excessive taxation and the vexatious laws governing movements—a daily burden in many countries, probably worst of all in the Belgian Congo, which developed a totalitarian system of control over lives and movements. The Belgian Congo was unusual in that it also kept the Western-educated people, called *évolués* (a revealing term also used in French Africa), on a tight leash. In Portuguese Africa the Salazar dictatorship destroyed freedoms among the African elites as it did among the Portuguese themselves, but before 1926 African elites had considerable freedom in Angola and Mozambique as in British and French territories. There are plenty of instances of harsh action against opponents of colonial rule, but in much of Africa what is striking is how much people could get away with. And unquestionably one reason for this was public opinion in Britain and France. Any arrest of a literate person working with other literate people could lead to questions in the House of Commons or the Chamber of Deputies, and further protests at the heart of the empire. For Mandated Territories the League of Nations could also deter drastic action against protesters, but it was only a minor additional deterrent.

So a good deal of activity opposed to the colonial order, provided it did not lead to violence, was possible in British West Africa and also in South Africa, where despite increasingly harsh legislation, enough law and justice remained for the ANC and the Communist Party to do a great deal. There was considerable liberty for anti-colonial activists under French rule in Madagascar and some in Dahomey, and some under British rule in Kenya, which was the main object of anti-colonial criticisms in Britain in the inter-war era. In considering the role of people in Europe, it should be noted that Kenyatta in Britain was the representative of the Kikuyu Central Association in Kenya. Similarly the Duala protesters, going further than most others and calling plainly for self-government in 1929, appointed Ganty of the LDRN as their representative in Europe; and one of the Gold Coast delegations sent to England in 1934 reported back to Wallace Johnson and his fellow activists in the Gold Coast.

So the scene of action was already in Africa by the 1930s. In fact a change can be seen then, involving more activity, many more people and more organisation back in Africa. Regarding North Africa Abun-Nasr (pp. 341-4) has written of a transition "from anti-colonialism to nationalism" in Tunisia between 1919 and 1934, and this fairly sums up a change that can be discerned. Discussion of the nature and meaning of "nationalism" has been avoided in this book, as explained in Chapter Two, because it is a study of *opposition*, which did not necessarily involve any clear ideas of what constitutes a "nation", though the word "national" was often used and many of the African anti-colonial activists called themselves nationalists and were called so by others. But in Tunisia the Neo-Destour was a recognisable nationalist party, as much as other parties so called anywhere, by the mid-1930s, and soon a popular and powerful one. Among Algerians the ENA had stood out even earlier by calling openly for independence, but it was after 1936 that it became a force to reckon with in the home country as well as in France. For sub-Saharan Africa the change from limited protest and campaigning activity, located in both Africa and the West but with activists in the West playing a big role, to large-scale nationalist organisation concentrated in the homelands was to come later, but it was presaged in Wallace Johnson's nationalist campaign in Sierra Leone in 1938-39. It was of course to leave some scope for activity by campaigners in the West, including European anti-colonialists, for many years.

The anti-colonial movements and activists within Africa at the height of the colonial era certainly influenced later generations of Africans. Wallace Johnson was respected as a pioneer nationalist in Sierra Leone, and Padmore's influence on Kwame Nkrumah is well known, while Kenyatta went on to become President of Kenya himself. In Europe the African, Caribbean and European anti-colonialists of the inter-war era certainly had an impact in publicising events in the colonies and ensuring that punishment of dissidents there was at least restrained. This was important, but did they also have an effect on the general public's attitude to empire? That is hard to say. They did draw attention to issues regarding colonial rule, but African anti-colonial movements were much less known to the British public than Gandhi and his movement in India. Maybe the stronger critics of empire did sow doubts in British and French minds before 1939. Twenty years later, certainly, the public in both countries was largely ready to give up the colonial empires without much hesitation.

BIBLIOGRAPHY

9 April 1938: Le "Procès" Bourguiba, Tunis: Editions SAEP, 1967.

Abbas, Ferhat *La Nuit coloniale*, Paris: Julliard, 1962.

Abd al-Rahim, M. *Imperialism and Nationalism in the Sudan*, Khartoum University Press and London: Ithaca Press, 1986.

Abd el-Krim et la République du Rif: Actes du colloque international d'études historiques et sociologiques 18-20 janvier 1973 (no editor named; Charles-André Julien headed the committee sponsoring the seminar), Paris: Maspéro, 1976.

Abun-Nasr, J.M. *A History of the Maghrib*, CUP 1971, 1975.

Adams, C.C. *Islam and Modernism in Egypt*, OUP, 1933.

Adejunmobi, M. *J.J. Rabearivelo, Literature and Lingua Franca in Colonial Madagascar*, New York: Peter Long, 1996.

Adi, H. "West African Students in Britain, 1900-60: The Politics of Exile", pp. 107-28 in D. Killingray (ed.), *Africans in Britain*, London: Frank Cass, 1994.

——— *West Africans in Britain 1900-1960: Nationalism, Pan-Africanism amd Communism*, London: Lawrence & Wishart, 1998.

Afigbo, A.E. *The Warrant Chiefs*, Harlow: Longman, 1972 .

Ageron, C.-R. *L'Anticolonialisme en France de 1871 à 1914*, Paris: Presses Universitaires de France, 1973.

——— "Les socialistes français et la guerre du Rif", in *Abd el-Krim et la République du Rif: Actes du colloque international d'études historiques et sociologiques 18-20 janvier 1973*, Paris: Maspéro, 1976, pp. 273-301.

——— "Emigration et politique: L'Etoile nord-africaine et le Parti du peuple algérien", appendix to Messali Hadj, *Les mémoires de Messali Hadj*, edited posthumous memoirs, Paris: Editions J.-C. Lattès, 1982, pp. 273-97.

———— "L'Association des étudiants musulmans nord-africains en France durant l'entre-deux-guerres: contribution à l'étude du nationalisme maghrébin", *Revue Française d'Histoire d'Outremer* vol. LXX, nos. 258-9, 1983, pp. 25-56. Ahmed, Jamal M. *The Intellectual Origins of Egyptian Nationalism*, OUP for Royal Institute of International Affairs (London), 1960.

Ahmed, E. and S. Schaar "M'hamed Ali: Tunisian Labor Organizer", pp. 191-204 in E. Burke III (ed.), *Struggle and Survival in the Modern Middle East*, London: Tauris, 1933.

Akpan, M.B. "Liberia and the Universal Negro Improvement Association: The Background to the Abortion of Garvey's Scheme for African Colonization", *Journal of African History* vol. XIV, no. 1, 1973, pp. 105-27.

———— *African Resistance in Liberia: the Vai and the Gola-Bandi*, Bremen: Liberia Working Group, 1988.

Allworth, E. (ed.) *Central Asia: A Century of Russian Rule,* Columbia University Press, 1967.

Almeida-Topor, Hélène d' "Les populations dahoméennes et le recrutement militaire pendant la première guerre mondiale", *Revue Française d'Histoire d'Outremer* Vol. LX no. 219, 1973, pp. 196-241.

Alpert, Michael *A New International History of the Spanish Civil War*, Basingstoke: Macmillan, 1994.

Anderson, J. *This was Harlem: A Cultural Portrait, 1900-1950*, New York: Farrar, Strauss and Giroux, 1981, 1982.

Anthony, F.R. *Sawpit Boy*, Freetown: published by author, 1980.

Archer-Straw, P. *Negrophilia: Avant-Garde Paris and Black Culture in the 1920s*, Thames & Hudson, 2000.

Asante, S.K.B. *Pan-African Protest: West Africa and the Italo-Ethiopian Crisis 1934-1941*, London: Longman, 1977.

———— entry on Awooner-Renner in *Dictionary of African Biography*, New York 1977, pp. 208-9.

Assimeng, J.M. "Sectarian Allegiance and Political Authority: the Watch Tower Society in Zambia, 1907-35", *Journal of Modern African Studies* vol. 8 no. 1, 1970, pp. 97-112.

Augagneur, V. *Erreurs et brutalités coloniales*, Paris: Editions Montaigne, 1927.

Austen, R.A. and J. Derrick *Middlemen of the Cameroons Rivers*, CUP, 1999.

BIBLIOGRAPHY

Austen, R.A. and R. Headrick "Equatorial Africa under Colonial Rule", pp. 27-94 in D. Birmingham and P.M. Martin (eds), *History of Central Africa*, Volume Two (Longman, 1983).

Ayandele, E.A. *Holy Johnson, Pioneer of African Nationalism, 1836-1917*, New York: Humanities Press, 1970.

Azikiwe, B.N. "In Defense of Liberia", *Journal of Negro History* vol. XVII no. 1, January 1932, pp. 30-50.

Azikiwe, Nnamdi *My Odyssey*, London: C. Hurst & Co., 1970.

Balandier, G. *Sociologie des Brazzavilles noires*, Cahiers de la NFSP, Paris: Armand Colin, 1955.

Baldwin, K. "The Russian Routes of Claude McKay's Internationalism", Ch. 4 in M. Matusevich (ed.), *Africa in Russia, Russia in Africa: Three Centuries of Encounters*, Trenton, NJ: Africa World Press, 2007.

Balfour, S. *Deadly Embrace: Morocco and the Road to the Spanish Civil War*, OUP 2002.

Barooah, Nirode K. *Chatto: The Life and Times of an Indian Anti-Imperialist in Europe*, New Delhi: OUP, 2004.

Beck, A. "Some Observations on Jomo Kenyatta in Britain, 1929-1930", *Cahiers d'Etudes Africaines* vol. VI, 2me cahier, 1966, pp. 308-29.

Beloff, Max *The Foreign Policy of Soviet Russia 1929-1941*, OUP, 1947.

Bennigsen, A. and C. Quelquejay *Les mouvements nationaux chez les Musulmans de Russie: Le "Sultangalievisme" au Tatarstan*, Paris: Mouton, 1960.

Berman, B. "Ethnography as Politics, Politics as Ethnography: Kenyatta, Malinowski, and the Making of *Facing Mount Kenya*", *Canadian Journal of African Studies* vol. 30 no. 3, 1996, pp. 313-44.

Bernard-Duquenet, N. *Le Sénégal et le Front populaire*, Paris: Harmattan, 1985.

Berque, J. *Egypt: Imperialism and Revolution*, London: Faber & Faber, 1972.

Bessis, J. *La Méditerranée fasciste: L'Italie mussolinienne et la Tunisie*, Paris: Karthala, 1981.

Biondi, J.-P. *Les Anticolonialistes (1881-1962)*, Paris: Laffont, 1992.

Birmingham, D. and P.M. Martin (eds), *History of Central Africa*, 2 vols, Harlow: Longman, 1983.

Blachère, R. "L'Insurrection rifaine, préfiguration des émancipations maghrébines", pp. 159-66 in *Abd el-Krim et la République du Rif: Actes du colloque international d'études historiques et sociologiques 18-20 janvier 1973*, Paris: Maspéro, 1976.

A. Blakely, "African Imprints on Russia : An Historical Overview", Ch. 2 in M. Matusevich (ed.), *Africa in Russia, Russia in Africa: Three Centuries of Encounters*, Trenton, NJ: Africa World Press, 2007.

Bontinck, F. "Mfumu Paul Panda Farnana 1888-1930, premier (?) nationaliste congolais", pp. 591-610 in V.Y. Mudimbe (ed.), *La Dépendance de l'Afrique et les moyens d'y remédier*, Actes du Congrès International des Etudes Africaines de Kinshasa, Paris: Berger-Levrault and ACCT, 1980.

Bradford, H. *A Taste of Freedom: The ICU in Rural South Africa 1924-1930*, Yale University Press, 1987.

Brandon, R. *Surreal Lives: The Surrealists 1917-1945*, Basingstoke: Macmillan, 2000.

Branson, N. *History of the Communist Party of Great Britain 1927-1941*, London: Lawrence & Wishart, 1985.

Brittain, V. *Testament of Friendship: The Story of Winifred Holtby*, London: The Book Club, 1941.

Brockway, F. *Inside the Left*, London: Allen & Unwin, 1942.

——— *The Colonial Revolution*, London and St Alban's: Hart-Davis, MacGibbon, 1973.

Brown, G. *Maxton*, Edinburgh: Mainstream Publishing Co., 1986, p. 201

Brown, I. (ed.) *The Economies of Africa and Asia in the Inter-War Depression*, Routledge 1989.

Buell, R.L. *The Native Problem in Africa*, New York: Macmillan, 1928, 2 vols.

Buhle, Paul *C.L.R. James: The Artist as Revolutionary*, London and New York: Verso, 1988.

Bunting, Brian *Moses Kotane, South African Revolutionary*, London: Inkululeko Publications, 1975.

Burke III, E. (ed.) *Struggle and Survival in the Modern Middle East*, London: Tauris, 1933.

Burnham, P. *The Politics of Cultural Difference in Northern Cameroon*, Edinburgh University Press for International African Institute, 1996.

Bush, Barbara *Imperialism, Race and Resistance: Africa and Britain, 1919-1945*, London and New York: Routledge, 1999.

Callaghan, J. *Rajani Palme Dutt: A Study in British Stalinism*, London: Lawrence & Wishart, 1993.

Callahan, M. *Mandates and Empire: The League of Nations and Africa, 1914-1931*, Portland, OR: Sussex Academic Press, 1999.

Callinicos, A. *Trotskyism*, Milton Keynes: Open University Press, 1990, pp. 62-3.

Carew Hunt, R.N. "Willi Muenzenberg", pp. 72-87 in *St Antony's Papers* No. 9, International Communism, 1960, ed. D. Footman, London: Chatto & Windus.

Carter, D.T. *Scottsboro: A Tragedy of the American South*, revised edition Baton Rouge and London: Louisiana State University Press, 1979.

Casely Hayford, J.E. *Gold Coast Native Institutions*, 1903.

Cell, J.W. (ed.) *By Kenya Possessed: The Correspondence of Norman Leys and J.H. Oldham 1918-1926*, University of Chicago Press, 1976.

Chafer, T. and A. Sackur (eds) *French Colonial Empire and the Popular Front: Hope and Disllusion*, Basingstoke: Macmillan, 1999.

————— *Promoting the Colonial Idea: Propaganda and Visions of Empire in France*, Basingstoke: Macmillan, 2001.

Challaye, Félicien *Le Congo français: la question internationale du Congo*, Paris: Félix Alcan, 1909.

Chenoufi, M. "Le rôle des mouvements d'étudiants tunisiens de 1900 à 1975", pp. 147-64 in *Le rôle des mouvements d'étudiants africains dans l'évolution politique et sociale de l'Afrique de 1900 à 1975* (no editor), Paris: Editions UNESCO/Harmattan, 1993.

Chisholm, A. *Nancy Cunard*, New York: Knopf, 1979, Harmondsworth: Penguin, 1981.

Citino, R. *Germany and the Union of South Africa in the Nazi Period*, New York, Westport and London: Greenwood Press, 1991.

Clarke J.H. *et al.* (eds) *Black Titan: W.E.B. Du Bois*, Boston: Beacon Press, 1970.

Clarke, P.B. *West Africa and Islam*, Edward Arnold, 1982.

Cleveland, W.L. *Islam against the West*, University of Texas Press and London: Al Saqi, 1985.

Cline, C. *E.D. Morel 1873-1924: The Strategies of Protest*, Belfast: Blackstaff Press, 1980.

Clough, M.S. *Fighting Two Sides: Kenyan Chiefs and Politicians, 1918-1940*, Niwot, CO: University Press of Colorado, 1990.

Cohen, R., Introduction to A.T. Nzula, I.I. Potekhin and A.Z. Zusmanovich, *Forced Labour in Colonial Africa*, London: Zed Press, 1979.

Cole, M., *The Story of Fabian Socialism*, London: Heinemann, 1961.

Cole, P.D. *Modern and Traditional Elites in the Politics of Lagos*, CUP 1975.

Coleman, J.S. *Nigeria: Background to Nationalism*, University of California Press, 1958.

Conklin, Alice L. *A Mission to Civilize: the Republican Idea of Empire in France and West Africa, 1895-1930*, Stanford, CA: Stanford University Press, 1997.

Connor, Walker *The National Question in Marxist-Leninist Theory and Strategy*, Princeton University Press, 1984.

Conquest, R. *The Harvest of Sorrow: Soviet Collectivization and the Terror-Famine*, Hutchinson, 1986.

Coury, Ralph M. *The Making of an Egyptian Arab Nationalist: The Early Years of Azzam Pasha, 1893-1936*, Reading: Ithaca Press, 1998.

Cowley, J. "West Indian Gramophone Recordings in Britain, 1927-1950" (ch. 17) in R. Lotz and O. Pegg (eds), *Under the Imperial Carpet: Essays in Black History 1786-1950*, Crawley: Rabbit Press, 1986.

Cromwell, A.M. *An African Victorian Feminist: The Life and Times of Adelaide Smith Casely Hayford 1868-1960*, London: Frank Cass, 1986.

Cronon, E.D. *Black Moses*, Madison: University of Wisconsin Press, 1955.

Crowder M. (ed.) *West African Resistance: The Military Response to Colonial Occupation*, London: Hutchinson, 1978;

Crowder, M. «West Africa and the 1914-18 War», *Bulletin de l'IFAN* (Dakar) Series B, Vol. XXX no. 1, January 1968, pp. 227ff.

——— *The Flogging of Phinehas McIntosh: A Tale of Colonial Folly and Injustice, Bechuanaland 1933*, Yale University Press, 1988.

Cummings-John, C.A. *Constance Agatha Cummings-John: Memoirs of a Krio Leader*, with introduction and annotation by LaRay Denzer, Sam Bookman for Humanities Research Centre, Ibadan, 1995.

Cunard, Nancy (collector and editor), *Negro: An Anthology*, 1970 edition edited and abridged with introduction by Hugh Ford, New York: Frederick Ungar, 1970.

Cutter, C.H. "The Genesis of a Nationalist Elite: The Role of the Popular Front in the French Soudan (1936-1939)", pp. 107-39 in G. Wesley Johnson (ed.), *Double Impact: France and Africa in the Age of Imperialism*, Westport, CT: Greenwood Press, 1985.

Davico, R. "La guérilla libyenne, 1911-1932", pp. 402-39 in *Abd el-Krim et la République du Rif: Actes du colloque international d'études historiques et sociologiques 18-20 janvier 1973*, Paris: Maspéro, 1976.

Davidson, A. and I. Filatova "African History: A View from behind the Kremlin Wall", Ch. 5 in M. Matusevic (ed.), *Africa in Russia, Russia in Africa: Three Centuries of Encounters*, Trenton, NJ: Africa World Press, 2007.

Davidson, A., I. Filatova, V. Gorodnov and S. Jones (eds) *South Africa and the Communist International: A Documentary History*, London: Frank Cass, 2003.

Debrunner, H.W. *Presence and Prestige: Africans in Europe* (Basel: Basler Afrika Bibiliographen, 1918).

Denzer, LaRay "I.T.A. Wallace-Johnson and the West African Youth League: A Case Study in West African Radicalism", PhD, Birmingham, 1973.

Derrick, J. "A Militant 'Prince' from Borno," *Savanna*, Zaria, vol. 7 no. 2, 1978, pp. 178-9.

——— "Douala under the French Mandate, 1916 to 1936," PhD, London, 1979, pp. 261-5.

——— "The 'Germanophone' Elite of Douala under French Administration", *Journal of African History* vol. 21 no. 3, 1980.

——— "The "Native Clerk" in Colonial West Africa", *African Affairs* vol. 82 no. 326, January 1983.

——— "The Dissenters: Anti-Colonialism in France, c. 1900-40,» pp. 53-68 in T. Chafer and A. Sackur (eds), *Promoting the Colonial Idea: Propaganda and Visions of Empire in France*, Basingstoke: Macmillan, 2001.

Dewitte, P. *Les Mouvements nègres en France 1919-1939*, Paris: Harmattan 1985.

——— "Le Paris noir de l'entre-deux-guerres", pp. 157-69 in A. Kaspi and A. Marès, *Le Paris des étrangers*, Paris: Imprimerie Nationale, 1989.

Dewitte, P. "Regards blancs et colères noires", *Hommes et Migrations* no. 1132, May 1990, pp. 3-14.

Dhondy, Farrukh *CLR James: Cricket, the Caribbean, and World Revolution*, London: Weidenfeld and Nicolson, 2001.

Dictionary of African Biography, New York, 1977

Dictionary of Labour Biography, ed. J.M. Bellamy and J. Saville, Basingstoke: Macmillan, 1984.

Diop, Birago, *La Plume rabutée*, Paris: Présence Africaine, 1978.

Domenichini, J.-P. "Jean Ralaimongo (1884-1943), ou Madagascar au seuil du nationalisme", *Revue Française d'Histoire d'Outremer* vol. LVI, no. 204, 3rd quarter, 1969, pp. 236-87.

Draper, T. *American Communism and Soviet Russia*, New York: Viking Press and London: Macmillan, 1960

Drechsler, H. *"Let Us Die Fighting": The Struggle of the Herero and Nama against German Imperialism (1884-1915)*, London: Zed Press, 1980.

Duffield, I. "The Business Activities of Duse Mohammed Ali," *Journal of the Historical Society of Nigeria* vol. IV no. 4, June 1969, pp. 571-600.

——— "John Eldred Taylor and West African Opposition to Indirect Rule", *African Affairs* vol. 70 no. 280, July 1971, pp. 252-68.

Duffy, J. *A Question of Slavery*, OUP 1967.

Duse Mohammed Ali, *In the Land of the Pharaohs*, London: Stanley Paul & Co., 1911; reprinted 1968 London: Frank Cass, with new introduction by Khalil Mahmud.

Echenberg, M. *Colonial Conscripts: The Tirailleurs Sénégalais in French West Africa, 1857-1960*, Portsmouth, NH: Heinemann and London: James Currey, 1991.

Edgar R. (ed.), *The Travel Notes of Ralph J. Bunche, 28 September 1937-1 January 1938*, Athens, OH: Ohio University Press.

Edgar, R. "Garveyism in Africa", *Ufahamu* vol. VI no. 3, 1976, pp. 31-57.

——— "Notes on the Life and Death of Albert Nzula", *International Journal of African Historical Studies* vol. 16 no. 4, 1983.

Edsman, B.M. *Lawyers in Gold Coast Politics c. 1900-1945*, Uppsala, 1979.

Edwards, Brent Hayes *The Practice of Diaspora : Literature, Translation and the Rise of Black Internationalism*, Cambridge, MA: Harvard University Press, 2003.

Ellis, E.R. *Echoes of Distant Thunder*, New York: Coward, McCann and Geoghegan, 1975.

Elphick, R. and R. Davenport (eds and compilers), *Christianity in South Africa: A Political, Social and Cultural History*, Oxford: James Currey and Cape Town: D. Philip, 1997.

Emery, L.F. *Black Dance from 1619 to Today*, Dance Books, 1972, 1988.

Esedebe, P.O. *Pan-Africanism: The Idea and the Movement, 1776-1991*, 2nd ed. Washington: Howard University Press, 1994.

Eudin, X.J. and R.C. North, *Soviet Russia and the East 1920-1927: A Documentary Survey*, Stanford, CA: Stanford University Press, 1957.

Evans, N. "Across the Universe: Racial Violence and the Post-War Crisis in Imperial Britain, 1919-25", *Immigrants and Minorities* vol. 13 nos. 2 & 3, July/November 1994, pp. 59-88.

Evans, Richard J. *The Coming of the Third Reich*, Allen Lane, 2003.

Evans-Pritchard, E.E. *The Sanusi of Cyrenaica*, OUP, 1949.

Fieldhouse, D.K. *Merchant Capital and Economic Decolonization: The United Africa Company, 1929-1987*, Oxford: Clarendon Press, 1994.

Flint, John E. "Macmillan as a Critic of Empire: The Impact of an Historian on Colonial Policy", Ch. 10 in H. Macmillan and S. Marks (eds), *W.M. Macmillan, Historian and Social Critic*, Temple Smith for the Institute of Commonwealth Studies, 1989.

Frost, D, ed. *Immigrants and Minorities* vol. 13 nos. 2 & 3, July/November 1994, special issue on "Ethnic Labour and British Imperial Trade: A History of Ethnic Seafarers in the UK".

Frost, D. "Racism, Work and Unemployment: West African Seamen in Liverpool 1880s-1960s", *Immigrants and Minorities* vol. 13 nos. 2 & 3, July/November 1994, pp. 22-33.

Fuglestad, F. "Les Révoltes des Touareg du Niger (1916-17)", *Cahiers d'Etudes Africaines* vol. XIII, 1973, 2me cahier, pp. 82-120.

——— "La grande famine de 1931 dans l'Ouest nigérien: Réflexions autour d'une catastrophe naturelle," *Revue Française d'Histoire d'Outremer* LXI, 1974, pp. 18-33.

——— *A History of Niger 1850-1960*, CUP 1983, pp. 126-31.

Funk, R. "Three Afro-American Singing Groups" (ch. 11), in R. Lotz and O. Pegg (eds), *Under the Imperial Carpet: Essays in Black History 1786-1950*, Crawley: Rabbit Press, 1986.

Fyfe, C. *A History of Sierra Leone*, Oxford University Press, 1962.

——— and D. Killingray, "A Memorable Gathering of Sierra Leoneans in London, 1919", *African Affairs* vol. 88 no. 350, January 1989, pp. 41-6.

Gailey, H.A. *The Road to Aba*, University of London Press, 1971.

Gallisot, R. "Le parti communiste et la guerre du Rif", pp. 237-57 in *Abd el-Krim et la République du Rif: Actes du colloque international d'études historiques et sociologiques 18-20 janvier 1973*, Paris: Maspéro, 1976.

Gann, L.H. and P. Duignan *Colonialism in Africa, 1870-1960*, 5 vols., Cambridge University Press, 1975.

Garigue, P. "The West African Students' Union", *Africa* vol. XXIII no. 1, January 1952, pp. 53-69.

Garvey, Amy Jacques (compiler) *The Philosophy and Opinions of Marcus Garvey*, 1923 and 1925, 2 vols. combined in new edition Dover, MA: The Majority Press, 1986.

Gaspard, F. "'Viollette l'Arabe'", *L'Histoire* no. 140, January 1991, special issue, "Le temps de l'Algérie Française", pp. 68-72.

Gautherot, Gustave "Le Bolchévisme en Afrique", *Renseignements Coloniaux* no. 7, 1930, supplement to *L'Afrique Française* vol. 40, no. 7, July 1930, pp. 418-29.

Geiss, Immanuel *The Pan-African Movement*, tr. Ann Keep, London: Methuen, 1974.

Gellner, E. *Nations and Nationalism*, Oxford: Blackwell, 1983.

Ghomsi, E. "Résistance africaine à l'impérialisme européen: le cas des Doualas du Cameroun", *Afrika-Zamani*, no. 4, July 1975.

Gilroy, Paul, *The Black Atlantic: Modernity and Double Consciousness*, Cambridge, MA: Harvard UP 1993.

Glendinning, Victoria, *Leonard Woolf: A Life*, London and New York: Simon & Schuster, 2006.

Goldschmidt Jr, A. "The Egyptian Nationalist Party: 1892-1919", pp. 308-33 in P.M. Holt (ed.), *Political and Social Change in Modern Egypt: Historical Studies from the Ottoman Conquest to the United Arab Republic*, London: Oxford University Press, 1968.

Goldstein, D. *Libération ou annexion: aux chemins croisés de l'histoire tunisienne 1914-1922*, Tunis: Maison Tunisienne de l'Edition, 1978.

Gopal, S. *Jawaharlal Nehru: A Biography: Vol. One: 1889-1947*, London: Jonathan Cape, 1975.

Greaves, C.D. *The Life and Times of James Connolly*, London: Lawrence & Wishart, 1961.

Green, J. "Afro-American Symphony: Popular Black Concert Hall Performers 1900-1940", Ch. 2 (pp. 39-41), in P. Oliver (ed.), *Black Music in Britain*, Open University Press, 1990.

Gromyko, A.N. (ed.) *The October Revolution and Africa*, trans. G. Glagoleva, Moscow: Progress Publishers, 1983, pp. 20-21.

Groves, R. "Noel, Conrad le Despenser Roden", *Dictionary of Labour Biography*, Vol. II, pp. 276-86.

Grundlingh, A. *Fighting their Own War: South African Blacks and the First World War*, Johannesburg: Ravan Press, 1987.

Guérin, D. *Ci-gît le colonialisme*, Paris and The Hague: Mouton, 1973.

Guillermaz, J. *A History of the Chinese Communist Party*, New York: Random House, 1972.

Gundara, J.S. and I. Duffield (eds) *Essays on the History of Blacks in Britain from Roman Times to the Mid-Twentieth Century*, Aldershot: Avebury, 1992.

Gupta, P.S. *Imperialism and the British Labour Movement, 1914-1964*, London : Macmillan, 1975.

Gupta, S.D. *Comintern, India and the Colonial Question, 1920-1937*, Calcutta, K.P. Bagchi & Co., 1980.

Guy, J. *The Heretic: A Study of the Life of John William Colenso 1814-1883*, Pietermaritzburg: University of Natal Press, 1983.

———— *The View Across the River: Harriette Colenso and the Zulu Struggle against Imperialism*, Oxford: James Currey and Charlottesville: University Press of Virginia, 2001.

Haithcox, J.P. *Communism and Nationalism in India: M.N. Roy and Comintern Policy 1920-1939*, Princeton University Press, 1971.

Halstead, J.P. *Rebirth of a Nation: The Origins and Rise of Moroccan Nationalism, 1912-1944*, Cambridge, MA: Harvard Univerity Press, 1967.

Hancock, W.K. *Smuts: The Fields of Force*, CUP, 1968.

———— *Survey of British Commonwealth Affairs, Vol. I, Problems of Nationality 1918-1936*, OUP 1937.

Hargreaves, A.G. *The Colonial Experience in French Fiction: A Study of Pierre Loti, Ernest Psichari and Pierre Mille*, Basingstoke: Macmillan, 1981.

Hargreaves, J. *Prelude to the Partition of West Africa*, London: Macmillan, 1963.

———— "Maurice Delafosse in the Pan-African Congress of 1919," *International Journal of African Historical Studies*, vol. 1 no. 2, 1968, pp. 233-41.

———— *West Africa Partitioned*, London/Basingstoke: Macmillan, Vol. I, 1974, vol. 2, 1985.

———— "The Comintern and Anti-Colonialism: New Research Opportunities," *African Affairs* vol. 92, no. 367, April 1993, pp. 255-61.

Harris, J.H. *Dawn in Darkest Africa*, 1912.

Harrison, C. *France and Islam in West Africa, 1860-1960*, Cambridge University Press, 1988.

Harrison, J.P. *The Long March to Power: A History of the Chinese Communist Party, 1921-72*, New York: Praeger, 1972.

Harrison, S. *Sylvia Pankhurst: A Crusading Life,* London: Aurum Press, 2003.

Haywood, H. *Negro Liberation,* New York: International Publishers, 1948.

Herd, N. *1922: The Revolt on the Rand,* Johannesburg: Blue Crane Books, 1966.

Hind, R.J. *Henry Labouchere and the Empire,* London: Athlone Press, 1972.

Hindson, D. *Pass Controls and the Urban African Proletariat,* Johannesburg: Ravan Press, 1987.

Hobson, J.A. *Imperialism: A Study,* London: George Allen & Unwin (1902, revised ed. 1938).

Hochschild, A. *King Leopold's Ghost,* Boston: Houghton Mifflin, 1998.

Hodeir, C. and M. Pierre *L'Exposition Coloniale,* Brussels: Complexe, 1991.

Hoisington Jr, William A. *The Casablanca Connection: French Colonial Policy, 1936-1943,* Chapel Hill and London: University of North Carolina Press.

Holmes, C. *John Bull's Island,* Basingstoke: Macmillan, 1988.

Hooker, J.R. *Black Revolutionary: George Padmore's Path from Communism to Pan-Africanism,* New York: Praeger, 1970.

Hopkirk, P. *Setting the East Ablaze,* London: John Murray, 1984.

――― *On Secret Service East of Constantinople: the Plot to Bring Down the British Empire,* London: John Murray, 1994.

Howe, S. *Anticolonialism in British Politics: The Left and the End of Empire,* Oxford: Clarendon Press, 1993.

Hoyt, Edwin P. *Paul Robeson,* Cassell 1967, pp. 74-7.

Hughes, A. and A. Perfect "Trade Unionism in The Gambia", *African Affairs* vol. 88 no. 363, October 1989, pp. 549-72.

Hunt, Davis E. Jr "John L. Dube: A South African Exponent of Booker T. Washington", *Journal of African Studies* (University of California, Los Angeles), vol. 2 no. 4, 1975-76, pp. 497-528.

Hyde, D. *I Believed,* London: Pan Books, 1953.

Hymans, J.L. *Leopold Sedar Senghor,* Edinburgh University Press, 1971.

Ingham, E.G. *Sierra Leone After a Hundred Years,* London: Seeley & Co., 1894.

Isichei, E. *A History of the Igbo People,* London: Macmillan, 1976.

Ismael, Tareq Y. and Rifa'at El-Sa'id, *The Communist Movement in Egypt 1920-1988,* Syracuse University Press, 1990.

Isoart, P. "Le Mouvement ouvrier européen et l'Occident face à la guerre du Rif", pp. 173-217 in *Abd el-Krim et la République du Rif: Actes du collo-*

que international d'études historiques et sociologiques 18-20 janvier 1973, Paris: Maspéro, 1976.

Jabavu, D.D.T. "Native Unrest in South Africa", *The International Review of Missions* vol. XI no. 42, April 1922, pp. 249-59.

Jackson, J. *The Popular Front in France: Defending Democracy, 1934-38,* CUP 1988.

Jacobs, Dan N. *Borodin: Stalin's Man in China,* Cambridge, MA: Harvard University Press, 1981.

James, C.L.R. "Black Intellectuals in Britain", pp. 154-63 in B. Parekh (ed.), *Colour, Culture and Consciousness,* London: Allen & Unwin, 1974.

———— *At the Rendezvous of Victory,* selected writings and speeches, London: Allison & Busby, 1984.

———— *The Black Jacobins,* 1938, Penguin re-edition 2001.

Jankowski, J.P. *Egypt's Young Rebels: "Young Egypt": 1933-1952,* Stanford, CA: Hoover Institution Press, 1975.

Jarrett-Macauley, Delia *The Life of Una Marson 1905-65,* Manchester University Press, 1998.

Jaugeon, R. "Les sociétés d'exploitation au Congo et l'opinion française de 1890 à 1906", *Revue Française d'Histoire d'Outremer* vol. XLVIII, 3rd-4th quarter 1961, pp. 353-437.

Jeeves, A.H. *Migrant Labour in the South African Mining Economy: The Struggle for the Gold Mines' Labour Supply 1890-1920,* Kingston and Montreal: McGill-Queen's University Press, 1985.

Jenkins, Ray "Gold Coasters Overseas, 1880-1919: With Specific Reference to Their Activities in Britain", *Immigrants and Minorities* Vol. 4 no. 3, November 1985, pp. 5-42.

Jenkinson, J. "The 1919 Race Riots in Britain: A Survey", in R. Lotz and O. Pegg (eds), *Under the Imperial Carpet: Essays in Black History 1780-1950,* Crawley: Rabbit Press, 1986, pp. 182-207.

Johanningsmeier, E. "Communists and the Black Freedom Movements in South Africa and the United States: 1919-1950", *Journal of Southern African Studies* vol. 30 no. 2, June 2004, pp. 155-80.

Johnson, G. Wesley (ed.) *Double Impact: France and Africa in the Age of Imperialism, Westport,* CT: Greenwood Press, 1985.

Johnson, G. Wesley *The Emergence of Black Politics in Senegal: The Struggle for Power in the Four Communes, 1900-1920,* Stanford, CA: Stanford University Press, 1971.

Joseph, R.A. "The German Question in French Cameroun, 1919-1939", *Comparative Studies in Society and History* vol. 17 no. 1, January 1975, pp. 65-90.

Julien, C.-A. with M. Morsy *Une pensée anticoloniale: positions 1914-1979*, Paris: Sindbad, 1979.

Jusu, B.M. "The Haidara Rebellion of 1931", *Sierra Leone Studies* New Series no. 3, December 1954, pp. 147-53.

Kadalie, C. *My Life and the ICU*, reprinted with introduction by S. Trapido, London: Frank Cass, 1970.

Kala-Lobe, I. "The Greatness and Decline of Mun'a Moto", *Présence Africaine* no. 37, 2nd quarter 1971, English version, pp. 69ff.

Kamel Pacha, Moustafa *Egyptiens et Anglais*, Paris: Perrin et Cie, 1906.

Kamoche, J.D. *Imperial Trusteeship and Political Evolution in Kenya, 1923-1963*, Washington: University Press of America, 1981.

Karis, T. and G.M. Carter (eds) *From Protest to Challenge: A Documentary History of African Politics in South Africa 1882-1964, Vol. I: Protest and Hope 1882-1934* (by Sheridan Johns III), Stanford, CA: Hoover Institution Press, 1972.

Karsani, Awad al- "The Establishment of Neo-Mahdism in the Western Sudan 1920-1934", *African Affairs* vol. 86 no. 344, July 1987, pp. 385-404.

Kaspi, A. and A. Marès *Le Paris des étrangers*, Paris: Imprimerie Nationale, 1989.

Keddie, N.R. "The Pan-Islamic Appeal: Afghani and Abdülhamid II", *Middle Eastern Studies* vol. 3 no. 1, October 1966, pp. 46-67.

Kelsey, E.W. *Friends of the Indians 1655-1917*, Philadelphia, 1917.

Kennedy, M.D. *A Short History of Communism in Asia*, London: Weidenfeld & Nicolson, 1957.

Kenyatta, Jomo *Facing Mount Kenya*, London: Secker & Warburg, 1938.

Khaled, Emir *La Situation des musulmans d'Algérie*, Algiers: Editions du Trait-d'Union, 1926, edited with introduction by Nadya Bouzar Kasbadji, reprint Algiers: Office des Publications Universitaires, 1987.

Kharchich, M. "Left Wing Politics in Lyons and the Rif War", *Journal of North African Studies* vol. 2 no. 3, winter 1997, pp. 34-45.

Khoury, Philip S. *Syria and the French Mandate: The Politics of Arab Nationalism*, London: I.B. Tauris, 1987.

Killingray, D. (ed.) *Africans in Britain*, London: Frank Cass, 1994.

Killingray, D. "Repercussions of World War I in the Gold Coast", *Journal of African History* Vol. XIX no. 1, 1978, pp. 39-59.

Kimble, D. *Politics in Ghana 1850-1928*, Oxford: Clarendon Press.

King, K. "James E.K. Aggrey: Collaborator, Nationalist, Pan-African», *Canadian Journal of African Studies* vol. 3 no. 3, 1969, pp. 511-30.

Koulakssis, A. and G. Meynier *L'Emir Khaled premier za'im? Identité algérienne et colonialisme français*, Paris: Harmattan, 1987.

Kublin, H. *Asian Revolutionary: The Life of Sen Katayama*, Princeton University Press 1964.

Lacouture, Jean and Dominique Chagnollaud, *Le Désempire: Figures et thèmes de l'anticolonisme*, Paris: Denoël, 1993.

Lamine Gueye, Amadou *Itinéraire Africain,* Paris: Présence Africaine, 1966, pp. 52-3.

Lane, T. "The Political Imperatives of Bureaucracy and Empire: The Case of the Coloured Alien Seamen Order, 1925", pp. 104-29 in *Immigrants and Minorities* vol. 13 nos. 2 & 3, July/November 1994, special issue on "Ethnic Labour and British Imperial Trade: A History of Ethnic Seafarers in the UK", ed. D. Frost.

Langley, J.A. *Pan-Africanism and Nationalism in West Africa 1900-1945*, OUP, 1973.

———— *Ideologies of Liberation in Black Africa 1856-1970*, London: Rex Collings, 1979.

Lee, F. *Fabianism and Colonialism: The Life and Political Thought of Lord Sydney Olivier*, London: Defiant Books, 1988.

Lejri, M-S. *Evolution du mouvement national tunisien,* 2 vols, Tunis: Maison Tunisienne de l'Edition, 1974.

Lenin, V.I. *Imperialism: The Highest Stage of Capitalism*, 1916, republished with Introduction by N. Lewis and J. Malone, London: Pluto Press, 1996.

Lewis, W. Arthur *Labour in the West Indies*, London: Fabian Society, 1938, reprinted London: Beacon Books, 1977 (with afterword by Susan Craig).

Leys, Norman *Kenya*, London: Hogarth Press, 1924.

———— *A Last Chance in Kenya*, London: Hogarth Press, 1931.

Liauzu, C. *Aux Origines des Tiers-mondismes: colonisés et anticolonialistes en France 1919-1939*, Paris: Harmattan, 1982.

Lilly, M. *The National Council for Civil Liberties: The First Fifty Years*, Macmillan, 1984.

Little, K. *Negroes in Britain: A Study of Racial Relations in British Society*, Kegan Paul, Trench, Trubner & Co., 1947.

Longrigg, S.H. *Syria and Lebanon under French Mandate*, OUP, 1958, reprinted 1972.

Lotz, R. and O. Pegg (eds), *Under the Imperial Carpet: Essays in Black History 1780-1950*, Crawley: Rabbit Press, 1986.

Lotz, R.E. "Will Garland's Negro Operetta Company", ch. 10 in R. Lotz and O. Pegg (eds), *Under the Imperial Carpet: Essays in Black History 1786-1950,* Crawley: Rabbit Press, 1986.

Löwy, M. "Marxism and the National Question", pp. 136-60 in R. Blackburn (ed.) *Revolution and Class Struggle: A Reader in Marxist Politics*, Hassocks, Sussex: The Harvester Press, 1978.

Lugard, F. *The Dual Mandate in British Tropical Africa*, 1922, reprinted London: Frank Cass, 1965.

Lynch, H. *Edward Wilmot Blyden, Pan-Negro Patriot, 1832-1912*, London: Oxford University Press, 1967.

MacDonald, C.A. "Radio Bari: Italian Wireless Propaganda in the Middle East and British Countermeasures 1934-38", *Middle Eastern Studies* vol. 13, no. 2, pp. 195-207.

MacDonald, J. Ramsay *Labour and the Empire*, London: George Allen, 1907, reprinted with introduction by P. Cain, London: Routledge/Thoemmes, 1998 ("The Empire and its Critics, 1899-1939" series).

Macdonald, R.J. "Dr. Harold Arundel Moody and the League of Coloured Peoples, 1931-1941: A Retrospective View", *Race* (London), vol. XIV no. 3, January 1973, pp. 291-319.

——— "'The Wisers who are Far away': The Role of London's Black Press in the 1930s and 1940s", pp. 150-72 in J.S. Gundara and I. Duffield (eds), *Essays on the History of Blacks in Britain from Roman Times to the Mid-Twentieth Century*, Aldershot: Avebury, 1992

MacKenzie, J.R. *Propaganda and Empire: The Manipulation of British Public Opinion 1880-1960*, Manchester University Press, 1984.

MacMillan, A. *The Red Book of West Africa*, Collingridge, 1920, reprint London: Frank Cass, 1968.

Macmillan, H. and S. Marks (eds), *W.M. Macmillan, Historian and Social Critic*, Temple Smith for the Institute of Commonwealth Studies, 1989.

Macmillan, M. "Macmillan, Indirect Rule and *Africa Emergent*", ch. 11 in H. Macmillan and S. Marks (eds), *W.M. Macmillan, Historian and Social Critic*, Temple Smith for the Institute of Commonwealth Studies, 1989.

Madariaga, M.-R. de "Le parti socialiste espagnol et le Parti communiste d'Espagne face à la revolution rifaine", *Abd el-Krim et la République du Rif: Actes du colloque international d'études historiques et sociologiques 18-20 janvier 1973*, Paris: Maspéro, 1976, pp. 308-66.

Maddox, T.R. *Years of Estrangement: American Relations with the Soviet Union, 1933-1941*, Tallahassee: University Presses of Florida, 1980.

Mahsas, A. *Le Mouvement révolutionnaire en Algérie de la 1re guerre mondiale à 1954*, Paris: Harmattan, 1979.

Makonnen, Ras *Pan-Africanism from Within*, recorded and edited by K. King, Nairobi: OUP, 1973.

Malmsten, N.R. "The British Labour Party and the West Indies, 1918-39", *Journal of Imperial and Commonwealth History* vol. V no. 2, 1977, pp. 177-205.

Manga Mado, H. *Complaintes d'un Forçat*, Yaounde: CLE, 1970.

Mann, K. *Marrying Well*, Cambridge University Press, 1985.

Marchal, J. *E.D. Morel contre Léopold II: L'Histoire du Congo 1900-1910*, 2 vols., Paris: Harmattan, 1996.

Marks, S. *Reluctant Rebellion: the 1906-8 Disturbances in Natal*, Oxford: Clarendon Press, 1970.

Marques, A.H. de Oliveira *History of Portugal, Vol. II: From Empire to Corporate State*, New York and London: Columbia University Press, 1972.

Martin, M.-L. *Kimbangu*, English translation Oxford: Basil Blackwell, 1975.

Martin, Wolf-Peter "The 'Negro Question' and the Comintern", paper given at the "Africa in the World" conference, 50th Anniversary Civic Celebration at Manchester commemorating the 1945 Pan-African Congress, in October 1995.

Massard-Guilbaud, G. *Des Algériens à Lyon de la grande guerre au Front populaire*, CIEMI: Harmattan, 1995.

Mathurin, O.C. *Henry Sylvester Williams and the Origins of the pan-African Movement, 1869-1911*, Westport, CT and London: Greenwood Press, 1976.

Matusevich, M. (ed.) *Africa in Russia, Russia in Africa: Three Centuries of Encounters*, Trenton, NJ: Africa World Press, 2007.

Mayer, T. "Egypt and the General Islamic Conference of Jerusalem in 1931", *Middle Eastern Studies* 18, 3, July 1982, pp. 311-22.

McCarthy, M. *Generation in Revolt,* Heinemann 1953.

McClellan, W. "Africans and Black Americans in the Comintern Schools, 1925-1934", *International Journal of African Historical Studies* Vol. 26 no. 2, 1993, pp. 371-90.

———— "Black Hajj to "Red Mecca": Africans and Afro-Americans at KUTV, 1925-1928", Ch. 3 in M. Matusevic (ed.), *Africa in Russia, Russia in Africa: Three Centuries of Encounters,* Trenton, NJ: Africa World Press, 2007.

McCracken, John *Politics and Christianity in Malawi 1875-1940,* new edition Blantyre: Christian Literature Association in Malawi, 2000.

McDermott K. and J. Agnew, *The Comintern: A History of International Communism from Lenin to Stalin,* Basingstoke: Macmillan, 1996.

McKay, Claud *Banjo,* New York: Harvest, 1929, new edition New York: Harcourt Brace Jovanovich, 1957.

———— *A Long Way from Home,* 1937, reprinted 1970 New York: Harcourt, Brace & World, Inc.

McMeekin, Sean *The Red Millionaire: A Political Biography of Willi Münzenberg, Moscow's Secret Propaganda Tsar in the West,* New Haven and London: Yale University Press, 2003.

Meek, C.K., W.M. Macmillan and E.R.J. Hussey *Europe and West Africa: Some Problems and Adjustments,* OUP 1940.

Meintjes, J. *General Louis Botha: A Biography,* London: Cassell, 1970.

Meriwether, James H. *Proudly We Can be Africans: Black Americans and Africa, 1935-1961,* Chapel Hill: University of North Carolina Press, 2002.

Merle, Marcel *L'anticolonialsme européen de Las Casas à Marx,* Paris: Armand Colin, 1969.

Messali Hadj *Les mémoires de Messali Hadj,* edited posthumous memoirs, Paris: Editions J.-C. Lattès, 1982.

Michel, M. *L'Appel à l'Afrique: Contributions et réactions à l'effort de guerre en A.O.F. 1914-1919,* Paris: Publications de la Sorbonne, 1982.

Molema, M.S. *The Bantu Past and Present,* Edinburgh: W. Green & Son, 1920.

Moon, P. *Gandhi and Modern India,* London: English Universities Press, 1968.

Moore, Richard B. "Du Bois and Pan-Africa", pp. 187- 212 in J.H. Clarke *et al.* (eds), *Black Titan*, Boston: Beacon Press, 1970.

Morel, E.D. *Red Rubber,* London, 1906, 3rd Edition London: Fisher Unwin, 1907.

Morewood, S. *The British Defence of Egypt 1935-1940: Conflict and Crisis in the Eastern Mediterranean*, London: Frank Cass, 2005.

Mortimer, E. *The Rise of the French Communist Party 1920-1947*, London: Faber & Faber, 1984.

Moume Etia, L. *Les Années Ardentes*, Paris: Jalivres, 1991.

Murray-Brown, J. *Kenyatta*, London: Allen & Unwin, 1972.

Nehru, J. *An Autobiography*, John Lane The Bodley Head, 1936.

Nouschi, A. *La naissance du nationalisme algérien*, 1914-1954, Paris: Minuit, 1962.

Nworah, K.D. "The Aborigines' Protection Society, 1889-1909: A Pressure Group in Colonial Policy", *Canadian Journal of African Studies* Vol. V no. 1, 1971, pp. 74-91.

Nzabakomada-Yakoma, R. *L'Afrique centrale insurgée: La Guerre du Kongo-Wara 1928-1931*, Paris: Harmattan, 1986.

Nzula, A.T., I.I. Potekhin and A.Z. Zusmanovich, *Forced Labour in Colonial Africa,* published in Russian 1933, English version London: Zed Press, 1979.

Ofosu-Appiah, L.H. *The Life and Times of Dr J.B. Danquah*, Accra: Waterville Publishing House, 1974.

Olcott, M.B. *The Kazakhs*, Stanford, CA: Hoover Institution Press, 1987.

Oliver, Paul (ed.) *Black Music in Britain*, Open University Press, 1990,

Olivier, Sydney *White Capital and Coloured Labour,* London: Hogarth Press, 1929.

Olusanya, G.O. "The Lagos Branch of the National Congress of British West Africa", *Journal of the Historical Society of Nigeria* vol. IV no. 2, June 1968, pp. 321-33.

———— *The West African Students' Union and the Politics of Decolonisation, 1925-1958*, Ibadan: Daystar, 1982.

Omu, F.I. *Press and Politics in Nigeria 1880-1937*, Longman, 1978.

Osuntokun, A. *Nigeria in the First World War*, London: Longman, 1979.

Ottley, Roi *No Green Pastures,* John Murray, 1952.

Oved, G. *La Gauche Française et le Nationalisme marocain 1905-1955*, Paris: Harmattan, 1984, 2 vols.

Owona, A. "La Curieuse figure de Vincent Ganty", *Revue Française d'Histoire d'Outremer* vol. LVI no. 204, 1969, pp. 199-235.

Padmore, George *The Life and Struggles of Negro Toilers*, Hamburg: ITUC-NW, 1931.

——— *How Britain Rules Africa*, London: Wishart Books, 1936.

——— *Africa and World Peace*, 1937, reprint London: Frank Cass, 1972.

——— *Pan-Africanism or Communism?* Dennis Dobson, 1956.

Pakenham, T. *The Scramble for Africa, 1876-1912*, London: Abacus, 1992.

Pankhurst, R. *Sylvia Pankhurst, Artist and Crusader, An Intimate Portrait*, London: Virago, 1979.

Parekh B. (ed.) *Colour, Culture and Consciousness*, London: Allen & Unwin, 1974.

Parpart, J.L. *Labor and Capital on the African Copperbelt*, Philadelphia: Temple University Press, 1983.

Pelling, H. *The British Communist Party*, 1958, reprint London: A. and C. Black, 1975.

Pennell, C.R. *A Country with a Government and a Flag*, London: Menas Press, 1986.

Plaatje, Sol *Native Life in South Africa*, 1916, reprint Harlow: Longman, 1987.

Porter, B. *Critics of Empire*, London: Macmillan, 1968.

——— *The Absent-Minded Imperialists: Empire, Society, and Culture in Britain*, OUP 2004.

Post, K. *Arise Ye Starvelings*, The Hague: Martinus Nijhoff, 1978.

Powers, R.G., *Secrecy and Power: The Life of J. Edgar Hoover*, Hutchinson, 1987.

Pretorius H. and F. Jafta "'A Branch Springs Out': African Initiated Churches," Ch. 12, pp. 211-26 in R. Elphick and R. Davenport (eds and compilers), *Christianity in South Africa: A Political, Social and Cultural History*, Oxford: James Currey and Cape Town: D. Philip, 1997.

Price, R. *An Imperial War and the British Working Class*, London: Routledge & Kegan Paul, 1972.

Pugh, P. *Educate, Agitate, Organize: 100 Years of Fabian Socialism*, London: Methuen, 1984.

Quinn-Judge, S. *Ho Chi Minh: The Missing Years*, London: Hurst & Co., 2003.

Rampersad, A. *The Life of Langston Hughes, Vol. I: 1902-1941, I, Too, Sing America,* OUP 1986, pp. 216-20.

Randrianja, S. *Société et luttes anticoloniales à Madagascar (1896 à 1946),* Paris: Karthala, 2001.

Ranger, T.O. (ed.), *Aspects of Central African History,* London: Heinemann, 1968.

Ranger, T.O. "African Politics in Twentieth-Century Southern Rhodesia", Ch. 9 in T.O. Ranger (ed.), *Aspects of Central African History,* London: Heinemann, 1968.

———— "The Nineteenth Century in Southern Rhodesia", chapter 6 in T.O. Ranger (ed.), *Aspects of Central African History,* London: Heinemann, 1968.

Rathbone, R. *Murder and Politics in Colonial Ghana,* New Haven: Yale University Press, 1993

Reed-Anderson, Paulette, *Rewriting the Footnotes: Berlin and the African Diaspora,* Berlin: Die Ausländerbeauftragte des Senats, 2000, in German and English

Rich, P. "W.M. Macmillan, South African Segregation and Commonwealth Race Relations, 1919-1938", ch. 9 in H. Macmillan and S. Marks (eds), *W.M. Macmillan, Historian and Social Critic,* Temple Smith for the Institute of Commonwealth Studies, 1989.

Rivet, D. "Le Commandement français et ses réactions vis-à-vis du mouvement rifain, 1924-1926", pp. 101-36 in *Abd el-Krim et la République du Rif: Actes du colloque international d'études historiques et sociologiques 18-20 janvier 1973,* Paris: Maspéro, 1976.

Robeson, Paul *Here I Stand,* London: Cassell, 1958, p. 37.

Robinson, Cedric J. *Black Marxism: The Making of the Black Radical Tradition,* Chapel Hill and London: University of North Carolina Press, 1983.

———— "Black Intellectuals at the British Core: 1920s-1940s", pp. 173-201 in J.S. Gundara and I. Duffield (eds) *Essays on the History of Blacks in Britain from Roman Times to the Mid-Twentieth Century,* Aldershot: Avebury, 1992.

Rohdie, S. "The Gold Coast Aborigines Abroad", *Journal of African History* vol. VI no. 3, 1965, pp. 389-411.

Romero, P.W. *E. Sylvia Pankhurst: Portrait of a Radical,* New Haven: Yale University Press, 1987.

Rose, P. *Jazz Cleopatra: Josephine Baker in Her Time*, Chatto & Windus, 1989.

Roux, E. *S.P. Bunting, A Political Biography*, published by the author, Cape Town, 1944.

———— *Time Longer than Rope*, London: Gollancz, 1948.

Roy, M.N. *M.N. Roy's Memoirs*, published posthumously in 1964, Bombay: Allied Publishers Private Ltd., with introduction by E.D. Parikh and epilogue by V.B. Karnik.

Rudin, H. *Germans in the Cameroons*, Yale University Press, 1938, reprint 1968.

Rüger, A. "Die Duala und Der Kolonialmacht 1884-1914", Vol. 2, pp. 184-257 in H. Stöcker (ed.), *Kamerun unter Deutsche Kolonialherrschaft*, Berlin: Rütten und Loening, Vol. 1 1960, Vol. 2 1968.

Rye, H. "The Southern Syncopated Orchestra", ch. 15 in R. Lotz and O. Pegg (eds), *Under the Imperial Carpet: Essays in Black History 1786-1950*, Crawley: Rabbit Press, 1986.

———— "Fearsome Means of Discord: Early Encounters with Black Jazz", ch. 3 of P. Oliver (ed.), *Black Music in Britain*, Open University Press, 1990.

Salifou, A. *Kaocen ou la révolte sénoussiste*, Niamey: Centre Nigérien de Recherches en Sciences Humaines, 1973.

Sanchez Diaz, R. "La Pacification espagnole", pp. 75-80 in *Abd el-Krim et la République du Rif: Actes du colloque international d'études historiques et sociologiques 18-20 janvier 1973*, Paris: Maspéro, 1976.

Sanderson, G.N. *England, Europe and the Upper Nile, 1882-1899: A Study in the Partition of Africa*, Edinburgh University Press, 1965.

Saul, Mahir and Patrick Royer *West African Challenge to Empire: Culture and History in the Volta-Bani Anticolonial War*, Athens, OH: Ohio University Press and Oxford: James Currey, 2001.

Sautter, G. "Notes sur la construction du chemin de fer Congo-Océan (1921-1934)", *Cahiers d'Etudes Africaines* vol. VII, 1967, 2me cahier, pp. 219-99.

Savage, D.C. "Jomo Kenyatta, Malcolm MacDonald and the Colonial Office 1938-39: Some Documents from the P.R.O.", *Canadian Journal of African Studies*, 3, 3, 1969, pp. 615-32.

Saville, J. "Bridgeman, Reginald Francis Orlando (1884-1968)", *Dictionary of Labour Biography*, ed. J.M. Bellamy and J. Saville, Basingstoke: Macmillan, 1984, vol. VII, pp. 25-40.

Scott, James C. *Domination and the Arts of Resistance: Hidden Transcripts*, Yale University Press 1990.

Segrè, C.C. *Fourth Shore: The Italian Colonization of Libya*, University of Chicago Press 1974.

Sekyi, K. *The Blinkards*, London: Heinemann 1974.

Sen, S.K. *The House of Tata (1839-1939)*, Calcutta: Progressive Publishers, 1975.

Shannon, M.W. *Jean Price-Mars, the Haitian Elite and the American Occupation, 1915-35*, Basingstoke: Macmillan, 1996.

Sharwood Smith, B. *But Always as Friends: Northern Nigeria and the Cameroons, 1921-1957*, London: Allen & Unwin, 1969.

Shepperson G. and T. Price *Independent African*, Edinburgh University Press, 1958.

Sherwood, Marika *Pastor Daniels Ekarte and the African Churches Mission, Liverpool, 1931-1964,* London: Savannah Press, 1994.

Simmons, A. *Modern Mauritius: The Politics of Decolonisation*, Bloomington: Indiana University Press, 1982.

Simon, J. *L'Etoile nord-africaine (1926-1937),* Paris: Harmattan, 2003, pp. 69-83.

Simons, J. and R. *Class and Colour in South Africa 1850-1950*, London: IDAF, 1983.

Sinda, M. *André Matsoua: fondateur du mouvement de libération du Congo,* Paris: ABC, 1978.

Sivan, E. *Communisme et nationalisme en Algérie 1920-1962*, Paris: Presses de la FNSP, 1976.

Spiegler, J. "Aspects of Nationalist Thought among French-Speaking West Africans 1921-1939", DPhil, Oxford, 1968.

Spitzer, L. *The Creoles of Sierra Leone*, Madison and London: University of Wisconsin Press, 1974.

———— and L. Denzer "I.T.A. Wallace Johnson and the West African Youth League", *International Journal of African Historical Studies* vol. VI no. 3, 1973, pp. 413-52 and vol. VI no. 4, pp. 565-601.

Squires, Mike *Saklatvala: A Political Biography*, London: Lawrence & Wishart, 1990.

Stapleton, C. "African Connections: London's Hidden Music Scene", Ch. 5 (pp. 91-3), in P. Oliver (ed.), *Black Music in Britain*, Open University Press, 1990.

Steene, D.V. *God's Irregular: Arthur Shearley Cripps*, SPCK, 1973.

Stöcker, H. (ed.) *Kamerun unter Deutsche Kolonialherrschaft*, Berlin: Rütten und Loening, Vol. 1 1960, Vol. 2 1968.

Stora, B. "La Gauche socialiste, révolutionnaire, et la question du Maghreb au moment du Front populaire (1935-1938)", *Revue Française d'Histoire d'Outremer* vol. LXX, 1983, no. 258-9, 1st-2nd quarters, pp. 57-79.

—— *Dictionnaire biographique de militants nationalistes algériens 1926-1954: E.N.A., P.P.A., M.T.L.D.*, Paris: Harmattan, 1985.

—— Stora, B. "Les Algériens dans le Paris de l'entre-deux-guerres", in A. Kaspi and A. Marès, *Le Paris des étrangers*, Paris: Imprimerie Nationale, 1989, pp. 141-55.

Subbotin, V.A. *et al.* "Political Independence – An Important Achievement of the African Peoples", pp. 19-29 in A.N. Gromyko (ed.), *The October Revolution and Africa*, trans. G. Glagoleva, Moscow: Progress Publishers, 1983.

Sundiata, I.K. *Black Scandal: America and the Liberian Labor Crisis, 1929-1936*, Philadelphia: Institute for the Study of Human Issues, 1980.

Suret-Canale, J. *French Colonialism in Tropical Africa 1900-1945*, London: C. Hurst and New York: Pica Press, 1971 (translation by T. Gottheiner of *L'Afrique noire*, vol. II: *L'Ere coloniale 1900-1945*, Paris: Editions Sociales, 1964).

Thatcher, I.D. *Trotsky*, London: Routledge, 2003.

Theobald, A.B. *Ali Dinar: Last Sultan of Darfur, 1898-1916*, London: Longmans, Green & Co., 1965.

Thomas, M. *The French Empire between the Wars: Imperialism, Politics and Society*, Manchester University Press, 2005.

Thomas, R. "La Politique socialiste et le problème colonial de 1905 à 1920", *Revue Française d'Histoire d'Outremer* Vol. XLVII, 2nd quarter, 1960, pp. 213-45.

Thu Trang-Gaspard *Ho Chi Minh à Paris (1917-1923)*, Paris: Harmattan, 1992.

Thuku, Harry with assistance from Kenneth King *An Autobiography*, Nairobi: OUP, 1970.

Ubah, C.N. "British Measures against Mahdism at Dumbulwa in Northern Nigeria, 1923: A Case of Colonial Overreaction", *Islamic Culture* vol. L no. 3, July 1976, pp. 169-83.

Vail L. and L. White *Capitalism and Colonialism in Mozambique: A Study of Quelimane District,* Heinemann 1980.

Valtin, J. *Out of the Night,* Heinemann 1941.

Van Onselen, C. *Chibaro: African Mine Labour in Southern Rhodesia 1900-1933,* London: Pluto Press, 1976.

Vanderstraeten, L.-F. *La Répression de la révolte des Pende au Kwango en 1931,* Brussels: Académie Royale des Sciences d'Outremer, 2000.

Vaughan, David A. *Negro Victory,* Independent Press Ltd, 1950.

Vigné d'Octon, Paul *La gloire du sabre* (1900), reprinted Paris: Quintette, 1984.

Vinson. R.J., ""Sea Kaffirs": "American Negroes" and the Gospel of Garveyism in Early Twentieth-Century Cape Town", *Journal of African History* 47, 2006, pp. 281-303.

Visram, R. *Ayahs, Lascars and Princes,* London: Pluto Press, 1986.

Wagner, G. *The Chocolate Conscience,* London: Chatto & Windus, 1987.

Walshe, P. *The Rise of African Nationalism in South Africa: The African National Congress 1912-1952,* London: C. Hurst & Co., 1970.

Weinstein, B. *Gabon: Nation-Building on the Ogooue,* Cambridge, MA and London: MIT Press, 1966.

—— *Eboué,* New York: OUP, 1972.

White, John *Black Leadership in America: from Booker T. Washington to Jesse Jackson,* London: Longman, 1985.

Whitehead, R. "The Aborigines' Protection Society and the Safeguarding of African Interests in Rhodesia, 1889-1930", DPhil, Oxford, 1975.

Wilks, I. *Asante in the Nineteenth Century: The Structure and Evolution of a Political Order,* CUP 1975.

Willan, B. *Sol Plaatje: South African Nationalist 1876-1932,* London: Heinemann, 1984.

Williams, Eric *Inward Hunger: The Education of a Prime Minister,* Andre Deutsch, 1969.

Wilson, E.T. *Russia and Black Africa before World War II,* New York: Holmes & Meier, 1974.

Wilson, H.S. (ed.) *Origins of West African Nationalism,* London: Macmillan.

Wiser, W. *The Crazy Years: Paris in the Twenties,* Thames & Hudson, 1983.

Wolf, J. *Les secrets du Maroc espagnol: l'épopée d'Abd-el-Khaleq Torres,* Paris: Balland, 1994.

Wolters, R. *Du Bois and his Rivals*, Columbia, MO and London: Missouri University Press, 2002.

Woolf, L. *Empire and Commerce in Africa: A Study in Economic Imperialism*, London: Allen & Unwin, 1920.

——— *Downhill All the Way*, London: Hogarth Press, 1967.

Wylie, D. "Norman Leys and McGregor Ross: A Case Study in the Conscience of African Empire 1900-39," *Journal of Imperial and Commonwealth History* vol. V no. 3, May 1977, pp. 294-309.

Wyse, A.J.G. "The 1926 Railway Strike and Anglo-Krio Relations: An Interpretation", *International Journal of African Historical Studies* vol. 14 no. 1, 1981, pp. 93-123.

——— *H.C. Bankole-Bright and Politics in Colonial Sierra Leone, 1919-1958*, CUP, 1990.

Zenkovsky, S.A. *Pan-Turkism and Islam in Russia*, Cambridge, MA: Harvard University Press, 1960.

Zinsou, E.D. and Luc Zouménou *Kojo Tovalou Houénou, Précurseur, 1887-1936: pannégrisme et modernité*, Paris: Maisonneuve et Larose, 2004.

Zmerli, S. *Les Successeurs*, Tunis: Maison Tunisienne de l'Edition, 1967.

Zoctizoum, Y. *Histoire de la Centrafrique, Vol. I, 1879-1959*, Paris: Harmattan, 1983.

INDEX

AFRICA'S 'AGITATORS'

Tamakloe, B.E.A. 308, 333
Tananarive 235, 348
Tanganyika 8, 46, 210
Tangier 264, 266
Tashkent 105-6
taxation 27, 60, 68, 233, 255, 306-7
Taylor, J. Eldred 24, 89, 93
Tempête sur le Maroc 265-7
Tessaoua 159-60
Tetuan 366
Tha'alibi, Abdelaziz al- 26, 63-4, 104, 267, 358
Thälmann, Ernst 199-200
The Truyen, Nguyen 141, 411
Thomas, Peter J.C. 89, 333
Thompson, Kojo 306-7, 315, 316
Thorez, Maurice 154, 157, 326, 330, 354
Thuku, Harry 77, 208, 293, 397
Tijaniyya 80, 163-4
Tlemcen 165, 270, 351
Togo 46, 70, 146, 233-4, 372
Torres, Abd al-Khaliq 266, 362-3, 365-7
Tours congress (SFIO) 108
Tovalou Houénou, Marc Kodjo 141-6, 222
Trade Union Congress (TUC) 394
trade unionism 74-5, 118-19, 134-5, 188, 190, 199-206, 308-9, 329, 348, 349, 360, 417, 394, 395, 402
Transkei 88
Transvaal 14, 20, 190
Trinidad 22, 198, 334-5, 395, 414
Tripolitania 51, 62-3
Trotsky, Lev 134, 281, 287, 413
Trotskyists 363-4, 413, 415
Tuareg 52

Tunisia 26-7, 52, 63-4, 104, 129, 133-5, 158, 160-3, 169, 175, 249, 259, 269, 316-17, 339, 342, 343, 355, 358-9, 366, 368, 369, 372
Turkestan, *see* Central Asia
Turkey 25, 27, 51-2, 55, 56, 63, 81, 259, 266, 281
Tuskegee Institute 19-20, 194

Ubangi-Shari 36, 237, 238, 239-40
Uganda 34, 210
Ukraine 255, 280
Union Congolaise 93, 221
Union des Travailleurs Nègres (UTN) 273, 285-6, 322-4
Union Intercoloniale 126-30, 137-40, 151, 157, 167, 175
Union of Democratic Control (UDC) 54-5, 99, 336, 392
United Africa Company 72
United South African National Party 327
Universal Negro Improvement Association (UNIA) 82-8, 122, 145, 193
USA 19-20, 51, 54, 57, 82-9, 108, 109, 110, 111, 119, 120-2, 145, 193-7, 214-15, 242, 289-91, 329-30, 418
USSR, *see* Soviet Union

Vaillant-Couturier, Paul 127, 129, 182, 220, 340
Valtin, Jan (Richard Krebs) 254, 260
Vandervelde, Emile 43
Vaughan, James Churchill 316, 333
Vietnam 127, 141
Vigné d'Octon 39-40, 45, 132
Viollette, Maurice 250-1, 352-3
Viollis, Andrée 318, 340, 350, 411

482